Essentials of Management blends current and traditional topics and organizes them around the functional, or process, approach to the study of management. Although other approaches have been developed, the functional approach remains a general framework, flexible enough to incorporate many viewpoints about management.

This book is written for newcomers to the field of management and for experienced managers seeking updated information and a review of the fundamentals. It also written for the many professionals and technical people who work closely with managers and who take their turn at performing some management work. An example would be the member of a cross-functional team who is expected to have the perspective of a general manager.

Based on extensive research about curriculum needs, the design of *Essentials of Management* addresses itself to the needs of introductory management courses and supervision courses offered in educational and work settings. Earlier editions of the text were used in the study of management in colleges and universities, as well as in career schools in such diverse programs as hospitality and tourism management. The book can also be used as a basic resource for management courses that rely heavily on lecture notes, handouts, and videos rather than an encyclopedia-like text.

ASSUMPTIONS UNDERLYING THE BOOK

The approach to synthesizing knowledge for this book is based on the following five assumptions:

1. A strong demand exists for practical and valid information about solutions to managerial problems. The information found in this text reflects the author's orientation toward translating research findings, theory, and experience into a form useful to both the student and the practitioner.
2. Managers and professionals need both interpersonal and analytical skills to meet their day-to-day responsibilities. Although this book concentrates on managing people, it also provides ample information about such topics as decision making, job design, organization structure, effective inventory management, and information technology.
3. The study of management should emphasize a variety of large, medium, and small work settings, as well as profit and not-for-profit organizations. Many

students of management, for example, intend to become small-business owners. Examples and cases in this book therefore reflect diverse work settings, including retail and service firms.

4. Effective managers and professionals generally focus on productivity, quality, and teamwork. These three factors are therefore noted frequently throughout the text.

5. Introductory management textbooks tend to become unrealistically comprehensive. Many introductory texts today are more than 800 pages long. Such texts overwhelm students who attempt to assimilate this knowledge in a single quarter or semester. The goal with *Essentials of Management* was to develop a text that realistically—in terms of time and amount of information—introduces the study of management.

FRAMEWORK OF THE BOOK

The first four chapters present an introduction to management. Chapter 1, "The Manager's Job," explains the nature of managerial work with a particular emphasis on managerial roles and tasks. Chapter 2, "International Management and Cultural Diversity," describes how managers and professionals work in a multicultural environment. Chapter 3, "Information Technology and the Internet," describes how information technology, including the Internet and e-commerce, influences the manager's job. Chapter 4, "Ethics and Social Responsibility," examines the moral aspects of management.

The next three chapters address the subject of planning. Chapter 5, "Essentials of Planning," presents a general framework for planning—the activity underlying almost any purposeful action taken by a manager. Chapter 6, "Problem Solving and Decision Making," explores the basics of decision making, with an emphasis on creativity and other behavioral aspects. Chapter 7, "Quantitative Techniques for Planning and Decision Making," describes several adjuncts to planning and decision making such as break-even analysis, PERT, and production-scheduling methods used for both manufacturing and services.

Chapters 8–10 focus on organizing, culture, and staffing. Chapter 8, "Job Design and Work Schedules," explains how jobs are laid out and work schedules arranged to enhance productivity and customer satisfaction. Chapter 9, "Organization Structure, Culture, and Change," explains how work is organized from the standpoint of the organization, how culture profoundly influences an organization, and how to cope with and capitalize on change. Chapter 10, "Staffing and Human Resource Management," explains the methods by which people are brought into the organization, trained, and evaluated.

The following three chapters, on leading, deal directly with the manager's role in influencing group members. Chapter 11, "Leadership," focuses on different approaches to leadership available to a manager and on the personal characteristics associated with leadership effectiveness. Chapter 12, "Motivation," describes what managers can do to increase or sustain employee effort toward achieving work goals. Chapter 13, "Communication," deals with the complex problems of accurately sending and receiving messages. Chapter 14, "Teams, Groups, and Teamwork," explains the nature of teams and how managers can foster group members' working together cooperatively.

The next two chapters, on controlling, each deal with an important part of keeping performance in line with expectations. Chapter 15, "Essentials of Control," presents an overview of measuring and controlling performance. It also describes how managers work with a variety of financial measures to monitor performance. Chapter 16, "Managing Ineffective Performers," describes current approaches to dealing with substandard performers, with an emphasis on elevating performance.

The final chapter in the text, Chapter 17, "Enhancing Personal Productivity and Managing Stress," describes how personal effectiveness can be increased by developing better work habits and time management skills and keeping stress under control. A major theme of the chapter is that good work habits help prevent and manage stress.

PEDAGOGICAL FEATURES

Essentials of Management is designed to aid both students and instructors in expanding their interest in and knowledge of management. The book contains the following features:

- Learning objectives coordinate the contents of each chapter. They preview the major topics and are integrated into the text by indicating which major topics relate to the objectives. The end-of-chapter Summary of Key Points, based on the chapter learning objectives, pulls together the central ideas in each chapter.
- An opening case example illustrates a major topic to be covered in the chapter.
- Management in Action, Organization in Action, and similar features present a portrait of how specific individuals or organizations practice an aspect of management covered in the chapter.
- Concrete, real-world examples with which the reader can readily identify are found throughout the text. Many examples are original, while others relate research information from published magazines, newspapers, and journals.
- Exhibits, which include figures, tables, and self-assessment quizzes, aid in the comprehension of information in the text.
- Key terms and phrases highlight the management vocabulary introduced in each chapter with definitions that appear in the margin.
- Questions at the end of each chapter assist learning by encouraging the reader to review and reflect on the chapter objectives.
- Skill-building exercises, including Internet activities, appear at the end of each chapter.
- Case problems also located at the end of each chapter can be used to synthesize the chapter concepts and simulate the practice of management.

New to the Sixth Edition

A number of significant changes and additions have been incorporated into this edition. A brief listing of these changes here is followed by a more detailed look.

- All 17 chapters contain new information where appropriate.
- More than half the end-of-chapter cases are new.
- All but two of the chapter-opening cases are new.
- About 90 percent of the Management in Action and Organization in Action boxes are new. The several boxes retained from the previous edition have been updated.
- Two "critical thinking" questions follow the regular questions at the end of the chapters. The purpose of these questions is to encourage a creative approach to a management issue, and to direct the student toward research.

- About half the Internet-skill building activities are new, and are intended to be more challenging than in the previous edition.
- More references to information technology and e-commerce are made throughout the text.
- A new Chapter 3 addresses the many changes that information technology and the Internet bring to the management field.
- About one-third of skill-building exercises are new.
- Many more cases and examples about not–for-profit organizations and government agencies are included in this edition.

Visit the Web Site

The Web site address for *Essentials of Management,* Sixth Edition, is http://dubrin. swcollege.com.

New in the Chapters

Several of the most important additions from substantially revised chapters are highlighted here.

Chapter 2
This chapter focuses on international management and cultural diversity. New information includes an expanded discussion of the problem of human rights violations, an exhibit on the pros and cons of globalization, and a self-quiz on cross-cultural skills and attitudes.

Chapter 3
This new chapter expands and consolidates the description of information technology, the Internet, and e-commerce. The ramifications of the Internet are divided into its impact on customers and other external relationships versus its impact on internal operations. Information is also presented about the wireless environment for managers and professionals.

Chapter 4
As part of the study of ethics, this chapter now includes a section about cyberethics and netiquette, or acceptable behavior for using the Internet and e-mail in particular.

Chapter 5
The planning chapter now includes information about how managers incorporate the Internet into their planning. As emphasized by Michael Porter, strategy is more important than ever in the Internet age. As margins are squeezed, a company must find a strategy that distinguishes itself from competitors.

Chapter 8
The discussion of job design talks about the increasing flexibility of job descriptions are becoming more flexible. Part of this flexibility is *job crafting*, or how workers modify their jobs to fit their personal preferences and capabilities. A major purpose of job crafting is to make the job more meaningful or enriched.

Chapter 9
The section on organization change now includes a description of disruptive technology, or how companies sometimes lose sight of small emerging markets served by a company with new technologies. Many students enjoy the challenge of identifying potential disruptive technologies.

Chapter 10
A new underlying theme to the chapter on human resource management is how human resource interventions, such as the right benefits, can improve employee retention. Retention continues to grow as a major focus of human resource management.

Chapter 11
To help the student personalize the vast topic of leadership, a new section explores how skills contribute to leadership. These many skills include sizing up the situation to employ the best leadership approach, and developing a mission statement that inspires others to perform well.

Chapter 12
An important addition to the chapter on motivation is an easy-to-follow case history of how a manufacturer used behavior modification to improve safety conditions in the plant. This insert provides an accessible supplement to technical explanations of motivation. Equity theory now appears in the chapter as well.

Chapter 13
The information about communication barriers in this chapter now includes a description of dishonest dialog, or not pinpointing the real problem in dealing with others. The chapter also contains new information about communication to fit a global environment, such as forming a global communications advisory team.

Chapter 15
An important control topic remains how to control and cut costs. The chapter includes a meaty sampling of ways to trim costs, divided into three categories: people, material and equipment, and money management.

New Topics Added to the Text

- Expanded explanation of entrepreneurship (Chapter 1)
- How poor interpersonal skills lead to executive failure (Chapter 1)
- Expanded discussion of the evolution of management thought including the information technology era (Chapter 1)
- Presentation of U.S.—international trade in goods and services and the Web site where more information can be found (Chapter 2)
- Expanded discussion of human rights violations (Chapter 2)
- Importance of environmentally friendly policies for multinational corporations (Chapter 2)
- Exhibit of pros and cons of globalization (Chapter 2)
- Self-quiz on cross-cultural skills and attitudes (Chapter 2)
- The wireless environment for managers and professionals (Chapter 3)

- The impact of the Internet on customers and other external relationships (Chapter 3)
- The impact of the Internet on internal operations (Chapter 3)
- Corporate espionage (Chapter 4)
- Cyberethics (Chapter 4)
- Domination as a business strategy (Chapter 4)
- Navigation for e-customers as a business strategy (Chapter 5)
- Appropriate physical surroundings for creativity (Chapter 6)
- Forecasts of the impact of the Internet (Chapter 7)
- Job crafting and job design (Chapter 8)
- The contributions of project managers (Chapter 9)
- Disruptive technology and organizational change (Chapter 9)
- Focus on retention in relation to human resource management (Chapter 10)
- Impairment testing (Chapter 10)
- Business or executive coaching for leaders (Chapter 11)
- Separate analysis of leadership skills (Chapter 11)
- Risk taking and thrill seeking (Chapter 12)
- Applying behavior modification to safety training (Chapter 12)
- Equity theory and job motivation (Chapter 12)
- Dishonest dialog (Chapter 13)
- Communication for a global environment (Chapter 13)
- Listening traps (Chapter 13)
- Virtual teams (Chapter 14)
- Stages of group development (Chapter 14)
- Loosening controls and creativity (Chapter 15)
- Cost-cutting suggestions organized into categories (Chapter 15)
- Boosting the self-confidence of difficult workers (Chapter 16)
- Emotional labor (faking emotion for customers) (Chapter 17)

Brand-New Internet Skill-Building Exercises

Every chapter contains an Internet-based skill-building exercise designed to connect students to Web sites that will boost their knowledge of management topics and issues.
- Researching the Quality of a Company's Management by Exploring the Company Web Site (Chapter 1)
- Making Internet Purchase Decisions (Chapter 3)
- Ethical Product Promotion (Chapter 4)
- Trends in Excess Inventory (Chapter 7)
- Success Factors for Flextime (Chapter 8)
- Analyzing an Organization Structure (Chapter 9)
- Charisma Tips from the Net (Chapter 11)
- Recognition Programs (Chapter 12)
- Analyzing Profit Margins (Chapter 15)

Self-Quizzes

Not only will students enjoy taking the self-quizzes, they will also learn about their strengths and areas for improvement in the process. Your students will benefit from taking the following:
- Cross-Cultural Skills and Attitudes (Chapter 2)

- The Ethical Reasoning Inventory (Chapter 4)
- How Involved Are You? (Chapter 8)
- Understanding Your Bureaucratic Orientation (Chapter 9)
- What Style of Leader Are You, or Would You Be? (Chapter 11)
- My Approach to Motivating Others (Chapter 12)
- Listening Traps (Chapter 13)
- Team Skills Inventory (Chapter 14)
- The Self-Sabotage Questionnaire (Chapter 16)
- Procrastination Tendencies (Chapter 17)
- The Stress Questionnaire (Chapter 17)

Brand-New Action Inserts

Students will find one Management in Action or Organization in Action insert in every chapter. Practically all inserts are completely new or an update of an insert from the fifth edition. A sampling follows:
- The Stable Hand of Charles F. Knight at Emerson Electric (Chapter 1)
- Kodak Boosts Chinese Film Factory (Chapter 2)
- Adding an *e* to Rx (Chapter 3)
- Kim Polese, Information Technology Pacesetter (Chapter 3)
- The Ecology-Friendly Tire Recyclers (Chapter 4)
- Amazon.com Develops Strategy to Lead the Internet Revolution (Chapter 5)
- Craig Conway Makes Tough Decisions at PeopleSoft (Chapter 6)
- Managers Attempt to Cope with an Inventory Glut (Chapter 7)
- Financial Consultant Runs Virtual Business (Chapter 8)
- The Contribution of Project Managers (Chapter 9)
- U.S. Postal Service Adapts to Disruptive Technology (Chapter 9)
- Soft-Skills Training Receives Attention (Chapter 10)
- The High-Flying Captain Deborah McCoy (Chapter 11
- Foamex Management Uses Behavior Modification to Improve Safety Training (Chapter 12)
- Deal Makers Prefer the Human Touch (Chapter 13)
- Nortel Networks Takes the Plunge into Virtual Teams (Chapter 14)
- IT Maintenance Systems at United Airlines (Chapter 15)
- Karyl Innis Helps the "Smart Buts" (Chapter 16)

Brand-New End-of-Chapter Cases

Twenty-two of the cases in the sixth edition are brand new, as follows:
- J.C. Penney Chief Plans a Running Start (Chapter 1)
- Hold On to Our Bilingual Workers (Chapter 2)
- Can We Wire the Avon Ladies? (Chapter 3)
- Is the Internet Draining Our Productivity? (Chapter 3)
- Napster Challenges the Music Business (Chapter 4)
- Vulture Time for E-Tailers (Chapter 5)
- High Hopes at Kellogg (Chapter 5)
- The Thinking Expedition (Chapter 6)
- The San Juan Snow House (Chapter 6)
- Imbalances at Family Services (Chapter 7)
- Our Best Cashiers Leave Too Soon (Chapter 8)

- The Culture War at DaimlerChrysler (Chapter 9)
- The Reluctant Information Sharers (Chapter 9)
- Labor Squeeze at Brittany Meadow (Chapter 10)
- "Carly" Attempts a Big Overhaul at HP (Chapter 11)
- Rewards and Recognition at Tel-Service (Chapter 12)
- The Scrutinized Team Member Candidate (Chapter 13)
- The Speed Team at IBM (Chapter 14)
- Building Cooperation at Ambitech (Chapter 14)
- The Squeeze at Palm (Chapter 15)
- The Preoccupied Business Analyst (Chapter 16)
- The Meridian Workers Go Surfing (Chapter 17)

INSTRUCTIONAL RESOURCES

Essentials of Management is accompanied by comprehensive instructional support materials.

- *Instructor's Manual with Test Bank and Transparency Masters.* The instructor's manual (ISBN: 0-324-11469-9) provides resources to increase the teaching and learning value of *Essential of Management.* The *Manual* contains "Chapter Outline and Lecture Notes," of particular value to instructors whose time budget does not allow for extensive class preparation.

  For each chapter, the *Manual* provides a statement of purpose and scope, outline and lecture notes, lecture topics, comments on the end-of-chapter questions and activities, responses to case questions, an experiential activity, and an examination. The examination contains twenty-five multiple-choice questions, twenty-five true/false questions, and three essay questions.

  The *Manual* contains two comprehensive cases that will be useful for instructors who wish to integrate the topics covered within the course. In addition, instructions are provided for the use of Computer-Aided Scenario Analysis (CASA). CASA is a user-friendly technique that can be used with any word-processing software. It allows the student to insert a new scenario into the case and then to re-answer the questions based on the new scenario. CASA helps to develop creative thinking and an awareness of contingencies or situational factors in making managerial decisions.

  A set of transparency masters that duplicates key figures in the text is included in the manual.

- *Examview.* The examinations presented in the *Manual* are also available on disk with the test generator program, Examview (ISBN: 0-324-11471-0). This versatile software package allows instructors to create new questions and edit or delete existing questions from the test bank.

- *Study Guide.* The *Study Guide* (ISBN: 0-324-11468-0) that accompanies the sixth edition of *Essentials of Management* is a real asset to students. For each text chapter, the *Study Guide* includes an overview, the objectives and key terms, an expanded study outline, and review questions—matching, multiple-choice, true/false, and fill-in. Each chapter also contains an application exercise that requires use of the concepts presented in the text chapter.

- *PowerPoint Slides.* A set of 150 professionally prepared *PowerPoint* slides (ISBN: 0-324-11470-2) accompanies the test. This slide package is designed for easy classroom use and includes reproductions of many of the exhibits found in the text.

A NOTE TO THE STUDENT

The information in the general preface is important for students as well as instructors. Here I offer additional comments that will enable you to increase the personal payoffs from studying management. My message can be organized around several key points.

- *Management is not simply common sense.* The number one trap for students in studying management is to assume that the material is easy to master because many of the terms and ideas are familiar. For example, just because you have heard the word *teamwork* many times, it does not automatically follow that you are familiar with specific field-tested ideas for enhancing teamwork.
- *Managerial skills are vital.* The information in the course for which you are studying this text is vital in today's world. People with formal managerial job titles such as supervisor, team leader, department head, or vice president are obviously expected to possess managerial skills. But many other people in jobs without managerial titles also benefit from managerial skills. Among them are administrative assistant, customer-service representative, and inventory-control specialist.
- *The combination of managerial, interpersonal, and technical skills leads to outstanding career success.* A recurring myth is that it is better to study "technical" or "hard" subjects than management because the pay is better. In reality, the people in business making the higher salaries are those who combine technical skills with managerial and interpersonal skills. Executives and business owners, for example, can earn incomes rivaled only by leading professional athletes and entertainment personalities.
- *Studying management, however, has its biggest payoff in the long run.* Entry-level management positions are in short supply. Management is a basic life process. To run a major corporation, manage a restaurant or a hair salon, organize a company picnic, plan a wedding, or run a good household, management skills are an asset. We all have some knowledge of management, but formally studying management can multiply one's effectiveness.

Take advantage of the many study aids in this text and the *Study Guide*. You will enhance your learning or management by concentrating on such learning aids as the chapter objectives, summaries, discussion questions, self-quizzes, skill-development exercises, and glossary. Carefully studying a glossary is an effective way of building a vocabulary in a new field, Studying the glossary will also serve as a reminder of important topics. Activities such as the cases, discussion questions, and skill-building exercises facilitate learning by creating the opportunity to think through the information. Thinking through information, in turn, leads to better comprehension and long-term retention of information. The *Study Guide* will provide excellent review and preparation for examinations.

ACKNOWLEDGMENTS

Any project as complex as this text requires a team of dedicated and talented people to see that it gets completed effectively. Many reviewers made valuable comments during the development of this new edition as well as the previous five editions of the text. I appreciate the helpful suggestions of the following colleagues:

xii

Thelma Anderson
Montana State University–Northern

Tom Birkenhead
Lane Community College

Genie Black
Arkansas Tech University

Brenda Britt
Fayetteville Technical Community College

Michel Cardinale
Palomar College

Gary Clark
North Harris College

Jose L. Curzet
Florida National College

Rex Cutshall
Vincennes University

Robert DeDominic
Montana Tech University

Robert Desman
Kennesaw State College

Kenneth Dreifus
Pace University

Ben Dunn
York Technical College

Thomas Fiock
Southern Illinois University at Carbondale

Dan Geeding
Xavier University

Shirley Gilmore
Iowa State University

Philip C. Grant
Hussen College

Randall Greenwell
John Wood Community College

David R. Grimmett
Austin Peay State University

Robert Halliman
Austin Peay State University

Paul Hegele
Elgin Community College

Thomas Heslin
Indiana University

Peter Hess
Western New England College

Nathan Himelstein
Essex County College

Judith A. Horrath
Lehigh Corbon Community College

Lawrence H. Jaffe
Rutgers University

B. R. Kirkland
Tarleton State University

Margaret S. Maguire
SUNY–Oneonta

Patrician Manninen
North Shore Community College

Noel Matthews
Front Range Community College

Christopher J. Morris
Adirondack Community College

Ilona Motsiff
Trinity College of Vermont

David W. Murphy
University of Kentucky

Ronald W. Olive
New Hampshire Technical College

George M. Padilla
New Mexico State University–Almogordo

J. E. Pearson
Dabney S. Lancaster Community College

Joseph Platts
Miami-Dade Community College

Larry S. Potter
University of Maine–Presque Isle

Thomas Quirk
Webster University

Jane Rada
Western Wisconsin Technical College

James Riley
Oklahoma Junior College

Robert Scully
Barry University

Gary Tilley
Surry Community College

William Searle
Asnuntuck Community Technical College

Bernard Weinrich
St. Louis Community College

William Shepard
New Hampshire Technical College

Blaine Weller
Baker College

Lynn Suksdorf
Salt Lake Community College

Alex Wittig
North Metro Technical College

John J. Sullivan
Montreat College

Thanks also to the members of the South-Western Marketing and Management Team who worked with me on this edition: executive editor for management John Szilagi, acquisitions editor for management Joe Sabatino, developmental editor Emma Guttler, production editor Starratt Alexander, designer Rik Moore, and photo editor Deanna Ettinger. The contribution of Theresa Curtis is also noted. Writing without loved ones would be a lonely task. My thanks therefore go to my family, Drew, Douglas, Gizella, Melanie, Rosie, and Clare.

Andrew J. DuBrin

ABOUT THE AUTHOR

Andrew J. DuBrin is a Professor of Management in the College of Business at the Rochester Institute of Technology, where he teaches courses and conducts research in management, organizational behavior, leadership, and career management. He has also served as department chairman and team leader in previous years. He received his Ph.D. in Industrial Psychology from Michigan State University. DuBrin has business experience in human resource management and consults with organizations and individuals. His specialties include career management leadership and management development. DuBrin is an established author of both textbooks and trade books, and he also contributes to profressional journals, magazines, newspapers, and online shows. He has written textbooks on management, leadership, organizational behavior, and human relations. His trade books cover many current issues, including charisma, team play, office politics, overcoming career self-sabotage, and preventing workplace problems.

Brief contents

PART 1   Introduction to Management

   1   The Manager's Job   1
   2   International Management and Cultural Diversity   29
   3   Information Technology and the Internet   59
   4   Ethics and Social Responsibility   85

PART 2   Planning

   5   Essentials of Planning   111
   6   Problem Solving and Decision Making   137
   7   Quantitative Techniques for Planning and Decision Making   171

PART 3   Organizing

   8   Job Design and Work Schedules   197
   9   Organization Structure, Culture, and Change   221
   10   Staffing and Human Resource Management   255

PART 4   Leading

   11   Leadership   285
   12   Motivation   317
   13   Communication   349
   14   Teams, Groups, and Teamwork   379

PART 5   Controlling

   15   Essentials of Control   409
   16   Managing Ineffective Performers   441

PART 6   Managing for Personal Effectiveness

   17   Enhancing Personal Productivity and Managing Stress   467

   Glossary   491
   Index   501

Contents

PART 1 **Introduction to Management**

1 **The Manager's Job** 1
Who Is a Manager? 2
Types of Managers 4
The Process of Management 5
The Seventeen Managerial Roles 8
Five Key Managerial Skills 13
Development of Managerial Skills 15
The Evolution of Management Thought 16

2 **International Management and Cultural Diversity** 29
International Management 30
Challenges Facing the Global Managerial Worker. 35
Methods of Entry into World Markets 40
The Scope and Competitive Advantage of Managing Diversity . . . 45
Organizational Practices to Encourage Diversity 49

3 **Information Technology and the Internet** 59
Information Technology and the Manager's Job. 60
The Positive and Negative Consequences of Information
   Technology 61
The Impact of the Internet on Customer and Other
   External Relationships 67
The Effects of the Internet on Internal Operations 71
Success Factors in an E-Business 76

4 **Ethics and Social Responsibility** 85
Business Ethics 86
Social Responsibility. 94
Benefits Derived from Ethics and Social Responsibility 102

Contents

PART 2   Planning

5   **Essentials of Planning** 111
   The Contribution of Planning 112
   A General Framework for Planning 112
   Strategic Planning and Business Strategies 117
   The Development of Business Strategy. 120
   Operating Plans, Policies, Procedures, and Rules 128
   Management by Objectives: A System of Planning and Review. . . 130

6   **Problem Solving and Decision Making** 137
   Nonprogrammed Versus Programmed Decisions 138
   Steps in Problem Solving and Decision Making. 139
   Influences on Decision Making. 144
   Creativity in Managerial Work 150
   Group Problem Solving and Decision Making 159

7   **Quantitative Techniques for Planning and Decision Making** 171
   Forecasting Methods. 172
   Gantt Charts and Milestone Charts. 176
   Program Evaluation and Review Technique 178
   Break-Even Analysis. 182
   Decision Trees 184
   Inventory Control Techniques 186
   Pareto Diagrams for Problem Identification 190

PART 3   Organizing

8   **Job Design and Work Schedules** 197
   Basic Concepts of Job Design. 198
   Job Involvement, Enlargement, and Rotation 205
   Job Crafting and Job Design 206
   Ergonomics and Job Design. 207
   Modified Work Schedules and Job Design. 209

9   **Organization Structure, Culture, and Change** 221
   Bureaucracy as a Form of Organization 222
   Departmentalization 224
   Modifications of the Bureaucratic Organization. 228
   Delegation, Empowerment, and Decentralization. 233
   Organizational Culture 235
   Managing Change 241

10   **Staffing and Human Resource Management** 255
   The Staffing Model 256
   Legal Aspects of Staffing. 256
   Strategic Human Resource Planning. 259
   Recruitment 260
   Selection 262
   Orientation, Training, and Development 271

Performance Appraisal 274
Compensation 277

PART 4   Leading

1 1   Leadership 285
The Link Between Leadership and Management 286
The Leadership Use of Power and Authority 288
Characteristics, Traits, and Behaviors of Effective Leaders 291
Leadership Styles 296
Transformational and Charismatic Leadership 303
The Leader as a Mentor 306
Leadership Skills 308

1 2   Motivation 317
The Relationship Between Motivation, Performance,
    and Commitment 318
Motivation Through Need Satisfaction 320
Motivation Through Goal Setting 325
Behavior Modification 327
Motivation Through Financial Incentives 331
Expectancy Theory 337
Equity Theory and Job Motivation 339

1 3   Communication 349
The Communication Process 350
Nonverbal Communication in Organizations 352
Organizational Channels and Directions of Communication 355
Barriers to Communication 359
Overcoming Barriers to Communication 362
How to Conduct an Effective Meeting 369
Organizational Politics and Interpersonal Communication 370

1 4   Teams, Groups, and Teamwork 379
Types of Teams and Groups 380
Characteristics of Effective Work Groups 386
Stages of Group Development 389
Roles for Team and Group Members 391
Managerial Actions for Building Teamwork 392
Being an Effective Team Player 393
Potential Contributions and Problems of Teams and Groups 395
Resolving Conflict within Teams and Groups 398

PART 5   Controlling

1 5   Essentials of Control 409
Controlling and the Other Management Functions 410
Types and Strategies of Control 411
Steps in the Control Process 413

Contents

Nonbudgetary Control Techniques 417
Budgets and Budgetary Control Techniques. 418
Managing Cash Flow and Cost Cutting 423
Information Systems and Control 428
Characteristics of Effective Controls 431

16 Managing Ineffective Performers 441
Factors Contributing to Ineffective Performance 442
The Control Model for Managing Ineffective Performers 446
Coaching and Constructive Criticism 453
Employee Discipline 454
Dealing with Difficult People, Including Cynics 457
Termination 460

PART 6   Managing for Personal Effectiveness

17 Enhancing Personal Productivity and Managing Stress 467
Improving Your Work Habits and Time Management 468
Understanding and Reducing Procrastination 474
The Nature of Stress and Burnout 478
Stress Management Techniques 482

Glossary 491
Index 501

The Manager's Job

In the command center at siteROCK Corp., based in Emeryville, California, eight workers tap on keyboards and watch rows of overhead screens spew out data on the performance of their customers' Web sites. One young professional suddenly yells out to a coworker across the room, who races over to help troubleshoot. According to siteROCK's "two-person rule," two heads reduce human error.

Dave Lilly, siteROCK's chief operating officer, beams as he watches through soundproof glass. Lilly was brought in to provide more professional management to the firm. The duo quickly runs through procedures laid out in 30 thick binders to pinpoint the Web site's problem. The activity follows a tight script based on the 53-year-old Lilly's six years in the military, part of them as a chief engineer of a nuclear submarine. The goal: to engineer human reliability, using military processes to create teamwork, orderliness, and quick resolutions in an often chaotic business. "If processes can work on a nuclear submarine where you have 19-year-olds taking orders from 22-year-olds, they'll work anywhere," he says.

You might not think that a small high-technology firm should be run like a nuclear submarine. Nevertheless, the siteROCK example sends an important message about managers and management. Almost any firm can benefit from a systematic approach to managing work and people. Management is the force behind all business activities, and helps firms of all sizes run more smoothly. Management pulls together resources to accomplish important objectives.

The alternative to placing effective managers in charge of an operation is chaos. Poor management (and leadership) is one of the major

1

OBJECTIVES

After studying this chapter and doing the exercises, you should be able to:

1 Explain the term *manager*, and identify different types of managers.

2 Describe the process of management, including the functions of management.

3 Describe the various managerial roles.

4 Identify the basic managerial skills and understand how they can be developed.

5 Identify the major developments in the evolution of management thought, along with several best management practices.

Chapter 1

reasons that many businesses of various sizes fail. These firms lack people who can tie together loose ends and accomplish important goals. When business firms fail because of competitive pressures or a lagging economy, it is often the case that knowledgeable management could have overcome the problem. Many founders of high-tech start-ups hired professional managers to steer their firms through the challenges of a competitive marketplace. Professional managers are often brought in after the high-tech firm's initial growth spurt to address problems such as fending off the competition and out-of-control expenses that often surface after the firm's early success.[1]

---

1   WHO IS A MANAGER?

Explain the term *manager*, and identify different types of managers.

manager

A person responsible for the work performance of group members.

management

The process of using organizational resources to achieve organizational objectives through planning, organizing and staffing, leading, and controlling.

A **manager** is a person responsible for the work performance of group members. A manager holds the formal authority to commit organizational resources, even if the approval of others is required. For example, the manager of an H&R Block income tax and financial service outlet has the authority to order the repainting of the reception area. The income tax and financial services specialists reporting to that manager, however, do not have that authority.

The concepts of manager and managing are intertwined. From the viewpoint of Peter Drucker, a noted management authority, management is the specific practice that converts a mob into an effective, goal-directed, and productive group.[2] The term **management** in this book refers to the process of using organizational resources to achieve organizational objectives through the functions of planning, organizing and staffing, leading, and controlling. These functions represent the broad framework for this book and will be described later. In addition to being a process, the term *management* is also used as a label for a specific discipline, for the people who manage, and for a career choice.

Levels of Management

Another way of understanding the nature of a manager's job is to examine the three levels of management shown in Exhibit 1-1. The pyramid in this figure illustrates progressively fewer employees at each higher managerial level. The largest number of people is at the bottom organizational level. (Note that the term *organizational level* is sometimes more precise than the term *managerial level*, particularly at the bottom organizational level, which has no managers.)

Top-Level Managers

top-level managers

Managers at the top one or two levels in the organization.

Most people who enter the field of management aspire to become **top-level managers**—managers at the top one or two levels in an organization. Top-level managers are empowered to make major decisions affecting the present and future of the firm. Only a top-level manager, for example, would have the authority to purchase another company, initiate a new product line, or hire hundreds of

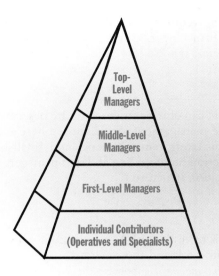

Chairman of the board, CEO, president, vice president, COO (chief operating officer), CFO (chief financial officer), CIO (chief information officer)

Director, branch manager, department chairperson, chief of surgery, team leader

Supervisor, office manager, crew chief

Tool-and-die maker, cook, word processing technician, assembler

Note: Some individual contributors, such as financial analysts and administrative assistants, report directly to top-level managers or middle managers.

employees. Top-level managers are the people who give the organization its general direction; they decide where it is going and how it will get there. The terms *executive* and *top-level manager* can be used interchangeably.

Middle-Level Managers

Middle-level managers are managers who are neither executives nor first-level supervisors, but who serve as a link between the two groups. Middle-level managers conduct most of the coordination activities within the firm, and they disseminate information to upper and lower levels. The jobs of middle-level managers vary substantially in terms of responsibility and income. A branch manager in a large firm might be responsible for more than 100 workers. In contrast, a general supervisor in a small manufacturing firm might have 20 people reporting to him or her. Other important tasks for many middle-level managers include helping the company undertake profitable new ventures and finding creative ways to reach goals. Quite often the middle-level manager conducts research on the Internet to gather ideas about market trends and improving work methods.

First-Level Managers

Managers who supervise operatives are referred to as **first-level managers,** first-line managers, or supervisors. Historically, first-level managers were promoted from production or clerical positions into supervisory positions. Rarely did they have formal education beyond high school. A dramatic shift has taken place in recent years, however. Many of today's first-level managers are career school graduates who are familiar with modern management techniques. The current emphasis on productivity and quality has elevated the status of many supervisors.

To understand the work performed by first-level managers, reflect back on your first job. Like most employees in entry-level positions, you probably reported to a first-level manager. Such a manager might be supervisor of newspaper carriers, dining room manager, service station manager, maintenance supervisor, or department manager in a retail store. Supervisors help shape the attitudes

middle-level managers

Managers who are neither executives nor first-level supervisors, but who serve as a link between the two groups.

first-level managers

Managers who supervise operatives (also known as first-line managers or supervisors).

of new employees toward the firm. Newcomers who like and respect their first-level manager tend to stay with the firm longer. Conversely, new workers who dislike and disrespect their first supervisor tend to leave the firm early.

TYPES OF MANAGERS

The functions performed by managers can also be understood by describing different types of management jobs. The management jobs discussed here are functional and general managers, administrators, entrepreneurs and small-business owners, and team leaders. (The distinction between line and staff managers will be described in Chapter 9 about organization structure.)

Functional and General Managers

Another way of classifying managers is to distinguish between those who manage people who do one type of specialized work and those who manage people who engage in different specialties. *Functional managers* supervise the work of employees engaged in specialized activities, such as accounting, engineering, information systems, food preparation, marketing, sales, and telephone installation. A functional manager is a manager of specialists and of their support team, such as office assistants.

General managers are responsible for the work of several different groups that perform a variety of functions. The job title "plant general manager" offers insight into the meaning of general management. Reporting to the plant general manager are various departments engaged in both specialized and generalized work, such as plant manufacturing, plant engineering, labor relations, quality control, safety, and information systems. Company presidents are general managers. Branch managers also are general managers if employees from different disciplines report to them.

Six key tasks form the foundation of every general manager's job. These tasks are:[3]

1. *Shaping the work environment:* Setting up performance standards
2. *Crafting a strategic vision:* Describing where the organization is headed
3. *Allocating resources:* Deciding who gets how much money, people, material, and access to the manager
4. *Developing managers:* Helping prepare people for their first and more advanced managerial jobs
5. *Building the organization:* Helping solve important problems so the organization can move forward
6. *Overseeing operations:* Running the business, spotting problems, and helping solve them

The six tasks of a general manager highlight many of the topics contained in the study of management. These tasks will therefore be reintroduced at various places in this book.

Administrators

An *administrator* is typically a manager who works in a public (government) or nonprofit organization rather than in a business firm. Among these managerial positions are hospital administrator and housing administrator. Managers in all types of educational institutions are referred to as administrators. The fact that individual contributors in nonprofit organizations are sometimes referred to as administrators often causes confusion. An employee is not an administrator in the managerial sense unless he or she supervises others.

Entrepreneurs and Small-Business Owners

Millions of students and employees dream of turning an exciting idea into a successful business. Many people think, "If Michael Dell started Dell computers from his dormitory room and he is the wealthiest man in Texas today, why can't I do something similar?" Success stories such as Dell's kindle the entrepreneurial spirit. An **entrepreneur** is a person who founds and operates an innovative business.

    Researcher Michael H. Morris defines entrepreneurship along three dimensions: innovativeness, risk taking, and proactiveness. Each of these dimensions or aspects can occur in different degrees. Entrepreneurs vary in how innovative they are, how much risk they take, and how proactive (initiative taking) they are.[4] After the entrepreneur develops the business into something bigger than he or she can handle alone or without the help of a few people, that person becomes a general manager. Remember the story about siteROCK? Top management hired a chief operating officer, which suggests that the entrepreneurial firm became too big for the founder to lead without adding a key manager.

    Similar to an entrepreneur, the owner and operator of a small business becomes a manager when the firm grows to include several employees. **Small-business owners** typically invest considerable emotional and physical energy into their firms. Note that entrepreneurs are (or start as) small-business owners, but that the reverse is not necessarily true. You need an innovative idea to be an entrepreneur. Simply running a franchise that sells sub sandwiches does not make a person an entrepreneur, according to the definition presented here.

Team Leaders

A major development in types of managerial positions during the last decade is the emergence of the **team leader**. A manager in such a position coordinates the work of a small group of people, while acting as a facilitator or catalyst. Team leaders are found at several organizational levels, and are sometimes referred to as project managers, program managers, process managers, and task force leaders. Note that the term *team* could also refer to an executive team, yet a top executive almost never carries the title *team leader*. You will be reading about team leaders throughout this text.

THE PROCESS OF MANAGEMENT   **2**

A helpful approach to understanding what managers do is to regard their work as a process. A process is a series of actions that achieves something—making a profit or providing a service, for example. To achieve an objective, the manager uses resources and carries out four major managerial functions. These functions are planning, organizing and staffing, leading, and controlling. Exhibit 1-2 illustrates the process of management.

Resources Used by Managers

Managers use resources to accomplish their purposes, just as a carpenter uses resources to build a patio. A manager's resources can be divided into four types: human, financial, physical, and informational.

---

entrepreneur
A person who founds and operates an innovative business.

small-business owner
An individual who owns and operates a small business.

team leader
A manager who coordinates the work of a small group of people, while acting as a facilitator and catalyst.

Describe the process of management, including the functions of management.

EXHIBIT 1-2

The Process of Management

The manager uses resources and carries out functions to achieve goals.

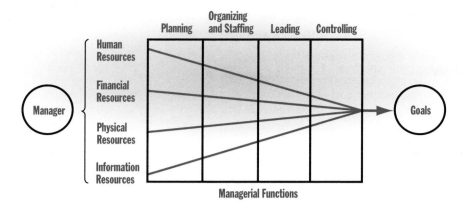

Source: Ricky W. Griffin, *Management,* 4e, Copyright © 1993 by Houghton Mifflin Co., p. 6. Used with permission.

Human resources are the people needed to get the job done. Managers' goals influence which employees they choose. A manager might set the goal of delivering automotive supplies and tools to auto and truck manufacturers. Among the human resources she chooses are manufacturing technicians, sales representatives, information technology specialists, and a network of dealers.

Financial resources are the money the manager and the organization use to reach organizational goals. The financial resources of a business organization are profits and investments from stockholders. A business must occasionally borrow cash to meet payroll or to pay for supplies. The financial resources of community agencies come from tax revenues, charitable contributions, and government grants.

Physical resources are a firm's tangible goods and real estate, including raw materials, office space, production facilities, office equipment, and vehicles. Vendors supply many of the physical resources needed to achieve organizational goals.

Information resources are the data that the manager and the organization use to get the job done. For example, to supply leads to the firm's sales representatives, the sales manager of an office supply company reads local business newspapers to learn about new firms in town. These newspapers are information resources. Jeffrey R. Immelt, the CEO of General Electric Corp., surfs the Internet regularly to learn about developments in the industry, thus using the Net as an information resource.

The Four Managerial Functions

Exhibit 1-2 shows the four major resources in the context of the management process. To accomplish goals, the manager performs four managerial functions. These functions are planning, organizing and staffing, leading, and controlling.

Planning

Planning involves setting goals and figuring out ways of reaching them. Planning, considered the central function of management, pervades everything a manager does. In planning, a manager looks to the future, saying, "Here is what we want to achieve, and here is how we are going to do it." Decision making is usually a component of planning, because choices have to be made in the process of finalizing plans. The importance of planning expands as it contributes heavily to performing the other management functions. For example, managers must make plans to do an effective job of staffing the organization. Planning is also part of marketing. For example, cereal maker Kellogg Corp. established plans to diversify further into the snack food business to reach its goal of expanding market share.

Organizing and Staffing

Organizing is the process of making sure the necessary human and physical resources are available to carry out a plan and achieve organizational goals. Organizing also involves assigning activities, dividing work into specific jobs and tasks, and specifying who has the authority to accomplish certain tasks. Another major aspect of organizing is grouping activities into departments or some other logical subdivision. The staffing function ensures the availability of necessary human resources to achieve organizational goals. Hiring people for jobs is a typical staffing activity. Staffing is such a major activity that it is sometimes classified as a function separate from organizing.

Leading

Leading means influencing others to achieve organizational objectives. As a consequence, it involves energizing, directing, persuading others, and creating a vision. Leadership involves dozens of interpersonal processes: motivating, communicating, coaching, and showing group members how they can reach their goals. Leadership is such a key component of managerial work that management is sometimes seen as accomplishing results through people. The leadership aspect of management focuses on inspiring people and bringing about change, whereas the other three functions focus more on maintaining a stable system.

Controlling

Controlling generally involves comparing actual performance to a predetermined standard. Any significant difference between actual and desired performance would prompt a manager to take corrective action. He or she might, for example, increase advertising to boost lower-than-anticipated sales.

A secondary aspect of controlling is determining whether the original plan needs revision, given the realities of the day. The controlling function sometimes causes a manager to return to the planning function temporarily to fine-tune the original plan. In recent years Amazon.com planned to improve its customer service by expanding its number of distribution centers. However, not enough revenue and profits were generated to support all of these new centers, so a readjustment was made and Amazon closed several of these centers.

The Management in Action on page 9 describes an executive who is widely respected for his ability to carry out the process of management. As you read the insert, identify which functions of management are illustrated.

The Functions Emphasized at Different Levels of Management

One important way in which the jobs of managers differ is in the relative amounts of time spent on planning, organizing and staffing, leading, and controlling. Executives ordinarily spend much more time on strategic (high-level and long-range) planning than do middle- or first-level managers.[5] Lower-level managers are more involved with day-by-day and other short-range planning.

One notable difference in time allocation is that, compared to middle managers and executives, first-level managers and team leaders spend more time in face-to-face leadership of employees, as Exhibit 1-3 shows. Exhibit 1-4 reveals

EXHIBIT 1-3

Time Spent on Supervising Individuals at the Three Levels of Management*

First-level supervisors place the most importance on dealing directly with group members.

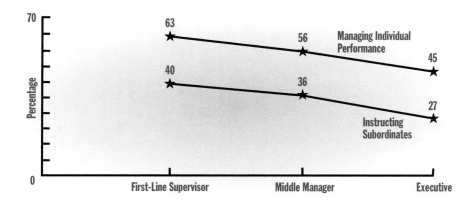

*Numbers refer to the percentage of managers who said the task was of "the utmost" or "considerable" importance.

Source: Allen I. Kraut et al., "The Role of Manager: What's Really Important in Different Management Jobs," *The Academy of Management Executive*, November 1989, p. 287.

EXHIBIT 1-4

Time Spent on Monitoring the Business Environment*

Executives place the most importance on monitoring the environment.

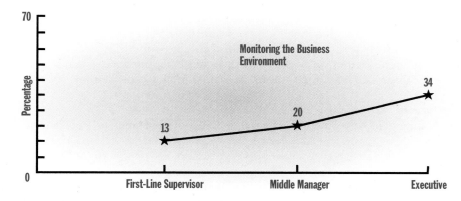

*Numbers refer to the percentage who said the task was of "the utmost" or "considerable" importance.

Source: Kraut et al., "The Role of the Manager," p. 288.

that executives spend most of their time monitoring the business environment. Such monitoring is a form of controlling. By analyzing what is going on in the outside world, the manager can help the firm compete effectively.

3 THE SEVENTEEN MANAGERIAL ROLES

Describe the various managerial roles.

role

An expected set of activities or behaviors stemming from a job.

To further understand the manager's job, it is worthwhile to examine the various roles managers play. A **role**, in the business context, is an expected set of activities or behaviors stemming from a job. Henry Mintzberg conducted several landmark studies of managerial roles.[6] Other researchers extended his findings.[7] In the sections that follow, the roles delineated by these researchers are associated with the major managerial functions to which they most closely pertain. (Roles and functions are closely related. They are both activities carried out by people.) The description of the 17 roles should help you appreciate the richness and complexity of managerial work. These roles are described next and listed in Exhibit 1-5.

Management *in Action*

The Stable Hand of Charles F. Knight at Emerson Electric

When asked to identify top-notch executives in corporate America, business school professors frequently mention Charles "Chuck" F. Knight, the chairman and CEO of Emerson Electric Co. Having held this position for 27 years, Knight is one of the longest-running CEOs in American business today. "Knight is at the helm of a managerial process that is a thing of beauty," says Stuart I. Greenbaum, dean of the John M. Olin School of Business at Washington University.

Emerson Electric Co. was founded in 1890 in St. Louis, Missouri, as a manufacturer of electric motors and fans. The people of St. Louis, like most Americans, were skeptical of electricity, which appeared to be a dangerous and unreliable energy source. As the company grew, it expanded its product line by attaching electric motors to new products such as sewing machines, dental drills, player pianos, and hair dryers. Emerson's first big commercial success was an electric fan.

Under Knight, Emerson evolved into a major global enterprise. The company produces technologically advanced products used in such markets as telecommunications, electronics, heating, ventilating and air conditioning, and process controls. Emerson has 31,000 employees in 82 facilities, and annual sales of about $1 billion.

Knight attributes some of his success to the management system set up by his predecessor, Wallace R. "Buck" Persons. When Knight took over, Persons had been the highest-ranking executive at Emerson for 19 years. Knight believes that Persons instilled in him a dedication to the basics, especially continuous cost-cutting and a culture of being open to employee ideas. Taking these lessons seriously,

Knight targets cost cuts of seven percent a year and conducts meetings with his staff regularly. Knight says that these principles allow him to keep alive the 42-year growth streak started under Persons.

Knight says he learned to set high goals for himself from his father, Lester Knight, who ran a successful consulting firm in Chicago. To teach his son the value of work and independence, Lester often sent him to do manual labor in distant lands, once sending the teenager to a tool and dye shop in Germany.

Chuck Knight's boyhood lessons paid off in the sense that he sets tough standards for employees and runs tight operations. His quick-changing temper, however, can be a problem for company employees. Stories circulate throughout the company about Knight's tongue lashings and door slamming. "He's tough as nails and he's demanding, but it's always about business and never personal," says Albert E. Suter, the chief administrative officer at Emerson. Suter remembers watching Knight dressing down an ill-prepared manager. "But later, he put his arm around him and gave him a pep talk."

At 64, Knight plans to end his career in the near future. For the past three years, he and Emerson's board have been searching for a successor. Knight says that the process at Emerson has always been more important than the person occupying the position. Also, Knight is in no hurry. "The board has not pressured me," he says. And as long as the consistent pattern of earnings keeps up, it's not likely it will.

Source: Darnell Little, "A Knight Who Is Not Errant," *Business Week,* July 24, 2000, p. 80; http://www.emersonelectric.com/about_emhistory.htm.

EXHIBIT 1-5

The Seventeen Managerial Roles

Planning
1. Strategic planner
2. Operational planner

Organizing and Staffing
3. Organizer
4. Liaison
5. Staffing coordinator
6. Resource allocator
7. Task delegator

Leading
8. Figurehead

9. Spokesperson
10. Negotiator
11. Coach
12. Team builder
13. Team player
14. Technical problem solver
15. Entrepreneur

Controlling
16. Monitor
17. Disturbance handler

Planning

Two managerial roles—strategic planner and operational planner—relate to the planning function.

1. *Strategic Planner.* Top-level managers engage in strategic planning, usually assisted by input from others throughout the organization. Specific activities in this role include (a) setting a direction for the organization, (b) helping the firm deal with the external environment, and (c) developing corporate policies.

2. *Operational Planner.* Operational plans relate to the day-to-day operation of a company or unit. Two such activities are (a) formulating operating budgets and (b) developing work schedules for the unit supervised. Middle-level managers are heavily involved in operational planning; first-level managers are involved to a lesser extent.

Organizing and Staffing

Five roles that relate to the organizing and staffing function are organizer, liaison, staffing coordinator, resource allocator, and task delegator.

3. *Organizer.* As a pure organizer, the manager emerges in activities such as (a) designing the jobs of group members; (b) clarifying group members' assignments; (c) explaining organizational policies, rules, and procedures; and (d) establishing policies, rules, and procedures to coordinate the flow of work and information within the unit.

4. *Liaison.* The purpose of the liaison role is to develop and maintain a network of work-related contacts with people. To achieve this end, the manager (a) cultivates relationships with clients or customers; (b) maintains relationships with suppliers, customers, and other persons or groups important to the unit or organization; (c) joins boards, organizations, or public service clubs that might provide useful, work-related contacts; and (d) cultivates and maintains a personal network of in-house contacts through visits, telephone calls, e-mail, and participation in company-sponsored events.

5. *Staffing Coordinator.* In the staffing role, the manager tries to make sure that competent people fill positions. Specific activities include (a) recruiting and hiring staff; (b) explaining to group members how their work performance

will be evaluated; (c) formally evaluating group members' overall job performance; (d) compensating group members within the limits of organizational policy; (e) ensuring that group members are properly trained; (f) promoting group members or recommending them for promotion; and (g) terminating or demoting group members.

6. *Resource Allocator.* An important part of a manager's job is to divide resources in the manner that best helps the organization. Specific activities to this end include (a) authorizing the use of physical resources (facilities, furnishings, and equipment); (b) authorizing the expenditure of financial resources; and (c) discontinuing the use of unnecessary, inappropriate, or ineffective equipment or services.

7. *Task Delegator.* A standard part of any manager's job is assigning tasks to group members. Among these task-delegation activities are (a) assigning projects or tasks to group members; (b) clarifying priorities and performance standards for task completion; and (c) ensuring that group members are properly committed to effective task performance.

Leading

Eight identified managerial roles relate to the leadership function. These roles are figurehead, spokesperson, negotiator, coach, team builder, team player, technical problem solver, and entrepreneur.

8. *Figurehead.* Figurehead managers, particularly high-ranking ones, spend some of their time engaging in ceremonial activities or acting as a figurehead. Such activities include (a) entertaining clients or customers as an official representative of the organization, (b) being available to outsiders as a representative of the organization, (c) serving as an official representative of the organization at gatherings outside the organization, and (d) escorting official visitors.

9. *Spokesperson.* When a manager acts as a spokesperson, the emphasis is on answering inquiries and formally reporting to individuals and groups outside the manager's organizational unit. As a spokesperson, the manager keeps five groups of people informed about the unit's activities, plans, and capabilities. These groups are (a) upper-level management, (b) clients and customers, (c) other important outsiders (such as labor unions), (d) professional colleagues, and (e) the general public. Usually, top-level managers take responsibility for keeping outside groups informed.

10. *Negotiator.* Part of almost any manager's job is trying to make deals with others for needed resources. Three specific negotiating activities are (a) bargaining with supervisors for funds, facilities, equipment, or other forms of support, (b) bargaining with other units in the organization for the use of staff, facilities, and other forms of support; and (c) bargaining with suppliers and vendors about services, schedules, and delivery times.

11. *Coach.* An effective manager takes time to coach group members. Specific behaviors in this role include (a) informally recognizing employee achievements; (b) offering encouragement and reassurance, thereby showing active concern about the professional growth of group members; (c) providing feedback about ineffective performance; and (d) giving group members advice on steps to improve their performance.

12. *Team Builder.* A key aspect of a manager's role is to build an effective team. Activities contributing to this role include (a) ensuring that group members

are recognized for their accomplishments (by issuing letters of appreciation, for example); (b) initiating activities that contribute to group morale, such as giving parties and sponsoring sports teams; and (c) holding periodic staff meetings to encourage group members to talk about their accomplishments, problems, and concerns.

13. *Team Player.* Three behaviors of the team player are (a) displaying appropriate personal conduct, (b) cooperating with other units in the organization, and (c) displaying loyalty to superiors by fully supporting their plans and decisions.

14. *Technical Problem Solver.* It is particularly important for first- and middle-level managers to help group members solve technical problems. Two such specific activities related to problem solving are (a) serving as a technical expert or advisor and (b) performing individual contributor tasks, such as making sales calls or fixing software problems on a regular basis. The managers most in demand today are those who combine a technical specialty with knowledge of other areas.

15. *Entrepreneur.* Managers who work in large organizations have some responsibility for suggesting innovative ideas or furthering the business aspects of the firm. Three entrepreneurial role activities are (a) reading trade publications and professional journals and searching the Internet to keep up to date; (b) talking with customers or others in the organization to keep abreast of changing needs and requirements; and (c) getting involved in activities outside the unit that could result in performance improvements within the manager's unit. These activities might include visiting other firms, attending professional meetings or trade shows, and participating in educational programs.

Controlling

One role, that of monitor, fits the controlling function precisely, because the term *monitoring* is often used as a synonym for *controlling*. The role of disturbance handler is categorized under controlling because it involves changing an unacceptable condition to an acceptable stable condition.

16. *Monitor.* The activities of a monitor are (a) developing systems that measure or monitor the unit's overall performance, (b) using management information systems to measure productivity and cost, (c) talking with group members about progress on assigned tasks, and (d) overseeing the use of equipment and facilities (for example, telephones and office space) to ensure that they are properly used and maintained.

17. *Disturbance Handler.* Four typical activities of a disturbance handler are (a) participating in grievance resolution within the unit (working out a problem with a labor union, for example); (b) resolving complaints from customers, other units, and superiors; (c) resolving conflicts among group members; and (d) resolving problems about work flow and information exchange with other units. Disturbance handling might also be considered a leadership role.

Managerial Roles Currently Emphasized

Managerial work has shifted substantially away from the controller and director role to that of coach, facilitator, and supporter. As reflected in the position of team leader, many managers today deemphasize formal authority and rank. Instead, they work as partners with team members to jointly achieve results. Managers today emphasize horizontal relationships and deemphasize vertical (top-down) relationships. Exhibit 1-6 presents a stereotype of the difference between the role of the modern and the traditional manager. We encourage you not to think that traditional (old) managers are evil, while new managers are good.

The Influence of Management Level on Managerial Roles

A manager's level of responsibility influences which roles he or she is likely to engage in most frequently, as shown in Exhibit 1-3 and 1-4. (Recall that roles are really subsets of functions.)

Information about the influence of level on roles comes from research conducted with 228 managers in a variety of private-sector service firms (such as banks and insurance companies) and manufacturing firms. The roles studied were basically those described in this chapter. One clear-cut finding was that, at the higher levels of management, four roles were the most important: liaison, spokesperson, figurehead, and strategic planner. Another finding was that the role of leader is critical at the first level of management.[8]

FIVE KEY MANAGERIAL SKILLS

4

To be effective, managers need to possess technical, interpersonal, conceptual, diagnostic, and political skills. The sections that follow will first define these skills and then comment on how they are developed. Whatever the level of management, a manager needs a combination of all five skills.

Identify the basic managerial skills and understand how they can be developed.

Technical Skill

Technical skill involves an understanding of and proficiency in a specific activity that involves methods, processes, procedures, or techniques. Technical skills include the ability to prepare a budget, lay out a production schedule, prepare a

Old Manager	New Manager
Thinks of self as manager or boss	Thinks of self as sponsor, team leader, or internal consultant
Follows the chain of command	Deals with anyone necessary to get the job done
Works within a set organizational structure	Changes organizational structures in response to market change
Makes most decisions alone	Invites others to join in decision making
Hoards information	Shares information
Tries to master one major discipline, such as marketing or finance	Tries to master a broad array of managerial disciplines
Demands long hours	Demands results
Manages group members	Works for group members

EXHIBIT 1-6

Traditional versus Modern Managerial Roles

"Old" managers and "new" managers see things differently.

Source: Adapted from Brian Dumaine, "The New Non-Managers," *Fortune,* February 22, 1991, p. 81; Joe McGavin, "You're a Good Manager If You . . ." *Manager's Edge,* September 1998, p. 7; "Control Is Not Leadership," *Executive Leadership,* November 2000, p. 1.

spreadsheet analysis, and demonstrate a piece of electronic equipment. A well-developed technical skill can facilitate the rise into management. For example, Bill Gates of Microsoft Corp. launched his career by being a competent programmer.

Interpersonal Skill

Interpersonal (or human relations) skill is a manager's ability to work effectively as a team member and to build cooperative effort in the unit. Interpersonal skills are more important than technical skills in getting to the top. Communication skills are an important component of interpersonal skills. They form the basis for sending and receiving messages on the job.

Many managers at all levels ultimately fail because their interpersonal skills do not match the demands of the job. Have you ever worked for a manager who was so rude and insensitive that he or she damaged morale and productivity? Douglas Ivester, formerly the Chairman and CEO at Coca-Cola Corporation, is an example of a manager whose poor interpersonal skills ultimately contributed to his downfall. (A slide in the sale of Coca-Cola products also facilitated Ivester's resignation.) Although he possessed expert financial skills, Ivester was accused of being overcontrolling, inflexible, and rude toward employees and customers. One example of insensitivity took place after dozens of Belgian school-children became ill after drinking Coke products. Ivester maintained what appeared to be an arrogant silence for more than a week before visiting Belgium to apologize.[9]

An important subset of interpersonal skills for managers is **multiculturalism**, or the ability to work effectively and conduct business with people from different cultures. Closely related is the importance of bilingualism for managers as well as other workers. Being able to converse in a second language represents an important asset in today's global and multicultural work environment.

multiculturalism

The ability to work effectively and conduct business with people from different cultures.

Conceptual Skill

Conceptual skill is the ability to see the organization as a total entity. It includes recognizing how the various units of the organization depend on one another and how changes in any one part affect all the others. It also includes visualizing the relationship of the individual business to the industry; the community; and the political, social, and economic forces of the nation as a whole. For top-level management, conceptual skill is a priority because executive managers have the most contact with the outside world.

Conceptual skill continues to increase in importance for managers as today's business environment forces them to rethink substantially how work is performed. For example, many organizations are shifting away from departments and toward processes. Instead of a group of specialists performing work under the direction of an authoritarian manager, people work together in teams as generalists.

Drucker emphasizes that the only comparative advantage of the developed countries is in the number of knowledge workers (people who work primarily with concepts). Educated workers in underdeveloped countries are just as smart as those in developed countries, but their numbers are smaller. According to Drucker and many other authorities, the need for knowledge workers and conceptual knowledge will continue to grow.[10]

Diagnostic Skill

Managers are frequently called on to investigate a problem and then to decide on and implement a remedy. Diagnostic skill often requires other skills, because managers need to use technical, human, conceptual, or political skills to solve the problems they diagnose. Much of the potential excitement in a manager's job centers on getting to the root of problems and recommending solutions. An office supervisor, for example, might attempt to understand why productivity has not increased in his office despite the installation of the latest office technology.

Political Skill

An important part of being effective is the ability to obtain power and prevent others from taking it away. Managers use political skill to acquire the power necessary to reach objectives. Other political skills include establishing the right connections and impressing the right people. Furthermore, managers high in political skill possess an astute understanding of people, along with a fundamental belief that they can control the outcomes of their interactions with people. This feeling of mastery often reduces the stress associated with interacting with people.[11]

Political skill should be regarded as a supplement to job competence and the other basic skills. Managers who overemphasize political skill at the expense of doing work of substance focus too much on pleasing company insiders and advancing their own careers. Too much time invested in office politics takes time away from dealing with customer problems and improving productivity.

DEVELOPMENT OF MANAGERIAL SKILLS

This text is based on the assumption that managerial skills can be learned. Education for management begins in school and continues in the form of training and development programs throughout a career. Examples of such programs include a seminar about how to be an effective leader or a workshop about e-commerce.

Developing most managerial skills is more complex than developing structured skills such as computing a return on investment ratio or retrieving e-mail messages. Nevertheless, you can develop managerial skills by studying this text and doing the exercises, which follow a general learning model:

1. *Conceptual knowledge and behavioral guidelines.* Each chapter in this text presents useful information about the practice of management, including step-by-step procedures for a method of group decision making called the nominal group technique.
2. *Conceptual information demonstrated by examples.* Brief descriptions of managers and professionals in action, including small-business owners, are presented throughout the text.
3. *Skill-development exercises.* The text provides an opportunity for practice and personalization through cases and self-assessment exercises. Self-quizzes are included because they are an effective method of helping you personalize the information.
4. *Feedback on skill utilization, or performance, from others.* Feedback exercises appear at several places in the text. Implementing some of these managerial skills outside of the classroom will provide additional opportunities for feedback.

Experience is obviously important in developing management skills. Yet experience is likely to be more valuable if it is enhanced with education. Take an analogy to soccer. A person learning soccer might read and watch on video the proper way to kick a soccer ball. With this education behind her she now kicks the ball with the side of her foot instead of toe first. She becomes a competent kicker by combining education and experience. People often make such statements as "You can't learn to be a manager (or leader) from a book." However, you can learn managerial concepts from a book, or lecture, and then apply them. People who move vertically in their careers usually have both education and experience in management techniques.

A key reason for continuing to develop managerial skills is that the manager's job is more demanding than ever, and the workplace keeps changing. A recent analysis states that managers today are being promoted faster and at younger ages than ever. A manager is likely to work in an intense, pressure-filled environment requiring many skills. Companies forced to keep up with competition are driving the demand for managers with updated skills. Rapid changes, such as developing an e-commerce presence, require managers to continually develop new skills.[12]

5 | THE EVOLUTION OF MANAGEMENT THOUGHT

Identify the major developments in the evolution of management thought, along with several best management practices.

Management as a practice has an almost unlimited history. Visualize a group of prehistoric people attempting to develop a device that would help transport heavy objects. Given a modern label, the caveperson suggesting this development is the head of product research and development. The project of building the curious new circular device was turned over to a group of people who had hands-on access to raw material. Because the developers of the wheel did not constitute a business enterprise, they handed over the technology of the wheel to all interested parties. Also, in prehistoric times, patents were not available.

Management as a formal study, in comparison to a practice, began in the 1700s as part of the Industrial Revolution. Here we take a brief historical look at management, covering both historical developments and various approaches to understanding it. The anchor points to our discussion are as follows:

1. Classical approach (scientific management and administrative management)
2. The human resources approach
3. Quantitative approaches to management
4. The systems perspective
5. The contingency approach
6. The information technology approach

All of these approaches are mentioned briefly here, but also appear in later sections of the book. For example, the study of leadership and motivation stems from both the classical and human resources approaches. The historical approaches laid the foundation for understanding and practicing management.

Classical Approach to Management

The study of management became more systematized and formal as a by-product of the Industrial Revolution that took place from the 1700s through the 1900s. The classical approach to management encompasses scientific management and administrative management.

The focus of **scientific management** was on the application of scientific methods to increase individual workers' productivity. An example would be

scientific management

The application of scientific methods to increase individual workers' productivity.

assembling a washing machine with the least number of wasted motions and steps. Frederick W. Taylor, considered the father of scientific management, was an engineer by background. He used scientific analysis and experiments to increase workers' ouputs. Other key contributors to scientific management were Henry Gantt and Frank and Lillian Gilbreth. (Gantt charts for scheduling activities are still used today.)

Administrative management was concerned primarily with how organizations should be managed and structured. The French businessman Henri Fayol and the German scholar Max Weber were the main contributors to administrative management. Based on his practical experience, Fayol developed 14 management principles through which management engaged in planning, organizing, commanding, coordinating, and controlling. Weber suggested that bureaucracy is the best form of organization, because it makes highly efficient management practices possible.

The core of management knowledge lies within the classical school. As its key contributions it studies management from the framework of planning, organizing, leading, and controlling—the framework chosen in this text. The classical school provides a systematic way of managing people and work that has proven useful over time and represents its major strength. Its major limitation is that it sometimes ignores differences among people and situations. For example, some of the classical principles for developing an organization are not well suited to fast-changing situations.

The Human Resources Approach

The **human resources approach to management** emphasizes improving management through the psychological makeup of people. In contrast to the largely technical emphasis of scientific management, a common theme of the human resources approach focuses on the need to understand people. The human resources (or behavioral) approach has profoundly influenced management, and a portion of this book is based on behavioral theory. Typical human resource topics include leadership, motivation, communication, teamwork, and conflict.

The most direct origins of the human resources approach are set in the 1930s through the 1950s. Yet earlier scholars, such as Robert Owen and Mary Parker Follett, also wrote about the importance of the human element. Working in the textile industry in Scotland in the early 1800s, Owen criticized fellow managers for failing to understand the human element in the mills. He contended that showing concern for workers resulted in greater profitability while at the same time reducing hardship for workers. Owen reported that efforts to pay careful attention to the human element often resulted in a 50 percent return on his investment.[13]

Follett focused her attention on the importance of groups in managing people. Although she published her works during the period of scientific management, Follett did not share Taylor's view that organizations should be framed around the work of individuals. In contrast, she argued that groups were the basis on which organizations should be formed. Follett explained that, to enhance productivity and morale, managers should coordinate and aid the efforts of work groups.[14]

Three cornerstones of the human resources approach are the Hawthorne studies, Theory X and Theory Y, and Maslow's need hierarchy. These developments contributed directly to managers' understanding of the importance of human relations on the job. Yet again, practicing managers have probably always

administrative management
The use of management principles in the structuring and managing of an organization.

human resources approach to management
A perspective on management that emphasizes managing people by understanding their psychological makeup and needs.

known about the importance of human relations. The prehistoric person who developed the wheel probably received a congratulatory pat on the back from another member of the tribe!

The Hawthorne Studies

The purpose of the first study conducted at the Hawthorne plant of Western Electric (an AT&T subsidiary located in Cicero, Illinois) was to determine the effects of changes in lighting on productivity.[15] In this study, workers were divided into an experimental group and a control group. Lighting conditions for the experimental group varied in intensity from 24 to 46 to 70 footcandles. The lighting for the control group remained constant.

As expected, the experimental group's output increased with each increase in light intensity. But unexpectedly, the performance of the control group also changed. The production of the control group increased at about the same rate as that of the experimental group. Later, the lighting in the experimental group's area was reduced. The group's output continued to increase, as did that of the control group. A decline in the productivity of the control group finally did occur, but only when the intensity of the light was roughly the same as moonlight. Clearly, the researchers reasoned, something other than illumination caused the changes in productivity.

An experiment was then conducted in the relay assembly test room over a period of six years, with similar results. In this case, relationships among rest, fatigue, and productivity were examined. First, normal productivity was established with no formal rest periods, and a 48-hour week. Rest periods of varying length and frequency were then introduced. Productivity increased as the frequency and length of rest periods increased. Finally, the original conditions were reinstated. The return to the original conditions, however, did not result in the expected productivity drop. Instead, productivity remained at the same high level.

One interpretation of these results was that the workers involved in the experiment enjoyed being the center of attention. Workers reacted positively because management cared about them. The phenomenon is referred to as the **Hawthorne effect.** It is the tendency of people to behave differently when they receive attention because they respond to the demands of the situation. In a work setting, employees perform better when they are part of any program, whether or not that program is valuable. Another useful lesson learned from the Hawthorne studies is that effective communication with workers is critical to managerial success.

Hawthorne effect

The phenomenon in which people behave differently in response to perceived attention from evaluators.

Theory X and Theory Y of Douglas McGregor

A widely quoted development of the human resources approach is Douglas McGregor's analysis of the assumptions managers make about human nature.[16] Theory X is a set of traditional assumptions about people. Managers who hold these assumptions are pessimistic about workers' capabilities. They believe that workers dislike work, seek to avoid responsibility, are not ambitious, and must be supervised closely. McGregor urged managers to challenge these assumptions about human nature because they are untrue in most circumstances.

Theory Y, the alternative, poses an optimistic set of assumptions. These assumptions include the idea that people do accept responsibility, can exercise self-control, possess the capacity to innovate, and consider work to be as natural as rest or play. McGregor argued that these assumptions accurately describe human nature in far more situations than most managers believe. He therefore proposed that these assumptions should guide managerial practice.

Maslow's Need Hierarchy

Most readers are already familiar with the need hierarchy developed by psychologist Abraham Maslow. This topic will be presented in Chapter 12 in discussions about motivation. Maslow suggested that humans are motivated by efforts to satisfy a hierarchy of needs, ranging from basic needs to those for self-actualization, or reaching one's potential. The need hierarchy prompted managers to think about ways of satisfying a wide range of worker needs to keep them motivated.

The primary strength of the human resources approach is that it encourages managers to take into account the human element. Many valuable methods of motivating employees are based on behavioral research. The primary weakness of the human resources approach is that it sometimes leads to an oversimplified view of managing people. Managers sometimes adopt one behavioral theory and ignore other relevant information. For example, several theories of motivation pay too little attention to the importance of money in people's thinking.

Quantitative Approaches to Management

The **quantitative approach to management** is a perspective on management that emphasizes the use of a group of methods in managerial decision making, based on the scientific method. Today, the quantitative approach is often referred to as management science or operations research (OR). Frequently used quantitative tools and techniques include statistics, linear programming, network analysis, decision trees, and computer simulations. These tools and techniques can be used when making decisions regarding inventory control, plant-site locations, quality control, and a range of other decisions where objective information is important. Several quantitative approaches to decision making are found in Chapter 6 (planning) and Chapter 7 (problem solving and decision making).

Frederick Taylor's work provided the foundation for the quantitative approach to management. However, the impetus for the modern-day quantitative approach was the formation of operations research teams to solve a range of problems faced by the Allied forces during World War II. Examples of the problems considered by the OR team included the bombing of enemy targets, the effective conduct of submarine warfare, and the efficient movement of troops from one location to another. Following World War II, many industrial applications were found for quantitative approaches to management. The approach was facilitated by the increasing use of computers. A representative problem tackled by a quantitative approach to management would be to estimate the effect of a change in the price of a product on the product's market share.

The primary strength of the quantitative approach to management is that it enables managers to solve complex problems that cannot be solved by common sense alone. For example, management science techniques are used to make forecasts that take into account hundreds of factors simultaneously. A weakness of management science is that the answers it produces are often less precise than they appear. Although quantitative approaches use precise methods, much of the data is based on human estimates, which can be unreliable.

The Systems Perspective

The **systems perspective** is a way of viewing problems more than it is a specific approach to management. It is based on the concept that an organization is a

quantitative approach to management

A perspective on management that emphasizes use of a group of methods in managerial decision making, based on the scientific method.

systems perspective

A way of viewing aspects of an organization as an interrelated system.

19

system, or an entity of interrelated parts. If you adjust one part of the system, other parts will be affected automatically. For example, suppose you offer low compensation to job candidates. According to the systems approach, your action will influence your product quality. The "low-quality" employees who are willing to accept low wages will produce low-quality goods. Exhibit 1-2, which showed the process of management, reflected a systems viewpoint.

Another aspect of systems theory is to regard the organization as an open system, one that interacts with the environment. As illustrated in Exhibit 1-7, the organization transforms inputs into outputs and supplies them to the outside world. If these outputs are perceived as valuable, the organization will survive and prosper. The feedback loop indicates that the acceptance of outputs by society gives the organization new inputs for revitalization and expansion. Managers can benefit from this diagram by recognizing that whatever work they undertake should contribute something of value to external customers and clients.

Two other influential concepts from the systems perspective are entropy and synergy. **Entropy** is the tendency of a system to run down and die if it does not receive fresh inputs from its environment. As indicated in Exhibit 1-7, the organization must continually receive inputs from the outside world to make sure it stays in tune with, or ahead of, the environment. **Synergy** means that the whole is greater than the sum of the parts. When the various parts of an organization work together, they can produce much more than they could working independently. For example, a few years ago product developers at Chrysler Corporation (before the merger with Daimler) thought about building a combination sedan and van called the PT Cruiser. The developers consulted immediately with manufacturing, engineering, purchasing, and dealers to discuss the feasibility of their idea. Working together, the units of the organization produced a highly successful product launch in a tightly competitive market.

The Contingency Approach

The **contingency approach to management** emphasizes that there is no single best way to manage people or work in every situation. A method that leads to high productivity or morale under one set of circumstances may not achieve the same results in another. The contingency approach is derived from the study of leadership and organization structures. With respect to leadership, psychologists developed detailed explanations of which style of leadership would work best in

entropy

A concept of the systems approach to management that states that an organization will die without continuous input from the outside environment.

synergy

A concept of the systems approach to management that states that the whole organization working together will produce more than the parts working independently.

contingency approach to management

A perspective on management that emphasizes that no single way to manage people or work is best in every situation. It encourages managers to study individual and situational differences before deciding on a course of action.

EXHIBIT 1-7

A Systems View of Organization

A systems perspective keeps the manager focused on the external environment.

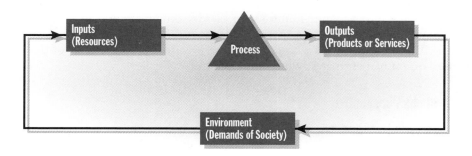

20

which situation. An example would be for the manager to give more leeway to competent group members. Also, the study of organization structure suggests that some structures work better in different environments such as a team structure being best for a rapidly changing environment. Common sense also contributes heavily to the contingency approach. Experienced managers know that not all people and situations respond identically to identical situations. The contingency approach is emphasized throughout this book.

The strength of the contingency approach is that it encourages managers to examine individual and situational differences before deciding on a course of action. Its major problem is that it is often used as an excuse for not acquiring formal knowledge about management. If management depends on the situation, why study management theory? The answer is because a formal study of management helps a manager decide which factors are relevant in a given situation.

The Information Technology Era

The information technology era had relatively modest beginnings in the 1950s with the use of electronic data processing to take over the manual processing of large batches of data and numbers. By the late 1980s, the impact of information technology and the Internet began to influence how managers manage work and people. A recent report by two economists concluded that the impact of the Internet on business is similar to the impact of electricity at the beginning of the twentieth century.[17] Can you visualize what it must have been like to work in an office or factory without electricity?

The impact of information technology and the Internet on the work of managers is so vast that it receives separate attention in Chapter 3. Information technology modified managerial work in the following ways:

- Managers often communicate with people, even sending layoff notices, by e-mail rather than by telephone or in person.
- Many managers organize their sales and marketing efforts differently by using the Internet to conduct most transactions.
- Managers run their organizations more democratically because through e-mail they receive input from so many workers at different levels in the organization.

Best Management Practices

Be careful not to dismiss the evolution of management thought with historical information that is no longer relevant. Practicing managers can use all six major developments in management thought. An astute manager selects information from the various schools of thought to achieve good results in a given situation. Visualize Dave Lilly making siteROCK more efficient and effective. He relied on the classical school of management in implementing highly systematic procedures for repairing Web sites. At the same time his initiatives to build teamwork reflect the human resources approach to management.

To give you a preliminary idea of what outstanding managers are doing these days to manage people and organize work, see Exhibit 1-8. All of these practices will be covered at various points in the text.

EXHIBIT 1-8

Eight Key Managerial Practices of Successful Organizations

1. **Employment security.** Workers do not feel a constant threat of being downsized or fired for flimsy reasons.

2. **High standards in selecting personnel.** The company attracts a large number of applicants and strives to find highly qualified candidates for all positions.

3. **Extensive use of self-managed teams and decentralized decision making.** Workers are organized into teams with the authority to make decisions. Managers throughout the company can make many decisions independently.

4. **Comparatively high compensation based on performance.** Paying employees better than the competition leads to success, as does paying employees based on their own performance or that of the department or company.

5. **Extensive employee training.** The most successful companies invest in training as a matter of faith, because they believe that a well-trained workforce contributes to profits in the long run.

6. **Reduction of status differences between higher management and other employees.** Successful firms take steps to deemphasize status differences among individuals and groups that make some people feel less valued. Examples include calling everyone an "associate" and decreasing differences in compensation among levels of workers.

7. **Information sharing among managers and other workers.** Sharing information about such matters as financial performance and company plans helps build trust among employees. Having ready access to useful information also helps many workers perform their job better.

8. **Promotion from within.** Loyalty is enhanced when employees believe that they have a shot at being promoted to good jobs within the company.

Source: Adapted from Jeffrey Pfeffer, *The Human Equation* (Boston: Harvard Business School Press, 1998), pp. 64–98; Pfeffer, "Producing Sustainable Competitive Advantage through the Effective Management of People," *Academy of Management Executive,* February 1995, pp. 64–65.

SUMMARY OF KEY POINTS

To facilitate your study and review of this and the remaining chapters, the summaries are organized around the learning objectives.

1 **Explain what the term *manager* means, and identify different types of managers.** A manager is a person responsible for work performance of other people. Management is the process of using organizational resources to achieve specific objectives through the functions of planning, organizing and staffing, leading, and controlling. Organizational levels consist of top-level managers, middle-level managers, first-level managers, and individual contributors. Categories of managers include functional managers (who deal with specialties within the firm) and general managers, administrators (typically managers in nonprofit firms), entrepreneurs (those who start innovative businesses), small-business owners, and team leaders.

2 **Describe the process of management, including the functions of management.** To accomplish organizational goals, managers use resources and carry out the basic management functions. Resources are divided into four categories: human, financial, physical, and informational. Top-level managers emphasize high-level planning, whereas first-level managers concentrate on person-to-person leadership. Executives place more emphasis on monitoring the environment than do managers in the other two levels.

3 **Describe the various managerial roles.** The work of a manager can be divided into 17 roles that relate to the four major functions. Planning roles include strategic planner and operational planner. Organizing and staffing calls for the organizer, liaison, staffing coordinator, resource allocator, and task delegator roles. Leading roles include figurehead, spokesperson, negotiator, coach, team builder, team player, technical problem solver, and entrepreneur. Controlling involves the monitor and disturbance handling roles. Managerial work has shifted substantially away from the controller and director role to that of coach, facilitator, and supporter. Top-level managers occupy more external roles than do lower-ranking managers.

4 **Identify the basic managerial skills and understand how they can be developed.** Managers need interpersonal, conceptual, diagnostic, and political skills to accomplish their jobs. An effective way of developing managerial skills is to follow a general learning model. The model involves conceptual knowledge, behavioral guidelines, following examples, skill development exercises, and feedback. Management skills are also acquired through a combination of education and experience.

5 **Identify the major developments in the evolution of management thought, along with several best man-** **agement practices.** Management practice has an almost unlimited history, whereas the formal study of management began as part of the Industrial Revolution. The major developments in management thought and the history of management are (1) the classical approach (scientific management and administrative management); (2) the human resources approach; (3) quantitative approaches to management; (4) the systems approach; (5) the contingency approach; and (6) the information technology era. The best practices of managers today include elements of the six major developments in management thought.

KEY TERMS AND PHRASES

Manager, *2*

Management, *2*

Top-level managers, *2*

Middle-level managers, *3*

First-level managers, *3*

Entrepreneur, *5*

Small-business owner, *5*

Team leader, *5*

Role, *8*

Multiculturalism, *14*

Scientific management, *16*

Administrative management, *17*

Human resources approach to management, *17*

Hawthorne effect, *18*

Quantitative approach to management, *19*

Systems perspective, *19*

Entropy, *20*

Synergy, *20*

Contingency approach to management, *20*

QUESTIONS

Here, as in other chapters, the questions and cases can be analyzed by groups or individuals. We strongly recommend using some small-group discussion to enhance learning.

1. Define the term *manager* . How is it defined in this chapter? What would you add or delete if creating your own definition?

2. Why are top-level managers in business firms often paid as much as professional athletes and movie stars, with many executives being paid more than $10 million per year?

3. In recent years, many employers seek out technically trained job candidates who also have studied manage-

ment. What advantages do you think employers see in a technical person studying management?

4. Why might the role of the "new" manager require a higher level of interpersonal skill than that required by the "old" manager?

5. Why do large companies encourage many of their employees to "think like entrepreneurs"?

6. During weather emergencies, such as a severe ice storm, some companies send out an alert that only "essential" employees should report to work. Explain why managers should or should not stay home on such emergency days.

7. How do students use the four management functions to accomplish their goal of graduating?

CRITICAL THINKING QUESTIONS

1. What is the average total compensation of top-level managers in the top 50 U.S. firms? (*Business Week* and *Fortune* are excellent sources of this information.) What do your results suggest about the value of top executives in our society?

2. Why is "management" regarded by some people as an essential life skill?

SKILL-BUILDING EXERCISE 1-A: Identifying Managerial Roles

Interview a manager at any level in any organization, including a retail store or restaurant. Determine which of the 17 managerial roles the manager you interview thinks apply to his or her job. Find out which one or two roles the manager thinks are the most important. Be ready to discuss your findings in class.

SKILL-BUILDING EXERCISE 1-B: Managerial Skills for Conducting a Project

Form a group of about six students. Your task is to plan a substantial project such as developing an e-business or creating a fund-raising campaign. Include both general and specific tasks necessary to achieve your goals. As you formulate your plans, identify the managerial skills you will need to accomplish the work. For each skill you mention, provide a specific example of why the skill is necessary. For instance, in developing an Internet business you will need the technical competence to work your way through the system. You will also need interpersonal skills to attract the right employees and motivate them.

INTERNET SKILL-BUILDING EXERCISE: Quality of Management

Visit the Web sites of three well-known companies such as GE, Microsoft, or Hewlett-Packard (HP). A quick way to find the Web sites of many companies is to simply put www before the company name, and .com after, such as www.ge.com. Through the Web site, uncover whatever information you can about the quality of the company's management. See whether you can dig up information about the education of the executive team, human resource practices (such as the type of employee benefits), profitability, and so forth. You might find some revealing information by visiting the section of the site reserved for employee recruitment. Write a two-paragraph summary of your evaluation of the quality of management in each company.

CASE PROBLEM 1-A: J. C. Penney Chief Plans a Running Start

Three months into his job at J. C. Penney Co., Allen Questrom delivers a spiel and he is sticking to it. It's the Questrom way: Dole out the broad vision and repeat it until everyone gets it right. He was giving Penney employees two to five years to turn the ship around. He doesn't plan to do it alone. He is not making any guarantees, but he's comfortable being captain.

"A business isn't run by one person. It's run by teams," said Penney's chairman and chief executive officer during an interview at the company's Plano, Texas, headquarters. "My job is to set the objectives and get people to understand them and execute them." He is asking employees who are helping to rebuild the Penney organization to rethink everything. A major challenge Questrom faces is that some critics think that Penney's fashions are tired and its prices too high.

Questrom joined Penney in September from Barneys New York, but is best known for his long tenure at Federated Department stores. He brought that company out of bankruptcy and acquired the Macy's and Broadway chains, which gave Federated a strong market share up and down both coasts. The veteran retailer has been charming employees, customers, and creditors for years. Particularly impressive has been his ability to turn around prestigious stores that fell on hard times. In addition to Federated, Questrom helped revive Neiman Marcus and Barneys.

Questrom says he believes in the J. C. Penney brand and he is trying to get back to Penney's roots as the department store of choice for middle-income Americans. (Penney also owns the Eckerd drugstore chain.) But he is not sentimental, nor is he wedded to ideas that do not work. In November 2000, Penney reported its first loss from operations in the history of the company. The retailer, which is almost 100 years old, is being called a dinosaur. Questrom has this to say about the task he faces:

I spend time thinking about getting this company in order. What difference does it make if it's 100 or 10 or 20? What's meaningful to me is whether our stores are current. I would like this company to be successful on its 100th anniversary. I've only been here a few months, and I see a very loyal but an unhappy group of people.

Questrom says the only way to boost morale is to start making money again. Profit will take care of the stock price as well. Penney's market value has declined to about $3 billion from a peak of $20 billion two years ago. Since the mid-1990s, the retailer lost customers to discount chains such as Target and Wal-Mart and to moderate-priced retailers including Kohl's and Old Navy, as they expanded nationwide. Becoming profitable is going to be painful because it means change, Questrom said. To offer competitive prices to shoppers, the company needs a more competitive cost structure, which means cutting costs.

Questrom said Penney department stores must have the right assortment of merchandise at competitive prices. The only way to do that is to centralize the buying decisions. Headquarters picks and delivers the merchandise, and store personnel focus on running the stores. Penney fell behind its competitors when it failed to centralize sooner, Questrom said. It is no longer efficient to have 1,150 stores each making that many decisions about merchandise. It is slow, expensive, and confusing to the customers. It also prevents the company from developing a national message.

Questrom said that some of the immediacy of having vendors knocking on your door every day was lost when the company moved to Dallas from New York in 1988. "We have to be aware of what's happening in the fashion world and bring that to middle America at great values." He is considering adding offices in New York and Los Angeles to put Penney merchandisers closer to the biggest concentration of vendors.

One of Questrom's first moves was to close 44 of Penney's 1,000 stores and lay off some 5,000 staff, taking a restructuring charge of $275 million. "We're looking at the entire organization and looking at getting rid of things we wouldn't have if we were just starting out as a new company." Another part of Questrom's turnaround plan is to recruit outsiders to key positions to help enliven the Penney corporate culture. He is also remodeling stores to make them less cluttered and better lit. Questrom looks forward to the challenge of helping revive Penney. He says, "I've been involved most of my life in turnaround situations. I look at this as another mountain to climb."

Retail analysts think that the biggest challenge at Penney is to redefine what the brand is about. Questrom emphasizes that the company caters to the broad middle market, where the bulk of consumers are found. Penney's national presence, along with a good catalog and online business are also assets. Analysts at Morningstar.com were particularly harsh about the problems facing Penney and Questrom: "The company's problems are nothing short of humongous, and include an inefficient supply chain, outdated apparel offerings, a stodgy brand name, and a money-losing drugstore operation."

Department stores have not been viewed in the retail industry as a growth business. But even this mature concept can operate in a profitable way, Questrom said. "Federated and May (Department Stores) can grow earnings 12 percent to 15 percent a year, which is a lot more money than the Amazon.coms can do," he said.

Discussion Questions

1. Which managerial functions is Questrom carrying out or planning to carry out?
2. Which managerial roles is Questrom carrying out or planning to carry out?
3. As a personal advisor to Allen Questrom, suggest what you think needs to be done to improve J. C. Penney's market share of the department store business?
4. Based on whatever current information you can locate, how successful has Questrom been in helping make J. C. Penney more profitable?

Source: "Penney's Chief Ready to Rebuild," Knight Ridder, January 2, 2001; Stephanie Anderson, "Can an Outsider Fix J. C. Penney?" *Business Week,* February 12, 2001, pp. 56–58; http://www.jcpenney .com; http://news/Wire/O,12302837,00.html.

CASE PROBLEM 1-B: Managing The Gap

The Gap Inc. has earned the reputation as the most popular and profitable specialty clothing chain in the United States today. Sales at The Gap and its affiliates, GapKids, Banana Republic, and Old Navy, are currently running at close to $11 billion annually. Earnings were $900 million in a recent year. The company currently has about 3,100 stores in five countries. The two top executives at The Gap are president Mickey S. Drexler and its founder and chairman Donald G. Fisher.

The formula behind The Gap's extraordinary success is "good style, good quality, good value." Store sites are carefully selected by Fisher, and each Gap store is clean and well lit. Gap stores make it possible for consumers to shop easily and quickly. The atmosphere at the stores leads employees to fuss over details such as cleaning floors and, at GapKids, rounding the corners of the fixtures to prevent puncture wounds. The company boasts a high-tech distribution system that keeps the Gap outlets stocked with fresh merchandise.

Fisher, regarded as low-key and conservative in personal style, enjoys working on the details of site selection, store construction, and clothing manufacturing. Drexler, in contrast, makes most of the major merchandising decisions.

Several years ago Drexler simplified the way The Gap did business. He replaced executives who relied too heavily on complicated quantitative research. He preferred executives who relied quickly on intuition in selecting merchandise and deciding when to pull slow sellers from the shelves.

Both Drexler and Fisher have pushed heavily for quality. The company has placed its own quality inspectors in many of the manufacturing sites around the world that make clothing for The Gap label. The company designs its own clothing, chooses its own materials, and monitors manufacturing carefully.

At one time Drexler supervised every major design decision, and he still keeps close tabs on design. He characteristically roams around the stores, dropping in unexpectedly on employees to praise or criticize projects in design, advertising, and merchandising. For these reasons, Drexler has been described as a hands-on president.

Drexler devotes considerable time and energy to fixing problems. When Drexler was hired in 1983, The Gap's merchandise wasn't compelling, the stores were drab, and the competition was also selling private labels. Drexler swung into action. He dumped all the private labels except the Gap line. He hired new designers, upgraded the quality of the clothes, and overhauled the appearance of the stores. A retail analyst said, "You really have to give Mickey credit for reinventing the whole company. It was one of the great turnarounds in retail history." Drexler's strategy was to give the store's everyday products a brand image.

Despite impressive successes between 1983 and 1991, new problems arose that required fixing. The competition jumped on The Gap's bandwagon and started selling basics. In 1992, The Gap's stock price dropped by one-half. From that point through 1995, growth was flat. Even Drexler was concerned that the chain was losing its spark, so a new fix was in order. Drexler gambled with a new approach to discount marketing.

The gamble took the form of Old Navy, a trendy discount store with stylish, yet low-priced clothing. Old Navy stores have exposed pipes and raw concrete floors. Some of the clothing is showcased in old grocery-store refrigerator cases that once displayed frozen foods and similar items. T-shirts are shrink-wrapped like packages of ground beef or sausages. Old Navy was an instant success, due in part to a trend whereby it is chic to buy good merchandise at a discount.

To further strengthen The Gap, Drexler decided to make it more like Coca-Cola and McDonald's in terms of omnipresence and large market share. The Gap went on another expansion surge that included Banana Republic, Old Navy, and GapKids. An upstart is Gap-to-Go, with a menu of 21 basic Gap items that can be ordered by fax and delivered to the home or office by the end of the day. Gap Online was another piece of the turnaround.

The management team at The Gap faced new challenges again in 2000. A major problem was a slowdown in sales. Children-oriented clothing at Old Navy stores was selling slower than anticipated. Old Navy stores were drawing customers away from the core Gap stores with lower prices for similar merchandise. Drexler analyzed that The Gap erred by trying to chase down the latest youth fashions. He said to a group of financial analysts, "When we get tricky and young and gimmicky at The Gap we lose." A general slowdown in the economy was hurting Gap, along with most other retailers.

Drexler's strategy is to emphasize a snappy new line of basic jeans, khakis, and shirts—seen by others as a return to Gap's core business. In addition, The Gap planned more clothing suitable for the parents of its major customer group. Another part of Gap's rebound strategy is to keep increasing the number of U.S. stores to about 3,250 by the end of 2001. A fund manager commented about Drexler, "He's turned around Gap before, but I don't know if the charm will hold again this time."

At the beginning of 2001, Drexler also faced the challenge of changing his management team. Six top executives were either released or quit in one year, increasing the workload for the rest of the top managers. Drexler said he was "making appropriate management changes to ensure we have the best talent to lead our business forward." The most controversial aspect of the departures was eliminating the position of the executive vice president and chief operating officer. Drexler took over some of these responsibilities, despite his strengths being concentrated in marketing.

Trend spotters were also concerned about The Gap because it focused on basic clothing while fashion trends, particularly for young people, were moving toward sexier, more glamorous clothing, such as embroidery on jeans. The most stunning criticism of The Gap, including the Banana Republic, is that it combined high prices and unpopular fashions.

Despite these gloomy predictions about The Gap, Drexler has his supporters. For example, Gordon Segal, founder and CEO of Crate & Barrel, said that he would buy Gap stock. Segal contended, "You never bet against a great merchant, and Mickey Drexler is a great merchant."

The changes Drexler has implemented over the years support the grand strategy of making The Gap the Gillette and Coca-Cola of the apparel business.

Discussion Questions

1. Identify the managerial skills of Drexler and Fisher as revealed in the preceding case.
2. Which approaches to management thought are illustrated by the management techniques of the two Gap executives?
3. Which management functions can be identified in the preceding case?
4. Which managerial skills does Drexler emphasize?

Source: Russell Mitchell, "The Gap," *Business Week,* March 9, 1992, pp. 58–64; Nina Monk, "Gap Gets It," *Fortune,* August 3, 1998, pp. 68–82; Louise Lee, "A Widening Gap at the Top," *Business Week,* December 18, 2000, pp. 72–74; Louise Lee, "Can Gap Put It All Together Again?" *Business Week,* August 14, 2000, pp. 58–60.

ENDNOTES

1. Ben Elgin, "Running the Tightest Ships on the Net," *Business Week,* January 29, 2001, p. 125.

2. Peter F. Drucker, *The Frontiers of Management* (New York: Truman Talley Books, Dutton, 1986), p. 1.

3. Andrall E. Pearson, "Six Basics of General Managers," *Harvard Business Review,* July–August 1989, pp. 94–101.

4. Michael H. Morris, *Entrepreneurial Intensity: Sustainable Advantages for Individuals, Organizations, and Societies* (Westport, CT: Quorum Books, 1998).

5. Allen I. Kraut et al., "The Role of the Manager: What's Really Important in Different Management Jobs," *The Academy of Management Executive,* November 1989, pp. 286–293.

6. This research is reported in Henry Mintzberg, *The Nature of Managerial Work* (New York: Harper & Row, 1973).

7. Kenneth Graham, Jr., and William L. Mihal, *The CMI Managerial Job Analysis Inventory* (Rochester, NY: Rochester Institute of Technology, 1987); Jeffrey S. Shippman, Erich Prien, and Gary L. Hughes, "The Content of Management Work: Formation of Task and Job Skill Composite Classifications," *Journal of Business and Psychology,* Spring 1991, pp. 325–354.

8. Cynthia M. Pavett and Alan W. Lau, "Managerial Work: The Influence of Hierarchical Level and Functional Specialty," *Academy of Management Journal,* March 1983, pp. 170–177.

9. John Greenwald, "Springing a Leak," *Time,* December 20, 1999, pp. 80–82.

10. Peter F. Drucker, "The Future Has Already Happened," *Harvard Business Review,* September–October 1997, p. 22.

11. Pamela L. Perrewé et al., "Political Skill: An Antidote for Workplace Stressors," *Academy of Management Executive,* August 2000, p. 120.

12. "Managers Face Greater Demands," Knight Ridder, July 30, 2000.

13. Robert Owen, *A New View of Society* (New York: E. Bliss and F. White, 1825), p. 57.

14. Mary Parker Follett, *The New State: Group Organization of the Solution of Popular Government* (New York: Longmans Green, 1918), p. 28.

15. E. J. Roethlisberger and W. J. Dickson, *Management and the Worker* (Cambridge, MA: Harvard University Press, 1939).

16. Douglas McGregor, *The Human Side of Enterprise* (New York: McGraw-Hill, 1960), pp. 33–57.

17. Martin Brooks and Zakhi Wahhaj, *Is the Internet Better Than Electricity?* Goldman Sachs report cited in Gary Hamel, "Inside the Revolution—Edison's Curse," *Fortune,* March 5, 2001, p. 176.

International Management and Cultural Diversity

Mark Weber has grown accustomed to the German style of working. "There is a much faster pace; things are very much on time," says Weber, an executive at NexPress Solutions LLC, a German-American joint venture. "Decisions are made more quickly, and you have to be in better mental shape. Some people find that unnerving."

Weber, chief operating officer for NexPress, also has become used to Germans turning off the overhead lights and opening the blinds. "In Germany, we are used to open windows," says 30-year-old Judith Metelka, who grew up there and came to New York almost two years ago to work for Heidelberg Digital, which owns half of NexPress along with Eastman Kodak Co. "We are not used to working under air conditioning, going to shopping malls and grocery stores with sealed-in air."[1]

These differences between the U.S. and German work pace and physical environment illustrate a major theme of this chapter. In today's multicultural workplace, successful managers (as well as many other workers) must be able to adapt to the preferences and work styles of people from different cultures. In this situation, an American manager had to adapt to a faster work pace. In many other situations, workers from other cultures must adapt to U.S. customs.

In this chapter we describe major aspects of the international and culturally diverse environment facing managers. Among the topics covered are methods of entry into the global marketplace, success factors in globalization, and the advantages and disadvantages of going global. We also highlight cultural diversity including its competitive advantage and

OBJECTIVES

After studying this chapter and doing the exercises, you should be able to:

1 Appreciate the importance of multinational corporations in international business.

2 Recognize the importance of sensitivity to cultural differences in international enterprise.

3 Identify major challenges facing the global managerial worker.

4 Explain various methods of entry into world markets.

5 Pinpoint success factors in the global marketplace, and several positive and negative aspects of globalization.

6 Describe the scope of diversity and the competitive advantage of a culturally diverse workforce.

7 Summarize organizational practices to encourage diversity.

Chapter 2

the skills required to become a multicultural manager. Globalization and cultural diversity are such major forces in the workplace that they receive some attention throughout our study of management.

1

Appreciate the importance of multinational corporations in international business.

INTERNATIONAL MANAGEMENT

An important environmental influence on the manager's job is the internationalization of business and management. Approximately 10 to 15 percent of all jobs in the United States are dependent upon trade with other countries. In general, as business becomes more global, the manager must adapt to the challenges of working with organizations and people from other countries. Even keeping time zone differences clearly in mind and converting back and forth between the metric and decimal (American) system challenges many people.

The Multinational Corporation

multinational corporation (MNC)

A firm with operating units in two or more countries in addition to its own.

The heart of international trade is the **multinational corporation (MNC)**, a firm with units in two or more countries in addition to its own. An MNC has headquarters in one country and subsidiaries in others. However, it is more than a collection of subsidiaries that carry out decisions made at headquarters. A multinational corporation sometimes hires people from its country of origin (expatriates) for key positions in facilities in other countries. At other times, the MNC will hire citizens of the country in which the division is located (host-country nationals) for key positions.

transnational corporation

A special type of MNC that operates worldwide without having one national headquarters.

The **transnational corporation** is a special type of MNC that operates worldwide without having one national headquarters. The transnational executive thinks in terms of the entire world, rather than looking upon operations in other countries as being "foreign operations." The food giant Nestlé operates throughout the world, yet is registered as a Swiss company.

In the globalization movement, many large companies have merged with each other, leaving a smaller number of competitors in key industries. In the oil sector, Exxon and Mobil merged. In the automotive sector Ford took over the automotive operations of Volvo and Jaguar, along with a few other manufacturers of luxury vehicles. Recent research suggests that these megamergers often fail to meet their expectations in terms of improved efficiency and profits.[2] A glaring example is that the merger of Daimler-Benz and Chrysler contributed to major losses for these companies three years after joining forces.

The accompanying Management in Action illustrates the successful penetration of a well-known multinational corporation into a foreign market. Notice the MNC works closely to help the affiliate rather than simply buying the operation.

Two key issues in international business and management are (1) government agreements about trade, and (2) correctly identifying the company of origin of a manufactured product. The first issue, in particular, has been one of the most challenging for many nations.

Management *in Action*

Kodak Boosts Chinese Film Factory Performance

Workers in Eastman Kodak Co.'s new film-making factory in Xiamen, China, get a lesson in western ways of business every time they open their paychecks. The plant's 1,220 employees receive only 90 percent of their salaries on a regular basis. They have to earn the remaining 10 percent by collectively meeting a series of stiff environmental and performance goals every six months.

The unprecedented pay-for-performance program represents an important building block in the success of Kodak's first new film plant anywhere in more than 30 years. Kodak management says the idea is to inspire creativity, hard work, and cooperation—important attributes because many of the workers came from state-owned enterprises where jobs were virtually guaranteed.

Kodak realized the opportunity to build a new site as part of its 1998 alliance with the Chinese government. The company agreed to purchase majority stakes in and restructure three state-owned photographic enterprises. One of those was Xiamen Fuda Co., a struggling firm that produced China's fourth or fifth best-selling film. Kodak paid more in taxes in the first six months of operations than Fuda had in the previous 14 years, according to city officials. Kodak was allowed by the government to hire only the workers it needed. It gave jobs to about 650 former Fuda employees and then went outside the company to fill the balance of its workforce with other Chinese workers.

A motivated workforce is critical as Kodak seeks to build the Xiamen factory into the main supplier of low-cost consumer film for the burgeoning Chinese and Asian photographic markets. "It is important to us that they know their job is not an entitlement," said Paul A. Walrath, general manager of the Xiamen factory. "Kodak is in the business of making money."

The company is spending a lot to help employees understand. They received average pay increases of about 30 percent when they went to work for Kodak, although many would say they are working twice as hard. Some employees saw their pay triple.

To help boost the Xiamen operation, Kodak also installed state-of-the-art equipment and manufacturing processes, and enlisted career engineers from its domestic and international operations to help with design, installation, training, and startup. The investment has paid off handsomely. The plant began operating ahead of schedule, and came in under its construction budget of about $600 million. Since opening the plant, Kodak's consumer film has grown to become China's best seller.

The pace of achievement at the plant has surprised veteran Kodakers. For instance, recently the staff at the plant produced marketable batches of consumer film in its first weekend of coating operations. The accomplishment sent cheers up and hugs all around in the site's control room.

Yet not everyone in Kodak is celebrating. The Xiamen factory is the source of some tension in Kodak Park, the company's major U.S. plant. Executives say workers have told them again and again they expect to lose their jobs to lower-paid counterparts in China. Company management says those fears are misplaced. The Xiamen plant will be busy for a long time supplying China and other Asian markets. Also, the Xiamen operation is good for the domestic company because it creates demand for chemicals, film base, and other materials made only in the United States.

Source: Ben Rand, "Kodak's New Plant: Company Builds a Modern Film Factory on Incentives," Rochester, New York, *Democrat and Chronicle*, June 25, 2000, p. 3, special report.

Trade Agreements Among Countries

The North American Free Trade Agreement (NAFTA) establishes liberal trading relationships among the United States, Canada, and Mexico.[3] The pact also calls for the gradual removal of tariffs and other trade barriers on most goods produced and sold in the United States. NAFTA became effective in Canada, Mexico, and the United States as of January 1, 1994. The agreement creates a giant trading zone extending from the Arctic Ocean to the Gulf of Mexico. NAFTA forms the world's second largest free trade zone, bringing together 365 million consumers in the three countries. The largest free trade zone is the European Economic Union.

Many companies benefit from NAFTA because of better access to the two other countries in the pact. Many U.S. companies have expanded sales of industrial and consumer products to Canada and Mexico. These products include computers, film, and machine tools. As a result of NAFTA, Canadian and Mexican firms have sold more products to the United States. More Canadian and Mexican beer now flows in the United States, as well as the sale of electronic products and furniture. Much of the surge in the Mexican auto industry can be attributed to the substantial drop in tariffs between the United States and Mexico. (Mexico assembles autos for the U.S. market.)

The North American Free Trade Agreement is not without its critics. Many labor union representatives argue that NAFTA threatens jobs of American workers. For example, the International Union of Electronic Workers (IUE) protests actions of General Electric Co. During an aggressive round of cost cutting, GE demanded deep price cuts from its suppliers. To help suppliers meet these challenging goals, several GE business units, including aircraft engines and power systems, urged suppliers to move to low-cost Mexico. The industrial giant already employs 35,000 workers in Mexico, and the number continues to climb. The shift to operations in Mexico is part of GE's strategy to lower costs by expanding in low-wage countries.[4]

The European Union (EU) is a 15-nation alliance that virtually turns member countries into a single marketplace for ideas, goods, services, and investment strategies. The EU trades with member nations, the United States and Canada, and other countries throughout the world. In addition, Japanese firms are now investing extensively in Europe.

A major step for the European Union is its monetary union in which 11 countries traded their national money for currency called the Euro. For two years prior to the debut in 2002 of the Euro as the single currency, the Euro was used concurrently with member countries' own currency. Also bank accounts, credit cards, and prices were measured in Euros. The Euro fluctuates in value, but frequently has been close to parity with the U.S. dollar making it easier for Americans and Europeans to think in Euros. As a Portuguese server said to a business traveler, "Your lunch is 7 U.S. dollars, 7 Euro dollars, or 1,645 escudos. Your choice." To help improve the profile of the Euro, the European Central Bank hired a French public relations firm to develop the slogan, "The EURO. OUR money."[5]

The World Trade Organization liberalizes trade among many nations throughout the world. (The WTO was previously referred to as the General Agreement on Tariffs and Trade, or GATT.) The idea is to lower trade barriers, thereby facilitating international trade. The WTO cut tariffs and other barriers on 8,000 categories of manufactured goods. The WTO now has about 130 member countries, which accounts for about 95 percent of world trade. Lower trade barriers eliminate the artificially high prices consumers previously paid for imported goods.

One issue in facilitating trade is that global trade liberalization leads to continuous job cuts and downward pressures on wages in industrialized nations. The concern about global trade contributing to worker exploitation is so strong that riots frequently take place outside the meetings of the WTO. Rioters regularly pelt security workers with rocks and smash the windows of American-owned stores, or U.S. franchises abroad. McDonald's restaurants are a frequent target because McDonald's symbolizes American trade overseas.

The counterargument to objections to overseas trade is that free trade, in the long run, creates more job opportunities by making it possible to export more freely. A related argument is that when companies shift manufacturing to low-wage countries, the companies can remain more cost competitive. As a consequence of globalizing production, the companies stay in business and keep more domestic workers employed.

What Constitutes a Domestic Product?

A side issue related to multinational corporations and free trade is what constitutes a foreign versus a domestic product. More specifically, an emotional issue is the meaning of the label "Made in USA." A good example is an American-made computer. Many of its components were probably manufactured in several Asian countries. The widely used ViewSonic PC monitor is made in Korea even though ViewSonic Corporation is based in California.

The Federal Trade Commission (FTC) forbids companies from using the label if an item produced exceeds more than a small amount of foreign content. Yet the FTC had proposed guidelines that allow merchandise with as little as 75 percent U.S. parts to read "Made in the USA." Labor unions and some lawmakers oppose the changed guidelines, because they believe the changes would encourage U.S. corporations to send jobs overseas. The FTC now requires at least 90 percent American parts for a product to be labeled "Made in the USA."

Sensitivity to Cultural Differences

The guiding principle for people involved in international enterprise is sensitivity to cultural differences. **Cultural sensitivity** is awareness of local and national customs and their importance in effective interpersonal relationships. Ignoring the customs of other people creates a communications block that can impede business and create ill will. For example, Americans tend to be impatient to close a deal while businesspeople in many other cultures prefer to build a relationship slowly before consummating an agreement. Exhibit 2-1 presents a sampling of cultural differences that can affect business.

Cultural sensitivity is also important because it helps a person become a **multicultural worker**. Such an individual is convinced that all cultures are equally good, and enjoys learning about other cultures. Multicultural workers are usually people who have been exposed to more than one culture in childhood. Being multicultural leads to being accepted by a person from another culture. According to Gunnar Beeth, a *multilingual* salesperson can explain the advantages of a product in other languages, but it takes a multicultural salesperson to motivate foreigners to buy.[6]

Candidates for foreign assignments generally receive training in the language and customs of the country they will work in. Intercultural training exercises include playing the roles of businesspeople from a different culture. The aircraft engine unit of General Electric Co. is one of many companies preparing people for the international work environment. Groups of middle-level engineers and managers receive cross-cultural training, including training in foreign language skills. Although not all of these managers are scheduled to live abroad, the train-

2

Recognize the importance of sensitivity to cultural differences in international enterprise.

cultural sensitivity
Awareness of local and national customs and their importance in effective interpersonal relationships.

multicultural worker
An individual who is aware of and values other cultures.

EXHIBIT 2-1

Cultural Mistakes to Avoid in Selected Regions and Countries

EUROPE

Great Britain	• Asking personal questions. The British protect their privacy.
	• Thinking that a businessperson from England is unenthusiastic when he or she says, "Not bad at all." English people understate positive emotion.
	• Gossiping about royalty
France	• Expecting to complete work during the French two-hour lunch.
	• Attempting to conduct significant business during August—les vacances (vacation time).
	• Greeting a French person for the first time and not using a title such as "sir" or "madam" (or monsieur, madame, or mademoiselle).
Italy	• Eating too much pasta, as it is not the main course.
	• Handing out business cards freely. Italians use them infrequently.
Spain	• Expecting punctuality. Your appointments will usually arrive 20 to 30 minutes late.
	• Making the American sign of "okay" with your thumb and forefinger. In Spain (and many other countries) this is vulgar.
Scandinavia (Denmark, Sweden, Norway)	• Being overly rank conscious. Scandinavians pay relatively little attention to a person's place in the hierarchy.

ASIA

| All Asian countries | • Pressuring an Asian job applicant or employee to brag about his or her accomplishments. Asians feel self-conscious when boasting about individual accomplishments, and prefer to let the record speak for itself. In addition, they prefer to talk about group rather than individual accomplishment. |

Japan	• Shaking hands or hugging Japanese (as well as other Asians) in public. Japanese consider the practices to be offensive.
	• Not interpreting "We'll consider it" as a no when spoken by a Japanese businessperson. Japanese negotiators mean no when they say, "We'll consider it."
	• Not giving small gifts to Japanese when conducting business. Japanese are offended by not receiving these gifts.
China	• Using black borders on stationary and business cards. Black is associated with death.
	• Giving small gifts to Chinese when conducting business. Chinese are offended by these gifts.
Korea	• Saying "no." Koreans feel it is important to have visitors leave with good feelings.
India	• Telling Indians you prefer not to eat with your hands. If the Indians are not using cutlery when eating, they expect you to do likewise.

MEXICO AND LATIN AMERICA

Mexico	• Flying into a Mexican city in the morning and expecting to close a deal by lunch. Mexicans build business relationships slowly.
Brazil	• Attempting to impress Brazilians by speaking a few words of Spanish. Portuguese is the official language of Brazil.
Most Latin American countries	• Wearing elegant and expensive jewelry during a business meeting. Most Latin Americans think people should appear more conservative during a business meeting.

Note: A cultural mistake for Americans to avoid when conducting business in most countries outside the United States and Canada is to insist on getting down to new business quickly. North Americans in small towns also like to build a relationship before getting down to business.

ing is designed to help them work effectively with people from another culture. The importance of such training was revealed by a study that found that 30 percent of placements in foreign countries were unsuccessful. These mistakes were due primarily to the employees' failures to adjust properly to a new culture.[7] (See Exhibit 2-1.)

Another approach to developing cross-cultural sensitivity is to recognize cross-cultural differences in managerial styles. These differences are cultural stereotypes applicable to many managers from the same country. As in all aspects of human behavior, considerable individual differences can be observed among managers from the same culture. National stereotypes of management styles, as revealed by the research of Geert Hofstede and his collaborators, are as follows:[8]

Germany: German managers are expected to be primarily technical experts, or meisters, who assign tasks and help solve difficult problems. (Although Hofstede's observations may be true at middle and first levels of management, top-level German managers, like their counterparts in other countries, are heavily involved in making major decisions that affect the entire organization.)

Japan: Japanese managers rely on group consensus before making a decision, and the group controls individual behavior to a large extent. Japanese managers are perceived as more formal and businesslike, and less talkative and emotional than their American counterparts. (Although many Japanese managers do strive for consensus, many others are authoritarian and maintain tight control over the organization.)

France: French managers, particularly in major corporations, are part of an elite class, and they behave in a superior, authoritarian manner.

The Netherlands: Dutch managers emphasize equality and consensus and do not expect to impress group members with their status. Dutch managers give group members ample opportunity to participate in problem solving.

The Overseas Chinese: Many managers from China work in Pacific Rim countries such as Taiwan, Hong Kong, Singapore, Malaysia, and the Philippines. In companies managed by Chinese, major decisions are made by one dominant person, quite often of advanced years. The Chinese manager maintains a low profile.

CHALLENGES FACING THE GLOBAL MANAGERIAL WORKER

Managerial workers on assignment in other countries, as well as domestic managers working on international dealings, face a variety of challenges. Rising to these challenges can be the difference between success and failure. Among the heaviest challenges are economic crises, balance of trade problems, collecting money, the liability of being a foreigner, human rights violations, culture shock, and differences in negotiating style, and piracy.

Identify major challenges facing the global managerial worker.

Economic Crises in Other Countries

A major threat to the international manager is dealing with economic crises that originate in other countries yet have a negative impact on his or her country. For example, the Asian crisis went on for about two years before softening in the fall of 1999. Many observers trace the origins of this crisis to Thailand's devaluation of its currency in July 1997. At the same time, stock prices and the real estate market fell and the banking system was severely weakened. Currency markets also fell in other Southeast Asian countries including Japan, South Korea, and the Philippines.

Japan's crisis received the most publicity because it is the world's second largest economy, trailing only the United States. A major cause of Japan's recession was a mountain of bad debt and losses in real estate values. Nonperforming bank loans were the most striking feature of the bad debt. Of concern to managers involved in both domestic and international trade, the Asian crisis spread rapidly to Russia and Latin America. As a result the world economy was threatened with recession. For example, it became more difficult to export to Asian countries whose economies were suffering.

Economies run in cycles, and the Asian crisis had improved a little by 2000. One analysis of the recovery indicates that the crisis forced countries such as Japan, Korea, and Vietnam to liberalize trade and other policies. Also, Japanese operations in Asia emerged stronger and more efficient than before the crisis because of cost cutting and a renewed emphasis on selling to the world at large.[9] Japan, however, has yet to return to its best economic times.

Closely tied in with an economic crisis is the challenge to international business created by inflation and currency devaluation. If the currency of a country suddenly gains in value, it may be difficult to export products made in that country. The strengthening of the U.S. dollar during the period of the new millennium made it more difficult for some countries to purchase U.S. goods and services. For example, the Canadian dollar fell to about 65 cents against the U.S. dollar in mid 2001. Canadian tourism in the United States dipped slightly, whereas U.S. tourism in Canada increased. (A hotel room for $100 Canadian would only cost $65 U.S. In contrast a hotel room for $100 U.S. would cost $154 Canadian!)

During the same period the surging value of the yen against the U.S. dollar posed a threat to Japan's economic recovery. (A U.S. dollar is worth about 105 yen.) The problem is that the strong yen makes Japanese exports more expensive and less competitive in other countries. As a consequence, earnings are reduced for export-oriented Japanese companies. One of the measures Japan took to cope with the strong yen was to manufacture in countries with weaker currencies, such as Thailand.

Balance of Trade Problems

balance of trade

A measure of the dollar volume of a country's exports relative to its imports over a specified time period.

A concern at the broadest level to an international manager is a country's **balance of trade**, the difference between exports and imports in both goods and services. Many people believe that it is to a country's advantage to export more than it imports. Yet in 2000, the total international deficit in goods and services for the United States was $369.7 billion. The trade deficit can be attributed to many factors, such as the preference for Americans to purchase lower-priced goods and to take vacations in foreign countries rather than the United States, as well as a strong U.S. dollar. Exhibit 2-2 presents some interesting facts about the trade deficit.

An individual manager might want to contribute to the national economy by exporting more than importing. In an effort to accomplish this goal, the manager might have to find ways to cut costs on products or services offered for export. An alternative would be to design products or services so attractive they would sell well despite their relative high price in foreign markets. Examples include American movies and Harley-Davidson motorcycles.

Collecting Money

A more specific financial problem facing the international manager can be collecting money from overseas customers. The most common way to get paid is through a letter of credit, a document issued by a bank. It guarantees a company will get paid as soon as it can provide documents showing that the goods or services were delivered as promised. Even with a letter of credit serious delays in

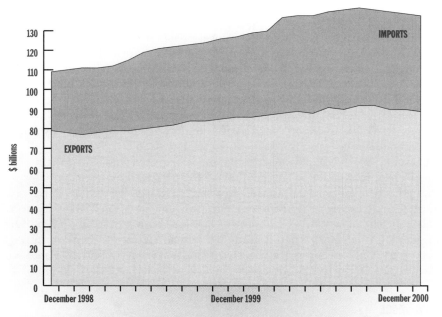

EXHIBIT 2-2

U.S. International Trade in Goods and Services Highlights

The U.S. continues to purchase more goods and services from other countries than they purchase from us, creating a trade deficit for the United States.

37

Source: *FTD Web Master*, Foreign Trade Division, U.S. Census, Washington, DC 20233.

	U.S. $ (in billions)
Deficit with China	83.3
Deficit with Japan	81.3
Deficit with Western Europe	59.8
Deficit with all other countries combined	<u>145.3</u>
Total international deficit in goods and services	369.7

Source: http://www.census.gov/indicator/www/ustrade.html.

getting paid can develop. Getting money out of Eastern Europe, China, and Russia, for example, can be difficult.

Sometimes a country will forbid the export of money, forcing the seller to spend the money in the foreign country. A company sending machine parts to one country might have to use its proceeds to purchase that country's product, and then resell the product in another country. For example, a company might purchase furniture in the overseas country with the proceeds from selling its own product, and then sell the furniture back home or in another country. Another reason it can be difficult to receive payments in these countries is that some companies are controlled by criminals. They accept shipment of the goods, but then refuse to pay and threaten anyone who attempts to collect payment.

Liability of Being a Foreigner

When doing business abroad, a company faces costs from factors such as as an unfamiliar environment, and cultural, political, and economic differences. It is also difficult to coordinate activities across geographic boundaries. A study of Western and Japanese banks suggested that an effective way to overcome the challenges of being foreign is simply to use a firm's best businesses and managerial practices abroad.[10]

Human Rights Violations

International managers face potential ethical problems when their customers and suppliers reside in countries where human rights are violated. Should a U.S. rug distributor purchase carpets from a supplier that employs 10-year-old children who work 11 hours a day for the equivalent of $4 U.S.? Should a U.S. shoe manufacturer buy components from a country that uses political prisoners as free labor? Ethical issues require careful thought, especially when they are not always clear-cut. To a child in an underdeveloped country, receiving $4 per day can mean the difference between malnutrition and adequate food.

The subject of human rights violations is complicated and touchy. Multinational corporations based in the United States are often accused of profiting from the fruits of labor of employees exploited in less-developed countries. However, at several garment industry sweatshops found in New York City and Los Angeles, illegal aliens work 12 hours per day for about $1 per hour. The United States sets high standards when it comes to human rights in other countries. Yet, according to Amnesty International, these standards are frequently violated within its own borders,[11] including the death penalty.

Culture Shock

culture shock

Physical and psychological symptoms that can develop when a person is placed in a foreign culture.

Many managers and professionals on overseas assignments face **culture shock**. The condition refers to a group of physical and psychological symptoms that may develop when a person is abruptly placed in a foreign culture. Among them are excessive hand washing and concern for sanitation, fear of physical contact with others, fear of being mugged, and strong feelings of homesickness.[12] Culture shock contributes to the relatively high rate of expatriates (employees sent to another country) who return home early because they are dissatisfied with their assignments. Somewhere between 16 percent and 50 percent of these international workers return early. Based on research into successful and unsuccessful expatriate assignments, two researchers found that certain human resource practices could help make overseas assignments more satisfying. These same practices, outlined next, also help reduce culture shock for the expatriates and their families:

- Give families realistic information about their assignments and language training.
- Arrange company-sponsored social functions for employees and families as an opportunity to interact with nationals from the host company.
- Provide family members back home with e-mail or other information technology advances such as teleconferencing.
- Provide job search assistance for spouses who want to work overseas.
- Assist with obtaining work permits or visas for spouses.
- Offer continuing education benefits packages that will finance either local or correspondence courses.[13]

Differences in Negotiating Style

A recurring challenge in other countries, as indicated in Exhibit 2-1, is that the international managerial worker may have to use a different negotiation style. A do-or-die attitude is often self-defeating. American negotiators, for example, often find that they must be more patient, use a team approach, and avoid being too informal. Patience is a major factor in negotiating outside the United States. Asian negotiators are willing to spend many days negotiating a deal. Much of their nego-tiating activity seems to be ceremonial (including elaborate dining) and unrelated to the task. Americans can be frustrated by this protracted process.

Although members of another culture spend a long time working a deal, they may still take a tough stance. As a key example, foreign firms seeking access to the Chinese market of 1.2 billion people face extraordinary demands by Chinese state planners. These planners demand that the foreign country hand over valuable technology and job-generating investments, especially in strategically important area such as autos, aerospace, and electronics. Companies that refuse these demands lose out to competitors.[14]

A study conducted by Jeanne Brett and Tetsushi Okumura provides more evi-dence about the challenges of cross-cultural negotiation. The two researchers examined the influence of cultural differences in negotiating style between Amer-ican and Japanese managers. The purpose of the study was to learn how negotia-tors' value differences might affect mutual gains in intercultural negotiation. The study results indicated that differences in cultural values and norms between U.S. and Japanese negotiators influence both the negotiating tactics and outcomes of negotiation. For example, the cultural values of individualism versus collectivism are expressed as differences in negotiators' levels of self-interest. (Individualism refers to concern for one's own welfare, whereas collectivism refers to a concern for group welfare.) Negotiators who have a strong individualistic orientation are likely to emphasize self-interest when entering into negotiations. A highly indi-vidualistic negotiator might be more concerned about winning an order than arriving at a price that would be most beneficial to his or her firm.

A specific experiment demonstrated that people negotiating with others from their own culture were more likely to achieve mutual gains, as when Americans negotiated with Americans or Japanese negotiated with Japanese. Mutual gains were less likely when negotiating across cultures—when Americans negotiated with Japanese.[15]

Piracy of Intellectual Property Rights and Other Merchandise

In international business, considerable revenue is lost when firms in other countries illegally copy and sell products. Furthermore, these imitations (or "knock-offs") might be sold in the domestic market as well, depriving the firm of additional rev-enue. Managers must address the reality of unauthorized third-party sales of imita-tions of their product. Products widely reproduced illegally include fine watches, perfume, videocassettes, CDs, clothing with high-status brand names, and software. Losses due to counterfeit software alone cost companies an estimated $3 billion in each of the three major markets of Asia/Pacific, Europe, and North America.[16]

China is a major producer of nonauthorized copies of products. The practice of piracy is widely accepted within the country. It also takes place on a substantial scale in Europe. (Product pirates can be found in a manager's own country as well.) A case in point occurred in Cambridge, England, several years ago. John Staud, the owner of PolyMould, and his 25 employees were printing the most-in-demand software disks, including Microsoft's Office and Windows NT, and shipping them throughout Europe. (Unauthorized copies of this type often come with stolen cer-tificates of authenticity and forged user manuals.) With the help of Microsoft detec-tives, German customs authorities finally intercepted a shipment from Staud's plant, and seized $60 million worth of pirated disks. Staud was arrested and eventually sentenced to four years in jail for illegally copying and selling software.[17]

4   METHODS OF ENTRY INTO WORLD MARKETS

Explain various methods of entry into world markets.

Firms enter the global market in several different ways, and new approaches continue to evolve. At one time a small firm relied on importer-exporters or distributors to enter the world market. Now even some home-based businesses sell worldwide through an established Web site. The initial entry mode used to penetrate a foreign market must be chosen carefully because of its potential effects on the success of the venture. Another factor is the difficulty in changing the mode without considerable loss of time and money.[18] Eight methods of entry into world markets are described next.

1. *Exporting.* Goods produced in one country are then sold for direct use or resale to one or more companies in foreign countries. Many small firms specialize in helping companies gain entry into foreign markets through exporting. An overseas distributor can be quite helpful, but one must be chosen carefully. Current research suggests than an in-person visit to a prospective overseas distributor eliminates many problems.[19]

2. *Licensing.* Companies operating in foreign countries are authorized to produce and market products or services with specific territories on a fee basis. A franchise arrangement, such as a U.S. citizen operating a Subway store in Madrid, would fit this category.

3. *Local warehousing and selling.* Goods produced in one country are shipped directly to storage and marketing facilities of the parent company or subsidiary in one or more foreign countries. Many products, including radios and pocket calculators, are manufactured by Asian companies and shipped directly to U.S. companies, such as Tandy Corporation, for distribution in the United States.

4. *Local assembly and packaging.* In this arrangement, components rather than finished products are shipped to company-owned facilities in other countries. There assembly is completed and the goods are marketed. Trade regulations sometimes require that a large product, such as a mainframe computer, be assembled locally rather than shipped from the exporting country as a finished product.

   An example of local assembly and packaging by U.S. companies is the use of maquiladoras. A **maquiladora**, a manufacturing plant in Mexico close to the U.S. border, is a plant established specifically to assemble American products. The U.S. owners of maquiladoras pay no import tax on components. When maquiladora products are exported to the United States, they are taxed only on the value added in Mexico.

   The maquiladora industry was established for two main purposes. First, it gave U.S. businesses the opportunity to use high-quality, inexpensive labor. (The average pay of a maquiladora worker is one-third that of a U.S. worker.) Second, it provided many economically disadvantaged northern Mexicans an opportunity for a relatively high-paying job and good working conditions. General Motors is one U.S. company making extensive use of maquiladoras. The explosive growth of the Mexican auto industry mentioned in the discussion of NAFTA has been facilitated by maquiladoras.

5. *Strategic alliance.* Instead of merging formally with a firm of mutual interest, a company in one country pools resources with one or more foreign companies. Alliances are so common today that the current era has been referred to as the "age of alliance capitalism."[20] A major reason for the willingness to form alliances is the enormous expense and effort necessary for a single organization

maquiladora

A manufacturing plant close to the U.S. border that is established specifically to assemble American products to accomplish a full range of business activities. In a joint venture, the companies in alliance produce, warehouse, transport, and market products. Profits or losses from these operations are shared in some predetermined proportion. The advanced camera system that combines film and digital photography is a joint venture among five of the world's leading photo companies.

6. *Direct foreign investment.* The most advanced stage of multinational business activity takes place when a company in one country produces and markets products through wholly owned facilities in foreign countries. Toyota Motor Co. and Ford Motor Co., two well-known multinational corporations, conduct business in this manner. Direct foreign investments are greatly facilitated by forming **transnational teams**, work groups composed of multinational members whose activities span multiple countries. The group is composed of workers representing each company in the venture, whose intent is to help the companies pursue a global business strategy.[21] An example of a transnational team is representatives of the European and North American divisions of GM working together to build and sell the Chevy Tahoe. Teamwork is important because the Tahoe components are built in several countries, and the vehicle has some export sales.

   Research with 25 Dutch companies suggests a factor contributing to whether a company expands internationally through a foreign investment rather than an acquisition. Companies that already operate in diverse markets are more likely to start a new venture in another country rather than acquire another company.[22]

7. *Global merger.* An increasingly frequent method of gaining entry to foreign markets, or increasing business activity in these markets, is to merge with a foreign company. You can find an example of a global merger almost weekly by reading the business section of the newspaper. An example of a highly successful global merger is San Francisco-based Barclays Global Investors (BGI). A merger of four multinational corporations in 1996 made BGI one of the world's largest institutional investment managers with clients in more than 20 countries. Half of all mergers fail, and the failure rate for global mergers is even higher because of cultural differences. A senior executive at BGI comments about mergers:

   > If you're going to do it, you have to invest very heavily in mitigating all the forces that work against it. Essentially, mergers have very tribal characteristics to them. You're asking different tribes to come together as a nation, and you'd better find out why it's in their mutual interest to do so. Otherwise, they'll use the opportunity of the merger to express their differences.[23]

8. *Global start-up.* A **global start-up** is a small firm that comes into existence by serving an international market. By so doing, the firm circumvents the previous methods. Logitech, Inc., the leading manufacturer of the computer mouse, is one of the most successful global start-ups. The company was founded in 1982 by a Swiss and two Italians who wanted to have an international company from the start. Logitech began with headquarters, manufacturing, and engineering in California and Switzerland and then established facilities in Taiwan and Ireland. Founders of global start-ups have one key characteristic in common: some international experience before going global.[24]

   Selling through the Internet facilitates creating a global start-up, particularly in the European market. Given that English is the universal language of

transnational teams
A work group composed of multinational members whose activities span multiple countries.

global start-up
A small firm that comes into existence by serving an international market.

business, it is possible to sell to European customers with Web sites in English. However, adding several other language options to the Web site facilitates sales. European usage of the Internet, including PCs installed in the home, is increasing rapidly. Television hookups to the Net are also increasing rapidly, facilitating the sale of consumer products such as jewelry, clothing, and sporting goods. Europeans now have available cellular telephones with small screens for Web access. Online business (or e-commerce) in Europe continues to expand rapidly.

Of the methods of entry into the global marketplace, exporting offers the least protection for the company doing business in another country. Each successive step through global mergers offers more protection against political and economic risks. Multinational firms run the risk that the firm in the other country may drop its affiliation and sell the product on its own. The affiliate thus becomes a competitor. To avoid this risk, direct foreign investment is recommended as the best way to protect the company's competitive advantage. The advantage is protected because the manager of a foreign subsidiary can control its operation.

Global start-ups offer similar protection to direct foreign investment. A problem, however, arises because the cost of attempting to sell through a Web site is small, both domestic and foreign competitors can readily copy your idea. Note that selling through the Web can be expensive if you hook up with a major portal such as Yahoo! or Excite, which require a commission and other fees to sell products or services.

5 Success Factors in the Global Marketplace

Pinpoint success factors in the global marketplace, and several positive and negative aspects of globalization.

Success in international business stems from the same factors that lead to success at home. The ultimate reason for the success of any product or service is its ability to satisfy customer needs. Additional strategies and tactics, however, are required for success in the global marketplace. It is important to recognize that internationalization of business is not always successful. Most of these strategies and tactics logically extend the topics discussed previously in this chapter.

Think Globally, Act Locally

A competitive enterprise combines global scale and world-class technology with deep roots in local markets. Local representatives of the firm behave as though their primary mission is to serve the local customer. A study of multinational corporations operating in China reinforces the importance of focusing on the local market. When exporting from China, foreign firms' main goal often is exporting what they produce, such as DVD players exported into Europe and North America. MNCs implementing a local market focus face the challenge of adapting a product to local trends and preferences. However, if the economy of the local market improves, the MNC may benefit from targeting a large and growing market—in this case China. The most profitable firms in the study were those that focused on the local Chinese market.[25]

Diversify into Similar Product Markets

Diversification into product markets similar to markets currently served may result in several competitive advantages. First, managers understand their customer. Second, the structural characteristics of the new industry are likely to be familiar, which facilitates responding to competitive challenges. Third, some of the firm's current skills may be transferred to the new product or market. A fast-food chain might diversify into a fast-food item that is popular in another culture.[26] For instance, Burger King might sell tacos in its restaurants in Mexico.

Be Familiar with Local Business Concepts, Laws, and Customs

Success in foreign markets is contingent upon close familiarity with the local scene. U.S. companies with established maquiladoras have discovered the importance of this principle. For example, a unique aspect of Mexican law comes into play when an officially recognized labor union declares a strike. All employees, including managers, must leave the building, and red and black flags are hung at entrances to the plant. Furthermore, employees receive full pay for all the time they are out on a legal strike.

Recruit Talented Nationals

A major success factor in building a business in another country is to hire talented citizens of that country to fill important positions. Greg Green, the human resources director for Sunglass Hut International offers three words of advice: network, network, network. One way to network would be to make a list of other companies from your country that are already established in your destination country.[27]

Western firms have the best chance of penetrating the perplexing Japanese market if they hire top Japanese talent. After the host-company nationals are hired, they must be taught the culture of the parent company. By teaching the overseas managers the values and traditions of the firm, those managers can better achieve corporate objectives.

At times the prevailing management style in the host country may not fit the parent company culture. Teaching the culture then becomes even more important. An example follows:

> Chicago-based Tellabs Inc., a manufacturer of telecommunications products, opened a branch in Munich, Germany. Tellabs had an informal and flexible culture in which all employees had access to senior management. The German culture was much more informal. Laura Bozich, the regional director for Central Europe, was sent to Munich to explain the corporate culture to the newly hired manager.[28]

Research and Assess Potential Markets

Another basic success strategy in international markets is to acquire valid information about the firm's target market. Trade statistics usually provide a good starting point. If the company manufactures long-lasting light bulbs, it must find out where such bulbs sell the best. Basic trade data are often available at foreign embassies, banks with international operations, and departments of commerce.

Hire or Develop Multicultural Workers

A contributing factor to success in global markets is to hire multicultural workers. Multiculturalism enhances acceptance of a firm by overseas personnel and customers. Included in multiculturalism is the ability to speak the language of the target (or host) country. Even though English is the official language of business and technology, overseas employees should develop the right foreign language skill. Being able to listen to and understand foreign customers speaking in their native language about their requirements may reveal nuances that would be missed by having them speak in English. Showing that one has made an effort to learn the native language can earn big dividends with employees, customers, prospective customers, bankers, and government officials. To be impressive, however, it is important to go beyond the most basic skill level.

To help workers and their family members become multicultural, many companies offer cultural training. Programs of this nature usually include key components such as those offered by the Eaton Consulting Group.[29]

> *Culture profiles.* Workers on assignment in other countries are taught the differences and similarities of the home- and host-country cultures.
> *Cultural adaptation.* This section explains the theory of the culture shock curve, alerting families to the typical time frame when culture shock emerges, describing the symptoms and tactics for coping with the problem.
> *Logistical information.* Culture trainers explain such details as the etiquette of gift giving, who to call in an emergency, how to write a check, and how to obtain money from the bank back home.
> *Application.* This section applies the cross-cultural information to the roles the employees will assume in the new location. The trainer will identify the adjustments the international worker may need to be successful performing a familiar function in the context of the host country.

Joerg Schmitz, a global management training expert, shares an illuminating example of the impact of culture on an employee's job performance: "The U.S. culture is extraordinarily task oriented. Northern Europe is perhaps the closest to the type of task orientation you'll find in the United States. But about every other country in the world is relationship oriented."[30] Expatriates must understand this observation as they work hard to build rapport and gain credibility with business colleagues in other cultures.

Adopt Environmentally Friendly Policies

An emerging success factor in the global marketplace focuses on a company's policies concerning the environment. Companies need to find ways to synchronize economic growth with protecting the natural environment. Shaker A. Zahar, among others, has observed that economic development in many parts of the world has been accomplished at a substantial cost to the physical environment. Some companies fail to develop policies and adopt workplace reforms that protect the natural environment and resources.[31]

A company that pursues the ideals of a *green economy* (one that is environmentally friendly) will therefore gain some competitive advantage in the global market. For instance, many Eastern European countries lag in terms of the equipment necessary to protect the environment against toxins from industrial waste. A multinational company that set up an environmentally friendly manufacturing site in Romania might attract customers who appreciated top management's concern for the environment.

Understand Competitors, Potential Partners, and Diverse Members of the Management Team

The most comprehensive strategy for success in international business is to thoroughly analyze and understand the people upon whom success depends. Understanding competitors includes such information as their managerial values and strategy, and predicting the type of products and services they will offer in the future. Understanding partners in an overseas alliance includes figuring out what they expect to gain from the relationship. Understanding the diverse members of your management team means knowing their culture and work experiences.[32]

The Advantages and Disadvantages of Globalization

Many managers and scholars believe that globalization of business is both inevitable and highly desirable. Yet for other managers, business owners, and individual workers, the internationalization of the workplace has created more problems than opportunities. Many of the advantages and disadvantages of global-ization depend upon an individual's vantage point. An executive in an MNC might receive a generous bonus because shifting a call center to Mexico saves the company $5 million per year in labor costs. As a consequence she welcomes glob-alization. The middle-aged call center supervisor who lost his enjoyable, well-paying job and is now a greeter at a discount department store would view globalization more negatively. Exhibit 2-3 outlines the major pros and cons of globalization.

THE SCOPE AND COMPETITIVE ADVANTAGE OF MANAGING DIVERSITY   6

The globalization of business means that the managerial workers must be able to deal effectively with people from other countries. At the same time it is important to deal effectively with different cultural groups within one's own country and

Describe the scope of diver-sity and the competitive advantage of a culturally diverse workforce.

Advantages	Disadvantages
Productivity grows more quickly when countries produce goods and services in which they have a comparative advantage. Living standards go up faster.	Millions of Americans have lost jobs due to imports or production shifts abroad. Most find lower-paying jobs. One-quarter of laid-off workers are still job hunting three years later.
Global competition and cheap imports set a ceiling on prices, so inflation is less likely to be too high.	Millions of others fear losing their jobs, especially at those companies operating under competitive pressure.
An open economy spurs innovation with fresh ideas from abroad.	Workers face paycut demands from employers, which often threaten to export jobs.
Export jobs often pay more than other jobs.	Service and white-collar jobs are increasingly vulnerable to operations moving offshore.
U.S. managers can invest in many different countries to seek the best return on their capital.	U.S. employees can lose their comparative advantage when companies build advanced factories in low-wage countries, making them as productive as those at home.
Workers become broader in their outlook and profit from the opportunity to become multicultural, including foreign travel.	Profits and executive salaries increase while workers toil in overseas sweatshops. Many of these workers are vulnerable to human rights violations.
With many jobs shipped overseas, talent is freed up within the United States, which can be reskilled and used elsewhere in a tight labor market.	National pride is hurt as many Americans lament, "Nothing is 'made in the USA' any longer. We used to be such a great country."

EXHIBIT 2-3

The Pros and Cons of Globalization

Source: Adapted from Aaron Bernstein, "Backlash Behind the Anxiety Over Globalization," *Business Week*, April 24, 2000, p. 41; Charlene Marmer Solomon, "Moving Jobs to Offshore Markets: Why It's Done and How It Works," *Workforce*, July 1999, pp. 51–52.

diversity

A demographic and/or cultural mixture of people with different group identities within the same work environment.

company. Both the international and domestic workforces are diverse. In the present context, **diversity** refers to a mixture of people with different group identities within the same work environment. The term *diversity* includes two subtypes, demographic and cultural.

Demographic diversity refers to the mix of group characteristics of the organization's workforce. Demographic characteristics include such factors as age, sex, religion, physical status, and sexual orientation. *Cultural diversity* refers to the mix of cultures and subcultures to which the organization's workforce belongs. Among these cultures are the Hispanic culture, the deaf culture, the Muslim culture, the Jewish culture, the Native American culture, and the Inuit (Eskimo) culture. It is possible for people with the same demographic characteristics not to share the same cultural characteristics. A deaf person who went to school with hearing people, whose parents are hearing, and most of whose friends can hear, may be deaf from a demographic standpoint, yet the person does not identify with the deaf culture. Following common practice, in this text the term *diversity* is used to reflect both demographic and cultural diversity.

Here and in the next section, we study diversity in the workplace from four perspectives: (1) the scope of diversity, (2) its competitive advantage, (3) organizational practices for capitalizing on diversity, and (4) an analysis of how the English language is used to unify people in business. Before reading further, take the self-quiz about cross-cultural skills and attitudes presented in Exhibit 2-4.

EXHIBIT 2-4

Cross-Cultural Skills and Attitudes

Various employers and cross-cultural experts believe the following skills and attitudes are important for relating effectively to coworkers in a culturally diverse environment.

	Applies to Me Now	Not There Yet
1. I have spent some time in another country.	____	____
2. At least one of my friends is deaf, blind, or uses a wheelchair.	____	____
3. Currency from other countries is as real as the currency from my own country.	____	____
4. I can read in a language other than my own.	____	____
5. I can speak in a language other than my own.	____	____
6. I can write in a language other than my own.	____	____
7. I can understand people speaking in a language other than my own.	____	____
8. I use my second language regularly.	____	____
9. My friends include people of races different from my own.	____	____
10. My friends include people of different ages.	____	____
11. I feel (or would feel) comfortable having friends with a sexual orientation different from mine.	____	____
12. My attitude is that although another culture may be different from mine, that culture is equally good.	____	____
13. I would be willing to (or already do) hang art from various countries in my home.	____	____
14. I would accept (or have already accepted) a work assignment of more than several months in another country.	____	____
15. I have a passport.	____	____

Interpretation: If you answered "Applies to Me Now" to 10 or more of the questions, you most likely function well in a multicultural work environment. If you answered "Not There Yet" to 10 or more of the questions, you need to develop more cross-cultural awareness and skills to work effectively in a multicultural work environment. You will notice that being bilingual gives you at least five points on this quiz.

Source: Adapted from Ruthann Dirks and Janet Buzzard, "What CEOs Expect of Employees Hired for International Work," *Business Education Forum*, April 1997, pp. 3–7; Gunnar Beeth, "Multicultural Managers Wanted," *Management Review*, May 1997, pp. 17–21.

The Scope of Diversity

Improving cross-cultural relations includes appreciating the true meaning of diversity. To appreciate diversity, a person must go beyond tolerating and treating people from different racial and ethnic groups fairly. Valuing diversity means respecting and enjoying a wide range of cultural and individual differences. To be diverse is to be different in some measurable way. Although the diversity factor is *measurable* in a scientific sense, it may not be *visible* on the surface. Upon meeting a team member, it may not be apparent that the person is diverse from the stand-point of being dyslexic, color-blind, gay, lesbian, or vegetarian. However, all these factors are measurable.

As just implied, some people are more visibly diverse than others because of physical features or disabilities. Yet the diversity umbrella is supposed to include everybody in an organization. In recent years, many white males have expressed an interest in being included in diversity programs. Some white males believe that they experience reverse discrimination in favor of women and minorities.[33] The goal of a diverse organization, then, is for persons of all cultural backgrounds to achieve their full potential, not restrained by group identification, such as sex, nationality, or race.[34]

Exhibit 2-5 presents a broad sampling of the ways in which work associates can differ from one another. Studying this list can help you anticipate the types of differences in cultural as well as individual factors. Individual factors are also important because people can be discriminated against for personal characteristics as well as group factors. Many men and women, for example, believe they are held back from promotion because they choose to wear long hair.

The Competitive Advantage of Diversity

Encouraging diversity within an organization helps an organization achieve social responsibility goals. Also, diversity brings a competitive advantage to a firm. Before diversity can offer a competitive advantage to a firm, it must be woven into

47

EXHIBIT 2-5
The Diversity Umbrella

Diversity has evolved into a wide range of group and individual characteristics.

- Race
- Sex or gender
- Religion
- Age (young, middle-aged, and old)
- Generation differences, including attitudes (e.g., baby boomers versus net generation)
- Ethnicity (country of origin)
- Education
- Abilities
- Mental disabilities (including attention deficit disorder)
- Physical disabilities (including hearing status, visual status, able-bodied, wheelchair user)
- Values and motivation
- Sexual orientation (heterosexual, homosexual, bisexual, transsexual)
- Marital status (married, single, cohabitating, widow/widower)
- Family status (children, no children, two-parent family, single parent, grandparent, same-sex parents)
- Personality traits
- Functional background (area of specialization, such as marketing, HR)
- Technology interest (high-tech, low-tech, technophobe)
- Weight status (average, obese, underweight, anorexic)
- Hair status (full head of hair, bald, wild hair, tame hair, long hair, short hair)
- Style of clothing and appearance (dress up, dress down, professional appearance, casual appearance, tattoos, body piercing)
- Tobacco status (smoker versus nonsmoker, chewer versus nonchewer)
- Additions to the list _____

the fabric of the organization. This stands in contrast to simply having a "diversity program" offered periodically by the human resources department. Instead, the human resource efforts toward accomplishing diversity becomes part of organizational strategy. The potential competitive (or bottom-line) benefits of cultural diversity, as revealed by research and observations, are described next:[35]

1. *Managing diversity well offers a marketing advantage, including increased sales and profits.* A representational workforce facilitates reaching a multicultural market. Allstate Insurance Company invests considerable effort into being a culturally diverse business firm. More than coincidentally, Allstate is now recognized as the nation's leading insurer of African Americans and Hispanics. A study of racial diversity and business strategy in banking indicates that cultural diversity adds value and, within the proper context, contributes to a competitive advantage for the firm. The proper context, however, means a bank with a growth strategy. Racial diversity does not increase profits for firms with a downsizing strategy.[36]

2. *Effective management of diversity can reduce costs.* More effective management of diversity may increase job satisfaction of diverse groups, thus decreasing turnover and absenteeism and their associated costs. A diverse organization that welcomes and fosters the growth of a wide variety of employees will retain more of its minority and multicultural employees. Also, effective management of diversity helps avoid costly lawsuits over discrimination based on age, race, or sex. In 1996, Texaco paid $175 million to settle a racial discrimination lawsuit filed by some of the company's African-American employees. Profiting from its errors, Texaco has since then become a model for diversity.[37]

3. *Companies with a favorable record in managing diversity are at a distinct advantage in recruiting talented people.* Those companies with a favorable reputation for welcoming diversity attract the strongest job candidates among women and racial and ethnic minorities. A shortage of workers gives extra impetus to diversity. During a tight labor market, companies cannot afford to be seen as racist, sexist, ageist, or even antiunion.

4. *Workforce diversity can provide a company with useful ideas for favorable publicity and advertising.* A culturally diverse workforce, or advertising agency, can help a firm place itself in a favorable light to targeted cultural groups. During Kwanzaa, the late December holiday celebrated by many African Americans, McDonald's Corp. has run ads aimed at showing its understanding of and respect for African Americans' sense of family and community. For such ads to be effective, however, the company must also have a customer-contact workforce that is culturally diverse. Otherwise the ads would lack credibility.

5. *Workforce heterogeneity may also offer a company a creativity advantage.* Creative solutions to problems are more likely when a diverse group attacks a problem due to the variety of perspectives that contribute to creative alternatives. Raymond V. Gilmartin, the chairman and CEO of the pharmaceutical giant Merck & Company, notes that a homogeneous workforce is likely to exclude some superior individuals. The executive says, "Whether it is in the labor force or in the marketplace, competitive advantage in a business like ours rests on innovation. To succeed, we must bring together talented and committed people with diverse perspectives—people who can challenge one another's thinking, people who collectively approach problems from multiple points of view. We will continue, therefore, to cast the widest net in our search for talent—because it's the smart thing to do."[38]

Gilmartin's comments hint at an important consideration: whether a diversity strategy will lead to competitive advantage. A study was conducted with 93 African-American business students who rated three different scenarios about diversity programs. A justified program contained this statement:

> Diversity is especially critical in the product development division because a large segment of the market consists of women and minorities. Recent research has shown that successfully implemented diversity programs increase a firm's competitive advantage in these markets. Therefore, you are the applicant chosen to fill this particular position.

According to the results of the experiment, diversity programs that are justified in terms of a business purpose will lead to positive attitudes and opinions. In contrast, diversity programs that lack tangible results such as improved marketing or creativity contribute to negative attitudes and lack of commitment.[39] (The nonjustified scenario in the experiment gave no reason for the diversity initiative.) The implication for managers is that diversity initiatives should be explained in terms of tangible business purposes to achieve the best results.

ORGANIZATIONAL PRACTICES TO ENCOURAGE DIVERSITY   **7**

The combined forces of the spirit of the times and the advantages of valuing diversity spark management initiatives to manage diversity well. Exhibit 2-6 provides details about five business firms with the best record of hiring, promoting, and retaining minority group members. (Being a member of a minority group is but one dimension of diversity.) Three representative practices that enhance diversity management are (1) corporate policies about diversity, (2) the establishment of employee network groups, and (3) diversity training.

Summarize organizational practices to encourage diversity.

EXHIBIT 2-6

Five Major Companies with Excellent Performance in Managing Diversity

Company	% Minority Officials and Managers	Comment on Diversity Practices
Levi Strauss & Company	35.3	One of first companies to integrate factories in the South, it also pioneered a program to buy supplies from minority-owned businesses.
Dole Food	36.6	This food company boasts a higher percentage of minority managers than any other company on this list of 50. It is also tops for Asians. Four in 10 employees are of Asian descent.
U.S. Postal Service	30	Delivers on diversity by bringing in people of color—about half of new hires are minorities—and helping them move up through special career management programs.
Xerox	23.4	The company continues to excel in diversity, including a better-than-average minority representation (20%) among its 50 highest paid.
Hilton Hotels	27.8	Senior diversity vice president reports directly to the CEO. As in other service firms, diversity is especially marked at the entry level. About 62% of new hires are minorities.

Source: "America's 50 Best Companies for Minorities," *Fortune*, July 10, 2000, pp. 190–200.

49

Corporate Policies Favoring Diversity

Many companies formulate policies that encourage and foster diversity. A typical policy is "We are committed to recruiting, selecting, training, and promoting individuals based solely on their capabilities and performance. To accomplish this goal, we value all differences among our workforce." A study conducted by *Working Woman* magazine and the YWCA indicated that such policies do lead to effective management of diversity. Survey participants included top managers and business owners, a variety of managers, and nonsupervisory professionals. The respondents indicated that a commitment to diversity was most likely to succeed if the company established a corporate diversity policy. In companies that had been successful in achieving diversity, 47 percent had a stated policy, versus 28 percent that did not have one.[40]

To create a culturally and demographically diverse organization, some companies monitor recruitment and promotions to assure that diverse people are hired and promoted into key jobs. Two such companies in the restaurant business are Shoney's and Advantica (owner of the Denny's chain). Both firms formerly faced charges of racial discrimination but now occupy positions on *Fortune*'s list as leading companies for minorities. The policy of both firms is to promote qualified minority group members into key jobs, such as regional manager. Part of policy-making also ties managers' bonuses to diversity goals, as is done by 38 of the 50 best companies for minorities.[41] The accompanying Management in Action illustrates how a well-established company applies policy to facilitate diversity.

Management *in Action*

Valuing Cultural Diversity at Pitney Bowes

The history and culture of Pitney Bowes demonstrate the value and uniqueness of each individual, and the ability to leverage that diversity into strategic business results. The company has received many awards in the area of effective diversity management, including being named among the top three companies for executive women by *Working Woman* magazine in 1998, and receiving the Catalyst Award in 1994. The representation of women at all levels of employment in our company exceeds industry averages, and over 40 percent of direct reports to our chair are women.

Pitney Bowes is fortunate to have a heritage of "doing the right thing" and the ability to creatively address complex business opportunities—two direct results of our efforts to leverage the diversity of our workforce.

According to chair and CEO Michael Critelli, "Pitney Bowes is nationally recognized for our innovative and resourceful leadership in promoting diversity. Our global agenda emphasizes a strategic commitment to diversity in several areas: One, minority- and women-owned businesses are among the most imaginative in turning obstacles into business opportunities. Two, the most strategic way for us to realize our business objectives is to leverage our unique and diverse workforce. It is the talent and productivity of our people that will sustain our competitive leadership now and well into the 21st century."

Source: "Strength Through Diversity for Bottom-Line Success," Special Advertising Section, *Working Woman,* March 1999, p. 68; http://www.pitneybowes.com.

Employee Network Groups

A company approach to recognizing cultural differences is to permit and encourage employees to form **employee network groups**. The network group is composed of employees throughout the company who affiliate on the basis of group characteristics such as race, ethnicity, gender, sexual orientation, or physical ability status. Group members typically have similar interests, and look to groups as a way of sharing information about succeeding in the organization. Although some human resource specialists are concerned that network groups can lead to divisiveness, others believe they play a positive role.

Bank One gives financial support to minority employees' networking groups, such as payments for flyers, meal meetings, and hotel gatherings. At 3M Corporation, employee network groups serve as advisors to business units. For example, the company's network group for employees with disabilities is often consulted by 3M product development groups. Company network groups also help their organizations recruit through such means as providing links to minority group members in the community.[42]

Diversity Training

Cultural training, as described in the section about international business, aims to help workers understand people from another culture. Understanding can lead to dealing more effectively with them as work associates or customers. **Diversity training** has a slightly different purpose. It attempts to bring about workplace harmony by teaching people how to get along better with diverse work associates. Quite often the program is aimed at minimizing open expressions of racism and sexism. All forms of diversity training center around increasing people's awareness of and empathy for people who are different from themselves.

Diversity training sessions focus on the ways that men and women, or people of different races, reflect different values, attitudes, and cultural background. These sessions can vary from several hours to several days. Sometimes the program is confrontational, sometimes not. As described by diversity consultant H. Roosevelt Thomas Jr., the objectives of diversity training include one or more of the following:[43]

- Fostering awareness and acceptance of individual differences
- Helping participants understand their own feelings and attitudes about people who are "different"
- Exploring how differences might be tapped as assets in the workplace
- Enhancing work relations between people who are different from each other.

An essential part of relating more effectively to diverse groups is to empathize with their point of view. To help training participants develop empathy, representatives of various groups explain their feelings related to workplace issues. During one of these training sessions a Chinese woman said she wished people would not act so shocked when she is assertive about her demands. She claimed that many people she meets at work expect her to fit the stereotype of the polite, compliant Chinese woman.

Many different exercises are used in diversity training. In one exercise, a nationality is mentioned, such as Italian. All group members then describe what comes to mind when the nationality "Italian" is mentioned. Later, the group discusses how their stereotypes help and hinder diversity.

employee network groups

Employees within a company who affiliate on the basis of race, ethnicity, gender, sexual orientation, or physical ability to discuss ways to succeed in the organization.

51

diversity training

Training that attempts to bring about workplace harmony by teaching people how to get along better with diverse work associates.

A new trend in diversity training is cross-generational diversity, or relating effectively to workers much older or younger than you. Wendy's International, Inc., with the help of a consultant, has developed training programs that raise awareness of generational issues. Allen Larson, director of management resources, says "Since generational cohorts help form people's attitudes toward work, employees of different generations who must work together may find that their work styles conflict with those of coworkers."[44]

Cultural diversity programs encounter several potential problems. The diversity trainers and participants are sometimes too confrontational and express too much hostility. Companies find that when employees are too blunt during these sessions, it may be difficult to patch up interpersonal relations in the work group later on. Another concern about diversity training is that it exaggerates stereotypes in order to promote understanding.[45]

In recent years, mentoring of minority group members has been effective in fostering some of the goals of diversity training. Many companies rely on both informal mentoring and formal mentoring (assigning a mentor to a person) as a way to help women and people of color advance in their careers. A survey of successful minority executives indicated that 48 percent of the respondents said they had a role model who guided them toward early career goals. The role model/mentors were primarily the same ethnic, racial, or cultural origin. A sponsor of the survey said, "Minority executives believe that mentors are very helpful in advocating for upward mobility and teaching them how to navigate through the corporation."[46]

The English Language as a Force for Unity

Although differences among people are important to business firms around the world, international workers have to communicate effectively with each other. To compete globally, more and more European businesses are making English their official language. In this way, workers of different European nationalities can communicate with each other. In many Asian countries also, English is widely used in business. The majority of managerial, professional, technical, and support positions in Europe require a good command of English.

One reason English maintains the edge as the official language of business in so many countries is that English grammar is less complex than that of many other languages. The Internet, and information technology in general, with its heavy emphasis on English, is another force for making English the language of business. A cartoon in *Fortune* summarizes the heavy presence of English in the e-world. Two men wearing business suits and carrying briefcases are talking to each other with the Eiffel Tower in the background. One man says to the other, "Oui, j'adore [French for "Yes, I love"] e-commerce start-ups!"[47]

Although English may have emerged as the official language of business, the successful international manager needs to be multicultural. Furthermore, if business associates throughout the world are fluent in their native tongue as well as English, command of a second language remains an asset for North Americans.

SUMMARY OF KEY POINTS

 Appreciate the importance of multinational corporations in international business. Multinational corporations (MNCs) are the heart of international business. The continued growth of the MNC has been facilitated by the North American Free Trade Agreement, the World Trade Organization, and the European Union. The globalization of business has led to controversy about what constitutes an American product.

2 **Recognize the importance of sensitivity to cultural differences in international enterprise**. The guiding principle for people involved in international enterprise is sensitivity to cultural differences. Candidates for foreign assignments generally receive training in the language and customs of the country in which they will work. Another approach to developing cross-cultural sensitivity is to recognize national differences in managerial styles.

3 **Identify major challenges facing the global managerial worker**. Challenges facing global managerial workers include economic crises in other countries (such as the recent Asian crisis) such as fluctuating money values, balance of trade problems, collecting money, the liability of being a foreigner, human rights violations, culture shock, differences in negotiating style, and piracy of intellectual property rights and other merchandise.

4 **Explain various methods of entry into world markets.** Firms enter global markets via the following methods: exporting, licensing, local warehousing and selling, local assembly and packaging, strategic alliance, direct foreign investment, global merger, and global start-up.

5 **Pinpoint success factors in the global marketplace, and several positive and negative aspects of globalization**. Success factors for the global marketplace

include (a) think globally, act locally, (b) diversify into similar product markets, (c) be familiar with local business concepts, laws, and customs, (d) recruit talented nationals, (e) research and assess local markets, (f) hire or develop multicultural workers, including offering cultural training, (g) adopt policies that are environmentally friendly, and (h) understand your competitors, potential partners, and the diverse members of the management team. Many of the advantages and disadvantages of globalization depend upon an individual's point of view. For example, profits may increase at the cost of many workers' jobs.

6 **Describe the scope of diversity and the competitive advantage of a culturally diverse workforce**. To be diverse is to be different in some measurable, but not necessarily visible way. The diversity umbrella is supposed to encompass everybody in the organization, including white males. Diversity often brings a competitive advantage to a firm including the following: marketing advantage, lowered costs due to turnover and absenteeism, improved recruitment, useful ideas for publicity and advertising, and a creativity advantage.

7 **Summarize organizational practices to encourage diversity**. Three representative practices that enhance diversity management are corporate policies about diversity, the establishment of employee network groups, and diversity training including mentoring of minority group members.

KEY TERMS AND PHRASES

Multinational corporation (MNC), *30*

Transnational corporation, *30*

Cultural sensitivity, *33*

Multicultural worker, *33*

Balance of trade, *36*

Culture shock, *38*

Maquiladora, *40*

Transnational teams, *41*

Global start-up, *41*

Diversity, *46*

Employee network groups, *51*

Diversity training, *51*

QUESTIONS

1. Why do top-level executives from many corporations insist that their firm cannot survive without foreign sales and foreign manufacturing?

2. Identify a profit-making enterprise that does not have to be bothered with international trade, and for whom international competition is not a threat.

3. Assume than an American manager is sent abroad to manage a division in another country. Explain whether

that manager should change styles to fit the preferred management style in that country.

4. How can a management team justify dealing with a subcontractor based in a country in which human rights are being widely violated?

5. What would be the potential disadvantage of a firm attempting to conduct all of its international business through e-commerce?

6. What steps can you take, starting this week, to ready yourself to become a multicultural worker?

7. Suppose an African-American couple opens a restaurant that serves African cuisine, hoping to appeal mostly to people of African descent. The restaurant is a big success, yet the couple finds that about 40 percent of its clientele is Caucasian. Should the restaurant owners then hire several Caucasians so the employee mix will match the customer mix?

CRITICAL THINKING QUESTIONS

1. Get together in a group to identify five *positive* cultural stereotypes, meaning that you are predisposed to thinking that a member of a specific cultural group has a particularly strong quality. How might this positive stereotype sometimes work against the person in terms of job assignments?

2. Check U.S. Department of Commerce data, or other sources, to identify the three largest trading partners of the United States. The results may surprise you.

SKILL-BUILDING EXERCISE: Evaluating a Multicultural Digital Assistant

You and several of your classmates are part of a task force to help develop the multicultural skills of your workforce. You have been placed on this assignment because your transnational corporation conducts business in 17 different countries, with a total of six different languages. Today you are asked to evaluate the feasibility of a digital device to enhance the multicultural and foreign language skills of your workforce. The product description is as follows:

Next time you find yourself linguistically challenged, whip out the **Universal Translator UT 106** *from Ectaco Inc. Here's how it works: Simply speak the desired phrase into the unit's built-in microphone. The palm-size machine uses speech-to-speech technology to translate the phrase into one of six languages. Then the translator talks back, providing the correct pronunciation via a built-in speaker.*

Easy to use, the unit can store 2,000 sentences in French, German, Italian, Portuguese, Russian, and Spanish. And you can go to the Web and download additional phrases. Bravo! The Universal Translator UT 106 retails for about $200. Visit Ectaco on the Web (http://www.ectaco.com).

Discuss the merits of the Universal Translator for helping your workforce become more multicultural, and reach a conclusion about equipping your international workers with the Translator. As part of your evaluation, visit the company Web site. See whether you can obtain a demonstration that can be played through the speakers connected to your computer and monitor.

Source: Product description from http://www.ectaco.com and *Fast Company*, March 2000, p. 80.

INTERNET SKILL-BUILDING EXERCISE: Becoming Multicultural

A useful way of developing skills in a second language, and learning more about another culture, is to create a "bookmark" or "favorite" written in your target language. In this way, each time you go on the Internet on your own computer, your cover page will contain fresh information in the language you want to develop. To get started, use a search engine like Yahoo or Excite that offers choices in several languages. Enter a key word like "newspaper" or "current events" in the search probe. Once you find a suitable choice, enter the edit function for "Favorites" or "Bookmarks" and insert that newspaper as your cover page. For example, imagine that French were your choice. The Yahoo France search engine might have brought you to www.france2.fr. This Web site keeps you abreast of French and international news, sports, and cultural events—written in French. Now every time you access the Internet, you can spend five minutes becoming multicultural. You can save a lot of travel costs and time using the Internet to help you become multicultural.

CASE PROBLEM 2-A: The Tale of a Cultural Translator

Gunnar Beeth works in seven languages throughout Europe, from his own executive search firm, IMA-CONSULT S.A. in Brussels, Belgium. He observes that joint ventures between Western and Japanese companies usually run into a series of small conflicts that escalate over the years. The small conflicts often become big emotional battles, due mainly to cultural differences. Beeth tells the tale of how one company he worked for as a director of international operations attempted to avoid a culture clash primarily through the activities of one employee:

George Schreiber was an installation engineer responsible for starting up our equipment. The company needed to send a person to train the new Japanese employees in the unique technology. Schreiber accepted a two-year contract for a temporary transfer to Japan. Before departing he was first sent to an intensive course in Japanese. Schreiber did not belong to the management group in the American company but had a solid understanding of the technical products, their installation, and use. On this basis he was highly qualified for training the Japanese engineers.

Schreiber quickly became well accepted by the Japanese employees. The Japanese managers perceived that the nonassertive Schreiber was no threat to their management careers, despite representing the U.S. owner. So they did not hesitate to ask his advice on a large number of matters, some outside his expertise but within his sharply developed common sense. The engineers throughout the company appreciated Schreiber's frequent help with a multitude of problems they encountered in the beginning. Soon the engineers began consulting Schreiber on almost any problem they faced. The support workers in the office were eager to help this nice American bachelor improve his wretched spoken Japanese.

The joint venture became profitable ahead of schedule, and was thriving and growing. Schreiber's first two-year contract came to an end. By that time he had learned Japanese customs. His spoken Japanese improved to a satisfactory level. He drank green tea at all hours, ate rice at all meals, and liked to sleep on Japanese tatami mats instead of a bed. He had become "tatamized."

Schreiber was offered a second two-year contract, which he accepted immediately. Other contracts followed for the joint venture. The venture soon had more than 100 Japanese

employees, and the Japanese engineers soon surpassed Schreiber in the intricacies of the new equipment, which changed rapidly. As a consequence, Schreiber had nothing left to teach them in technical matters. Instead of returning to the American company, or finding new employment, Schreiber became a cultural translator.

When a message arrived from the American headquarters and the capable Japanese joint-venture president felt offended, he stormed into Schreiber's small office and threw the message in front of him, fuming. George read the message and explained calmly that the American had not really meant it in the way such a message would be understood in Japan.

For communication from Japan to the United States, the written English of one of the Japanese secretaries was quite adequate. But at times something far more important than good English was needed. At one time the American auditors demanded an explanation for two expense items. One issue was why the Japanese company spent $46,534 on 874 December holiday presents. Another was why the Japanese affiliate continued to keep a chemist on the payroll whose specialty had become obsolete a year earlier.

When the Western managers came traveling to Japan, Schreiber accompanied them to ensure that they didn't do or say anything too stupid, from the Japanese viewpoint. Whenever they did, he corrected them at once: "What you really mean is . . ." And he did the same thing from the opposite direction. He prevented many conflicts from arising, and he smoothed over small conflicts before they became big, emotional, and costly.

Discussion Questions

1. How justifiable is it to keep a full-time employee on the payroll as a "cultural translator"?
2. Placing yourself in George Schreiber's role, how would you explain to the auditor, the money spent on the holiday gifts and the salary paid to the obsolete engineer?
3. What alternatives can you recommend to renewing Schreiber's contract for a third term?

Source: Adapted from Gunnar Beeth, "Multicultural Managers Wanted," *Management Review*, May 1997, p. 17.

CASE PROBLEM 2-B: Hold on to Bilingual Workers

Jaime Ornelas's Spanish-language skills and technology know-how helped him go global. Ornelas, a chemical engineer by training, who has been stationed all over the world, said he's an example of how bilingual skills—and the cultural

lessons that come with them—can be a huge plus for tech workers.

"It's important in the sense of making sure there's no miscommunication in terms of anecdotes and idioms," said

Ornelas, who now works as a cost and financial planning analyst at Texas Instruments in Dallas. "But more importantly, it's the notion that you have the ability to see things from a different perspective."

Ornelas was born in Mexico City, attended college and graduate school in Texas, and then held chemical engineering jobs in Waco, Mexico City, and San Antonio. While working in San Antonio, he switched to financial planning, becoming an expert in compliance with environmental regulations. At Texas Instruments, he helps the environmental and safety groups meet government standards.

With such a varied background, Ornelas learned a lot about how different cultures interact. Not only can bilingual tech workers communicate around the world, but they can also help companies understand the cultural backgrounds of their global partners and their employees, he said.

That's exactly the help that Lois Melbourne needs. She's president of Irving, Texas-based TimeVision Inc., a software company that makes organizational charting programs for human resources departments. TimeVision already has customers in Europe and wants to expand in Latin America. But it needs technology-savvy Spanish speakers for customer support and sales help.

"In our job postings, we say 'multilingual preferred.' But because the job market is so tight, we hire quality people regardless of that requirement," she said. "To find somebody with all those skills would be almost too good to be true."

Melbourne said her company is so eager to sell to Latin America that one bilingual employee is teaching Spanish at lunchtime. "Not having the bilingual employees really slows us down," she said.

Other tech companies say they also need bilingual workers to help serve the growing Spanish-speaking market in the United States. Studies indicate that almost half of all Hispanic households are online.

Angelo Ioffreda, a spokesperson for America Online Inc. said that most jobs at tech companies that require Spanish skills are in customer service, sales, and marketing.

Steve Adams, a spokesperson for Dallas-based Internet America Inc., said that his company actively searches for bilingual tech support experts. "We have trouble holding on to them," he said. "There's such a demand for people with bilingual skills."

Discussion Questions

1. What does the information provided by the people in this case reveal about the relationship between cultural diversity within a firm and its ability to compete effectively in international business?

2. What suggestions can you offer the companies mentioned to attract and retain Spanish-speaking employees?

3. As an executive in one of the companies mentioned in the case, which of the following two strategies would you choose to have a larger number of Spanish-speaking employees? (a) teach Spanish to technology-skilled workers, or (b) teach technology to Spanish-speaking workers? Explain your reasoning.

Source: Adapted from Crayton Harrison, "Tech Companies Hunting for Bilingual Employees," Knight Ridder, October 15, 2000.

ENDNOTES

1. Richard Mullins, "World at Work," Rochester, New York, *Democrat and Chronicle,* September 17, 2000, p. 1E.
2. Pankaj Ghemawat and Fariborz Ghadar, "The Dubious Logic of Megamergers," *Harvard Business Review,* July–August 2000, pp. 64–72.
3. "North American Free Trade Agreement," Microsoft® Encarta® Online Encyclopedia 2000, http://encarta.msn.com.© 1997–2000 Microsoft Corporation. All rights reserved.
4. Aaron Bernstein, "Welch's March to the South," *Business Week,* December 6, 1999, pp. 74, 78.
5. "Slogan to Increase Profile of the Euro," The Associated Press, March 2, 2001.
6. Gunnar Beeth, "Multicultural Managers Wanted," *Management Review,* May 1997, p. 17.
7. Marvina Shilling, "Avoid Expatriate Culture Shock," *HR Magazine,* July 1993, p. 58.
8. Geert Hofstede, "Cultural Constraints in Management Theories," *The Academy of Management Executive,* February 1993, pp. 81–94; David C. Thomas and Elizabeth C. Ravlin, "Responses of Employees to Cultural Adaptation by a Foreign Manager," *Journal of Applied Psychology,* February 1995, p. 138.
9. Emily Thornton, "Japan's Asian Comeback," *Business Week,* November 1, 1999, pp. 58–59.
10. Srilata Zaheer, "Overcoming the Liability of Foreignness," *Academy of Management Journal,* April 1995, pp. 341–363.
11. "Amnesty International Latest Press Releases," http://www.web.amnesty.org/web (accessed March 1, 2001); John Hanchette, "Report: U.S. Firms Trading in Torture," Gannett News Service, February 27, 2001.
12. Harry C. Triandis, *Culture Shock and Social Behavior* (New York: McGraw-Hill, 1994), p. 263.
13. Margaret A. Shaffer and David A. Harrison, "Expatriates' Psychological Withdrawal from International Assignments: Work, Nonwork, and Family Influences," *Personnel Psychology,* Spring 1998, p. 114.
14. Paul Blustein, "China Plays Rough: 'Invest and Transfer Technology, or No Market Access,'" *The Washington Post,* October 25, 1997, p. C1.
15. Jeanne Brett and Tetsushi Okumura, "Inter- and Intracultural Negotiations: U.S. and Japanese Negotiators," *Academy of Management Journal,* October 1998, pp. 495–510.
16. Stephen Baker and Inka Resch, "Piracy! How Microsoft Cracked a Counterfeiting Ring in Europe—and How It's Stepping Up the Fight," *Business Week,* July 26, 1999, pp. 90–94.
17. Baker and Resch, "Piracy!" p. 90.
18. Rodney C. Shrader, "Collaboration and Performance in Foreign

Markets: The Case of Young High-Technology Manufacturing Firms," *Academy of Management Journal*, February 2001, p. 45.

19. Eugene H. Fram and Riad A. Ajami, "International Distributors and the Role of U.S. Top Management: A Requirement for Export Competitiveness," *Journal of Business and Industrial Marketing*, 1998:4, pp. 33–44.

20. Shrader, "Collaboration and Performance in Foreign Markets," p. 45.

21. Charles C. Snow et al., "Use Transnational Teams to Globalize Your Company," *Organizational Dynamics*, Spring 1996, p. 52.

22. Harry G. Barkema and Freek Vermeylen, "International Expansion through Start-Up or Acquisition: A Learning Perspective," *Academy of Management Journal*, February 1998, pp. 7–26.

23. Charlene Marmer Solomon, "Corporate Pioneers Navigate Global Mergers," *Global Workforce* (Supplement to *Workforce*), September 1998, p. 14.

24. Benjamin M. Oviatt and Patricia Phillips McDougal, "Global Start-Ups: Entrepreneurs on a Worldwide Stage," *The Academy of Management Executive*, May 1995, p. 30.

25. Yigang Pan and Peter Chi, "Financial Performance and Survival of Multinational Corporations in China," *Strategic Management Journal*, 20, 1999, pp. 359–374.

26. Michael A. Hitt and R. Duane Ireland, "Building Competitive Strength in International Markets," *Long Range Planning*, February 1987, pp. 115–122.

27. Valerie Frazee, "Handling Recruiting as a Business Traveler," *Global Workforce* (Supplement to *Workforce*), July 1998, p. 22.

28. Charlene Marmer Solomon, "Learning to Manage Host-Country Nationals," *Personnel Journal*, March 1995, p. 61.

29. Valerie Frazee, "Send Your Expats Prepared for Success," *Global Workforce* (Supplement to *Workforce*), March 1999, p. 8.

30. Frazee, "Send Your Expats," p. 8.

31. Shaker A. Zahra, "The Changing Rules of Global Competitiveness in the 21st Century," *Academy of Management Executive*, February 1999, p. 39.

32. Michael A. Hitt et al., "Understanding Strategic Intent in the Global Marketplace," *The Academy of Management Executive*, May 1995, p. 18.

33. Gillian Flynn, "White Males See Diversity's Other Side," *Workforce*, February 1999, pp. 52–55.

34. Joan Crockett, "Winning Competitive Advantage Through a Diverse Workforce," *HRfocus*, May 1999, p. 9.

35. The general framework here is based on Orlando C. Richard, "Racial Diversity, Business Strategy, and Firm Performance: A Resource-Based View," *Academy of Management Journal*, April 2000, pp. 164–177; Crockett, "Winning Competitive Advantage," *HRfocus*, pp. 9–10; "Diversity: A 'New' Tool for Retention," *HRfocus*, June 2000, pp. 1, 14–15.

36. Richard, "Racial Diversity," pp. 164–177.

37. Kenneth Labich, "No More Crude at Texaco," *Fortune*, September 6, 1999, pp. 205–212.

38. Raymond V. Gilmartin, "Diversity and Competitive Advantage at Merck," *Harvard Business Review*, January–February 1999, p. 146.

39. Orlando C. Richard and Susan L. Kirby, "Organizational Justice and the Justification of Work Force Diversity Programs," *Journal of Business and Psychology*, Fall 1999, pp. 109–118.

40. Harris Collingwood, "Who Handles a Diverse Workforce Best," *Working Woman*, February 1996, p. 25.

41. Stephanie N. Mehta, "What Minority Employees Really Want," *Fortune*, July 10, 2000, p. 186.

42. "Banks Sow Diversity: Industry Initiatives Help Them Attract, Keep Minority Workers," Rochester, New York, *Democrat and Chronicle*, September 12, 2000, p. 10D; Patricia Digh, "Well-Managed Employee Networks Add Business Value," *HR Magazine*, August 1997, pp. 67–72.

43. R. Roosevelt Thomas, Jr., *Beyond Race and Gender: Unleashing the Power of Your Total Work Force by Managing Diversity* (New York: AMACOM, 1991), p. 25.

44. Joanne M. Glenn, "Wendy's International, Inc.—Managing Cross-Generational Diversity," *Business Education Forum*, February 2000, p. 16.

45. Gillian Flynn, "The Harsh Reality of Diversity Programs," *Workforce*, December 1998, p. 27.

46. Jerry Langdon, "Minority Executives Benefit from Mentors," Gannett News Service, December 7, 1998. See also Letty C. Hardy, "Mentoring: A Long-Term Approach to Diversity," *HRfocus*, July 1988, p. S11.

47. Justin Fox, "The Triumph of English," *Fortune*, September 18, 2000, pp. 209–212.

Information Technology and the Internet

Diamond Technology Partners Inc. (http://www.diamtech.com), is an e-commerce services company with 800 employees. *Time Digital* designated the firm as one of the top 10 digital workplaces. *Time* defines a digital workplace as an employer that lets high technology work for you while you work for the company.

Only half the people who work for Diamond live anywhere near its Naperville, Illinois, headquarters. The rest, says partner David Baker, "can live anywhere we want." Baker lives in Austin, Texas, but he works "out of my computer bag, which my wife fondly calls my 'office.'"

Diamond makes this footloose culture viable by providing laptops (some with webcams for videoconferencing), a state-of-the-art voice-mail system that receives faxes and routes them to remote locations, and a "hoteling" system, which allows employees to reserve office space in Naperville as needed. On a recent visit there, Baker was shocked to find himself assigned to a desk with a pen-and-pencil holder. "I didn't use it," he says. "I had no idea what to put in it."[1]

The story about Diamond Technology Partners illustrates the extent to which information technology pervades the modern office. Not only do employees stay linked to technology within the office, through wireless devices they can continue to work while on a patio or stuck in a snowstorm. This chapter highlights how information technology, including the Internet, influences the manager's job. Although the Internet is part of information technology, it is described separately here because of its profound impact on both the manager's job and the

OBJECTIVES

After studying this chapter and doing the exercises, you should be able to:

1 Summarize the demands information technology places on the manager's job.

2 Describe positive and negative consequences of information technology for the manager.

3 Discuss the impact of the Internet on customer and other external relationships.

4 Explain the effects of the Internet on internal company operations.

5 Pinpoint factors associated with success in e-business.

Chapter 3

conduct of business. Your present knowledge of information technology, including computers, provides the necessary technical background for understanding this chapter.

1   INFORMATION TECHNOLOGY AND THE MANAGER'S JOB

Summarize the demands information technology places on the manager's job.

Information technology changes the work methods of workers in a wide variety of jobs. For example, office workers are rarely out of touch with their computers, and clerks in auto supply stores use computerized databases to search for the availability of replacement parts. Managerial workers also feel the profound influence of information technology. In this section we look at the heavy demand information technology places on managers, as well as the specific impact of wireless devices.

Increased Demands Placed on Managers

From the perspective of work methods, the landscape of a manager's job looks substantially different. Instead of handing work to an office assistant, the manager now types, sends, and receives his or her own messages, and makes appointments on a palm-sized computer. Our concern here, however, is with the broader implications of the changes created by information technology. As analyzed by Michael Hitt, management today must build an organization that constantly transforms itself because information technology increases competition.[2] For instance, the manager of a travel agency must now compete with the many online sources for purchasing airplane and hotel reservations.

Managers must develop and respond continuously to new technologies, new types of businesses, and new people in the form of employees and customers. Information technology itself changes so rapidly that managers must adapt themselves to the changes, and help others adapt. For example, managers expect and prepare for productivity dips while workers adapt to a new company-wide software system.

Another general issue with technology, including information technology, is how the development and spread of the new technology increases the importance of innovating to remain competitive. The continuous development of technology decreases product life cycles, creating more pressure on managers and workers involved in the development and manufacture of products.

Information and communications technology is at the center of the technological revolution. This technology is used in most business firms and provides an integral part of many systems, such as inventory control. Information technology makes globalization more practical because it allows ready access to employees all over the world at nominal cost. The same technology makes it feasible to customize many industrial products by combining special features with standard features, such as a Saturn automobile or Dell computer to meet your personal preferences.[3]

The sampling of technological changes just mentioned illustrates why information technology pushes managers into a continuous learning mode. Even if the manager is not an expert on how to use information technology to customize mass-produced products, the manager still requires a working understanding of the process. Otherwise, he or she will seem foolish when asked questions.

The Wireless Environment

A specific, direct consequence of information technology comes from managers' use of wireless communication devices to facilitate their work from different locations. For almost a century, managers used wired telephones to stay in touch with the office. In the modern environment, a rapidly evolving number of devices give managers more constant access to the office and to customers. Cellular telephones and laptop computers are standard in the manager's toolkit. Managers typically use three other information technology devices to stay in touch with employees and customers, and current business information:

1. *Personal digital assistant (hand-held PC).* Aside from the standard functions of a small computer such as accessing e-mail and linking to the PC at the office, many managers input databases into their palm-sized computer. The databases can be strictly business-related with customer and supplier information. Databases in hand-held PCs also include regularly updated lists of restaurants, movies, and plays. Personal digital assistants have screens the size of playing cards, and can display simple graphic images. Most hand-held PCs also offer organizers to help boost productivity.
2. *Web-enabled cell phones.* In addition to hooking up to the Web, these tiny devices transmit and receive both voice messages and data. Some of these models support voice activation so the manager on the go can issue a voice command like, "Yahoo.com" to reach a search engine. The Web phone enables e-mail, and many incorporate two-way pagers with instant messaging.
3. *E-mail pager.* This small device combines e-mail and paging to allow sending messages back and forth, much like the messaging function of many e-mail systems. A message can typically contain up to 500 characters of text. An e-mail pager is most valuable for a manager who needs to be in touch with people who would find phone conversations difficult to hear, such as customers at a construction site or in a subway. Note that the e-mail pager is likely to be included on a Web phone.

To use the three mobile devices just mentioned effectively, the manager must be able to tolerate a miniaturized keyboard and have sharp vision. Also note that not every manager finds these devices comfortable or productive. For example, paper-based desk planners are still preferred by many managers and professionals over personal digital assistants. And many managers can wait until they return to the office to obtain information from e-mail and the Internet so they can enjoy the comforts of a large monitor.

THE POSITIVE AND NEGATIVE CONSEQUENCES OF INFORMATION TECHNOLOGY   2

Information technology is integrated into the everyday work of first-level and middle-level managers and staff professionals. Top-level managers also rely on PCs to conduct their work. Furthermore, executives who depend on office assistants to access their e-mail, or open Web pages, are becoming a rarity. The new generation of executives is information tech-savvy. Here we look at both the advantages and disadvantages of information technology as part of the manager's job.

Describe the positive and negative consequences of information technology for the manager.

Positive Consequences of Information Technology for the Manager

An information technology revolution that did not help managers, other workers, and organizations perform better, would not last. The following description of the positive consequences of IT emphasizes its benefits to managerial work. Exhibit 3-1 outlines these potential advantages.

Improved Productivity and Teamwork

A major justification for installing information technology is its capability for improving productivity. Information technology facilitated much of the slimming down of organizations in recent years. A reduction in staffing leads to increased productivity providing that the sales volume remains constant or improves. For example, most banks found they could reduce the number of branches and consolidate customer service into centralized call centers.

Small business owners can increase their productivity in many ways by exploiting information technology. An advanced application of IT is using online services to find sources of investment capital. The business owner posts a message to which potential investors (venture capitalists) respond. Finding investors online can be quicker than extensive letter-writing and telephone-calling campaigns.

Information technology enhances teamwork by allowing team members to maintain frequent contact with each other through e-mail and pagers. Even if the group cannot hold an in-person meeting, team members can give electronic feedback to each other's ideas. Furthermore, with extensive use of IT, teammates can work in geographically dispersed locations. (The virtual office will be described later.)

Increased Competitive Advantage

Effective use of information technology can give a firm a competitive advantage. Judicious use of *infotech* enables companies to conduct business in ways that would be impossible without such technology. How one company in the energy field gained control of another illustrates this point. Jack L. Messman, the CEO of Union Pacific Resources Group Inc., launched a hostile takeover of Pennzoil Co. Before taking action he compiled every piece of available data on Pennzoil's fields throughout the world. Using computer programs that help locate hidden oil and natural gas, he concluded that Penzoil had more reserves than it realized. As a result he made a more aggressive takeover offer. "Technology is what's driving this business today," says Messman, a former computer company executive turned oilman.[4]

Today, not using modern information technology makes a company noncompetitive. Imagine how embarrassing it would be for a company to have neither a Web site nor e-mail for interacting with customers and suppliers. Today, even low-tech establishments like restaurants and sub shops often have Web sites and e-mail addresses.

EXHIBIT 3-1

Positive Consequences of Information Technology for the Manager

Information technology can help the manager work smarter.

1. Improved productivity and teamwork
2. Increased competitive advantage
3. Improved customer service and supplier relationships
4. Enhanced communication and coordination, including the Virtual Office
5. Quick access to vast information
6. Enhanced analysis of data and decision making
7. Greater empowerment and flatter organizations
8. Saved time through employee self-service

Improved Customer Service and Supplier Relationships

Advances in information technology, including networking, can lead to improved customer service and smoother working relationships with suppliers. Customer service improves when service representatives can immediately access information to resolve a customer problem. USAA, a large financial services firm, provides a model for the industry in terms of prompt service. The company sells insurance directly to the public, without the use of external sales representatives or insurance agents. Policyholders can call an 800 number to receive immediate answers to complex questions such as how much rates will increase if a 16-year-old family member becomes a licensed driver.

Supplier relationships can be more productive when suppliers and purchasers are part of the same network. Large retailers such as Wal-Mart authorize some of their suppliers to ship and stock goods based on electronic messages sent from point of purchase to the suppliers' computers. When inventory gets low on a fast-moving item, supplies are replenished automatically without a retail store official having to make a phone call or send a letter.

Another development to improve customer services is the **extranet**, a secure section of a Web site that only visitors with a password can enter. Many financial services firms use an extranet to allow customers to manage accounts and trade stocks on line. The extranet is also used to share inventory or customer information with suppliers, send information to vendors, and sell products and services.

extranet
A Web site that requires a password to enter.

Enhanced Communication and Coordination, Including the Virtual Office

Nowhere is the impact of information technology on the manager's job more visible than in communication and coordination. By relying on information technology, managers can be in frequent contact with group members without being physically present. They can also be part of the **virtual office**, in which employees work together as if they were part of a single office despite being physically separated. Highly coordinated virtual office members form a *virtual team*. Such teams are groups of geographically separated coworkers who are assembled using information technology to accomplish a task.

virtual office
An arrangement whereby employees work together as if they were part of a single office despite being physically separated.

Virtual teams rarely meet face-to-face. They are sometimes established as temporary structures to accomplish a specific task such as developing a company-wide mentoring program. At other times virtual teams assume an ongoing responsibility such as providing input for the future direction of the organization.[5]

The virtual office and virtual teams conduct much of the work through *cybermeetings,* a gathering of participants in scattered locations using videoconferencing or e-mail. A videoconference enables people to see and hear each other through real-time video. Cybermeetings can accommodate from 4 to 200 people. Large firms often establish their own videoconferencing centers, whereas smaller firms typically rent a center as needed.

Frequent contact with company employees, customers, and suppliers enhances coordination. The alternative is for the manager to communicate primarily when back at the office. A high-tech manager is never away from the office—even if he or she would like to be!

Quick Access to Vast Information

Information technology gives managers quick access to vast amounts of information. A careful library researcher could always access vast amounts of business-related information. Advances in information technology, however, allow for fingertip access if the manager has the right computer skills. For example, a sales manager might want a targeted list of prospects for her company's new pool tables. She uses an electronic database to locate sporting goods stores in her region, ranking them by revenue and zip code to streamline her sales strategy.

A major contributor to accessing information quickly is the **company intranet**, a Web site for company use only. Ford Motor Company estimates saved billions of dollars over a few years by using its intranet. Ford's intranet connects more than 120,000 workstations around the world to thousands of Web sites. The Web sites contain proprietary information like market research, analyses of components, and rankings of the most effective suppliers. All vehicle teams have their own Web sites, enabling team members to post questions and progress reports, point out bottlenecks, and resolve quality problems. Sharing all this information has helped Ford reduce the cycle time on new models from 36 months down to 24 months. Using the intranet, the manager can achieve better results such as cost savings and quicker model introductions.[6]

Enhanced Analysis of Data and Decision Making

Closely related to gathering a wider array of information, IT allows for better analysis of data and decision making. Managers at business firms of all sizes now analyze data better to improve efficiency. A before-and-after example follows:

> Years ago, Pink Jeep Tours, a Sedona, Arizona, company that offers guided Jeep tours through nearby red-rock formations, booked tours by entering basic customer information into a DOS-based program and then scheduling and organizing tour lengths and party sizes on magnetic boards. Unfortunately, if someone brushed up against the boards, magnets would come tumbling off, tour guides wouldn't have a clue as to which parties were scheduled when, and chaos would ensue. Then the company installed a Windows-based reservations system that electronically schedules each day's tours.[7]

Another way in which information technology helps managers make better decisions is through computer-assisted decision making. Among the variety of software designed for such purposes, the most directly relevant for most managers is **decision-making software**. It is any computer program that helps a decision maker work through problem-solving and decision-making steps. Such software usually asks the user questions about values, priorities, and the importance attached to factors such as price and quality.

The decision-making process used in these programs is referred to as "intuitive" because the programs rely more on human judgment than on quantitative analysis. The intent of the programs is to improve the quality of decisions rather than to just make computations or generate data. A decision-making program might help a traffic manager decide whether to make a large shipment by truck, railroad, or airplane.

Greater Empowerment and Flatter Organizations

The widespread use of information technology gives more workers access to information they need for decision making. As a result, more workers can be empowered to make decisions. Fewer layers of management are needed to act as information conduits. Instead, workers at lower levels access information directly through computer networks. Information technology therefore provides line employees with the documents they need to perform their jobs more effectively and make decisions on their own.

---

company intranet

A Web site designed only for company employees, often containing proprietary information.

64

decision-making software

Any computer program that helps a decision maker work through problem-solving and decision-making steps.

Saved Time Through Employee Self-Service

A final important way in which information technology benefits managers happens when employees are able to serve themselves in some areas rather than requiring managerial or staff assistance. Managers are freed from the need to supervise routine activities. Also, from the standpoint of top management, fewer managers and staff support need to be hired.

A notable example of information technology-based employee self-service is the electronic travel and expense reporting (T&E) system used at Cisco Systems Inc. Employees submit expense reports through an intranet and browser. When an employee logs on to the system, it registers charges from his or her corporate American Express card. The employee then adds out-of-pocket expenses and the system generates a travel and expense report. Within four days, the employee receives the reimbursement by direct deposit to his or her bank. Expense reports submitted by paper took 21 days for reimbursement at Cisco.

Another advantage to the company is that the system can spot discrepancies and send the e-form back to the employee for clarification. A suspicious form can be routed for audit approval. However, after all the proper information is in place, the system can generate the credit card payments to American Express and cash reimbursements to the employee.

By automating the process, Cisco auditors boosted the number of claims they can review from 19,000 to 35,000. The firm saves money by paying off credit card debt faster. Additionally, the cost of processing an expense report went from upwards of $25 to $3.

Cisco now uses many of the same self-service techniques to improve its internal travel reservation system. Jennifer Loftin, manager of T&E automation, says, "It's letting managers and employees focus on high-value activities."[8]

Negative Consequences of Information Technology

Information technology continues to make extraordinary contributions to organizational productivity. Nevertheless, the same exciting technology produces some unintended negative consequences. Even when these negative consequences do not affect the manager directly, he or she usually plays a major role in dealing with the consequences. For example, if extensive use of information technology deteriorates customer service, the manager faces angry customers and discouraged employees. Awareness of these potential problems can help managers prevent them from occurring. One subtle problem occurs when managers or other employees become **computer goof-offs**. They spend so much time attempting new computer routines and accessing information of questionable value that they neglect key aspects of their jobs. Many managers, for example, would prefer to surf the Internet for low-value information than to confront an employee about a discipline problem.

Surfing the Net needlessly on company time may involve accessing a sports site, such as http://www.ESPN.com, shopping online, or viewing pornography. A study by Elron Software (http://www.elronsoftware.com) found that 62 percent of firms with Internet access saw some traffic on pornographic Web sites. In addition to draining productivity, displaying pornography on company computer monitors could lead to sexual harassment charges. Elron offers software that can block out sites, as well as track where employees are spending their time online.[9]

Vault.com conducted a survey about Internet surfing that asked workers themselves about their surfing habits. The top four types of sites for surfing on

computer goof-offs

Employees who spend so much time attempting new computer routines and accessing information of questionable value that they neglect key aspects of their job.

company time were reading the news (72%), making travel arrangements (45%), making purchases (40%), and conducting a job search (37%). Only 4 percent said they visited pornographic sites.[10]

Computer goofing off in extreme form leads to an *online addiction*, in which the person spends so much time surfing the Internet on and off the job that productivity and interpersonal relationships suffer. For the addicted, the Internet becomes the most important satisfaction in life. A number of students suffer from online addiction, often not attending class because they have stayed up all night surfing the Internet. Some psychologists specialize in treating online addiction, and many support groups are available.

techno–obsessives

Individuals obsessed with technological devices.

Closely related to online addicts are **techno–obsessives**, people who cannot detach from technology and keep information technology devices poised for immediate use in the office and elsewhere. They keep on hand devices such as cellular telephones, palm-sized computers, and laptop computers. A study showed that 29 percent of e-mail users feel anxious about important messages that may be waiting for them.[11]

As you will read in Chapter 8, information technology contributes to the repetitive motion disorders found in the workplace. In addition to well-designed workplaces, improved technology may decrease repetitive motion disorders. Voice recognition systems enable computer users to dictate commands into word processors, thereby cutting back on keyboarding. The software is cumbersome at present because it has to be adapted to an individual user's speech patterns, including pronunciation and accents. Dictation software now allows for continuous speech, rather than pauses between words as in the past. Two such programs are Dragon NaturallySpeaking and IBM Viavoice. But watch out for the "Wreck a nice beach" problem. (Repeat "Wreck a nice beach" a few times until you get the joke.)

A problem of considerable magnitude comes from the deterioration in customer service that sometimes accompanies information technology. Many banks, for example, force customers with a service problem to call an 800 number rather than allowing them to deal with a branch representative. A voice-response system instructs the customer to punch in lengthy account numbers and make choices from a complicated menu. The process is time-consuming and impersonal, and difficult for customers unfamiliar with information technology. A related problem occurs when highly automated customer-service operations appear unfriendly and detached.

Sometimes the firms most committed to high-technology experience chaotic customer service systems. A business reporter described customer service struggles with Sprint PCS, a fast-growing wireless communication company. In one instance, a customer care advocate placed on hold for 17 minutes a customer with a billing inquiry. When asked for assistance with high unexplainable charges, the customer care advocate asked for help himself by calling a representative from the fraud department. The representative then placed the customer care advocate on hold. The second advocate then calls a third representative who puts her on hold. So three holds were taking place simultaneously. The irate reporter concluded, "That right there is customer service in the new economy. It has become a slow, dissatisfying tangle of telephones, computers, Web sites, e-mail, and people that wastes time at a prodigious rate, produces far more aggravation than service. . . ."[12]

As implied in the discussion of wireless communication, information technology results in *wired managerial workers*. Being electronically connected to the office at all times leads many managers and professionals to complain that their employers expect them to be always available for consultation. Many managers, for example, are expected to bring pagers, laptop computers, and cellular telephones on vacation so they can respond to inquiries from the office and customers.

THE IMPACT OF THE INTERNET ON CUSTOMER AND OTHER EXTERNAL RELATIONSHIPS

The Internet profoundly affects how business is conducted. Developments of similar magnitude include electricity, the railroad, and the interstate highway system. As a consequence, the Internet also influences managerial work, especially the technical problem-solver role of a manager who might be contributing ideas about such work as marketing, purchasing, and information systems. Even when managers are not directly involved in such specialized activities, they are still concerned with making decisions about the Internet. Here we look at four ways in which the Internet affects external relationships: e-commerce marketing, e-commerce purchasing, integrating the old and new economies, and living with increased visibility.

The Marketing Side of E-Commerce

The biggest impact on business comes from selling many goods and services to other businesses and consumers over the Internet. Companies that sell exclusively over the Internet are sometimes referred to as *pure players*, such as dot.com companies with no physical stores or distribution centers. Pure players are much less stable than companies who use the Internet only as one method for marketing goods and services. The Management in Action on page 70 illustrates how a well-established company can improve its marketing and customer service by engaging in e-commerce. The company also uses the Internet for e-tailing, which is the direct customer side of e-commerce, much like ordering a CD from barnesandnoble.com. Observe how the company prepares its customers for ordering online.

Eighty percent of business conducted on the Net today takes place between firms (B2B, or business-to-business) rather than by individual consumers. Among the many estimates about the scope of e-commerce is that business-to-business sales will total $6.8 trillion in 2004, accounting for 10 percent of all such sales. However, the influence of the Internet on marketing is far greater than sales conducted online. Jupiter Communications found that 68 percent of online buyers first research products online and then purchase them from a physical store, catalog, or some other offline channel. (These data refer mostly to retail shoppers but also apply to companies making purchases.) Jupiter predicts that in 2005, online consumers will spend more than $632 billion offline as a direct result of research they conduct online.[13]

A specific example of the interrelationship between online and offline selling might occur in this manner: A person reads a print ad about a Web site, visits the Web site to learn about a specific product, and then visits the store to make the purchase.

E-commerce affects managerial work in two major ways. First, the manager must be familiar with e-commerce to suggest strategies for marketing over the Internet and resolving problems. Second, managers who formerly worked directly with salespeople (such as coaching and motivating) may have fewer subordinates. One **Web master** might replace 50 face-to-face salespeople. The manager, with fewer people to supervise, would spend more time developing business strategy and perhaps interacting with a few major customers. Exhibit 3-2 presents some technical details managers need to know in working with e-commerce.

Discuss the impact of the Internet on customer and other external relationships.

3

67

Web master

An individual responsible for the creation and maintenance of a company's Website.

EXHIBIT 3-2

E-Business Essentials

For a thriving e-business, a company needs to consider some or all of the products described next.

- **Enterprise Servers.** For heavy-traffic Web sites, a dedicated server is a must. These big-iron behemoths typically include Pentium III Xeon chips, enormous hard drives, and remote management systems. The key word is scalability, so the server can grow as a business grows.
- **Broadband Access.** Consumers and businesses want high-speed access to the Web. Networking kits enable every computer in the office to share a single Web connection. The units are designed for use by novices who do not have their own tech support teams.
- **Small Business Servers.** Servers can be used for more than Web sites. Dedicated appliances, called eServers, are available for storage, e-mail, Web hosting, and more. The devices can recognize each other, so if one goes down, another can provide backup.
- **Nonstop Service.** Customers have no patience with unreliable sights. Guarantee uptime with an uninterruptible power supply (UPS). These devices range from simple wall units that provide a few minutes of backup to more thorough support.
- **M-Commerce.** Mobile commerce is the new wave thanks to Web-enabled cell phones. New models contain internal microbrowsers that can display sites written for Wireless Application Protocol (WAP).
- **Site Analysis.** Prepare your sight for launch and keep it running smoothly with analysis software. Such software and other tools simulate traffic on a site to assess how well your server will hold up and to predict when you will need more power.
- **Hosting.** A site-hosting service gets a site up and running and takes care of the maintenance on its own servers. Most hosts offer free software for building e-commerce sites, and many can help register a site with search engines and set up a merchant account for credit card processing.
- **Digital Imaging.** Online vendors must strike a balance between rich, detailed images of the products for sale and a Web page that will load quickly enough to keep impatient customers on-site. Startups can often manage with a moderately priced digital camera, then use image-editing software to trim down the file sizes.

Source: "Setting Up Shop," *Fortune Technology Guide*, Summer 2000, pp. 44–45.

The Purchasing Side of E-Commerce

An important consequence of e-commerce is that it sometimes enables companies to purchase more efficiently than they could by speaking to sales representatives or purchasing through catalogs over the telephone. A growing number of companies encourage both customers and suppliers to conduct business with them over the Internet. For example, a company cannot stay on the General Electric approved supplier list unless the company is willing to accept orders and inquiries online.

An online marketplace called OrderZone.com provides a representative example of how companies purchase over the Internet. Eight industrial suppliers merged forces to form OrderZone, including W. W. Grainger, a large supplier of pipe fittings, lightbulbs, ladders, and other maintenance, repair, and operations products. Customers buy from a merged catalog that contains more than 100,000 items. Customers then receive just one invoice, which is proving to be a big pay-off. OrderZone gives the suppliers in the group marketing information about their common pool of customers. The marketing insight includes purchasing behavior such as the combination of items customers tend to buy together. The managers of the suppliers who join OrderZone can use the marketing information to run special offers, create new product combinations, and adjust prices to keep inventories in balance.[14]

Companies realize smaller transaction costs and a time savings by purchasing over the Net. As a result, product prices tend to be lower than purchasing through sales representatives or catalogs. The purchaser can also ask questions online about products and services. A good starting point for any company wanting to purchase over the Internet would be to visit http://www.yahoo.com/business. The manager or professional can quickly locate companies that offer the product or service he or she needs, and then make inquiries.

Purchasing over the Net saves time because purchasing agents spend less time talking to and being entertained by sales representatives. Nevertheless, e-commerce has not completely eliminated the human touch in business. Many big deals are still made over lunch and on the golf course, and executives tend to purchase from people they like. Furthermore, many well-established companies that have worked hard to develop their brand name refuse to join buyer exchanges. The established companies are concerned that online buying often results in the lowest bidder (sometimes an unknown supplier) getting the sale. A company with a good reputation would prefer that customers stay loyal to them based on high product quality and after-sale service.

Integrating the New Economy with the Old Economy

Managers at all levels face the challenge of how to integrate the traditional way of doing business (the old economy) with e-business (the new economy). In Net-speak, it is the difference between bricks and clicks. During the initial surge of e-businesses, many Internet-based companies regarded traditional business firms as virtually obsolete. Many predicted that establishments like shopping malls, automobile dealers, and companies that sold hard-copy greeting cards would soon go the way of the dinosaurs. Furthermore, companies that acted as brokers between business firms and suppliers would soon be *vaporized* (tough talk for being run out of business). By early 2000, that prediction turned into a realization that the vast majority of companies relying strictly on the Internet for sales could not earn a profit, and continued to sustain enormous losses. About 90 percent of dot-com pure players went out of business.

The reality: Well-established companies that integrated e-commerce into their marketing and internal operations became the biggest beneficiaries of the Net revolution. Among the many old economy companies prospering with e-commerce one finds Wal-Mart, Kmart, Office Depot, Hewlett-Packard, and GE.

Wells Fargo & Co., founded in 1852 to help finance the California gold rush, provides an illuminating example of a traditional company that capitalized on e-commerce without sacrificing its roots. Wells Fargo formed a successful Internet-banking team for big-business customers. The team works in close partnership with Internet start-ups. The young staff members in the small Internet firms bring ingenuity and a sense of urgency that the big bank could not muster on its own. In contrast, Wells Fargo with $222 billion in assets and long history of banking expertise, contributes strengths that a small Internet start-up could not muster on its own. Wells Fargo leads online consumer banking with nearly 2 million account holders using the Web. The bank is slowly growing its online corporate-banking business. Wells Fargo now has about 200 Web-related projects under way.[15]

An issue often raised in getting the right mixture of bricks and clicks is whether the Internet portion of the business should be a separate company. In making some

Management *in Action*

A d d i n g   a n   e   t o   R x

For 60 years, Wright & Filippis (http://www.firsttoserve.com, Rochester Hills, Michigan) set the standard for prosthetics (artificial limbs), orthopedic devices, and home medical equipment. The firm also enjoys a reputation as one of the most respected providers of products and services for physical rehabilitation.

Now, the company wants to extend its reputation for customer service through e-business initiatives that let patients and health care professionals purchase products and services over the Internet. This goal means greater convenience and higher-quality health-care for patients, as well as reduced costs and streamlined processes for health-care providers. It also means competitive advantage for Wright & Filippis, and the ability to redeploy customer service reps to focus on more profitable activities.

"We saw a clear opportunity to use e-business to serve our customers and run our company more effectively," says Jeff Mastej, director of organizational improvement. "It's an excellent example of using technology to achieve business goals."

Company Database

The company runs its e-business application on Unisys servers and tightly integrates e-business activities with back-end systems, including the customer database. The database provides a key piece of the e-business puzzle because Wright & Filippis captures and maintains crucial medical information about its customers.

"Of primary importance is that the e-business application be tightly integrated with our database," says John Pincura, IT director for the company. This integration allows the company to take advantage of the rich store of information it has already amassed. In addition, "It means we don't have to add IT staff or another level of expertise," Pincura explains. "We can move into

e-business while using the knowledge base we already have."

The database also comes into play as the company serves its broad range of clients. First and foremost are the end consumers, the patients who use its products and services. But Wright & Filippis also works directly with insurance companies, physicians, physical therapists, hospital discharge planners, and other medical professionals.

Better Service = Better Care

The first customers Wright & Filippis targeted with its online sales initiative were purchasers of diabetic supplies. Such supplies include alcohol swabs, lancing devices, test strips, and other products used in testing blood sugar levels. "This is a high-volume business for us," Pincura explains, "so it made sense to look at it as our first e-business activity."

It also represents an area where online sales can quickly deliver a high level of customer service. Customers could order most supplies through a drugstore, but it would involve making upfront payments, filling out forms, and submitting information to insurance companies. Wright & Filippis handles that entire process for its customers. And its staff of nurses, pharmacists, nutritionists, and other medical professionals are available for consultation.

Wright & Fillipis believes it can use e-business to raise the bar higher. In the past, customers placed orders by leaving a voice-mail message or speaking directly with a customer service rep. This process becomes time-consuming if, as is often necessary, customers need to adjust quantities as their prescriptions change. Further, many customers are retirees who have winter homes in warmer climates and change their shipping addresses frequently.

Allowing customers to place orders online streamlines the process significantly. Customers still engage in an initial consultation to set up an account, provide necessary information, and confirm that they know how to use the products. After that point, however, they can place online orders at their convenience. The system automatically processes the order, generates shipping instructions, schedules the shipment, issues a confirmation number, and takes care of all the details that make online sales work.

"Because diabetes is a chronic condition, ordering supplies is something our customers do on a regular basis," points out Pincura. "So this recurring benefit will save them a tremendous amount of time and effort." The e-business solution also offloads the company's

busy call center, which handles about 500 calls per day. In this way employees can be redeployed to focus on new ways to serve customers.

Mastej says, "E-business is about more than technology. You need to think about it from a variety of perspectives: how customers will use the system, how employees will use the systems, things like compliance with regulations, logistics, and distribution, transaction processing. All those things need to be in place to be successful."

Source: Eric Schoeniger, "Adding an *e* to Rx," *UNISYS Exec*, 23, no. 1 (2001), pp. 36–38.

concession to this idea, Wells Fargo houses its Internet operations in separate, trendy offices. Many executives assume that certain aspects of traditional business, such as the protectiveness of its present customers, will smother any Internet initiative. Ranjay Gulati and Jason Garino argue that executives do not have to make an either-or choice when it comes to their clicks versus bricks-and-mortar strategies. Instead, they should seek the right degree of integration, as done by Wells Fargo.[16]

Living with Increased Visibility

An unanticipated consequence of the Internet is a different kind of visibility than in the past to which companies must adjust. People who like or dislike the organization can disseminate this information over the Internet. Several current Web sites encourage consumers to voice their complaints. Negative comments on the Web can be dismissed as the work of jealous people or kooks, but the exposure carries the potential to badly hurt the corporate image. Companies recognize the need for risk and damage control in a variety of scenarios. For example, management at some large companies purchases a set of potential negative domain names, such as www.companyname.sucks.org. In this way, the critics will not be able to launch such a site.

To counteract the downside of increased visibility, management must work extra hard to create fans and to deal openly with the issues that make people dislike you. Suppose a company subcontracts the manufacture of a clothing line to a company that hires prison labor at low wages under punitive working conditions. The company addresses the issue by setting higher standards for subcontractors to minimize negative publicity over the Net.[17]

THE EFFECTS OF THE INTERNET ON INTERNAL OPERATIONS

Working in an Internet environment affects internal operations as well as relationships with outsiders. Doing business on the Internet is far more complicated than

4

Explain the effects of the Internet on internal company operations.

simply taking orders over an electronic catalog. E-commerce often brings about changes in the way in which a company operates. Here we look at several issues influenced by the Internet environment: revamping operations, a squeeze on profits and pressure toward cost control, monitoring work and employee surveillance, dealing with instability and chaos, data mining, and outsourcing of information technology.

Revamping Operations

The Internet ushered in a new era and transforms the way in which businesses operate internally. Using the Internet, many companies changed their methods of distributing goods, of collaborating inside the company, and of dealing with suppliers. Technology companies pioneered this use of the Net to overhaul their operations. For instance, at Intel, Web-based automation freed up 200 sales clerks from tediously entering orders. Instead of laying off these workers, Intel made them responsible for analyzing sales trends and taking good care of customers.

A specific example of how the Internet transforms operations can be found at Ingram Micro, the biggest PC distributor. Ingram teamed up with Solectron, a major contract manufacturer of high-technology equipment. Ingram custom-makes PCs inexpensively for brand-name computer companies. Instead of the PC companies handling orders and manufacturing, Ingram and Solectron perform the task for them. The Web-based system speeds up communication and decreases assembly times. The PC companies continue to design and market their products, and handle quality assurance. The difference in operations comes from their alliance with Ingram. "Customers are doing business with a virtual company," says Ingram president Jeffrey R. Rodek.[18]

Exhibit 3-3 presents a step-by-step analysis of the Web-based process for customizing an order for a PC.

Squeeze on Profits and Pressure Toward Cost Control

The changing flow of information created by the Internet tipped the balance of power from sellers to buyers. In the past, sellers had almost all the information about profit margins and manufacturer's true costs. Industrial buyers and individual consumers can now use the Web to uncover information about costs that puts them on the same level as professionals. Many prospective car purchasers today walk into dealer's offices with copies of factory invoices showing the true dealer cost of a given car model. The dealer can no longer claim, "We are giving you this car at $50 over dealer cost," unless it is true.

Given that the buyer knows so much about costs, the seller must offer products with lower profit margins than in the past. The manager is therefore responsible for controlling costs in any sensible way possible including reducing turnover, minimizing expenditures, and using the Internet for purchasing! To reduce costs, one manager decided to discontinue the practice of allowing company employees to accumulate frequent flyer miles when they traveled on company business. Instead, the company would keep the miles, thus getting some company airplane trips for free.

Monitoring Work and Employee Surveillance

Automation in the workplace not only changes how employees labor, it changes the ability of management to measure and monitor the work, and the

EXHIBIT **3-3**
The Internet Supply Chain

73

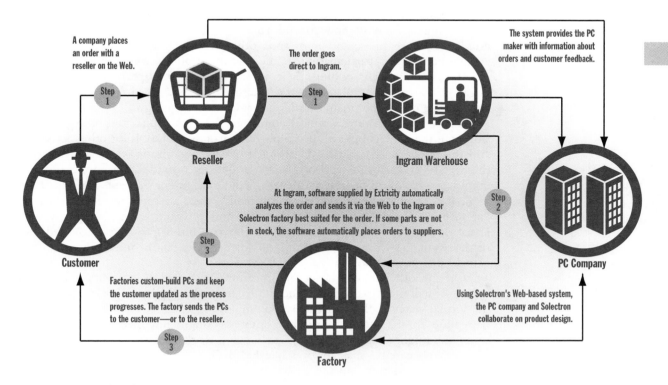

A company places an order with a reseller on the Web.

The order goes direct to Ingram.

The system provides the PC maker with information about orders and customer feedback.

Step 1

Step 1

Reseller

Ingram Warehouse

At Ingram, software supplied by Extricity automatically analyzes the order and sends it via the Web to the Ingram or Solectron factory best suited for the order. If some parts are not in stock, the software automatically places orders to suppliers.

Step 2

Customer

Step 3

PC Company

Factories custom-build PCs and keep the customer updated as the process progresses. The factory sends the PCs to the customer—or to the reseller.

Using Solectron's Web-based system, the PC company and Solectron collaborate on product design.

Step 3

Factory

Source: Solectron Corp., Ingram Micro Inc., and Extricity Inc.

workers. In many jobs—especially in manufacturing and the more mechanical service industries—employees are increasingly held to standards derived from metering or measuring the work. Management also has new responsibilities and tools to oversee employee behavior in the wired workplace.

Computer automation in telemarketing and telephone support call centers illustrates how far advances of information technology have taken us from the days of the rotary phone and dog-eared phone book. In telemarketing, information on prospective customers is collected, collated, and massaged to generate more precise targeting. Computers manage call setup, placing calls, and only connecting the call with a telemarketer once a live person answers on the other end.

Although computer-managed and measured work can result in greatly improved efficiency and productivity, it can also lead to employee anxiety, and negative effects on morale. Once average call profiles are understood—for example, "It should take only 25 seconds to make the pitch and request preferred method of payment"—employees can be pushed to adhere to standards, or docked for failing to maintain a given pace, reducing the work to the same sort of mechanistic grind encountered on demanding factory assembly lines.

Beyond the monitoring of basic performance, workplace surveillance is expanding to encompass any number of facets of employee activity in the workplace. As technology blurs the lines between home and work, between personal and professional activities, such surveillance may spill outside the confines of the traditional office environment as well. In November 2000, the U.S. Central Intelligence Agency (CIA) announced the results of an investigation of more than 100 employees for their participation in unauthorized and inappropriate communications using agency systems for informal networking. In the aftermath, four employees were fired, and numerous others reprimanded or demoted. Some agency contractors participating in the communications were stripped of their clearances, effectively ending their jobs. None of the participants allegedly engaged in security violations—the transgression was in violating policies on appropriate use of the organization's information technology.

Although far from the typical employer, the CIA found itself in a common situation: use versus abuse of the employees' professional tools for other activities, and the question of what to do about it. Many organizations, the CIA among them, take a hard-line approach: the employer provides the tools, and the employer calls the shots. Given that the employer might be liable for any abuse (e.g., if an employee sends harassing e-mails), such attempts to clearly separate "appropriate" and "inappropriate" use by policy would seem a simple way to lessen risk. (According to *Business Week*, Chevron and Microsoft both settled sexual harassment lawsuits for $2.2 million apiece as a result of internally circulated e-mails that created hostile work environments.)

On the other hand, the communications taking place over any company's networks will most likely be a blend of professional and personal. The appearance of "virtual water cooler" chat between employees separated by distance, and perhaps time zones, but with common interests, ought not surprise us. (Banning some uses might also drive employees to invent workarounds—a great many users of free Web-based e-mail services like Hotmail, now a part of Microsoft, do so because of restrictions on use of company-provided e-mail. Of course many of those users may be accessing their Hotmail accounts from their company-provided Web browser.)

Many companies deploy tools to monitor employees' use of company Internet connections and the traffic passing over internal networks. Products like Websense's Employee Internet Management tools (http://www.websense.com) monitor and block inappropriate Internet traffic such as logging employee visits to Web porn sites or sports sites. Raytheon's SilentRunner (http://www.silentrunner.com) intercepts internal network traffic and construct maps of communications flows. A manager might employ SilentRunner to detect corporate espionage, such as an employee attempting to send restricted documents out to other parties, but the product can equally well map out an organization's "virtual communities," to show who's talking to whom.

Websense claims that its products are used by more than 14,000 organizations worldwide, including half of the *Fortune* 500. One can imagine why: according to an International Data Corporation survey, some 30 to 40 percent of employee Internet surfing is not business related. In 2001, the American Management Association (http://www.amanet.org) conducted a survey of employer policies and practices in workplace monitoring and surveillance. The survey found more than 60 percent of respondents monitored company Internet connections, with nearly half storing and reviewing company e-mail.

Not all employers are moving toward a crackdown on employee use of organizational resources for private purposes, and expanding the use of surveillance tools. In 2001, federal judges on the U.S. 9th Circuit Court of Appeals directed that monitoring of their own employees' use of computers and the Internet be turned off as unnecessarily invasive.

Dealing with Instability and Chaos

The Internet creates a major challenge for managers who must deal with an unstable and sometimes chaotic environment. Although managers are no strangers to change, the volatile Internet environment requires even more adaptation. A major instability associated with the Internet comes in the form of extensive layoffs in Internet-based businesses. In December 2000 alone, 10,000 Internet workers lost their jobs. By early 2001, even the leading supplier of infrastructure for the Internet, Cisco Systems, experienced widespread layoffs because of slumping sales.[19] As a result of the layoffs, managers must deal with such confusion as reassigning the work of the laid-off employees to survivors, and dealing with rumors about future layoffs.

A substantial internal challenge created by the collapse of so many Internet-based companies is what to do with used Internet equipment that suddenly enters the market. Companies that manufacture the equipment must now adjust their inventories because of the competing used equipment. For example, when ZipLink folded, it placed on the auction block a Cisco router that usually sells for $150,000 retail, and for $11,000 when refurbished. Under auction, the router sold for $1,850.[20]

Even when business is good, the Internet revolution creates instability because managers generally face smaller profit margins. As described earlier, the Internet makes comparison shopping easier. The more efficient the Internet becomes, the greater the squeeze on the profit margins of e-businesses. As a result, the manager must look for creative ways to trim costs. Or, the company can offer a product so unique, and valuable that price is not a significant factor in making a decision to buy. Other factors squeeze profit margins as well, including the expense of establishing elaborate hardware, software, and order fulfillment systems required of Internet companies. By mid-2001, the number one e-tailer, Amazon.com, was still not profitable despite annual sales of $2.8 billion.[21]

Data Mining

The automation of business means that the process of just doing business generates actionable information. With most everything reduced to a capturable electronic form, companies find themselves sitting atop mountains of data. The term **data mining** describes the extraction of useful analyses from the raw mass of business transactions and other information.

data mining

The extraction of useful analyses from the mass of information available to firms.

In her book, *In the Age of the Smart Machine*, Harvard Business School professor Shoshanna Zuboff described a bank that observed that even though its primary (originally, sole) business focused on the lending and borrowing of money, it was accumulating something more: a knowledge of trends and patterns in the lending and borrowing of money. The bank began to broaden its offerings to include financial consulting. Many businesses in other sectors also find that the information they handle as a consequence of one aspect of the business can drive whole new business lines.

Commerce steadily evolves toward greater quantifiability—think how ubiquitous consumer product bar code scanning has become in the quarter century since its introduction in a handful of grocery stores. The value of collected data increases as it becomes more comprehensive and complete.

Outsourcing Information Technology

For many companies, the *outsourcing* of information technology services makes sense. At its simplest, outsourcing represents a decision to rent or lease services, rather than owning a staff to provide them internally. Outsourcing offers both benefits and drawbacks; the manager in a company relying on the outsourcing of IT services will need to appreciate how it differs from a more traditional, organic approach to doing business.

A common basis for a decision to outsource recognizes that information technology management is not a core competency. A company in the business of making soap, or soup, or semi-trucks spreads itself thin by trying to stay on the cutting edge of a rapidly changing IT industry.

Recruiting and retention of IT-savvy staff presents a particular problem in government. Some federal agencies attempt to keep qualified staff on board with additional compensation (e.g., defining new job categories for IT workers, and stretching traditional civil service wage scales), but outsourcing is a growing trend. Even the National Security Agency, which collects communications intelligence around the world and which was once known as the "no such agency" for its secrecy during the Cold War, entered a $2 billion contract giving the private sector management of its less mission-critical systems. That 10-year contract also entails the transfer of at least 750 employees from NSA, to the contractor, Computer Sciences, Corp.

In IT particularly, but in business more generally, employees expect far more fluidity in their careers. While the previous generation might have put in a 35-year career working for a single large employer, like General Motors, a more typical current career path might include participation in mergers (e.g., when GM bought Electronic Data Systems), experiencing the consequences of outsourcing. (e.g., as GM transferred its IT management to EDS) and divestment of business units (e.g., the public offering of Delphi, once GM's auto parts subsidiary).

Outsourcing of IT-related services is much easier in the Internet environment, a near-ubiquitous platform. Any application that can be delivered to a Web browser can also be delivered from outside or inside the company, from down the hall in the IT or accounting department, from across town or across the country, or from a strategic outsourcing partner, and so on.

5 SUCCESS FACTORS IN AN E-BUSINESS

Pinpoint factors associated with success in e-business.

To help synthesize the vast amounts of information about the impact of the Internet, here we list six factors that contribute to success in e-business. Factors that contribute to success in any type of business, such as offering high-quality products that customers want, also apply.[23]

1. *Develop an excellent call center to allow for the human touch.* Despite conducting business over the Internet, many customers want to follow up with telephone calls. Several online brokers found that telephone traffic actually increases after online trading is initiated. Many customers want to follow up online inquiries with human beings. Customers often seek the type of clarification that is difficult to obtain by asking questions online.
2. *Keep customers informed about order progress.* The online transaction is not completed until the customer receives the order and is satisfied. If the company experiences shipping delays, it should notify the customer.

3. *Constantly monitor and update the e-business system.* "There's nothing more annoying to a customer than going through the buying process and not being able to close the transaction," says Sam Taylor of onlineretailpartners.com. "It's very tiring for them to have to re-input the information."[24] Many order systems turn out to be much more complex than their developers realize, and executing an order can be complicated and time-consuming.

4. *Mix bricks and clicks.* The most successful players in e-tailing give customers the opportunity to purchase online, in stores, and by telephone. Among the many successful companies that offer multiple channels for customers to make purchases are Gateway Computer, Wal-Mart, Kmart, and Eddie Bauer.

5. *Develop a global presence.* Customers throughout the world like to shop on American Web sites, which provides a unique opportunity to U.S. companies. Although the U.S. firm must adapt to local tastes and laws, back office, distribution, and marketing functions translate well overseas. Three U.S.-based companies with highly successful European operations are eBay, Yahoo!, and E★TRADE.

6. *Adopt a positive attitude toward change.* A company that makes a successful shift to e-commerce must be willing to experiment with a new way of doing business, invest heavily in e-ventures, and challenge the usual way of doing business.

The accompanying Management in Action illustrates the workings of a moderately successful e-business, whose chief executive stays focused on a product line that helps other e-businesses operate smoothly.

Despite the many positive changes brought about by the Internet revolution, some of its promises fell short. The vast majority of consumers prefer to shop in physically real stores, most automobile dealers don't pay much attention to auto prices listed on the Internet, and personal contacts still dominate high-level business. The Internet supplements and enhances traditional business activity but does not replace the practice of management.

Management *in Action*

Kim Polese, Information Technology Pacesetter

Stylish and poised Kim Polese is chair and chief strategy officer of Marimba, located in Mountain View, California. A few years ago, photos of the technology executive appeared on the cover of every industry magazine and several business magazines. Polese was a member of the core team responsible for launching Java for Sun Microsystems. When she left the company in 1996 to form a new company called Marimba, many predicted she would guide the company to the tech world's summit.

"There was a tremendous amount of attention and pressure on us when we left Sun, and some huge expectations," says Polese, who cofounded Marimba with three engineers from the Java team at Sun. "We had a few missteps at the beginning. These were some of the scariest times for us. You know, the world expected us to be the next Netscape, so we had to shut that out and focus."

78

Polese refers to Marimba's infrastructure technology as plumbing for the Internet. "It's not sexy technology, but Cisco does plumbing, and we would love to be as unsexy as them," she says. "Unsexy" though it may be, Marimba's mission is valuable. The company defines itself as "a leading supplier of Internet infrastructure management solutions." Think of them as data cops in an information-driven world. Documents, software, or support—almost anything that travels over a network, according to Marimba—must rely on the network's integrity. That's where Marimba comes in.

According to research analyst, Frank Gillett, Marimba is a viable company. "They make a useful product, but their challenge is to be nimble enough to adapt to a world with no personal computers and put their products in the wireless futures of cell phones, handhelds, and Palms."

For 39-year-old Polese, starting her own company was always about creating something special that would make her mark in the world. "I know it's old fashioned, but I've always had the long-term approach to Marimba," says Polese. "People look at the day-to-day fluctuations of the stock, and what's been lost is the reality that it takes years to build a successful company. I understand that you have to put in the hard work and that substance is more important than style. I think smart investors understand that too."

When Marimba grew to more than 280 employees, Polese hired John Olsen, an experienced executive manager, as CEO. Polese took the new title of chair and chief strategy officer. She says, "I was trying to do everything, and one person can't handle that. We needed to broaden and deepen our management team. I don't care about my title or ego. I just care about building a successful company. Now I can focus on where the company is going and what products are needed, which is what I need to do, versus working on human resource or payroll issues."

While talking about earlier stages in her career, Polese commented, "Working at Sun was great training for me because as a product manager you are in one sense a mini-CEO. It was a great place to start a career. There are very intelligent people there, and the bar is raised high."

The project she mentioned eventually became Java, which went on to change everything, and Polese became the ubiquitous face of the new technology and the techno-geeks' favorite download. From the time she came on board, she and the engineers worked for three years on Java. It was an isolated team with the feel and camaraderie of a start-up. After Java's launch and incredible success for Sun they wanted to keep the adrenaline flowing—so why not for themselves?

"We didn't want to start a company just because it was the cool thing to do," she says. "We wanted to see if we had something that we could get funded." Each cofounder kicked in $15,000, and for the first six months they toiled on borrowed computers in a defunct stationary store in downtown Palo Alto. A leading venture capital firm soon pitched in $4 million in first-round funding, and Marimba suddenly had a payroll and started hiring.

"I want to leave a legacy—something that matters and benefits people," says Polese, who volunteers her time to nonprofit organizations. "People get focused on making money, and they achieve that and then feel empty.

"I'm frustrated when I see people start a company and then turn around and sell it for the cash. I admire people like Bill Gates who had the doggedness to persevere and build something that is successful and will last."

Source: Thomas Melville, "Surviving the Spotlight," *Success,* February–March 2001, pp. 34–36.

SUMMARY OF KEY POINTS

1 **Summarize the demands information technology places on the manager's job.** Management must build an organization that constantly transforms itself as information technology increases competition. To remain competitive requires innovation. Information and communications technology is at the center of the technological revolution and also makes globalization more practical because of ready access to employees everywhere. In general, information technology places managers in a continuous learning mode. Wireless communication devices facilitate work from different locations.

2 **Describe the positive and negative consequences of information technology for the manager.** Information technology helps the manager work smarter in such ways as improved productivity and teamwork, gaining competitive advantage, improved customer service and supplier relationships, enhanced communication including the virtual office, quick access to vast information, enhanced analysis of data and decision making, greater empowerment and flatter organizations, and time saved through employee self-service.

Negative consequences of information technology include goofing off by computer, online addictions, facilitating techno-obsessive behavior, repetitive stress disorder, poor customer service, and wired managerial workers.

3 **Discuss the impact of the Internet on customer and other external relationships.** The biggest impact of the Internet on business comes from selling many goods and services to other businesses over the Internet. Eighty percent of business conducted on the Net today occurs between firms (B2B). The manager must be familiar with e-commerce to help develop strategy, and the manager may work with a reduced staff because of online selling. E-commerce sometimes enables companies to purchase more efficiently than they could

through other channels. Managers face the major challenge of how to integrate the traditional way of doing business (the old economy) with e-business (the new economy). Relying strictly on Internet sales is rarely profitable. Well-established companies that integrate e-commerce into their marketing and internal operations have benefited the most from the Net revolution.

Using the Internet, many companies changed their methods of distributing goods, of collaborating inside the company, and of dealing with suppliers. Buyers' power makes it more difficult to charge higher prices, forcing companies to more carefully control costs. The Internet can create an unstable and chaotic environment with which managers must deal. Companies also experience increased visibility, particularly from angry consumers.

4 **Explain the effects of the Internet on internal company operations.** The Internet affects companies in a number of ways, beginning with a revamping of operations, such as changing the method of distributing goods. The Net also squeezes profits and exerts pressure toward cost control. Companies now require increased capacity to monitor work and conduct employee surveillance. The Internet also creates more instability and chaos that require management attention, but it facilitates data mining as well. For many companies, information technology is a function frequently outsourced.

5 **Pinpoint factors associated with success in e-business.** Successful e-businesses provide an excellent call center to allow for the human touch and keep customers informed about order progress. The e-business system requires constant monitoring and updating. Other strategies e-businesses can employ include mixing bricks and clicks, developing a global perspective, and adopting a positive attitude toward change.

KEY TERMS AND PHRASES

Extranet, *63*

Virtual office, *63*

Company intranet, *64*

Decision-making software, *64*

Computer goof-off, *65*

Techno-obsessive, *66*

Web master, *67*

Data mining, *75*

QUESTIONS

1. What do you regard as the most important way in which a manager can use information technology?
2. What is your reaction to the opinion that the Internet is simply another tool for conducting business?
3. To what extent has business travel been reduced because so many business firms are buying and selling over the Internet?
4. Many retailing experts predict that retail stores will never die because online shopping cannot replace the experience of visiting a store. What aspects of visiting a store make it preferable to shopping online for so many people?
5. Several large e-tailers state that their policy is to not accept telephone customer inquiries. How does a customer then resolve a problem that is unresolved by e-mail and a no-telephone-call policy?
6. Among the biggest failures in e-tailing are companies that sell furniture. What are some of the problems associated with selling furniture online?
7. An increasing number of companies subcontract their call centers and pay other companies to handle their customer service by telephone. Describe the advantages and disadvantages of this practice.

CRITICAL THINKING QUESTIONS

1. You have been assigned to head a group charged with establishing policy on employee use of PCs and company networks. Who might stakeholders be, and whose views would you seek out in developing such a policy?
2. What latitude ought to be given to commercial employers and other organizations (e.g., a university, providing IT services to a large student and faculty community) in conducting monitoring and surveillance? How does surveillance of user activity complement and contrast with policy enforcement tools—like those offered by Websense—that block undesired activity?

SKILL-BUILDING EXERCISE: Cost Reduction Through Information Technology

Work in small groups to identify 10 tangible ways that a manager can use information technology to reduce costs. For each item on your list, explain precisely the way in which information technology will reduce costs. Take into account all types of information technology from a desk-top printer to the Internet. A team leader from each group might present the team's findings to the rest of the class.

INTERNET SKILL-BUILDING EXERCISE: Computer Surveillance

Surveillance of computer and network use is a contentious policy issue in terms of the workplace and in law enforcement and national security. Find documents and discussion on the question of computer surveillance on the Web sites of these policy and lobbying organizations and informational sites: The Electronic Privacy Information Center (EPIC) at http://www.epic .org; The Electronic Frontier Foundation (EFF) at http://www.eff .org; The Center for Democracy and Technology (CDT) at http://www.cdt.org; and The Computers, Freedom and Privacy Conference at http://www.cfp.org. Why do you think these organizations oppose computer surveillance? What arguments do they make to support their cases? How active are government entities, such as the U.S. Congress and the relevant federal executive branch agencies, in addressing surveillance issues?

CASE PROBLEM 3-A: Can We Wire the Avon Ladies?

The setting is the Tomas & Mack Center in Los Vegas. A crowd of 13,000 mostly middle-aged women await the on-stage appearance of Avon Products CEO, Andrea Jung. With the attire of a movie star, the 41-year-old Jung strides on the stage to wild applause. Jung keeps the crowd alive with statements such as, "Avon is first and foremost about you. I stand here before you and promise you that will never change." She vows that Avon will become as dominant in the beauty business as Walt Disney is in entertainment.

"We will change the future of women around the world,"

continues Jung. As the audience rises to a standing ovation, Jung declares, "I love you all."

Jung needs the support of as many Avon ladies as possible, because the company faces a critical turning point. Founded in 1886, Avon pioneered door-to-door selling, yet its basic direct sales model seems antiquated. About three-quarters of American women work outside the home, making them unavailable for the Avon Lady during the day. Sales growth in the domestic market has been about 5 percent per year for the last decade, with annual sales of approximately $5.5 billion. The Latin American and Asian markets, however, play a major role in sustaining profits for Avon. The company's 3 million independent sales representatives in 137 countries include 500,000 Avon ladies in the United States. Examples of their products include Hydrafinish Lipcolor for $7 each and Anew Retroactive Age Reversal Cream for $24 each.

One of Jung's major challenges is to reconcile the growth of e-tailing with the company's Old Economy direct-sales business model. Outsiders wonder whether even a talented and charismatic leader like Jung can rise to the challenge. Investment portfolio manager Larry D. Coats says, "Anytime you expand your business beyond your existing universe of operations, you have risk. The key is in the execution—the careful, thoughtful, and deliberate execution."

Jung's plan is to rebuild Avon from the ground up into a company that does much more than sell beauty products door-to-door and at home parties. The Avon that Jung envisions will one day be the source for anything a woman would want to buy. Also, she wants to give busy women a choice in their method of purchasing: through an Avon rep, in a store, or online.

Avon previously avoided traditional retail outlets out of concern for its sales representatives. A company experiment with shopping mall kiosks showed success in attracting young customers who had never purchased an Avon product before. To overcome sales rep opposition, the company now franchises the kiosks to Avon ladies.

Jung looks toward the Web as the biggest channel for expansion. Yet she ponders how to incorporate the Avon ladies into marketing online. Reps still produce about 98 percent of the company's revenue, though the top 20 percent of producers account for approximately 80 percent of the sales. "If we don't include them in everything we do, then we're just another retail brand, just another Internet site, and I don't see the world needing more of those."

To move the Web strategy along, Jung set aside $60 million to build a Web site focused around the reps and the Avon catalog. For $15 a month, any rep can become an *e-representative* who can sell online and earn commissions ranging from 20 percent to 25 percent for orders shipped direct, or 30 percent to 50 percent for orders they deliver in person. Today most reps still fill out 40-page paper forms in No. 2 pencil and send them in by mail or fax. The cost of processing that order is 90 cents, in comparison to 30 cents over the Web. Chief operating officer Susan Kropf says, "Anything we can get off of paper has a significant cost advantage to us."

Concern about competing with sales reps held back Avon management from moving aggressively into online sales. When management printed its Web address on catalogs, the reps were outraged. Many covered the address with their own stickers. The reps also criticized the company for selling online while prohibiting reps from setting up their own sites. Representatives are now authorized to use Avon's Web template to launch their own sites to reach more customers.

Jung recognizes that more online sales are inevitable for Avon, but still recognizes the nature of the Avon business. "I don't believe that in the future sitting alone in front of the Internet is how people are going to conduct their lives," says Jung. "What we do is about relationships, affiliations, being with other people. That is never going to go out." So far about 12,000 of the 500,000 U.S. reps have signed up to sell online.

Discussion Questions

1. What is your recommended Internet strategy for Avon products?

2. Why not lay off all the Avon ladies and sell Avon products by Internet, in stores, and over toll-free numbers exclusively? (Remember, many Avon ladies are earning 50 percent commissions.)

3. What is your evaluation of the effectiveness of www.avon.com as a method of selling Avon products? Is the site a good replacement for the Avon lady? How does the Avon site compare to www.eve.com and www.Sephora.com?

4. Find an Avon customer among your contacts, and get her (or his) opinion of the effectiveness of online sales for Avon products.

Source: Nanette Byrnes, "The New Avon Lady," *Business Week*, September 18, 2000, pp. 136–148; Danielle Kost, "The Soft Sell," *Rochester Democrat and Chronicle*, December 24, 2000, pp. 1E, 4E.

CASE PROBLEM 3-B: Is the Internet Draining Our Productivity?

Casey Bauman is the founder and CEO of Orderfulfillment .com, a company that processes orders for a large number of e-tailers. About 75 percent of his clients are pure players whose only business is selling consumer products over the Internet, such as beauty aids supplied by other companies. The other 25 percent of the company's clients are bricks-and-mortar retailers who also sell merchandise over the Internet. Many companies find that outsourcing order fulfillment is less expensive than developing and staffing their own order-fulfillment centers.

Bauman's firm continues to grow steadily, as many dot.com companies and traditional retailers look for ways to reduce staffing and information technology expenses. Order-fulfillment employs 51 full-time workers and 23 part-time workers. Part-time employees handle most of the order-taking activity between midnight and 7 A.M.

Despite the robustness of his business, Bauman looks toward enhancing the productivity of his own firm. One of his specific concerns is that his order-fulfillment specialists are spending too much time surfing the Internet. An occasional spot-check by Bauman revealed that many images appeared on the monitor screens that are unrelated to order fulfillment.

To verify his suspicions about too much surfing on company time, Bauman hired an Internet detective, Troy Muldoon, to come in and investigate Orderfulfillment's server logs. These logs record all Internet activity on a network, indicating who visited what Web site, the duration of the visit, what the visitors searched for, and where they went next.

Muldoon went through the logs, piecing together patterns of nonbusiness activity on the Internet. Thirty percent of the staff was visiting news sites including sports news, 25 percent visited pornographic sites, and 20 percent were shopping during working hours. Several staff members came in on weekends to catch up with their work, but then spent several hours surfing the Web for recreation.

Muldoon informed Bauman of his findings. "I see a familiar pattern here," said Muldoon. "I'll give you your company-specific findings. But before overreacting, I want to share some data with you collected by Vault.com."

Here is the printout Muldoon prepared for Bauman.

The Twelve Most Frequent Methods of Cyberloafing*

72%	Read the news
45%	Make travel arrangements
40%	Make purchases
37%	Conduct job searches
37%	Visit special interest sites
34%	Check stocks
28%	Coordinate social events
26%	Instant message
13%	Download music
11%	Play games
9%	Chat
4%	Visit pornographic sites

*At least what they admit to.

Source: September 2000 vault.com survey, adapted in Alan Cohen, "No Web for You," *Fortune Small Business,* October 2000, p. 56.

"You'll note that the people who responded to the Vault.com survey were light on visits to pornographic sites. That's good for their employers, because visiting porn sites can lead to complaints about sexual harassment. You appear to be more at risk."

Bauman responded, "This information is very helpful. It appears that we have a real productivity drain here at Orderfulfillment. Maybe I'll block Internet access, or threaten my employees with severe punishments if they surf on company time.

"Hold on Casey," said Muldoon. "You don't want to make an overcorrection. You have to take into account factors such as the natural tendency of employees to find ways to goof off. If employees call home to touch base with family members, would you block telephone access? What about the smokers who step outside the building for 10 minutes? Do you punish them?

"I want to work with you to get productivity on track, but not damage morale."

Bauman replied, "You've given me some good ideas to work on. I need to think through this productivity problem a little more."

Discussion Questions

1. In what way are the Internet detective's findings related to employee productivity?
2. What actions, if any, do you think Bauman should take?
3. What is your evaluation of the ethics of a company hiring an outsider to investigate the server logs?
4. Based on your personal experiences, how accurate is the Vault.com study about Internet surfing?

ENDNOTES

1. Flora Tartakovsky, "The Top 10 Digital Workplaces," *Time Digital,* October 2000, p. 35.
2. Michael A. Hitt, "The New Frontier: Transformation of Management for the New Millennium," *Organizational Dynamics,* Winter 2000, p. 15.
3. Hitt, "The New Frontier," p. 12.
4. Gary McWilliams, "Technology Is What's Driving This Business," *Business Week,* November 3, 1997, p. 146.
5. Anthony M. Townsend, Samuel M. DeMarie, and Anthony R. Hendrickson, "Virtual Teams: Technology and the Workplace of the Future," *Academy of Management Executive,* August 1998, p. 18.
6. Mary J. Cronin, "Ford's Intranet Success," *Fortune,* March 30, 1998, p. 158.
7. Heather Page, "Wired for Success," *Entrepreneur,* May 1997, p. 132.
8. Samuel Greengard, "Technology Finally Advances HR," *Workforce,* January 2000, pp. 38–39.
9. "Ask Success," *Success,* August 1998, p. 26.
10. "The Dirty Dozen: Where Workers Go When You're Not Looking," Vault.Com survey, September 2000.

11. Yankelovich Partners survey reported in Mildred Culp, "Are You 'Techno-Obsessive'? Step Back," *Passage Media,* August 23, 1998.
12. Charles Fishman, "But Wait You Promised," *Fast Company,* April 2001, p. 118.
13. Peter Haapaniemi, "The Truth about E-Business," *Unisys Exec (unysys.com/execmag),* November–December 2000, p. 26.
14. "The Website Is the Business," *Fortune Technology Guide,* Winter 2001, pp. 148–149.
15. George Anders, "Power Partners," *Fast Company,* September 2000, pp. 148–150; http://www.wellsfargo.com.
16. Ranjay Gulati and Jason Garino, "Get the Right Mix of Bricks and Clicks," *Harvard Business Review,* May–June 2000, pp. 107–114.
17. Esther Dyson, "Mirror, Mirror, on the Wall," *Harvard Business Review,* September–October 1997, pp. 24–25.
18. Steve Hamm and Marcia Stepanek, "From Reengineering to E-Engineering," *Business Week e.biz,* March 22, 1999, p. 16.
19. Michael J. Mandel and Robert D. Hof, "Rethinking the Internet," *Business Week,* March 26, 2001, p. 118.
20. John Shinal, "Dead Dot-Coms Can Still Cause Havoc," *Business Week,* March 12, 2001, p. 50.
21. Mandel and Hof, "Rethinking the Internet," p. 117.
22. Esther Dyson, "Mirror, Mirror, on the Wall," *Harvard Business Review,* September-October 1997, pp. 24–25.
23. "Three Overlooked Keys to E-Commerce Success," *What's Working Online,* Special Issue, 2001, p. 1; Amy Wilson Sheldon, "Strategy Rules," *Fast Company,* January 2001, pp. 165–166; Rosabeth Moss Kanter, "The Ten Deadly Sins of Wanna-Dots," *Harvard Business Review,* January 2001, p. 91; "American E-Tailers Take Europe by Storm," *Business Week,* August 7, 2000, pp. 54–55; Suzanne Koudsi, "Attention Kmart Bashers," *Fortune,* November 13, 2000, pp. 213–222.
24. "Three Overlooked Keys to E-Commerce Success," p. 1.

Ethics and Social Responsibility

Suppose you strolled through Ton Yang Indonesia (TYI) shoe factory, an 8,500-worker complex of hot, dingy buildings outside of Jakarta. Company president Jung Moo Young would show you all the improvements he has made in the past two years. He did so at the behest of his biggest customer, Reebok International, Ltd., to mollify protests by Western activists who accuse the U.S. athletic shoemaker of using sweatshops.

Last year, Jung bought new machinery to apply a water-based solvent to paste on shoe soles instead of toluene, which may be hazardous to workers who breathe it all day. He installed a new ventilation system and chairs with back supports. Ton Yang Indonesia spent $2 million of its own money to satisfy Reebok. (The company has $100 million in annual sales.) Much to Jung's surprise, the workers have become more productive.[1]

The anecdote about the Indonesian shoe factory illustrates how some multinational companies are making strides in encouraging their subcontractors to improve sweatshop conditions in their factories. Many people argue that considerable progress still needs to be made. Nevertheless companies like Reebok are aware that being socially responsible is an important part of remaining a profitable business.

The purpose of this chapter is to explain the importance of ethics and social responsibility. To accomplish this purpose we present various aspects of ethics and social responsibility. We also present guidelines to help managerial workers make ethical decisions and to conduct socially responsible acts.

OBJECTIVES

After studying this chapter and doing the exercises, you should be able to:

1 Identify the philosophical principles behind business ethics.

2 Explain how values relate to ethics.

3 Identify factors contributing to lax ethics, and common ethical temptations and violations.

4 Apply a guide to ethical decision making.

5 Describe the stakeholder viewpoint of social responsibility and corporate social performance.

6 Present an overview of social responsibility initiatives.

7 Summarize the benefits of ethical and socially responsible behavior, and how managers can create an environment that fosters such behavior.

Chapter 4

1   BUSINESS ETHICS

Identify the philosophical principles behind business ethics.

ethics

The study of moral obligation, or separating right from wrong.

moral intensity

The magnitude of an unethical act.

Understanding and practicing good business ethics is an important part of a manager's job. One of the many reasons ethics are important is that customers and suppliers prefer to deal with ethical companies. **Ethics** is the study of moral obligation, or separating right from wrong.

Although many unethical acts are illegal, others are legal and issues of legality vary by nation. An example of an illegal unethical act in the United States is giving a government official a kickback for placing a contract with a specific firm. An example of a legal, yet unethical, practice is giving such a large gift to a corporate employee for signing a sales contract that the "gift" (such as a home entertainment center) could be considered a kickback.

A useful perspective in understanding business ethics emphasizes **moral intensity**, or the magnitude of an unethical act.[2] When an unethical act is not of large consequence, a person might behave unethically without much thought. However, if the act is of large consequence, the person might refrain from unethical or illegal behavior. For example, a manager might make a photocopy of an entire book or copy someone else's software (both unethical and illegal acts). The same manager, however, might hesitate to dump toxins into a river.

Business ethics will be mentioned at various places in this text. Here we approach the subject from several perspectives: philosophical principles, values, contributing factors to ethical problems, common ethical problems, and a guide to ethical decision making. To better relate the study of ethics to yourself, take the self-quiz presented in Exhibit 4-1.

Philosophical Principles Underlying Business Ethics

A standard way of understanding ethical decision making is to know the philosophical basis for making these decisions. When attempting to decide what is right and wrong, managerial workers can focus on (1) consequence; (2) duties, obligations, and principles; or (3) integrity.[3]

Focus on Consequences

When attempting to decide what is right or wrong, people can sometimes focus on the consequences of their decision or action. According to this criterion, if no one gets hurt, the decision is ethical. Focusing on consequences is often referred to as *utilitarianism*. The decision maker is concerned with the utility of the decision. What really counts is the net balance of good consequences over bad. An automotive body shop manager, for example, might decide that using low-quality replacement fenders is ethically wrong because the fender will rust quickly. To focus on consequences, the decision maker would have to be aware of all the good and bad consequences of a given decision. The body-shop manager would have to estimate such factors as how angry customers would be whose cars were repaired with inferior parts, and how much negative publicity would result.

Focus on Duties, Obligations, and Principles

Another approach to making an ethical decision is to examine one's duties in making the decision. The theories underlying this approach are referred to as *deontological*, from the Greek word *deon*, or duty. The *deontological* approach is based on universal principles such as honesty, fairness, justice, and respect for persons and property.

Rights, such as the rights for privacy and safety, are also important. From a deontological perspective, the principles are more important than the consequences. If a given decision violates one of these universal principles, it is automatically unethical even if nobody gets hurt. An ethical body shop manager might think, "It just isn't right to use replacement fenders that are not authorized by the auto-

EXHIBIT 4-1

87

The Ethical Reasoning Inventory

Describe how much you agree with each of the following statements, using the following scale: disagree strongly (DS); disagree (D); neutral (N); agree (A); agree strongly (AS). Circle the answer that best fits your level of agreement.

	DS	D	N	A	AS
1. When applying for a job, I would cover up the fact that I had been fired from my most recent job.	5	4	3	2	1
2. Cheating just a few dollars in one's favor on an expense account is OK if the person needed the money.	5	4	3	2	1
3. Employees should inform on each other for wrongdoing.	1	2	3	4	5
4. It is acceptable to give approximate figures for expense account items when one does not have all the receipts.	5	4	3	2	1
5. I see no problem with conducting a little personal business on company time.	5	4	3	2	1
6. I would fix up a purchasing agent with a date just to close a sale.	5	4	3	2	1
7. To make a sale, I would stretch the truth about a delivery date.	5	4	3	2	1
8. I would flirt with my boss just to get a bigger salary increase.	5	4	3	2	1
9. If I received $100 for doing some odd jobs, I would report it on my income tax returns.	1	2	3	4	5
10. I see no harm in taking home a few office supplies.	5	4	3	2	1
11. It is acceptable to read the e-mail and fax messages of coworkers even when not invited to do so.	5	4	3	2	1
12. It is unacceptable to call in sick to take a day off, even if only done once or twice a year.	1	2	3	4	5
13. I would accept a permanent, full-time job even if I knew I wanted the job for only six months.	5	4	3	2	1
14. I would check company policy before accepting an expensive gift from a supplier.	1	2	3	4	5
15. To be successful in business, a person usually has to ignore ethics.	5	4	3	2	1
16. If I were physically attracted to a job candidate, I would hire him or her over another candidate.	5	4	3	2	1
17. I tell the truth all the time on the job.	1	2	3	4	5
18. Software should never be copied, except as authorized by the publisher.	1	2	3	4	5
19. I would authorize accepting an office machine on a 30-day trial period, even if I knew I had no intention of making a purchase.	5	4	3	2	1
20. I would never accept credit for a coworker's ideas.	1	2	3	4	5

Scoring and interpretation: Add the numbers you have circled to obtain your score.

90–100   You are a strongly ethical person who may take a little ribbing from coworkers for being too straight-laced.

60–89   You show an average degree of ethical awareness, and therefore should become more sensitive to ethical issues.

41–59   Your ethics are underdeveloped, but you have at least some awareness of ethical issues. You need to raise your level of awareness about ethical issues.

20–40   Your ethical values are far below contemporary standards in business. Begin a serious study of business ethics.

mobile manufacturer. Whether or not these parts rust quickly is a secondary consideration."

Focus on Integrity (Virtue Ethics)

The third criterion for determining the ethics of behavior focuses on the character of the person involved in the decision or action. If the person in question has good character, and genuine motivation and intentions, he or she is behaving ethically. The ingredients making up character will often include the two other ethical criteria. One might judge a person to have good character if she or he follows the right principles and respects the rights of others.

The decision maker's environment, or community, helps define what integrity means. You might have more lenient ethical standards for a person selling you a speculative investment than you would for a bank vice president who accepted your cash deposit.

The virtue ethics of managers and professionals who belong to professional societies can be judged readily. Business-related professions having codes of ethics include accountants, purchasing managers, and certified financial planners. To the extent that the person abides by the tenets of the stated code, he or she is behaving ethically. An example of such a tenet would be for a financial planner to be explicit about any commissions gained from a client accepting the advice.

When faced with a complex ethical decision, a manager would be best advised to incorporate all three philosophical approaches. The manager might think through the consequences of a decision, along with an analysis of duties, obligations, principles, and intentions.

Tim Berry, the president of Palo Alto Software in Eugene, Oregon, exemplifies a manager who believes that integrity contributes to his success. Part of his integrity is expressed in refusing to lie. "There were times I felt at a disadvantage with people who lacked integrity," he admits. "But I've found the truth always pays off in the long term, even if it hurts in the short term." Berry learned to appreciate the power of integrity while working as a consultant for Apple Computer, early in his career. He observed as other consultants made generous promises, only to back out or fail to deliver. Berry says that clients might be fooled temporarily, but dishonest consultants lost clients quickly.[4]

2 _____ Values and Ethics

Explain how values relate to ethics.

Values are closely related to ethics. Values can be considered clear statements of what is critically important. Ethics become the vehicle for converting values into actions, or doing the right thing. For example, a *clean environment* is a value, whereas *not littering* is practicing ethics.[5] Many firms contend that they "put people before profits" (a value). If this assertion were true, a manager would avoid actions such as delaying payments to a vendor just to hold on to money longer, or firing a group member for having negotiated a deal that lost money.

A person's values also influence which kind of behaviors he or she believes are ethical. An executive who strongly values profits might not find it unethical to raise prices more than are needed to cover additional costs. Another executive who strongly values family life might suggest that the company invest money in an on-premises child-care center.

Values are important because the right values can lead to a competitive advantage. According to business writer Perry Pascarella, winning executives see values as a competitive tool that enables their organizations to respond quickly and appropriately. These executives invest time in nurturing values they think will help the organization, including honesty, integrity, teamwork, and risk taking. Another key value is satisfying the customer.[6] A contributing factor to the success of Lands' End (remember the ad in Chapter 3) is that associates are taught to try extra hard to please customers.

The concept of **ethically centered management** helps put some teeth into an abstract discussion of how values relate to ethics. Ethically centered management emphasizes that the high quality of an end product takes precedence over its scheduled completion. At the same time, it sets high quality standards for dealing with employees and managing production. Robert Elliott Allinson believes that many work-related catastrophes can be attributed to a management team that is not ethically centered. One such example was the failure of the Hubbell telescope to function property in outer space because of a flaw in a mirror. (The problem was later corrected.)

According to Allinson, management acted irresponsibly by not emphasizing the importance of quality control and clearly designating officials to be in charge of quality. Also, top management at NASA disowned responsibility for finding out and ensuring that the end product was problem-free and of highest quality.[7]

The concept of ethically centered management is helpful in understanding what went wrong in the many serious accidents involving Ford Explorer sport utility vehicles (SUV) equipped with two different models of Firestone tires. The outer treads of the tires sometimes peeled off, causing the driver to lose control of the vehicle. By fall 2000, more than 1,100 incident reports and 57 lawsuits had been filed against Firestone. The first lawsuits were filed against Firestone involving tires on the Ford Explorer. Evaluations by Bridgestone/Firestone Inc. emphasize that is the interaction (combined effect) of the Firestone tires with the Ford Explorer in particular that caused the tire failures and vehicle turnovers. Explorers had been involved in 16,000 rollover mishaps over a 10-year period since the vehicle was introduced, yet less than 10 percent of those accidents involved tread separation from the tire casing.

First reports of the tire failure surfaced in the press in Saudi Arabia in 1998. Ford responded in several months by approving a tire recall in Saudi Arabia. Within one year, Ford recalled tires in Thailand and Malaysia, prompting the company to persuade Firestone to launch a study of why the failure was occurring. Soon Firestone recalled 6.6 million tires. In August of 2000, the National Highway Traffic Safety Association labeled 1.4 million more tires as defective. The number of fatalities associated with the tires rose to 88, and injuries to 250. Venezuela launched a criminal probe into an alleged cover-up by Ford and Firestone.

Firestone officials pointed out that the lower level of air pressure that Ford recommended for the tires—26 pounds per square inch (psi), compared with Firestone's suggested 30 psi—may have contributed to the tire separations. However, other explanations for the problems have been offered such as poor quality control at the Decatur, Illinois, plant where many of the faulty tires were manufactured. A government investigator also charged that Firestone and Ford knew for several years that they had a serious problem, but decided to continue equipping the Ford Explorers with the faulty tires. If Firestone and Ford indeed glossed over the tread separation and vehicle rollover problems, management was far from being ethically centered.[8]

ethically centered management

An approach to management that emphasizes that the high quality of an end product takes precedence over its scheduled completion.

89

3

Identify factors contributing to lax ethics, and common ethical temptations and violations.

Contributing Factors to Ethical Problems

Individuals, organizations, and society itself must share some of the blame for the prevalence or unethical behavior in the workplace. Major contributors to unethical behavior are an individual's greed and gluttony, or the desire to maximize self-gain at the expense of others.

Another major contributor to unethical behavior is an organizational atmosphere that condones such behavior. According to one study, even employees with high ethical standards may stray in a climate that rewards unethical behavior. A firm's official code of ethics may not coincide with its actual climate. It is the firm's top executives who set the company's moral tone.[9]

A more recent study on unethical employees found similar results. One-third of employees admitted to having stolen from their employer. The most frequent forms of theft were misuse of the employee-discount privilege and theft of company merchandise or property. The researchers concluded that a perceived management climate more lenient than the norm for management is accompanied by employee attitudes that are more protheft. The opposite was also true: a management climate strongly opposed to theft leads to stronger antitheft attitudes by employees.[10]

moral laxity

A slippage in moral behavior because other issues seem more important at the time.

A third case of unethical behavior is **moral laxity**, a slippage in moral behavior because other issues seem more important at the time. The implication is that the businessperson who behaves unethically has not carefully planned the immoral behavior but lets it occur by not exercising good judgment. Many workplace deaths fit into this category. More than 300 people were killed and about 900 injured when a shopping mall collapsed in Seoul, South Korea. Officials blamed the disaster on shoddy construction and negligence by executives of the shopping complex. Police said that the executives knew the floor was crumbling hours before the disaster. Nevertheless, they decided not to close and left the premises without warning anyone.[11]

Unethical behavior is often triggered by pressure from higher management to achieve goals. One study found that 56 percent of all workers feel some pressure to act unethically or illegally. Forty-eight percent of workers surveyed admitted they had engaged in one or more unethical or illegal actions during the year. Among the most common ethical violations were (1) cutting corners on quality, (2) covering up incidents that would make them look bad, (3) deceiving customers, (4) lying to a supervisor or group member, and (5) taking credit for a coworker's idea.[12] A contributing factor to these five types of unethical behavior is that the person has an incentive for being unethical. For example, if a worker cuts corners on quality, thereby saving the company money (at least in the short run), he or she might be rewarded for good performance.

Although emphasis on corporate training programs in ethics increases, illegal and unethical behavior on the job continues to be a major problem. A survey of 2,390 working adults by KPMG, a consulting and advisory group, reinforces the study just mentioned. Among the study highlights were as follows:

- Seventy-six percent of workers say they have witnessed unethical or illegal behavior by coworkers in the past year. The misconduct included theft, harassment and discrimination, lying, mishandling of confidential information, and cutting corners.
- Of those who saw misconduct, 49 percent considered it serious enough to damage public trust in their company if it ever became public knowledge.
- Sixty-one percent suspected that higher-ups caught doing something unethical or illegal would be disciplined less severely than would lower-ranking workers.

- Fifty-three percent of the employees surveyed believed their managers would not protect them from retaliation if they turned in an ethical violator.[13]

Although these findings might suggest that unethical and illegal behavior is on the increase, another explanation is possible. Workers today might be more observant of ethical problems, and more willing to note them on a survey. Even if people are more aware of ethical problems, self-interest continues to be a factor that influences ethics. An experiment with 75 graduate business students showed that people are willing to misrepresent the truth if given an incentive. The students were enrolled in a negotiation class, and participated in a negotiation exercise. The negotiation involved dissolving a partnership formed by two people, with a conflict over trying to figure out the value of two products. Of the participants, 55 percent misrepresented their true estimates of the value of the product to an arbitrator. (The incentive is that the negotiator would receive a $100 prize instead of a $1 prize if the overstimate were accepted.)[14]

A new explanation for the cause of unethical behavior emphasizes the strength of relationships among people as a major factor.[15] Assume that two people have close ties to each other, such as having worked together for a long time, or knowing each other both on and off the job. As a consequence, they are likely to behave ethically toward each other on the job. In contrast, if a weak relationship exists between the two people, either party is more likely to engage in an unethical relationship. The owner of an auto service center is more likely to behave unethically toward a stranger passing through town than a long-term customer. The opportunity for unethical behavior between strangers is often minimized because individuals typically do not trust strangers with sensitive information or valuables.

Ethical Temptations and Violations

Certain ethical mistakes, including illegal actions, recur in the workplace. Familiarizing oneself with these behaviors can be helpful in managing the ethical behavior of others as well as monitoring one's own behavior. A list of commonly found ethical temptations and violations, including criminal acts, follows:[16]

1. *Stealing from employers and customers.* Employee theft costs U.S. and Canadian companies about $60 billion annually. Retail employees steal goods from their employers, and financial service employees steal money. Examples of theft from customers includes airport baggage handlers who steal from passenger suitcases, and bank employees, stockbrokers, and attorneys who siphon money from customer accounts.
2. *Illegally copying software.* A rampant problem in the workplace is making unauthorized copies of software for either company or personal use. Similarly, many employees make illegal copies of videos, books, and magazine articles instead of purchasing these products.
3. *Treating people unfairly.* Being fair to people means equity, reciprocity, and impartiality. Fairness revolves around the issue of giving people equal rewards for accomplishing the same amount of work. The goal of human resource legislation is to make decisions about people based on their qualifications and performance—not on the basis of demographic factors such as gender, race, or age. A fair working environment is where performance is the only factor that counts (equity). Employer-employee expectations must be understood and met (reciprocity). Prejudice and bias must be eliminated (impartiality).

conflict of interest

A situation that occurs when one's judgment or objectivity is compromised.

4. *Sexual harassment.* Sexual harassment involves making compliance with sexual favors a condition of employment, or creating a hostile, intimidating environment related to sexual topics. Harassment violates the law and is also an ethical issue because it is morally wrong and unfair. A study of about 750 women who worked for either a private firm or a university revealed that 65 percent had been sexually harassed at least once during the last 24 months. Furthermore, sexual harassment led to problems of psychological well-being such as dissatisfaction with work. After being harassed, women also tended to be absent and tardy more frequently.[17] Sexual harassment is such a widespread problem that most employers take steps to prevent the problem. Exhibit 4-2 describes actions employers can take to protect themselves against harassment charges.

5. *Conflict of interest.* Part of being ethical is making business judgments only on the basis of the merits in a situation. Imagine that you are a supervisor who is romantically involved with a worker within the group. When it came time to assigning raises, it would be difficult for you to be objective. A **conflict of interest** occurs when your judgment or objectivity is compromised.

6. *Divulging confidential information.* An ethical person can be trusted by others not to divulge confidential information unless the welfare of others is at stake. The challenge of dealing with confidential information arises in many areas of business, including information about performance-appraisal results, compensation, personal problems of employees, disease status of employees, and coworker bankruptcies.

7. *Misuse of corporate resources.* A corporate resource is anything the company owns, including its name and reputation. Assume that a man named Jason Hedgeworth worked for Microsoft Corporation. It would be unethical for him to establish a software consulting company and put on his letterhead

EXHIBIT 4-2

A Corporate Tip Sheet on Sexual Harassment

The U.S. Supreme Court has given companies guidelines on how to protect themselves against sexual harassment charges. Most of these suggestions reflect actions that many companies already employ to prevent and control sexual harassment.

- Develop a zero-tolerance policy on harassment, and communicate it to employees.
- Ensure that victims can report abuses without fear of retaliation.
- Take reasonable care to prevent and promptly report any sexually harassing behavior.
- When defending against a charge of sexual harassment, show that an employee failed to use internal procedures for reporting abusive behavior.
- Publicize antiharassment policies aggressively and regularly—in handbooks, on posters, in training sessions, and in reminders in paychecks.
- Give supervisors and employees real-life examples of what could constitute offensive conduct.
- Ensure that workers do not face reprisals if they report offending behavior. Designate several managers to take these complaints so that employees do not have to report the problem to their supervisor, who may be the abuser.
- Train managers at all levels in sexual harassment issues.
- Provide guidelines to senior managers explaining how to conduct investigations that recognize the rights of all parties involved.
- Punishment against harassers should be swift and sure.

Source: Adapted from information in Susan B. Garland, "Finally, a Corporate Tip Sheet on Sexual Harassment," *Business Week,* July 13, 1998, p. 39; Jonathan A. Segal, "Prevent Now or Pay Later," *HRMagazine,* October 1998, pp. 145–149.

"Jason Hedgeworth, software designer, Microsoft Corporation." Using corporate resources can fall into the gray area, such as whether to borrow a laptop computer to prepare income taxes for a fee.

8. *Greed, gluttony, and avarice.* An ethical temptation, particularly among top-level executives, is to misuse corporate resources in an extravagant, greedy manner. The temptation is greater for top executives because they have more control over resources. Examples of the greedy use of corporate resources include using the corporate jet for personal vacations for oneself, friends, and family members; and paying for personal items with an expense account. A case in point is Lars Bildman, the former chief executive of Astra-USA, a drug company. He bilked the company out of $1 million, including having his house renovated by contrac-tors who were doing work for his company. Bildman instructed the contractors to bury the costs of renovating his home in their bill for legitimate work for Astra.[18]

9. *Corporate espionage.* A growing unethical practice is to collect competitive information to the extent that it constitutes spying on competitors. Among the common forms of spying are computer hacking, bribing present employees to turn over trade secrets, and prying information from relatives of workers with useful information. Another controversial practice is *dumpster diving,* or digging through the garbage of competitors or rivals to uncover trade secrets or derogatory information. Oracle Corp. is one of several well-known companies that publicly admitted to spying. Oracle chairman Larry Ellison, hired detectives to dig up information on archrival Microsoft including rifling through Microsoft dumpsters.[19]

Outright stealing of information about rivals is obviously unethical. A less obvious form of espionage would be to leave your company, join a competitor, and then reveal key insider information about the first company to your new employer.

10. *Poor cyberethics.* The Internet creates new potential for unethical behavior, thereby making it important for all employees to resist the temptation of practicing poor cyberethics. One example of questionable ethics would be to send a giant e-mail file containing your opinion about a nonwork-related issue to everyone in your

---

- Observe the Golden Rule in cyberspace: Treat others as you would like to be treated.
- Act responsibly when sending e-mail or posting messages to a discussion group. Do not use language or photographs that are racist, sexist, or offensive. Be careful when using humor or sarcasm as they can be misunderstood.
- Respect the privacy of others. Do not read other individuals' e-mail or access their personal files without permission.
- Help maintain the security of your local system and the Internet by taking precautions when downloading files to avoid introducing a virus. Do not engage in hacking. Protect your account number, password, and access codes.
- Respect intellectual property rights. Do not use or copy software you have not paid for. Give proper credit for other people's work—do not plagiarize work from the Net.
- Observe the rules of your school or employer. Most schools have Acceptable Use Policies that outline responsible behavior on the Net.
- Conserve resources. Do not add to network congestion by downloading huge files, sending long-winded e-mail messages, or engaging in spamming.
- Protect your personal safety. Never give personal information, such as your phone number or address, to strangers on the Internet. Report any concerns to a network administrator.

Source: Adapted from "Netiquette Tips," *Keying In,* November 2000, p. 4.

EXHIBIT 4-3

Netiquette Tips

company. As a consequence the servers would be blocked from conducting legitimate company business. Exhibit 4–3 presents suggestions for practicing good cyberethics and netiquette. (Etiquette is related to ethics because gross etiquette, such as widely distributing racist or sexist jokes, borders on being unethical.)

4

Apply a guide to ethical decision making.

A Guide to Ethical Decision Making

A practical way of improving ethical decision making is to run contemplated decisions through an ethics test when any doubt exists. The ethics test presented next was used at the Center for Business Ethics at Bentley College as part of corporate training programs. Decision makers are taught to ask themselves:[20]

1. *Is it right?* This question is based on the deontological theory of ethics that there are certain universally accepted guiding principles of rightness and wrongness, such as "thou shall not steal."
2. *Is it fair?* This question is based on the deontological theory of justice, implying that certain actions are inherently just or unjust. For example, it is unjust to fire a high-performing employee to make room for a less competent person who is a personal friend.
3. *Who gets hurt?* This question is based on the utilitarian notion of attempting to do the greatest good for the greatest number of people.
4. *Would you be comfortable if the details of your decision were reported on the front page of your local newspaper or through your company's e-mail system?* This question is based on the universalist principle of disclosure.
5. *Would you tell your child (or young relative) to do it?* This question is based on the deontological principle of reversibility, referring to reversing who carries out the decision.
6. *How does it smell?* This question is based on a person's intuition and common sense. For example, underpaying many accounts payable by a few dollars to save money would "smell" bad to a sensible person.

A decision that was obviously ethical, such as donating some managerial time for charitable organizations, would not need to be run through the six-question test. Neither would a blatantly illegal act, such as not paying employees for work performed. But the test is useful for decisions that are neither obviously ethical nor obviously unethical. Among such gray areas would be charging clients based on their ability to pay and developing a clone of a successful competitive product.

Another type of decision that often requires an ethical test is choosing between two rights (rather than right versus wrong).[21] Suppose a blind worker in the group has personal problems so great that her job performance suffers. She is offered counseling but does not follow through seriously. Other members of the team complain about the blind worker's performance because she is interfering with the group achieving its goals. If the manager dismisses the blind worker, she might suffer severe financial consequences. (She is the only wage earner in her family.) However, if she is retained the group will suffer consequences of its own. The manager must now choose between two rights, or the lesser of two evils.

5

Describe the stakeholder viewpoint of social responsibility and corporate social performance.

SOCIAL RESPONSIBILITY

Many people believe that firms have an obligation to be concerned about outside groups affected by an organization. **Social responsibility** is the idea that firms have obligations to society beyond their economic obligations to owners or stockholders and also beyond those prescribed by law or contract. Both ethics and social responsibility relate to the goodness or morality of organizations. However, business ethics is a narrower concept that applies to the morality of an individual's decisions and behaviors. Social responsibility is a broader concept that relates to an organization's impact on society, beyond doing what is ethical.[22] To behave in a socially responsible way, managers must be aware of how their actions influence the environment.

An important perspective is that many socially responsible actions are the by-products of sensible business decisions. For instance, it is both socially responsible and profitable for a company to improve the language and math skills of entry-level workers. Literate and numerate entry-level workers for some jobs may be in short supply, and employees who cannot follow written instructions or do basic math may be unproductive.

An expanded view of social responsibility regards organizations as having a **corporate social consciousness**. The term refers to a set of consciously held shared values that motivate and guide individuals to act in a responsible way. As part of being responsible, the interests of the corporation are balanced against its accountability for the effect of its actions upon society, the environment, and other interested parties. A company with a strong corporate social consciousness would be profitable, pay high wages, attract high-quality job candidates, and be admired by the general public and the government. Companies who fit this description include Southwest Airlines, Charles Schwab, J. M. Smucker, and Kinko's.[23]

A practical problem in having a corporate social consciousness is that not all interested parties agree on what constitutes responsible behavior. Target stores might have many customers who believe that citizens have a constitutional right to defend themselves with handguns against intruders to their home. To this group of customers, a retailer with a corporate social consciousness would sell handguns to the public. Another customer group might believe strongly in tight gun controls. To this group, Target *not* selling handguns to the public would reflect corporate social consciousness.

Wal-Mart has struggled continuously with how to avoid controversy about what products are stocked on its shelves. Top management wants to act with a strong social consciousness, but also wants to please as many consumer groups as possible and remain profitable. Based on its enormous size and reach, Wal-Mart has played an unwanted role as a sort of national conscience. The company has been accused of being a promoter of demon rum and slave labor, and a friend and ally of the environment. A Wal-Mart senior executive says, "The watchword for all our people is 'Do what is right.' That's what we really preach and teach, and we want, but there's so much gray."[24] Two of Wal-Mart's difficult merchandising decisions were to sell (1) hunting rifles, but not handguns, and (2) tabloid newspapers like the *National Enquirer,* but not adult magazines like *Penthouse.*

This section will examine three aspects of social responsibility: (1) the stockholder versus stakeholder viewpoints of social responsibility, (2) corporate social performance, and (3) a sampling of social responsibility initiatives.

Stockholder Versus Stakeholder Viewpoints

The **stockholder viewpoint** of social responsibility is the traditional perspective. It holds that business firms are responsible only to their owners and stockholders. The job of managers is therefore to satisfy the financial interests of the stockholders. By so doing, says the stockholder view, the interests of society will be

---

social responsibility
The idea that firms have obligations to society beyond their obligations to owners or stockholders and also beyond those prescribed by law or contract.

corporate social consciousness
A set of consciously held shared values that guide decision making.

stockholder viewpoint
The traditional perspective on social responsibility that a business organization is responsible only to its owners and stockholders.

served in the long run. Socially irresponsible acts ultimately result in poor sales. According to the stockholder viewpoint, corporate social responsibility is therefore a by-product of profit seeking.

The **stakeholder viewpoint** of social responsibility contends that firms must hold themselves responsible for the quality of life of the many groups affected by the firm's actions. These interested parties, or stakeholders, include those groups composing the firm's general environment. Two categories of stakeholders exist. Internal stakeholders include owners, employees, and stockholders; external stakeholders include customers, labor unions, consumer groups, and financial institutions. Exhibit 4-4 depicts the stakeholder viewpoint of social responsibility.

Another way of framing the stakeholder perspective is that society grants authority to business leaders, shareholders, employees, and customers. Yet according to an *iron law*, in the long run those parties who do not use their power in an acceptable manner will lose that power. Under extreme misuse of power, the government might intervene, such as declaring a company to be an illegal monopoly. Microsoft has fought charges for years that it abused its power by bullying other companies into using its products, and not using competitors' products.[25]

Many organizations regard their various stakeholders as partners in achieving success, rather than as adversaries. The organizations and the stakeholders work together for their mutual success. For example, Ford Motor Company owns 49 percent of the Hertz rental car company, which is also a major Ford customer. An example of a company partnership with a labor union is the establishment of joint committees on safety and other issues of concern to employees.

Part of understanding the stakeholder viewpoint is to recognize that not all stakeholders are the same. Instead, they can be differentiated along three dimensions. Some stakeholders are more powerful than others, such as the United Auto Workers (UAW) union being more powerful than a small group of protesters.

stakeholder viewpoint

The viewpoint on social responsibility contending that firms must hold themselves responsible for the quality of life of the many groups affected by the firm's actions.

96

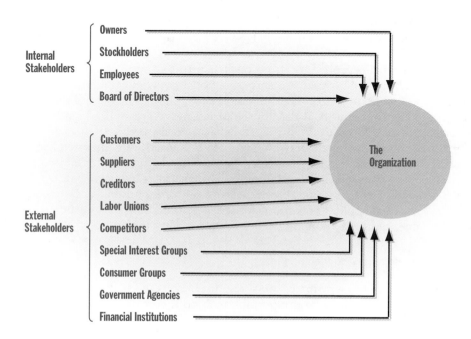

EXHIBIT 4-4

The Stakeholder Viewpoint of Social Responsibility

An organization has to satisfy the interests of many groups.

Internal Stakeholders
- Owners
- Stockholders
- Employees
- Board of Directors

External Stakeholders
- Customers
- Suppliers
- Creditors
- Labor Unions
- Competitors
- Special Interest Groups
- Consumer Groups
- Government Agencies
- Financial Institutions

The Organization

Some stakeholders are more legitimate than others, such as the UAW, which is a well-established and legal entity. Some stakeholders are more urgent than others because they require immediate attention. A group of protesters chaining themselves to a company fence because they believe the company is polluting the ground, would require immediate attention.[26]

Corporate Social Performance

Corporate social performance is the extent to which a firm responds to the demands of its stakeholders for behaving in a socially responsible manner. After stakeholders have been satisfied with the reporting of financial information, they may turn their attention to the behavior of the corporation as a good citizen in the community. One way of measuring social performance is to analyze the company's annual report in search of relevant statistical information.

corporate social performance

The extent to which a firm responds to the demands of its stakeholders for behaving in a socially responsible manner.

Two accounting professors interested in social responsibility scanned the annual reports of the top 100 corporations on the Fortune 500 list. The corporations were involved in a variety of industries including chemicals, health, petroleum, manufacturing, foods, electronics, aerospace, and information technology.[27] The analysis most closely tied to social performance was the disclosure of environmental measures, with the following rates of activity being reported:

- Pollution measures, 74%
- Contributions to crime prevention, 0%
- Contributions to the homeless, 10%
- Contributions to AIDS treatment and substance abuse programs, 10%
- Contributions to the arts, 17%
- Contributions to education, 44%

As particular causes become more popular, they tend to gather more corporate support. For example, if the study in question were repeated today, AIDS treatment and prevention would show a higher percentage of support.

Another consequence of social performance is that a group of mutual funds purchase stocks only of companies the fund manager believes to have good social performance. At the same time the fund manager does not purchase the stocks of companies it believes to have poor social performance. The Domini Social Equity Fund is an example of such a socially responsible mutual fund. Fund manager Amy Domini, screens out the industries in disfavor with most advocates of social responsibility: alcohol, tobacco, weapons, gambling, and nuclear power. Domini also screens for good social behavior, such as generous charitable giving. Domini describes her approach in these terms: "We do a stakeholder analysis based on information that's ascertainable without the company's help, about employees, consumers, suppliers, and the natural environment. For example, we can find out if a company gives 1.5% of pretax profits to charity for three years in a row."[28]

Domini also mentions that it would be too difficult to avoid purchasing stocks from every corporation that sells products manufactured in sweatshops, because that would likely involve throwing out every single corporation. (Domini is probably referring to consumer-products companies, and not industrial companies.)

Another approach to measuring corporate social performance is to observe how a company responds to social issues by examining programs in greater detail. The next section describes corporate activities in relation to a variety of social issues.

6 Social Responsibility Initiatives

Present an overview of social responsibility initiatives.

Creating opportunities for a diverse workforce, as described in Chapter 2, is an important social responsibility initiative. Here we describe positive corporate responses to other important social issues. A firm that takes initiatives in these areas can be considered socially responsible. The six social responsibility initiatives described here are: environmental management, work/life programs, social leaves of absence, community redevelopment projects, acceptance of whistle blowers, and compassionate downsizing.

Environmental Management

Many companies take the initiative to preserve the natural environment in a way that pleases environmental groups. As a result, the company works in partnership with a group intent on such purposes as preserving forests or a species of fish or animal. For example, Southern California Edison developed a guidebook to train company employees to recognize sensitive habitats and endangered species. The guidebook became so popular with environmental groups that it was published through an alliance with the Audubon Society. Another example is Ciba-Geigy, the chemical company. It initiated worldwide dialog with a large number of environmental organizations. As a result of these dialogs, Ciba became involved with a coalition of 11 business firms and associations that develops solutions to many of the problems of hazardous waste cleanup.[29]

Another key aspect of environmental management is to prevent pollution rather than control wastes after they have surfaced. For example, a company might eliminate the use of mercury in electrical switches and instead substitute a metal such as copper that is less toxic to the environment. The concern is that when the switch is discarded, the highly poisonous mercury could eventually work its way into the ground. Recycling also helps prevent pollution because recycled products are resources in use rather than resources decaying in dumps or land fills. The accompanying Management in Action describes a constructive approach to one of the major recycling challenges facing the industrialized world.

Work/Life Programs

Organizations take a major social responsibility initiative when they establish programs that help employees balance the demands of work and personal life. The intent of a work/life program is to help employees lead a more balanced life, and be more satisfied and productive on the job. Exhibit 4-5 lists a variety of work/life

EXHIBIT 4-5

A Variety of Work/Life Programs

- Flexible work schedules
- Child-care resource and referral
- Part-time options
- Compressed workweek
- Telecommuting
- Job sharing among two or more employees
- Elder-care resource and referrals
- Elder-care case management and assessment
- Subsidy for emergency care for dependents
- "Family sick days" that permit employees to stay home and care for sick children or relatives
- Arrangements for school counselors to meet with parents on site during regular working hours

- Electric breast pumps for mothers of young children who want to return to work and continue breastfeeding
- Maintenance worker on company payroll whom employees can hire for household tasks, by paying only for supplies
- Laundry service, including ironing, on company premises
- Concierge service in which company employee runs a variety of errands for employees
- Postal service
- Automatic teller machines
- On-site fitness centers including massages

Management *in Action*

The Ecology-Friendly Tire Recyclers

Mike Potts wasn't motivated by an environmental ethic when he placed shredded rubber made from recycled tires beneath the jungle gym he built for his children. "My prime concern was safety," said Potts, who paid $600 for 2½ tons of the safety surface for his Tampa, Florida, home.

Whatever his intention, Potts was helping the growth of an industry that gives new meaning to the term e-commerce—when "e" stands for ecology-minded. Whether in playground surfaces, fuel alternatives, automobile parts, or indoor flooring, 64 percent of the 270 million tires thrown away per year in the United States, wind up in dozens of retail and industrial products, according to the Scrap Tire Management Council. The rest are retreaded and sold overseas, or put in landfills.

The largest market for recycled tires comes from "tire-derived fuel," used in power plants, paper mills, and cement kilns. It accounts for two-thirds of the recycled tire industry's raw materials. Demand for this alternative fuel enabled GreenMan Technologies of Lynnfield, Massachusetts, to report a profit of $4.7 million several years ago. The company expects to process 17 million tires per year into 2-inch fuel chips. GreenMan president Bob Davis said that each tire contains about 2½ gallons of fuel oil.

Davis, a self-proclaimed "practical environmentalist," said that the tire recycling industry is still in it embryonic stage. However, Sonoma County Stable and Livestock, a firm based in California, has been selling 500 custom-made, inch-thick rubber mats per month since the early 1990s. The mats make it easier to clean horse stables and help protect the animal's legs. "Your horse's legs are his life," says Stable and Livestock owner Lindy Giannecchinni, who sells the matting for $1.63 per square foot.

Human habitats and business establishments also provide a market for flooring made from recycled tires. Ads for stylish rubber flooring that come in dozens of colors and patterns appear in glossy design magazines. As Bob Krinick, president of Task Floors in New York City put it, "What started out 15 years ago in gymnasium floors has gone kind of mainstream."

Ample raw material is available for the tire recyclers. The 500 million tires piled up in landfills across the United States are an environmentalist's nightmare, because they can catch fire easily and can burn out of control, emitting noxious chemicals into the air and releasing oils harmful to water sources. The basic building blocks of many products made from recycled tires are minuscule rubber granules, known as "crumb." A common method of mincing tires into usable crumb entails freezing and pulverizing them, and separating unwanted fiber and steel from the rubber.

Dodge-Regupol Inc., of Lancaster, Pennsylvania, collects old tires, crumbs them, and then turns them into products including rubber flooring and automobile tires. The company has 150 employees, who turn out products made from more than 2 million tires annually. One of Dodge-Regupol's clients is General Motors, which uses 5.8 million pounds of recycled rubber annually in 35 different parts along the production line, including brake pedal pads and radiator baffles.

"We're doing it because it makes economic sense," said Wendy Lange, a GM engineer, about the company's drive to use recycled material.

Source: "Recyclers Shape Old Tires into Hot Commodities," The Associated Press, May 26, 2000.

programs. The most popular of these programs remains flextime, or flexible work schedules. (Chapter 8 describes flexible work schedules in more detail.) Flextime has grown in popularity because evidence suggests that it reduces turnover, improves morale, and helps recruit talent.

Hewlett-Packard has offered flextime options for 40 years. HP allows managers and employees to develop the best flextime options to suit their needs. Schedules might include staggered start times, or working four 10-hour days or 80 hours in nine days. Kathy Burke, Global Worklife Program manager for HP believes that giving employees the freedom and power to create schedules that accommodate their work/life balance needs makes them more productive. She says, "HP employees face a lot of stress on the job. Giving them flextime options allows them to meet their personal commitments while staying committed."[30]

Social Leaves of Absence

social leave of absence

An employee benefit that gives select employees time away from the job to perform a significant public service.

Some companies offer employees paid leaves of absence, of anywhere from several weeks to six months, to help them prevent burnout. A **social leave of absence**, however, gives select employees time away from the job to perform a significant public service. For example, American Express Travel-Related Services allows employees with 10 or more years of service to take up to six months to contribute to the community. Obtaining a leave of absence is competitive. Candidates for the leave fill out an application that describes the employee's plans and qualifications for performing the community work. As with other firms offering social leaves, the community work must be integrated into the department's work plans.

The social good performed by the person on leave often takes the form of lending business expertise to a nonprofit agency. For example, a corporate controller develops a financial plan for a youth agency. At other times the social leave is to perform work indirectly related to one's professional expertise, such as a human resources professional volunteering as a high-school drug counselor for six months.[31]

Community Redevelopment Projects

As a large-scale social responsibility initiative, business firms invest resources in helping rebuild distressed communities. Investment could mean constructing offices or factories in an impoverished section of town, or offering job training for residents from these areas. The Prudential Insurance Company helps rebuild inner cities by investing money in ventures such as grocery stores, housing, and entertainment. The New Jersey Performing Arts Center is one of their investment projects.

Peter Goldberg, president of the Prudential Foundation, explains the rationale for community redevelopment projects: "The future well-being of this company, this industry, and of corporate America is very much intertwined with the health and well-being of American society."[32]

A specific goal of some community redevelopment projects is to replace a crime-ridden development with new housing that is associated with less crime and more community pride. A project of this nature took place in Atlanta, Georgia, when developer Thomas G. Cousins bought Atlanta's East Lake Golf Club in 1993. The club was located across the street from a crime-ridden public housing project called East Lake Meadows. Cousins's plan was for the club to serve as an economic anchor to transform the entire East Lake neighborhood. After recruiting 55 corporate members including IBM, GE, and Georgia Pacific, the club reopened in 1996. Among the projects undertaken by Cousins's foundation are a golf academy, a new YMCA, and a charter school—all for East Lake children. The 550 crime-ridden units of East Lake Meadows have been replaced with 542 new townhouses. Half of the units are public housing, and half are rented at market rates. After several years of operation, crime has decreased and housing prices in adjoining neighborhoods have increased 30 percent.

Cousins hopes that his model will spur corporate America to rebuild public housing nationwide. Despite the promise of this social responsibility initiative, it does have its drawbacks. Tenants may be forced out of their homes to make way for new development, which cannot accommodate all previous tenants.[33]

Acceptance of Whistle Blowers

A **whistle blower** is an employee who discloses organizational wrongdoing to parties who can take action. Whistle blowers are often ostracized and humiliated by the companies they hope to improve, by such means as no further promotions or poor performance evaluations. More than half the time, the pleas of whistle blowers are ignored. A representative example of whistle blowing and its negative consequences for the individual took place at the Department of Energy radioactive materials clean-up program. Stephen Buckely, who became a pizza deliverer, said he was fired from his position as an environmental protection specialist because he objected to wasteful and expensive procedures. He objected to a department policy that extensive 300-page environmental impact studies be routinely conducted even though, in his opinion, less expensive procedures would work. Buckely said he was fired because top management at the Energy Department was upset. He is not alone. An independent government agency that investigates and prosecutes illegal workplace practices received 814 complaints of reprisals against whistle blowers in one year.[34]

Only an organization with a strong social conscience would embrace employees who inform the public about its misdeeds. Yet some companies are becoming more tolerant of employees who help keep the firm socially responsible by exposing actions that could harm society.

whistle blower
An employee who discloses organizational wrongdoing to parties who can take action.

Compassionate Downsizing

To remain competitive and provide shareholders with a suitable return on investment, about 80 percent of large organizations have undergone **downsizing**. Downsizing is the slimming down of operations to focus resources and boost profits or decrease expenses. Downsizings occur regularly worldwide among companies of all sizes, yet the size of layoffs are more substantial during business downturns. For example, during the first three months of 2001, U.S. companies laid off 138,800 workers, nearly the population of Tallahassee, Florida. Among the layoffs announced were 26,000 by DaimlerChrysler, 18,000 by Motorola, about 7,000 by Cisco, and 1,700 by both Dell and Hewlett-Packard.[35] Information technology facilitated downsizing during this period because most companies had already invested heavily in IT equipment and personnel. It then became time to use the information technology to automate transactions, eliminate intermediaries, and streamline production.[36]

The focus here is on the social responsibility aspects of downsizing. Chapter 9 views downsizing as a strategy for improving organizational effectiveness. Compassionate downsizing would include the following considerations:

- Ponder whether downsizing is worthwhile from a financial perspective. A study of more than 3,000 companies over a 15-year period suggests that

downsizing
The slimming down of operations to focus resources and boost profits or decrease expenses.

layoffs may not produce expected results. Unless the downsizing was accompanied by selling company assets, such as a division, the financial performance of the firm usually did not improve. Among the costs associated with downsizing are severance pay, supplements to early retirement plans, turnover among the survivors, and reduced productivity stemming from low morale.[37]

- Redeploy as many workers as possible by placing them in full-time or temporary jobs throughout the organization, where their skills and personality fit. Several companies have turned surplus workers into sales workers to generate new business for the firm. During one downturn in international sales at Lincoln Electric, 54 factory workers were redeployed as salespeople who grossed $10 million in sales the first year. Up through 2001, the company has still not laid off any workers because of a business downturn. Workers are guaranteed a job, but as a trade-off get neither paid sick days nor holidays and pay their own health insurance.[38]

- Provide outplacement services to laid-off employees, thereby giving them professional assistance in finding a new position or redirecting their careers. (The vast majority of employers do provide outplacement services to laid-off workers.)

- Provide financial and emotional support to the downsized worker. Included here is treating employees with respect and dignity rather than escorting them out the door immediately after the downsizing announcement. Many companies already provide severance pay and extended health benefits to the laid-off workers. Financial assistance with retraining is also helpful.

- Give hope to the more qualified employees who were laid off by reassuring them they will be on the top of the list if a job recall does take place in the future.

7   BENEFITS DERIVED FROM ETHICS AND SOCIAL RESPONSIBILITY

Summarize the benefits of ethical and socially responsible behavior, and how managers can create an environment that fosters such behavior.

Highly ethical behavior and socially responsible acts are not always free. Investing in work/life programs, granting social leaves of absence, and telling customers the absolute truth about potential product problems may not have an immediate return on investment. Nevertheless, recent evidence suggests that high ethics and social responsibility are related to good financial performance. Here we look at evidence and opinions about the advantages of ethics and social responsibility.

A study was conducted about the impact of discovered unethical behavior on the performance of a company's stock. The researchers found that unethical behavior that is discovered and publicized has a negative impact on the stock price for an appreciable period of time. Unethical behavior, therefore, decreases a firm's wealth.[39] An example of this type of unethical behavior would be a cellular telephone company charged with hiding evidence about the health risks of cell phone use. As a result many shareholders sell their shares, and other investors lose interest in buying stock in the company.

The relationship between profits and social responsibility works two ways in another perspective. More profitable firms can better afford to invest in social responsibility initiatives, and these initiatives in turn lead to more profits. Sandra A. Waddock and Samuel B. Graves conducted a large-scale study that supports the two-way conclusion. The researchers analyzed the relationship between corporate social performance and corporate financial performance for 469 firms, spanning 13 industries, for a two-year period. Many different measures of social and financial performance were used.

Researchers found that levels of corporate social performance were influenced by prior financial success. This result suggests that financial success creates enough money left over to invest in corporate social performance. The study also found that good corporate social performance contributes to improved financial performance as measured by return on assets and return on sales. Waddock and Graves concluded that the relationship between social and financial performance may be a *virtuous circle*, meaning that corporate social performance and corporate financial performance feed and reinforce each other.[40]

Being ethical also helps avoid the costs of paying huge fines for being unethical. So many firms have been fined for unethical and illegal activities, it is almost unfair to select one as an example. However, the $180 million in fines Texaco Corporation paid for discriminating against people of color illustrates the gravity of the problem.

A big payoff from socially responsible acts is that they often attract and retain socially responsible employees and customers. A recent analysis of a group of studies suggests a specific level of corporate social responsibility investment maximizes profit, while also satisfying stakeholder demand for social responsibility on the part of the company. Cost-benefit analysis is useful in calculating how much to invest in corporate social responsibility (CSR). In making these calculations, a CEO might decide that spending $250,000 per year on such activities as feeding the poor, having onsite dependent care, and giving money to charity improves the firm's financial performance. Beyond that point, the CSR investment loses money for the company.[41]

Creating an Ethical and Socially Responsible Workplace

Establishing an ethical and socially responsible workplace is not simply a matter of luck and common sense. Top-level managers, assisted by other managers and professionals, can develop strategies and programs to enhance ethical and socially responsible attitudes and behavior. We turn now to a description of several of these initiatives.[42]

Formal Mechanisms for Monitoring Ethics

Forty-five percent of companies with 500 or more employees have ethics programs of various types. Large organizations frequently set up ethics committees to help ensure ethical and socially responsible behavior. Committee members include a top management representative plus other managers throughout the organization. An ethics and social responsibility specialist from the human resources department might also join the group. The committee establishes policies about ethics and social responsibility, and may conduct an ethical audit of the firm's activities. In addition, committee members might review complaints about ethical violations.

The Lockheed Martin Corporation's ethics and compliance program has received much favorable publicity. A contributing factor to its formation was that in the mid-1980s the company had a series of ethics scandals in its role as a defense contractor to the U.S. government. (Among the problems was a product substitution not in agreement with the contract.) Several elements of the Lockheed-Martin program follow:

- *Don't be condescending.* Employees should be empowered to raise questions about ethical violations based on their own understanding of right and wrong.

- *Make ethics training mandatory. Mandatory* means for every employee, the CEO included.
- *Address ethical dilemmas that employees have faced in the past.* A key part of the training program can be to use the examples to illustrate how to deal with these dilemmas in the future.
- *Develop multiple channels for raising questions and voicing concerns.* These mechanisms include a toll-free hotline, a formal ethics office at the corporate level, and a culture that welcomes discussion of ethical issues.
- *Allow for voicing concerns anonymously.* Many employees fear reprisals if they identify ethical problems in their company.
- *Act decisively on legitimate ethical problems reported by employees.* Demonstrate to employees that the company's commitment to good ethics is serious.

Written Organizational Codes of Conduct

Many organizations use written ethical codes of conduct as guidelines for ethical and socially responsible behavior. Such guidelines continue to grow in importance because workers in self-managing teams have less supervision than previously. Some general aspects of these codes require people to conduct themselves with integrity and candor. Here is a statement of this type from the Johnson & Johnson (medical and health supplies) code of ethics:

> We believe our first responsibility is to the doctors, nurses, and patients, to mothers and fathers and all others who use our products and services. In meeting these needs everything we do must be of high quality.

Other aspects of the codes might be specific, such as indicating the maximum gift that can be accepted from a vendor. In many organizations, known code violators are disciplined.

Widespread Communication About Ethics and Social Responsibility

Extensive communication about the topic reinforces ethical and socially responsible behavior. Top management can speak widely about the competitive advantage of being ethical and socially responsible. Another effective method is to discuss ethical and social responsibility issues in small groups. In this way the issues stay fresh in the minds of workers. A few minutes of a team meeting might be invested in a topic such as "What can we do to help the homeless people who live in the streets surrounding our office?"

Lockheed Martin has an ethics communication program labeled "Top-Down Cascade Training." The chairman of the board trains the managers directly reporting to him, who in turn train their staff. Eventually, all 200,000 employees hear the same core message about ethics delivered at annual training sessions.

Leadership by Example

A high-powered approach to enhancing ethics and social responsibility is for members of top management to behave in such a manner themselves. If people throughout the firm believe that behaving ethically is "in" and behaving unethically is "out," ethical behavior will prevail. Visualize a scenario in which a group of key people in an investment banking firm vote themselves a $3 million year-end bonus. Yet to save money, entry-level clerical workers earning $8 an hour are denied raises. Many employees might feel that top management has a low sense of ethics, and therefore that being ethical and socially responsible is not important.

Encourage Confrontation About Ethical Deviations

Unethical behavior may be minimized if every employee confronts anyone seen behaving unethically. For example, if you spotted someone making an unauthorized copy of software, you would ask the software pirate, "How would you like it if you owned a business and people stole from *your* company?" The same approach encourages workers to ask about the ethical implications of decisions made by others in the firm.

Training Programs in Ethics and Social Responsibility

Many companies now train managerial workers about ethics. Forms of training include messages about ethics from executives, classes on ethics at colleges, and exercises in ethics. These training programs reinforce the idea that ethically and socially responsible behavior is both morally right and good for business. Much of the content of this chapter reflects the type of information communicated in such programs. In addition, Skill-Building Exercise 4-A represents the type of activity included in ethical training programs such as those given at CitiCorp.

SUMMARY OF KEY POINTS

1 **Identify the philosophical principles behind business ethics.** When deciding on what is right and wrong, people can focus on consequences; duties, obligations, and principles; or integrity. Focusing on consequences is called utilitarianism, because the decision maker is concerned with the utility of the decision. Examining one's duties in making a decision is the deontological approach and is based on universal principles such as honesty and fairness. According to the integrity (or virtue) approach, if the decision maker has good character and genuine motivation and intentions, he or she is behaving ethically.

2 **Explain how values relate to ethics.** Ethics becomes the vehicle for converting values into action, or doing the right thing. A firm's moral standards and values also influence which kind of behaviors managers believe are ethical. According to ethically centered management, the high quality of an end product takes precedence over meeting a delivery schedule. Catastrophes can result when management is not ethically centered.

3 **Identify factors contributing to lax ethics, and common ethical temptations and violations.** Major contributors to unethical behavior are greed and gluttony, and an organizational atmosphere that condones unethical behavior. Other contributors are moral laxity (other issues seem more important at the time), and pressure from higher management to achieve goals. Incentives for being unethical, such as being rewarded for cutting

back on quality, can contribute to low ethics, as can weak relationships among people.

Recurring ethical temptations and violations, including criminal acts, include the following: stealing from employers and customers, illegally copying software, treating people unfairly, sexual harassment, conflict of interest, divulging confidential information, and misusing corporate resources. Greed, gluttony, and avarice among top executives is a separate category of ethical problems. Two other problems are corporate espionage and poor cyberethics.

4 **Apply a guide to ethical decision making.** When faced with an ethical dilemma, ask yourself: Is it right? Is it fair? Who gets hurt? Would you be comfortable with the deed exposed? Would you tell your child to do it? How does it smell?

5 **Describe the stakeholder viewpoint of social responsibility and corporate social performance.** Social responsibility refers to a firm's obligations to society. Corporate consciousness expands this view by referring to values that guide and motivate individuals to act responsibly. The stakeholder viewpoint of social responsibility contends that firms must hold themselves accountable for the quality of life of the many groups affected by the firm's actions. Corporate social performance is the extent to which a firm responds to the demands of its stakeholders for behaving in a socially responsible way.

6 **Present an overview of social responsibility initiatives.** Creating opportunities for a diverse workforce is a major social responsibility initiative. Also important are environmental management, work/life programs, social leaves of absence, community redevelopment projects, acceptance of whistle blowers, and compassionate downsizing.

7 **Summarize the benefits of ethical and socially responsible behavior, and how managers can create an environment that fosters such behavior.** High ethics and social responsibility are related to good financial performance, according to research evidence and opinion. Also, more profitable firms can invest in good corporate social performance. Being ethical helps avoid big fines for being unethical, and ethical organizations attract more employees. Initiatives for creating an ethical and socially responsible workplace include (a) formal mechanisms for monitoring ethics, (b) written codes of conduct, (c) communicating about the topic, (d) leadership by example, (e) confrontation about ethical deviations, and (f) training programs.

KEY TERMS AND PHRASES

Ethics, *86*

Moral intensity, *86*

Ethically centered management, *89*

Moral laxity, *90*

Conflict of interest, *92*

Social responsibility, *95*

Corporate social consciousness, *95*

Stockholder viewpoint, *95*

Stakeholder viewpoint, *96*

Corporate social performance, *97*

Social leave of absence, *100*

Whistle blower, *101*

Downsizing, *101*

QUESTIONS

1. Why should managers study ethics and social responsibility?
2. Review several articles about the antitrust charges made against Microsoft and its executive team. Based on this information, what do you think of the ethics of Bill Gates and his colleagues?
3. Give examples of rights that you think every employee is entitled to.
4. What do you think of *cookies* (software devices that furnish information about the preferences of people who visit a particular Web site)? Do you think it is ethical for companies to use information from such devices?
5. Would you or your family members be willing to pay 25 percent more for most of your clothing so manufacturers would not feel compelled to use sweatshops? Explain your reasoning.
6. According to several religious and community leaders, companies can become more socially responsible by allowing homeless people to stay overnight in the office lobby. The need is particularly urgent when it is extremely cold outside. The companies are also urged to serve basic meals. What is your evaluation of the merits of making office lobbies shelters for the homeless during extreme weather conditions?
7. Suppose a person makes extensive use of work/life benefits offered by the company. How might using these benefits frequently have a negative effect on his or her career?

CRITICAL THINKING QUESTIONS

1. Get together with a group of people and rank the occupations listed next in terms of your perception of their ethical reputation. The most ethical occupation receives a rank of one. (The list that follows is presented in random order.) Use the average rank of the group members if consensus is not reached.
   ___ Cosmetic (plastic) surgeon
   ___ Computer programmer
   ___ Business executive, major firm
   ___ Criminal lawyer
   ___ Veterinarian for domestic animals
   ___ Business school professor
   ___ Family court judge
   ___ Small-business owner
   ___ New car sales representative
   ___ Stockbroker/financial consultant

2. Search the print media or the Internet for an example of an act of high social responsibility by a business firm. Explain why you think the actions taken by the firm reflect high social responsibility.

SKILL-BUILDING EXERCISE 4-A: Ethical Decision Making

Working in small groups, take the following two ethical dilemmas through the six steps for screening contemplated decisions. You might also want to use various ethical principles in helping you reach a decision.

SCENARIO 1: TO RECYCLE OR NOT

Your group is the top management team at a large insurance company. Despite information technology making paper less necessary, your firm still generates tons of paper each month. Customer payments alone account for truckloads of envelopes each year. The paper recyclers in your area contend that they can hardly find a market any longer for used paper, so they will

be charging you just to accept your paper for recycling. Your group is wondering whether to continue to recycle paper.

SCENARIO 2: JOB APPLICANTS WITH A PAST

A state (or provincial) government official approaches your bank asking you to hire three people soon to be released from prison. All were found guilty of fraudulently altering computer records for personal gain in a bank. The official says these people have paid their debt to society and that they need jobs. Your company has three openings for computer specialists. All three people obviously have good computer skills. Your group is wondering whether to hire them.

INTERNET SKILL-BUILDING EXERCISE: Ethical Product Promotion

Search the Internet for an advertisement or similar promotional information about a food supplement or beauty product, such as wrinkle remover. Note carefully whether the information is provided by the company or the individual that manufactures or sells the product, or by an objective third party. Give your opinion on the ethics of the person making the

claim. For example, attempt to evaluate the honesty of the claims. Use the six-step guide to ethical decision making to help you in your ethical evaluation.

For help getting started, go to the Paula Begoun Web site at http://www.cosmeticscop.com.

CASE PROBLEM 4-A: Napster Challenges the Music Business

Shawn Fanning, the person who founded Napster at age 20, is transforming the way people think about technology and the Internet, along with music and intellectual property rights. Fanning began his famous journey with a laptop computer, some solitude, and 60 consecutive hours of heavy thinking. His accomplishment, the file-sharing application labeled Napster, has turned into an icon for either the free exchange of information or a massive violation of intellectual property rights.

Fanning's Napster, which was released in September 1999 on a Web site with cofounder Sean Parker, enables everyone to trade music and other files over the Net easily, and without paying a fee to anyone. Indignant media companies and recording artists have alleged that the file sharing trespasses on their copyrighted material. The result has been a major legal battle with the Recording Industry Associates of America. The lawyers and judges continue to work on the legality of Napster, even as individuals all over the world acquired music for free, while debating the merits of what they were doing.

According to Fannon, his primary intent was to create a program that allowed computer users to swap music files directly off the hard drives of other users. In this way they could circumvent a centralized server loaded with music files

that would make sharing a much slower process. Although Fanning had been told that computer users would not want strangers to have access to their hard drives, he was convinced that people would want to share. From Fanning's perspective, he was doing something quite similar to the CD swapping carried out among his college buddies.

Fanning was on target. Napster became the fastest growing Web site in history. Data provided by Media Metrix, an online tracking service, indicate that the number of unique users of Napster rose from slightly over 1 million in February 2000, to about 6.7 million in August of the same year.

Using technology already available, such as instant messaging, file sharing, and search engines, Fanning developed one of the most powerful Internet applications in the Web's history. According to *Success* magazine, Napster technology, with its peer-to-peer file sharing, could turn the Internet into more of a conduit for PC owners seeking and disseminating information.

The Napster technology may have applications far beyond sharing music. For example, scientists working on the Human Genome Project discussed with Fanning building a program for exchanging their valuable data. Given that the information about genes would be too extensive to store in a single database, the scientists could use peer-to-peer file sharing to instantly keep up with the rapidly accumulating data.

Before getting involved with more exotic applications of Napster technology, Fanning must deal with more fundamental issues. A big concern is potential security hazards that accompany allowing other users direct access to your hard drive. An even bigger challenge is the Recording Industry Association of America's assertion that Napster allows users unauthorized trading of copyrighted material.

Fanning's defense is that Napster is not guilty of any copyright violation because the company does not keep any of the illegal files on its servers. Yet as expressed by Lars Ulrich, drummer for the band Metallica, "Why would people pay for music if they get it for free?"

A milestone in Napster history took place when Shawn Fanning accepted a dinner invitation from Thomas Middelhoff, the 47-year-old chairman of Bertelsmann, the world's third largest media conglomerate. Middlehoff sought an agreement with Fanning because Napster's online music sharing was costing the music industry many millions of dollars in lost sales. Under the agreement, Napster will develop a business model that will allow for record companies and artists to be paid for their music.

To help Napster overcome the formidable technological hurdles involved, Bertelsmann opened a $50 million line of credit that can be expanded. The technological challenge is to find a way to keep the music accessible to Net users, yet retain the copyright protection. The music sharing service in the future will probably charge a monthly fee of about $5, giving members direct access to the highest-quality downloads.

Should the new model be in place, the Bertelsmann subsidiary BMG Entertainment will make its music catalog available and no longer participate in the copyright infringement lawsuit against Napster. Bertelsmann is attempting to persuade his counterparts at Time Warner, Sony, Universal, and EMI to follow his lead.

Bertelsmann envisions the world's largest community of online music enthusiasts, which could also eventually share books, movies, and videos as well. The community could easily reach 38 million computer users worldwide.

Bertelsmann's plan came closer to implementation in March 2001 when a U.S. Court district judge ordered Napster to block all copyright songs identified by the major music labels. The music companies were required to provide Napster with the song, artist name, and file name associated with the copyrighted tunes. This requirement has been difficult because the song titles and artists' names are frequently misspelled in the digitized music files that Napster users exchange. As a result, the filtering software misses many copyrighted files.

Industry watchers say Napster obtained a partial victory by avoiding a complete court-ordered shutdown. Napster CEO Hank Barry said, "We will continue to seek a settlement with the record companies and to prepare our new membership-based service." Napster signed a preliminary accord in September 2001 to pay the music industry $26 million for past copyright infringements and $10 million in future royalties. The stage was thereby set for Napster to re-launch as a subscription music download by December 2001.

Discussion Questions

1. What are the ethical issues involved with the Napster file sharing program?

2. What is your opinion of the likely success of the business model that would charge users about $5 per month to share music files?

3. If you were a music industry executive at a competitor of Bertelsmann, such as Sony or EMI, would you go along with the proposed Napster deal?

Source: Steven V. Brull, Dennis K. Berman, and Mike France, "Inside Napster: How the Music-Sharing Phenom Began, Where It Went Wrong, and What Happens Next," *Business Week,* August 14, 2000, pp. 112–120; Spencer Ante, "Shawn Fanning's Struggle," *Business Week,* May 1, 2000, pp. 197–198; Thomas Melville, "Renegade Revolutionary: Shawn Fanning," *Success,* December–January 2001, pp. 26–28; Frank Gibney Jr., "Napster Meister," *Time,* November 13, 2000, pp. 58–62; "Napster Ordered to Honor Copyrights," The Associated Press, March 7, 2001; Greg Wright, "Reformed Napster to Return in December," Gannett News Service, October 8, 2001.

CASE PROBLEM 4-B: Multinational Sweatshops

One night in December a few years ago, a desperate Chinese man appeared at military police headquarters in Bergamo, Italy, pleading for help. His 25-year-old wife, Deng Singmei, an illegal immigrant, had to escape slave-like working conditions in a garment sweatshop near Milan. However, the Chinese gangsters who had arranged her illegal passage to Italy for $25,000, captured her at gunpoint. Deng was supposed to work until her debt was repaid. The police tapped her husband's phone to trace the calls from the mobsters, and five days later they freed a raped and beaten Deng.

Deng's kidnapping turned out to be a vital breakthrough for the police. Building on information gathered from Deng's incarcerated tormentors, Italian officials launched a nationwide investigation. After 16 months of undercover work, "Operation Sunrise" climaxed with raids on sweatshops in 28 cities from Milan to Rome. The raids broke up a criminal network of some 200 gangsters in China, Russia, and Italy involved in bringing Chinese immigrants to Italy. The immigrants were forced to work 12 to 16 hours per day in textile, apparel, shoe, and leather factories for little or no pay. Similar raids have revealed other illegal sweatshops, some finding children as young as 11 working 20 hours per day.

A similar raid took place several years earlier in the United States. Based on a tipoff, U.S. federal agents raided an El Monte, California, garment manufacturer. Evidence was found that that the company held 75 Thai immigrants behind barbed wire and paid them $1 per hour. The names of several larger retailers were found on the boxes in the grimy, poorly lit shop. Among the names were Sears and Dayton Hudson. Company officials agreed to meet with the U.S. Department of Labor to discuss ways to combat the use of sweatshops.

The representatives explained that they had no idea of the deplorable conditions at the El Monte manufacturer. Furthermore, they promised to adopt a statement of principles requesting that their suppliers adhere to federal labor laws.

The Department of Labor estimates that 20,000 small U.S. garment makers supply the one-half of the country's clothing that is not imported. Many of these firms require their employees to work under cramped, poorly ventilated, and unsafe conditions. A Labor Department spot check of 69 garment-making firms in Southern California uncovered health and safety violations in all but seven of them. The workers are mostly female immigrants who earn an average of $8 an hour. Wages are just over the federal poverty level. However, they are comparable to pay for many jobs in the service industry, and well above the minimum wage.

Several years ago, Robert L. Mettier, the president of apparel at Sears, wanted fellow retailers to find ways to combat the problems of suppliers who use sweatshops or who subcontract to sweatshops. The executive vice president of a giant retailer on the verge of insolvency looks at the problem from a different perspective: "We simply cannot afford to hire inspectors. We won't knowingly do business with a company that hires slave labor. Yet if you close down all these alleged sweatshops, a lot of families will go hungry. An $8 per hour steady job is decent extra money for a low-income family. A lot of people are lined up looking for these jobs. Yet with the pressure the Department of Labor is putting on us, we'll have to think of some official position on this issue."

David R. Henderson, a research fellow with the Hoover Institute, observes that a low-paying job in Honduras or in Los Angeles's garment district may seem horrible to many people. Yet for many adults and children, it represents their best option. He believes that you do not make somebody better off by taking away the best of her bad options. An apparel worker in Honduras told a reporter: "This is an enormous advance, and I give thanks to the *maquila* (factory) for it. My monthly income is seven times what I make in the countryside."

Some Honduran girls allegedly make about 35 cents an hour at 70-hour-per-week jobs. Assuming a 50-week year, the girl can earn more than $1,200 per year. Yet the per capita income in Honduras is about $75 per person. The clothing made in these Honduran factories is often done on a subcontract basis for an American firm. Or sometimes the Honduran subcontractor makes components of clothing, such as coat liners, that are later assembled into the final garments in an American shop.

In 1999, three well-known multinational corporations released information about their garment factories to placate groups concerned about sweatshops. Nike Inc. looked to appease student protestors by revealing the locations of 42 of its 365 factories. By so doing they reversed its long-standing position that identifying the factories would put the company at a competitive disadvantage. Reebock International Ltd. then released the first independent factory audit conducted by human rights groups. The audit involved two Indonesian plants. A few days later, Liz Claiborne Inc. did the same by releasing a candid report on working conditions in a Guatemalan factory. Soon thereafter Mattel Inc. published a comprehensive review of eight plants in four countries, using hundreds of specific labor standards.

The three audits marked the first time companies have allowed truly independent auditors with expertise in labor issues to comb through their factories and then make the unpleasant findings public. Following these audits, an industry-wide inspection system fell into place. One example is the Fair Labor Association, a monitoring group made up of industry and human rights representatives created by a presidential task force.

Human rights and student groups have maintained steady pressure on the Fair Labor Association. In 1999, the United Students Against Sweatshops developed an even stricter monitoring scheme. The student group's demands for closer monitoring were prompted in part by a group called Press for Change that surveyed 2,300 workers at five Nike factories outside Jakarta, Indonesia, employing 45,000 workers. More than half of the workers said they had seen colleagues yelled at or mistreated. A third said they had been compelled to work overtime.

Mattel Inc. has rigorously pursued approaches to improving working conditions throughout its sphere of influence. The toymaker has appointed an outside group to create a monitoring system, requiring factories to meet hundreds of precise standards. A team of 50 Mattel managers and outside experts has drawn up standards for five countries where Mattel manufactures toys. The group lays out everything from how many toilets are required per worker to how many calories company cafeterias should serve workers daily.

Discussion Questions

1. Explain whether retailers have a social responsibility to inspect vendors for possible violation of wage and safety laws.

2. Who are the stakeholders involved in companies that rely on sweatshops for their manufacturing?

3. Have the inspections authorized by several leading consumer-products companies now taken care of their social responsibility obligations with regard to sweatshops?

4. What is your position about an $8 per hour job being a good opportunity for many workers?

Source: Adapted from "Workers in Bondage," *Business Week,* November 27, 2000, pp. 147–160; "Look Who's Sweating Now," *Business Week,* October 16, 1995, pp. 96–98; "The Case for Sweatshops," *Fortune,* October 28, 1996, pp. 48, 52; Aaron Bernstein, "Sweatshops: No More Excuses," *Business Week,* November 9, 1999, pp. 104–106.

ENDNOTES

1. "A World of Sweatshops," *Business Week,* November 6, 2000, p. 84.
2. Thomas M. Jones, "Ethical Decision Making by Individuals in Organizations," *Academy of Management Review,* April 1991, p. 391.
3. Linda K. Treviño and Katherine A. Nelson, *Managing Business Ethics: Straight Talk About How to Do It Right* (New York: Wiley, 1995), pp. 66–70; Laurie Tone Hosmer, "Trust: The Connecting Link Between Organizational Theory and Philosophical Ethics," *Academy of Management Review,* April 1995, pp. 396–397.
4. "Software Executive Puts Integrity First," *Executive Leadership,* April 2001, p. 3.
5. H. D. Karp quoted in "Ethics Is 'Doing the Right Thing,' So How Do You Know What's Right?" *Marriott Executive Memo, 8* (1), 1996, p. 4.
6. Perry Pascarella, "Winners Supply New Leaders," *Management Review,* November 1997, p. 52.
7. Robert Elliott Allinson, "A Call for Ethically Centered Management," *The Academy of Management Executive,* February 1995, pp. 73–74.
8. "Anatomy of a Recall," *Time,* September 11, 2000, pp. 28–32; Joann Muller, David Welch, and Jeff Green, "Would You Buy One?" *Business Week,* September 25, 2000, pp. 46–47.
9. "Lax Moral Climate Breeds White-Collar Crime Wave," *Personnel,* January 1988, p. 7.
10. John Kamp and Paul Brooks, "Perceived Organizational Climate and Employee Counterproductivity," *Journal of Business and Psychology,* Summer 1991, p. 455.
11. "24 Extracted from Mall Ruins after 4 Days," Associated Press, July 2, 1995.
12. Samuel Greengard, "50% of Your Employees Are Lying, Cheating, and Stealing," *Workforce,* October 1997, p. 46.
13. Brian Sharp, "Reports of Unethical Job Behavior on the Increase," Gannett News Service, June 12, 2000.
14. Ann E. Tenbrunsel, "Misrepresentation and Expectations of Misrepresentation in an Ethical Dilemma: The Role of Incentives and Temptation," *The Academy of Management Journal,* June 1998, pp. 330–339.
15. Daniel J. Brass, Kenneth D. Butterfield, and Bruce C. Skaggs, "Relationships and Unethical Behavior: A Social Network Perspective," *The Academy of Management Review,* January 1998, pp. 14–31.
16. The first seven items on the list are from Treviño and Nelson, pp. 47–57; "Spy vs. Spy Is a High-Stakes Corporate Duel," Associated Press, July 1, 2000; "Cyberethics: Teaching Internet Ethics, *Keying In,* November 2000, pp. 1, 3, 5–7.
17. Kimberly T. Schneider, Suzanne Swan, and Louise F. Fitzgerald, "Job-Related and Psychological Effects of Sexual Harassment in the Workplace: Empirical Evidence from Two Organizations," *Journal of Applied Psychology,* June 1997, pp. 401–415.
18. Mark Maremount, "Sex, Lies, and Home Improvements," *Business Week,* March 31, 1997, p. 40.
19. "Spy vs. Spy Is a High-Stakes Corporate Duel," Associated Press, July 1, 2000.
20. James L. Bowditch and Anthony F. Buono, *A Primer on Organizational Behavior,* 5th ed. (New York: Wiley, 2001), p. 4.
21. Joseph L. Badaracco, Jr., *Defining Moments: When Managers Must Choose Between Right and Wrong* (Boston: Harvard Business School Press, 1997).
22. Keith A. Lavine and Elina S. Moore, "Corporate Consciousness: Defining the Paradigm," *Journal of Business and Psychology,* Summer 1996, p. 401–413.
23. Robert Levering and Milton Moskowitz, "The 100 Best Companies to Work For," *Fortune,* January 8, 2001, pp. 148–168.
24. Bill Saporito, "Wrestling with Your Conscience," *Time,* November 15, 1999.
25. Bradley R. Agle, Ronald K. Mitchell, and Jeffrey A. Sonnenfeld, "What Matters to CEOs? An Investigation of Stakeholder Attributes and Salience, Corporate Performance, and CEO Values," *Academy of Management Journal,* October 1999, p. 522.
26. Ronald K. Mitchell, Bradly R. Agle, and Dona J. Wood, "Toward a Theory of Stakeholder Identification and Salience: Defining the Principle of Who and What Really Counts," *Academy of Management Review,* October 1997, p. 869.
27. Jane Park and Adnan Abdeen, "Are Corporations Improving Efforts at Social Responsibility?" *Business Forum,* Summer–Fall 1994, pp. 26–30.
28. "A Fund That Tracks the Do-Gooder Index," *Business Week,* May 1, 2000, p. 208.
29. Gail Dutton, "Green Partnerships," *Management Review,* January 1996, pp. 24–26.
30. Sarah Fister Gale, "Formalized Flextime: The Perk That Brings Productivity," *Workforce,* February 2001, pp. 38–42.
31. "Time for a Sabbatical?" *HRfocus,* July 1995, p. 10.
32. Samuel Greengard and Charlene Marmer Solomon, "The Fire This Time," *Personnel Journal,* February 1994, p. 60.
33. "How Green Is My Alley?" *Business Week,* April 19, 1999, pp. 123–124.
34. Larry Reynolds, "A New Social Agenda for the New Age," *Management Review,* January 1993, p. 40.
35. "The Axman Cometh," *Fortune,* April 2, 2001, p. 101.
36. "The New Economy's Cruel Math," *Business Week,* February 5, 2001, p. 42.
37. James R. Morris, Wayne F. Cascio, and Clifford E. Young, "Downsizing After All These Years: Questions and Answers About Who Did It, How Many Did It, and Who Benefited from It," *Organizational Dynamics,* Winter 1999, pp. 78–87; Assa Birati and Tziner Aharon, "Cost-Benefit Analysis of Organizational Interventions: The Case of Downsizing," *Journal of Business and Psychology,* Winter 2000, p. 285.
38. Marlene Piturro, "Alternatives to Downsizing," *Management Review,* October 1999, p. 38; Daniel Eisenberg, "Where People Are Never Let Go," *Time,* June 18, 2001, p. 40.
39. Research reported in *Positive Leadership,* sample issue, March 2001, p. 5.
40. Sandra A. Waddock and Samuel B. Graves, "The Corporate Social Performance–Financial Performance Link," *Strategic Management Journal,* Spring 1997, pp. 303–319.
41. Larry Reynolds, "A New Social Agenda for the New Age," *Management Review,* January 1993, p. 40.
42. Abagail McWilliams and Donald Siegel, "Corporate Social Responsibility: A Theory of the Firm Perspective," *Academy of Management Review,* January 2001, p. 125.
43. Dayton Fandray, "The Ethical Company," *Workforce,* December 2000, p. 76; John Davidson, "The Business of Ethics," *Working Woman,* February 1998, pp. 68–70; Susan J. Harrington, "What Corporate America Is Teaching About Ethics," *The Academy of Management Executive,* February 1991, p. 21.

Essentials of Planning

Several years ago, analysts and investors concluded that Howard Schultz, the CEO of Starbucks Corp., was practically lost in cyberspace. Schultz and his management team were busy developing an Internet plan for Starbucks that would turn the coffee shop chain's Web site into a "lifestyle portal" by partnering with gourmet food sellers and home furnishing stores.

While Schultz was exploring cyberspace, trouble was surfacing in the bricks-and-mortar cafés. Delayed store openings and underforecast sales at existing cafés were suppressing earnings. Because Schultz spent most of his time chatting about his Internet strategy during a meeting with investors, they concluded that Schultz's online plans were distracting him. The next day, Starbucks' stocked plunged 25 percent. Seven months later, Schultz reintensified his effort in expanding coffee shops. For year 2000 alone, Schultz planned to add about 450 U.S. outlets. More overseas expansion was also planned.

Schultz did not completely abandon the Internet, but focused instead on pumping up store sales by stocking more sandwiches, gifts, and other noncoffee merchandise. Starbucks decided to limit the Internet effort to partnerships and minority stakes in other e-merchants. "Our management team is 100 percent focused on growing our core business without distraction or dilution from any other initiative," says Schultz.[1]

The shift away from dabbling in e-commerce, and back toward doing what Starbucks does best (operating coffee shops) illustrates one of the many business strategies covered in this chapter—sticking to core

OBJECTIVES

After studying this chapter and doing the exercises, you should be able to:

1 Document how planning contributes to business success.

2 Summarize a general framework for planning and apply it to enhance your planning skills.

3 Describe the nature of business strategy.

4 Explain how business strategy is developed, including SWOT analysis.

5 Identify 12 different business strategies.

6 Explain the use of operating plans, policies, procedures, and rules.

7 Present an overview of management by objectives.

Chapter 5

competencies. By virtue of planning, including using a basic strategy, businesspeople manage the future instead of being guided by fate.

The purpose of this chapter is to describe the planning function in such a way that you can use what you learn to plan more effectively as a manager or individual contributor. First the chapter looks at the value of planning and a framework for its application. You will also learn about high-level, or strategic planning, including how strategy is developed and the types of strategy that result from strategic planning. We then describe operating plans, policies, procedures, and rules, and a widely used method for getting large numbers of people involved in implementing plans: management by objectives.

1   THE CONTRIBUTION OF PLANNING

Document how planning contributes to business success.

Planning is important because it contributes heavily to success and gives you some control over the future. According to one analysis, the value of planning is in the process itself. By planning, you set aside your daily tasks and deadlines so you can enlarge your mental focus and see the bigger picture.[2] More specifically, planning often leads to improvement in productivity, quality, and financial results.

Extensive research evidence supports the value of planning, as revealed by an analysis of 26 studies. Companies that engaged in strategic (high-level and long-range) planning achieved better financial results. They also did a better job of fitting into their environment, such as an automotive company adapting to changing preferences for vehicles. Planning also contributed to corporate growth.[3]

Despite the many advantages of planning, it can interfere with the spontaneity necessary for success. Astute businesspeople often seize opportunities as they occur, even if they are not part of any plan. For example, a report cited the contribution of red wine in lowering cholesterol among French people. Several wineries in the United States seized this marketing opportunity by rapidly increasing the production of red wine. Another problem is that planning can create blinders designed to focus direction and block out peripheral vision. As management theorist Henry Mintzberg says, "Setting oneself on a predetermined course in uncharted waters is the perfect way to sail straight into an iceberg."[4]

An effective antidote to the disadvantages of planning is to allow some slack in your plan for capitalizing on the unexpected. For example, in planning a job search, leave room to explore opportunities you did not envision in your plan.

2   A GENERAL FRAMEWORK FOR PLANNING

Summarize a general framework for planning and apply it to enhance your planning skills.

Planning is a complex and comprehensive process involving a series of overlapping and interrelated elements or stages, including strategic, tactical, and operational planning. **Strategic planning** establishes master plans that shape the destiny of the firm. When Wal-Mart decided to expand beyond the United States and Canada into Europe and Asia, that represented strategic planning. (Strategic planning and business strategies will be described later in the chapter.) A second type of planning is needed to support strategic planning, such as how to select expansion sites in Europe and Asia. **Tactical planning** translates strategic plans into specific goals and plans that are most relevant to a particular organizational unit.

A third type of planning is aimed more at day-to-day operations or the nuts and bolts of doing business. **Operational planning** identifies the specific procedures and actions required at lower levels in the organization. If your local Wal-Mart wanted to add produce, such as vegetables, to its merchandise, operational plans would have to be drawn. In practice, the distinction between tactical planning and operational planning is not clear cut. However, both tactical plans and operational plans must support the strategic plan such as the globalization of Wal-Mart.

The framework presented in Exhibit 5-1 summarizes the elements of planning. With slight modification the model could be applied to strategic, tactical, and operational planning. A planner must define the present situation, establish goals and objectives, forecast aids and barriers to goals and objectives, develop action plans to reach goals and objectives, develop budgets, implement the plans, and control the plans.

This chapter will examine each element separately. In practice, however, several of these stages often overlap. For example, a manager might be implementing and controlling the same plan simultaneously.

strategic planning
A firm's overall master plan that shapes its destiny.

tactical planning
Planning that translates a firm's strategic plans into specific goals by organizational unit.

operational planning
Planning that requires specific procedures and actions at lower levels in an organization.

113

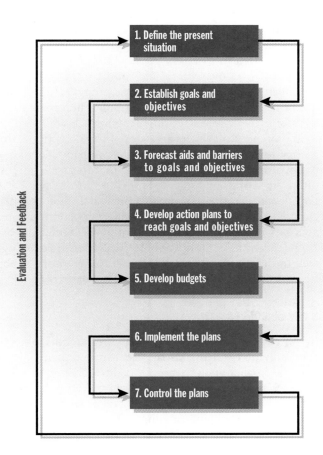

EXHIBIT 5-1

A Framework for Planning

Planning at its best is a systematic process.

The planning steps are not always followed in the order presented in Exhibit 5-1. Planners frequently start in the middle of the process, proceed forward, and then return to an earlier step. This change of sequence frequently happens because the planner discovers new information or because objectives change. Also, many managers set goals before first examining their current position.

To illustrate the general framework for planning we turn to Wal-Mart, whose plan is to globally dominate the retail industry. Former president and CEO David Glass said, "Our priorities are that we want to dominate North America first, then South America and then Asia and then Europe."[5] The plan for global domination would proceed approximately as described next, without presenting confidential company information.

Define the Present Situation

Knowing where you are is critical to establishing goals for change. Wal-Mart top management knows it is already the world's largest retailer: it is three times as large as Sears, its closest competitor. The plan toward global domination is well under way. By 2001 Wal-Mart passed 100 million customers served per week outside the United States through more than 1,000 retail outlets in Mexico, Puerto Rico, Canada, Argentina, Brazil, China, Korea, Germany, and the United Kingdom. Wal-Mart employs more than 885,000 associates in the United States and 225,000 internationally. H. Lee Scott, Jr. and other managers investigate whether the company has sufficient funds to keep on expanding overseas. The answer is affirmative: Continue with plans for global domination.

Defining the present situation includes measuring success and examining internal capabilities and external threats. Wal-Mart management must therefore engage in two more activities to complete this first step. *Success* in this situation would mean that new stores overseas would soon contribute a positive cash flow to the company. *Internal capabilities* refer to the strengths and weaknesses of the firm, or organizational unit, engaging in planning. The capabilities of Wal-Mart are extensive. Among them are a world-recognized brand name, thousands of experienced and competent managers and specialists, exceptional financial health, and a reputation for low prices. In addition, the company has achieved considerable success in global markets. And the "Made in America" label is appealing to consumers around the world.

External threats and opportunities include several tough competitors such as France's Carrefour and the Netherlands SHV Makro, economic crises, and sudden currency fluctuations in other countries. Another potential threat is that some communities do not want to be dominated by Wal-Mart. Predicting which products will sell well in different cultures could lead to inventory problems. Finding local talent with retailing knowledge could also be a problem.

Establish Goals and Objectives

The second step in planning is to establish goals and identify objectives that contribute to the attainment of goals. (Goals are broader than objectives, whereas objectives function as smaller goals that support the bigger goals.) Being a carefully planned enterprise, Wal-Mart already has precise goals and objectives. Total global domination itself can be regarded as an overall goal or strategic goal. Specific goals for the intermediate future include opening 80 retail outlets outside the United States in countries where Wal-Mart already has stores. Among these countries are

Argentina, Brazil, China, South Korea, and Mexico. Another goal is for one-third of Wal-Mart sales and earnings to come from the international division by 2003. Objectives to support these goals would include establishing target dates for opening stores in the various countries, stocking the shelves and warehouses, and advertising in the target countries.

Forecast Aids and Barriers to Goals and Objectives

As an extension of defining the present situation, the manager or other planner attempts to predict which internal and external factors will foster or hinder attainment of the desired ends. President and CEO H. Lee Scott, Jr. and other Wal-Mart managers and professionals rely on past experience and intuition about the feasibility of further penetration into the global market. Market research also is used to assess demand for giant, one-stop retailers in the various countries. The Wal-Mart team concludes that its many present successes in the international market make further expansion a likely success.

Despite the optimistic forecast, Wal-Mart faces some barriers. One is economic instability, such as the Asian crisis of 1998 and the downturn in 2000–2001. Sudden changes in currency valuation, such as the rapidly changing value of the Mexican peso in recent years, can create pricing problems. Another barrier to success is making accurate predictions about seasonal demands when getting started in a foreign country. An example is that when the company opened its first superstore in Brazil in November 1995, managers there were overwhelmed when sales were quadruple those in the United States. In general, it is difficult to predict accurately the type of Wal-Mart that best fits each location. One tricky factor is predicting the best ratio of locally made goods to those imported from the United States.

Develop Action Plans to Reach Goals and Objectives

Goals and objectives are only wishful thinking until action plans are drawn. An **action plan** consists of the specific steps necessary to achieve a goal or objective. The Wal-Mart planners must figure out specifically how they will acquire or rent the real estate necessary to build their stores, wholesale clubs, and supercenters. Teams have to be assembled to research specific countries and cities such as a suburb of Sydney, Australia. Action plans also have to be drawn for meeting with local government officials and citizens' groups to obtain necessary approvals for launching a Wal-Mart. Many local groups have opposed a Wal-Mart presence in their town. Two of hundreds of possible action plans would be:

action plan
The specific steps necessary to achieve a goal or objective.

- Consult with construction companies in Caracas, Venezuela, to determine whether they can accomplish the work needed to be done, when we need it done, and at the price we are willing to pay.
- Hire a local translator to ensure none of our signs translated from English into the native language will in any way be considered an insult, a vulgar term, or a cultural blooper of any type.

Develop Budgets

Planning usually results in action plans that require money to implement. For example, Wal-Mart spends about $14 million to open each store in another country.

Money must be budgeted for advertising after the store opens, and for real estate taxes. A formal budget would indicate how much money a manager can afford to spend on each action plan. A company like Wal-Mart has deeper pockets than most firms, with 2001 profits of about $8 billion from $205 billion in sales. Nevertheless, all expenditures are accounted for by a budget. Some action plans require almost no cash outlay, such as speaking to customers in retail outlets overseas about their preferences. The purpose of these talks would be to assess how well Wal-Mart serves the needs of customers in a given country. The feedback can be useful in planning expansion in the same country.

Implement the Plans

If the plans developed in the previous five steps are to benefit the firm, they must be put to use. A frequent criticism of planners is that they develop elaborate plans and then abandon them in favor of conducting business as usual. One estimate is that 70 percent of the time when CEOs fail, the major cause of failure is poor execution, not poor planning. Poor execution in this study included not getting things done, being indecisive, and not delivering on commitments.[6] Wal-Mart executives are particularly strong at implementation. They move ahead relentlessly, learning from mistakes such as having too few American-made goods in a foreign location.

Control the Plans

Planning does not end with implementation, because plans may not always proceed as conceived. The control process measures progress toward goal attainment and indicates corrective action if too much deviation is detected. The deviation from expected performance can be negative or positive. Site purchase and construction expenditures could run overbudget or underbudget. After a given store opens, sales could be higher or lower than anticipated. Higher sales than anticipated could mean inventory shortages (such as getting caught short on Hispanic Barbie Dolls), which might hurt goodwill in launching a new store.

In Exhibit 5-1, note the phrase "Evaluation and Feedback" on the left. The phrase indicates that the control process allows for the fine tuning of plans after their implementation. One common example of the need for fine tuning is a budget that has been set too high or too low in the first attempt at implementing a plan. A manager controls by making the right adjustment.

Make Contingency Plans

contingency plan

An alternative plan to be used if the original plan cannot be implemented or a crisis develops.

Many planners develop a set of backup plans to be used in case things do not proceed as hoped. A **contingency plan** is an alternative plan to be used if the original plan cannot be implemented or a crisis develops. (The familiar expression "Let's try plan B" gets at the essence of contingency planning.) A hurricane or typhoon could wreck a local economy as Wal-Mart is about to enter that country. Or a sudden outburst from local merchants could create an unfavorable climate for the giant retailer. If Wal-Mart discovers that the timing is poor to enter a given country, the executive team might be able to attain the expansion goal by shifting focus to another country. If plans for a store in Caracas must be changed suddenly, Wal-Mart might decide instead to quickly plan an opening in Quito, Ecuador.

Contingency plans are often developed from objectives in earlier steps in planning. The plans are triggered into action when the planner detects, however early in the planning process, deviations from objectives. Construction projects, such as building a retail supercenter, are particularly prone to deviations from completion dates because so many different contractors and subcontractors are involved.

STRATEGIC PLANNING AND BUSINESS STRATEGIES

3
117

The framework for planning can be used to develop and implement strategic plans, as well as tactical and operational plans. The output of one aspect of strategic planning by Wal-Mart was globalization, or the penetration of international markets. The emphasis of strategic planning in the current era is to help the firm move into emerging markets, or invent the future of the firm.

Describe the nature of business strategy.

Strategic planning should result in managerial workers throughout the organization thinking strategically and wondering about how the firm adapts to its environment and how it will cope with its future. A strategically minded worker at any level would think, "How does what I am doing right now support corporate strategy?" The help-desk worker at Hewlett-Packard might say to himself, "Each time I help a customer solve a problem I am contributing to the strategy of having the highest-quality products in all the markets we serve." To sensitize you to the realities of business strategies, the Management in Action on page 119 illustrates the type of strategic thinking behind Amazon.com.

Business strategy is a complex subject that can be viewed from a variety of perspectives. Here we look at business strategy from three major perspectives: its nature, how it is developed, and a sampling of the various types of strategy in use.

The Nature of Business Strategy

What constitutes business strategy has been described in dozens of ways. A **strategy** is the organization's plan, or comprehensive program, for achieving its vision, mission, and goals in its environment. An explanation of business strategy developed by Michael Porter, a leading authority, provides useful guidelines for managers who need to develop strategy. According to Porter, true business strategy has four components as outlined in Exhibit 5-2 and described next.[7]

strategy
The organization's plan, or comprehensive program, for achieving its vision, mission, and goals.

Strategy Involves More Than Operational Effectiveness
A starting point in understanding the nature of business strategy is to understand that it involves more than operational effectiveness or being efficient. In recent years many firms in the private and public sector have become more efficient through such means as downsizing, performing work more efficiently, and outsourcing (paying outsiders to perform some activities). Although the improvements in operations may often be dramatic, they rarely lead to sustainable improvements in profitability. As many top-level executives have said, "You can't cost-cut your way to growth." Strategy essentially involves performing activities differently, such as 1-800-MATTRESS, the company that pioneered selling mattresses over the phone. Being able to purchase a mattress over the phone is a convenience that adds value to the purchase of a mattress.

Strategy Rests on Unique Activities
Competitive strategy means deliberately choosing a different set of activities to deliver a unique value. An often cited example is Southwest Airlines. They offer

EXHIBIT 5-2

The Nature of Strategy

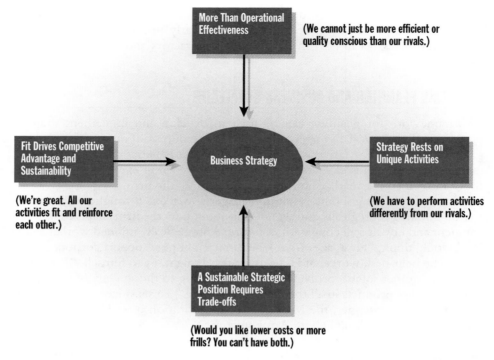

Source: Adapted from Michael E. Porter, "What Is Strategy?" *Harvard Business Review,* November–December 1998, pp. 61–78.

short-haul, low-cost, direct service between midsized cities and secondary airports in large cities. Southwest's frequent departures and low fares attract price-conscious customers who would otherwise travel by car or bus. Southwest customers willingly forego the frill of in-flight meals to save money and have a wide choice of flight departures. All Southwest activities focus on delivering low-cost, convenient service on its routes. By doing away with added features such as meals and interline transfer of baggage, the airline can achieve gate turnarounds in about 15 minutes. Planes can then be airborne more of the time, allowing for more frequent flights. By using automated ticketing, passengers can bypass travel agents, which saves Southwest money on commissions. Another unique activity is flying only 737 aircraft, which boosts the efficiency of maintenance.

A Sustainable Strategic Position Requires Trade-Offs

After a firm finds a strategic position (or place in the market), it can best sustain it by making trade-offs with other positions. Trade-offs are necessary when activities are incompatible. A good example is shopping through the Internet. If you want the convenience of shopping anytime and from your home or office, you sacrifice interacting with a sales associate who can answer your questions. Another trade-off with e-commerce (and shopping by phone) is that defective or ill-fitting merchandise has to be repacked and shipped back to the manufacturer. Repacking and reshipping is more inconvenient for many people than, for example, driving back to the merchant with a computer that doesn't work.

Management *in Action*

Amazon.com Develops Strategy to Lead the Internet Revolution

In the early days of Amazon.com, founder and chief executive Jeff Bezos evaded questions about when his company would earn a profit. Today, Bezos talks regularly about money and profits when interacting with members of the press. For the first five years, Amazon.com lost $1.74 billion and borrowed $2 billion. Each year as sales have surged, so have losses. Part of Bezos's plan to become profitable included slashing spending, revamping the corporate culture, laying off employees, and hiring old-economy whizzes to teach him Six Sigma (a demanding quality standard) and inventory management. Bezos predicted that the company would turn a profit by the end of 2002.

Several years ago a Merrill Lynch analyst said that, freed of the costs and problems of physical stores, Amazon could become the most profitable retailer in history. The same analyst contended that Amazon's losses were really investments in building a great company.

"Our initial strategy was very focused and unidimensional," says Bezos. "It was GBF [get big fast]. We put that on our shirts at the company picnic: They said GET BIG FAST, and on the back, EAT ANOTHER HOTDOG." The strategy was simple and enticing: Once Amazon got big enough, the efficiencies of a virtual store would kick in, and Amazon would start making money. GBF also meant, more or less, spend at will. Any expense was justifiable, as long as it helped the company grow. No formal budget existed. Employees simply spent what they needed to keep sales up. If it cost $100 to ship a $10 order, so be it. One former Amazon employee recalls sending items out regularly by messenger service to make sure customers didn't cancel orders.

The push to find customers has paid off. Amazon now has more than 20 million customers, and repeat purchases make up 73 percent of its sales, which makes renting space on its Web site of high potential value. As Bezos says, "When you reach a certain critical mass of customers, you very quickly have a long line of people who want to associate with you."

Launches of its virtual stores were lavish. Over the course of two years Amazon has opened 31 new businesses—selling toys, electronics, cars, kitchen appliances, and so on. Amazon also bought stakes in ten others. In one year those new stores lost $300 million. To avoid being unable to deliver on a hot item, such as a George Forman grill, Amazon overbought on inventory. The strategy of GBF created havoc in the warehouses. As the company keeps adding new products, balancing demand and inventory becomes increasingly difficult. Amazon built seven distribution centers in the United States so the company could sell to large numbers of customers at below-average selling costs.

By late 2000, the Amazon strategy shifted from "Get big fast" to "Make some great cash, baby." Instead of looking for ways to grow sales, employees look for ways to save money. Now every division must carefully account for what it spends. Each meets weekly to go over its numbers. Executives must also write operating plans that outline specific financial deadlines and target precise sales goals and profit margins. To learn the basics of P&Ls, balance sheets, and cash flow analysis, Amazon employees now take Finance 101 courses offered at the Seattle headquarters. When they completed it, they take Finance 102. With the new discipline in place, the books/music/video division actually turned a profit in the third quarter of 2000, earning $25 million on $400 million in sales.

Another part of Amazon's business model is to earn money by getting paid about a month before it pays suppliers. Amazon charges credit cards as soon as buyers click but doesn't have to pay suppliers until about 45 days later, enabling Amazon to earn interest on the *float*.

Bezos makes the case that Amazon is fundamentally different from a regular retailer. As he describes his strategy: "The foundation of e-commerce is technology, as opposed to the foundation for retail commerce, which is real estate. As real estate becomes more and more expensive, technology gets cheaper and cheaper. That's the fundamental analysis for e-commerce."

In the real world, Bezos argues, every time Wal-Mart opens a new store, it has a brand-new set of costs: new rent, sales staff, electricity bill, cash registers, and so on. When Amazon, on the other hand, opens up a virtual store, it has none of these costs. Over the past few years the company has paid upfront to build its basic foundation—the Web site, distribution centers, servers, and customer-service centers. That foundation serves as an e-tailing mold, so Amazon can sell just about anything—electronics, kitchen appliances, shovels—without incurring a bundle of new costs. If Target, on the other hand, wanted to start selling lawnmowers, it

would have to pay for more space and sales staff. Amazon just has to tack a new tab onto its Web site.

The counterargument to the Amazon expansion strategy is that some products are difficult and cumbersome to sell over the Net. The shipping costs are enormous for a product like a home theater system; service technicians must be hired, and most people want local service on big-ticket items. Furthermore, many name brand manufacturers will not sell directly to an e-tailer, so Amazon must buy from resellers. (The manufacturers do not want to alienate physical retail stores.) An analyst put it this way, "Let's face it: This company is a retailer, and the margins just aren't that great."

Asked to describe the Amazon of the future, he says, "Our mission is to be the earth's most customer-centric company. We will be the worldwide standard of what it means to be a customer-obsessed company."

Source: Katrina Brooker, "Beautiful Dreamer," *Fortune*, December 18, 2000, pp. 234–244; Robert D. Hof, "Suddenly, Amazon's Books Look Better," *Business Week*, February 21, 2000, pp. 78–84.

Fit Drives Both Competitive Advantage and Sustainability

Strategy includes efficiently combining activities related to making a product or service. The chain of company activities fit and support each other to form an effective system. Bic Corporation is an example of the *fit* aspect of strategy. The company sells a narrow line of standard, low-priced ballpoint pens to the major customer markets (retail, commercial, promotional) through practically every available channel. Bic targets the common need for a low-price, acceptable pen throughout the markets it serves. The company gains the benefit of consistency across nearly all activities, meaning that they do not have to have different equipment or staff to conduct their business with different customer groups. Bic achieves fit by a product design that emphasizes ease of manufacturing, manufacturing plants designed for low-cost, large-scale purchasing to minimize material costs, and in-house parts production whenever cost effective.

4   THE DEVELOPMENT OF BUSINESS STRATEGY

Explain how business strategy is developed, including SWOT analysis.

Business strategy develops from planning. Strategic planning encompasses those activities that lead to the statement of goals and objectives and the choice of strategies to achieve them. The final outcomes of strategic planning are statements of vision, mission, strategy, and policy. A **vision** is an idealized picture of the future of the organization. The **mission** identifies the firm's purpose and where it fits into the world. Specifying a mission answers the question, "What business are we really in?" A mission is more grounded in present-day realities than is a vision, but some companies use the terms interchangeably. A firm's mission may not be apparent to the casual observer. For example, Godiva Chocolates (the company that produces high-priced chocolate sold in separate displays in retail outlets) would appear to be in the candy business. In reality, their real mission places them in the luxury and pampering business. Exhibit 5-3 presents a few examples of company vision and mission statements.

Planning alone does not create strategy. Corporate values also influence strategy because well-managed organizations tend to develop strategy to fit what the people in power think is important. If the company highly values innovation, it will not adopt a strategy of being successful by imitating (or benchmarking) other successful products. Piaget, for example, has remained successful for more than 200 years by staying with its own high-quality watches, and not imitating other trends in the watch industry.

Under ideal circumstances a firm arrives at strategy after completing strategic planning. In practice, many firms choose a strategy prior to strategic planning. Once the firm has the strategy, a plan is developed to implement it. A chief executive might say, "Let's compete by becoming the most recognizable company in our field." The executive team would then develop specific plans to implement that strategy, rather than strategic planning leading to the conclusion that brand recognition would be an effective strategy. For many medium-sized and small organizations it is strategy first, followed by planning.

Three major approaches to developing strategy are gathering multiple inputs, analyzing the realities of the business situation, and doing a SWOT analysis. All three of these approaches are consistent with, and extensions of, the basic planning model presented in Exhibit 5-1.

Gathering Multiple Inputs to Formulate Strategy

Strategic managers and leaders are often thought of as mystics who work independently and conjure up great schemes for the future. In reality, many strategic leaders arrive at their ideas for the organization's future by consulting with a wide range of parties at interest. Strategy theorist Gary Hamel advises executives to make the strategy creation process more democratic. He reasons that imagination is scarcer than

vision

An idealized picture of the future of an organization.

mission

The firm's purpose and where it fits into the world.

121

EXHIBIT 5-3

Sample Vision and Mission Statements

Microsoft: "To give people the power to do anything they want, anywhere they want, and on any device, whether it's on a PC or on a Web phone."

McCormick & Company Inc.: "The primary mission of McCormick & Company Inc. is to expand its worldwide leadership position in the spice, seasoning, and flavoring market."

Vietnam Airlines: "The strategic vision for Vietnam Airlines in the next 10 to 20 years is to become one of the best airlines in the region, to operate efficiently, and to become even better at meeting the increasing requirements of the society for air transportation."

Bombardier: "Bombardier's mission is to be the leader in all the markets in which it operates. This objective will be achieved through excellence in design, manufacturing, and marketing in the fields of transportation equipment, aerospace, recreational products, financial services, and services related to its products and core competencies."

Roth Staffing Companies: "We are the preeminent staffing-services company, recognized as a creative industry leader, equally fulfilling the diverse needs of our customers, staffing associates, and coworkers."

resources. As a consequence, "We have to involve hundreds, if not thousands, of new voices in the strategy process if we want to increase the odds of seeing the future."[8]

A positive example of using multiple inputs to formulate strategy is J. S. Smucker Co., the manufacturer of high-quality jams and jellies. President Richard K. Smucker enlisted a team of 140 employees (7 percent of the workforce) who devoted nearly half of their time to a major strategy exercise for more than six months. Instead of having only the 12 top-level company executives working on the strategy, the 140 team members were used as ambassadors to solicit input from 2,000 employees. Strategy formulation was necessary because the company was in a bind as it struggled to grow in a mature market. Smucker developed a dozen new product initiatives that doubled its revenues in five years. One of these initiatives was an alliance with Brach & Brock Confections Inc. to produce Smucker's jelly-beans, the first of several cobranded products. The idea stemmed from a team of workers who would ordinarily not participate in strategy formulation.[9]

A caution about the Smucker example is that some strategy theorists would dismiss the example as incrementalism rather than true strategic leadership such as moving the company into a new business or reinventing the future. Yet from a practical standpoint, pointing a company in a direction that will double its revenues despite competing in a mature business is effective strategic management.

Analyzing the Realities of the Business Situation

To develop effective strategy, the strategist must make valid assumptions about the environment. When the assumptions are incorrect, the strategy might backfire. Let's get preposterous for a moment. Assume that Wal-Mart regards e-commerce as the wave of the future, and therefore halts its plans to achieve globalization by opening retail outlets throughout the world. Instead, Wal-Mart develops Web sites so people from all over the world can purchase everything from dish detergent to soccer balls over the Web. Worldwide sales do increase, but by such a small amount that profits are barely effected. The wrong assumption is that potential Wal-Mart customers throughout the world own computers, are online, and have credit cards. The globalization strategy fails because assumptions about the potential customer base were flawed.

Greyhound Lines, Inc., is an example of a company that almost went bankrupt by making false assumptions about its customer base. To boost sales, the company attempted to apply an airline reservation system and promotional efforts to the bus business. However, bus travelers are so different demographically from airplane travelers that the system failed miserably. For example, more than 80 percent of people who made reservations through a toll-free reservations system were no-shows.[10] Intercity bus travelers much prefer to just show up at the ticket office about one hour before departure time.

Accurately analyzing the environment in terms of understanding customers, potential customers, production capability, and the relevant technology is a time-consuming and comprehensive activity. Yet for strategy to work well, the manager has to understand both the external environment and the capabilities of the firm, as already implied from the basic planning model. Exhibit 5-4 presents a series of questions the strategist is supposed to answer to accurately size up the environment. Finding valid answers to these questions will often require considerable interviewing, including interviewing groups of consumers, and information gathering.

SWOT analysis

A method of considering the strengths, weaknesses, opportunities, and threats in a given situation.

Conducting a SWOT Analysis

Quite often strategic planning takes the form of a **SWOT analysis**, a method of considering the strengths, weaknesses, opportunities, and threats in a given situa-

EXHIBIT 5-4

A Strategic Inventory

The purpose of the *strategic inventory* is to help a manager relate ideas about strategy to his or her own organization. By finding answers to these questions, the manager is likely to do a better job of sizing up the competition, the customers, and the technology necessary to compete effectively. The manager will often need the assistance of others in finding answers to these challenging questions.

Defining the Boundaries of the Competitive Environment
- What are the boundaries of our industry? What market do we serve? What products or services do we provide?
- Who are our customers? Who has chosen not to buy from us? What is the difference between these two groups?
- Who are our competitors? Which firms do not compete with us? What makes one firm a competitor and not the other?

**Defining the Key Assumptions Made About the Environment,
Customers, Competition, and the Capabilities of the Firm**
- Who is our customer? What product or service features are important to that customer? How does the customer perceive us? What kind of relationship do we have with the customer?
- Who are our competitors? What are their strengths and weaknesses? How do they perceive us? What can we learn from our competitors?
- Who are our potential competitors? New entrants? What changes in the environment or their behavior would make them competitors?
- What is the industry's value chain (points along the way in which value is added)? Where is value added? What is the industry's cost structure? How does our firm compare? How about the cost structure of our competitors?
- What technologies are important in our industry? Product technologies? Delivery and service technologies? How does our firm compare? How about our competitors?
- What are the key factors of production? Who are the suppliers? Do we rely on just a few suppliers and sources? How critical are these relationships to our success? How solid are these relationships?
- What are the bases for competition in our industry? What are the key success factors? How do we measure up on these success factors? How do our competitors measure up?
- What trends and factors in the external environment are important in our industry? How are they likely to change? What is likely to be the time period for the changes?
- Are we able, in assessing our knowledge and assumptions, to clearly separate fact from assumption?
- Which of the preceding assumptions are the most important in terms of the impact on our business?

**Examining the Process for Reviewing and Validating
Our Key Assumptions and Premises**
- Do we have a process already established? Have responsibilities been assigned? Are periodic reviews planned and scheduled?

Source: Adapted from Joseph C. Picken and Gregory G. Dess, "Right Strategy—Wrong Problem," *Organizational Dynamics,* Summer 1998, p. 47.

tion. Elements of a SWOT analysis are included in the general planning model, and in using the strategic inventory to size up the environment. Given SWOT's straightforward appeal, it has become a popular framework for strategic planning. The framework, or technique, can identify a niche the company has not already exploited. To illustrate the use of the model, we return to Piaget, one of the world's finest watch makers. The price range of Piaget watches is between $7,000 and $20,000. (No, the last figure is not a typographical error.) Assume that top executives at Piaget are thinking about finding another niche by manufacturing luxury pens in the $200 to $500 range. Some of their thinking in regard to a SWOT analysis might proceed as follows:

Strengths. *What are good points about a particular alternative? Use your judgment and intuition; ask knowledgeable people.* Selling luxury pens appears to be a reasonable fit with the watch line because a luxury pen is often worn as jewelry. People who just want a writing instrument could settle for a Bic or competitive brand. The profit margins on luxury pens are quite good, and they are not likely to be deeply discounted in department stores or discount stores. We can also maintain low inventories until we assess the true demand. As our sales representatives and distributors receive orders, we can manufacture the pens quickly.

Weaknesses. *Consider the risks of pursuing a particular course of action, such as getting into a business you do not understand.* If only a handful of companies manufacture luxury pens, it could be because it is a tough market to crack. (We will need to do some market research here.) Another risk is that we will cheapen the Piaget name. The average price of a Piaget product is now about $11,000. With a brand of luxury pens, a person could take home a Piaget brand product for about $400, which could result in a scaling down of our image. Another problem is that we are not presently linked to all the distribution channels that sell luxury pens, such as office supply stores. We might have to rely on new distributors to get us into that channel.

Opportunities. *Think of the opportunities that welcome you if you choose a promising strategic alternative. Use your imagination and visualize the opportunities.* The opportunities could be quite good in terms of snob appeal. Maybe large numbers of consumers would welcome the opportunity to carry a Piaget anything in their shirt pocket, handbag, or attaché case. Many of the people who become Piaget luxury pen customers might want to take a step up to become a Piaget watch owner.

Threats. *Every alternative has its downside, so think ahead to allow for contingency planning. Ask people who have tried in the past what you are attempting now. But don't be dissuaded by the naysayers, heel draggers, and pessimists. Just take action.* Several manufacturers of high-end products in jewelry, clothing, and automobiles have cheapened their image and lost market share when they spread their brand name too thin. Following this approach, we could wind up having Piaget pens, wallets, and handbags. At that point the high prestige of the Piaget brand would be at risk.

As a result of this SWOT analysis, Piaget sticks to its knitting (or watch making) and continues to make world-class watches. Do you think they are making the right decision? Or do you think the brand equity (value of the brand name) warrants putting the Piaget label on another product?

A Variety of Business Strategies

Identify 12 different business strategies.

The nature of strategy and how it is developed may appear complex. Yet strategy statements themselves, as expressed by managers and planners, are usually straightforward and expressed in a few words, such as "We will be cost leaders." A variety of business strategies have already been mentioned in this and previous chapters. To help you appreciate what strategy means in practice, here we look at

124

a sampling of current strategies, as listed in Exhibit 5-5. Keep in mind that businesspeople are likely to have a less precise and less scientific meaning of strategy than do strategy researchers.

Find and Retain the Best People

A foundation strategy for becoming and remaining a successful organization is to find and retain highly competent people. Such people will help the organization develop products and services that are in demand, and will find ways to reduce costs and behave ethically. Top management at Microsoft attributes most of its success to hiring only intelligent, motivated job candidates. *Fast Company* magazine calls this strategy, *peoplepalooza,* and offers this advice to modern business executives:

> Yes, you need an Internet strategy. Sure, you've got to stay on the good side of Wall Street. But when it comes to building great companies, the most urgent business charge is finding and keeping great people. In an economy driven by ideas and charged by the Web, brainpower is the real source of competitive advantage.[11]

Cost Leadership

The cost leader provides a product or service at a low price in order to gain market share. Wal-Mart and Kmart are masters at cost leadership because their massive buying power enables them to receive huge price concessions from suppliers. In recent years Kmart was losing market share to Wal-Mart. The Kmart CEO fought back by reintroducing a symbol of cost leadership, the Blue Light Special.[12] The purpose of the flashing blue light is to direct customers to unadvertised bargains. A cost leadership strategy can create ethical problems because of what suppliers must do to cut costs, such as having goods manufactured at sweatshops.

Southwest Airlines is another well-known company that emphasizes cost leadership. In addition to the low-cost maneuvers mentioned earlier in this chapter, the company uses one aircraft type to simplify training and maintenance. Also, you will not find such luxuries as a Southwest airport club.[13]

Domination

A blatant business strategy is to be such a dominant player in the field that other companies have difficulty competing with you. At one time IBM had an 80 percent share of the computer industry based on the company's powerful marketing, manufacturing, and product development. Today, Exxon Mobil exemplifies the domination strategy, having the highest annual sales of any U.S.-based corporation. The company's net income of $17.7 billion in 2000 was the most ever earned by a corporation.

1. Finding and keeping the best people	7. Redefining the industry
2. Cost leadership	8. High speed
3. Domination	9. Global diversification
4. Product or differentiation	10. Diversification of goods and services
5. Imitation	11. Sticking to core competence
6. Strategic alliances (alliance capitalism)	12. Navigation for e-customers

EXHIBIT 5-5

A Variety of Business Strategies

Exxon's domination is not solely based on its overwhelming size and wealth, or its central position in the oil industry upon which much of the world depends. A visitor to Exxon headquarters observes, "Exxon is a machine and it grinds its own way. They have only one way of doing things: the most efficient, with the least risk. They want to see the studies. If the studies are yours, they want to redo them. They have a clear line of sight to the target."[14]

A potential problem with a domination strategy is that too many managers and other workers become complacent and smug. Several well-known companies that executed a domination strategy were eventually challenged by smaller competitors. Among these former dominators were GM, IBM, Sears & Roebuck, and Motorola.

Product Differentiation

A differentiation strategy attempts to find a niche or offer a product or service perceived by the customer as different from available alternatives. Krispy Kreme produces a unique donut (extra soft and tasty) that allows the company to capture a niche in a world with many alternative brands of donuts available. Computer maker Gateway is another firm that uses a product differentiation strategy. The core of chairman and CEO Theodore W. Waitt's strategy is to capture customers early on and keep them generating incremental revenues through a variety of services. After a customer purchases a PC, Gateway attempts to lock in these customers through financing, Internet access, and a personalized portal that leads to Gateway's e-commerce sites. A key part of the differentiation strategy is gateway.net, an Internet-access service.[15]

Imitation

If you cannot be imaginative, why not imitate the best? Benchmarking (or modeling the best practices of other companies) has given a new impetus to the imitation strategy. The entire industry of PC clones is based on an imitation strategy. Amazon.com was the first organization to sell virtually any book title in print over the Internet. As such, the company competed directly with bookstores with physical locations. Giant bookseller Barnes & Noble quickly imitated this successful approach to selling books and music in its Web shopfront http://www.barnesandnoble.com. Borders Books also developed an online shopping outlet, but sold its site to Amazon.com in 2001. The imitation strategy is not always successful!

Strategic Alliances

A widely used business strategy is to form alliances, or share resources, with other companies to exploit a market opportunity. A strategic alliance is also referred to as alliance capitalism because capitalism is carried out by collaborating with other companies, including competitors. A major factor contributing to the growth of alliances is the enormous costs and time involved in developing and distributing products if a company starts from zero. Many business executives see the object of an alliance as creating value for both sides, rather than a short-term means of filling in gaps in capabilities. The drug company, Warner-Lambert, holds this perspective. Several years ago Warner-Lambert formed an alliance with Pfizer Pharmaceuticals to jointly market a new drug developed by the former. The Warner-Lambert director of strategic alliances said, "We live by the concept of co-destiny. We believe that our destinies are intertwined, so what is good for our business ally is good for us."[16]

Redefining the Industry

To be a true leader, an organization must change the nature of the industry or change the rules of the game. Dell Computer exemplifies redefining an industry by finding ways to eliminate distributors in selling computers. Selling first by telephone, and then via the Internet, the company is credited with helping to define Internet commerce. The company sold about $1 billion of equipment on its Web site alone in 1998. A money manager said about Dell's accomplishments: "Think about it. Going directly to customers. Eliminating the middleman. Selling over the Internet. Wouldn't a Chrysler like to do that? Wouldn't everybody want to do business like that?"[17]

High Speed

Satisfy customer needs more quickly and you will make more money. High-speed managers focus on speed in all of their business activities, including speed in product development, sales response, and customer service. Knowing that "time is money," they choose to use time as a competitive resource. It is important to get products to market quickly because the competition might get there first. Part of Domino's Pizza's original success was based on getting pizzas delivered more quickly than competitors. The strategy had to be modified slightly when too many deliverers sacrificed auto safety to enhance delivery speed. Dell Computer relies on high speed as part of its strategy. A custom order placed at 9 A.M on Wednesday can be on a delivery truck by 9 P.M. on Thursday.

Global Diversification

A widely practiced business strategy is to diversify globally in order to expand business. Global diversification has already been described here in relation to Wal-Mart. The information about international business in Chapter 2 also describes global diversification, which gives a business firm a much larger potential customer base. Without global diversification, many American companies would be much less profitable. An astonishing 80 percent of the sales of Coca-Cola are *outside* the United States.

Diversification of Goods and Services

"Don't put all your eggs in one basket" is a standard business strategy. One of the many reasons that diversification is an effective strategy is that it serves as a hedge in case the market for one group of products or services softens. In recent years sales of traditional Nike products such as basketball shoes have softened. Nike has responded by investing considerable resources into promoting its soccer products around the world. For example, Nike paid $200 million to sponsor Brazil's national team. The Nike strategy of product diversification is simultaneously a strategy of global diversification.

Sticking to Core Competencies

It may be valuable to not put all your eggs in one basket, but also guard against spreading yourself too thin. Many firms of all sizes believe they will prosper if they confine their efforts to business activities they perform best—their core competencies. You will recall the initial description in this chapter about the chief executive at Starbucks deciding to back away from Internet activities and reconcentrate on the coffee shops. Starbucks is part of a recent trend in which companies that have diversified later sell off acquired assets in order to refocus on their core business. For instance, Xerox Corporation sold its European business that financed large purchases, which enabled Xerox to concentrate on selling document and digital products and services. (Xerox also needed the cash from the sale to pay off debt.)

Sticking to a core competency can also help a company remain independent because focusing on what the company does best often boosts profits. Increased profits, in turn, lead to a higher stock price that makes the company less likely to be bought by another company. Several years ago Mellon Bank sold off lagging businesses—credit cards, ATM servicing, and most mortgages. In this way Mellon was able to concentrate on its core competency: managing money for wealthy clients through several upscale subsidiaries.[18]

Focus

In a focus strategy, the organization concentrates on a specific regional or buyer market. To gain market share, the company uses either a differentiation or a cost leadership approach in a targeted market. Some companies have several products or services catering to a buyer market, such as vitamins for seniors, but it does not constitute a full focus strategy. Wright & Filippis, the medical supply company described in Chapter 3, is a good example of a successful focus strategy. The company's target buyer group consists of those people requiring prosthetics, orthopedic devices, and home medical equipment. It would be extremely rare for anyone outside their target group to purchase their equipment. (Okay, a medical school might buy an occasional prosthetic.)

Navigation for E-Customers

Strategy guru Michael E. Porter explains that many managers believe that the Internet makes strategy obsolete. In reality, strategy is more important than ever in the Internet age. Because the Internet typically weakens profitability, it is more important than ever for a company to find a strategy that distinguishes it from competitors.[19] (The Internet weakens profitability because purchasers have more choices and can comparison shop readily.) A specific strategy for the Internet and e-commerce is **navigation**, techniques for helping consumers more around within the Web.

navigation

A specific strategy that provides techniques for helping consumers move around within the Web.

Navigation is three-dimensional. *Reach* deals with access and connection. It refers to how many customers an e-merchant can connect with and how many products it can offer to those customers. For example, http://www.walmart.com comes up strong here because of its vast offerings. *Richness* refers to the depth of information that a business firm gives to or collects about customers. Purchasing exchanges that supply extensive product information, and also carefully track customer purchasing patterns, have richness. *Affiliation* is about whose interests the business represents. The affiliation is typically on the part of the seller, yet some e-commerce firms shift the affiliation to the purchaser by representing him or her. One company, http://www.priceline.com, affiliates with the customer as it helps them choose among suppliers such as hotels and airlines. An effective Internet strategy offers customers reach, richness, and affiliation.[20]

6   OPERATING PLANS, POLICIES, PROCEDURES, AND RULES

Explain the use of operating plans, policies, procedures, and rules.

Strategic plans are formulated at the top of the organization. Four of the vehicles through which strategic plans are converted into action are operating plans, policies, procedures, and rules.

Operating Plans

Operating plans are the means through which strategic plans alter the destiny of the firm. Operating plans involve organizational efficiency (doing things right), whereas strategic plans involve effectiveness (doing the right things). Both strategic and operational plans involve such things as exploring alternatives and evaluating the effectiveness of the plan. In a well-planned organization, all managers take responsibility for making operating plans that mesh with the strategic plans of the business. Operational plans (a term used synonymously with *operating plans*) provide the details of how strategic plans will be accomplished. In many firms, suggestions to be incorporated into operating plans stem from employees at lower levels.

Operating plans focus more on the firm than on the external environment. To illustrate, the strategic plan of a local government might be to encourage the private sector to take over government functions. One operating unit within the local government might then formulate a plan for subcontracting refuse removal to private contractors and phasing out positions for civil-service sanitation workers.

Operating plans tend to be drawn for a shorter period than strategic plans. The plan for increasing the private sector's involvement in activities conducted by the local government might be a 10-year plan. In contrast, the phasing out of government sanitation workers might take two years.

operating plans
The means through which strategic plans alter the destiny of the firm.

129

Policies

Policies are general guidelines to follow in making decisions and taking action; as such, they are plans. Many policies are written; some are unwritten, or implied. Policies, designed to be consistent with strategic plans, must allow room for interpretation by the individual manager. One important managerial role is interpreting policies for employees. Here is an example of a policy and an analysis of how it might require interpretations.

policies
General guidelines to follow in making decisions and taking action.

> Policy: When hiring employees from the outside, consider only those candidates who are technically competent or show promise of becoming technically competent and who show good personal character and motivation.

A manager attempting to implement this policy with respect to a given job candidate would have to ask the following questions:

- What do we mean by "technical competence"?
- How do I measure technical competence?
- What do we mean by "show promise of becoming technically competent"?
- How do I rate the promise of technical competence?
- What do we mean by "good personal character and motivation"?
- How do I assess good personal character and motivation?

Policies are developed to support strategic plans in every area of the firm. Many firms have strict policies against employees accepting gifts and favors from vendors or potential vendors. For example, many schools endorse the Code of Ethics and Principles advocated by the National Association of Educational Buyers. One of the specific policies states that buyers should "decline personal gifts or gratuities which might in any way influence the purchase of materials."

Procedures

procedures

A customary method for handling an activity. It guides action rather than thinking.

Procedures are considered plans because they establish a customary method of handling future activities. They guide action rather than thinking, in that they state the specific manner in which a certain activity must be accomplished. Procedures exist at every level in the organization, but they tend to be more complex and specific at lower levels. For instance, strict procedures may apply to the handling of checks by store associates. The procedures for check handling by managers may be much less strict.

Rules

rule

A specific course of action or conduct that must be followed. It is the simplest type of plan.

A **rule** is a specific course of action or conduct that must be followed; it is the simplest type of plan. Ideally, each rule fits a strategic plan. In practice, however, many rules are not related to organizational strategy. When rules are violated, corrective action should be taken. Two examples of rules follow:

- Any employee engaged in an accident while in a company vehicle must report that accident immediately to his or her supervisor.
- No employee is authorized to use company photocopying machines for personal use, even if he or she reimburses the company for the cost of the copies.

The next section describes a program that thousands of organizations use to apply the principles and techniques of planning and goal setting.

7

Present an overview of management by objectives.

MANAGEMENT BY OBJECTIVES: A SYSTEM OF PLANNING AND REVIEW

management by objectives (MBO)

A systematic application of goal setting and planning to help individuals and firms be more productive.

Management by objectives (MBO) is a systematic application of goal setting and planning to help individuals and firms be more productive. An MBO program typically involves people setting many objectives for themselves. However, management frequently imposes key organizational objectives upon people. An MBO program usually involves sequential steps, which are cited in the following list. (Note that these steps are related to those in the basic planning model shown in Exhibit 5-1.)

1. *Establishing organizational goals.* Top-level managers set organizational goals to begin the entire MBO process. Quite often these goals are strategic. A group of hospital administrators, for example, might decide upon the strategic goal of improving health care to poor people in the community. After these broad goals are established, managers determine what the organizational units must accomplish to meet these goals.
2. *Establishing unit objectives.* Unit heads then establish objectives for their units. A cascading of objectives takes place as the process moves down the line. Objectives set at lower levels of the firm must be designed to meet the general goals established by top management. Lower-level managers and operatives provide input because a general goal usually leaves considerable latitude for setting individual objectives to meet that goal. The head of inpatient admissions might decide that working more closely with the county welfare department must be accomplished if the health-care goal cited earlier in this list is to be met. Exhibit 5-6 suggests ways to set effective goals.
3. *Reviewing group members' proposals.* At this point, group members make proposals about how they will contribute to unit objectives. For example, the assistant

EXHIBIT 5-6

Guide to Establishing Goals and Objectives

131

Effective goals and objectives have certain characteristics in common. Effective goals and objectives

- **Are clear, concise, and unambiguous.** An example of such an objective is "Reduce damaged boxes of photocopying paper during April 27 to April 30 of this year."
- **Are accurate in terms of the true end state or condition sought.** An accurate objective might state, "The factory will be as neat and organized as the front office after the cleanup is completed."
- **Are achievable by competent workers.** Goals and objectives should not be so high or rigid that the majority of competent team members become frustrated and stressed by attempting to achieve them.
- **Include three difficulty levels: routine, challenging, and innovative.** Most objectives deal with routine aspects of a job, but they should also challenge workers to loftier goals.
- **Are achieved through team-member participation.** Subordinates should participate actively in setting objectives.
- **Relate to small chunks of accomplishment.** Many objectives should concern small, achievable activities, such as uncluttering a work area. Accomplishing small objectives is the building block for achieving larger goals.
- **Specify what is going to be accomplished, who is going to accomplish it, when it is going to be accomplished, and how it is going to be accomplished.** Answering the what, who, when, and how questions reduces the chance for misinterpretation.

to the manager of inpatient admissions might agree to set up a task force to work with the welfare department. Each team member is also given the opportunity to set objectives in addition to those that meet the strategic goals.

4. *Negotiating or agreeing.* Managers and team members confer together at this stage to either agree on the objectives set by the team members or negotiate further. In the hospital example, one department head might state that he or she wants to reserve 10 beds on the ward for the exclusive use of indigent people. The supervisor might welcome the suggestion but point out that only five beds could be spared for such a purpose. They might settle for setting aside seven beds for the needy poor.

5. *Creating action plans to achieve objectives.* After the manager and team members agree upon objectives, action plans must be defined. Sometimes the action plan is self-evident. For example, if your objective as a sales manager is to hire three new telemarketers this year, you would begin by consulting with the human resources department.

6. *Reviewing performance.* Performance reviews are conducted at agreed-upon intervals (a semiannual or annual review is typical). Persons receive good performance reviews to the extent that they attain most of their major objectives. When objectives are not attained, the manager and the team member mutually analyze what went wrong. Equally important, they discuss corrective actions. New objectives are then set for the next review period. A new objective for one hospital manager, for example, is to establish a task force to investigate the feasibility of establishing satellite health-care facilities in poor sections of town. Because establishing new objectives is part of an MBO program, the process of management by objectives can continue for the life of an organization.

Hewlett–Packard is one of many companies that implement management by objectives to improve organizational performance. Its Web site, http://www.hp.com, explains its general approach to MBO: "Individuals at each level contribute to company goals by developing objectives which are integrated with their manager's and those of other parts of HP. Flexibility—and innovation in recognizing alternative approaches to meeting objectives—provide effective means of meeting customer needs."

SUMMARY OF KEY POINTS

1 Document how planning contributes to business success. One value of planning is the process of self-examination itself. Extensive research shows that planning contributes to financial success and corporate growth.

2 Summarize a general framework for planning and apply it to enhance your planning skills. A generalized planning model can be used for strategic planning, tactical planning, and operational planning. The model consists of seven related and sometimes overlapping elements: defining the present situation; establishing goals and objectives; forecasting aids and barriers to goals and objectives; developing action plans; developing budgets; implementing the plan; and controlling the plan. Contingency plans should also be developed.

3 Describe the nature of business strategy. A current explanation of business strategy emphasizes four characteristics. First, strategy involves more than operational effectiveness. Second, strategy rests on unique activities. Third, a sustainable strategic position requires trade-offs. Fourth, fit among organizational activities drives both competitive advantage and sustainability.

4 Explain how business strategy is developed, including a SWOT analysis. Business strategy usually develops from planning, and is also influenced by values. Gathering multiple inputs is important in developing strategy. Strategists must also analyze the realities of the business situation to guard against false assumptions about customers, production capability, and the relevant technology. Strategy development often begins with a SWOT analysis, which considers the strengths, weaknesses, opportunities, and threats in a given situation.

5 Identify 12 different business strategies. Strategy development leads to many different strategies, including the following: finding and keeping the best people; cost leadership; domination; product differentiation; imitation; strategic alliances (alliance capitalism); redefining the industry; high speed; global diversification; diversification of goods and services; sticking to core competence; and navigation for e-customers. These strategies are not mutually exclusive, and several are often used in combination.

6 Explain the use of operating plans, policies, procedures, and rules. Operating plans provide the details of how strategic plans will be accomplished or implemented. They deal with a shorter time span than do strategic plans. Policies are plans set in the form of general statements that guide thinking and action in decision making. Procedures establish a customary method of handling future activities. A rule sets a specific course of action or conduct and is the simplest type of plan.

7 Present an overview of management by objectives. Management by objectives (MBO) is the most widely used formal system of goal setting, planning, and review. In general, it has six elements: establishing organizational goals, establishing unit objectives, obtaining proposals from group members about their objectives, negotiating or agreeing to proposals, developing action plans, and reviewing performance. After objectives are set, the manager must give feedback to team members on their progress toward reaching the objectives.

KEY TERMS AND PHRASES

Strategic planning, *113*

Tactical planning, *113*

Operational planning, *113*

Action plan, *115*

Contingency plan, *116*

Strategy, *117*

Vision, *121*

Mission, *121*

SWOT analysis, *122*

Navigation, *128*

Operating plans, *129*

Policies, *129*

Procedures, *130*

Rule, *130*

Management by objectives (MBO), *130*

QUESTIONS

1. In what way does planning control the future?
2. How can you use the information in this chapter to help you achieve your career and personal goals?
3. Why do managers whose work involves strategic planning typically receive much higher compensation than those involved with operational planning?
4. How realistic is Microsoft's vision? ("To give people the power to do anything they want, anywhere they want, and on any device, whether it's on a PC or on a Web phone.")
5. Which of several business strategies is likely to be the most relevant for a hospital?
6. Identify three Web sites whose *affiliation* is more with the consumer than with the supplier of the product or service.
7. Give an example of how a rule could fit the corporate strategy of "high speed."

CRITICAL THINKING QUESTIONS

1. Dig around to find the vision of your school. What do you think of this vision? Do you think the administration is bringing this vision into reality? If you could change this vision, what would you change?
2. What is wrong with the common expression, "plan ahead"?

SKILL-BUILDING EXERCISE: Conducting a SWOT Analysis

In this chapter you have read the basics of conducting a SWOT analysis. Now gather in small groups to conduct one. Develop a scenario for a SWOT analysis, such as the group starting a chain of coffee shops, pet-care service centers, or treatment centers for online addictions. Or, conduct a SWOT analysis for reorganizing a company from being mostly hierarchical to one that is mostly team based. Because most of your data are hypothetical, you will have to rely heavily on your imagination. Group leaders might share the results of the SWOT analysis with the rest of the class.

INTERNET SKILL-BUILDING EXERCISE: Business Strategy Research

The purpose of this assignment is to find three examples of business strategy by searching the Internet. A good starting point is to visit http://www.prnewswire.com. After copying down several strategic statements (or transferring them to a floppy disk or your hard drive) compare them to the section of this chapter called "A Variety of Business Strategies." Attempt to match the company statement about its strategy to a type of strategy listed in the chapter. If you cannot find the information you need in the publicity releases found in http://www.prnewswire.com, research companies you are curious about by inserting their name in a search engine, such as http://www.apple.com.

CASE PROBLEM 5-A: Vulture Time for E-Tailers

Inside an office park on the outskirts of Silicon Valley, not far from the local cemetery, an increasingly common death ritual is under way: A dot-com liquidator is poking through the remains of a start-up. In one room, dozens of computers sit idle in rows of deserted cubicles. Through a back door that leads past a metal detector a high-security warehouse, two women hunch over a table, tallying up what's left of Miadora, Inc., an online jewelry retailer that folded several weeks earlier. Patrick Byrne grins as he watches them pull trays of glittering merchandise from the refrigerator-size safes that line the walls.

Another woman plucks a necklace out of one of the safes. It's a strand of champagne Tahitian pearls with 18-karat-gold settings studded with diamonds. Mr. Byrne is buying the piece from Miadora's creditors for approximately $10,000 or about half what he estimates Miadora paid for it. "We'll sell it to the customer at $19,000 so we can say, 'You're getting a better deal for it than the jeweler.'" Byrne says.

Byrne's company, Overstock.com Inc., employs about 70 people and buys goods from distressed Web start-ups, manufacturers, and other sources at anywhere between 30 percent and 50 percent of their wholesale cost. Then it uses the Internet to sell the very same stock, offering the goods to consumers at less than the original retailer's cost. Overstock, might, for example, pay $25 for an item that wholesales for $50 and retails for $100. The closely held Salt Lake City company can then sell the item for $45 and still pocket a tidy sum on the transaction.

So far, the formula hasn't added up to an overall profit. Overstock, which started out using faxes, rather than the Web, as its primary marketing tool, has incurred losses of $22 million since its inception in 1998. Byrne, its chief executive officer, expects the company to be profitable by January 2001, when the company's sales will be enough to offset the cost of running and marketing the business.

Since acquiring a majority stake in Overstock in May 1999, Byrne has invested $15 million of his own money in the business, which has been growing rapidly. Before the Overstock venture, Byrne had amassed a $100 million portfolio as CEO of High Plains, a personal investment fund through which he bought Overstock.com. Overstock is now the 25th most-visited shopping site among those who surf the Web from work, according to Internet traffic-tracking service Nielsen/Netratings. The company sells about $1 million a week of merchandise ranging from stereo speakers to luxury handbags. And Byrne says sales should approach $50 million this year.

Byrne is pursuing failed Internet retailers more eagerly than most liquidators. In September, his company paid $3.7 million for the inventory of ToyTime.com, Inc., an operation that went under recently. He says that the goods in the warehouse had an estimated retail value of about $11.5 million. Last month, Overstock bought another Internet liquidator, Gear.com Inc., which specializes in sporting goods. Byrne said he recently bid 30 cents on the wholesale dollar for 25,000 Stetsons, baseball caps, and other headgear being sold by the creditors of eHats Inc., an Internet retailer that filed for bankruptcy protection early this year.

Before becoming an e-tailing liquidator, Byrne specialized in the liquidation of a variety of businesses. One of his biggest successes came in the early 1990s, when Byrne and a group of investors that included his father and two brothers, purchased New Dartmouth Bank, a collection of five failed New Hampshire savings banks. On its investment of $7 million, Byrne's family reaped a $20 million profit when the banks were later sold to another institution. Buying Internet retailers is "like buying that bank in New Hampshire," says Byrne. "It's the same principle."

Byrne has little sympathy for failing Internet retailers. "I think a sophomore economics student could have told you why these business models are garbage," he says. As for venture capitalists, they "have no understanding of what will make a good business," he adds, they just "try to pick what's going to be hot in six months."

Byrne found out about Miadora's deep financial problem through Joanne Dalebout, Overstock's jewelry buyer. On the day the company closed in September, Byrne drove to its headquarters in San Mateo, where employees, some in tears, were still boxing up their belongings. He says he scribbled, "I have cash" on the back of his business card and asked an employee to deliver it to Miadora's CEO. About 10 days later, Miadora accepted his offer.

Byrne is always on the alert for signs of weakness at other dot-coms. As he and Dalebout talk shop with Richard Canglia, Miadora's vice president of operations, Canglia mentions that the Web site of Adornis.com, an Irish jewelry retailer with offices in Greenwich, Connecticut, is no longer accessible. Byrne and Dalebot exchange glances. "Interesting," Dalebout says.

"Oh, you gonna get a plane ticket?" Canglia asks Byrne with a chuckle. "This is like the grim reaper here." Byrne says he has since bid less than 40 cents on the dollar for Adornis's inventory.

Canglia says he bears no grudge against Byrne, saying the liquidator is paying a fair price and helping out Miadora's creditors. Still, Canglia adds: "No one wants to see his car pulling up in the parking lot."

Some of Miadora's suppliers are concerned. Last month, Dalebout got calls from jewelry designers seeking to buy back pieces they had sold to Miadora. They are worried that

Overstock's discounts will hurt their relationship with full-price retailers, but Byrne says he isn't going to sell the items back.

Byrne routinely scours a Web site that keeps track of dot-com deaths. He recently posted an appeal there for failing companies to contact him. However, the rapid pace of Byrne's acquisitions has created challenges for Overstock's operations team. Among the tasks are to build high-security cages for precious jewelry. A variety of merchandise including toys like Barbie DeLuxe Dreamhouses, occupy a football-field size section of floor space.

Byrne thinks most e-tailers will fail eventually, with the exception of standouts such as Amazon.com. Executives within Overstock acknowledge that the supply of wounded dot-coms won't last forever, but Overstock has other sources of inventory, including manufacturers and traditional retailers. While the trend lasts, Overstock plans to exploit it.

Dalebout says she sometimes feels guilty about preying on failing dot-coms. Byrne says scavenging isn't a moral issue to him. "I say, 'Fella, you're in this position because you're in this position—I didn't put you there. I'm cleaning up the mess."

Discussion Questions

1. Which specific business strategy best fits the activities of Overstock?
2. In what way is Overstock management really using an imitation strategy?
3. What business strategy do you recommend so that Overstock does not become another failed dot-com?

Source: Nick Wingfield, "Dot-Com Liquidator: New Breed of Vulture Gets Fat on Remains of 'E-Tailers'," *The Wall Street Journal*, November 14, 2000, pp. A1, A8.

C A S E   P R O B L E M   5 - B :   High Hopes at Kellogg

In April 1999 Carlos Gutierrez, a career Kellogg executive who rose quickly through the ranks, took over as chief executive of the world's largest cereal maker. Friends and analysts hoped that his rare combination of youth and experience would spark a much-needed turnaround. The change came after a year of disappointing earnings and stock performance for the company whose best-known brands include Corn Flakes and Rice Krispies.

An analyst said, "Kellogg so badly needed change that any change probably was for the better. Gutierrez is young, he's articulate, and he's ambitious. These are all qualities that have not necessarily been part of Kellogg management."

When his promotion to CEO was first announced in January 1999, Gutierrez said his goal would be to build sales and profits. "I am convinced that the key to growth for our company and the category is investment—in product innovation, in franchise-building marketing, and in the accelerated expansion of our convenience foods and business," said Gutierrez.

That sentiment was a welcome change to financial analysts who had long criticized Kellogg for its lack of innovation and reluctance to spend money to build up its brands. At one time the undisputed leader in the U.S. cereal market, Kellogg now clings to a small lead over No. 2 cereal maker General Mills in the battle for market share. A food industry analyst said, "All signs indicate that this guy has the ability and the strategy. However, I think personally that the ready-to-eat cereal segment in the United States is going to remain very challenging for the next two years. I really think they are going against the wind a little bit."

A former Kellogg executive said about Gutierrez, "He is

involved, engaged and very hands-on. He will get into the details. He is not somebody who is just going to sit up on top and look down and hope."

Two years after taking over the corner office, the loyal Kellogg executive is struggling with the idea that the old battle plan is failing. The uneasy truth is that Kellogg sells something that doesn't fit easily into America's eat-on-the-run lifestyle. The people who do sit down for breakfast often choose cheaper, bagged cereal, or toast, or bagels instead. At the same time, rival General Mills Inc., has countered the trend by offering new versions of familiar brands such as Cheerios. The company has also introduced innovative snack foods, such as Go-Gurt, yogurt in a tube. Kellogg has been slower to come up with new ideas, and has also lost market share when it reduced advertising to save money and boost earnings.

To help improve the company outlook, Gutierrez has cut costs, shuffled management, offered customers more discount coupons, and pressured Kellogg's scientists to develop new products. He has also done what none of his predecessors dared: closed the original 93-year old Corn Flakes plant, laying off more than 500 employees. Although he found the plant closing difficult, Gutierrez believed that shutting down the factory was good for the company.

Recognizing that the recovery steps he took so far were not substantial enough, Gutierrez did something more radical. He invested $4.4 billion to buy Keebler Foods, maker of Cheez-Its and a variety of crackers and cookies. In a single act, the cereal veteran has transformed Kellogg into a $10 billion snack-foods company. Kellogg now derives just 40 percent of its sales from breakfast cereals, down from 75 percent before the acquisition. The purchase of Keebler also helped quiet critics who think Kellogg is averse to taking risks.

The next step is to make the Keebler deal work. Acquiring the cracker-and-cookie company gives Kellogg two crucial advantages: faster-growing food categories and a more efficient delivery system. In the past it took Kellogg six to eight weeks to roll out new products from warehouses to retailers. Now the company can use Keebler's in-house distribution system to put new items on store shelves faster, which allows Kellogg to take more chances with new products. "Failure is a lot less expensive," he says.

Discussion Questions

1. What strategy do you recommend Gutierrez use to improve Kellogg even further?
2. What is your evaluation of the wisdom of Kellogg acquiring Keebler for $4.4 billion?
3. Should Kellogg stay in the cereal business? Explain your reasoning.

Source: Emily Kaiser, "Little-Known Kellogg CEO Faces Challenge," Reuters story, April 22, 1999, available at http://foxmarketwire.com/042299/k.sml; "Thinking Out of the Cereal Box," *Business Week*, January 15, 2001, pp. 54–55.

ENDNOTES

1. Adapted from Louise Lee, "Now, Starbucks Uses Its Bean: The Java Giant Bets on More Bricks and Mocha, Less Web," *Business Week*, February 14, 2000, p. 92.
2. "The Real Value of Planning," *Working Smart*, January 1995, p. 1.
3. C. Chet Miller and Laura B. Cardinal, "Strategic Planning and Firm Performance: A Synthesis of More than Two Decades of Research," *The Academy of Management Journal*, December 1994, pp. 1649–1665.
4. Henry Mintzberg, "The Strategy Concept II: Another Look at Why Organizations Need Strategies," *California Management Review*, January 1987, p. 26.
5. Quoted in Lorrie Grant, "Wal-Mart Yearns for Global Market Domination," Gannett News Service, November 8, 1998; "Wal-Mart Spoken Here," *Business Week*, June 23, 1997, pp. 138–145; http://www.walmartstores.com/newsstand/ataglance.html; "Inside the 500," *Fortune*, April 16, 2001, p. F-1.
6. Ram Charan and Geoffrey Colvin, "Why CEOs Fail," *Fortune*, June 21, 1999, p. 70.
7. Michael E. Porter, "What is Strategy?" *Harvard Business Review*, November–December 1996, pp. 61–78; Richard M. Hodgetts, "A Conversation with Michael E. Porter: A 'Significant Extension' Toward Operational Improvement and Positioning," *Organizational Dynamics*, Summer 1999, pp. 24–33.
8. John A. Byrne, "Three of the Busiest New Strategists," *Business Week*, August 26, 1996, p. 50.
9. John A. Byrne, "Strategic Planning: After a Decade of Gritty Down-sizing, Big Thinkers Are Back in Corporate Vogue," *Business Week*, August 26, 1996, p. 52.
10. Joseph C. Picken and Gregory G. Dess, "Right Strategy—Wrong Problem," *Organizational Dynamics*, Summer 1998, p. 35.
11. Bill Breen and Anna Mudio, "Peoplepalooza," *Fast Company*, January 2001, pp. 80–81.
12. Joann Muller, "Kmart's Bright Idea," *Business Week*, April 9, 2001, pp. 50–52.
13. Wendy Zeller, "Southwest: After Kelleher, More Blue Skies," *Business Week*, April 2, 2001, p. 45.
14. Anthony Bianco, "Exxon Unleashed," *Business Week*, April 9, 2001, p. 60.
15. Steven V. Brull, "A Net Gain for Gateway?" *Business Week*, July 19, 1999, pp. 77–78.
16. Andrew C. Inkpen and Kou-Quing Li, "Joint-Venture Formation: Planning and Knowledge-Gathering for Success," *Organizational Dynamics*, Spring 1999, p. 36.
17. Quoted in Andy Serwer, 'Michael Dell Rocks,' *Fortune*, May 11, 1998, p. 60.
18. Peter Galuszka, "Lenders Living Alone and Liking it," *Business Week*, April 5, 1999, p. 94.
19. Michael E. Porter, "Strategy and the Internet," *Harvard Business Review*, March 2001, p. 63.
20. Philip Evans and Thomas S. Wurster, "Getting Real About Virtual Commerce," *Harvard Business Review*, November–December 1999, pp. 84–98.

Problem Solving and Decision Making

When the CEO of office furniture manufacturer Steelcase asked a team of 27 vice presidents to abandon their private offices and move into a bullpen, he expected resistance. As company environments director Joyce Bromberg recalls, "People were dragged kicking and screaming" into the Leadership Community, an executive floor with few walls, where some assistants work in larger spaces than their bosses. To ease the transition, a full-scale version of the proposed space was mocked up for users to tour and make suggestions before construction began.

To encourage teamwork, "community members"—as the VPs and their assistants are known—are issued laptop computers and cellular telephones so they can gather in the multimedia information center or choose from one of 50 collaborative spaces and work centers. Portability is the key because many vice presidents' functional teams are located in buildings across town, where the executives use minimal "touch-down" workspaces and hold information catch-up "mixers" each morning.

In addition to encouraging teamwork, the Steelcase executives find that the ready flow of information among them makes problem solving easier. Many problems are quickly solved during the mixers that might have taken a long time by exchanging e-mail messages, or setting up a series of meetings. Some Steelcase managers and staff professionals can point to creative ideas that came to them by bouncing ideas off each other and their assistants.

After a few months in the new quarters, 53 percent of workers said that they sensed a clear direction from company management—up from

OBJECTIVES

After studying this chapter and doing the exercises, you should be able to:

1 Differentiate between nonprogrammed and programmed decisions.

2 Explain the steps involved in making a non-programmed decision.

3 Understand the major factors that influence decision making in organizations.

4 Understand the nature of creativity and how it contributes to managerial work.

5 Describe organizational programs for improving creativity.

6 Implement several suggestions for becoming a more creative problem solver.

7 Appreciate the value and potential limitations of group decision making.

Chapter 6

43 percent. "We're aligned as a team," says VP of design Ann Jarvis, who has been with the company for 22 years. She says none of the vice presidents would even consider going back into a private office.[1]

---

problem

A discrepancy between ideal and actual conditions.

decision

A choice among alternatives.

As illustrated by the revamped office space at Steelcase, managers are finding new ways of enhancing communication, as well as improving the process of solving problems and finding creative ideas. This chapter explores how managerial workers solve problems and make decisions individually, and in groups. A **problem** is a discrepancy between ideal and actual conditions. For example, a hospital might have too many beds unoccupied. The ideal would be to have an occupancy rate of 90 percent or greater. A **decision** is choosing among alternatives, such as affiliating with more doctors so as to receive more patient referrals.

Problem solving and decision making are required to carry out all management functions. For example, when managers control, they must make a series of decisions about how to solve the problem of getting performance back to standard. Understanding decision making is also important because decision making contributes to job satisfaction. Jobs allowing for more decision-making authority are generally more satisfying.

Another important perspective on decision making sees it at the heart of management. A distinguishing characteristic of a manager's job is the authority to make decisions. The Management in Action on page 141 lists some of the most important decisions ever made by managers in business.

1

Differentiate between nonprogrammed and programmed decisions.

NONPROGRAMMED VERSUS PROGRAMMED DECISIONS

Managerial workers face a variety of decisions. Some decisions, known as **nonprogrammed decisions** (or nonroutine decisions), are difficult because they occur infrequently. In contrast, **programmed decisions** are repetitive, or routine, and made according to a specific procedure.

nonprogrammed decision

A decision that is difficult because of its complexity and the fact that the person faces it infrequently.

A problem that has not taken the same form as in the past or is extremely complex or significant calls for a nonprogrammed decision. A complex problem contains many elements. Significant problems affect an important aspect of an organization such as the introduction of a new service. Virtually all strategic decisions are nonprogrammed.

A well-planned and highly structured organization reduces the number of nonprogrammed decisions. It does so by formulating hundreds of policies to help managers know what to do when faced with a given problem. In contrast, many small firms do not offer much guidance about decision making.

programmed decision

A decision that is repetitive, or routine, and made according to a specific procedure.

Handling a nonprogrammed problem properly requires original thinking. The skill required for decision making varies inversely with the extent to which it is programmed. Highly routine decisions require minimum decision-making skill; highly nonroutine decisions require maximum skill.

Managers and nonmanagers also make many small, uncomplicated decisions involving alternatives that are specified in advance. Procedures specify how to handle these routine, programmed decisions. Here is an example: A person who earns $26,000 per year applies to rent a two-bedroom apartment. The manager makes the decision to refuse the application on the basis of an established rule that families with annual incomes of $39,000 or less may not rent in the building.

Under ideal circumstances, top-level management concerns itself almost exclusively with nonroutine decisions, and lower-level management handles all routine ones. In reality, executives do make many small, programmed decisions in addition to nonprogrammed ones. Some executives sign expense account vouchers and answer routine correspondence. Middle managers and first-level managers generally make both routine and nonroutine decisions, with first-level managers making a higher proportion of routine decisions. A well-managed organization encourages all managers to delegate as many nonprogrammed decisions as possible.

STEPS IN PROBLEM SOLVING AND DECISION MAKING

2

Learning how to solve problems and make decisions properly is important because, according to a long-term study, being systematic about decision making helps avoid bad decisions. Paul C. Nutt studied 356 decisions in medium to large organizations in the United States and Canada. About one quarter of the decisions were made in a public agency, one quarter in nonprofit firms, and one half in private companies. One half of these decisions failed, such as a bank dropping Saturday service and losing customers as a result. Most instances of decision-making failure were attributed to poor tactics, including not exploring enough alternatives, and not obtaining enough input from group members.[2]

Explain the steps involved in making a nonprogrammed decision.

Problem solving and decision making can be regarded as an orderly process, similar to the planning model described in Chapter 5. Yet not every effective solution or decision is the product of an orderly process. The key principle is that managers find better solutions to complex problems—and therefore make better major, or nonprogrammed, decisions—when they follow an orderly process. Drawing a consistent distinction between problem solving and decision making is difficult because they are part of the same process. The basic purpose of making a decision is to solve a problem, but you must analyze the problem prior to making the decision. A broader and grander purpose of decision making is to move the organization forward, to seize opportunities, and to avoid problems.

As shown in Exhibit 6-1, and described next, problem solving and decision making can be divided into steps.

Identify and Diagnose the Problem

Problem solving and decision making begin with the awareness that a problem exists. In other words, the first step in problem solving and decision making is identifying a gap between desired and actual conditions. At times, a problem is imposed on a manager, such as when customer complaints increase. At other times, he or she has to search actively for a worthwhile problem or opportunity. For example, a sales manager actively pursued a problem by conducting an audit to find out why former customers stopped buying from the company.

Indicators of Problems
Identifying problems requires considerable skill. Managers may become aware of a problem by noticing one of four typical indicators.[3]

1. *Deviation from past performance.* If performance figures are down, a problem almost surely exists. Common problem indicators are declining sales, increased employee turnover, higher scrap rates, increased customer complaints, and an increased number of bad checks cashed.

EXHIBIT 6-1

Steps in Problem Solving and Decision Making

Managers who are thorough in their decision making will often proceed through the steps shown here.

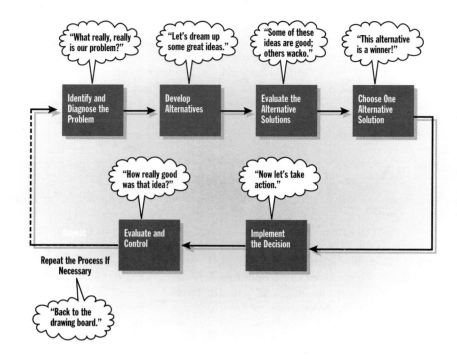

2. *Deviations from the plan.* When the results you hoped to attain with a plan are not forthcoming, you have a problem. This type of problem identification requires you to see a deviation from anticipated *future* performance. The possibility exists that the established plan was unduly optimistic.

3. *Criticism from outsiders.* Managers sometimes become aware of problems by hearing complaints from individuals and groups who are not employees of the firm. These sources of criticism include customers, government regulators, and stockholders.

4. *Competitive threats.* The presence of competition can create problems for an organization. Compaq Computer, for example, has slashed its prices in recent years to compete with lower-priced brands.

Diagnosis

A thorough diagnosis of the problem is important because the real problem may be different from the one that a first look suggests. The ability to think critically helps a person get at the real problem. To diagnose a problem properly, you must clarify its true nature. An important part of the decision process for making the right diagnosis is how you frame the problem. According to J. Edward Russo, framing puts you on the right track by defining what must be decided, and separating out what is important. A classic example of the right frame is the development of the Gillette Sensor for Women razor. Gillette management asked Jill Shurtleff, an industrial designer on their staff, to investigate the women's shaving market. The designer put herself on the right track by rejecting the frame that had previously been used in developing shavers for women—start with a man's razor and then modify it for women. Instead, Shurtleff focused on how women shave and developed a razor that became the greatest success ever in its product category.[4]

Management *in Action*

Eleven of the Greatest Management Decisions Ever Made

Many people consider good decision making to be the essence of management. So a business writer for *Management Review* asked experts for their nominations of the 75 greatest decisions ever made. All these decisions were successful and had a major impact. Here we list 11 of these decisions related directly to business rather than to government or religion. For example, we excluded Queen Isabella's decision to sponsor Christopher Columbus's voyage to the new world in 1492. Each decision's rank among 75 is listed in brackets.

1. **Walt Disney** listened to his wife and named his cartoon mouse Mickey instead of Mortimer. Entertainment was never the same after Mickey and Minnie debuted in "Steamboat Willie" in 1928 (1).
2. **Frank McNamara,** in 1950, found himself in a restaurant without money, prompting him to come up with the idea of the Diners Club Card. This first credit card changed the nature of buying and selling throughout the world (5).
3. **Thomas Watson, Jr.,** of IBM, decided in 1962 to develop the System/360 computer, at a cost of $5 billion. Although IBM's market research suggested it would sell only two units worldwide, the result was the first mainframe computer (7).
4. **Robert Woodruff** was president of Coca-Cola during World War II when he committed to selling bottles of Coke to members of the armed services for a nickel a bottle, starting around 1941. The decision led to enormous customer loyalty, including the fact that returning soldiers influenced family members and friends to buy Coca-Cola (12).
5. **Jean Nidetch,** in 1961, was put on a diet in an obesity clinic in New York City. She invited six dieting friends to meet in her

Queens apartment every week. The decision created Weight Watchers and the weight-loss industry (20).
6. **Bill Gates,** in 1981, decided to license MS/DOS to IBM, while IBM did not require control of the license for all non-IBM PCs. The decision laid the foundation for Microsoft's huge success and a downturn in IBM's prestige and prominence (21).
7. A **Hewlett-Packard** engineer discovered in 1979 that heating metal in a specific way caused it to splatter. The management decision to exploit this discovery launched the ink-jet printer business, and laid the groundwork for more than $6 billion in revenue for HP (25).
8. **Sears, Roebuck and Co.,** in 1905, decided to open its Chicago mail-order plant. The Sears catalogue made goods available to an entirely new customer base, and also provided a model for mass production (40).
9. **Ray Kroc** liked the McDonald brothers' stand that sold hamburgers, french fries, and milk shakes so much that he decided to open his own franchised restaurant in 1955 and form McDonald's Corp. Kroc soon created a giant global company and a vast market for fast food (58).
10. **Procter & Gamble,** in 1931, introduced its brand management system, which showcased brands and provided a blueprint that management has followed ever since (62).
11. **Michael Dell** made the decision in 1986 to sell PCs direct and build them to order. Others in the industry are now trying to imitate Dell Computer's strategy (73).

Source: Based on information in Stuart Crainer, "The 75 Greatest Management Decisions Ever Made," *Management Review*, November 1998, pp. 16–24.

Develop Alternative Solutions

The second step in decision making is to generate alternative solutions. In this intellectually freewheeling aspect of decision making, all kinds of possibilities are explored, even if they seem unrealistic. Often the difference between good and mediocre decision makers is that the former do not accept the first alternative they think of. Instead, they keep digging until they find the best solution. When Jeff Bezos, the founder of Amazon.com was searching for a way to commercialize the Internet, he made a list of the top 20 mail-order products. He then looked for where he could create the most value for customers, and finally decided on the alternative of selling books.[5]

Often the problem solver will find a creative alternative solution to the problem. At other times, a standard solution will work adequately. For example, one small-business owner needing money to expand the business might choose the standard alternative of borrowing money from a bank. Another small business owner might attempt the creative alternative of raising money by investing profits in high-risk securities.

Evaluate Alternative Solutions

The next step involves comparing the relative value of the alternatives. The problem solver examines the pros and cons of each one and considers the feasibility of each. Some alternatives may appear attractive, but implementing them would be impossible or counterproductive.

Comparing relative value often means performing a cost and savings analysis of each alternative. Alternatives that cost much more than they save are infeasible. The possible outcome of an alternative should be part of the analysis. If an unsatisfactory outcome is almost a certainty, the alternative should be rejected. For example, if a firm is faced with low profits, one alternative would be to cut pay by 20 percent. The outcome of this alternative would be to lower morale drastically and create high turnover, so a firm should not implement that alternative. High employee turnover is so expensive that it would override the cost savings.

One approach to examining the pros and cons of each alternative is to list them on a worksheet. This approach assumes that virtually all alternatives have both positive and negative consequences.

Choose One Alternative Solution

The process of weighing each alternative must stop at some point. You cannot solve a problem unless you choose one of the alternatives—that is, make a decision. Several factors influence the choice. A major factor is the goal the decision should achieve. The alternative chosen should be the one that appears to come closest to achieving it.

Despite a careful evaluation of alternatives, ambiguity remains in most decisions. The decisions faced by managers are often complex, and the factors involved in them are often unclear. Even when quantitative evidence strongly supports a particular alternative, the decision maker may be uncertain. Human resource decisions are often the most ambiguous because making precise predictions about human behavior is so difficult. Deciding which person to hire from a list of several strong candidates is always a challenge.

Implement the Decision

Converting the decision into action is the next major step. Until a decision is implemented, it is not really a decision at all. Many strategic decisions represent wasted effort because nobody is held responsible for implementing them. Much of a manager's job involves helping subordinates implement decisions.

A fruitful way of evaluating the merit of a decision is to observe its implementation. A decision is seldom a good one if people resist its implementation or if it is too cumbersome to implement. Suppose a firm tries to boost productivity by decreasing the time allotted for lunch or coffee breaks. If employees resist the decision by eating while working and then taking the allotted lunch break, productivity will decrease. Implementation problems indicate that the decision to boost productivity by decreasing break time would be a poor one.

Evaluate and Control

The final step in the decision-making framework is to investigate how effectively the chosen alternative solved the problem. Controlling means ensuring that the results the decision obtained are the ones set forth during the problem identification step.

After gathering feedback, characterize the quality of the decision as optimum, satisficing, or suboptimum. Optimum decisions lead to favorable outcomes. **Satisficing decisions** provide a minimum standard of satisfaction. Such decisions are adequate, acceptable, or passable. Many decision makers stop their search for alternatives when they find a satisficing one. Accepting the first reasonable alternative may only postpone the need to implement a decision that really solves the problem. For example, slashing the price of a personal computer to match the competition's price can be regarded as the result of a satisficing decision. A longer-range decision might call for a firm to demonstrate to potential buyers that the difference in quality is worth the higher price.

Suboptimum decisions lead to negative outcomes. Their consequences are disruptive to the employees and to the firm. When you obtain suboptimum results, you must repeat the problem-solving and decision-making process.

Evaluating and controlling your decisions will help you improve your decision-making skills. You can learn important lessons by comparing what actually happened with what you thought would happen. You can learn what you could have improved or done differently and use this information the next time you face a similar decision.

Criticism of the Rational Decision-Making Model
So far, this chapter has presented the classical model of problem solving and decision making. The model regards the activities as an orderly and rational process. In reality, decision making is seldom logical and systematic. Michael Dell, for example, did not require a study to decide that selling computers by telephone had substantial consumer appeal. Instead, he used his marketing and business intuition to arrive at that conclusion.

Awareness that decision making is not always so orderly stems from the research of psychologist and economist Herbert A. Simon. He proposed that bounds (or limits) to rationality are present in decision making. These bounds are the limitations of the human organism, particularly related to the processing and

satisficing decision
A decision that meets the minimum standards of satisfaction.

143

bounded rationality

The observation that people's limited mental abilities, combined with external influences over which they have little or no control, prevent them from making entirely rational decisions.

144

heuristic

A rule of thumb used in decision making.

recall of information.[6] **Bounded rationality** means that people's limited mental abilities, combined with external influences over which they have little or no control, prevent them from making entirely rational decisions. Satisficing decisions result from bounded rationality.

You should strive to follow the orderly steps of problem solving and decision making. However, problems generally do not occur in isolation, and you may not have the time to carefully evaluate each alternative. The next section will discuss the factors that influence the decision-making process and how they affect the quality of decisions.

Partly because of bounded rationality, decision makers often use simplified strategies to choose an alternative solution, also known as **heuristics**. A heuristic becomes a rule of thumb in decision making. A widely used investing heuristic is as follows: The percent of equity in your portfolio should equal 100 minus your age, with the remainder being invested in fixed-income investments. A 25-year old would therefore have a portfolio consisting of 25 percent interest-bearing securities, such as bonds or money-market funds, and 75 percent in stocks. Heuristics help the decision maker cope with masses of information, but their oversimplification can lead to inaccurate or irrational decision making.

3   INFLUENCES ON DECISION MAKING

Understand the major factors that influence decision making in organizations.

Although most people can follow the decision-making steps described, not everybody can arrive at the same quality of decision. Decision-making ability varies from person to person, and other forces can hamper anyone from finding optimum solution. Exhibit 6-2 shows the factors that influence decision making.

EXHIBIT 6-2

Factors Influencing
Decision Making

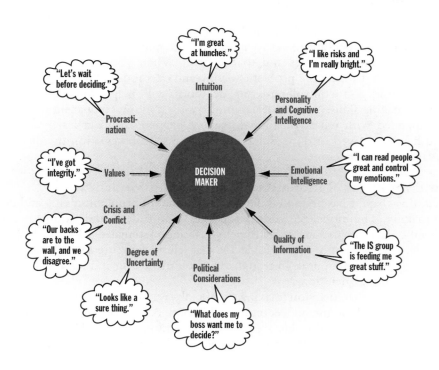

Intuition

Effective decision makers do not rely on analytical and methodological techniques alone. They also use their hunches and intuition. **Intuition** is an experience-based way of knowing or reasoning in which weighing and balancing evidence are done unconsciously and automatically. Intuition is also a way of arriving at a conclusion without using the step-by-step logical process. (Yet the intuitive person might be racing through the steps in his or her mind without realizing it.) The fact that experience contributes to intuition means that decision makers can become more intuitive by solving many difficult problems because accumulated facts are an asset to intuition.

As shown in one study, employees who use intuition more frequently tend to be more experienced, older, and often hold a managerial position. Executives need to rely on intuition more than others because their job focuses on the bigger picture as they deal with long-term rather than short-term issues.[7]

Intuition, of course, can be wrong. Because intuitions are stored information packaged in a new way, if faulty information is packaged, it makes the subsequent intuition faulty.[8] A company CEO decided to relocate headquarters from its current metropolitan setting to a rural area 40 miles away. His intuition told him that employees would much prefer rural tranquillity to urban congestion. The CEO's intuition was wrong. Many key employees quit rather than sacrifice the conveniences and excitement of working in the metropolitan area. As a check on your intuition, from time to time attempt to trace the reasons behind your decision. The CEO in question might have asked, "Now what evidence do I have that our best associates want to work in a rural location?"

The distinction between analytical and intuitive thinking is often traced to which half of the brain is dominant. The left half of the brain controls analytical thinking; the right half controls creative and intuitive thinking. Effective problem solvers achieve a balance between analytical and intuitive, or left-brain and right-brain thinking. Rather than operating independently of each other, the analytical and intuitive approaches should be complementary components of decision making.

Personality and Cognitive Intelligence

The personality and cognitive intelligence of the decision maker influence his or her ability to find effective solutions. The term *cognitive intelligence* refers to the traditional type of intelligence involved in solving difficult problems and doing well in school. Today psychologists recognize other types of intelligence also, such as being imaginative and adapting well to the environment, or having practical intelligence.

A particularly relevant personality dimension is a person's propensity for taking risks. A cautious, conservative person typically opts for a low-risk solution. An extremely cautious person may avoid making major decisions for fear of being wrong. Organizational pressures can also influence a person's propensity for risk taking. In a study conducted of the risk-taking attitudes of commercial loan officers in Norwest banks, a key finding indicated that company pressures for profitability appeared to influence the risk ratings borrowers received. Newer borrowers were more likely to receive overly favorable risk ratings by the loan officers. Also, larger loans tended to receive overly favorable assessments.[9]

In addition to being related to risk taking, cautiousness and conservatism influence **decisiveness**, the extent to which a person makes up his or her mind

intuition

An experience-based way of knowing or reasoning in which weighing and balancing evidence are done unconsciously and automatically.

145

decisiveness

The extent to which a person makes up his or her mind promptly and prudently.

promptly and prudently. Good decision makers, by definition, are decisive. Take the quiz presented in Exhibit 6-3 to examine your degree of decisiveness.

Perfectionism exerts a notable impact on decision making. People who seek the perfect solution to a problem are usually indecisive because they hesitate to accept the fact that a particular alternative is good enough. Self-efficacy, the feeling of being an effective and competent person on a specific task, also has an influence. Researchers note, for example, that having the right amount of gall contributes to innovative thinking.[10]

Rigid people encounter difficulty identifying problems and gathering alternative solutions. Mentally flexible people perform well in these areas. Optimism versus pessimism is another relevant personality dimension. Optimists are more likely to find solutions than pessimists are. Pessimists are more likely to give up searching, because they perceive situations as being hopeless.

Cognitive (or traditional) intelligence carries a profound influence in decision-making effectiveness. In general, intelligent and well-educated people are more likely to identify problems and make sound decisions than are those who have less intelligence and education. A notable exception applies, however. Some intelligent, well-educated people have such a fondness for collecting facts and analyzing them that they suffer from "analysis paralysis." One plant manager put it this way: "I'll never hire a genius again. They dazzle you with facts, figures, and computer graphics. But when they get through with their analysis, they still haven't solved the problem." An effective manager makes it clear to team members that decision making is more important than data collection. A manager can convey this message by acting as a good model.[11]

Emotional Intelligence

How effective you are in managing your feelings and reading other people can affect the quality of your decision making. For example, if you cannot control

EXHIBIT 6-3

How Decisive Are You?

Answer the following questions by placing a check in the appropriate space: N = never; R = rarely; Oc = occasionally; Of = often.

		N	R	Oc	Of
1.	Do you let the opinions of others influence your decisions?	—	—	—	—
2.	Do you procrastinate when it's time to make a decision?	—	—	—	—
3.	Do you let others make your decisions for you?	—	—	—	—
4.	Have you missed out on an opportunity because you couldn't make a decision?	—	—	—	—
5.	After reaching a decision do you have second thoughts?	—	—	—	—
6.	Did you hesitate while answering these questions?	—	—	—	—

Scoring and interpretation: Score one point for each "often" response, two points for each "occasionally," three points for each "rarely," and four points for each "never."

19–24   You are very decisive and probably have no problem assuming responsibility for the choices you make.

13–18   Decision making is difficult for you. You need to work at being more decisive.

12 or   You are going to have a big problem unless you learn to overcome your timidity. When a decision has to be made, face up to it and do it!

Source: Adapted from Roger Fritz, "A Systematic Approach to Problem Solving and Decision Making," *Supervisory Management*, March 1993, p. 4. Reprinted with permission of the American Management Association.

your anger you are likely to make decisions motivated by retaliation, hostility, and revenge. An example would be shouting and swearing at your team leader because of a work assignment you received. **Emotional intelligence** refers to qualities such as understanding one's own feelings, empathy for others, and the regulation of emotion to enhance living. This type of intelligence generally affects the ability to connect with people and understand their emotions. If you cannot read the emotions of others you are liable to make some bad decisions involving people, such as pushing your boss too hard to grant a request. Emotional intelligence contains five key factors, all of which can influence the quality of our decisions:[12]

1. *Self-awareness:* The ability to understand your moods, emotions, and needs, as well as their impact on others. Self-awareness also includes using intuition to make decisions you can live with happily. (A manager with good self-awareness knows whether he is pushing group members too hard.)
2. *Self-regulation:* The ability to control impulsiveness, calming down anxiety, and reacting with appropriate anger to situations. (A manager with high self-regulation would not suddenly decide to drop a project because she found the work frustrating.)
3. *Motivation:* A passion to work for reasons in addition to money or status. Also, drive, persistence, and optimism when faced with setbacks. (A manager with this type of motivation would make the decision to keep trying when faced with a serious obstacle such as a drastic budget cut.)
4. *Empathy:* The ability to understand and respond to the unspoken feelings of others. Also, the skill to respond to people according to their emotional reactions. (A manager with empathy would take into account the most likely reaction of group members before making a decision affecting them. Remember the manager who relocated the company to a rural area and lost some key personnel because of his decision?)
5. *Social skill:* Competency in managing relationships and building networks of support, and having positive relationships with people. (A manager with social skill would decide to use a method of persuasion that is likely to work with a particular group.)

Quality and Accessibility of Information

Reaching an effective decision usually requires high-quality, valid information. The ability to supply managers with high-quality information forms the major justification for information systems. Accessibility may be even more important than quality in determining which information is used or not used. Sometimes it takes so much time and effort to search for quality information that the manager relies on lower-quality information that is close at hand. One manager was researching the potential market for transformers in Ireland. After three hours of making telephone calls and digging through search engines without finding the information he needed, the manager finally relied on 10-year-old information his predecessor had used.

Closely related to quality and accessibility of information is the tendency to be influenced by the first information we receive when attempting to solve a problem or make a decision. **Anchoring** occurs during decision making when the mind gives too much weight to the first information it receives. Initial impressions, estimates, or data hold back, or anchor, later thoughts and judgments.[13] The manager who used the old information about the market for transformers in Ireland might be overly influenced by that information. Having been received first,

emotional intelligence

The ability to connect with people and understand their emotions.

anchoring

In the decision-making process, placing too much value on the first information received and ignoring later information.

the anchored information becomes the standard against which to judge other information. When an assistant brings in more current information about the Irish market for transformers that indicates a smaller market, the manager might think, "This information with the lower estimate is less important than the information I already have." Anchoring can therefore lead to wasting useful information received after the first information.

Another decision-making trap is overconfidence. The risk here comes from associating confidence with accuracy. The problem then arises because accuracy reflects what we know, whereas confidence reflects what we think we know. You can test your opinions by searching for information that challenges your beliefs or facts as a way to help combat the overconfidence trap and thereby avoid the natural tendency to look only for supporting information.[14]

Political Considerations

Under ideal circumstances, managers make organizational decisions on the basis of the objective merits of competing alternatives. In reality, many decisions are based on political considerations, such as favoritism, alliances, or the desire of the decision maker to stay in favor with people who wield power.

Political factors sometimes influence which data are given serious consideration in evaluating alternatives. The decision maker may select data that support the position of an influential person whom he or she is trying to please. For instance, one financial analyst, asked to investigate the cost-effectiveness of the firm owning a corporate jet, gave considerable weight to the "facts" supplied by a manufacturer of corporate jets. This information allowed her to justify the expense of purchasing the plane.

The *status quo trap* ties decisions to political factors. Failure to challenge the status quo often stems from worry that being critical will invite criticism from key people. Breaking away from the status quo requires action, and when we take action, we take responsibility, thus opening ourselves up to criticism.[15] A barrier many sales representatives face in selling against a dominant product in the industry results from managers' fear of being criticized if the new product fails. As one systems administrator said, "You can never get fired for buying Cisco." (The implication is that if the manager bought Internet equipment from a smaller competitor, he would risk being reprimanded.)

A study of the effectiveness of strategic decisions compared those made rationally versus those made mostly on the basis of politics. *Politics* as measured in this study referred to factors such as people being more concerned about their own goals than those of the organization, and the use of power and influence with group members. The study found that managers who collected information and used analytical techniques made more effective decisions than those who did not. It also found that managers who used power or pushed hidden agendas (both political tactics) were less effective than those who did not.[16] So in this study, political factors hampered good decision making. On the other hand, a person with professional integrity arrives at what he or she thinks is the best decision and then makes a diligent attempt to convince management of the objective merits of that solution.

Degree of Uncertainty

The more certain a decision maker is of the outcome of a decision, the more calmly and confidently the person will make the decision. Degree of certainty is divided into three categories: certainty, risk, and uncertainty. A condition of certainty exists when the facts are well known and the outcome can be predicted accurately. A retail store manager might predict with certainty that more hours of operation will lead to more sales. It might be uncertain, however, whether the increased sales would cover the increased expenses.

A condition of risk exists when a decision must be made based on incomplete, but accurate, factual information. Managers frequently use quantitative techniques to make decisions under conditions of risk. Suppose a promoter schedules a tour for a popular singing group. Some statistical information about costs and past ticket sales would be available. The promoter can, to an extent, calculate the risk by studying factual information from the past.

Effective managers often accept a condition of risk. A calculated risk is where the potential return is well worth the cost that will be incurred if the effort fails. Ronald L. Zarella, a General Motors marketing executive, was willing to take the risk several years ago of launching the Catera, a sporty new Cadillac designed to appeal to a hipper consumer group. The Catera has been a moderate success, thereby vindicating Zarella's risk-taking behavior.

Crisis and Conflict

In a crisis, many decision makers panic. They become less rational and more emotional than they would in a calm environment. Decision makers who are adversely affected by crisis perceive it to be a stressful event. As a consequence, they concentrate poorly, use poor judgment, and think impulsively. Under crisis, some managers do not bother dealing with differences of opinion because they are under so much pressure. A smaller number of managers perceive a crisis as an exciting challenge that energizes them toward their best level of problem solving and decision making. Larry Weinbach, the Unisys chief executive, is such a manager. He welcomed the opportunity to bring a failing organization back to health.

A recommendation for becoming more adept at making decisions under crisis conditions is to anticipate crises.[17] Visualize ahead of time how you will react to the situation. Visualization serves somewhat as a rehearsal for the real event. A hospital administrator might think to herself, "Here is what I would do if a patient dies during routine surgery, and the media grab hold of the story."

Conflict relates to crisis because both can be an emotional experience. When conflict is not overwhelming, and is directed at real issues, not personalities, it can be an asset to decision making. By virtue of opposing sides expressing different points of view, problems can be solved more thoroughly, which leads to better decisions. One study analyzed strategic decision making by top management teams in both the food-processing and furniture-making industries. The researchers found that the quality of a decision appears to improve with the introduction of conflict. However, the conflict often had the negative side effect of creating antagonistic relationships among some members of the management team.[18]

Values of the Decision Maker

Values influence decision making at every step. Ultimately, all decisions are based on values. A manager who places a high value on the personal welfare of employees tries to avoid alternatives that create hardship for workers and implements decisions in ways that lessen turmoil. Another value that significantly influences decision making is the pursuit of excellence. A manager who embraces the pursuit of excellence will search for the high-quality alternative solution.

Attempting to preserve the status quo is a value held by many managers, as well as others. People tend to cling to the status quo because by not taking action they can prevent making a bad decision.[19] If you value the status quo too highly, you may fail to make a decision that could bring about major improvements. At one company, the vice president of human resources received numerous inquiries about when the firm would begin offering benefits for domestic partners (of the opposite or same sex). The vice president reasoned that since the vast majority of employees rated the benefit package highly, a change was not needed. A few employees took their complaints about "biased benefits" to the CEO. The vice president of human resources was then chastised by the CEO for not suggesting an initiative that would keep the company in the forefront of human resources management. As you can see, preserving the status quo can sometimes lead to procrastination.

Procrastination

procrastinate

To delay in taking action without a valid reason.

Many people are poor decision makers because they **procrastinate**, or delay taking action without a valid reason. Procrastination results in indecisiveness and inaction and is a major cause of self-defeating behavior. Procrastination is a deeply ingrained behavior pattern. Yet research suggests it can be overcome by learning how to become self-disciplined.[20] Part of the process involves setting goals for overcoming procrastination and conquering the problem in small steps. For example, a person might first practice making a deadline for a decision over a minor activity such as ordering a box of copier paper. We will return to the problem of procrastination in Chapter 17.

Although too much procrastination may interfere with effective decision making, rapid decision making is not always the most effective. A recent survey (http://www.kepner-tregoe.com) concludes that decision making in the digital age is faster but not always better. When too much emphasis is placed on speed, financial data become less reliable, customer service might be compromised, and productivity suffers. Furthermore, critical information may not be shared, alternative solutions are dismissed too readily, and risks are ignored. Effective decision making still requires careful reflection, and approval from higher-level managers, and considerable politics to gain alliances.[21] Good decision makers recognize the balance between procrastination and impulsiveness.

Up to this point we have explored how decisions are made and characteristics that influence the decision-making situation. The accompanying Management in Action describes a person who is skilled at making tough decisions.

4

Understand the nature of creativity and how it contributes to managerial work.

CREATIVITY IN MANAGERIAL WORK

creativity

The process of developing novel ideas that can be put into action.

Creativity is an essential part of problem solving and decision making. To be creative is to see new relationships and produce imaginative solutions. **Creativity** can be defined simply as the process of developing novel ideas that can be put into action. By emphasizing the application of ideas, creativity is closely linked to innovation. To be innovative, a person must produce a new product, service, process, or procedure.

Without some creativity a manager cannot solve complex problems or contribute to any type of organizational breakthroughs. A new perspective on creativity helps illustrate the point that it is not a rarified talent of the privileged few.

Management *in Action*

C r a i g   C o n w a y   M a k e s   T o u g h   D e c i s i o n s   a t   P e o p l e S o f t

The rise and fall and rise again of enter-prise software developer PeopleSoft, Inc. is a story of a contrast in personalities. On the one hand is David A. Duffield, the founder and chief executive officer for 11 years. He established a friendly culture for employees and customers alike. Duffield wore comfy sweaters, signed e-mail with his initials DAD, and sup-ported a rock band comprised of employees. The company encouraged customers to vote on features they wanted to see in the next round of products.

PeopleSoft pioneered the market for pack-aged software that managed human resources. The company then added programs to handle finances, manufacturing, and inventory. Duffield led PeopleSoft up a growth curve that elevated its stock price, only to see its dominance end as the stock tumbled in 1999 when the market for giant corporate software packages flattened.

Tough guy and president, current CEO Craig A. Conway is forging a comeback for PeopleSoft. When Duffield hired Conway to run the company in 1999, he gave his succes-sor free rein to overhaul the company. Conway moved swiftly. Six of the company's top-level managers quit within six months. Customers who had never been asked to pay their bills on time started to receive reminders. On average, customers were taking 103 days between sale and payment. With pressure from Conway, the gap was reduced to 81 days. The company's profits and stock price both rose suddenly.

Much of PeopleSoft's growth has come from attracting new customers, rather than selling more software to companies that bought before. Conway's focus on new prod-uct development led to an array of new prod-ucts built for the Internet. Most of the new customers were attracted to these products. Conway also spearheaded a move to purchase Vantive Corporation, the second-largest maker of customer-management software, placing PeopleSoft directly in a hot software market. "I have to credit Conway with seeing the potential and bringing an intensity and focus that was lacking," says analyst Charles I. Phillips of Morgan Stanley Dean Witter.

"I would like to pretend that there's some secret formula for turning around a company," says Conway. "But there isn't. You just keep solving problems. You keep working your way through an equation until you're finished."

To bring PeopleSoft to a state of full recovery, Conway performs a balancing act. He keeps parts of Duffield's culture that make sense, like the pep rallies at a theater. However, the sloppiness that had gone unnoticed two years ago is no longer tolerated under Con-way's watch. By mid-2001, PeopleSoft was one of a handful of high-tech companies whose profits exceeded the expectation of Wall Street analysts. Furthermore, its stock tripled during a period when the average high-tech stock plunged 31 percent.

Source: "PeopleSoft's Hard Guy: By Bringing Discipline to the Company, CEO Conway Has Pulled It Back from the Brink," *Business Week*, January 15, 2001, pp. 76–77; "People Soft Avoids Tech Wreck," The Associated Press, May 27, 2001.

Stanford University creativity expert Michael L. Ray contends that creativity is closely tied to taking your work seriously. Ray describes creativity in these words:

When you're doing something that's really meaningful to you, that takes you to the core of who you are, when you're so involved in something that an earthquake could happen and you wouldn't even notice it, that's creativity. When you make the perfect golf shot, when you say exactly the right thing, when you hold a meeting that works especially well, that's creativity. Creativity is continuously being yourself and doing your work—and by that I mean work with a capital *W*, your purpose in life.[22]

Our discussion of managerial creativity focuses on the creative personality, the necessary conditions for creativity, the creative organization, creativity programs, and suggestions for becoming more creative.

Creative Aspects of a Manager's Job

A manager's workday consists of a collection of miscellaneous activities, from holding scheduled meetings and doing analytical work on a computer to engaging in impromptu conversations. Managers jump from task to task and from person to person. To fashion order from this potential chaos requires creative problem solving. Managers can display creativity in the way they arrange and rearrange, juggle schedules, collect and disseminate information and ideas, make assignments, and lead people.

An important point about creativity in managerial work is that many successful new business ideas are straightforward and uncomplicated. Examples include potato chips in a can (Pringles), mortgage brokering, and a gloved sweatshirt. Can you think of another simple, breakthrough idea in business?

The Creative Personality

Creative people tend to be more emotionally open and flexible than their less-creative counterparts. People who rarely exhibit creative behavior suffer from "hardening of the categories" and cannot overcome the traditional way of looking at things. In business jargon, creative people can *think outside the box*, or get beyond the usual constraints when solving problems.

Yet another way of characterizing creative thinkers is that they *break the rules*. An unusual example took place in relation to paying life insurance benefits. The rules say that the company pays benefits *after* a person dies. Yet Living Benefits, Inc., a New Mexico company, developed the idea of *viatical settlements*, the purchase of life insurance policies from terminally ill people. The policies are purchased at a discount, and the company collects the face amount of the policy when the person dies. The longer the person lives, the poorer the investment. Assume that a man with lung cancer is slowly dying. He holds a $300,000 life insurance policy and needs cash now to pay living expenses. A company such as Living Benefits buys the rights to his policy for $200,000. When the man dies, the company collects the $300,000 from the life insurance company. This example illustrates breaking the rules to meet an identified need.

Creative people also more easily make a paradigm shift. A **paradigm** consists of the perspectives and ways of doing things that are typical of a given context. For example, top management at Toys R Us was able to shift away from the paradigm that only Japanese-made toys can be sold in Japan.

Closely related to making paradigm shifts is the ability to think laterally. **Lateral thinking** spreads out to find many alternative solutions to a problem. **Vertical thinking**, in contrast, is an analytical, logical process that results in few answers. A problem requiring lateral thinking would be to specify a variety of

paradigm

The perspectives and ways of doing things that are typical of a given context.

lateral thinking

A thinking process that spreads out to find many alternative solutions to a problem.

vertical thinking

An analytical, logical process that results in few answers.

ways in which a small-business owner could increase income. A vertical thinking problem would be to calculate how much more money the small-business owner needs each month to earn a 10 percent profit.

Lateral thinking is thus divergent, while vertical thinking is convergent. Creative people think divergently. They can expand the number of alternatives to a problem, thus moving away from a single solution. Yet the creative thinker also knows when it is time to think convergently. For example, the divergent thinker might generate 25 ways to reduce costs. Yet at some point he or she will have to converge toward choosing the best of several cost-cutting procedures. For the lateral thinking problems presented next, compare your solutions to the ones given at the end of the chapter.[23]

> Kurt and Jessica were co-owners of a building, with both their names on the mortgage. The two people ended their business relationship, and decided to split their assets. Kurt wanted ownership of the building, and Jessica agreed. However, Kurt had to pay Jessica $25,000 for her share of the building. To come up with the $25,000 he needed a second mortgage. Five consecutive banks told Kurt the same story, "We cannot lend you a second mortgage so long as Jessica's name is on the first mortgage." Kurt replied, "Please help me. Jessica's name stays on the mortgage until I give her the $25,000." After weeks of mulling over the problem, Kurt finally solved his Catch-22 problem. What did he do?

Conditions Necessary for Creativity

Well-known creativity researcher Teresa M. Amabile summarized 22 years of research about the conditions necessary for creativity in organizations. Creativity takes place when three components join together: expertise, creative-thinking skills, and motivation.[24] Expertise refers to the necessary knowledge to put facts together. The more facts floating around in your head, the more likely you are to combine them in some useful way. The brothers who developed the gloved sweatshirt had some knowledge about how certain people need to keep their hands warm yet still have their fingers free. They also needed to know about retailing, along with many other factors.

Creative-thinking refers to how flexibly and imaginatively individuals approach problems. If you know how to keep digging for alternatives, and to avoid getting stuck in the status quo, your chances of being creative multiply. Persevering, or sticking with a problem to a conclusion, is essential for finding creative solutions. A few rest breaks to gain a fresh perspective may be helpful, but the creative person keeps coming back until a solution emerges. Quite often an executive will keep sketching different organization charts on paper or on the computer before the right one surfaces that will help the firm run smoothly.

The right type of motivation is the third essential ingredient for creative thought. A fascination with, or passion for, the task is more important than searching for external rewards. People will be the most creative when they are motivated primarily by the satisfaction and challenge of the work itself. Dineh Mohajer is the creative force behind Hard Candy, the cosmetics company. She became successful as a by-product of being passionate about making her own nail polish. Her intent was not to find a hobby that could lead to fame and fortune.

In addition to the internal conditions that foster creativity, two factors outside the person have a significant effect. An environmental need must stimulate the setting of a goal, which is another way of saying, "Necessity is the mother of invention." For example, an inventory control manager might be told, "We've got too much inventory in the warehouse. Reduce it by 75 percent, but do not lose money for us." No standard solution is available. The manager sets the goal of reducing the inventory, including working with the marketing department to accomplish the feat.

Enough conflict and tension to put people on edge also foster creativity. Creativity expert Mike Vance says, "Almost any company can benefit from irritants on the staff. Don't put too much emphasis on harmony—that can undermine the commitment to creativity."[25] In the inventory reduction problem, an irritant might challenge people by declaring that selling the old inventory through the same channels won't work. A new channel of distribution must therefore be sought. Being challenged in this way can stimulate creative thinking.

The Creative Organization

Another perspective on the conditions necessary for creativity is to recognize that certain managerial and organizational practices foster creativity. The most important characteristic of the creative organization is an atmosphere that encourages creative expression. A manager who encourages imaginative and original thinking, and does not punish people for making honest mistakes, is likely to receive creative ideas from group members. At the same time, supervision that is supportive of employees encourages creative expression. Among the specifics of being supportive are showing concern for employees' feelings and needs, and encouraging them to voice their concerns. It is also important for the supervisor to provide feedback that is informational rather than harsh, and to help employees with personal development.[26]

Six categories of activities summarize much of what is known about what managers can do to establish a creative atmosphere, as described next. Much of this information stems from Amabile's research, yet her findings have been supported and duplicated by others as well.[27]

1. *Challenge.* Giving employees the right type and amount of challenge is part of providing a creative atmosphere. Employees should be neither bored with the simplicity of the task, nor overwhelmed by its difficulty. A good creativity-inducer for a new sales representative might be for the manager to say, "How would you like to go through our ex-customer file, and attempt to bring back 5 percent of them? It would have a great impact on profits."

2. *Freedom.* To be creative, employees should have the freedom to choose how to accomplish a goal, but not which goal to accomplish. For example, creativity would be encouraged if a manager said to a group member, "I would like to improve our Internet service, and you figure out how." A creative result would be less likely if the manager said, "I would like you to improve our service, and you decide which service to improve and how to do it."

3. *Resources.* Managers need to allot time and money carefully to enhance creativity. Tight deadlines can get the creative juices flowing, but people still need enough time to let creative ideas swirl around in their heads. Employees also need large enough budgets to purchase the equipment and information necessary to get the job done. At one company, top management asked employees to be more creative and at the same time canceled subscriptions to trade magazines and limited book purchases. The result was that many readily accessible sources of good ideas dried up.

4. *Organizational support.* The organization as well as the manager must support creativity. Support can take such forms as giving recognition and financial rewards for successful new ideas. 3M has long been recognized as an organization that supports creativity. One of the leading companywide programs lets workers invest 15 percent of their time on their own projects. Such projects do not have to fit into the strategic business plan. One of the most successful projects to come from the program is Post-it® notes, a top-selling product in the United States.

5. *Encouragement of risk taking.* Employees are sometimes hesitant to make creative suggestions for fear of being zapped if their new idea fails when implemented. In contrast, if risk taking is encouraged by informing employees that it is okay to fail, more people will take chances. Neville Isdell, president of Coca-Cola's Greater Europe Group illustrates this point as follows: "We celebrated the 10th anniversary of the launch of the New Coke. We celebrated the failure because it led to fundamental learning and showed that it's okay to fail."[28]

6. *Positive managerial relationships.* A study conducted with 191 technical and professional employees in the research and development division at a U.S. chemical corporation found that a positive relationship with one's manager was associated with higher creativity, as measured by higher creativity ratings from the manager and more patent-disclosure forms. Receiving encouragement is part of a positive relationship. For people to sustain creative effort, they need to feel that their work matters to the employer. Just as the elementary school teacher says to the eight-year-old, "I love your drawing. Keep up the good work," the manager might say, "I love your idea for reducing shipping costs. Keep up the good work."

7. *Greater diversity in groups.* Managers can also cultivate creativity by establishing a group of people with diverse backgrounds. Intellectual diversity, in particular, fans the fire of creativity. A variety of perspectives leads to thinking outside the box and challenging existing paradigms. At the Xerox Palo Alto Research Center, an artist-in-residence program pairs an artist with a computer scientist. This diversity has resulted in several breakthroughs in multimedia technology.

8. *A cause, not a business.* When employees believe they are part of a grand purpose or cause, they are more likely to innovate. Employees at a pharmaceutical firm pursuing an anticancer drug might readily develop a cause-mentality. The same fervor is possible in other types of businesses. David Pottruck, the president and co-CEO of discount broker Charles Schwab, describes the cause that fires up Schwab employees: "We are the guardians of our customers' financial dreams."[29]

Organizational Programs for Improving Creativity

Another aspect of the creative organization is formal programs or mechanisms for creativity improvement. Four such mechanisms include creativity training, brainstorming, idea quotas, and suggestion programs.

Describe organizational programs for improving creativity.

Creativity Training
About 30 percent of medium-sized and large U.S. firms provide some sort of creativity training. An outstanding example is the Center for Creativity and Innovation at DuPont, which holds numerous events, including seminars on creative

pet-peeve technique

A creativity training (or problem-solving) exercise in which the group thinks up as many complaints as possible about every facet of the department.

brainstorming

A group method of solving problems, gathering information, and stimulating creative thinking. The basic technique is to generate numerous ideas through unrestrained and spontaneous participation by group members.

thinking techniques. A representative training exercise used in many firms is the **pet-peeve technique**. The group thinks up as many complaints as possible about every facet of the department. The group is encouraged to take the views of external and internal customers, competitors, and suppliers. The group is also encouraged to throw in some imaginary complaints. "No holds barred" is the rule. A complaint might be "We set up a work schedule to suit our own convenience, not that of the customer." In addition, participants can solicit feedback on themselves from coworkers or from the people they serve. The technique works best in an atmosphere of trust, and requires diplomacy when giving constructive feedback.

As with many creativity training exercises, the pet-peeve technique loosens people up and provides information for improving operations. Participants can laugh at their own weaknesses in a friendly setting. Laughter is important because humor facilitates creativity. The pet-peeve technique can also be used outside the training program, as a method for improving productivity, quality, and service.

Brainstorming

The best-known method of improving creativity is **brainstorming.** This technique is a method of problem solving carried out by a group. Group members spontaneously generate numerous solutions to a problem, without being discouraged or controlled. Brainstorming produces many ideas; it is not a technique for working out details. People typically use brainstorming when looking for tentative solutions to nontechnical problems. In recent years, however, many information systems specialists have used brainstorming to improve computer programs and systems. By brainstorming, people improve their ability to think creatively. To achieve the potential advantages of brainstorming, the session must be conducted properly. Another suggestion is to allow natural light into the brainstorming work space. A sterile, windowless room may not be conducive to idea generation.[30] Exhibit 6-4 presents the rules for conducting a brainstorming session.

Some types of business problems are well suited to brainstorming, such as coming up with a name for a new sports car, developing an idea for a corporate

EXHIBIT 6-4

Rules for Conducting a Brainstorming Session

RULE 1	Enroll five to eight participants. If you have too few people, you lose the flood of ideas; if you have too many, members feel that their ideas are not important, or too much chatter may result.
RULE 2	Give everybody the opportunity to generate alternative solutions to the problem. Have them call out these alternatives spontaneously. One useful modification of this procedure is for people to express their ideas one after another, to decrease possible confusion.
RULE 3	Do not allow criticism or value judgments during the brainstorming session. Make all suggestions welcome. Above all, members should not laugh derisively or make sarcastic comments about other people's ideas.
RULE 4	Encourage freewheeling. Welcome bizarre ideas. It is easier to tone down an idea than it is to think one up.
RULE 5	Strive for quantity rather than quality. The probability of discovering really good ideas increases in proportion to the number of ideas generated.
RULE 6	Encourage members to piggyback, or build, on the ideas of others.
RULE 7	Record each idea or tape-record the session. Written notes should not identify the author of an idea because participants may worry about saying something foolish.
RULE 8	After the brainstorming session, edit and refine the list of ideas and choose one or two for implementation.

logo, identifying ways to attract new customers, and making concrete suggestions for cost cutting. Brainstorming can also be conducted through e-mail, generally referred to as electronic brainstorming. In brainstorming by e-mail, group members simultaneously enter their suggestions into a computer. The ideas are distributed to the screens of other group members. Or ideas can be sent back at different times to a facilitator who passes the contributions along to other members. In either approach, although group members do not talk to each other, they are still able to build on each other's ideas and combine ideas. Electronic brainstorming researcher Keng L. Siau suggests that brainstorming via e-mail can increase both the quantity and quality of ideas. When participants do not face each other directly, they can concentrate more on the creativity task at hand, and less on the interpersonal aspects of interaction.[31]

Idea Quotas

An increasingly popular technique for encouraging creative input from employees is to set quotas for employee suggestions. Being creative therefore becomes a concrete work goal. Dana Corp., for example, sets a quota of two ideas per employee per month. All employees are involved, including the CEO and entry-level workers in manufacturing. Dana management favors ideas that help streamline problem areas. Employees are asked to make suggestions about quality, customer service, production control, office efficiency, and security. Monthly raffles are held to reward ideas with cash. Noncash rewards are also given. Employees receive a leather jacket for having submitted 100 ideas. Another part of the program is a sincere effort by management to implement 80 percent of the ideas.

Since Dana introduced the idea–quota system in one division seven years ago, the number of employee ideas from that division's 3,600 employees increased from 9,000 to 64,000. Division profitability has increased by 40 percent, and morale is at an all-time high.[32] We can assume that at least some of the increase in profitability and morale is attributed to the idea quotas.

Suggestion Programs

To encourage creative thinking, companies throughout the world use **suggestion programs**. They are a formal method for collecting and analyzing employee suggestions about processes, policies, products, and services. Suggestion programs have been around for many years. Unlike idea quotas, suggestion programs rely on voluntary submissions. Typically, the employee who makes a suggestion that is implemented receives a percentage of the savings resulting from it. Useful suggestions save money, earn money, or increase safety or quality. Pollution Prevention Pays is the name of a topic-specific suggestion system at 3M. Since its inception 25 years ago, some 4,200 projects have saved the company $750 million and kept 65,000 tons of pollution from entering the environment.[33] A more typical suggestion program is the one at American Airlines in which a group of mechanics received a $37,500 award for developing a tamper-proof security door.

Committees evaluate submissions and make awards in suggestion programs. These programs foster creativity by offering financial rewards and by conferring prestige on employees whose ideas are implemented. In addition, suggestion programs help get employees involved in the success of their organization.

Suggestion programs are sometimes criticized because they collect loads of trivial suggestions and pay small awards just to humor employees. One employee, for example, was paid $50 for suggesting that the firm dust light bulbs more frequently to increase illumination.

suggestion program

A formal method for collecting and analyzing employees' suggestions about processes, policies, products, and services.

Appropriate Physical Surroundings

Providing the correct physical environment for facilitating creativity merits increased attention. Consider how a room with a window might have a positive impact on creativity, as previously mentioned, and how open office space facilitates problem solving, as noted in the chapter opener. The general idea is that creativity is facilitated when the physical environment allows for the flow of ideas.

Sun Microsystems provides a representative example of how physical space can be configured to enhance collaboration, including the exchange of ideas. Consultants observed that engineers tended to gather briefly in office doorways and kitchens, and then walk away. This observation spawned the idea that physical spaces should be designed that encourage informal conversations but discourage the workers dispersing. As a result "Forum" spaces extend from the kitchens as open areas designed to encourage informal, chance encounters. Conference rooms are available for spontaneous meetings. Wooden benches, tables, and chairs for reflection and quiet work are provided on company grounds. "Sun rooms" are designed to allow ideas to incubate, and also include white boards along with recreational equipment like Ping-Pong tables.[34]

On the other hand, many workers need private space to do their best creative thinking. After developing a creative idea, the person might want to refine the idea by interacting with others. Yet the time for independent thinking, away from the buzz of the office, is important. Microsoft makes sure that employees required to do creative work have access to private space, as well as the opportunity for group interaction.

Self-Help Techniques for Improving Creativity

In addition to participating in organizational programs for creativity improvement, you can help yourself become more creative. Becoming a more creative problem solver and decision maker requires that you increase the flexibility of your thinking. Reading about creativity improvement or attending one or two brainstorming sessions is insufficient. You must also practice the methods described in the following sections. As with any serious effort at self-improvement, you must exercise the self-discipline to implement these suggestions regularly. Creative people must also be self-disciplined to carefully concentrate on going beyond the obvious in solving problems.

Implement several suggestions for becoming a more creative problem solver.

Ten Specific Creativity-Building Suggestions

To develop habits of creative thinking, you must regularly practice the suggestions described in the list that follows.[35]

1. Keep track of your original ideas by maintaining an idea notebook or computer file. Few people have such uncluttered minds that they can recall all their past flashes of insight when they need them.
2. Stay current in your field. Having current facts at hand gives you the raw material to link information creatively. (In practice, creativity usually takes the form of associating ideas that are unassociated, such as associating the idea of selling movie tickets with the idea of selling through vending machines.)
3. Listen to other people as another medium for gathering creative ideas you can use. Creative people rarely believe they have all the answers. The CEO of the company that includes Chili's restaurants introduced the fajita because he listened to the menu suggestion of a busperson.
4. Learn to think in the five senses, or in various combinations thereof, because

it enhances your perceptiveness of what might work. The concept is particularly applicable if you are developing a product or service that would be experienced in many ways, such as a restaurant, nightclub, or clothing. Suppose you were trying to think of a creative idea for an office party. Using the five-senses approach you would imagine what the setting would look like, how it would sound, what the food would taste like, how the decorations would feel, and the aroma of the party.

5. Improve your sense of humor, including your ability to laugh at your own mistakes. Humor helps reduce stress and tensions, and you will be more creative when you are relaxed.

6. Adopt a risk-taking attitude when you try to find creative solutions. You will inevitably fail a few times.

7. Develop a creative mental set; allow the foolish side of you to emerge. Creativity requires a degree of intellectual playfulness and immaturity. Many creative people are accomplished practical jokers.

8. Identify the times when you are most creative and attempt to accomplish most of your creative work during that period. Most people are at their peak of creative productivity after ample rest, so try to work on your most vexing problems at the start of the workday. Schedule routine decision making and paperwork for times when your energy level is lower than average.

9. Be curious about your environment. The person who routinely questions how things work (or why they do not work) is most likely to have an idea for improvement.

10. When faced with a creativity block, step back from the problem and engage in a less mentally demanding task for a brief pause, or even a day. Sometimes by doing something quite different, your perspective will become clearer and a creative alternative will flash into your head when you return to your problem. Although creative problem solvers are persistent, they will sometimes put a problem away for awhile so they can come back stronger.

Play the Roles of Explorer, Artist, Judge, and Lawyer
One method for improving creativity incorporates many of the suggestions discussed so far. It requires you to adopt four roles in your thinking. First, you must be an explorer. Speak to people in different fields to get ideas you can use. Second, be an artist by stretching your imagination. Strive to spend about 5 percent of your day asking "what if?" questions. For example, an executive in a swimsuit company might ask, "What if the surgeon general decides that since sunbathing causes skin cancer, we have to put warning labels on bathing suits?" Third, know when to be a judge. After developing some wild ideas, evaluate them. Fourth, achieve results with your creative thinking by playing the role of a lawyer. Negotiate and find ways to implement your ideas within your field or place of work. You may spend months or years getting your best ideas implemented.[36]

Despite all the positive things that have been said about creativity, when an organization does not want to disturb the status quo, being creative can work to a person's disadvantage. Also, creativity for its own sake can result in discarding traditional, but useful, ideas.

GROUP PROBLEM SOLVING AND DECISION MAKING   **7**

We have described how individuals go about solving problems and making decisions. However, most major, nonroutine decisions in organizations are made by groups. **Group decisions** result when several people contribute to a final decision.

Appreciate the value and potential limitations of group decision making.

group decision

The process of several people contributing to a final decision.

Because so much emphasis has been placed on teams in organizations and participative decision making, an increasing number of decisions are made by groups rather than individuals. Group decision making is often used in complex and important situations such as:

- Developing a new product, such as a car, or a service such as selling equipment replacement parts over the Internet
- Deciding which employees should be placed on a downsizing list
- Deciding whether to operate a company cafeteria with company personnel or to outsource the activity to a company that specializes in running company cafeterias.

The group problem-solving and decision-making process is similar to the individual model in one important respect. Groups often work on problems by following the decision-making steps shown in Exhibit 6-1. Many groups, however, tend to ignore formal sequencing.

We will examine the advantages and disadvantages of group decision making, describe when it is useful, and present a general problem-solving method for groups.

Advantages and Disadvantages of Group Decision Making

Group decision making offers several advantages over the same activity carried out individually. First, the quality of the decision might be higher because of the combined wisdom of group members. A second benefit is a by-product of the first. Group members evaluate each other's thinking, so major errors are likely to be avoided. The marketing vice president of a company that sells small appliances such as microwave ovens, toasters, and coffee pots decided the company should sell direct through e-commerce. Before asking others to begin implementing the decision, the executive brought up the matter for group discussion. A sales manager in the group pointed out that direct selling would enrage their dealers, thus doing damage to the vast majority of their sales. The marketing vice president then decided she would back off on direct marketing until a new product was developed that would not be sold through dealers.

Third, group decision making is helpful in gaining acceptance and commitment. People who participate in making a decision will often be more committed to the implementation than if they were not consulted. Fourth, groups can help people overcome blocks in their thinking, leading to more creative solutions to problems.

Group decision making also has some notable disadvantages. The group approach consumes considerable time and may result in compromises that do not really solve the problem. An intelligent individual might have the best solution to the problem, and time could be saved by relying on his or her judgment.

The explosion of the space shuttle Challenger presents a serious example of the disadvantages of group decision making. According to several analyses of this incident, NASA managers were so committed to reaching space program objectives that they ignored safety warnings from people both inside and outside the agency. An internal NASA brief reported that astronauts and engineers were concerned about agency management's groupthink mentality. (This term will be explained later.) Furthermore, the brief characterized NASA managers as having the tendency not to reverse decisions or heed the advice of people outside management. (The analysis of the style was made several years before the Challenger explosion.)[37]

Seriously flawed group decisions have occurred so frequently in government and business that they have been extensively analyzed and researched. Well-publicized flawed group decisions include the arms-for-hostage deal (an illegal arms sale to Iran to fund Contras in Nicaragua) and the decision by Chrysler Corporation executives to sell, as new cars, autos they had personally sampled. The illusion of newness was created by cleaning up the cars and turning back the odometers. Another example of a seriously flawed decision took place at several different telephone companies. The long-distance service of many individuals was switched to another company without the individuals' consent, a practice known as slamming. Several of these companies received heavy fines because of their illegal and unethical decisions.

Flawed decisions of the type just described have generally been attributed to **groupthink**, a psychological drive for consensus at any cost. Groupthink makes group members lose their ability to evaluate bad ideas critically. Glen Whyte believes that many instances of groupthink are caused by decision makers who see themselves as choosing between inevitable losses. The group believes that a sure loss will occur unless action is taken. Caught up in the turmoil of trying to make the best of a bad situation, the group takes a bigger risk than any individual member would.

groupthink
A psychological drive for consensus at any cost.

The arms-for-hostages decision was perceived by those who made it as a choice between losses. The continued captivity of American citizens held hostage by terrorist groups was a certain loss. Making an arms deal with Iran created some hope of averting that loss, although the deal would most likely fail and create more humiliation.[38]

Even though groupthink is classified here as a negative influence on group decision making, one study showed that some aspects of groupthink may facilitate performance. The participants in the study—108 employees who made up 30 teams in five large business firms—answered a questionnaire about crisis events they had faced within the past year. The results surprised researchers: Three symptoms of groupthink combined together enhanced team performance. The three specific symptoms include belief in inherent group morality, illusion of unanimity, and illusion of invulnerability.[39] Apparently having a strong faith in the group was associated with high group performance.

The negative aspects of groupthink can often be avoided if the team leader encourages group members to express doubts and criticisms of proposed solutions. It is helpful to show by example that you are willing to accept criticism. It is also important for someone to play the role of the devil's advocate. This person challenges the thinking of others by asking such questions as, "Why do you think so many consumers are so stupid that they won't recognize they have been switched to another long-distance phone company without their consent?"

When to Use Group Decision Making

Because group decision making takes more time and people than individual decision making, it should not be used indiscriminately. Group decision making should be reserved for nonroutine decisions of reasonable importance. Too many managers use the group method for solving such minor questions as "What should be on the menu at the company picnic?"

Aside from being used to enhance the quality of decisions, group decision making is often used to gain acceptance for a decision. If people contribute to a decision, they are more likely to be committed to its implementation.

A General Method of Group Problem Solving

When workers at any level gather to solve a problem, they typically hold a discussion rather than rely on a formal decision-making technique. These general meetings are likely to produce the best results when they follow the decision-making steps. Exhibit 6-5 recommends steps for conducting group decision making, which are quite similar to the decision-making steps presented in Exhibit 6-1.

In addition, a problem-solving group should also follow suggestions for conducting an effective meeting. Five of these suggestions particularly related to problem solving are:

1. *Have a specific agenda and adhere to it.* Meetings are more productive when an agenda is planned and followed carefully. People should see the agenda in advance so they can prepare for the session.
2. *Rely on qualified members.* Groups often arrive at poor solutions because the contributors do not have the necessary knowledge and interest. An uninformed person is typically a poor decision maker. Also, a person who attends a meeting reluctantly will sometimes agree to any decision just to bring the meeting to a close.
3. *Have the leader share decision-making authority.* A key attribute of an effective problem-solving meeting is a leader who shares authority. Unless authority is shared, the members are likely to believe that the hidden agenda of the meeting is to seek approval for the meeting leader's decision.
4. *Provide summaries for each major point.* Decision-making quality improves when members clearly understand the arguments that have been advanced for and against each alternative. Summarizing major points can help. Summaries also keep the meeting focused on major issues, because minor issues are excluded from the summary.
5. *Build consensus so the decision is more likely to be implemented.* When group decision making is really team decision making, obtaining general agreement is particularly important. The emphasis on a *team* rather than merely on a *group* signals a

EXHIBIT 6-5

Steps for Effective Group Decision Making

1. **Identify the problem.** Describe specifically what the problem is and how it manifests itself.
2. **Clarify the problem.** If group members do not perceive the problem in the same way, they will offer divergent solutions. Make sure everyone shares the same definition of the problem.
3. **Analyze the cause.** To convert "what is" into "what we want," the group must understand the causes of the specific problem and find ways to overcome them.
4. **Search for alternative solutions.** Remember that multiple alternative solutions can be found to most problems.
5. **Select alternatives.** Identify the criteria that solutions must meet, and then discuss the pros and cons of the proposed alternatives. No solution should be laughed at or scorned.
6. **Plan for implementation.** Decide what actions are necessary to carry out the chosen solution.
7. **Clarify the contract.** The contract is a restatement of what group members have agreed to do, and it includes deadlines for accomplishment.
8. **Develop an action plan.** Specify who does what and when to carry out the contract.
9. **Provide evaluation and accountability.** After the plan is implemented, reconvene to discuss its progress and hold people accountable for results that have not been achieved.

Source: Adapted from Andrew E. Schwartz and Joy Levin, "Better Group Decision Making," *Supervisory Management,* June 1990, p. 4.

particular emphasis on members working together smoothly and depending on each other. Consensus is most likely to happen when key points are discussed thoroughly and each member's input is asked for in reference to the point. It also helps to take at least a small part of each member's idea and incorporate it into the final decision. At one company, the group decided not to have a wellness center on company premises. A member from the human resources department was quite disturbed about the decision, and the team needed her concurrence. So the team leader incorporated her suggestion about having a jogging track in the woods near the office, thereby incorporating some of her thinking. The human resources member then supported the group decision.

A Specific Method of Group Problem Solving: The Nominal Group Technique

A manager who must make a decision about an important issue sometimes needs to know what alternatives are available and how people would react to them. An approach called the **nominal group technique (NGT)** has been developed to fit this situation. NGT is a group decision-making technique that follows a highly structured format. The term *nominal* means that, for much of the activity, the participants are a group in name only; they do not interact.

An appropriate candidate for NGT is the problem of deciding which plants of a multiplant firm should be closed because of declining demand for a product. This type of highly sensitive decision elicits many different opinions. Suppose Sherry McDivott, the company president, faces the plant-closing problem. A six-step decision process follows. It uses the nominal-group technique, as summarized in Exhibit 6-6.[40]

1. Group members (called the target group) are selected and assembled. McDivott includes her five top managers, each representing a key function of the business, and informs them in advance of the topic.

nominal group technique (NGT)

A group decision-making technique that follows a highly structured format.

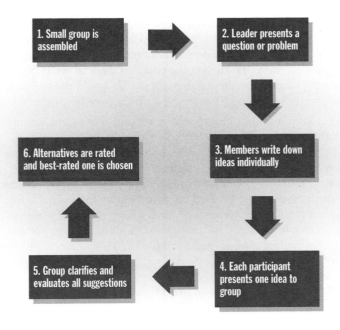

EXHIBIT 6-6

The Nominal Group Technique

Observe that when the group reaches Step 6, the job is completed except for implementation. An important purpose of the NGT is to find a high-quality solution to a problem that will result in an effective decision.

2. The group leader presents a specific question. McDivott tells the group, "Our board of directors says we have to consolidate our operations. Our output isn't high enough to justify keeping five plants open. Whatever we do, we must cut operating expenses by about 20 percent.

    "Your assignment is to develop criteria for choosing which plant to close. However, if the group can think of another way of cutting operating costs by 20 percent, I'll give it some consideration. I also need to know how you feel about the alternative you choose and how our employees might feel."

3. Individual members write down their ideas independently, without speaking to other members. Using notepads, the five managers write down their ideas about reducing operating costs by 20 percent.

4. Each participant, in turn, presents one idea to the group. The group does not discuss the ideas. The administrative assistant summarizes each idea by writing it on a flip chart. Here are some of the group's ideas:

    Alternative A. Close the plant with the most obsolete equipment and facilities. We all know that the Harrisburg plant is running with equipment built about 100 years ago. Close the plant in 60 days. Give employees six months of severance pay and assist them to find new jobs. Transfer the most outstanding staff to our other plants.

    Alternative B. Close the plant with the least flexible, most unproductive workforce. A lot of employees are likely to complain about this type of closing. But the rest of the workforce will get the message that we value productive employees.

    Alternative C. Forget about closing a plant. Instead, take our least productive plant and transfer all its manufacturing to our other four plants. Then, work like fury to get subcontracting business for the emptied-out plant. I think our employees and stockholders will be pleased if we take such a brave stance.

    Alternative D. We need a careful financial analysis of which plant is producing the lowest return on investment of capital, all factors considered. We simply close that plant. Employees will accept this decision because they all know that business is based on financial considerations.

    Alternative E. Closing one plant would be too much of a hardship on one group of people. Let's share the hardship evenly. Cut everybody's pay by 25 percent, eliminate dividends to stockholders, do not replace anybody who quits or retires for the next year, and ask all our suppliers to give us a 10 percent discount. These measures would be the starting point. We could then appoint a committee to look for other savings. If everybody pulls together, morale will be saved.

5. After each group member has presented his or her idea, the group clarifies and evaluates the suggestions. The length of the discussion for each of the ideas varies substantially. For example, the discussion about cutting salaries 25 percent and eliminating dividends lasts only 3 minutes.

6. The meeting ends with a silent, independent rating of the alternatives. The final group decision is the pooled outcome of the individual votes. The target group is instructed to rate each alternative on a 1-to-10 scale, with 10 being the most favorable rating. The ratings that follow are the pooled ratings (the sum of the individual ratings) received for each alternative. (50 represents the maximum score):
    Alternative A, close obsolete plant: 35
    Alternative B, close plant with unproductive workforce: 41

Alternative C, make one plant a subcontractor: 19
Alternative D, close plant with poorest return on investment: 26
Alternative E, cut everybody's pay by 25 percent: 4

McDivott agrees with the group's preference for closing the plant with the least productive, most inflexible workforce. Ultimately, the board accepts Alternative B. The best employees in the factory chosen for closing are offered an opportunity to relocate to another company plant.

NGT is effective because it follows the logic of the problem-solving and decision-making method and allows for group participation. It also provides a discipline and rigor that are often missing in brainstorming.

SUMMARY OF KEY POINTS

1 **Differentiate between nonprogrammed and programmed decisions.** Unique decisions are nonprogrammed decisions, whereas programmed decisions are repetitive or routine, and made according to a specific procedure.

2 **Explain the steps involved in making a nonprogrammed decision.** The recommended steps for solving problems and making nonprogrammed decisions call for a problem solver to identify and diagnose the problem, develop alternative solutions, evaluate the alternatives, choose an alternative, implement the decision, evaluate and control, and repeat the process if necessary.

3 **Understand the major factors that influence decision making in organizations.** People vary in their decision-making ability, and the situation can influence the quality of decisions. Factors that influence the quality of decisions are intuition, personality and cognitive intelligence, emotional intelligence, quality and accessibility of information, political considerations, degree of uncertainty, crisis and conflict, values of the decision maker, and procrastination.

4 **Understand the nature of creativity and how it contributes to managerial work.** Creativity is the process of developing novel ideas that can be put into action. Many aspects of managerial work, including problem solving and establishing effective work groups, require creativity. Creative people are generally more open and flexible than their less creative counterparts. They are also better able to make paradigm shifts, think laterally, and break the rules.

Creativity takes place when three components join together: expertise, creative-thinking skills, and internal motivation. Perseverance in digging for a solution is also important, and so is an environmental need that stimu-

lates the setting of a goal. Conflict and tension can also prompt people toward creativity. Certain managerial and organizational practices foster creativity. Above all, the atmosphere must encourage creative expression, including supportive supervision. To establish a creative atmosphere, managers can (a) provide the right amount of job challenge, (b) give freedom on how to reach goals, (c) provide the right resources, (d) support creativity by such means as rewards, (e) encourage risk taking, (f) foster positive and managerial relationships, (g) promote greater diversity in groups, and (h) create a cause, not a business.

5 **Describe organizational programs for improving creativity.** One organizational program for improving creativity is to conduct creativity training, such as a session that uses the pet-peeve technique. Brainstorming is the best-known method of improving creativity. The method can also be conducted by e-mail, known as electronic brainstorming. Giving employees idea quotas often enhances creativity, as do suggestion programs. Physical space should encourage interaction.

6 **Implement several suggestions for becoming a more creative problem solver.** Self-discipline improves creative thinking ability. Creativity-building techniques include staying current in your field, thinking in five senses, improving your sense of humor, and taking risks. A broad approach for improving creativity is to assume the roles of an explorer, artist, judge, and lawyer. Each role relates to a different aspect of creative thinking.

7 **Appreciate the value and potential limitations of group decision making.** Group decision making often results in high-quality solutions, because many people contribute. It also helps people feel more committed to the decision. However, the group approach consumes considerable time, may result in compromise solutions that do not really solve the problem, and may encourage groupthink. Groupthink occurs when consensus becomes so important that group members lose their ability to evaluate ideas. It is likely to occur when decision makers have to choose between inevitable losses. Yet, at times groupthink enhances performance.

General problem-solving groups are likely to produce the best results when the decision-making steps are followed closely. Other steps for conducting an effec-

tive meeting include (1) adhering to an agenda, (2) relying on qualified members, (3) sharing decision-making authority, and (4) providing summaries of major points.

The nominal group technique (NGT) is recommended for a situation in which a manager needs to know what alternatives are available and how people will react to them. Using the technique, a small group of people contribute written thoughts about the problem. Other members respond to their ideas later. Members rate each other's ideas numerically, and the final group decision is the value of the pooled individual votes.

KEY TERMS AND PHRASES

Problem, *138*

Decision, *138*

Nonprogrammed decision, *138*

Programmed decision, *138*

Satisficing decision, *143*

Bounded rationality, *143*

Heuristics, *143*

Intuition, *145*

Decisiveness, *145*

Emotional intelligence, *147*

Anchoring, *147*

Procrastinate, *150*

Creativity, *150*

Paradigm, *152*

Lateral thinking, *152*

Vertical thinking, *152*

Pet-peeve technique, *156*

Brainstorming, *156*

Suggestion program, *157*

Group decision, *160*

Groupthink, *161*

Nominal group technique (NGT), *163*

QUESTIONS

1. Describe a problem the construction manager for a new office building might face, and point to the actual and ideal conditions in relation to this problem.
2. In what way does the use of empowered teams influence the proportion of nonprogrammed decisions made by lower-ranking workers?
3. How might the use of Internet search engines help you make better decisions on the job?
4. Which one of the factors influencing decision making would likely give you the most trouble? What can you do to get this factor more in your favor?
5. Assume that the director of a social agency was exploring different alternatives for decreasing the number of homeless people in the area. Describe how a political factor might influence his or her decision making.
6. What is a potential disadvantage of giving employees prizes, such as a leather jacket for submitting 100 ideas in the idea quota program?
7. Describe the general approach a family of five might take to use the nominal group technique for deciding which vehicle to purchase.

CRITICAL THINKING QUESTIONS

1. Search for an example of a poor decision a company made. Try to uncover what went wrong in their decision-making process.
2. After studying this chapter, do you think a noncreative person can be successful in business? Explain.

SKILL-BUILDING EXERCISE: The Forced-Association Technique

A widely used method for releasing creativity is to make forced associations between the properties of two objects to solve a problem. Apply the method by working in small groups. One group member selects a word at random from a dictionary, textbook, or newspaper. Next, the group lists all the properties and attributes of this word. Assume you randomly chose the word *rock*. Among its attributes are "durable," "low-priced," "abundant in supply," "decorative," and "expensive to ship."

You then force-fit these properties to the problem you are facing. Your team might be attempting to improve the quality of an office desk chair. Reviewing the properties of the rock might give you the idea to make the seat covering more durable because it is a quality hot point.

Think of a problem of your own, or perhaps the instructor will assign one. Another possibility is to use as your problem the question of how to expand the market for snow tires. The groups might work for about 15 minutes. To make the technique proceed smoothly, keep up the random search until you hit a noun or adjective. Prepositions usually do not work well in the forced-association technique. Group leaders share their findings with the rest of the class.

INTERNET SKILL-BUILDING EXERCISE: Learning About Creativity Training

Use the Internet to learn more about what companies are doing to enhance employee creativity. Be specific when you make an entry in your search engine to avoid being deluged with a choice of Web sites far removed from your topic. A sample phrase to enter into your search engine would be "creativity training programs for business." When you have located one or two sites that give some details about a training program, compare the information you've found to the information in this chapter about creativity training. Note similarities and differences, and be prepared to discuss your findings in class.

CASE PROBLEM 6-A: The Thinking Expedition

"This is *NOT* a meeting. This is *NOT* a training session. This is *NOT* an exercise," shouts Rolf Smith, who is standing before the Face 2005 Team—22 chemical engineers, biologists, and project leaders from Procter & Gamble. Smith says, "This is an expedition. And there will be no whining. No sniveling. No excuses. Please take off your watches, and place them in this basket. We will give them back to you in five days." A former U.S. Air Force officer, 59-year-old Smith was known throughout the ranks as "Colonel Innovation."

The Challenge and Rationale for the Expedition

The 22 P&G employees from Hunt Valley, Maryland, are part of a company effort to double the company's revenue by 2005. The team's mandate is to develop new products that will redefine the future of cosmetics. Cathy Pagliaro, 34, an associate director of product development, is responsible for launching this expedition. She says, "Our CEO has declared that Organization 2005 is about three things: stretch, innovation, and speed. The challenge for our small group is to help make those words a reality. My department has a charter to do new and different things to help fulfill our revenue goal. The only way we can change is if we start to think differently."

Rolf Smith's job is to help the team to begin to think differently—and to turn what can feel at times like a crushing burden into a thrilling intellectual adventure. A thinking expedition combines creative problem solving with challenging outdoor experiential learning. According to Smith, "The days are intense, full, and demanding. There are no scheduled meals, and no scheduled breaks. We deliberately design the expedition to push people out of their 'stupid zone'—a place of mental and physical normalcy—so that they can start to think differently, explore what they don't know, and discover answers to mission critical problems."

Smith believes that breakthrough ideas come from the edge—that uncomfortable point at which levels of stress, tension, and exhaustion are pushed beyond the comfort zone. "People like to complain that they don't think well when they're tired or hungry. I take those people aside and tell them, 'That's the whole point. We don't want you to think well. We want you to think differently.'"

The Expedition Itself

"You are not who you were yesterday," Smith tells the members of the P&G team, now outfitted in safari vests. The first day of the expedition, which ended at 11:30 P.M., is now behind them. Team members have been briefed on the mission, the rules, and their roles. The main objective is not to solve the specific product development challenges that the team faces—no one is going to invent a new mascara or face cream in the next five days. Rather it is to define and refine the challenge itself ("the mess") that the team faces as it tries to invent new products.

Smith and the P&G team began working on the mess long before they arrived here. Each participant filled out an Expedition Visa, a detailed questionnaire with open-ended and fill-in-the-blank questions. The answers to the questions help Smith and his team leaders design the expedition. Cathy Pagliaro did not tell anyone what they were doing, where they were going, or what to expect. All she told them was to block off several days to go off-site. A lot of the people couldn't handle not knowing, but idea is to knock them out of the comfort zone.

To capture ideas, Smith uses blue slips—a piece of light blue paper measuring two and three-quarter inches by four and one-quarter inches (deliberately not three by five) that expedition members carry with them at all times. The key to capturing an idea, emphasizes Smith, is to write it down. The hundreds of blue-slip ideas that the Face 2005 Team will generate over its five days are gathered into the "Trail Ahead Travel Log." The written log is divided into sections that list the team's discoveries, results, vision, and concepts of operation, and how to keep the sense of expedition alive upon the return to the office. During the expedition Smith maintains a barrage of questions. Some are intentionally vague, and seemingly silly, such as "What's a thought that you've never thought before?"

On one hot, humid, and overcast day the agenda is rock-climbing. Harnessed, helmeted, and with all the appropriate legal waivers signed, the Face 2005 Team starts hiking down a narrow path in Virginia's Great Falls Park toward the Potomac River—and toward a sheer rock face at the water's edge.

It's dark as the team hikes back up the steep trail after hours of climbing. Some made it to the top of the cliff, others did not, and some fell off trying, avoiding serious injury or death via the safety ropes. Still, everyone is pumped. Despite groans from a blue-slip-fatigued group, Smith prompts the usual flurry with his pointed questions. One woman shares her insight: "We're conditioned to think that small steps aren't

good enough. But I realize that small steps are just what you need to get to the top."

The trip back down the mountain, called the "long trek home," represents the work required to turn the big ideas that were generated at the summit into useful action items that can be implemented when the team returns. During descent, team members are tired, they want to get home, and worse, they stop thinking. The danger is that they return to their organization with the "high" of climbing but without the "how" of getting things done differently.

The P&G team experienced several breakthroughs but also breakdowns. A 50-year-old research psychologist on the team wound up in the emergency room with severe rope burns on her hands. She tried a rope swing at 2 A.M. when she lacked the strength to hold on. At 11 A.M. on the second night, one of the teams within the overall team, acted so arrogant about its capabilities that tensions exploded in crying, pouting, yelling, finger pointing, and some door slamming.

Cathy Pagliaro thought that the blowout was one of her biggest take-aways. "The 'troublemakers' had no idea how they were being perceived," she says. "And the rest of the group was [angry] because they felt undervalued, cut off, and unappreciated. This stuff happens all the time in the real world of work. For me, there was no clearer way to demonstrate the power of differences among teams. And once you understand that power, you can leverage it when forming teams or tackling a problem."

Questions

1. What creativity principles does the thinking expedition illustrate?

2. How can a company justify a creativity improvement program that results in physical injury to even one member, and potential injury to many others?

3. How do you think going on a thinking expedition would benefit you?

Source: Adapted from Anna Muio, "Idea Summit," *Fast Company*, January–February 2000, pp. 150–164.

CASE PROBLEM 6-B: The San Juan Snow House

The tropical Caribbean island of San Juan, Puerto Rico, is expecting a white Christmas, on a cargo ship from Canada. An entrepreneur plans to ship 300 tons of snow from Quebec to San Juan. Families will be charged $30 each to build snow sculptures and wage snowball fights in a refrigerated event hall.

It's going to be like a dream for these people—to see real snow," said businessman Luis Guzman. He is spending $200,000 to import the snow from Fermont, Quebec. Residents of the small village of Fermont say they are baffled. "I

can't believe somebody would want our snow," said mayor Robert Belanger.

But in this former Spanish colony turned U.S. territory, Santa Claus is challenging the traditional Three Kings in popularity. And with Puerto Ricans paying $70 for U.S.-style fir Christmas trees imported from Canada, Guzman thinks people will pay for a bit of white Christmas.

"Everyone hears so much about the whole American winter—the Christmas carols, the snow, Santa Claus coming down the chimney," he said. "It's a beautiful tradition, and I think the people here want to share in it."

Workers in San Juan—where it is a humid 88 degrees Fahrenheit—were preparing the "snow house" in Luis Munoz Marin Park. Cooling machines and blowers backed by two generators create an artificial snowfall, Guzman said. Those who want to play will be equipped with plastic booties to keep the snow clean, and be allowed 15 minutes to frolic.

Discussion Questions

1. What problem is Guzman attempting to solve with his San Juan snow park?
2. To what extent is Guzman being creative?
3. How do you rate Guzman's chances for making a profit with his snow house?

Source: "Puerto Rico Gets Taste of Real Snow," The Associated Press, December 13, 2000.

ANSWER TO THE LATERAL THINKING PROBLEM

Kurt finally overcame his traditional mental set of going to a bank for a second mortgage. Instead, he called a financial services firm with a loan company. He had his second mortgage in ten days, gave Jessica her $25,000, and the two business partners parted on good terms.

ENDNOTES

1. Expanded from Craig Kellogg, "Offices that Work," *Working Woman*, February 1999, p. 59.
2. Paul C. Nutt, "Surprising but True: Half the Decisions in Organizations Fail," *Academy of Management Executive*, November 1999, pp. 75–90.
3. John M. Ivancevich, James H. Donnelly, Jr., and James L. Gibson, *Managing for Performance: An Introduction to the Process of Managing*, rev. ed. (Burr Ridge, IL: Irwin, 1983), pp. 83–84.
4. Russo is quoted in "Our Decision Can't Be 100% Right, but Our Decision Process Can," *Marriott Executive Memo*, Number 2, 1996, p. 2.
5. Joshua Quittner, "An Eye on the Future: Jeff Bezos Merely Wants Amazon.com to Be Earth's Biggest Seller of Everything," *Time*, December 27, 1999, p. 57.
6. Herbert A. Simon, "Rational Choice and the Structure of the Environment," *Psychological Review*, 63 (1956), pp. 129–138.
7. Roger Frantz, "Intuition at Work," *Innovative Leader*, April 1997, p. 4.
8. Lisa A. Burke and Monica K. Miller, "Taking the Mystery Out of Intuitive Decision Making," *Academy of Management Executive*, November 1999, p. 94.
9. Gerry McNamara and Philip Bromiley, "Decision Making in an Organizational Setting: Cognitive and Organizational Influences on Risk Assessment in Commercial Lending," *Academy of Management Journal*, October 1997, pp. 1063–1088.
10. Michael A. West and James L. Farr (eds.), *Innovation and Creativity at Work: Psychological and Organizational Strategies* (New York: Wiley, 1990).
11. Richard Sharwood Gates, "The Gordian Knot: A Parable for Decision Makers," *Management Review*, December 1990, p. 47.
12. Daniel Goleman, "What Makes a Leader?" *Harvard Business Review*, November–December 1998, pp. 92–102; Jennifer Laabs, "Emotional Intelligence at Work," *Workforce*, July 1999, pp. 68–71.
13. John S. Hammond, Ralph L. Keeney, and Howard Raffia, "The Hidden Traps in Decision Making," *Harvard Business Review*, September–October 1998, p. 48.
14. "Are You 90% Sure You'll Hit That Target? Check Out Your Knowledge Calibration," *Knowledge@Wharton*, January 31–February 13, 2001.
15. Hammond, Keeney, and Rafia, "The Hidden Traps," pp. 48–49.
16. James W. Dean, Jr., and Mark P. Sharfman, "Does Decision Process Matter? A Study of Strategic Decision-Making Effectiveness," *Academy of Management Journal*, April 1996, pp. 368–396.
17. Susan Heitler cited in "Think Fast!" *Working Woman*, September 2000, p. 90.
18. Allen C. Amason, "Distinguishing the Effects of Functional and Dysfunctional Conflict on Strategic Decision Making: Resolving a Paradox for Top Management Teams," *Academy of Management Journal*, February 1996, pp. 123–148.
19. Hammond, Keeney, and Raiffa, "The Hidden Traps," p. 50.
20. Andrew J. DuBrin, *Getting It Done: The Transforming Power of Self-Discipline* (Princeton, NJ: Peterson's/Pacesetter Books, 1995), pp. 49–71.
21. Survey cited in "Don't Always Trade Strategy for Speed," *Executive Leadership*, November 2000, p. 1.
22. "Let's Get Creative with Michael L. Ray, Ph.D., Professor of Creativity and Innovation, Stanford Business School," *Unisys Exec*, Number 1, 2001, p. 14.
23. Paul Sloane, *Lateral Thinking Puzzlers* (New York: Sterling Publishing, 1992).
24. Teresa M. Amabile, "How to Kill Creativity," *Harvard Business Review*, September–October 1998, pp. 78–79.
25. Quoted in Robert McGarvey, "Turn It On: Creativity Is Crucial to Your Business' Success," *Entrepreneur*, November 1996, p. 156.
26. Greg R. Oldham and Anne Cummings, "Employee Creativity: Personal and Contextual Factors at Work," *Academy of Management Journal*, June 1996, p. 611.
27. Amabile, "How to Kill Creativity," pp. 81-84; Oldham and Cummings, "Employee Creativity," pp. 607–634; Pamela Tierney, Steven M. Farmer, and George B. Graen, "An Examination of Leadership and Employee Creativity: The Relationship of Traits and Behaviors," *Personnel Psychology*, Autumn 1999, pp. 591–620; Dorothy Leonard and Walter Swap, *When Sparks Fly: Igniting Creativity in Groups* (Boston: Harvard Business School Press, 1999).
28. Gail Dutton, "Enhancing Creativity," *Management Review*, November 1996, p. 45.
29. Gary Hamel, "Reinvent Your Company," *Fortune*, June 12, 2000, p. 102.
30. "Future Edisons of America: Turn Your Employees into Inventors," *Working SMART*, June 2000, p. 2.
31. Keng L. Siau, "Electronic Brainstorming," *Innovative Leader*, April 1997, p. 3.
32. Southwood J. Morcott, in G. William Dauphinais and Colin Price (eds.), *Straight from the CEO: The World's Top Business Leaders*

Reveal Ideas That Every Manager Can Use (New York: Simon & Schuster, 1998).

33. Dutton, "Enhancing Creativity," p. 46.

34. Dorothy Leonard and Walter Swap, "Igniting Creativity," *Workforce*, October 1999, pp. 87–89.

35. Eugene Raudsepp, "Exercises for Creative Growth," *Success*, February 1981, pp. 46–47; Mike Vance and Diane Deacon, *Think Out of the Box* (Franklin Lakes, NJ: Career Press, 1995); "Test: Can You Laugh at His Advice?" (Interview with John Cleese), *Fortune*, July 6, 1998, pp. 203–204.

36. "Be a Creative Problem Solver," *Executive Strategies*, June 6, 1989, pp. 1–2.

37. Kenneth A. Kovach and Barry Render, "NASA Managers and Challenger: A Profile of Possible Explanation," *Personnel*, April 1987, p. 40.

38. Glen Whyte, "Decision Failures: Why They Occur and How to Prevent Them," *Academy of Management Executive*, August 1991, p. 25.

39. Jin Nam Choi and Myung Un Kim, "The Organizational Application of Groupthink and Its Limitations in Organizations," *Journal of Applied Psychology*, April 1999, pp. 297–306.

40. Andrew H. Van de Ven and Andrew L. Delbercq, "The Effectiveness of Nominal, Delphi, and Interacting Group Decision-Making Processes," *Academy of Management Journal*, December 1972, p. 606.

Quantitative Techniques for Planning and Decision Making

Vermont Crafters Inc., owned and operated by Russ Cortland and Maggie Cortland, has been in business since 1991. The small maker of handcrafted dining room and kitchen tables and chairs employs two full-time furniture makers. The workforce also includes several part-time employees who are hired as needed. Vermont Crafters' gross sales have been about $350,000 for the last several years. About one-half the sales are made directly to individuals, and the other half to furniture distributors.

Vermont Crafters was launched when the couple extended their furniture-making hobby into selling custom-made dining room sets to a few friends. As word about their fine designs and high quality spread, the couple found they could no longer meet demand by making furniture only at night and on weekends. So they both quit their corporate jobs to manufacture and sell Vermont Crafters furniture full time. They began advertising through display ads in home decoration magazines and local newspapers. Although the couple was eking out a living, they believed that the sales potential of Vermont Crafters was hardly being tapped.

While shoveling snow together one Sunday afternoon, Russ said to Maggie, "What would you think of our marketing our furniture on the Internet? You know, go modern with e-commerce." Maggie responded, "Could be a golden opportunity, but let me check with my friend Kathy Ramon, the marketing instructor."

One week later the couple had dinner with Ramon. She told them, "Sure, you could become the Internet giant of handcrafted furniture in two years. Or you could experience a serious profit drain that would put you out of business a couple of thousand dollars at a time. *E-tailing* is a

OBJECTIVES

After studying this chapter and doing the exercises, you should be able to:

1 Explain the use of forecasting techniques in planning.

2 Describe how to use Gantt charts, milestone charts, and PERT planning techniques.

3 Describe how to use break-even analysis and decision trees for problem solving and decision making.

4 Describe how to manage inventory by using materials requirement planning (MRP), the economic order quantity (EOQ), and the just-in-time (JIT) system.

5 Describe how to identify problems using a Pareto diagram.

Chapter 7

tricky business. Let me read you some information from Kenneth Cassar, an analyst from the research firm, Jupiter Communications. He notes that Internet retailing should reach $81 billion by 2004, with 81 million people making purchases. But Cassar also said that e-tailers of all categories face one common problem—a lack of profits.

"I agree with Cassar that site development is expensive. Sales and marketing is expensive. You need to create a strong awareness of your brand online. Before you two jump into e-tailing, let's figure out what the true costs are. You will also need to make an accurate forecast of how much furniture you will have to sell to cover your costs. I think you should go modern, but not at the expense of going bankrupt."[1]

The story about Vermont furniture makers illustrates an important point about managing a business. You sometimes need to use quantitative planning and decision-making techniques to help put you on the right track. In this case the couple, assisted by a marketing instructor, was looking to figure out how much sales volume they would need to cover their expenses from venturing into e-tailing. At the same time, they would need to make accurate forecasts about the increase in sales they could anticipate by selling over the Internet.

To make planning and decision making more accurate, a variety of techniques based on the scientific method, mathematics, and statistics have been developed. This chapter will provide sufficient information for you to acquire basic skills in several widely used techniques for planning and decision making. You can find more details about these techniques in courses and books about production and operations management and accounting. All these quantitative tools are useful, but they do not supplant human judgment and intuition. For example, a decision-making technique might tell a manager that it will take four months to complete a project. She might say, "Could be, but if I put my very best people on the project, we can beat that estimate."

As you read and work through the various techniques, recognize that software is available to carry them out. A sampling of appropriate software is presented in Exhibit 7-1. Before using a computer to run a technique, however, it is best to understand the technique and try it out manually or with a calculator. Such firsthand knowledge can prevent accepting computer-generated information that is way off track. Similarly, many people use spell checkers without a good grasp of word usage. The results can be misleading and humorous, such as "Each of our employees is assigned to a *manger*" or "The company picnic will proceed as scheduled *weather* or not we have good *whether*."

FORECASTING METHODS

Explain the use of forecasting techniques in planning.

All planning involves making forecasts, or predicting future events. Forecasting is important because if a manager fails to spot trends and react to them before the competition does, the competition can gain an invaluable edge. As noted in an

Forecasting Techniques	Decision Pro 3.0 (Vanguard Software); IMA FORECAST (Power-flex Software Systems, Inc.); PROCAST (Cube Software Limited); spreadsheet programs can also be used to make forecasts.
Gantt Charts and Milestone Charts	Milestones, Etc. is a project management, planning, scheduling, and Gantt charting program (KIDASA Software, Inc.), Gantt Charts (B-GUL)
PERT Diagrams	PERT Chart; EXPERT (both distributed by Microsoft Project); Program Evaluation and Review Technique (FOLDOC)
Break-Even Analysis	Alpha Plus, Inc. (Security Development Corporation); WinBreak Pro (Break-Even Feeder Analysis Agricultural Software)
Decision Trees	Decision Pro 3.0 (Vanguard Software)
Economic Order Quantity	Software would be superfluous, use pocket calculator.
Just-in-Time (JIT) Inventory Management	AGAMA Integrated Manufacturing Software (Manufacturing Information Systems, Inc.); XelusExtend (Xelus Inc.); AMICS Info-tech Systems, Inc. GetSmart Solutions 6.0 (SFI); OCI—Oblique Classifier 1 (Johns Hopkins University Computer Science Department)
All Techniques Combined	Enterprise software controls an entire company's operations, linking them together. The software automates finance, manufacturing, and human resources, incorporating stand-alone software such as that designed for PERT and break-even analysis. Enterprise software also helps make decisions based on market research. Specific types of enterprise software have several different names. (Three key suppliers are SAP, People-Soft, and Siebel.)

EXHIBIT 7-1

Software for Quantitative Planning and Decision-Making Techniques

173

Managers and professionals generally rely on computers to make use of quantitative planning and decision-making techniques. Examples of applicable software are presented at the left, and should be referred to for on-the-job-application of these techniques.

executive newsletter: "The handwriting is on the wall. The way your business reacts to newly emerging trends is perhaps the best barometer of your future success."[2] The forecasts used in strategic planning are especially difficult to make because they involve long-range trends. Unknown factors might crop up between the time the forecast is made and the time about which predictions are made. This section will describe approaches to and types of forecasting.

Qualitative and Quantitative Approaches

Forecasts can be based on both qualitative and quantitative information. Most of the forecasting done for strategic planning relies on a combination of both. *Qualitative* methods of forecasting consist mainly of subjective hunches. For example, an experienced executive might predict that the high cost of housing will create a demand for small, less-expensive homes, even though this trend cannot be quantified. One qualitative method is a **judgmental forecast**, a prediction based on a collection of subjective opinions. It relies on analysis of subjective inputs from a variety of sources, including consumer surveys, sales representatives, managers, and panels of experts. For instance, a group of potential home buyers might be asked how they would react to the possibility of purchasing a compact, less-expensive home.

Quantitative forecasting methods involve either the extension of historical data or the development of models to identify the cause of a particular outcome. A

judgmental forecast

A qualitative forecasting method based on a collection of subjective opinions.

time-series analysis

An analysis of a sequence of observations that have taken place at regular intervals over a period of time (hourly, weekly, monthly, and so forth).

174

widely used historical approach is **time-series analysis**. This technique is simply an analysis of a sequence of observations that have taken place at regular intervals over a period of time (hourly, weekly, monthly, and so forth). The underlying assumption of this approach is that the future will be much like the past. Exhibit 7-2 shows a basic example of a time-series analysis chart. This information might be used to make forecasts about when people would be willing to take vacations. Such forecasts would be important for the resort and travel industry.

Many firms use quantitative and qualitative approaches to forecasting. Forecasting begins with a quantitative prediction, which provides basic data about a future trend. An example of a quantitative prediction is the forecast of a surge in demand for handheld personal digital assistants (PDAs). (The PDA is a palm-size computer that can also record voice memos, function as a date book and calculator, and retrieve e-mail.) Next, the qualitative forecast is added to the quantitative forecast, somewhat as a validity check. For example, a quantitative forecast might predict that, if the current growth trend continues, every household in North America will contain two handheld personal digital assistants by 2006.

The quantitative forecast is then adjusted according to the subjective data supplied by the qualitative forecast. In this case, it could be reasoned that the growth trend was extrapolated too aggressively. In many instances, a quantitative forecast will serve as a validity check on qualitative forecasts because numerical data is more accurate than intuition.

Three errors or traps are particularly prevalent when making forecasts or estimates.[3] One is the *overconfidence trap*, whereby people overestimate the accuracy of their forecasts. A CEO might be so confident of the growth of her business that she moves the company into expensive new headquarters. Based on her confidence, she does not prepare contingency plans in case the estimated growth does not take place. A second problem is the *prudence trap*, in which people make cautious forecasts "just to be on the safe side." Being safe can mean taking extra measures just not to be caught short, such as a restaurant owner buying ten extra boxes of strawberries "just to be safe." If the strawberry desserts go unsold the owner is stuck unless he can make strawberry pudding for tomorrow's menu.

A third problem is the *recallability trap* whereby our forecasts are influenced by extremely positive or negative incidents we recall. If a manager vividly recalls

EXHIBIT 7-2

Time-Series Analysis Chart

A time-series analysis uses the past to make predictions.

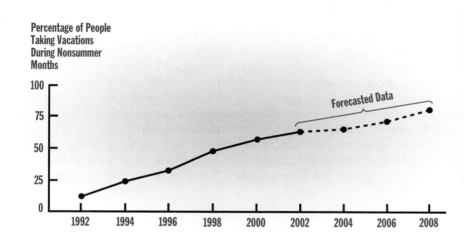

Percentage of People Taking Vacations During Nonsummer Months

success stories from global expansion to Singapore, he might overestimate the chances of succeeding in that country.

Being aware of these traps can help you take a more disciplined approach to forecasting. For example, to reduce the effect of the overconfidence trap, start by considering the extremes—the possible highs and lows. Try to imagine a scenario in which your forecast could be way too high or way too low and make appropriate adjustments if necessary. For a reality check, discuss your forecasts with other knowledgeable people. To become a good forecaster, you need to make a large number of predictions and then look for feedback on the accuracy of these predictions.

Types of Forecasts

Three types of forecasts are used most widely: economic, sales, and technological. Each of these forecasts can be made by using both qualitative and quantitative methods.

Economic Forecasting

No single factor is more important in managerial planning than predicting the level of future business activity. Strategic planners in large organizations rely often on economic forecasts made by specialists they hire. Planners in smaller firms are more likely to rely on government forecasts. However, forecasts about the general economy do not necessarily correspond to business activity related to a particular product or service.

A major factor in the accuracy of forecasts is time span: Short-range predictions are more accurate than long-range predictions. Strategic planning is long-range planning, and many strategic plans have to be revised frequently to accommodate changes in business activity. For example, a sudden recession may abort plans for diversification into new products and services.

Sales Forecasting

The sales forecast is usually the primary planning document for a business. Even if the general economy is robust, an organization needs a promising sales forecast before it can be aggressive about capitalizing on new opportunities. Strategic planners themselves may not be involved in making sales forecasts, but to develop master plans they rely on forecasts that the marketing unit makes. For instance, the major tobacco companies have embarked on strategic plans to diversify into a number of nontobacco businesses, such as soft drinks. An important factor in the decision to implement this strategic plan was a forecast of decreased demand for tobacco products in the domestic market. The cause for decreased demand will be health concerns of the public.

Technological Forecasting

A technological forecast predicts what types of technological changes will take place. Technological forecasts allow a firm to adapt to new technologies and thus stay competitive. For example, forecasts made in the late 1990s about the explosive growth of e-commerce have enabled many firms to ready themselves technologically for the future. Even if a lot of the activity is not yet profitable, the majority of industrial and consumer companies are now prepared to buy and sell over the Internet.

Exhibit 7-3 presents expert forecasts about the future of e-commerce. Several of the forecasts are short-range because they refer to trends that are already in place.

EXHIBIT 7-3

Forecasts of the Impact of the Internet

Financial Services
Most financial services can potentially be handled electronically. But so far, banks can't even figure out a good way of letting people pay bills online.

Entertainment
Much of entertainment can easily be digitized. But no one knows how to make money yet, and the technology is lagging.

Health Care
The benefits of shifting health-care transactions to the Web could be enormous. But so are institutional barriers such as many physicians sticking to writing prescriptions illegibly on paper pads.

Education
E-learning could cut the costs of education, but only at the price of making education more impersonal.

Government
Delivering information to citizens electronically has enormous appeal, but requires massive investments where the impact may be incremental.

Retailing
The glitzy Web sites caught all the attention. But dot-com success turned more on who had the best logistics.

Manufacturing
Web-enabled supply chains and intranets are important, but ultimately a manufacturer lives or dies on the quality of its goods.

Travel
Online travel sights are popular, but the ultimate constraint on travel is the physical capacity of the air and road systems.

Power
Online energy exchanges get the publicity, but power generation and transmission capabilities will have the bigger economic impact.

Source: Michael J. Mandel and Robert D. Hof, "Rethinking the Internet," *Business Week,* March 26, 2001.

2

Describe how to use Gantt charts, milestone charts, and PERT planning techniques.

GANTT CHARTS AND MILESTONE CHARTS

Two basic tools for monitoring the progress of scheduled projects are Gantt charts and milestone charts. Closely related to each other, they both help a manager keep track of whether activities are completed on time.

Gantt Charts

Gantt chart

A chart that depicts the planned and actual progress of work during the life of the project.

A **Gantt chart** graphically depicts the planned and actual progress of work over the period of time encompassed by a project. Gantt charts are especially useful for scheduling one-time projects such as constructing buildings, making films, and launching satellites. Charts of this type are also called time-and-activity charts, because time and activity are the two key variables they consider. Time is plotted on the horizontal axis, activities listed on the vertical axis.

Despite its simplicity, the Gantt chart is a valuable and widely used control technique. It also provides the foundation of more sophisticated types of time-related charts, such as the PERT diagram, which will be described later.

Exhibit 7-4 shows a Gantt chart used to schedule the opening of a small office building. Gantt charts used for most other purposes would have a similar format.

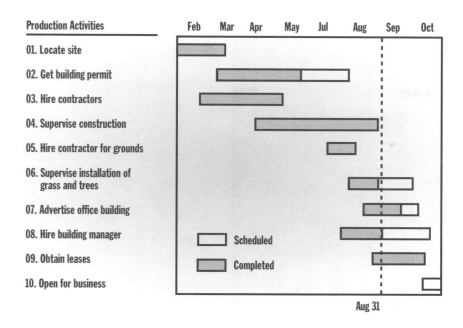

EXHIBIT 7-4

A Gantt Chart Used for
Opening a Small Office
Building

*A Gantt chart helps keep
track of progress on a project.*

177

At the planning phase of the project, the manager lays out the schedule by using rectangular boxes. As each activity is completed, the appropriate box is shaded. At any given time, the manager can see which activities have been completed on time. For example, if the building owner has not hired a contractor for the grounds by August 31, the activity would be declared behind schedule.

The Gantt chart presented here is quite basic. On most Gantt charts, the bars are movable strips of plastic. Different colors indicate scheduled and actual progress. Mechanical boards with pegs to indicate scheduled dates and actual progress can also be used. Some managers and specialists now use computer graphics to prepare their own high-tech Gantt charts.

Because Gantt charts are used to monitor progress, they also act as control devices. When the chart shows that the building permit activity has fallen behind schedule, the manager can investigate the problem and solve it. The Gantt chart gives a convenient overall view of the progress made against the schedule. However, its disadvantage is that it does not furnish enough details about the sub-activities that need to be performed to accomplish each general item.

Milestone Charts

A **milestone chart** is an extension of the Gantt chart. It provides a listing of the subactivities that must be completed to accomplish the major activities listed on the vertical axis. The inclusion of milestones, which are the completion of individual phases of an activity, adds to the value of a Gantt chart as a scheduling and control technique. Each milestone serves as a checkpoint on progress. In Exhibit 7-5, the Gantt chart for constructing a small office building has been expanded into a milestone chart. The numbers in each rectangle represent milestones. A complete chart would list each of the 33 milestones. In Exhibit 7-5 only the milestones for screening tenants and the opening date are listed.

milestone chart
An extension of the Gantt chart that provides a listing of the subactivities that must be completed to accomplish the major activities listed on the vertical axis.

EXHIBIT 7-5

A Milestone Chart Used for Opening a Small Office Building

Production Activities	Feb	Mar	Apr	May	Jul	Aug	Sep	Oct
01. Locate site	1 2 3							
02. Get building permit		4		5 6	7 8 9		10	
03. Hire contractors			11 12 13					
04. Supervise construction		14 15	16 17	18 19				
05. Hire contractor for grounds				20 21				
06. Supervise installation of grass and trees					22 23 24			
07. Advertise office building						25 26		
08. Hire building manager					27 28			
09. Obtain leases						29 30 31 32		
10. Open for business								33

Milestones to Be Accomplished

•
•
•

29. Speak to friends and acquaintances about space availability.

30. Put ad in local newspaper.

31. Conduct interviews with rental applicants and check credit history of best potential tenants.

32. Offer lease to most creditworthy candidates.

33. Have grand-opening celebration October 5.

PROGRAM EVALUATION AND REVIEW TECHNIQUE

program evaluation and review technique (PERT)

A network model used to track the planning activities required to complete a large-scale, nonrepetitive project. It depicts all of the interrelated events that must take place.

Gantt and milestone charts are basic scheduling tools, exceeded only in simplicity by a to-do list. A more complicated method of scheduling activities and events uses a network model. The model depicts all the interrelated events that must take place for a project to be completed. The most widely used network-modeling tool is the **program evaluation and review technique (PERT)**. It is used to track the planning activities required to complete a large-scale, nonrepetitive project.

A scheduling technique such as PERT is useful when certain tasks have to be completed before others if the total project is to be completed on time. In the small office building example, the site of the building must be specified before the owner can apply for a building permit. (The building commission will grant a permit only after approving a specific location.) The PERT diagram indicates such a necessary sequence of events.

PERT is used most often in engineering and construction projects. It has also been applied to such business problems as marketing campaigns, company relocations, and convention planning. Here we examine the basics of PERT, along with a few advanced considerations.

Key PERT Concepts

Two concepts lie at the core of PERT: event and activity. An **event** is a point of decision or the accomplishment of a task. Events are also called milestones. The events involved in the merger of two companies would include sending out announcements to shareholders, changing the company name, and letting customers know of the merger.

An **activity** is the physical and mental effort required to complete an event. One activity in the merger example is working with a public relations firm to arrive at a suitable name for the new company. Activities that have to be accomplished in the building example include supervising contractors and interviewing potential tenants.

Steps Involved in Preparing a PERT Network

The events and activities included in a PERT network are laid out graphically, as shown in Exhibit 7-6. Preparing a PERT network consists of four steps:

1. *Prepare a list of all the activities necessary to complete the project.* In the building example, these would include locating the site, getting the building permit, and so forth. Many more activities and subactivities could be added to this example.

event

In the PERT method, a point of decision or the accomplishment of a task.

activity

In the PERT method, the physical and mental effort required to complete an event.

179

INFORMATION FOR PREPARING THE PERT DIAGRAM

Event	Activity	Estimated Time in Weeks	Preceding Event
A	Locate site	5	None
B	Get building permit	30	A
C	Hire contractors	13	A
D	Supervise construction	30	C
E	Hire contractor for grounds	6	D
F	Supervise installation grass and trees	13	E
G	Advertise office building	8	B,F
H	Hire building manager	14	G
I	Obtain leases	8	G,H
J	Open for business	1	I

——▶ = Critical Path (thick arrow)

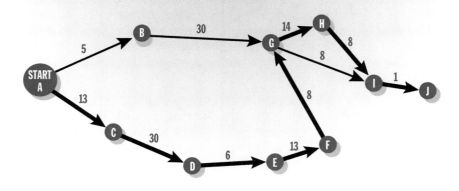

EXHIBIT 7-6

A PERT Network for Opening a Building

Each numeral in the diagram equals the expected time for an activity, such as 5 weeks to locate site (between circles A and B) and 13 weeks to supervise installation of grass and trees (between circles E and F). The critical path is the estimated time for all the activities shown above the thick arrows (13 + 30 + 6 + 13 + 8 + 14 + 8 + 1 = 93).

2. *Design the actual PERT network, relating all the activities to each other in the proper sequence.* Anticipating all the activities in a major project requires considerable skill and judgment. In addition, activities must be sequenced—the planner must decide which activity must precede another. In the building example, the owner would want to hire a grounds contractor before hiring a building manager.

3. *Estimate the time required to complete each activity.* This step must be done carefully because the major output of the PERT method is a statement of the total time required by the project. Because the time estimate is critical, several people should be asked to make three different estimates: optimistic time, pessimistic time, and probable time.

   Optimistic time (O) is the shortest time an activity will take if everything goes well. In the construction industry, the optimistic time is rarely achieved.

   Pessimistic time (P) is the amount of time an activity will take if everything goes wrong (as it sometimes does with complicated projects such as installing a new subway system).

   Most probable time (M) is the most realistic estimate of how much time an activity will take. The probable time for an activity can be an estimate of the time taken for similar activities on other projects. For instance, the time needed to build a cockpit for one aircraft might be based on the average time it took to build cockpits for comparable aircraft in the past.

expected time

The time that will be used on the PERT diagram as the needed period for the completion of an activity.

After the planner has collected all the estimates, he or she uses a formula to calculate the **expected time**. The expected time is the time that will be used on the PERT diagram as the needed period for the completion of an activity. As the following formula shows, expected time is an "average" in which most probable time is given more weight than optimistic time and pessimistic time.

$$\text{Expected time} = \frac{O + 4M + P}{6}$$

(The denominator is 6 because O counts for 1, M for 4, and P for 1.)

Suppose the time estimates for choosing a site location for the building are as follows: optimistic time (O) is 2 weeks; most probable time (M) is 5 weeks; and pessimistic time (P) is 8 weeks. Therefore,

$$\text{Expected time} = \frac{2 + (4 \times 5) + 8}{6} = \frac{30}{6} = 5 \text{ weeks}$$

critical path

The path through the PERT network that includes the most time-consuming sequence of events and activities.

4. *Calculate the **critical path**, the path through the PERT network that includes the most time-consuming sequence of events and activities.* The length of the entire project is determined by the path with the longest elapsed time. The logic behind the critical path is this: A given project cannot be considered completed until its lengthiest component is completed. For example, if it takes six months to get the building construction permit, the office-building project cannot be completed in less than one year, even if all other events are completed earlier than scheduled.

Exhibit 7-6 shows a critical path that requires a total elapsed time of 93 weeks. This total is calculated by adding the numerals that appear beside each thick line segment. Each numeral represents the number of weeks scheduled to complete the activities between each lettered label. Notice that activity completion must occur in the sequence of steps indicated by the direction of the arrows. In this case, if 93 weeks appeared to be an excessive length of time, the building owner would have to search for ways to shorten the process. For example, the owner might be spending too much time supervising the construction.

When it comes to implementing the activities listed on the PERT diagram, control measures play a crucial role. The project manager must ensure that all critical events are completed on time. If activities in the critical path take too long to complete, the overall project will not be completed on time. If necessary, the manager must take corrective action to move the activity along. Such action might include hiring additional workers, dismissing substandard workers, or purchasing more productive equipment.

Advanced Considerations in PERT

Considering that PERT is used for projects as complicated as building a new type of airliner, the process can become quite complex. In practice, PERT networks often specify hundreds of events and activities. Each small event can have its own PERT diagram. Many computer programs are available to help perform the mechanics of computing paths. The Open Plan software enables the user to handle projects with as many as 100,000 activities. Here we look at two concepts that are used in complex applications of PERT.

Refined Calculation of Expected Times
The optimistic, pessimistic, and most probable times should be based on a frequency distribution of estimates. Instead of using one intuitive guess as to these durations, somebody collects all available data about how long comparable activities took. For example: wiring a cockpit took seven weeks in ten different cases; six weeks in five cases; five weeks, in three cases; and so forth. The optimistic and pessimistic times are then selected as the lower and upper ten percentiles of the distribution of times. In other words, it is optimistic to think that an event will be completed as rapidly as suggested by the briefest 10 percent of estimates. Also, it is pessimistic to think that the event will be completed in the longest 10 percent of estimated times. (Remember, the *expected* time is calculated based on a weighted average of the optimistic, most probable, and pessimistic times.)

It is often difficult to obtain data for comparable activities, so quantified guesswork will be required. To illustrate, a project manager might guess, "If we attempted to drill a hole for oil through that ice cap 100 times, I think it would take us 60 days 25 times, 90 days 35 times, 110 days 5 times, and 130 days, 5 times." The guesses provided by this project manager might be combined with the guesses of another specialist before calculating the pessimistic, optimistic, and most probable times.

Resource and Cost Estimates
In addition to estimating the time required for activities, advanced applications of PERT estimate the amount of resources required. Before a building contractor would establish a price for erecting a building, it would be prudent to estimate how much and what types of equipment would be needed. It would also be essential to estimate how many workers of different skills would be required. Considering that payroll runs about two-thirds of the cost for manufacturing, miscalculating costs can eliminate profits.

The resource and cost estimates can be calculated in the same manner as time estimates. Resource and cost estimates can then be attached to events, thereby suggesting at which point in the project they will most likely be incurred. For example, the building contractor might estimate that siding specialists will not be needed until 90 days into the project.

3   BREAK-EVEN ANALYSIS

Describe how to use break-even analysis and decision trees for problem solving and decision making.

break–even analysis

A method of determining the relationship between total costs and total revenues at various levels of production or sales activity.

"What do we have to do to break even?" This question is asked frequently in business. Managers often find the answer through **break–even analysis**, a method of determining the relationship between total costs and total revenues at various levels of production or sales activity. Managers use break–even analysis because—before adding new products, equipment, or personnel—they want to be sure that the changes will pay off. Break–even analysis tells managers the point at which it is profitable to go ahead with a new venture.

Exhibit 7-7 illustrates a typical break-even chart. It deals with a proposal to add a new product to an existing line. The point at which the Total Costs line and the Revenue line intersect is the break-even point. Sales shown to the right of the break-even point represent profit. Sales to the left of this point represent a loss.

Break-Even Formula

The break-even point (BE) is the situation in which total revenues equal fixed costs plus variable costs. It can be calculated with several algebraic formulas. One standard formula is:

$$BE = \frac{TFC}{P - AVC}$$

EXHIBIT 7-7

Break-Even Chart for Adding a New Product to an Existing Line

A break-even chart indicates at what point a venture becomes profitable.

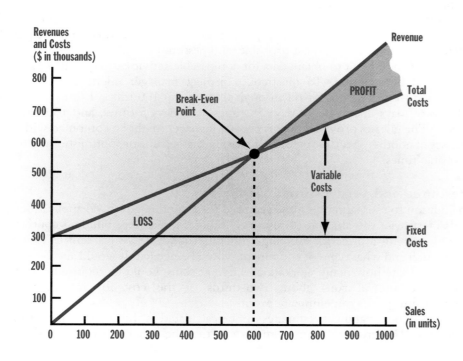

where

P = selling price per unit

AVC = average variable cost per unit, the cost that varies with the amount produced

TFC = total fixed cost, the cost that remains constant no matter how many units are produced

Another version of the preceding formula uses variable cost instead of average variable cost, and fixed cost instead of total fixed cost. Professor Ron Olive, however, believes that using AVC and TFC is more accurate from the standpoint of economics.[4]

The chart in Exhibit 7-7 is based on the plans of Vermont Crafters to sell furniture over the Internet. For simplicity, we provide data only for the dining room sets. The average selling price (P) is $1,000 per unit; the average variable cost (AVC) is $500 per unit, including Internet commission fees for sales made through major Web sites (portals). The total fixed costs are $300,000.

$$BE = \frac{\$300,000}{\$1,000 - \$500} = \frac{\$300,000}{\$500} = 600 \text{ units}$$

Under the conditions assumed and for the period of time in which these costs and revenue figures are valid, a sales volume of 600 dining room sets would be required for Vermont Crafters to break even. Any volume above that level would produce a profit and anything below it would result in a loss. (We are referring to Internet sales only. Sales through their customary channels would have to be figured separately.) If the sales forecast for dining room sets sold through e-commerce is above 600 units, it would be a good decision to sell on the Net. If the sales forecast is less than 600 units, Vermont Crafters should not attempt e-commerce for now. However, if the husband–and–wife team is are willing to absorb losses now to build for the long range, they might start e-commerce anyway. Break-even analysis would tell the couple how much money they are likely to lose. An encouraging note is that small operations like Vermont Crafters have typically profited from e-tailing.

Advantages and Limitations of Break-Even Analysis

Break-even analysis helps managers keep their thinking focused on the volume of activity that will be necessary to justify a new expense. The technique is also useful because it applies to a number of operations problems. Break-even analysis can help a manager decide whether to drop an existing product from the line, to replace equipment, or to buy rather than make a part.

Break-even analysis has some drawbacks. First, it is only as valid as the estimates of costs and revenues that managers use to create it. Second, the analysis is static in that it assumes no changes in other variables. The dynamic nature of business makes this assumption questionable. The third limitation of break-even analysis is potentially more serious. Exhibit 7-7 indicates that variable costs and sales increase together in a direct relationship. In reality, unit costs may decrease with increased volume. It is also possible that costs may increase with volume: Suppose that increased production leads to higher turnover because employees prefer not to work overtime.

Break-even analysis relates to decisions about whether to proceed or not to proceed. The next section will examine a more complicated decision-making technique that relates to the desirability of several alternative solutions.

DECISION TREES

decision tree

A graphic illustration of the alternative solutions available to solve a problem.

Another useful planning tool is called a **decision tree**, a graphic illustration of the alternative solutions available to solve a problem. Decision trees are designed to estimate the outcome of a series of decisions. As the sequences of the major decision are drawn, the resulting diagram resembles a tree with branches.

To illustrate the essentials of using a decision tree for making financial decisions, return to the building owner who used the Gantt and milestone charts. One major decision facing the owner is whether to open an office building only or open an office building with an attached conference facility (rented to the public as needed). According to data from a local real estate association, the probability of having a good first year is 0.6 and the probability of a poor one is 0.4.

Discussion with an accountant indicates that the payout, or net cash flow, from a good year with the building only would be $100,000. The payout from a poor first year with the same alternative would be a loss of $10,000. Both these figures are conditional because they depend on business conditions and tenants paying their rent. The owner and accountant predict that a good first year with the alternative of a building and public conference facility would be $150,000. A poor first year would result in a loss of $30,000.

expected value

The average return on a particular decision being made a large number of times.

Using this information, the manager computes the expected values and adds them for the two alternatives. An **expected value** is the average value incurred if a particular decision is made a large number of times. Sometimes the alternative would earn more, and sometimes less, with the expected value being the alternative's average return.

Expected value: Office building only	=	0.6 × $100,000	=	$60,000
		0.4 × −$10,000	=	−4,000
				$56,000

Expected value: Office building and conference facility	=	0.6 × $150,000	=	$90,000
		0.4 × −$30,000	=	−12,000
				$78,000

As Exhibit 7-8 graphically portrays, the decision tree suggests that the building and conference room will probably turn a first-year profit of $78,000. The building-only alternative is likely to show a profit of $56,000. Over one year, operating a building and public conference center would be $22,000 more profitable.

The advantage of a decision tree is that it can be used to help make sequences of decisions. After having one year of experience in running a building and conference center, the owner may think of expanding. One logical possibility for expansion would be to open a public warehouse for the use of small business firms and individuals. The building owner would now have more accurate information about the conditional values for an office building and conference room—the choice the owner made when opening his new enterprise. With one year of success with the office building and conference center, the probability of having a second good season might be raised to 0.8. With each successive year, the owner would have increasingly accurate information about the conditional values.

Following is an explanation of how the expected values are calculated for the new branch of the decision tree in question, shown in Exhibit 7-9.

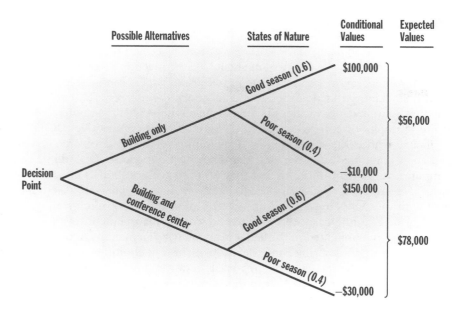

EXHIBIT 7-8

First-Year Decision Tree for Building Owner

		Conditional Values	Expected Values

Possible Alternatives | States of Nature

Building only

Good season (0.6) $100,000

Poor season (0.4) $56,000

−$10,000

Building and conference center

Good season (0.6) $150,000

Poor season (0.4) $78,000

−$30,000

Decision Point

Expected value: Office building and conference room	$= 0.8 \times \$180{,}000$	$= \$144{,}000$
	$0.2 \times -\$30{,}000$	$= \underline{-6{,}000}$
		$\$138{,}000$

Expected value: Office building and conference room, and warehouse	$= 0.6 \times \$200{,}000$	$= \$120{,}000$
	$0.4 \times -\$50{,}000$	$= \underline{-20{,}000}$
		$\$100{,}000$

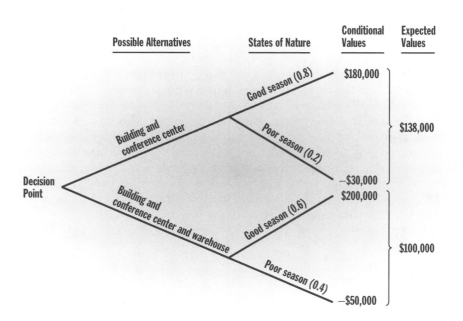

EXHIBIT 7-9

Second-Year Decision Tree for Building Owner

		Conditional Values	Expected Values

Possible Alternatives | States of Nature

Building and conference center

Good season (0.8) $180,000

Poor season (0.2) $138,000

−$30,000

Building and conference center and warehouse

Good season (0.6) $200,000

Poor season (0.4) $100,000

−$50,000

Decision Point

4

Describe how to manage inventory by using materials requirement planning (MRP), the economic order quantity (EOQ), and the just-in-time (JIT) system.

INVENTORY CONTROL TECHNIQUES

Managers of manufacturing and sales organizations face the problem of how much inventory to keep on hand. If a firm maintains a large inventory, goods can be made quickly, customers can make immediate purchases, or orders can be shipped rapidly. However, stocking goods is expensive. The goods themselves are costly, and the money tied up in inventory cannot be invested elsewhere. Dell Computers and Wal-Mart are examples of companies that owe some of their competitive advantage to their efficient management of inventory. Dell minimizes the need for large inventory by building a computer only after an order is received. Of course, Dell still keeps lots of computer components on hand, but they do not have warehouses filled with yet-to-be sold computers. Wal-Mart collaborates with its suppliers to keep shelves stocked with the right amount and quantity of merchandise to minimize inventory accumulation. The importance of effective inventory management to a company's financial health is highlighted in the accompanying Management in Action.

This section will describe three decision-making techniques used to manage inventory and control production: materials-requirement planning (MRP), the economic order quantity (EOQ), and the just-in-time (JIT) system.

Materials Requirement Planning

Manufacturing a finished product is complicated. It involves various production functions, including scheduling, purchasing, and inventory control. Many firms use a master plan to coordinate these production functions. **Materials requirement planning (MRP)** is a computerized manufacturing and inventory control system designed to ensure that materials handling and inventory control are efficient. The system is designed to manage inventories that come from components or raw materials to support scheduled production of finished goods. A manufacturer of dishwashers such as Maytag Corporation uses MRP because a dishwasher has many components, including electric motors, rubber belts, and sheet metal.

Materials requirement planning is important because the parts used in building a product such as dishwashers are needed at exact times in the production cycle. MRP helps smooth the parts-ordering cycle and provides immediate information about the inventory levels of critical parts.

Materials requirement planning has three major components. The *master production schedule* is the overall production plan for the completed products, such as dishwashers. This schedule is expressed in terms of timing and quantity of production. The *inventory record file* consists of information about the status of each item held in inventory. The *bill of materials* is a list of the components needed for each completed item. A bill of materials, for example, might list the many parts of a dishwasher. Materials requirement planning coordinates all this data and provides information to ensure that materials are available when needed.

Materials requirement planning makes an important contribution by reducing inventory levels and direct labor costs. For this system to work effectively accurate information is necessary, along with good cooperation among the individuals and groups involved.

materials requirement planning (MRP)

A computerized manufacturing and inventory control system designed to ensure that materials handling and inventory control are efficient.

economic order quantity (EOQ)

The inventory level that minimizes both administrative costs and carrying costs.

Economic Order Quantity

The **economic order quantity (EOQ)** is the inventory level that minimizes both administrative costs and carrying costs. The EOQ represents the reorder

Management *in Action*

Managers Attempt to Cope with an Inventory Glut

F red Hickey's influential newsletter, *The High Tech Strategist*, screamed several years ago that bloated inventories—particularly at high-tech companies—almost guarantee worsening economic times. Other experts are also worried about the inventory problem. "The inventory problem and supply chain are the No. 1 issues we have been working on," says info-tech investor Roger McNamee. Federal Reserve chief Alan Greenspan has zeroed in on glut, warning Congress, "We are observing the beginnings of what is probably a major inventory correction."

The fourth quarter of 2000 saw $67.1 billion of annualized business accumulation, growing 15 percent faster than in the first half of 2000. Mega-output plus rapidly declining demand equals massive inventory buildup. "It's the end result of multiple years of an unparalleled buildup in tech capacity," says Hickey. "Since 1995, capacity has been growing at 30% to 35% a year. We've created an overproduction machine."

Glut is everywhere. In autos, GM dealers now have an average of 101 days of cars and trucks on the lots in contrast to about 80 days historically. In construction, Georgia Pacific blamed a recent earnings shortfall on inventory glut. To help cope with the problem, management has slashed gypsum production by 34 percent and lumber output by 20 percent. In apparel and retail, Guess jeans recently announced an earnings restatement for the fourth quarter, in part because of excess inventory. Levi's and Burlington are suffering from inventory pile-up also. In steel, LTV recently cited a glut of steel as a contributing factor in its decision to file for Chapter 11 bankruptcy.

Infotech has the largest inventory oversupply. Inventories at Sony's electronics division grew 29 percent last year, to almost $8 billion, much of it being PCs and peripherals. Apple has too many iMacs. Chipmakers have stuffed storerooms also. At the end of its fiscal year 2000, the industry leaders reported $1.2 billion in inventory. The buildup represented more than a 100 percent increase in six months. Nortel Networks' inventory grew from $2.7 to $4.3 billion last year.

McNamee suggests that the solution to the problem could turn out to be another triumph of the new economy. "There is a whole new class of applications that addresses these supply-chain issues in real time," he says referring to newly developed software by companies like Agile and SeeCommerce. "This stuff lets companies and suppliers fly like the Blue Angels." If the sophisticated new technology doesn't work, managers might resort to Web sites, such as TradeOut.com and FastAsset.com, that serve as online marketplaces for unwanted inventory.

Source: Andy Server, "First Glut Check," *Fortune*, March 5, 2001.

---

quantity of the least cost. Carrying costs include the cost of loans, the interest foregone because money is tied up in inventory, and the cost of handling the inventory. EOQ is expressed mathematically as

$$EOQ = \sqrt{\frac{2DO}{C}}$$

where

> D = annual demand in units for the product
> O = fixed cost of placing and receiving an order
> C = annual carrying cost per unit (taxes, insurance, and other expenses)

Assume that the annual demand for Vermont Crafters coffee tables is 100 units and that it costs $1,000 to order each unit. Furthermore, suppose the carrying cost per unit is $200. The equation to calculate the most economic number of coffee tables to keep in inventory is:

$$
\begin{aligned}
\text{EOQ} &= \sqrt{\frac{2 \times 100 \times \$1,000}{\$200}} \\
&= \sqrt{\frac{\$200,000}{\$200}} \\
&= \sqrt{1,000} \\
&= 32 \text{ coffee tables (rounded figure)}
\end{aligned}
$$

Therefore, the owners of Vermont Crafters conclude that the most economical number of coffee tables to keep in inventory during the selling season is 32. (The assumption is that Vermont Crafters has a large storage area.) If the figures entered into the EOQ formula are accurate, EOQ calculations can vastly improve inventory management.

Just-in-Time System

just–in–time (JIT) system

A system to minimize inventory and move it into the plant exactly when needed.

An important thrust in manufacturing is to keep just enough parts and components on hand to fill current orders. The **just–in–time (JIT) system** is an inventory control method designed to minimize inventory and move it into the plant exactly when needed. The key principle of the system is to eliminate excess inventory by producing or purchasing parts, subassemblies, and final products only when—and in the exact amounts—needed. JIT helps a manufacturing division stay "lean." Imagine Vermont Crafters having raw wood delivered to its door within an hour or so after an order is received over the Internet. Just-in-time is generally used in a repetitive, single-product, manufacturing environment. However, the system is now also used to improve operations in sales and service organizations.

Philosophies

Three basic philosophies underlie the specific manufacturing techniques of JIT.[5] *First, setup time for assembly and cost must be reduced.* The goal of JIT is to make setup time and cost so low that small batch sizes are economical, even to the point of manufacturing just one finished product. *Second, safety stock is undesirable.* Stock held in reserve is expensive and hides problems, such as inefficient production methods. "Just in time" should replace "just in case." *Third, productivity and quality are inseparable.* JIT is only possible when high-quality components are delivered and produced. The goal of the JIT system is 100 percent good items at each manufacturing step.

Procedures and Techniques

Just-in-time inventory control is part of a system of manufacturing control. Therefore, it involves many different techniques and procedures. Seven of the major techniques and procedures are described in the list that follows.[6] Knowing them provides insight into the system of manufacturing used by many successful Japanese companies.

1. *Kanbans.* The JIT system of inventory control relies on *kanbans*, or cards, to communicate production requirements from the final point of assembly to the manufacturing operations that precede it. When an order is received for a product, a kanban is issued that directs employees to finish the product. The finishing department selects components and assembles the product. The kanban is then passed back to earlier stations. This kanban tells workers to resupply the components. Kanban communication continues all the way back to the material suppliers. In many JIT systems, suppliers locate their companies so they can be close to major customers. Proximity allows suppliers to make shipments promptly. At each stage, parts and other materials are delivered just in time for use.

2. *Demand-driven pull system.* The just-in-time techniques requires producing exactly what is needed to match the demand created by customer orders. Demand drives final assembly schedules, and assembly drives subassembly timetables. The result is a pull system—that is, customer demand pulls along activities to meet that demand.

3. *Short production lead times.* A JIT system minimizes the time between the arrival of raw material or components in the plant and the shipment of a finished product to a customer.

4. *High inventory turnover (with the goal of zero inventory and stockless production).* The levels of finished goods, work in process, and raw materials are purposely reduced. Raw material in a warehouse is regarded as waste, and so is idle work in process. (A person who applied JIT to the household would regard backup supplies of ketchup or motor oil as shameful!)

5. *Designated areas for receiving materials.* Certain areas on the shop floor or in the receiving and shipping department are designated for receiving specific items from suppliers. At a Toyota plant in Japan, the receiving area is about half the size of a football field. The designated spaces for specific items are marked with yellow paint.

6. *Designated containers.* Specifying where to store items allows for easy access to parts, and it eliminates counting. For example, at Toyota the bed of a truck has metal frame mounts for exactly eight engines. A truckload of engines means eight engines—no more, no less. No one has to count them.

7. *Neatness.* A JIT plant that follows Japanese tradition is immaculate. All unnecessary materials, tools, rags, and files are discarded. The factory floor is as neat and clean as the showroom.

Advantages and Disadvantages of the JIT Inventory System

Manufacturing companies have realized several benefits from adopting JIT. Just-in-time controls can lead to organizational commitment to quality in design, materials, parts, employee-management and supplier-user relations, and finished goods. With minimum levels of inventory on hand, finished products are more visible and defects are more readily detected. Quality problems can therefore be attacked before they escalate to an insurmountable degree. Low levels of inventory also shorten cycle times.

Despite the advantages just-in-time management can offer large manufacturers, it has some striking disadvantages. Above all, a just-in-time system must be placed in a supportive or compatible environment. JIT is applicable only to highly repetitive manufacturing operations such as car or residential furnace manufacturing.

190

Small companies with short runs of a variety of products often may suffer financial losses from just-in-time practices. One problem they have is that suppliers are often unwilling to promptly ship small batches to meet the weekly needs of a small customer.

Product demand must be predictable for JIT to work well. If customer demand creates a surge of orders, a tight inventory policy will not be able to handle this windfall. The savings from just-in-time management can be deceptive. Several manufacturers who used JIT discovered that their suppliers were simply building up inventories in their own plants and adding that cost to their prices.[7] Just-in-time inventory practices also leave a company vulnerable to work stoppages, such as a strike. With a large inventory of finished products or parts, the company can continue to meet customer demand while the work stoppage is being settled.

Just-in-time inventory control also presents ethical problems. The big company saves money by forcing the supplier to maintain expensive inventories, so it (the big company) can be served promptly. Another ethical concern about JIT occurs when a manufacturer ceases dealing with a supplier. The supplier will usually have to close the facility it built just to be in proximity to the manufacturer.

5   PARETO DIAGRAMS FOR PROBLEM IDENTIFICATION

Describe how to identify problems using a Pareto diagram.

Pareto diagram

A bar graph that ranks types of output variations by frequency of occurrence.

Managers and professionals frequently must identify the major causes of their problem, such as "What features of our product are receiving the most complaints from consumers?" or "Our agency is offering more services to the public than we can afford. Which services might we drop without hurting too many people?" One problem identification technique uses a **Pareto diagram**, a bar graph that ranks types of output variations by frequency of occurrence. Managers and workers often use Pareto diagrams to identify the most important problems or causes of problems that affect output quality. Identification of the "vital few" allows management or product improvement teams to focus on the major cause of a quality problem.

An example might be an investigation of laser printer failures. As Exhibit 7-10 shows, the cause of a problem is plotted on the *x*-axis (horizontal). The cumulative

EXHIBIT 7-10

A Pareto Analysis of Laser Printer Failure

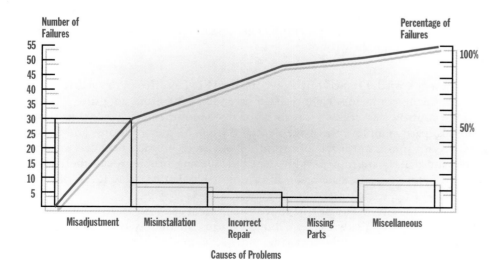

effects are plotted on the *y*-axis (vertical). In a Pareto diagram, the bars are arranged in descending order of height (or frequency of occurrence) from left to right across the *x*-axis. As a consequence, the most important causes are at the left of the chart. Priorities are then established for taking action on the few causes that account for most of the effect. According to the Pareto principle, generally 20 percent or fewer of the causes contribute to 80 percent or more of the effects. It is widely recognized, for example, that about 20 percent of the customers of an industrial company account for 80 percent of sales. And also, about 20 percent of customers account for about 80 percent of complaints.

A crisis management team of Ford managers and professionals did a Pareto analysis of problems with Bridgestone/Firestone tires used on the Ford Explorer. The Ford team analyzed the data based on tire sizes that had more than 30 reported warranty claims. The key results of their analysis, reported as follows, strongly support the Pareto principle:

> Of 2,498 complaints involving eight separate size categories, 2,030, or 81 percent, involved the 15-inch P235/75R15 models, which included the Firestone ATX and Wilderness tires. Of the 1,699 reported complaints of tread separations on 13 different size tires, 1,424, or 84 percent, were for the P234/75R15 series of tires used on Ford's Explorer and Bronco SUVs and its F-150 and Ranger pickup trucks.[8]

As you probably observed, one model created 81 percent of the problems, and another series 84 percent. Although, the 80/20 (Pareto) principle is a general guide, it is a close approximation of reality in many situations.

SUMMARY OF KEY POINTS

1 **Explain the use of forecasting techniques in planning.** All planning includes making forecasts, both qualitative and quantitative. A judgmental forecast makes predictions on subjective opinions. Time-series analysis is a widely used method of making quantitative forecasts. Three widely used forecasts are economic, sales, and technological.

2 **Describe how to use Gantt charts, milestone charts, and PERT planning techniques.** Gantt and milestone charts are simple methods of monitoring schedules that are particularly useful for one-time projects. Gantt charts graphically depict the planned and actual progress of work over the period of time encompassed by a project. A milestone chart lists the subactivities that must be completed to accomplish the major activities.

Managers use PERT networks to track complicated projects when sequences of events must be planned carefully. In a PERT network, an event is a point of decision or accomplishment. An activity is the physical and mental effort required to complete an event. To complete a PERT diagram, a manager must sequence all the events and estimate the time required for each activity. The expected time for each activity takes into account optimistic, pessimistic, and probable estimates of time. The critical path is the most time-consuming sequence of activities and events that must be followed to implement the project. The duration of the project is determined by the longest critical path. Frequency distributions are sometimes used to calculate expected times, and PERT can also be used to estimate resources and costs that will be needed.

3 **Describe how to use break-even analysis and decision trees for problem solving and decision making.** Managers use break-even analysis to estimate the point at which it is profitable to go ahead with a new venture. It is a method of determining the relationship between total costs and total revenues at various levels of sales activity or operation. Break-even analysis determines the ratio of total fixed costs to the difference between the selling price and the average variable cost for each unit. The results of break-even analysis are often depicted on a graph. Break-even analysis is based on an assumption of static costs.

A decision tree provides a quantitative estimate of the best alternative. It is a tool for estimating the outcome of a series of decisions. When the sequences of the major decisions are drawn, they resemble a tree with branches.

4 **Describe how to manage inventory by using materials requirement planning (MRP), the economic order quantity (EOQ), and the just-in-time (JIT) system.** Materials requirement planning (MRP) is a computerized manufacturing and inventory-control system designed to make materials handling and inventory control efficient. The economic order quantity (EOQ) is a decision-support technique widely used to manage inventory. The EOQ is the inventory level that minimizes both ordering and carrying costs. The EOQ technique helps managers in a manufacturing or sales organization decide how much inventory to keep on hand.

Just-in-time (JIT) inventory management minimizes stock on hand. Instead, stock is moved into the plant exactly when needed. Although not specifically a decision-making technique, JIT helps shape decisions about inventory. The key principle underlying JIT systems is the elimination of excess inventory by producing or purchasing items only when and in the exact amounts they are needed.

Just-in-time processes involve (1) *kanbans*, or cards for communicating production requirements to the previous operation, (2) a customer demand-driven system, (3) short production lead times, (4) high inventory turnover, (5) designated areas for receiving materials, (6) designated containers, and (7) neatness throughout the factory.

JIT inventory management is best suited for repetitive manufacturing processes. One drawback of JIT is that it places heavy pressures on suppliers to build up their inventories to satisfy sudden demands of their customers who use the system.

5 **Describe how to identify problems using a Pareto diagram.** Problems or causes of problems can often be identified by a problem identification technique called the Pareto diagram. The Pareto principle stems from the diagram, and suggests that about 20 percent or fewer of the causes contribute to 80 percent or more of the effects.

KEY TERMS AND PHRASES

Judgmental forecast, *173*

Time-series analysis, *174*

Gantt chart, *176*

Milestone chart, *177*

Program evaluation and review technique (PERT), *178*

Event, *179*

Activity, *179*

Expected time, *180*

Critical path, *180*

Break-even analysis, *182*

Decision tree, *184*

Expected value, *184*

Materials requirement planning, *186*

Economic order quantity (EOC), *186*

Just-in-time system, *188*

Pareto diagram, *190*

QUESTIONS

1. How could the information presented in this chapter help you make a better decisions as a manager?
2. Which of the techniques described in this chapter do you think would most likely be used by top-level managers?
3. What is the difference between a milestone chart and a to-do list?
4. Describe two possible job applications for a PERT network.

5. What similarities do you see between the purposes of break-even analysis and a decision tree?
6. Dell Computer, as well as several other companies, build a computer only after receiving an order. To what extent is building upon demand compatible with a just-in-time inventory system?
7. How might the Pareto principle apply to the profits an automobile company earns on the sales of its vehicles?

CRITICAL THINKING QUESTIONS

1. Find some information on the work of *futurists*. What is your evaluation of the potential contribution of these people to business forecasting?

2. Find evidence to support (or refute) the validity of the Pareto principle (the 80/20 principle). Do you agree or disagree with the evidence found? Why?

SKILL-BUILDING EXERCISE 7-A: Developing a PERT Network

Use the following information about a quality improvement project to construct a PERT diagram. Be sure to indicate the critical path with a dark arrow. Work individually or in small groups.

Event	Description	Time Required (units)	Preceding Event
A	Complete quality audit	6	none
B	Benchmark	15	A
C	Collect internal information	6	A
D	Identify performance problems	3	B, C
E	Identify improvement practices	7	D
F	Elicit employee participation	20	A
G	Implement quality program	6	E, F
H	Measure results	8	G

Source: Reprinted with permission from Raymond L. Hilgert and Edwin C. Leonard, Jr., *Supervision: Concepts and Practices of Management,* 6th ed. (Cincinnati: South-Western College Publishing, 1995), p. 191.

SKILL-BUILDING EXERCISE 7-B: Break-Even Analysis

On recent vacation trips to Juarez, Mexico, you noticed small stores and street vendors selling original art. The prices ranged from $3 to $25 U.S. A flash of inspiration hit you. Why not sell Mexican art back home to Americans, using a van as your store? Every three months you would drive the 350 miles to Mexico and load up on art. You anticipate receiving generous large-quantity discounts.

You would park your van on busy streets and nearby parks, wherever you could obtain a permit. Typically you would display the art outside the van, but on a rainy day people could step inside. Your intention is to operate your traveling art sale about 12 hours per week. If you could make enough money from your business, you could attend classes full-time during the day. You intend to sell the original painting at an average of $15 a unit.

Based on preliminary analysis, you have discovered that your primary fixed costs per month would be: $500 for payments on a van, $125 for gas and maintenance, $50 for insurance, and $45 for a street vendor's permit. You will also be driving down to Mexico every three months at $400 per trip, resulting in a $125 per month travel cost. Your variable costs would be an average of $5 per painting and 45¢ for wrapping each painting in brown paper.

1. How many paintings will you have to sell each month before you start to make a profit?
2. If the average cost of your paintings rises to $8, how many pieces of art will you have to sell each month if you hold your price to $15 per unit?

INTERNET SKILL-BUILDING EXERCISE: Trends in Excess Inventory

The Management in Action in the chapter described how during one period, many companies faced a serious inventory oversupply. Visit http://www.TradeOut.com and http://www.FastAsset .com to study patterns of surplus inventory. Figure out what types of equipment appear to have been overbuilt in contrast to demand. Look to see what kind of discounts a purchaser can find on several types of equipment. Do you notice telecommunications equipment available in large supply at big discounts? What conclusions do you reach about inventory management from visiting these two Web sites (or similar sites)?

CASE PROBLEM 7-A: Imbalances at Family Services

Gisela Sanchez is the director at Downtown Family Services, a social agency that provides various forms of assistance to low-income and no-income citizens in the northeast section of the city. Family Services receives funding from the city, state, and federal governments along with charitable contributions. Among the services the agency provides are family counseling, abortion counseling, home care for the infirm, and emergency shelters for battered or homeless people.

Seventeen professionals work at Family Services, including nurses and counselors, 19 paraprofessionals who assist the professionals, and a support staff of six people. Although the premises at Family Services are far from luxurious, the offices are adequately equipped with furniture, restrooms, break rooms, and office technology. The biggest problem facing the agency is an overworked staff, accompanied by complaints of burnout.

After the Christmas season, Sanchez was particularly worried about the haggard look of many staff members. As a preliminary step in dealing with the problem, Sanchez called a staff meeting at 4:30 two Fridays after the New Year. Sanchez served snacks and beverages. Sanchez began the meeting with these words: "I know you've been overworked, underpaid, and feel unappreciated, but I love you all. I think it's time to take some managerial action about our problems."

Gil Toomey, the director of social work, responded: "Oh, Gisela, are you going to merge us with another agency, and layoff duplicate positions?"

"Not at all Gil," responded Sanchez. "I want to know where we are spending the most of our time, what's dragging

us down, and how we can improve the situation. We've known for a long time we're spreading ourselves too thin."

"I sure feel spread too thin," said Marcie Beaudoin, the director of home-health care. My staff is also spread dangerously thin."

Sanchez then explained that she would like to analyze where the human resources are being used in the agency. She explained, "After we know what we are really doing with our time, we can develop a plan to ease the workload. The most we can hope for in the budget is to hire one new professional, and one paraprofessional. My suspicion is that a small number of our clients are draining us. Because of these needy people, we are not devoting enough attention to some other worthy clients."

Discussion Questions

1. Recommend a technique that Family Services can use to evaluate how much of their time is being spent on a relatively few number of clients.

2. After making this analysis and perhaps furnishing some illustrative data, explain what can be done about the situation.

3. How might forecasting techniques help Family Services do a better job of managing their workload?

CASE PROBLEM 7-B: Selling Snow Boards Just in Time

Sharon Prell is the general manager of three Sports Vancouver stores located in shopping malls around Vancouver, British Columbia. About 75 percent of their business stems from the sales of equipment and clothing for ice hockey, figure skating, and snow skiing. The other 25 percent of their business is derived mostly from swimming gear, and golf and tennis equipment.

Prell believes strongly that an important success factor in her business is maintaining the right inventory levels. She notes that she wants her stores to be stocked fully enough so as to excite and entice consumers. Yet she has data to prove that inventory piling up on the showroom floor or in the back room is costly.

Prell says, "If a customer asks for an item in his or her size or color that is not available in one store, we can often get that item in a hurry from one of our other stores. You might say I'm kind of a just-in-time inventory nut."

Two months after making that statement, the Sports Vancouver stores experienced a glorious winter season. Skates, skis, hockey sticks, pucks, and related clothing were being run up at the cash registers at a heartwarming clip. Sales of snow boards, however, boomed. Fifteen days before Christmas, the stores had sold out of every snow board in stock.

Frantic pleas to the snow board manufacturers brough in only an extra 25 snow boards. All were sold out in two more days. Prell then asked two competitors to lend them their inventory of snow boards. The competition, however, wanted to hold on to their dwindling stocks to satisfy their own customers.

The ski department manager kept a log of all the demand for snow boards that Sports Vancouver could not satisfy. By January 5, the figure was 250 boards. In discussing the problem with Prell, the ski department manager said, "Sharon, I think our just-in-time policy was implemented just in time to choke off what could have been a record season."

Prell responded, "I catch your dig, but this problem warrants further study. Losing money on unsold inventory is the problem on the other side of the ditch."

Discussion Questions

1. How might Prell prevent the snow board shortage problem (or a similar problem) in the future?

2. How might Press make more effective use of just-in-time inventory management?

3. How applicable would the economic quantity be to the snow board problem?

ENDNOTES

1. Case researched by Francesca Palladino, Rochester Institute of Technology, November 1998. The e-tailing facts are from data cited in Peter Haapaniemi, "The Truth about E-Business," November–December 2000, p. 26, available at *http://www.unisys.com/execmag.*
2. Daniel Levinas, "How to Stop the Competition from Eating Your Lunch," *Executive Focus*, May 1998, pp. 55–58.
3. John S. Hammond, Ralph L. Keeney, and Howard Raiffa, "The Hidden Traps in Decision Making," *Harvard Business Review*, September–October 1998, pp. 55–58.
4. Personal communication from Ron Olive, New Hampshire Technical College, May 17, 1992.
5. Ramon L. Aldag and Timothy M. Stearns, *Management,* 2d ed. (Cincinnati: South-Western College Publishing, 1991), pp. 645–646.
6. Lance Heiko, "Some Relationships Between Japanese Culture and Just-in-Time," *The Academy of Management Executive*, November 1989, pp. 319–321.
7. Doron P. Levin, "Is Auto Plant of the Future Almost Here?" *New York Times*, June 14, 1993, p. D8.
8. Bill Vlasic, "Tire Recall Rife with Blame, Tragedy," *The Detroit News*, March 9, 2000.

Job Design and Work Schedules

Continental Insurance Company wanted to increase productivity and breathe new life into a large insurance policy processing operation located in Glens Falls, New York. The location was the firm's most troublesome in terms of staffing. Furthermore, the unit generated no revenue, just expense. Management wanted to develop ways to get the work done, serve customers better, and also give employees more control over the work and how it gets accomplished.

To help accomplish these goals, the vice president for employee relations at the time, Anne M. Pauker, introduced Total Flex, a program that authorized employees to decide how and when they wanted to work. Top management did not specify core hours during which employees had to be present. However, employees had to keep in mind the hours that coverage was essential. Management then introduced Option 30 in order to meet demand for extended business hours, Saturdays included. The program did not include adding to staff or running up overtime expenses. Option 30 enabled employees to volunteer for a reduced, nontraditional work-hour schedule.

Eighty percent of employees in the Glens Falls location participated in alternative work arrangements, including Option 30. According to Pauker, "The productivity of this office was more than triple any other office in the company mainly because employee morale was uplifted thanks to management's new open-mindedness."

The turning point came when the company allowed employees to decide how and when they worked. The Glens Falls operation became Continental's most desirable operation.[1]

OBJECTIVES

After studying this chapter and doing the exercises, you should be able to:

1 Identify the major dimensions and different types of job design.

2 Describe job enrichment, including the job characteristics model.

3 Describe job involvement, enlargement, and rotation.

4 Explain how workers use job crafting to modify their jobs.

5 Illustrate how ergonomic factors can be part of job design.

6 Summarize the various modified work schedules.

Chapter 8

Not every company can achieve the same dramatic turnaround in productivity and satisfaction in an organizational unit as did Continental Insurance Company. Nevertheless, the principle is noteworthy: Modifying job design and work schedules can contribute to the success of an operation. Employers use a variety of job designs and work schedules to increase productivity and job satisfaction. Modifying job design and giving workers more control over schedules are the two major topics of this chapter.

To accomplish large tasks, such as building ships or operating a hotel, you must divide work among individuals and groups. Subdividing the overall tasks of an enterprise can be achieved in two primary ways. One way is to design specific jobs for individuals and groups to accomplish. The shipbuilding company must design jobs for welders, metal workers, engineers, purchasing agents, and contract administrators. In addition, many workers may be assigned to teams that assume considerable responsibility for productivity and quality. The other primary way of subdividing work assigns tasks to different units within the organization—units such as departments and divisions.

This chapter will explain basic concepts relating to job design, such as making jobs more challenging and giving employees more control over their working hours and place of work. We also look at how workers often shape their own jobs. The next chapter will describe how work is divided throughout an organization.

1   BASIC CONCEPTS OF JOB DESIGN

Identify the major dimensions and different types of job design.

job design

The process of laying out job responsibilities and duties and describing how they are to be performed.

Understanding how tasks are subdivided begins with **job design**. Managers use this process to lay out job responsibilities and duties and describe how they are to be performed in order to achieve an organization's goals. Each position in the organization serves a specific purpose. The importance of job design also comes from its potential for motivating workers. This section will describe several different types of job design, job specialization, and job enrichment, including the job characteristics model.

Four Different Types of Job Design

Michael Campion and his associates conducted extensive research in job design. Based on their results, they identified four approaches to job design: motivational, mechanistic, biological, and perceptual/motor.[2]

1. *The motivational approach.* A motivational approach to job design makes the job so challenging and the worker so responsible that the worker is motivated just by performing the job. Job enrichment and the job characteristics model, described later, are examples of this approach.
2. *The mechanistic approach.* The mechanistic approach to job design emphasizes total efficiency in performing a job. It assumes that work should be broken down into highly specialized and simplified tasks that involve frequent repetition of assignments. The section on "Job Specialization," describes the mechanistic approach. The mechanistic approach to job design developed out of scientific management and the work of Frederick W. Taylor (see Chapter 1).
3. *The biological approach.* Based on ergonomics, the biological approach to job design focuses on minimizing physical strain on the workers. It does so by reducing strength and endurance requirements and making improvements to upsetting noise and climate conditions. The biological approach results in less

discomfort, fatigue, and illness for workers. The ergonomic workstation shown later in this chapter is based primarily on the biological approach to job design.

4. *The perceptual/motor approach.* The perceptual/motor approach concentrates on mental capabilities and limitations. It considers the attention and concentration required by a job and ensures they stay within the capability of the least competent worker. For example, the instruction manual for a piece of equipment should not exceed the information-processing abilities of its least intelligent user. The perceptual/motor approach seeks to reduce mental stress, fatigue, training time, and chances for error.

Exhibit 8-1 summarizes research about the four types of job design. This table merits careful attention because it provides an overview of job design and lists the benefits and costs of each approach.

In practice, managers may blend these four approaches to job design to create a productive and satisfying job. For example, the job of information systems specialist might be primarily designed along motivational lines. Yet it might also take into account the perceptual/motor demands of working with a computer frequently.

Approach	Characteristics	Benefits	Costs
MOTIVATIONAL	*i* Variety	*i* Satisfaction	*i* Training
	i Autonomy	*i* Motivation	*i* Staffing difficulty
	i Significance	*i* Involvement	i Errors
	i Skill usage	*i* Performance	*i* Mental fatigue
	i Participation	d Absenteeism	*i* Stress
	i Recognition		*i* Mental abilities
	i Growth		*i* Compensation
	i Achievement		
	i Feedback		
MECHANISTIC	*i* Specialization	*d* Training	*d* Satisfaction
	i Simplification	*d* Staffing difficulty	*d* Motivation
	i Repetition	*d* Errors	*i* Absenteeism
	i Automation	*d* Mental fatigue	
	d Spare time	*d* Mental abilities	
		d Compensation	
BIOLOGICAL	*d* Strength requirements	*d* Physical abilities	*i* Financial costs
	d Endurance requirements	*d* Physical fatigue	*i* Inactivity
	i Seating comfort	*d* Aches & pains	
	i Postural comfort	d Medical incidents	
	d Environmental stressors		
PERCEPTUAL/ MOTOR	*i* Lighting quality	*d* Errors	*i* Boredom
	i Display and control quality	*d* Accidents	*d* Satisfaction
	d Information processing requirements	*d* Mental fatigue	
	i User-friendly equipment	*d* Stress	
		d Training	
		d Staffing difficulty	
		d Compensation	
		d Mental abilities	

i = increased
d = decreased

EXHIBIT 8-1

The Four Types of Job Design

Source: Adapted with permission from Michael A. Campion and Michael J. Stevens, "Neglected Aspects in Job Design: How People Design Jobs, Task-Job Predictability, and Influence of Training," *Journal of Business and Psychology,* Winter 1991, p. 175.

job description

A written statement of the key features of a job along with the activities required to perform it effectively.

job specialization

The degree to which a job holder performs only a limited number of tasks.

Before choosing a job design, managers and human resource professionals develop a job description. The **job description** is a written statement of the key features of a job, along with the activities required to perform it effectively. Sometimes a description must be modified to fit basic principles of job design. For example, the job description of a customer-service representative might call for an excessive amount of listening to complaints, thus creating too much stress. Exhibit 8-2 presents a job description of a middle-level manager.

Job Specialization

A major consideration in job design is how specialized the job holder must be. **Job specialization** is the degree to which a job holder performs only a limited number of tasks. The mechanistic approach favors job specialization. Specialists handle a narrow range of tasks especially well. High occupational level specialists include the stock analyst who researches companies in one or two industries and the surgeon who concentrates on liver transplants. Specialists at the first occupational level are usually referred to as *operatives*. An assembly-line worker who fastens two wires to one terminal is an operative.

A generalized job requires the handling of many different tasks. The motivational approach to job design favors generalized jobs. An extreme example of a top-level generalist is the owner of a small business who performs such varied tasks as making the product, selling it, negotiating with banks for loans, and hiring new employees. An extreme example of a generalist at the first (or entry) occupational level is the maintenance worker who packs boxes, sweeps, shovels snow in winter, mows the lawn, and cleans the lavatories.

Advantages and Disadvantages of Job Specialization

As its most important advantage, job specialization allows for the development of expertise at all occupational levels. When employees perform the same task repeatedly, they become highly knowledgeable. Many employees derive status and self-esteem from being experts at some task.

Specialized jobs at lower occupational levels require less training time and less learning ability, which can prove to be a key advantage when the available labor force lacks special skills. For example, McDonald's could never have grown so large if each restaurant needed expert chefs. Instead, newcomers to the workforce can quickly learn such specialized skills as preparing hamburgers and french fries. These newcomers can be paid entry-level wages—an advantage from a management perspective only!

Job specialization also has disadvantages. Coordinating the work force can be difficult when several employees do small parts of one job. Somebody must take

EXHIBIT 8-2

Job Description for Branch Manager, Insurance

Manages the branch office, including such functions as underwriting, claims processing, loss prevention, marketing, and auditing, and resolves related technical questions and issues. Hires new insurance agents, develops new business, and updates the regional manager regarding the profit-and-loss operating results of the branch office, insurance trends, matters having impact on the branch office function, and competitor methods. Makes extensive use of information technology to carry out all of these activities, including spreadsheet analyses and giving direction to establishing customer databases.

responsibility for pulling together the small pieces of the total task. Some employees prefer narrowly specialized jobs but the majority prefer broad tasks that give them a feeling of control over what they are doing. Although many technical and professional workers join the workforce as specialists, they often become bored by performing a narrow range of tasks.

Automation and Job Specialization

Ever since the Industrial Revolution, automation has been used to replace some aspects of human endeavor in the office and the factory. Automation typically involves a machine that performs a specialized task previously performed by people. Automation is widely used in factories, offices, and stores. Two automation devices in the store are optical scanners and the automatic recording of remaining inventory when a customer checks out. The computerization of the workplace represents automation in hundreds of ways, such as personal computers decreasing the need for clerical support in organizations. Today, only high-level managers have personal secretaries. Others rely on their computers to perform many chores. The fax machine has automated the delivery of many types of messages once sent by mail or messenger service. Similar to many machines, the fax machine is quite specialized. It doesn't respond to the request, "On your way back, pick up some bagels and donuts."

Job Enrichment and the Job Characteristics Model

Job enrichment is an approach to including more challenge and responsibility in jobs to make them more appealing to most employees. At its best, job enrichment gives workers a sense of ownership, responsibility, and accountability for their work. Because job enrichment leads to a more exciting job, it often increases employee job satisfaction and motivation. People usually work harder at tasks they find enjoyable and rewarding, just as they put effort into a favorite hobby. The general approach to enriching a job is to build into it more planning and decision making, controlling, and responsibility. Most managers have enriched jobs; most data entry specialists do not.

Characteristics of an Enriched Job

According to industrial psychologist Frederick Herzberg, the design of an enriched job includes as many of the characteristics in the following list as possible.[3] (Exhibit 8-3 summarizes the characteristics and consequences of enriched jobs.) The person holding the job must perceive these characteristics as part of the job. Research indicates that supervisors and group members frequently have different perceptions of job characteristics. For example, supervisors are more likely to think that a job has a big impact on the organization.[4] A worker who is responsible for placing used soft-drink cans in a recycling bin might not think his job is significant. Yet the supervisor might perceive the individual to be contributing to the social responsibility goal of creating a cleaner, less congested environment.

1. *Direct feedback.* Employees should receive immediate evaluation of their work. This feedback can be built into the job (such as the feedback that closing a sale gives a sales representative) or provided by the supervisor.
2. *Client relationships.* A job is automatically enriched when an employee has a client or customer to serve, whether that client is inside or outside the firm. Serving a client is more satisfying to most people than performing work solely for a manager.

201

2

Describe job enrichment, including the job characteristics model.

job enrichment
An approach to including more challenge and responsibility in jobs to make them more appealing to most employees.

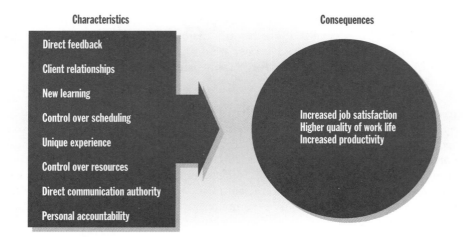

EXHIBIT 8-3

Characteristics and Consequences of an Enriched Job

202

Enriched jobs have eight distinguishing characteristics. A job holder who welcomes the challenge of the job characteristics listed in the box can expect the consequences listed in the circle.

Characteristics

Direct feedback

Client relationships

New learning

Control over scheduling

Unique experience

Control over resources

Direct communication authority

Personal accountability

Consequences

Increased job satisfaction
Higher quality of work life
Increased productivity

3. *New learning.* An enriched job allows its holder to acquire new knowledge. The learning can stem from job experiences themselves or from training programs associated with the job.

4. *Control over scheduling.* The ability to schedule one's own work contributes to job enrichment. Scheduling includes the authority to decide when to tackle which assignment and having some say in setting working hours.

5. *Unique experience.* An enriched job exhibits some unique qualities or features. A public-relations assistant, for example, has the opportunity to interact with visiting celebrities.

6. *Control over resources.* Another contribution to enrichment comes from some control over resources, such as money, material, or people.

7. *Direct communication authority.* An enriched job provides workers the opportunity to communicate directly with other people who use their output. A software specialist with an enriched job, for example, handles complaints about the software he or she developed. The advantages of this dimension of an enriched job are similar to those derived from maintaining client relationships.

8. *Personal accountability.* In an enriched job, workers take responsibility for their results. They accept credit for a job done well and blame for a job done poorly.

A highly enriched job with all eight of the preceding characteristics gives the job holder an opportunity to satisfy high-level psychological needs, such as self-fulfillment. Sometimes the jobs of managers are too enriched, with too much responsibility and too many risks. A job with some of these characteristics would be moderately enriched. An impoverished job has none.

Information technology workers are another occupational group that may suffer from overenriched jobs. Working with computers and software at an advanced level may represent healthy job enrichment for many workers—working directly with information technology gives a person direct feedback, new learning, and personal accountability. However, many other computer workers feel stressed by the complexity of information technology, the amount of continuous learning involved, and frequent hardware and software breakdowns beyond the control of the worker. According to Clare-Marie Karat, a psychologist at IBM who studies how humans interface with computers, the problem is simple: The engineers and computer scientists who design software and hardware lack sufficient knowledge about the needs and frustrations of computer users. Among the major frustrations of users are difficult-to-interpret error messages, and the difficulty in getting problems resolved when calling a help desk.[5] (To a computer whiz, these problems represent exciting and enriching challenges.)

The Job Characteristics Model of Job Enrichment

Expanding the concept of job enrichment creates the **job characteristics model**, a method of job enrichment that focuses on the task and interpersonal dimensions of a job.[6] As Exhibit 8-4 shows, five measurable characteristics of jobs improve employee motivation, satisfaction, and performance. These characteristics are:

1. *Skill variety:* The degree to which a job holds many skills to perform.
2. *Task identity:* The degree to which one worker completes a job from beginning to end, with a tangible and visible outcome.
3. *Task significance:* The degree to which work affects others in the immediate organization or the external environment.
4. *Autonomy:* The degree to which a job offers freedom, independence, and discretion in scheduling and in determining procedures involved in its implementation.
5. *Feedback:* The degree to which a job provides direct information about performance.

As Exhibit 8-4 reports, these core job characteristics relate to critical psychological states or key mental attitudes. Skill variety, task identity, and task significance lead to a feeling that the work is meaningful. The task dimension of autonomy leads quite logically to a feeling of responsibility for work outcomes.

job characteristics model

A method of job enrichment that focuses on the task and interpersonal dimensions of a job.

203

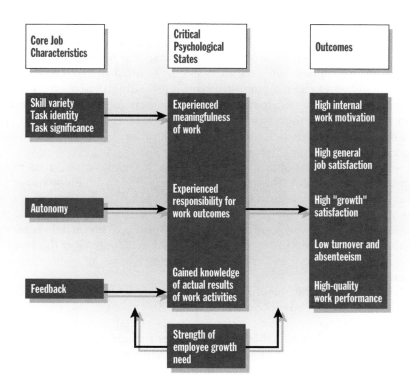

EXHIBIT 8-4

The Job Characteristics Model of Job Enrichment

Job enrichment can be made more precise and scientific by following the model presented here.

And the feedback dimension leads to knowledge of results. According to the model, a redesigned job must lead to these three psychological states for workers to achieve the outcomes of internal motivation, job satisfaction, low turnover and absenteeism, and high-quality performance.

The notation in Exhibit 8-4, *strength of employee growth need*, provides guidelines for managers. The link between the job characteristics and outcomes strengthens as workers want to grow and develop.

Guidelines for Implementing a Job Enrichment Program

Before implementing a program of job enrichment, a manager must first ask whether the workers need or want more responsibility, variety, and growth. Some employees already have jobs that are enriched enough. Many employees do not want an enriched job because they prefer to avoid the challenge and stress of responsibility. Brainstorming is useful in pinpointing changes that will enrich jobs for those who want enrichment.[7] The brainstorming group would be composed of job incumbents, supervisors, and perhaps an industrial engineer. The workers' participation in planning changes can be useful. Workers may suggest, for example, how to increase client contact.

Fresh insights into the type of workers likely to benefit from job enrichment (or any other motivational approach to job design) stem from a survey of 1,123 American workers sponsored by Shell Oil Co. The results show that workers generally fit into one of six categories:[8]

1. *Fulfillment seekers.* The majority of fulfillment seekers believe a good job is one that "allows me to use my talents and make a difference," rather than one that provides a good income and benefits. Most fulfillment seekers believe they have a career as opposed to a job, and the majority claim to be team players rather than leaders.
2. *High achievers.* The high achievers carefully plan their careers, have the highest level of education, and are the highest income group. Most are leaders who take initiative, and a majority hold managerial positions.
3. *Clock punchers.* These workers are the least satisfied of any group surveyed, with nearly all of them saying they have a job rather than a career. An overwhelming majority said they wound up in their job by chance, and nearly three quarters said they would make different career choices given another chance. Clock punchers have the lowest educational level and income of the six groups in the study.
4. *Risk takers.* Members of this group are the most willing to take risks to pursue large financial rewards. Risk takers are young people who enjoy moving from one employer to another in search of the best job, and are strongly motivated by money.
5. *Ladder climbers.* These company people appreciate the stability of staying with one firm a long time. Most prefer a stable income over the possibilities of great financial success, and consider themselves to be leaders rather than team players.
6. *Paycheck cashers.* The majority of paycheck cashers prefer jobs that provide good income and benefits over those that allow them to use their talents and make a difference. Members of this group are young. Although a majority say they will takes risks to achieve big financial success, an even larger number also want job security with one employer. Most paycheck cashers have limited education and prefer working in a large company or agency.

The groups most likely to want and enjoy enriched jobs are the fulfillment seekers, high achievers, risk takers, and perhaps ladder climbers. The less-enriched jobs are best assigned to clock punchers and paycheck cashers. Which one of the six types do you think best characterizes you now, or will in the future?

JOB INVOLVEMENT, ENLARGEMENT, AND ROTATION

3

205

Job enrichment, including the job characteristics model, requires a comprehensive program. Managers can also improve the motivational aspects of job design through less complicated procedures: job involvement, job enlargement, and job rotation. All three processes are built into the more comprehensive job enrichment.

Describe job involvement, enlargement, and rotation.

Job involvement is the degree to which individuals identify psychologically with their work. It also refers to the importance of work to a person's total self-image. If an insurance claims examiner regards his job as a major part of his identity, he experiences high job involvement. For example, at a social gathering the claims examiner would inform people shortly after meeting them, "I'm a claims examiner with Nationwide Insurance." The employee-involvement groups in quality management are based on job involvement. By making decisions about quality improvement, the team members ideally identify psychologically with their work. Exhibit 8-5 gives you an opportunity to think about job involvement as it applies to you.

job involvement
The degree to which individuals identify psychologically with their work.

EXHIBIT 8-5

How Involved Are You?

Indicate the strength of your agreement with the following statements by circling the number that appears below the appropriate heading: DS = disagree strongly; D = disagree; N = neutral; A = agree; AS = agree strongly. Respond in relation to a present job, the job you hope to have, or schoolwork.

	DS	D	N	A	AS
1. The major satisfaction in my life comes from my work.	1	2	3	4	5
2 Work is just a means to an end.	5	4	3	2	1
3. The most important things that happen to me involve my work.	1	2	3	4	5
4. I often concentrate so hard on my work that I'm unaware of what is going on around me.	1	2	3	4	5
5. If I inherited enough money, I would spend the rest of my life on vacation.	5	4	3	2	1
6. I'm a perfectionist about my work.	1	2	3	4	5
7. I am very much involved personally in my work.	1	2	3	4	5
8. Most things in life are more important than work.	5	4	3	2	1
9. Working full-time is boring.	5	4	3	2	1
10. My work is intensely exciting.	1	2	3	4	5

Score _____

Scoring and interpretation: Total the numbers circled, and then use the following guide to interpretation.

45–50   Your attitudes suggest intense job involvement. Such attitudes should contribute highly to productivity, quality, and satisfaction.

28–44   Your attitudes suggest a moderate degree of job involvement. To sustain a high level of productivity and quality, you would need to work toward becoming more involved in your work.

10–27   Your attitudes suggest a low degree of job involvement. It would be difficult to sustain a successful, professional career with such low involvement.

Source: Adapted from Myron Gable and Frank Dangello, "Job Involvement, Machiavellianism, and Job Performance," *Journal of Business and Psychology,* Winter 1994, p. 163.

job enlargement

Increasing the number and variety of tasks within a job.

Job enlargement refers to increasing the number and variety of tasks within a job. Because the tasks are approximately at the same level of responsibility, job enlargement is also referred to as *horizontal job loading*. In contrast, job enrichment is referred to as *vertical job loading*, because the job holder takes on higher-level job responsibility. The claims examiner would experience job enlargement if he were given additional responsibilities such as examining claims for boats and motorcycles as well as automobiles.

As responsibilities expand in job enlargement, job holders usually find themselves juggling multiple priorities. Two, three, four, or even more demands might be facing the worker. In one approach to handling multiple priorities, a job holder ranks them in order of importance and then tackles the most important one first. With this approach, the lowest-priority tasks may be neglected. With a more recommended approach, the job holder finishes the top-priority task, and then moves immediately to all other tasks. Top-priority items can be tackled again after the lesser tasks are completed. Yet if the manager or team leader insists that a specific task must be done immediately, it is good office politics to work on that task. Some catch-up time at night or on weekends might then be invested in work to avoid falling behind on other projects.

job rotation

A temporary switching of job assignments.

Job rotation is a temporary switching of job assignments. In this way employees develop new skills and learn about how other aspects of the unit or organization work. However, the potential advantages of job rotation are lost if a person is rotated from one dull job to another. A motivational form of job rotation would be for the claims examiner to investigate auto and small-truck claims one month, and large trucks the next. Job rotation helps prevent workers from feeling bored or in a rut.

Some employers take another approach to job rotation in which they share employees with another organization that has a different seasonal demand for workers. For example, AT&T in Maine made a sharing arrangement with L.L. Bean, the mail-order company whose peak business is during the holiday season. AT&T outdoor workers, such as line repair technicians, spend part of the winter picking and packing and answering telephones at L.L. Bean. Then, during the slower-selling summer season, some L.L. Bean employees hold down outdoor positions for AT&T.[9]

Job enlargement and job rotation offer similar advantages and disadvantages to the individual and the organization. Through job enlargement and job rotation, workers develop a broader set of skills making them more valuable and flexible. Pushed to extremes, however, job enlargement and rotation lead to feelings of being overworked.

4

JOB CRAFTING AND JOB DESIGN

Explain how workers use job crafting to modify their jobs.

In the traditional view of a job, a competent worker carefully follows a job description, and good performance means that the person accomplishes what is specified in the job description. A contemporary view sees a job description as only a guideline: the competent worker exceeds the constraints of a job description. He or she takes on constructive activities not mentioned in the job description.

The flexible work roles carried out by many workers contribute to the move away from tightly following job descriptions that are too rigid. An emerging trend finds companies hiring people "to work" rather than to fill a specific job slot. Both Amazon.com and Koch industries rarely use job descriptions. At Amazon, a person might still hold the same essential job, but three months later be performing entirely different work. The "Amazonian" might be working out a software glitch one day and helping lay out a new wing of a distribution center the next.[10]

Workers sometimes deviate from their job descriptions by modifying their job to fit their personal preferences and capabilities. According to the research of Amy Wrzesniewski and Jane E. Dutton, employees craft their jobs by changing the tasks they perform and their contacts with others to make their jobs more meaningful.[11] To add variety to her job, for example, a team leader might make nutritional recommendations to team members. The team leader alters her task of coaching about strictly work-related issues to also coaching about personal health. In this way, she broadens her role in terms of her impact on the lives of work associates.

Job crafting refers to the physical and mental changes individuals make in the task or relationship aspects of their job. Three common types of job crafting include (1) the number and types of job tasks, (2) the interactions with others on the job, and (3) one's view of the job. The most frequent purpose of crafting is to make the job more meaningful or enriched. A cook, for example, might add flair to a meal that was not required, just to inject a little personal creativity. Exhibit 8-6 illustrates these three forms of job crafting, including how crafting affects the meaning of work. After studying the exhibit think through whether you have ever engaged in job crafting.

job crafting

The physical and mental changes individuals make in the task or relationship aspects of their job.

ERGONOMICS AND JOB DESIGN

As mentioned in the biological approach to job design, a job should be laid out to decrease the chances that it will physically harm the incumbent. For example, jack-hammer operators are required to wear sound dampeners and kidney belts to minimize

Illustrate how ergonomic factors can be part of job design.

Form	Example	Effect on Meaning of Work
Changing number, scope, and type of job tasks	Design engineers engage in changing the quality or amount of interactions with people, thereby moving a project to completion.	Work is completed in a more timely fashion; engineers change the meaning of their jobs to be guardians or movers of projects.
Changing quality and/or amount of interaction with others encountered in the job	Hospital cleaners actively caring for patients and families, integrating themselves into the workflow of their floor units.	Cleaners change the meaning of their jobs to be helpers of the sick; they see the work of the floor unit as an integrated whole of which they are a vital part.
Changing the view of the job	Nurses take responsibility for all information and "insignificant" tasks that may help them to care more appropriately for a patient.	Nurses change the way they see the work to be more about patient advocacy, as well as high-quality technical care.

EXHIBIT 8-6

Forms of Job Crafting

Source: Adapted from Amy Wrzesniewski and Jane E. Dutton, "Crafting a Job: Revisioning Employees as Active Crafters of Their Work," *Academy of Management Review,* April 2001, p. 185.

cumulative trauma disorders

Injuries caused by repetitive motions over prolonged periods of time.

trauma. A hazard in the modern workplace is **cumulative trauma disorders**, injuries caused by repetitive motions over prolonged periods of time. These disorders now account for almost half of occupational injuries and illnesses in the United States.

Any occupation involving excessive repetitive motions, including bricklayer and meat cutter, can lead to cumulative trauma disorder. The use of computers and other high-tech equipment such as price scanners contributes to the surge in the number of cumulative trauma disorders. Extensive keyboarding places severe strain on hand and wrist muscles, often leading to *carpal tunnel syndrome*. This syndrome occurs when frequent bending of the wrist causes swelling in a tunnel of bones and ligaments in the wrist. The nerve that gives feeling to the hand is pinched, resulting in tingling and numbness in the fingers.

The symptoms of carpal tunnel syndrome are severe. Many workers suffering from the syndrome are unable to differentiate hot and cold by touch and lose finger strength. They often appear clumsy because they have difficulty with everyday tasks such as tying their shoes or picking up small objects. Treatment of carpal tunnel syndrome may involve surgery to release pressure on the median nerve. Another approach is anti-inflammatory drugs to reduce tendon swelling.

To help prevent and decrease the incidence of cumulative trauma disorders, many companies select equipment designed for that purpose. Exhibit 8-7 depicts a workstation based on ergonomic principles developed to engineer a good fit between person and machine. In addition, the following steps should be taken to prevent cumulative trauma disorders:[12]

- Analyze each job with an eye toward possible hazards on that job, including equipment that is difficult to operate.
- Install equipment that minimizes awkward hand and body movements. Try ergonomically designed keyboards to see whether they make a difference.
- Encourage workers to take frequent breaks, and rotate jobs so that repetitive hand and body movements are reduced.

EXHIBIT 8-7

An Ergonomically Designed Workstation

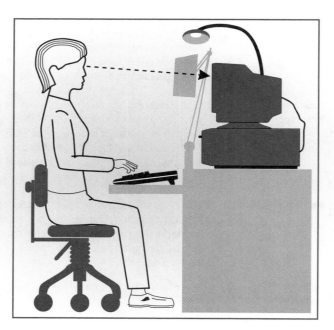

- Screen is below eye level.

- Elbows are on same level with the homekey row, keeping wrists and lower arms parallel to the floor.

- Back and thighs are supported.

- Upper legs are parallel to the floor.

- Feet are placed flat on the floor.

- Task lamp supplements adequate room lighting.

- Use voice recognition systems as a substitute for keyboarding where feasible, especially for repetitive functions. (However, guard against creating vocal chord strain from talking into the computer for long periods of time!)
- Make less use of the mouse by using more key commands. Overuse of the mouse can cause repetitive motion injury. Find ways to use the left hand more, such as for tapping function keys.

Workers must also recognize that if they spend many nonworking hours using a keyboard, they increase the probability of developing carpal tunnel syndrome.

Repetitive motion disorders, and other musculoskeletal disorders including tendonitis, sciatica, and lower-back pain are well-publicized ergonomic problems. Another recurring problem relates to uncomfortable noise levels. Although industrial noise problems are usually associated with manufacturing and mills, the constant buzz in offices can also create discomfort and physical problems.

An experiment was conducted in which 40 female clerical workers were assigned to a control (low-noise) group or to a high-noise group. The noise was a three-hour exposure to low-intensity noise designed to simulate open-office noise levels. Workers exposed to the noise experienced negative consequences, not experienced by the control (comparison) group. One effect was an increase in epinephrine, a hormone that enters the urine in response to stress. The group exposed to noise also performed more poorly on a puzzle given to participants. Also, the group exposed to noise made less use of work-furniture features designed to provide opportunities for postural adjustment during work.[13] In this way one ergonomics problem (noise) could lead to increased ergonomic problems (repetitive motion disorder and back problems).

MODIFIED WORK SCHEDULES AND JOB DESIGN

6

Summarize the various modified work schedules.

A key characteristic of job enrichment gives workers authority in scheduling their own work. Closely related is the widespread practice of giving workers some choice in deviating from the traditional five-day, 40-hour work week. A **modified work schedule** is any formal departure from the traditional hours of work, excluding shift work and staggered work hours. Yet shift work presents enough unique managerial challenges that it will be described here. Modified work schedules include flexible working hours, a compressed workweek, job sharing, an alternative workplace (such as working at home), and part-time work, including reduced hours.

modified work schedule

Any formal departure from the traditional hours of work, excluding shift work and staggered work hours.

Modified work schedules serve several important organizational purposes in addition to being part of job design. They potentially increase job satisfaction and motivation and attract workers who prefer to avoid a traditional schedule. Many single parents need flexible hours to cope with child care. Flexible working hours are popular with many employees. Working at home continues to gain popularity with a subset of the workforce. Yet, as companies continue to remain thinly staffed, employees show less willingness to volunteer for job sharing and part-time work. A prevailing attitude is to cling to a full-time job. Many workers also feel that not being seen around the office regularly might hurt their chances for promotion.

Flexible Working Hours

For about 28 million American employees, the standard eight-hour day with fixed starting and stopping times is a thing of the past. Instead, these employees exert some control over their work schedules through a system or informal arrangement of **flexible working hours**. The vast majority of workers with flexible working

flexible working hours

A system in which employees must work certain core hours but can choose their arrival and departure times.

hours adjust their working hours through informal agreements with their managers, rather than as part of a formal program.[14]

Employees with flexible working hours work certain core hours, such as 10:00 A.M. to 3:30 P.M. However, they are able to choose which hours they work from 7:00 A.M. to 10:00 A.M. and from 3:30 P.M. to 6:30 P.M. Exhibit 8-8 presents a basic model of flexible working hours. Time-recording devices frequently monitor employees' required hours for the week.

Flexible working hours are far more likely to be an option for employees on the nonexempt payroll. Such workers receive additional pay for work beyond 40 hours per week and premium pay for Saturdays and Sundays. Managers, professional-level workers, and salespeople generally have some flexibility in choosing their work hours. In addition, managers and professionals in corporations work an average of 55 hours per week, making concerns about fitting in a 40-hour-per-week flextime schedule irrelevant.

Many employers believe that flexible working hours enhance productivity for reasons such as decreasing employee absenteeism and stress. For example, Hewlett-Packard has offered flexible working options since the 1960s. HP leaves flextime arrangements largely up to employees and their managers, under the assumption that they will find the best solutions. Kathy Burke, Global Worklife Program manager for HP, believes that empowering employees to create schedules that accommodate their quest to balance work and family life makes them more productive. "HP employees face a lot of stress on the job," she says. "Giving them flextime options allows them to meet their personal commitments while staying committed."[15]

Many employees hesitate to use flexible working hours (as well as other work/life programs) for fear of being perceived as not strongly committed to the organization. A survey of Fortune 500 companies conducted by the Conference Board indicated that the flextime option is available at most companies, yet few employees choose the option. The reason is that too many managers question an employee's motives or commitment if he or she requests flexible working hours.[16] A major problem for the career-oriented employee who chooses flextime is that meetings might be held at times beyond the employee's scheduled quitting time. Suppose you have agreed to work from 7 A.M. until 4 P.M. on Thursday. The team leader schedules an important meeting at 4:30 for Thursday. You now face a conflict between taking care of personal obligations and appearing to be a dedicated worker.

Flextime often comes about after an employee requests the opportunity to participate in a program. Finding answers to the following questions can help the

EXHIBIT 8-8

A Typical Flexible-Working-Hours Schedule

Flexible working hours have a fixed core time in the middle.

Flexible Arrival Time	Fixed Core Time (designated lunch break)	Flexible Departure Time
7:00 AM 10:00 AM		3:30 PM 6:30 PM

Sample schedules: Early Schedule, 7:00–3:30
Standard Schedule, 9:00–5:30
Late Schedule, 10:00–6:30

manager evaluate a flextime request:[17] (The same questions also apply generally to other types of modified work schedules.)

1. *Does the nature of the job allow for a flexible schedule?* Employees who must turn around work quickly or respond to crises might not be good candidates for flexible working hours. Negative indicators for flextime also include other employees being inconvenienced by the altered schedule, and a job that requires frequent interaction with others.
2. *Will this individual work well independently?* Some employees thrive on working solo, such as being in the office at 6 A.M. or 7 P.M. Others lose momentum when working alone. Does the employee have a high level of initiative and self-motivation?
3. *Are you comfortable managing a flex-worker?* A manager who feels the need to frequently monitor the work of employees will become anxious when the employees are working by themselves during noncore hours.
4. *Can you arrange tasks so the employee will have enough to do when you or other workers are not present?* Some employees can find ways to make a contribution in the office alone, while others must be fed work in small doses.

As a member of a self-managing team a modern worker should be able to rise to the challenge of handling a flexible work schedule responsibly. Yet an effective manager must stay alert to possible differences in employee behavior.

Compressed Work Week

A **compressed work week** is a full-time work schedule that allows 40 hours of work in less than five days. The usual arrangement is 4–40 (working four 10–hour days). Many employees enjoy the 4–40 schedule because it enables them to have three consecutive days off from work. Employees often invest this time in leisure activities or part-time jobs. A 4–40 schedule usually allows most employees to take off Saturdays and Sundays. Important exceptions include police workers, hospital employees, and computer operators.

A compressed work week currently gaining some attention is the 9–80. The numerals signify 9-hour days and 80 hours worked every two weeks. Employees on 9–80 work nine-hour days from Monday through Thursday, and an eight-hour day on Friday. The following Friday is a day off.

Compressed work weeks are well liked by employees whose lifestyle fits such a schedule. However, the 4–40 week has many built-in problems. Many workers are fatigued during the last two hours and suffer from losses in concentration. From a personal standpoint, working for 10 consecutive hours can be inconvenient.

compressed work week

A full-time work schedule that allows 40 hours of work in less than five days.

The Alternative Workplace and Telecommuting

A major deviation from the traditional work schedule is the **alternative workplace,** a combination of nontraditional work practices, settings, and locations that supplements the traditional office. An estimated 24 million people in the United States work at home as corporate employees or for self-employment.[18] In addition to working at home, the alternative workplace can include working from a small satellite office, sharing an office or cubicle, or being assigned a laptop computer and a cellular phone as a substitute for a private work space. Here we concentrate on working at home because it represents the most substantial change in a work schedule.

alternative workplace

A combination of nontraditional work practices, settings, and locations that supplements the traditional office.

telecommuting

An arrangement with one's employer to use a computer to perform work at home or in a satellite office.

Telecommuting is an arrangement in which employees use computers to perform their regular work responsibilities at home or in a satellite office. Employees who telecommute usually use computers tied to the company's main office. People who work at home are referred to as *teleworkers.* The vast majority of people who work at home are either assigned a computer by the company or own their own computer and related equipment. Yet a person might do piecework at home, such as making garments or furniture, without using a computer.

In addition to using computers to communicate with their employer's office, telecommuters attend meetings on company premises and stay in contact by telephone and teleconferences. Some telecommuting programs are huge. The Mobility Initiative at IBM, for example, has resulted in 12,500 sales representatives giving up their dedicated work spaces. The sales representative's residence, along with an automobile trunk, becomes his or her office. IBM estimates it is saving $100 million annually on the cost of offices in its North America sales and distribution unit alone. Many small businesses operate with informal telecommuting programs.

Telecommuting makes possible a *virtual corporation* in which people work as a team even though they are physically separated. (Chapter 3 described this type of office.) Many virtual corporations are alliances of representatives from small companies working together to produce a product such as a book publisher subcontracting with copyeditors, visual artists, photographers, and a printer. At times, however, some of the people in the virtual corporation work out of their homes. The accompanying Management in Action illustrates how people working in different locations can join forces to achieve important business results.

Advantages of Telecommuting

Telecommuting can work well with self-reliant and self-starting employees who have relevant work experience. Work-at-home employees usually volunteer for such an arrangement. As a result, they are likely to find telecommuting satisfying. Employees derive many benefits from working at home, including easier management of personal life; lowered costs for commuting, work clothing, and lunch; much less time spent commuting; and fewer distractions such as office noise. Telecommuting offers the following advantages to the employer:[19]

1. *Increased productivity.* Surveys consistently show that telecommuting programs increase productivity, usually by at least 25 percent. Research contained in a Department of Labor (DOL) report concluded that teleworkers save their employers up to $10,000 per year in reduced absenteeism and retention costs. Another study found that telework reduces absenteeism costs by 63 percent, with average savings of more than $2,000 per employee. A survey of employees in the Mobility Initiative program at IBM revealed that 87 percent believe their productivity had increased significantly.

2. *Low overhead.* Because the employees provide some of their own office space, the company can operate with much less office space. Over a seven-year period, AT&T improved cash flow by $500 million by eliminating offices people no longer need, consolidating others, and reducing related overhead costs. A vice president of marketing research operations noted that, because of its work-at-home program, the company was able to greatly expand its client load without acquiring additional space. During a five-year period of IBM's Mobility Initiative program, real estate savings alone amounted to $1 billion. (IBM would probably have to sell $10 billion in equipment to earn the same amount of profit.)

Management *in Action*

Financial Consultant Runs Virtual Business

Like many entrepreneurs, Jeff Stello overflows with ideas about building businesses and making money. Bringing those ideas to reality, at times, can get a bit tricky. But the challenges haven't stopped the 40-year-old president and owner of IT Financial Inc., a financial management consulting company in Malvern, Pennsylvania, from trying.

At one time his client, Healthy PetCorp., a Trumbull, Connecticut, company that owns and manages animal hospitals, needed to draw up a business plan and operations manual for several hospitals it had acquired. The founders pulled together a management team of eight individuals, including Stello and several people working out of their homes, from around the country to write and edit the documents. At first, the team used e-mail to send files and communicate ideas. But the project got messy when team members began experiencing problems opening different file formats and tracking multiple versions of the document.

Stello found a solution to his dilemma. He chose the HotOffice Virtual Office Service from HotOffice Technologies Inc., a subscription-based solution that lets users store information on a centrally located server they can access via the Internet. HotOffice Virtual Office provided Stello's team with one easily accessible place to store, retrieve, and track the project's documents.

To Stello, the real benefit of building virtual teams is the reduction in travel time and costs involved in working with individuals in far-flung locations. Moving most of the work online makes it possible for Stello to manage, discuss, and work on tasks with people across the country with every little investment and people who work out of their homes can contribute equally to the project.

Source: Adapted from Heather Page, "Remote Control," *Entrepreneur*, October 1998, p. 146.

3. *Access to a wider range of employee talent.* Companies with regular work-at-home programs are usually deluged with résumés from eager job applicants. The talent bank includes parents (mostly mothers) with young children, employees who find commuting unpleasant, and others who live far way from their firms. The DOL regards telework as an option for disabled workers who traditionally have few opportunities in the workplace. The disabled workers may have talents that otherwise might been overlooked.

Disadvantages of Telecommuting

Work-at-home programs must be used selectively because they pose disadvantages for both employee and employer. The careers of telecommuters may suffer because they are not visible to management. Many telecommuters complain of the isolation from coworkers.

Also, telecommuters can be exploited if they feel compelled to work on company problems late into the night and on weekends. The many potential distractions at home make it difficult for some telecommuters to concentrate on work. Finally, telecommuters are sometimes part-time employees who receive limited benefits and are paid only for what they produce. As one telecommuter, a data entry specialist, said, "If I let up for an afternoon, I earn hardly anything."

Working at home can reinforce negative tendencies: It will facilitate a workaholic to work harder and longer, and it will give a procrastinator ample opportunity to delay work.[20]

Telecommuting programs can be disadvantageous to the employer because building loyalty and teamwork is difficult when so many workers are away from the office. Telecommuters who are not performing measured work are difficult to supervise—working at home gives an employee much more latitude in attending to personal matters during work time. Another problem is that the organization may miss out on some of the creativity that stems from the exchange of ideas in the traditional office.

Suggestions for Managers of Teleworkers

To maximize the advantages and minimize the disadvantages of telecommuting, managers should follow a few key suggestions:[21]

1. Choose the right type of work for working at home. If a job requires frequent monitoring, such as reviewing progress on a complex report, it is not well suited for telecommuting. Jobs requiring the use of complicated, large-scale equipment, such as medical laboratory work or manufacturing, cannot be done off premises. Work that requires clients or customers to visit the employee is best done on company premises. In general, positions with measurable work output are best suited for working at home.

2. Teleworkers should be chosen with care. Working at home is best suited for self-disciplined, well-motivated, and deadline-conscious workers. Make sure the telecommuter has a suitable home environment for telecommuting. The designated work area should be as separate from the household as possible and relatively free from distractions. Merrill Lynch insists that its teleworkers first participate in a training program about working at home. The program includes information about work habits and setting up an effective office at home.

3. Agree early on the number of days or months for telecommuting. The optimum number of days depends somewhat on the position and the worker. For corporate telecommuters, about two days per week of working at home is typical.

4. Clearly define productivity goals and deadlines. The more measurable the work output, such as lines of computer code or insurance claims forms processed, the better suited it is for telecommuting. Collect weekly data that relate to the results being achieved, such as orders filled or cases settled.

5. Keep in contact through a variety of means, including e-mail, telephone, phone meetings, and conference calls. Agree on working hours during which the teleworker can be reached. Remember, the manager is not disturbing the worker at home by telephoning that person during regularly scheduled working hours. Also, agree on how frequently the worker will be checking e-mail.

6. Use telecommuting as a reward for good performance in the traditional office. Poor performers should not be offered the opportunity to telecommute. Employees who volunteer to become telecommuters should only be accepted if they can demonstrate average or above-average performance records.

7. Make periodic visits to the workers at home, but give them appropriate lead time. During the visit look to see if equipment is being used in a way that is ergonomically sound. Field visits, as long as they are not perceived as spying, communicate the fact that teleworkers are an important part of the team.

Sharing Office Space and Hoteling

Another major aspect of the alternative workplace is for workers to share offices or cubicles, or have use of a shared office (similar to a hotel) only when on premises. Shared office space means simply that more than one employee is assigned to the same office or cubicle because their work schedules allow for such an arrangement. Among the factors allowing for sharing office space are complementary travel schedules, working different shifts, and working from home on different schedules. AT&T discovered that for some groups of employees, as many as six people could use the same desk and equipment formerly assigned to one. The company now has 14,000 employees in shared-desk arrangements. The savings on real estate costs can be enormous from sharing office space.

In *hoteling*, the company provides work spaces equipped and supported with typical office services. The worker who travels frequently might even be assigned a locker for personal storage. A computer system routes phone calls and e-mail as necessary. However, the office space, similar to a hotel (or rented temporary office space) is reserved by the hour, day, or week instead of being permanently assigned.[22]

From the perspective of top management, requiring workers to share office space or have no permanent office space provides an excellent method of cost control. From the perspective of many employees, not having a permanent office or cubicle can be an indignity and an inconvenience. As many workers lament, "I have no home." Years ago ambitious workers aspired toward having a corner office. Now they aspire toward having any office.

Job Sharing

About one-third of large companies that offer modified work schedules allow more than one employee to share the same job.[23] **Job sharing** is a work arrangement in which two people who work part-time share one job. The sharers divide up the job according to their needs. Each may work selected days of the work week. Or, one person might work mornings and the other work afternoons. The job sharers might be two friends, a husband and wife, or two employees who did not know each other before sharing a job. For complex jobs, the sharers may spend work time discussing it.

Job sharing is not an option valued by large numbers of employees. It appeals mostly to workers whose family commitments do not allow for full-time work. A typical job-sharing situation involves two friends who want a responsible position but can only work part time. A successful example of job sharing takes place at KLIF-AM radio in Dallas, Texas, where two women who are friends have set sales records while sharing a sales position at the station. Job sharing offers the employer an advantage in that two people working half time usually produce more than one person working full time, which is particularly noticeable in creative work. Also, if one employee is sick, the other is still available to handle the job for half the time.

Part-Time and Temporary Work

Part-time work is a modified work schedule offered by about two-thirds of employers. The category of part-time workers includes employees who work reduced weekly, annual, or seasonal hours and those who have project-based occasional work. For example, a marketing brand manager might work full days

job sharing

A work arrangement in which two people who work part time share one job.

on Mondays, Wednesdays, and Fridays. Many people, such as students and semi-retired people, choose part-time work because it fits their lifestyle. Also, many people work part time because they cannot find full-time employment.

Managers and professionals often fall into another category: employees who choose to reduce their working hours to allow more time for personal activities. Working fewer hours also helps avoid the potential stress associated with a demanding work schedule. For many professional workers, working 10 to 15 fewer hours per week would be a meaningful change. A recent analysis concluded that reduced hours for professional workers often produce beneficial effects in employee creativity, work quality, satisfaction, and retention.[24]

Temporary employment is at an all-time high, with some employers even hiring part-time managers, engineers, lawyers, and other high-level workers. Collectively, part-time and temporary employees constitute one-fourth to one-third of the workforce. Given that they are hired according to, or contingent upon, an employer's need, they are referred to as **contingent workers**. Some contingent workers receive modest benefits. Other contingent workers function as independent contractors who are paid for services rendered but do not receive benefits. A familiar example would be a plumber hired by a business owner to make a repair. The plumber sets the wage, and receives no benefits.

Many employees enjoy part-time work, which allows them to willingly trade off the low pay for personal convenience. Employers are eager to hire contingent workers to avoid the expense of hiring full-time workers. Paying limited or no benefits to part-time workers can save employers as much as 35 percent of the cost of full-time compensation. Also, contingent workers can be readily laid off if business conditions warrant. Some seasonally oriented businesses, such as gift-catalog sales firms, hire mostly part-time workers.

contingent workers

Part-time or temporary employees who are not members of the employer's permanent workforce.

Shift Work

To accommodate the needs of employers rather than employees, many workers are assigned to shift work. The purpose of shift work is to provide coverage during nonstandard hours. The most common shift schedules are days (7 A.M. to 3 P.M.), evenings (3 P.M. to 11 P.M.), and nights (11 P.M. to 7 A.M.). Manufacturing uses shift work to meet high demand for products without having to expand facilities. It is more economical to run a factory 16 or 24 hours per day than to run two or three factories eight hours per day. Service industries make even more extensive use of shift work to meet the demands of customers around the clock, such as in a hotel. Shift work is also necessary in public service operations such as police work, fire fighting, and health care.

Shift work involves more than a deviation from a traditional work schedule. It creates a lifestyle that affects productivity, health, family, and social life. Shift work unfortunately disrupts the natural rhythm of the body and creates job problems. Three times the average incidence of drug and alcohol abuse fosters an increased risk of errors and accidents. Many industrial catastrophes, such as ship wrecks, oil spills, and chemical leaks have taken place during the night ("graveyard") shift. Shift workers also experience difficulty in integrating their schedules with the social needs of friends and families.

With proper training, employees can adjust better to shift work. A shift-work consultant, for example, recommends: "Create healthy sleep environments by keeping rooms cool and eliminating daylight with dark shades and curtains or even styrofoam cutouts or black plastic taped to the window frame."[25]

SUMMARY OF KEY POINTS

1 **Identify the major dimensions and different types of job design.** Job design involves establishing job responsibilities and duties and the manner in which they are to be performed. Four approaches to job design are (1) the motivational approach, (2) the mechanistic approach (which emphasizes efficiency), (3) the biological approach (which emphasizes safety), and (4) the perceptual/motor approach. Each of these approaches has benefits and costs.

Job specialization is the degree to which a job holder performs only a limited number of tasks. Specialists are found at different occupational levels. Job specialization enhances workforce expertise at all levels and can reduce training time at the operative level. Specialization, however, can lead to problems. Coordinating the work of specialists can be difficult, and some employees may become bored. Automation, including robotics, contributes to job specialization. Robots perform many specialized tasks, including those that would be unsafe for humans. The computerization of the workplace represents automation in hundreds of ways, such as personal computers decreasing the need for clerical support.

2 **Describe job enrichment, including the job characteristics model.** Job enrichment is a method of making jobs involve more challenges and responsibility so they will be more appealing to most employees. The person holding the job must perceive these enriched characteristics of a job. An enriched job provides direct feedback, client relationships, new learning, scheduling by the employee, unique experience, control over resources, direct communication authority, and personal accountability.

Expanding on the idea of job enrichment creates the job characteristics model, which focuses on the task and interpersonal dimensions of a job. Five characteristics of jobs improve employee motivation, satisfaction, and performance: skill variety, task identity, task significance, autonomy, and feedback. These characteristics relate to critical psychological states, which in turn lead to outcomes such as internal motivation, satisfaction, low absenteeism, and high quality.

Implementing job enrichment begins by finding out which employees want an enriched job. The groups of employees most likely to want and enjoy enriched jobs can be classified as fulfillment seekers, high achievers, risk takers, and perhaps ladder climbers.

3 **Describe job involvement, enlargement, and rotation.** Job involvement reflects psychological involvement with one's work and how much work is part of the self-image. Job enlargement increases the number and variety of job tasks. Job rotation switches assignments and can contribute heavily to career development.

4 **Explain how workers use job crafting to modify their jobs.** The rigidness of some job descriptions does not fit the flexible work roles carried out by many workers. Following an emerging trend, many companies hire people "to work" rather than to fill a specific job slot. Another way of deviating from job descriptions is for workers to modify their job to fit their personal preferences and capabilities. Employees often craft their jobs by changing the tasks they perform and their contacts with others to make their jobs more meaningful.

5 **Illustrate how ergonomic factors can be part of job design.** Cumulative trauma disorders are injuries caused by repetitive motions over prolonged periods of time. Workstations can be designed to minimize these problems by such measures as supporting the back and thighs, and placing the feet flat on the floor. Uncomfortable noise levels present another ergonomic problem to be addressed.

6 **Summarize the various modified work schedules.** Work scheduling is another part of job design. A modified work schedule departs from the traditional hours of work. Modified work scheduling options include flexible working hours, a compressed work week, the alternative workplace and telecommuting, job sharing, and part-time and temporary work. Reduced working hours are a variation of part-time work.

KEY TERMS AND PHRASES

Job design, *198*

Job description, *200*

Job specialization, *200*

Job enrichment, *201*

Job characteristics model, *203*

Job involvement, *205*

Job enlargement, *206*

Job rotation, *206*

Job crafting, *207*

Cumulative trauma disorders, *208*

Modified work schedule, *209*

Flexible working hours, *210*

Compressed work week, *211*

Alternative workplace, *211*

Telecommuting, *212*

Job sharing, *215*

Contingent workers, *216*

QUESTIONS

1. In about 35 words write the job description for (a) a restaurant manager, or (b) the top executive at Dell Computer, or (c) the head coach of one of your favorite athletic teams.

2. A study showed that high-level mental ability is generally required to perform well in jobs designed by the motivational approach. Why might this conclusion be true?

3. Why is job rotation often more exciting to workers than job enlargement?

4. What are the benefits of frequent job rotation for a person who would like to become a high-level manager?

5. How might a customer service representative who works on the help desk for technical equipment *craft* his or her job?

6. How well suited would a work schedule of three 13⅓-hour days per week be for an employee whose job demanded considerable creativity?

7. From the standpoint of moving up in the company hierarchy, what might be a limitation of being a telecommuter for several years?

CRITICAL THINKING QUESTIONS

1. Would you be satisfied as a telecommuter? Why or why not?

2. Find evidence that indicates whether enriched jobs pay more than nonenriched jobs.

SKILL-BUILDING EXERCISE: The Ideal Home-Based Office

Gather into teams of about five people to design an ideal office at home for a professional worker. Take about 20 minutes to develop suggestions for the following aspects of a home office: (1) hardware and software, (2) equipment other than computers, (3) furniture, (4) ergonomics design, (5) office layout, and (6) location within home or apartment. Consider both productivity and job satisfaction when designing your office. After the designs are completed, the team leaders can present the design to the rest of the class.

INTERNET SKILL-BUILDING EXERCISE: Success Factors for Flextime

Many flextime programs succeed, whereas others fail. The following four Web resources describe successful flextime programs. As you browse through one or more of these sites, look for key factors that contributed to the success of the program.

Catalyst: http://www.catalystwomen.org/

Work in America Institute: http://www.workinamerica.org/

The Alliance of Work/Life Professionals: http://awlp.org/

The Boston College Center for Work and Family: http://www.be.edu/bc_org/avp/esom/executive

Source: "Flextime Web Resources," *Workforce*, February 2001, p. 42.

CASE PROBLEM 8-A: Our Best Cashiers Leave Too Soon

Larry Stockton is the human resources director for Alpha-Giant, a chain of 37 supermarkets in the northwestern United States. Alpha-Giant has purposely developed a niche that most supermarket chains have neglected, small-size supermarkets. Major supermarket companies find higher sales per square foot in larger-sized elaborate stores. Megastores generally prove even more profitable.

At the other extreme are the many small convenience stores that attract customers who want to make a few quick purchases without having to cope with walking through a giant store, and navigating through a large, congested parking lot. Alpha-Giant caters to the consumer group that wants to avoid shopping at a giant store, yet prefers a wider selection and lower prices than offered at convenience stores and mom-and-pop grocery stores. As Stockton notes, "Some of our steadiest customers are phobic about shopping in a mega-store, yet still appreciate the benefits of shopping at a supermarket."

Stockton's current project involves directing a task force to solve Alpha-Giant's major operational problem, the turnover among cashiers. About 70 percent of the cashiers quit within one year. Training new cashiers takes considerable time, and much productivity is lost during busy periods when a not-up-to-speed cashier is at the counter. Alpha-Giant managers have found it increasingly difficult to find qualified applicants for the positions. Many of the people applying for these positions lack the minimum communication skills necessary to create a favorable impression with the public. Many of the applicants with satisfactory communication skills lack the physical stamina required for the job.

Stockton and other members of the task force thoroughly investigated the possible reasons for the turnover. They found pay and benefits comparable to the competition. When cashiers left, they were unlikely to find higher-paying work. Very few of the cashiers who left complained about the working hours because they are given considerable choice. Many cashiers work part time, and purposely choose to work weekends and nights.

Stockton feels discouraged that higher-performing cashiers show a higher turnover rate than the lower-performers. As one store manager noted, "I worry when one of our cashiers is fast and makes very few errors. That guy or gal is a strong candidate to leave."

Another task force finding gives Stockton some ideas about where to look for a solution to the problem. Many of the cashiers note that they cannot tolerate the hundreds of repetitive actions required in their job. As Mandi Chang, a high-performing 18-year-old explained to a task force interviewer, "When I was learning how to handle all the keys and the codes, and bag properly, it was exciting. But after scanning what seems like 3,000 six packs of beer and soft drinks, and 5,000 cartons of milk in a few days, I'm like a zombie. Oh, my manager was nice and told me I could step away from the register every once and a while, and bag groceries on a busy line. But that's no fun. It's like I'm being downgraded."

Discussion Questions

1. Which job design alternative would you suggest for reducing turnover among the cashiers at Alpha-Giant?
2. How might the company enrich the job of cashiers?
3. How might job rotation and job enlargement be applied to help reduce dissatisfaction with the position of cashier?

Source: The company name has been changed to protect confidentiality.

CASE PROBLEM 8-B: Protecting the Computer Athletes

Pacifica Distributors supplies hundreds of grocery stores, drugstores, small retail stores, and hospitals with pharmaceutical and health products produced by companies that do not sell directly to large retailers like Kroger, Eckerd Drugs, and Kmart. Approximately 75 distribution specialists spend their entire work week stationed at computers. Although they interact with some customers by telephone, almost their complete day is spent at the keyboard. Many of the distribution specialists complain of pains in the hand, ocular fatigue, and headaches. During the last several years, at least three specialists have undergone surgery for carpal tunnel syndrome.

Problems of this type concern Jill Bertrand, the Pacifica vice president of human resources. Based on her concern, she studied a report prepared by Dr. Emil Pasacarelli, professor of clinical medicine at Columbia University College of Physicians and Surgeons. His report notes that people prone to computer injuries should regard themselves as computer athletes—training and cross-training to stay ahead of possible injuries. Pasacarelli wants workers to consider the following accommodations to make their workspace more ergonomically correct:

- Desks should ideally be between 23 and 28.5 inches from the floor, depending on the person's height.

- Ensure adequate knee clearance to accommodate full range of movement at the workstation.
- Use vertical CPU stands and monitor arms to provide extra workspace.
- Include an adjustable back rest and seat for good lumbar (lower-back) support from the chair.
- Chairs with five legs have more stability, and wheels allow for movement and adjustment.
- Reclining seatbacks and adjustable seat pans control the pressure on the back and thighs.
- Use a footrest for support when seat heights are adjusted for fixed-height workstations. They are also helpful for people who have short legs because they relieve pressure on the thighs.
- The top of the monitor screen should be slightly below eye level when sitting straight in a chair. The center of the screen should be about 20 degrees below eye level.
- Source documents should be at the same height and plane as the screen to avoid unnecessary neck and back movements.
- Filter screens on monitors can reduce glare.
- Monitor stands allow proper height adjustments of video displays and control glare.

- A detachable keyboard can be positioned for optimum ergonomically correct typing.

- Like desks, keyboards should be on work surfaces that stand between 23 and 28.5 inches from the floor, depending on the person's height. The top surface of the front-row keys should be no higher than 2 to 2.5 inches above the work surface.

- Keyboards should be level with thumb joints. Elbows should be positioned at a 90-degree angle and forearms kept parallel to the floor.

- Wrist rests or supports can help keep wrists in straight positions while allowing freedom of movement.

- Combinations of indirect and task light, plus natural light, are best. Indirect light alone can reduce eyestrain and fatigue.

- For close work, use task lighting that shines sideways onto the paper and doesn't create glare on the computer screen.

- Task lighting should illuminate source documents on a copy holder under a wide variety of general lighting conditions.

- Grids refract the light pattern of fluorescent lights and reduce glare, which can provide added comfort.

Bertrand scheduled a meeting with Gerry McKinsey, the CEO of Pacifica. She carefully reviewed the findings with him in person, after having sent the report for his review before the meeting. McKinsey said, "I think that a few of the ideas have merit, but I'm not in a big rush to have us implement all of those ideas. It would be very expensive to overhaul all our computer workstations. And no matter what we did, somebody would complain about headaches and wrist aches. You find these complaints in almost every workplace. We can't eliminate every small discomfort. We're a business enterprise, not an ergonomics laboratory."

With a concerned expression, Bertrand said, "Gerry, you might be taking these ergonomics problems too lightly. Many of the suggestions could be implemented quite inexpensively."

McKinsey said, "Maybe we'll take up this problem in a staff meeting in the next few months or so. Send me an e-mail as a reminder."

Discussion Questions

1. What is your evaluation of the practicality of the ergonomic suggestions contained in the report?

2. What impact would these suggestions have on your use of the computer?

3. How might Bertrand more effectively sell the merits of this report to McKinsey?

Source: The Pascarelli report is from "Athletic Accommodations," *Management Review*, February 1996, p. 27.

ENDNOTES

1. Genevieve Capowski, "The Joy of Flex," *Management Review*, March 1996, pp. 14–15; "Workplace Flexibility Works Better with Management Flexibility," *Marriott Executive Memo*, no. 8, 1994, p. 4.

2. Michael A. Campion and Michael J. Stevens, "Neglected Aspects in Job Design: How People Design Jobs, Task-Job Predictability, and Influence of Training," *Journal of Business and Psychology*, Winter 1991, pp. 169–192.

3. Frederick Herzberg, "The Wise Old Turk," *Harvard Business Review*, September–October 1974, pp. 70–80.

4. Marc C. Marchese and Robert P. Delprino, "Do Supervisors and Subordinates See Eye-to-Eye on Job Enrichment?" *Journal of Business and Psychology*, Winter 1998, pp. 179–192.

5. Stephen H. Widstrom, "A Computer User's Manifesto," *Business Week*, September 28, 1998, p. 18; Widstrom, "They're Mad as Hell Out There," *Business Week*, October 19, 1998, p. 32.

6. John Richard Hackman and Greg R. Oldham, *Work Redesign* (Reading, MA: Addison-Wesley, 1980), p. 77.

7. J. Barton Cunningham and Ted Eberle, "A Guide to Job Enrichment and Redesign," *Personnel*, February 1990, p. 59.

8. Sixtus Oeschsle, "Who We Are at Work: Six Types of Employee Attitudes," *Workforce*, November 1998 supplement, p. 10.

9. "Sharing Employees," *The Pryor Report*, September 1996, p. 9.

10. Shari Caudron, "Jobs Disappear: When Work Becomes More Important," *Workforce*, January 2000, pp. 30–32.

11. Amy Wrzesniewski and Jane E. Dutton, "Crafting a Job: Revisioning Employees as Active Crafters of Their Work," *The Academy of Management Review*, April 2001, pp. 179–201.

12. "Preventing Carpal Tunnel Syndrome," *HRfocus*, August 1995, p. 4; Neil Gross and Paul C. Judge, "Let's Talk," *Business Week*, February 23, 1998, pp. 61–72.

13. Gary W. Evans and Dana Johnson, "Stress and Open-Office Noise," *Journal of Applied Psychology*, October 2000, pp. 779–783.

14. Sarah Fister Gale, "Formalized Flextime: The Perk That Brings Productivity," *Workforce*, February 2001, p. 39.

15. Quoted in Gale, "Formalized Flextime," p. 41.

16. Survey reported in "Flextime Is Not Good If Nobody Uses It," *Positive Leadership*, October 1998, p. 5.

17. "A Time for Change? Maybe Not—Flextime Isn't for Everyone," *Working Smart*, September 1996, pp. 1–2.

18. John Yaukey, "Plugging into Office from Home," Gannett News Service, May 22, 2001; Joanne H. Pratt and Associates, available at http://www.joannepratt.com.

19. Mahlon Apgar, IV, "The Alternative Workplace: Changing Where and How People Work," *Harvard Business Review*, May–June 1998, p. 121; "What Is the Future of Telework?" *HRfocus*, March 2001, pp. 5–6; Jenny C. McCune, "Telecommuting Revisited," *Management Review*, February 1998, p. 12.

20. McCune, "Telecommuting Revisited," p. 13.

21. "Managing Telecommuters: Taking the Mystery Out of Tracking Work from Afar," *Executive Strategies*, March 1998, p. 6; "What Is the Future of Telework?" p. 6; Stephen L. Schilling, "The Basics of a Successful Telework Network," *HRfocus*, June 1999, p. 10.

22. Apgar, "The Alternative Workplace," pp. 124–125.

23. Survey reported in Diana Kunde, "Job Sharing: Best of Both Worlds," *Dallas Morning News*, October 6, 1997.

24. Rosalind Chait Barnett and Douglas T. Hall, "How to Use Reduced Hours to Win the War for Talent," *Organizational Dynamics*, Winter 2001, p. 207.

25. Ellen Hale, "Lack of Sleep Is Now Grounds for Filing Suit—Or Being Sued, " Gannett News Service, August 15, 1993.

220

Organization Structure, Culture, and Change

When describing why it had been difficult to get the giant chipmaker to move into new businesses and into the Internet age, Intel chief executive Craig R. Barrett offered the metaphor of Intel's microprocessor business as a creosote bush, a tall desert plant that drips poisonous oil, killing off all vegetation that attempts to grow anywhere near it. Microprocessors so dominated the company's strategy, Barrett explained, that other businesses could not sprout around it. Chips, he said, "are a dream business with wonderful margins and a wonderful market position. How could anything else compete here for resources and profitability?"

Barrett works to reshape Intel into a supplier of a full range of semiconductors for networking gear, information appliances, and PCs. His efforts move Intel toward radically different areas such as e-commerce, consumer electronics, Internet servers, and wireless telephones. "We're putting a new image on top of the big powerful chip monster that eats the world," Barrett says.

The old Intel dedicated itself to a single product (Intel inside). The core changes at Intel divide the company into five groups in order to better pursue new products and acquisitions. The groups are Computer Processors, Information Appliances, Intel Online Service, New Business Group, and Web-Hosting Business. However, the Computer Processors group still represents the heart of Intel's business. Processors and companion chips still contribute the vast majority of Intel's sales and profits, but the new divisions are poised to help the company grow.[1]

OBJECTIVES

After studying this chapter and doing the exercises, you should be able to:

1 Describe the bureaucratic form of organization and discuss its advantages and disadvantages.

2 Explain the major ways in which organizations are divided into departments.

3 Describe three modifications of the bureaucratic structure: the matrix structure; flat structures, downsizing, and outsourcing; and the horizontal structure.

4 Specify how delegation, empowerment, and decentralization spread authority in an organization.

5 Identify major aspects of organizational culture, including its management and control.

6 Describe key aspects of managing change including gaining support for change.

Chapter 9

The Intel story illustrates one of the major themes of this chapter—a company's success sometimes depends on the organizational structure it creates to meet the demands of the future. Intel continues to move away from an organization designed for a one-product company to a multidivision firm organized according to products and services.

In Chapter 8, we described how the tasks of an organization are divided into jobs for individuals and groups. Companies also subdivide work through an **organization structure**—the arrangement of people and tasks to accomplish organizational goals. The structure specifies who reports to whom and who does what. An organization structure resembles the framework of a building or the skeleton of the body.

This chapter explains three related aspects of total organizations or large subunits: how organizations subdivide work among their units, the culture (or general atmosphere) of organizations, and how to manage change.

organization structure

The arrangement of people and tasks to accomplish organizational goals.

1 BUREAUCRACY AS A FORM OF ORGANIZATION

Describe the bureaucratic form of organization and discuss its advantages and disadvantages.

bureaucracy

A rational, systematic, and precise form of organization in which rules, regulations, and techniques of control are specifically defined.

A **bureaucracy** is a rational, systematic, and precise form of organization in which rules, regulations, and techniques of control are specifically defined. Think of bureaucracy as the traditional form of organization, with other structures as variations of, or supplements to, bureaucracy. Do not confuse the word *bureaucracy* with bigness. Although most big organizations are bureaucratic, small firms can also follow the bureaucratic model. An example might be a small, carefully organized bank.

Principles of Organization in a Bureaucracy

The entire traditional, or classical, school of management contributes to our understanding of bureaucracy. Yet the essence of bureaucracy can be identified by its major characteristics and principles as listed next:

1. *Hierarchy of authority.* The dominant characteristic of a bureaucracy is that each lower organizational unit is controlled and supervised by a higher one. The person granted the most formal authority (the right to act) occupies the top place of the hierarchy. Exhibit 9-1 presents a bureaucracy as pyramid-shaped. The number of employees increases substantially as one moves down each successive level. Most of the formal authority concentrates at the top and decreases with each lower level.

unity of command

The classical management principle stating that each subordinate receives assigned duties from one superior only and is accountable to that superior.

2. *Unity of command.* A classic management principle, **unity of command**, states that each subordinate receives assigned duties from one superior only and is accountable to that superior. In the modern organization many people serve on projects and teams in addition to reporting to their regular boss, thus violating the unity of command.

3. *Task specialization.* In a bureaucracy, division of labor is based on task specialization (described in Chapter 8). To achieve task specialization, organizations designate separate departments, such as manufacturing, customer service, and information systems. Workers assigned to these organizational units employ specialized knowledge and skills that contribute to the overall effectiveness of the firm.

4. *Duties and rights of employees.* Bureaucracies are characterized by rules that define the rights and duties of employees. In a highly bureaucratic organization, each

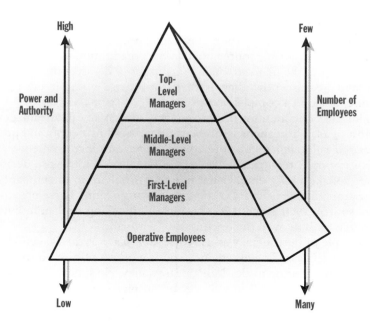

EXHIBIT 9-1

The Bureaucratic Form of Organization

In the bureaucratic organization structure people at the top of the organization have the most formal authority, yet many more employees occupy lower levels in the organization.

223

employee follows a precise job description, adheres to current policies and procedures in accessible manuals.

5. *Definition of managerial responsibility.* In a bureaucracy, the responsibility and authority of each manager is defined clearly in writing. Responsibility defined in writing lets managers know what is expected of them and what limits are set to their authority. This approach minimizes overlapping of authority and accompanying confusion.

6. *Line and staff functions.* A bureaucracy identifies the various organizational units as being line or staff. Line functions involve the primary purpose of an organization or its primary outputs. In a bank, line managers supervise work related to borrowing and lending money. Staff functions assist the line functions. Staff managers take responsibility for important functions such as human resources (or personnel) and purchasing. Although staff functions do not deal with the primary purposes of the firm, they plan an essential role in achieving the organization's mission.

Advantages and Disadvantages of Bureaucracy

Bureaucracy made modern civilization possible. Without large, complex organizations to coordinate the efforts of thousands of people, we would not have airplanes, automobiles, skyscrapers, universities, vaccines, or space satellites.

Many large bureaucratic organizations successfully continue to grow at an impressive pace. The leading giants include Exxon, Wal-Mart, Ford Motor Company, General Electric, and Southwest Airlines. A major argument in favor of bureaucracy holds that after abandoning the bureaucratic structure, many organizations suffer. Paul S. Adler observes that many firms that eliminate layers of management later discover that these downsized managers supplied precious skills and experience. Also, in an attempt to make their companies less bureaucratic, many executives eliminate policies, rules, and regulations. However, these procedures often embody an invaluable source of effective organizational practices. Adler says, "Having tossed out the manuals, many organizations discover that their employees are frustrated because now they have to improvise without even a common melody line let alone a complete score."[2]

Despite the contributions of bureaucracy, several key disadvantages come to mind. Most of all, a bureaucracy can be rigid in handling people and problems. Its well-intended rules and regulations sometimes create inconvenience and inefficiency. For example, requiring several layers of approval to make a decision causes the process to take a long time. Other frequent problems in the bureaucratic form of organization include frustration and low job satisfaction. These negative feelings arise from sources such as red tape, slow decision making, and an individual's limited influence on how well the organization performs.

An example of bureaucracy at its worst took place at the Ravenwood Hospital in Chicago, Illinois. The emergency room workers refused to treat a 15-year-old boy who lay bleeding to death in a nearby alley. He suffered a gunshot wound while playing basketball within steps of the hospital's entrance. The workers followed literally the hospital's policy of forbidding them from going outside of the emergency room to treat patients. A police officer who commandeered a wheelchair took the wounded boy inside the hospital, but it was too late.[3] (Here one might argue that the emergency room workers were at fault for ignoring common sense. A deeper analysis indicates a passive-aggressive behavior in the workers; they showed hostility by doing nothing.)

To examine your own orientation to the bureaucratic form of organization, take the self-quiz presented in Exhibit 9-2.

2   DEPARTMENTALIZATION

Explain the major ways in which organizations are divided into departments.

departmentalization

The process of subdividing work into departments.

Bureaucratic and other forms of organization subdivide the work into departments, or other units, to prevent total confusion. Can you imagine an organization of 300,000 people, or even 300, in which all employees worked in one large department? The process of subdividing work into departments is called **departmentalization**.

This chapter uses charts to illustrate four frequently used forms of departmentalization: functional, territorial, product-service, and customer. In practice, most organization charts show a combination of the various types. The most appropriate form of departmentalization is the one that provides the best chance of achieving the organization's objectives. The organization's environment is an important factor in this decision. Assume that a company needs to use radically different approaches to serve different customers. It would organize the firm according to the customer served. A typical arrangement of this nature sets up one department to serve commercial accounts and another department to serve the government.

Functional Departmentalization

functional departmentalization

An arrangement that defines departments by the function each one performs, such as accounting or purchasing.

Functional departmentalization defines departments by the function each one performs, such as accounting or purchasing. Dividing work according to activity is the traditional way of organizing the efforts of people. In a functional organization, each department carries out a specialized activity, such as information processing, purchasing, sales, accounting, or maintenance. Exhibit 9-3 illustrates an organization arranged on purely functional lines. The major subdivisions further

EXHIBIT 9-2

Understanding Your
Bureaucratic Orientation

Answer each question "mostly agree" (MA) or "mostly disagree" (MD). Assume the mental set of attempting to learn something about yourself rather than impressing a prospective employer.

	MA	MD
1. I value stability in my job.	_____	_____
2. I like a predictable organization.	_____	_____
3. I enjoy working without the benefit of a carefully specified job description.	_____	_____
4. I would enjoy working for an organization in which promotions were generally determined by seniority.	_____	_____
5. Rules, policies, and procedures generally frustrate me.	_____	_____
6. I would enjoy working for a company that employed 95,000 people worldwide.	_____	_____
7. Being self-employed would involve more risk than I'm willing to take.	_____	_____
8. Before accepting a position, I would like to see an exact job description.	_____	_____
9. I would prefer a job as a freelance landscape artist to one as a supervisor for the Department of Motor Vehicles.	_____	_____
10. Seniority should be as important as performance in determining pay increases and promotion.	_____	_____
11. It would give me a feeling of pride to work for the largest and most successful company in its field.	_____	_____
12. Given a choice, I would prefer to make $90,000 per year as a vice-president in a small company than $100,000 per year as a middle manager in a large company.	_____	_____
13. I would feel uncomfortable if I were required to wear an employee badge with a number on it.	_____	_____
14. Parking spaces in a company lot should be assigned according to job level.	_____	_____
15. I would generally prefer working as a specialist to performing many different tasks.	_____	_____
16. Before accepting a job, I would want to make sure that the company had a good program of employee benefits.	_____	_____
17. A company will not be successful unless it establishes a clear set of rules and regulations.	_____	_____
18. I would prefer to work in a department with a manager than to work on a team where managerial responsibility is shared.	_____	_____
19. You should respect people according to their rank.	_____	_____
20. Rules are meant to be broken.	_____	_____

Score: _____

Scoring and interpretation: Give yourself one point for each question you answered in the bureaucratic direction, then total your score.

1. Mostly agree	8. Mostly agree	15. Mostly disagree
2. Mostly agree	9. Mostly disagree	16. Mostly agree
3. Mostly disagree	10. Mostly agree	17. Mostly agree
4. Mostly agree	11. Mostly agree	18. Mostly agree
5. Mostly disagree	12. Mostly disagree	19. Mostly agree
6. Mostly agree	13. Mostly disagree	20. Mostly disagree
7. Mostly agree	14. Mostly agree	

15–20	You would enjoy working in a bureaucracy.
8–14	You would experience a mixture of satisfactions and dissatisfactions if working in a bureaucracy.
0–7	You would most likely be frustrated by working in a bureaucracy, especially a large one.

Source: Adapted and updated from Andrew J. DuBrin, *Human Relations: A Job Oriented Approach,* 5th ed. (Upper Saddle River, NJ: Prentice Hall, 1991), pp. 434–435.

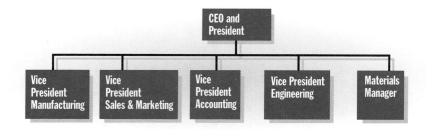

EXHIBIT 9-3

Functional Departmentalization with the Davenport Machine Company

Observe that each box below the level of CEO indicates an executive in charge of a specific function or activity, such as sales and marketing.

divide along their own functional lines as shown in Exhibit 9-4. The exhibit shows the functional organization within the materials management department.

The list of advantages and disadvantages of the functional organization, the traditional form of organization, reads the same as for bureaucracy. Functional departmentalization works particularly well when large batches of work have to be processed on a recurring basis and when the expertise of specialists is required.

Territorial Departmentalization

territorial departmentalization

An arrangement of departments according to the geographic area served.

Territorial departmentalization is an arrangement of departments according to the geographic area served. In this organization structure, all the activities for a firm in a given geographic area report to one manager. Marketing divisions often use territorial departmentalization; the salesforce may be divided into the northeastern, southeastern, midwestern, northwestern, and southwestern regions.

Territorial departmentalization that divides an organization into geographic regions generally works well for international business. Yet in a new global business trend, organizations develop a central structure that serves operations in various geographic locations. A case in point is Ford Motor Company. To economize, Ford merged its manufacturing, sales, and product development operations in North America, Europe, Latin America, and Asia.

A key advantage of territorial departmentalization allows for decision making at a local level, where the personnel are most familiar with the problems. Territorial departmentalization also presents some potential disadvantages. The arrangement can be quite expensive because of duplication of costs and effort. For instance, each region may build service departments (such as for purchasing) that

EXHIBIT 9-4

Functional Departmentalization Within a Department of the Davenport Machine Company

Observe that the materials management department, as with other departments, has its own functional structure.

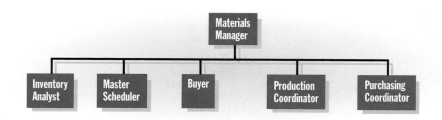

duplicate activities carried out at headquarters. A bigger problem arises if top-level management experiences difficulty controlling the performance of field units.

Product–Service Departmentalization

Product–service departmentalization is the arrangement of departments according to the products or services they provide. When specific products or services are so important that the units that create and support them almost become independent companies, product departmentalization makes sense.

Exhibit 9-5 presents a version of product–service departmentalization. Notice that the organization depicted offers products and services with unique demands of their own. For example, the business of manufacturing and selling airplane engines differ entirely from the business of developing real estate.

Organizing by product line offers numerous benefits because employees focus on a product or service, which allows each department the maximum opportunity to grow and prosper. Similar to territorial departmentalization, grouping by product or service helps train general managers, fosters high morale, and allows decisions to be made at the local level.

Departmentalization by product poses the same potential problems as territorial departmentalization. It can be expensive, because of duplication of effort, and top-level management may find it difficult to control the separate units.

Customer Departmentalization

Customer departmentalization creates an organization structure based on customer needs. When the demands of one group of customers differ significantly from the demands of another, customer departmentalization often results. Many insurance companies, for example, organize their efforts into consumer and commercial departments. Manufacturers of sophisticated equipment typically consist of different groups for processing government and commercial accounts. Customer departmentalization resembles product departmentalization, and sometimes the distinction between these two forms of organization blurs. For example, is a bank department that sells home mortgages catering to homeowners, offering a special service, or both?

product–service departmentalization

The arrangement of departments according to the products or services they provide.

227

customer departmentalization

An organization structure based on customer needs.

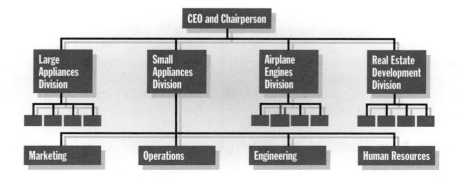

EXHIBIT 9-5

Product-Service Departmentalization

Notice that each division in a product-service form of organization is much like a company of its own. The small appliances division, for example, has all the main key functions: marketing, operations, engineering, and human resources.

3

MODIFICATIONS OF THE BUREAUCRATIC ORGANIZATION

Describe three modifications of the bureaucratic structure: the matrix structure; flat structures, downsizing, and outsourcing; and the horizontal structure.

To overcome some of the problems of the bureaucratic and functional forms of organization, several other organization structures have been developed. Typically, these nonbureaucratic structures supplement or modify the bureaucratic structure. Virtually all large organizations combine bureaucratic and less bureaucratic forms. This section describes three popular modifications of bureaucracy: the matrix organization; flat structures, downsizing, and outsourcing; and the horizontal structure. The team structure described in Chapter 8 can also be considered a modification of the bureaucratic design.

The Matrix Organization

project organization

A temporary group of specialists working under one manager to accomplish a fixed objective.

Departmentalization tends to be poorly suited to performing special tasks that differ substantially from the normal activities of a firm. **Project organization**, in which a temporary group of specialists works under one manager to accomplish a fixed objective, offers one widely used solution to this problem. Used most extensively in the military, aerospace, construction, motion picture, and computer industries, project management is so widespread that software has been developed to help managers plot out details and make all tasks visible. The accompanying Management in Action presents details about the challenging role of a project manager.

matrix organization

A project structure superimposed on a functional structure.

The best-known application of project management is the **matrix organization**, a project structure superimposed on a functional structure. Matrix organizations evolved to capitalize on the advantages of project and matrix structures while minimizing their disadvantages. The project groups act as minicompanies within the firm in which they operate. However, the group usually disbands after completing its mission. In some instances, the project proves so successful that it becomes a new and separate division of the company.

Exhibit 9-6 shows a popular version of the matrix structure. Notice that functional managers exert some functional authority over specialists assigned to the projects. For example, the quality manager occasionally meets with the quality specialists assigned to the projects to discuss their professional activities. The project managers hold line authority over the people assigned to their projects.

The project managers borrow resources from the functional departments, a feature that distinguishes the matrix from other organizational structures. Also, each person working on the project reports two superiors: the project manager and the functional manager. For example, observe the quality analyst in the lower right corner of Exhibit 9-5. The analyst reports to the manager of quality three boxes above him or her *and* to the project manager for the personal digital assistant located five boxes to the left.

Users of the matrix structure include banks, insurance companies, aerospace companies, and educational institutions. Colleges often use matrix structures for setting up special interest programs. Among them are African-American studies, adult education, and industrial training. A director who uses resources from traditional departments heads each of these programs.

Flat Structures, Downsizing, and Outsourcing

Three closely related approaches to simplifying an organization structure include creating flat structures, downsizing, and outsourcing. One major approach to making an

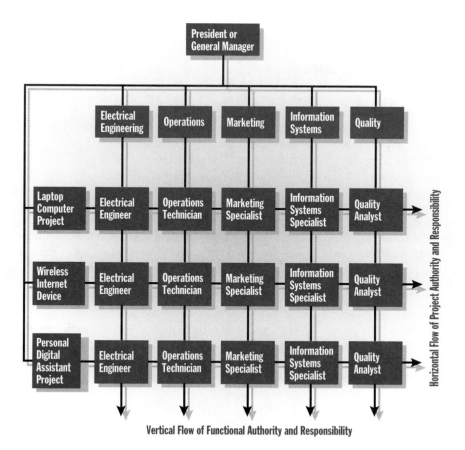

EXHIBIT 9-6

Matrix Organization
Structure in an Electronics
Company

*Personnel assigned to a
project all report to two
managers: a project head
and a functional manager.*

229

organization less bureaucratic reduces its number of layers. Both downsizing and out-sourcing (contracting work to other firms) typically lead to a flat structure.

Flat Structures

Organizations with a bureaucratic structure tend to accumulate many layers of management, and often too many employees in general. At times, staff groups outnumber the line groups. Top management may then decide to create a **flat organization structure**, a form of organization with relatively few layers. The last decade saw most large business corporations become flatter. GM reduced its previous 22 layers of management to about eight layers within most units of the company. A flat organization structure acts less bureaucratic for two reasons. First, fewer available managers review the decisions of other workers. Second, a shorter chain of command means that managers and workers at lower levels can make decisions more independently.

An important consequence of creating flat structures leaves the remaining managers with a larger **span of control**—the number of workers reporting directly to a manager. An exception occurs when a large number of individual contributors are laid off along with the managers. A large span of control works best with competent and efficient managers and group members. When group members do relatively similar work, the manager can supervise more people.

**flat organization
structure**

*A form of organization with
relatively few layers of
management, making it less
bureaucratic.*

span of control

*The number of workers
reporting directly to a
manager.*

Management *in Action*

The Contribution of Project Managers

Jonathan Gispan spent 38 years working as a project manager. Now he teaches the skill at a Lockheed Martin Corporation division. He believes that project managers have never been more critical. The project manager becomes the focal point of a complex relationship matrix that includes customers, workers, vendors, and bosses. Gispan says that project managers manage a project from start to finish, and also manage the people who make it happen.

The job requires a jack-of-all-trades who can both understand a problem and solve it. "Project managers must successfully manage the total life cycle of a project," says Gispan. "The job requires a super-organized person who knows how to get a project completed quickly and inexpensively and has the advanced communication skills necessary to work closely with vendors, project teams, and senior management.

"The current marketplace keeps you on your toes. Even though everything is changing at what seems like an overwhelming pace, it is best to view change as a motivator that allows you to keep pace with technology and get

better at your job. The idea is not merely to cope with change but to thrive on it. It is more of an attitude than anything else."

Project managers benefit from at least five to seven years in the trenches (performing technical work) that translate into a good technical base. But the project manager also requires a knowledge of how the business side of the equation works. Project managers need to be familiar with accounting methods as well as sales and marketing strategies. They must know how to manage a project so it makes a profit.

According to Gispan, a project manager can move up quickly. "After you've proven to management that you're organized and can manage several tasks, it won't be long before you are managing everything associated with a program. Get good at it and you'll move up the ranks from project manager to general manager where you are running several company businesses."

Source: Bob Weinstein, "Project Managers Have Never Been More Critical," *Rochester Democrat and Chronicle*, February 14, 1999, p. 1G.

Downsizing

In Chapter 4 we analyzed downsizing as it related to social responsibility. Downsizing can also be viewed as a way of simplifying an organization to make it less bureaucratic. Under ideal circumstances, downsizing also leads to better profits and higher stock prices. In fact, the motivation behind most downsizings of both assets (such as company divisions or buildings) and workers comes from the drive to reduce costs and increase profits. GE provides a historically significant example. During an 11-year period, the company reduced its workforce by more than 120,000 workers, while profits rose 228 percent and the price of GE stock reached all-time highs.[4] (From the standpoint of social responsibility, these financial gains exacted a substantial human cost.)

Under many circumstances, downsizing offers a small return compared to its costs. A study conducted with 2,136 firms that fired at least 5 percent of their employees at least once during the 15-year period of study found numerous instances in which downsizing improved a company's financial position. However, the research concluded that layoffs do not necessarily provide a quick fix that leads to productivity improvements and bigger profits. For many firms, the impact of downsizing on profits proved negligible in comparison to the magnitude of the layoffs. Employment downsizers in the study reduced their workforces by an average of 11 percent. Yet return on assets failed to increase, and actually continued to decline after the layoffs. By the second year after the layoffs, the return on assets rose to only .3 percent above the industry average.[5]

Two other researchers recommended that, before reducing human capital, management should undertake a careful financial analysis to evaluate the long-term net effect of such a step. Among the costs associated with downsizing that need to be considered the researchers mention severance pay, supplements to early retirement plans, disability claims, and lowered productivity resulting from possible decline in staff morale.[6]

Eliminating low-volume and no-value activities provides a starting point in effective restructuring. This *activity-based reduction* systematically compares the costs of a firm's activities to their value to the customer. In searching for low-value activity, workers monitor the output of others. *Keeping the future work requirements in mind* also contributes to effective restructuring. Letting go of people who will be an important part of the firm's future rarely provides an effective answer to overstaffing. *Sensible criteria should be used to decide which workers to let go.* In general, the poorest performers should be released first. Offering early retirement and asking for voluntary resignations also leads to less disruption.

An important strategy for helping layoff survivors refocus on their jobs includes *sharing information with employees*. Information sharing helps quell rumors about further reductions in force. *Listening to employees* can soften the shock of restructuring. Many survivors will need support groups and other sympathetic ears to express sorrow over the job loss suffered by coworkers. *Be honest with workers* by informing people ahead of time if layoffs are imminent or even a possibility. Workers should be told why layoffs are likely, who might be affected, and in what way. Employees want to know how the restructuring will help strengthen the firm and facilitate growth.[7]

Outsourcing

An increasingly common practice among organizations of all types and sizes is **outsourcing**, or having work performed for them by individuals or companies outside the organization. By outsourcing, a company can reduce its need for employees and physical assets and their associated costs. Many companies outsource work to geographic areas where workers receive lower wages. For example, a small company hires another company to manage its payroll and employee benefits, or a large manufacturing firm contracts for certain components or entire products to be made by another firm. Even IBM is a contractor for other employers: it makes the hard drives for other computer manufacturers or manages their computer systems. The outsourcing movement continues to grow through many small and medium-sized firms that perform stable work for larger organizations.

Public as well as private employers subcontract services. The City of Chicago subcontracts its information technology activities. The need for subcontracting IT became apparent when the municipal government could not effectively manage the demands placed on its information technology services. A staff of 20 could not keep up with helpdesk calls from 10,000 users. Also, practically no processes

outsourcing

The practice of hiring an individual or another company outside the organization to perform work.

guided the handling of IT purchases or managing of IT assets. New hardware sometimes sat on the loading dock so long it went out of warranty before it was installed. It became clear to CIO (chief information officer) Beth Boatman that outsourcing key IT functions such as the helpdesk, and management of user desktops and the computer network, offered the best way to improve performance.

Boatman and other managers decided to outsource their IT function to UNISYS, a major manufacturer of large computers and a service provider. Within four months, Boatman began seeing results. She recalls, "The network stabilized, standards for software and hardware were in place, and I was able to get back into our e-government initiatives—and out of the business of recruiting an IT staff."[8]

The Horizontal Structure (Organization by Process)

In the bureaucratic form of organization, people in various organization units are assigned specialized tasks such as purchasing, manufacturing, selling, and shipping. In another approach to organization structure, a group of people concerns itself with a process, such as filling an order or developing a new product. Instead of focusing on a specialized task, all team members focus on achieving the purpose of all the activity, such as getting a product in the hands of a customer. A **horizontal structure** is the arrangement of work by teams that are responsible for accomplishing a process. Exhibit 9-7 illustrates a horizontal structure, as do the projects shown in Exhibit 9-6. The employees take collective responsibility for customers.

As with other modifications of the bureaucratic structure, the horizontal structure coexists with vertical structures. The process teams offer a balanced focus so that employees direct their effort and attention toward adding value for the customer.[9] The UNISYS groups that provide IT services for clients use a horizontal structure because a project manager is responsible for making sure that client needs are met.

Switching from a vertical (task) emphasis to a horizontal (process) emphasis can be done through **reengineering**, the radical redesign of work to achieve substantial improvements in performance. Reengineering searches for the most efficient way to perform a large task. It emphasizes uncovering wasted steps, such as people handing off documents to one another to obtain their approval. E-commerce considerably reengineers the work of sales representatives. If goods are exchanged over the Internet, the need for industrial sales representatives shrinks.

horizontal structure

The arrangement of work by teams that are responsible for accomplishing a process.

reengineering

The radical redesign of work to achieve substantial improvements in performance.

EXHIBIT 9-7

A Horizontal Organization Structure

In a horizontal organization, even though specialists are assigned to the team, they are expected to understand each other's tasks, and perform some of those tasks as needed.

As a result of reengineering, work is organized horizontally rather than vertically. The people in charge of the process function as team leaders who guide the team toward completion of a core process such as new product development or filling a complicated order. Key performance objectives for the team would include "reduce cycle time," "reduce costs," and "reduce throughput time."

A major challenge in creating a horizontal structure comes in breaking the functional mindset. Workers naturally tend to think about performing their own specialty, which interferes with thinking about collaborating with others and taking collective responsibility.[10]

The push toward the horizontal structures and a *process mentality* should not be embraced without qualification, however. Having a *task mentality* remains important because expertise is still crucial in many endeavors. A building construction team, for example, still relies on highly proficient specialists such as mechanical and electrical engineers. Wouldn't you prefer to ride in an elevator that was designed by a highly proficient specialist?

All organization structures described so far in this chapter are influenced by information technology. Workers from various units throughout an organization can solve problems together through information networks without being concerned with "who reports to whom," as indicated by organization charts. Also, entry-level workers can leapfrog layers of management and communicate directly with senior executives through e-mail. However, now, as in the past, entry-level workers almost never telephone a member of upper management.

DELEGATION, EMPOWERMENT, AND DECENTRALIZATION   4

Collective effort would not be possible, and organizations could not grow and prosper, if a handful of managers did all the work themselves. In recognition of this fact, managers divide up their work. The division can be in one of two directions. Subdividing work in a horizontal direction, through the process of departmentalization, has already been described. The section that follows will discuss subdivision of work in the vertical direction, using the chain of command through delegation and empowerment, and decentralization.

Specify how delegation, empowerment, and decentralization spread authority in an organization.

Delegation of Responsibility

Delegation is an old concept that has been revitalized in the modern organization. It refers to assigning formal authority and responsibility for accomplishing a specific task to another person. If managers do not delegate any of their work, they are acting as individual contributors—not true managers. Delegation relates closely to **empowerment**, the process by which managers share power with group members, thereby enhancing employees' feelings of personal effectiveness. Delegation is a specific way of empowering employees, thereby increasing motivation.

A major goal of delegation is the transfer of responsibility as a means of increasing one's own productivity. At the same time, delegation allows team members to learn how to handle more responsibility and to become more productive. In downsized organizations, delegation becomes essential because of the increased workload of managers. As managers assume more responsibility, they must find ways to delegate more work. This feat requires imagination, because in a downsized firm support staff has usually been trimmed as well.

Even though a manager may hold a group member responsible for a task, final accountability belongs to the manager. (To be accountable is to accept credit or

delegation

Assigning formal authority and responsibility for accomplishing a specific task to another person.

empowerment

The process by which managers share power with group members, thereby enhancing employees' feelings of personal effectiveness.

blame for results.) If the group member fails miserably, the manager must accept the final blame; the manager chose the person who failed. As noted in an executive newsletter, "Nothing makes a worse impression than the whining manager who blames a staffer for mishandling a task."[11]

Delegation and empowerment lie at the heart of effective management. Following the eight suggestions presented next improves the manager's chance of increasing productivity by delegating to and empowering individuals and teams.[12] (Note that teams as well as individuals can be the unit of delegation and power-sharing, such as asking a team to find a way of filling orders more rapidly.)

1. *Assign duties to the right people.* The chances for effective delegation and empowerment improve when capable, responsible, well-motivated group members receive the delegated tasks. Vital tasks should not be assigned to ineffective performers.

2. *Delegate the whole task.* In the spirit of job enrichment, a manager should delegate an entire task to one subordinate rather than dividing it among several. So doing gives the group member complete responsibility and enhances motivation, and gives the manager more control over results.

3. *Give as much instruction as needed.* Some group members will require highly detailed instructions, while others can operate effectively with general instructions. Many delegation and empowerment failures occur because instruction was insufficient. Dumping is the negative term given to the process of dropping a task on a group member without instructions.

4. *Retain some important tasks for yourself.* Managers need to retain some high-output or sensitive tasks for themselves. In general, the manager should handle any task that involves the survival of the unit. However, which tasks the manager should retain always depend on the circumstances.

5. *Obtain feedback on the delegated task.* A responsible manager does not delegate a complex assignment to a subordinate, then wait until the assignment is complete before discussing it again. Managers must establish checkpoints and milestones to obtain feedback on progress.

6. *Delegate both pleasant and unpleasant tasks to group members.* When group members' assignments include a mixture of pleasant and unpleasant responsibilities, they tend to accept it as fair treatment. Few group members expect the manager to handle all the undesirable jobs. Managers also use a related approach in rotating undesirable tasks among group members.

7. *Step back from the details.* Many managers make poor delegators because they get too involved with technical details. If a manager cannot let go of details, he or she will never be effective at delegation or empowerment.

8. *Allow for spending money and using other resources.* Sharing power includes permitting others to spend money. People who have no budget of their own to control do not have much power. Having a budget, for even such small matters as ordering in dinner for an evening meeting, gives team members a feeling of power. Access to other resources, such as use of advanced information technology equipment and office temporaries, provides another meaningful form of empowerment.[13]

decentralization

The extent to which authority is passed down to lower levels in an organization.

Decentralization

Decentralization is the extent to which authority is passed down to lower levels in an organization. It comes about as a consequence of managers delegating work to lower levels. **Centralization** is the extent to which authority is retained at the top of the organization. In a completely centralized organization, one chief executive would retain all the formal authority. Complete centralization can exist only in a one-person firm. Decentralization and centralization lie on two ends of a continuum. No firm operates as completely centralized or decentralized.

The term *decentralization* generally refers to the decentralization of authority. However, the term also refers to decentralization by geography. A multidivision firm departmentalized on the basis of territory has a flat organization structure. A flat organization may often be referred to as decentralized, but the reference indicates geography, not authority. Unless so noted, this text uses the term *decentralization* in reference to authority.

How much control top management wants to retain determines how much to decentralize an organization. Organizations favor decentralization when a large number of decisions must be made at lower organizational levels, often based on responding to customer needs. GE favors decentralization in part because the company consists of a collection of different businesses, many with vastly different customer requirements. Division management is much more aware of these needs than are people at company headquarters.

In general, a centralized firm exercises more control over organization units than a decentralized firm. Top management that wants to empower people through such means as teams and horizontal structures must emphasize decentralization.

Many firms centralize and decentralize operations simultaneously. Certain aspects of their operations are centralized, whereas others are decentralized. Fast-food franchise restaurants such as Subway, Long John Silver's, and Wendy's illustrate this trend. Central headquarters exercises tight control over such matters as menu selection, food quality, and advertising. Individual franchise operators, however, make human resource decisions on their own.

centralization

The extent to which authority is retained at the top of the organization.

ORGANIZATIONAL CULTURE 5

Even though organization structure has sometimes been referred to as the "hard side" of understanding how a firm operates, an understanding of the "soft side" of an organization contributes to an understanding of how the organization operates. **Organizational culture (or corporate culture)** is the system of shared values and beliefs that actively influence the behavior of organization members. The term *shared* implies that many people are guided by the same values and that they interpret them in the same way. Values develop over time and reflect a firm's history and traditions. Culture consists of the customs of a firm, such as being helpful and supportive toward new employees and customers.

This section describes significant aspects of organizational culture: its dimensions, consequences, organizational learning, and knowledge management, and its management and control. To obtain a quick overview of what a culture can mean to an organization, see the accompanying Management in Action.

Identify major aspects of organizational culture, including its management and control.

organizational culture (or corporate culture)

The system of shared values and beliefs that actively influence the behavior of organization members.

Dimensions of Organizational Culture

The dimensions of organizational culture help explain the subtle forces that influence employee actions. Recognize that large units within an organization may have a different culture. For example, the culture of a company's lumber mill may be quite different from the culture of its marketing department. Seven dimensions significantly influence organizational culture.[14]

1. *Values.* Values provide the foundation of any organizational culture. The organization's philosophy expressed through values guides behavior on a day-to-day basis. Representative values of a firm might include concern for employee welfare, a belief that the customer is always right, a commitment to quality, or a desire to please stakeholders.

2. *Relative diversity.* The existence of an organizational culture assumes some degree of homogeneity. Nevertheless, organizations differ in terms of how much deviation can be tolerated. Many firms are highly homogeneous; executives talk in a similar manner and even look alike. Furthermore, those executives promote people from similar educational backgrounds and fields of specialty into key jobs. The diversity of a culture also reflects itself in the dress code. Some organizations insist on uniformity of dress, such as wearing a jacket and tie (for men) when interacting with customers or clients. Strongly encouraging all workers to conform to dress-down Fridays discourages diversity.

3. *Resource allocations and rewards.* The allocation of money and other resources exerts a critical influence on culture. The investment of resources sends a message to people about what is valued in the firm. If a customer-service department is fully staffed and nicely furnished, employees and customers can assume that the company values customer service.

4. *Degree of change.* The culture in a fast-paced, dynamic organization differs from that of a slow-paced, stable one. Top-level managers, by the energy or lethargy of their stance, send signals about how much they welcome innovation. The degree of change also influences whether a culture can take root and how strong that culture can be.

5. *A sense of ownership.* The movement toward employee stock ownership in companies creates an ownership culture and inspires workers to think and act like owners. An ownership culture increases loyalty, improves work effort, and aligns worker interests with those of the company. An ownership culture can be reflected in such everyday actions as conserving electricity, making gradual improvements, and not tolerating sloppiness by coworkers. An ownership culture can backfire, however, if employee wealth stays flat or decreases as a result of stock ownership.[15]

6. *An attitude of caring.* One distinctive aspect of an organization culture comes from the extent to which people care for each other, including managers caring for employees and employees caring for each other. Caring refers generally to being concerned about the welfare and rights of other people. Hatim Tyabji, the CEO of VeriFone Inc., explains how the culture of caring is expressed in his company: "We are constantly searching for ways to create a degree of empathy in the VeriFone family. Whether people are single or married, whether they have children or they're living with their parents—unless their personal support system is excited about VeriFone, unless they feel a part of Verifone, then VeriFone will fail."[16]

7. *Strength of the culture.* The strength of the culture, or how much influence it exerts, emerges partially a by-product of the other dimensions. A strong culture guides employees in everyday actions. It determines, for example, whether an employee will inconvenience himself or herself to satisfy a customer. Without a strong culture, employees are more likely to follow their own whims—they may decide to please customers only when convenient. Unfortunately, strong cultures may develop a cult-like, atmosphere in which employees become more attached to the firm than to their outside life. The corporation takes over as the major source of satisfying emotional needs.[17]

Some members of an organization remain unaware of the dimensions of their culture, despite being influenced by it. Sometimes a visitor can best observe a dimension of culture and how it controls behavior. A consultant told one CEO that "strong differentiation between executives and other workers" was a notable characteristic of the firm. The CEO denied the characterization until the consultant pointed out that managers at the rank of vice president and above always kept their jackets on. Also, lower-ranking employees addressed them by their last name. Lower-ranking managers usually removed their jackets, and were addressed by their first name by most workers.

These dimensions represent a formal and systematic way of understanding organizational culture. In practice, people use more glib expressions in describing culture, as illustrated in Exhibit 9–8.

Consequences and Implications of Organizational Culture

The attention to organizational culture stems from its pervasive impact on organizational effectiveness. Exhibit 9–9 outlines several key consequences of organizational culture.

The right organizational culture contributes to *gaining competitive advantage and therefore achieving financial success.* A study of 34 firms investigated the relationship between a high involvement/participative culture and financial performance. Firms perceived by employees to link individual efforts to company goals showed higher returns on investments and sales than firms without such links.[18] The consistently strong performance of Southwest Airlines can be partially attributed to its human and fun-loving culture.

EXHIBIT 9-8

Brief Descriptions of Selected Organizational Cultures

Company employees and industry analysts typically describe an organization's culture in several words as in the following:

Amazon.com Loose and easy, exemplified by a liberal dress and appearance code. (Body piercing is welcome.) A customer service director tells the temporary employment agencies, "Send us your freaks."

Exxon/Mobil Exxon half is reserved, stuffy, buttoned-down, focused on the numbers, controlled, and disciplined. Mobil half is feisty, aggressive, risk taking.

Daimler/Chrysler Daimler half is an analytical, methodical, disciplined, buttoned-down, engineering-driven bureaucracy with conservative styling. Chrysler half is more impulsive and intuitive, focusing on speedy product development and flashy design.

IBM (particularly in marketing and engineering) Controlling, powerful, smug, and still hierarchical despite mammoth efforts by chairman Louis Gerstner to make IBM more egalitarian and less traditional and conservative. IBM now encourages employees to wear a wide range of clothing to the office.

Microsoft Adventuresome, creative, worships intelligence, smug, feelings of superiority, and commitment to control its industry. Emphasizes problem-solving ability and creativity much more than rank in decision making.

Southwest Airlines Preoccupied with customer satisfaction, job satisfaction, and laughter on company time, but intolerant of negative attitudes toward work or customers. Employees attend company meetings and social events after normal working hours, without extra compensation.

Sources: Adapted from "The First Global Car Colossus," *Business Week*, May 18, 1998, p. 42; "amazon.com: The Wild World of E-Commerce," *Business Week*, December 14, 1998, p. 110.

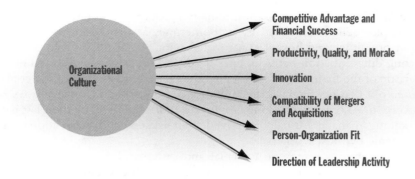

EXHIBIT 9-9

Consequences and Implications of Organizational Culture

238

Although organizational culture is a soft concept, it has many hard consequences.

The right organizational culture can *enhance productivity, quality, and morale.* A culture that emphasizes productivity *and quality* encourages workers to be more productive and quality conscious. The strong link between productivity and competitive advantage comes from the heavy contribution productivity makes toward gaining on the competition. For example, CEO Charles Christos Cotsakos created a unique culture at E★Trade, the online stockbroker, characterized by a "lust for being different," which propels the professional staff to work unusually hard. The culture emphasizes high enthusiasm and bizarre behavior with such stunts as having workers wear propeller beanies. Cotsakos believes that a remarkable culture is crucial for achieving corporate success.[19] A culture that values the dignity of human beings fosters high morale and job satisfaction.

A corporate culture that encourages creative behavior contributes to innovation, as described in Chapter 6 about problem solving and decision making. In an article, Gary Hamel identified specific features of a culture that inspire innovation, including setting high expectations, creating a cause that workers can be passionate about, encouraging radical ideas, and allowing talented people in the company to easily transfer to different business areas within the firm. Also, innovators must be paid exceptionally well. As Hamel states, "Entrepreneurs won't work for peanuts, but they'll work for a share of the equity, a piece of the action."[20]

A reliable predictor of success in merging two or more firms is compatibility of their respective cultures. When the cultures clash, such as a mechanistic firm merging with an organic one, the result can be negative synergy. To soften any possible culture barriers, top management at Cisco Systems makes every acquisition (more than 60 through year 2001) feel that it is part of the company. When Chrysler and Daimler/Benz merged in 1999, on the other hand, their cultures clashed considerably, creating many transition problems. Examples of the culture clash included American executives objecting to the German executives spending so lavishly on hotel suites and meals. Another problem arose because American managers drew salaries up to four times higher than their German counterparts. (See Case 9-A for more details.)

Individuals can contribute to their own success by finding a good *person-organization fit,* an organization that fits his or her personality. Similarly, an organization will be more successful when the personalities of most members fit its culture. One study measured organizations on such dimensions as stability, experimenting, risk taking, and rule orientation. Researchers then compared the preferences of professional employees regarding culture to the culture of their firms and found good person-organization fit resulted in more commitment and higher job satisfaction.[21]

Organizational culture powerfully influences the *direction of leadership activity.* Top-level managers spend much of their time working with the forces that shape the attitudes and values of employees at all levels. Leaders in key roles establish what type of culture is needed for the firm and then shape the existing culture to match that ideal, which is why outsiders are sometimes brought in to head a company. When Michael Armstrong joined AT&T as its top executive, he acted quickly to shake up a culture that was too smug about competition. Armstrong also eliminated company chauffeur privileges for many managers because he thought they had developed an imperial attitude. Charles D. Morgan, the top executive at Axicom Corp. sums up the link between culture and company leadership in these words: "Your culture should be everything you do as a business. It should be how you solve problems, build products and work in teams. For the CEO and other leaders, it's about how you lead."[22]

Organizational Learning, Knowledge Management, and Culture

Understanding organizations and their cultures requires an examination of how well they learn. An effective organization engages in continuous learning by proactively adapting to the external environment. In the process, the organization profits from its experiences. Instead of repeating the same old mistakes, the organization learns. A **learning organization** is skilled at creating, acquiring, and transferring knowledge. It also modifies its behavior to reflect new knowledge and new insights.[23]

Learning organizations find ways to manage knowledge more productively and encourage organizational members to share information. IBM defines **knowledge management** as the ways and means by which a company leverages its knowledge resources to generate business value. More simply, knowledge management involves "getting the right knowledge to the right people at the right time."[24]

The position of *chief knowledge officer* (CKO) in many large firms indicates the importance of organizational learning and knowledge management. Behind the rise of these positions lies the growing realization that companies can no longer base the key to business success on physical assets, but must consider intellectual assets as well. An often-expressed opinion states that intellectual capital (the sum of ideas that give an organization a competitive edge) provides the most decisive form of organization wealth. An example of intellectual capital would be a pharmaceutical firm's knowledge about which type of consumers actually use their medicines.

Key tasks for most knowledge officers involve collecting knowledge from employees throughout the company, often using software such as Lotus Notes and an intranet. In addition, the CKO provides external knowledge and research, and makes certain that knowledge is spread as widely as possible throughout the organization. Most organizations employ many people with useful knowledge, such as how to solve a particular problem. Because this information may be stored solely in the person's brain, other workers who need the information do not know who possesses it. Systematizing such knowledge develops a sort of corporate yellow pages.

In addition to the specialized work of the chief knowledge officer in a learning organization, managers also manage knowledge. He or she should actively contribute to knowledge management. Firms that fail to codify and share knowledge lose the knowledge of workers who leave. Shared knowledge, such as knowing who the real decision makers are within a particular customer's business, can be retained. In a learning organization, considerable learning takes place in teams as members share expertise.

learning organization

An organization that is skilled at creating, acquiring, and transferring knowledge.

knowledge management

The ways and means by which a company leverages its knowledge resources to generate business value.

Another key characteristic of a learning organization teaches people to realize that whatever they do in their job can have an effect on the organizational system. For example, a manufacturing worker who finds a way to reduce costs can help the sales department win a large order by selling at a lower price.

Organizational learning is related to culture, because the culture must support learning for it to take place. An emphasis on learning and knowledge management gradually becomes part of the organizational culture. The concept of knowledge management (KM) continues to gain considerable momentum, as organizations become increasingly dependent on useful knowledge to stay competitive.

Managing and Controlling the Culture

A major responsibility of top management is to shape, manage, and control the organizational culture. After a new CEO is appointed, the person typically makes a public statement to the effect: "My number-one job is to change the culture." The executive would then have to use his or her best leadership skills to inspire and persuade others toward forming a new culture. Many executives, for example, attempt to move the culture in the direction of higher creativity and risk taking.

Another general way of changing an organization's culture involves organization development, a set of specialized techniques for transforming an organization. These techniques include conducting surveys about the need for change, and then involving many people in making the desirable changes. In addition to working with an organization development consultant to bring about cultural change, a manager might do the following:

- Serve as a role model for the desired attitudes and behaviors. Leaders must behave in ways consistent with the values and practices they wish to see imitated throughout the organization. Deere & Co. is going through a major cultural change in which customer needs are satisfied through mass customization. For a strongly traditional company to undergo such change, considerable new training is necessary. Top managers at Deere both set up teams for training and participate in the training sessions themselves.[25]
- Educate from the top down. At Axicom Corp., a manufacturer of data products, Charles D. Morgan, the company leader (the company has no executive titles) sat down with his direct reports to begin an education process that eventually cascaded down to the business units and teams. When Axicom eliminated all executive titles, Morgan had to deal with some senior vice presidents who liked having titles.[26]
- Establish a reward system that reinforces the culture, such as giving huge suggestion awards to promote an innovative culture.
- Select candidates for positions at all levels whose values mesh with the values of the desired culture. At Sony Corporation all new hires must demonstrate that they care about quality (such as having produced something of quality as a hobby) in order to be hired.
- Sponsor new training and development programs that support the desired cultural values. Among many examples, top management at Levi Strauss wants to support a culture favoring diversity. Training programs in valuing differences therefore receive high levels of encouragement from Levi Strauss executives.

MANAGING CHANGE

"The only constant is change" is a cliché frequently repeated in the workplace. To meet their objectives, managers must manage change effectively on an daily basis. As one business writer notes,

> Change today happens suddenly, unexpectedly, unpredictably. It occurs in companies the way that we see it occur in biological systems or in technological breakthroughs: Change is sudden, nonlinear, and constant. Its amplitude and direction can't be forecast. Killer apps [applications] can come from anywhere; new competitors are lurking everywhere. Markets emerge, flourish, inspire imitators, breed competitors, and disappear overnight.[27]

Change in the workplace relates to any factor with an impact on people, including changes in technology, organization structure, competition, human resources, and budgets. An example of a heavy-impact change for many firms and their workers is the shift to e-business, as described in Chapter 3. One of the many changes created by e-business is the upgraded roles of some workers. Instead of earning a living with routine transactions, to survive they must now offer value-added advice. For example, stockbrokers cannot earn a good living by simply conducting trades, and travel agents cannot survive by booking airline and hotel reservations alone.[28]

The following description of managing change contains six components: (1) change at the individual versus organizational level; (2) a model of the change process; (3) resistance to change; (4) gaining support for change; (5) the role of disruptive technology in change; and (6) bringing about planned change through quality programs such as Six Sigma. Knowledge of these components helps in managing change that affects oneself and others.

Creating Change at the Individual Versus Organizational Level

Many useful changes in organizations take place at the individual and small group level, rather than at the organizational level. Quite often individual contributors, middle-level managers, and team leaders identify a small need for change and make it happen. For example, the division head at Dayton-Hudson decided that tools with pink handles were not attractive to the modern woman. As a result the manager discontinued pink handles on tools for women, and sales to women surged.

One study researched the effective change brought about by individuals in a variety of organizations. Each of the more than 100 participants was identified as a "mover and shaker," someone who brought about constructive change. Constructive change included, for example, modifying a software product so as to open new markets. A common characteristic of these people who brought about change was a greater focus on results than on trying not to offend anyone. At the same time they concentrated more on exerting individual initiative than on blending into the group.[29]

Change at the organizational level receives much more attention than the small, incremental changes brought about by individuals. One of these major changes has already been described: changing the organizational culture. Later we describe how Six Sigma changes an organization. Change at the organizational level can be regarded as change in the fundamental way in which the company operates, such as moving from a government-regulated utility to a competitive organization. A current analysis suggests that for total organizational change to take place, every employee must be able and eager to rise to the challenge of change. Organizational change requires getting individuals at every level involved—such as the thousands of Sears employees helping to bring about the new image (the softer side) of Sears.[30]

The Unfreezing-Changing-Refreezing Model of Change

Psychologist Kurt Lewin developed a three-step analysis of the change process.[31] His unfreezing-changing-refreezing model is widely used by managers to help bring about constructive change. Many other approaches to initiating change stem from this simple model, which is illustrated in Exhibit 9-10. *Unfreezing* involves reducing or eliminating resistance to change. As long as employees oppose a change, it will not be implemented effectively. To accept change, employees must first deal with and resolve their feelings about letting go of the old. Only after people have dealt effectively with endings can they readily make transitions.

Changing, or moving on to a new level, usually involves considerable two-way communication, including group discussion. According to Lewin, "Rather than a one-way flow of commands or recommendations, the person implementing the change should make suggestions. The changee should be encouraged to contribute and participate." *Refreezing* includes pointing out the success of the change and looking for ways to reward people involved in implementing the change.

Bill Ochalek, a manager in the automobile design group at GM, perceives the need for unfreezing design specialists to better enable them to bring about significant changes in auto design. Ochalek believes you learn the most from interacting with people who are the least like you. To counter the insularity of GM designers, he lobbied to get his team into the outside world. Members of the design team went to work inside various car dealerships and visited companies in different industries. The team stopped attending auto shows and started going to Internet conferences, consumer-electronics trade shows, and toy fairs. All these activities were intended to help the designers change their traditional ways of thinking.[32]

Resistance to Change

Before a company's managers can gain support for change, they must understand why people resist change. People resist changes for reasons they think are important, the most common being the fear of an unfavorable outcome, such as less

EXHIBIT 9-10
The Change Process

To bring about change, you have to break old habits, create new ones, and solidify the new habits.

money or personal inconvenience. People also resist change for such varied reasons as not wanting to break well-established habits. Change may also be unwelcome because it upsets the balance of an activity, such as the old system of visiting customers in person instead of the new system of strictly electronic communication.[33]

Personality factors also contribute to resistance to change. For example, a rigid person might be more naturally disposed to maintaining the status quo. In a study of how well 514 managers in six different organizations responded to change, researchers compared the personality factors of positive self-concept and risk tolerance to how well the managers coped with change. Coping, as measured by both self-reports and independent observations by others who worked with the managers showed a high correlation to positive self-concept.[34] In short, if you feel good about yourself and you like to take risks, you can cope better with change.

Even when people do not view a change as potentially damaging, they may sometimes cling to a system they dislike rather than change. According to folk wisdom, "People would rather deal with the devil they know." Workers may also resist change based on weaknesses in the proposed changes that may have been overlooked or disregarded by management.

> A sales manager resisted her company's proposal to shift a key product to dealer distribution. She explained that dealers would give so little attention to the product that sales would plunge. Despite her protests, the firm shifted to dealer distribution. Sales of the product did plunge, and the company returned to selling through sales representatives.

Gaining Support for Change

Gaining support for change, and therefore overcoming resistance, is an important managerial responsibility. Let us look at ten techniques for gaining support for change.

1. *Invest time in planning the change.* Effective managers invest time in planning a change before implementation begins. If possible, the people affected by the change should help in the planning. A change consultant advises, "One of the biggest mistakes American organizations make is that they do not take the time required to develop a comprehensive change plan and to get buy-in from the people who will be affected by the change."[35]
2. *Allow for discussion and negotiation.* Support for change can be increased by discussing and negotiating the more sensitive aspects of the change. It is important to acknowledge the potential hardships associated with the change, such as longer working hours or higher output to earn the same compensation. The two-way communication incorporated into the discussion helps reduce some employee concerns. Discussion often leads to negotiation, which further involves employees in the change process.
3. *Allow for participation.* To overcome resistance to change, allow people to participate in the changes that will affect them. In applying this concept, a manager can allow employees to set their own rules to increase compliance. A powerful participation technique is to encourage people who already favor the change to help in planning and implementation. These active supporters of the change will be even more strongly motivated to enlist the support of others.
4. *Point out the financial benefits.* Given that so many employees express concern about the financial effects of work changes, it is helpful to discuss these effects

openly. If employees will earn more money as a result of the change, this fact can be used as a selling point. For example, a company owner told his employees, "I know you are inconvenienced and upset because we have cut way back on secretarial support. But some of the savings will be invested in bigger bonuses for you." Much of the grumbling subsided.

5. *Avoid change overload.* Too much change too soon leads to negative stress. Too many sweeping changes in a brief period of time, or simultaneous change also causes confusion, and it leads to foot dragging about the workplace innovation. The more far-reaching the innovation, such as restructuring a firm, the greater the reason for not attempting other innovations simultaneously.

6. *Gain political support for change.* Few changes get through organizations without the change agent's forming alliances with people who will support his or her proposals. Often it means selling the proposed changes to members of top-level management before proceeding down the hierarchy. It is much more difficult to create change from the bottom up. When you do start from the bottom, it is important to find a backer—someone who can sell your plan to the senior team. Change efforts wither away without someone smart enough and skilled enough to convince the opposition. For example, it took a skilled change agent to get GM to restyle the venerable Buick whose customer base was slowly shrinking.[36]

7. *Allow for first-hand observation of successful change.* Support for change can sometimes be overcome by giving workers an opportunity to see first-hand an example of a model of the change in question.[37] Suppose, for example, top management decides that the company should shift to a virtually paperless company without secretarial assistance. Many managers and staff professionals would be quite skeptical. If feasible, it would be helpful for a small team of company skeptics to visit a company like VeriFone that has become a paperless office. Seeing is believing, and also helps overcome resistance to change.

8. *Reduce uncertainty* When top-level management initiates a large-scale program of organization change, such as organizational restructuring, a merger, or a downsizing, considerable confusion and uncertainty run through the company. Negative rumors about the change surface, making support for the change difficult to find. Based on in-depth interviews of managers involved in change, Nicholas DiFonzo and Prashant Bordia concluded that communicating effectively helps workers deal with the changes. The wrong way to communicate about the changes is to delay the announcement of change and to handle information in a secretive fashion. By communicating openly about the changes, even with incomplete information, management can reduce uncertainty among workers. Fewer rumors often mean decreased resistance to change.[38]

9. *Ask effective questions to involve workers in the change.* An *effective question* moves people toward a goal or objective instead of dwelling on what might have gone wrong. The effective question focuses on what is right rather than wrong, thereby offering encouragement. As in active listening, effective questions are open-ended. They also ask *what* or *how* rather than *why*, thereby decreasing defensiveness. (E.g., "How is the software installation coming along?" rather than "Why hasn't the new software been installed?") Effective questions are also you-oriented; they focus on the person who is supposed to implement the change. Two examples of effective questions are:

"How would you describe your progress so far?"

"What kind of support do you need to ensure your success?"[39]

10. *Build strong working relationships.* The better the working relationship with workers, the less the resistance.[40] Factors in a good working relationship include trust and mutual respect. Building strong working relationships also helps reduce fear about the changes in process. For example, workers might ordinarily fear that a new system of performance evaluation will result in smaller salary increases. With a good working relationship with management, this fear may be reduced somewhat.

Disruptive Technology and Organizational Change

Imagine that you are an executive at a profitable regional airline. You learn that a startup company called JetYou is selling jet packs that enable people to fly within a 500-mile radius without having to purchase an airline ticket or visit an airport. You laugh at the idea of a jet pack as a serious competitor. But gradually one-half of your customers shift to JetYou instead of flying commercially. JetYou blindsided you with **disruptive technology**. This phenomenon generally refers to large successful companies losing sight of small emerging markets served by a company with new technologies. In essence, a large industry leader is subject to attacks from a shoestring startup.[41] So now you think to yourself, "Should we get into the jet pack business?"

Disruptive technologies create an entirely new market by introducing a new kind of product or service. The product or service is inferior in terms of what the best customers demand. (Flying 200 miles in the rain by jetpack rather than seated in an airplane might be considered inferior service.) Charles Schwab's initial entry as a bare-bones stock brokerage firm was a disruptive technology for big brokerage firms like Merrill Lynch. Early PCs were a disruptive innovation in comparison to mainframes and minicomputers. Full-service brokerage firms said, "Who would want to buy investments without full professional advice?" Mainframe manufacturers at first said, "Why bother with those junkie toys with slim profit margins?" However, discount brokers and PCs occupy dominant positions in the fields of financial services and computers.

Disruptive technology and innovations also affect health care. Less complex alternatives to expensive health care include off-the-shelf eyeglasses (sold in stores for about 100 years) and angioplasty instead of open–heart surgery. Health-care providers other than physicians, including nurse practitioners and physician's assistants, can provide services in less-expensive decentralized settings. In the past, these services could previously be provided only by expensive specialists in centralized, inconvenient locations.[42] Note carefully that not all physicians think these disruptive innovations contribute to the best interests of patients.

A new technology or start-up can create havoc for an organization. Several larger, well-established firms have been able to cope with innovation. Dayton-Hudson, for example, is the only department store company to be successful in the discount business. Dayton-Hudson staved off the competition by founding the Target Stores division. Clayton M. Christensen and Michael Overdorf offer three approaches for meeting the challenge of disruptive change:

1. Create new organization structures within the existing corporation in which new processes can be developed. An example might be a traditional book publisher developing a project team in a remote location to develop electronic books.
2. Spin out an independent organization from the existing organization and develop within it the new processes and values required to solve the problem.

disruptive technology

Innovations by small or lesser-known companies that create an entirely new market and jeopardize the position of industry leaders by introducing a new kind of product or service.

Hewlett-Packard finally met with success in the ink-jet printer business when it transferred the ink-jet unit to a separate division in Vancouver, British Columbia.

3. Acquire another company whose processes and values closely match the requirements of furnishing the new product or service. Cisco Systems routinely purchases start-ups with a technology that could threaten their business, such as improved software for linking computers together.[43]

The accompanying Organization in Action provides an illuminating description about how a firm you have probably used regularly is adapting to disruptive technology.

total quality management (TQM)

A management system for improving performance throughout a firm by maximizing customer satisfaction, making continuous improvements, and relying heavily on employee involvement.

Six Sigma and Planned Change

The shift to a more quality-conscious firm can be classified as a total systems approach to organization change. Defined with some focus, **total quality management (TQM)** is a management system for improving performance throughout a firm by maximizing customer satisfaction, making continuous

Organization *in Action*

The U.S. Postal Service Adapts to Disruptive Technology

Wary of losing its lucrative bill and payment delivery business to the Internet, the Postal Service decided to offer one-stop bill paying via computer. Many Americans have grown comfortable paying bills electronically, and now they will be able to do all their business at a single site using a password.

It does not matter whether the bill is from the electric or telephone company, the local hardware store, or the dentist's office. Postmaster General Henderson predicts that "the generation that has grown up with PCs will move to transacting business on the Internet."

The service, made available in April 2000, provided new customers with six months of free service. People interested in the service, USPSeBillPay, can get details and sign up at http://www.usps.gov. The post office worked with CheckFree Corp. and YourAccounts.Com, a division of Output Technology Solutions, to develop the system. Companies send bills electronically, which individuals can then pay electronically. If someone wants to make a payment

to a company that does not have an electronic connection to the service, the post office will simply issue a check.

After the initial six months of free service, customers can choose from two plans. "Pay Everyone," at $6 a month, includes 20 payments and costs 40 cents for each additional payment. "Pay As You Go" costs $2 a month, plus 40 cents per payment.

The U.S. Postal Service entry into Internet bill-paying services is part of a larger trend toward using technology to compete and be more efficient. Other automation at the Postal Service includes the use of robots for simple tasks that do the work of six people in less time. These results from continuous efforts help the Postal Service stay competitive in the midst of rapidly changing technologies.

Source: "Postal Service Offers Bill Paying Over the Internet," The Associated Press, April 6, 2000; Danielle Kost, "The Letter Factory," *Rochester Democrat and Chronicle*, January 21, 2001, pp. 1E, 6E.

improvements, and relying heavily on employee involvement. Defined more broadly, total quality management "is a fundamental change in the organization's culture to one that includes a focus on the customer, an environment of trust and openness, formation of work teams, breaking down of internal barriers, team leadership and coaching, shared power, and communication improvement."[44]

Although the term *TQM* is rarely used, and many people consider the quality movement to have passed, having high-quality goods and services is considered a necessary minimum to compete effectively. Most customers today require high quality standards from vendors. One such standard is *six sigma*, or 3.4 errors in 1 million opportunities. (The figure is derived from the area under the normal curve from −6 to +6 standard deviations from the mean.) A number of organizations formalized this quality standard as company-wide programs for attaining high quality. With capital first letters, Six Sigma also refers to a philosophy of driving out waste and improving quality and the cost and time performance of a company. Three examples of companies with Six Sigma programs are GE, Honeywell, and Motorola Corp.

Six Sigma is regarded as a data-driven method for achieving near-perfect quality, with an emphasis on preventing problems. The approach stresses statistical analysis and measurement in design, manufacturing, and the entire area of customer-oriented activities. Six Sigma also contains a strong behavioral aspect, with a focus on motivating people to work together to achieve higher levels of productivity. As with all programs of organizational improvement, top management commitment is vital. Six Sigma can also be viewed as a fusion of technical and social systems because of the emphasis on both technical programs and creating a culture of quality. Six Sigma teams carry out most of an organization's quality improvement efforts.[45]

Six Sigma, as with other quality programs, can help an organization achieve reliable products and services. However, good quality alone does not attract large numbers of customers and job candidates. Motorola ran into difficulty selling its high-quality analog cellular telephones because most consumers preferred digital phones. Products that offer passion, fun, and excitement (such as the Chrysler PT Cruiser) draw more attention than flawless construction. A final note: Remember that an exciting product of high quality outperforms an exciting product of low quality. The Jaguar auto suffered from low quality for years despite its high status appeal. After by Ford Motor Company bought Jaguar, it overhauled manufacturing procedures in pursuit of higher quality. The waiting list for the S-type V8 Jaguar sedan soon numbered 20,000.

SUMMARY OF KEY POINTS

1 Describe the bureaucratic form of organization and discuss its advantages and disadvantages. The most widely used form of organization is the bureaucracy, a multilevel organization in which authority flows downward and rules and regulations are carefully specified. Bureaucracies can be highly efficient organizations that are well suited to handling repetitive, recurring tasks. However, they may be rigid in terms of rule interpretation, and they may result in decision-making delays.

2 Explain the major ways in which organizations are divided into departments. The usual way of subdividing effort in organizations, particularly in bureaucracies,

is to create departments. Four common types of departmentalization are functional, territorial, product–service, and customer.

3 Describe three modifications of the bureaucratic structure: the matrix structure; flat structures, downsizing, and outsourcing; and the horizontal organization. The matrix organization consists of a project structure superimposed on a functional structure. Personnel assigned to the projects within the matrix report to a project manager, yet they report to a functional manager also. Flat organizations have fewer layers than traditional hierarchies, and are often the result of downsizings. They are created for such purposes as reducing personnel costs and speeding up decision making. Downsizing can also be looked upon as a way of simplifying an organization to make it less bureaucratic. Unless downsizing is done carefully, it can backfire in terms of increasing efficiency. By outsourcing, a company can reduce its need for employees and physical assets, and associated payroll costs.

Another approach to organization structure is to organize horizontally, or for a group of people to concern themselves with a process, such as filling an order or development of a new product. Team members focus on their purpose rather than their specialty, and take collective responsibility for customers. Switching from a task to a process emphasis can often be done through reengineering.

4 **Specify how delegation, empowerment, and decentralization spread authority in an organization.** Delegation is assigning formal authority and responsibility for accomplishing a task to another person. Delegation fosters empowerment. The manager remains accountable for the result of subordinates. Effective delegation includes assigning duties to the right people and obtaining feedback on the delegated task. Decentralization stems from delegation. It is the extent to which authority is passed down to lower levels in an organization. Decentralization sometimes refers to geographic dispersion.

5 **Identify major aspects of organizational culture, including its management and control.** Seven key dimensions of organizational culture are values, relative diversity, resource allocation and rewards, degree of change, a sense of ownership, an attitude of caring, and the strength of culture. Culture has important consequences and implications for factors such as competitive advantage, productivity, quality, and morale. How well an organization learns (or profits from its experiences) and manages knowledge is also part of its culture. Top management is responsible for shaping, managing, and controlling culture. Although culture is slow to change, the manager can lead the firm through organization development. The manager can also act as a role model and reward behaviors that fit the desired cultural values.

6 **Describe key aspects of managing change, including gaining support for change.** Change can take place at the individual and small group levels as well as the organizational level. A model of change suggests that the process has three stages: unfreezing attitudes, followed by attitude change, then refreezing to point out the success of the change. People resist change for reasons they think are important, the most common being the fear of an unfavorable outcome.

Ten techniques for gaining support for change are as follows: invest time in planning the change; allow for discussion and negotiation; allow for participation; point out the financial benefits; avoid change overload; gain political support for change; allow for first-hand observation of successful change; reduce uncertainty; ask effective questions to involve workers in the change; and build strong working relationships.

Disruptive technology occurs when large successful companies lose sight of small emerging markets served by a company with new technologies. The new technology creates havoc for the more established firm. Total quality management, including Six Sigma programs, is an important organizational change strategy.

KEY TERMS AND PHRASES

Organization structure, *222*

Bureaucracy, *222*

Unity of command, *222*

Departmentalization, *224*

Functional departmentalization, *224*

Territorial departmentalization, *226*

Product–service departmentalization, *227*

Customer departmentalization, *227*

Project organization, *228*

Matrix organization, *228*

Flat organization structure, *229*

Span of control, *229*

Outsourcing, *231*

Horizontal structure, *232*

Reengineering, *232*

Delegation, *233*

Empowerment, *233*

Decentralization, *234*

Centralization, *235*

Organizational culture (or corporate culture), *235*

Learning organization, *239*

Knowledge management, *239*

Disruptive technology, *245*

Total quality management (TQM), *246*

QUESTIONS

1. Why do some people particularly enjoy working in a bureaucracy?
2. Small and medium-sized companies are often eager to hire people with about five years of experience working in a large, successful bureaucratic firm like IBM or Ford Motor Company. What might be the reason behind the demand for these workers with experience in a bureaucracy?
3. Community and student organizations occasionally attempt to run their activities without placing any one person in charge, including holding meetings without a head. Almost inevitably, the members become frustrated and little work gets accomplished. What do these inci-

dents of frustration and failure tell you about organization structure?
4. What is the basis for departmentalization in the last hospital you visited, read about, or saw on television?
5. Describe the culture of an organization you are familiar with such as your employer or the school in which you are taking this course. Use the dimensions of organizational culture to help you build your description.
6. What can first- and middle-level managers, as well as team leaders, do about shaping the culture of a firm?
7. How can a manager tell whether an employee is resisting change?

CRITICAL THINKING QUESTIONS

1. Managers who value rank and status often prefer working in a traditional bureaucracy rather than a modern team-based organization. Why?
2. Many career counselors believe that you are more likely to succeed in an organization in which you fit the culture. How could you determine before joining an organization whether you fit its culture?

SKILL-BUILDING EXERCISE: Designing a Flat Organization

You and your teammates are assigned the task of creating a flatter structure for the organization depicted in Exhibit 9-11. Draw a new organization chart, with each box carefully labeled. Explain what happens to any managers who might be downsized and why your new structure is an improvement.

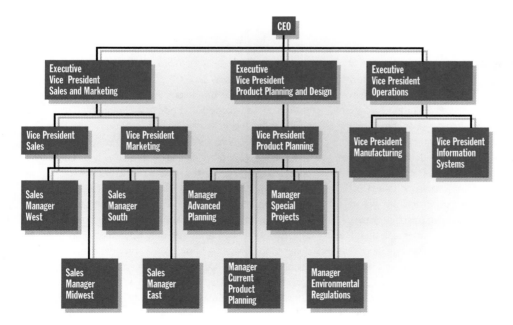

EXHIBIT 9-11

Company Organization Chart Before Downsizing

INTERNET SKILL-BUILDING EXERCISE: Analyzing an Organization Structure

Organization structures come in all shapes and sizes. The Internet provides examples of the different types of structures. One approach to finding examples is to use search phrases such as "example of organization structure." Another approach is to visit the Web site of a company of your choosing. Sometimes going to the company annual report will lead to an organization chart. (However, it might be necessary to visit the sites of several companies to find an organization chart.) If you do not find the organization structure laid out on the Web site, you might send the company an e-mail message, asking for a copy of the company organization chart. Once you have found an example of organization structure, try classifying it by structural type (or types).

CASE PROBLEM 9-A: The Culture War at DaimlerChrysler

On November 17, 1998, DaimlerChrysler co-chairs Jürgen Schrempp and Robert J. Eaton celebrated the first day of their newly merged company stock. The two executives, along with many others, held high expectations for creating a powerful new auto behemoth with a global reach. Yet quickly bringing together two such different companies in one year proved to be a difficult task. Thomas T. Stallkamp is keenly aware of the problems. His inability to integrate smoothly the auto units of Chrysler and Mercedes cost him his job just nine months into the merger. Stallkamp says, "You can't ignore culture."

Stallkamp became aware of the many problems early in the merger. Daimler Benz employees, for example, flew first class, in keeping with the company's luxury image. At Chrysler, only top officers could fly first class. Daimler Benz executives, while working on the merger, spent lavishly on hotels, restaurants, and fine wines. Chrysler officials were much more frugal. Like many other seemingly ordinary issues, the travel and entertainment policy became a sore point and took more than six months to resolve.

Bickering over small issues consumed precious time that could have been invested in bigger issues, such as how to squeeze cost savings out of the merger. Stallkamp believes that Schrempp was impatient for progress. "Jürgen is very fast on integrating. He's not very much into detail on that, though," says Stallkamp who had the job of handling details.

From the beginning, Stallkamp argued that a successful merger would require the two companies to abandon their own business cultures and create a new distinct one. But the ensuing territorial disputes bogged down the creation of a new culture. Some issues that should have been handled easily were sent up to the company's management board to resolve. Two such issues referred to the board were labor relations problems and emission-control policies, which became disruptive and difficult-to-resolve disputes.

Instead of trying to blend the best of each company culture, he said, "It became a question of comparing the styles of the two and picking one." In late 1999, Schrempp and Eaton decided to put the brakes on the integration and to operate each of the three automotive units—the old Chrysler, Mercedes, and the commercial truck business—separately. Stallkamp fully supported the decision, believing that favorable cultural changes would eventually take place.

Attempts at integrating the cultures focused on getting people from two different organizational cultures to work smoothly. Daimler Benz is generally thought to be methodical, disciplined, buttoned-down, hierarchical, and engineering-driven. The company favors conservative vehicle styling. The Chrysler half is more impulsive, intuitive, and free-wheeling, with a focus on speedy product development and flashy design.

In November 1999, Chrysler vice president James P. Holden was named to replace Stallkamp as president of DaimlerChrysler's U.S. operations. One of his main responsibilities was to bring about the merger synergies promised when the merger first took place. Holden, who majored in political science then business, was considered a highly competent executive with leadership skills, mechanical skills, and computer expertise.

Morale in U.S. operations in particular began to decline as employees watched a parade of well-respected executives depart from Chrysler headquarters in Auburn Hills, Michigan. Investors became concerned that the Daimler and Chrysler divisions were operating as essentially two companies, despite managers from the American and German companies visiting each other regularly. Potential savings from combined purchasing materialized slowly because of Chrysler's and Daimler's different specifications for materials such as steel.

By December 2000, Jürgen Schrempp continued his domination of what he had originally proposed as a merger of equals. He decided that the U.S. managers were not good enough to serve on his board, or to hold the top position in the Chrysler division. Schrempp fired Chrysler president James Holden, and brought in a Mercedes veteran, Dieter Zetsche, after the U.S. automaker had lost $512 million in the third quarter. Outside analysts predicted a Chrysler loss of $2 billion for 2001. The losses, along with layoffs of 20,000 workers took place despite rosy forecasts by Holden. Zetsche fired three Chrysler executives, including the head of sales and marketing, his first day on the job. Despite these setbacks, in February 2001 Schrempp predicted that the Chrysler division would be profitable again in 2003.

Listed among its many problems, Chrysler bungled its hottest product, the stylish PT Cruiser. They had enough production capacity to meet only two-thirds of the demand for the sensationally successful hybrid retro minivan/station wagon.

The hard feelings between the Americans and the Germans became more acute when Schrempp made a remark to the *Financial Times* that the notion of a merger of equals was always fictitious: "If I had gone and said Chrysler would be a division, everybody on their side would have said, 'There is no way we'll do this deal.'" Schrempp later apologized.

In another attempt to create a true merger, Zetsche started a program of Mercedes sharing components with Chrysler. New rear-wheel versions of the Chrysler Concorde and 300M (scheduled for production in 2004 and 2005, respectively) will include Mercedes electronics, transmissions, and seat frames among other parts.

Discussion Questions

1. In what way are differences in culture contributing to the problems between Chrysler and Daimler?
2. What advice can you offer top management at Daimler-Chrysler to work as a more unified company?
3. What advice can you offer Jürgen Schrempp to be a more effective executive?

Source: Joann Muller, "Lessons from a Casualty of the Culture Wars," *Business Week*, November 29, 1999, p. 198; Muller, "Man with a Plan: DaimlerChrysler's CEO Is Forcing Out Key U.S. Execs—at What Cost?" *Business Week*, March 29, 1999, p. 50; Frank Gibney Jr., "Purging Chrysler," *Time*, December 4, 2000, pp. 58–60; Alex Taylor III, "Can the Germans Rescue Chrysler?" *Fortune*, April 30, 2001.

CASE PROBLEM 9-B: The Reluctant Information Sharers

The Flagstaff Marketing Group specializes in marketing assistance for business firms. Most of their accounts are small and medium-sized firms without large marketing staffs of their own. The Flagstaff Group often helps a client market a product by finding prospective customers and developing a marketing slogan. One client, a manufacturer of foot-powered scooters, sought advice on opening a new market. Flagstaff helped them market their product to city dwellers as a vehicle for going to work. The marketing theme was "Scoot Your Way to Success." Sales quadrupled for the scooter manufacturer.

Flagstaff also has several large firms as clients. For these firms, Flagstaff offers specialized expertise that the client firm may lack. For example, Flagstaff develops company logos and names that help give a firm a distinctive identity, such as finding a new name for a company after a merger or spin-off, such as Avitar, the information technology services division of a manufacturing company.

Peter Flagstaff, the founder of the firm, worries lately that his firm develops ideas inefficiently. He said to Lindsay Gibson, the executive vice president at Flagstaff, "I keep hearing the same discussions over and over about solving a particular client problem. The account executives keep sifting through the alternatives that others have done before. People don't capitalize on all the good problem solving that has taken place in the past. We go through the same agonizing process of dealing with similar problems."

Gibson replied, "Are you suggesting that we should offer canned solutions to clients so we could save lots of time?"

"Not at all," responded Peter. "We could at least save some time and offer similar types of assistance to clients that we offered to other clients in the past. I'll give you a good example. Reggie Whitson recently had a pet-clothing manufacturer for a client. The client wanted to expand the market for items like dog raincoats, dog shoes for cold weather, and a luxury line of dog sweaters for special occasions. So Reggie spent a week researching dog clothing before coming up with some recommendations for his client.

"If Reggie could have picked up some ideas in-house, he could have saved time and still found good ideas more quickly. Also, if he had spent less time, the client would not have been so shocked by the large fee."

Looking perplexed, Lindsay said, "But how would Reggie have known about who had tackled a similar client problem in the past?"

Peter jumped in, "Lindsay, you have pinpointed the problem. We have done a poor job of systematically pooling all that great information in our heads. Not only do we reinvent the wheel, we reinvent the idea that a wheel would be useful.

"I'm proposing that we find a way of sharing knowledge that will pay big dividends for the firm. The major consulting firms have developed pretty effective systems of knowledge management and knowledge sharing in recent years.

"I'm not implying that we hire somebody to be our chief knowledge officer or that we invest $500,000 in sophisticated software. I just want us to do a better job of sharing ideas with each other."

"I've got an idea," said Lindsay. "Let's schedule a combination dinner and focus group for the professional staff. The subject will be why we aren't doing a better job of information sharing."

Among the comments that emerged from the dinner/focus group were the following:

GARY: I would like to share more of my experiences with the other account executives. I'm concerned though about the good of the firm. Suppose I give some of my best ideas to another account exec, and then he or she leaves the firm. My good ideas are fed right to the competition.

BRENDA: Unlike Gary, I have no hesitancy in sharing ideas. The problem is the time involved. We were encouraged at one time to do a write-up of how we solved unusual client problems. The task proved to be busywork. We had to follow a complicated format. Maybe we should use a briefer method of recording good ideas.

SHARON: I'm not opposed to sharing ideas, but it makes me a little self-conscious. To ask someone else for ideas suggests that I'm not so creative myself. Take that dog-clothing account. If I asked others for ideas, it would have been like I can't think of any good ideas for promoting dog clothing myself.

JASON: As long as we are all being brutally honest here, let me get to the heart of the problem. We're creative types. Our careers depend on having good ideas. After you share an idea with another exec the idea becomes public knowledge. It loses its originality. So therefore if you use that idea again, you are no longer creative because other account execs are using it.

ANNE: Jason has a point. Teamwork is nice but you still have to look out for *numero uno*. Sure I have warm, fuzzy feelings toward top management and the other account executives. Yet I'm still evaluated by Flagstaff in terms of my originality.

Peter Flagstaff said to the group, "Thank you for being so candid. I see a few glimmers of hope in terms of knowledge sharing in our firm. But this is just the start of a continuing dialogue. We have a long way to go to manage knowledge well at Flagstaff marketing."

Discussion Questions

1. What suggestions can you offer Peter Flagstaff and Lindsay Gibson to improve knowledge sharing at the Flagstaff Marketing Group?

2. How valid are the points made by the account executives for not doing a better job sharing information?

3. What cultural changes might be needed at Flagstaff to improve knowledge sharing?

ENDNOTES

1. Amy Reinhardt, "The New Intel: Craig Barrett Is Leading the Chip Giant into Riskier Terrain," *Business Week*, March 13, 2000, pp. 110–124.

2. Paul S. Adler, "Building Better Bureaucracies," *Academy of Management Executive*, November 1999, pp. 26–37.

3. "When Senselessness Reigns," *Rochester Democrat and Chronicle*, May 25, 1998, p. 8A.

4. Donald L. Barlett and James B. Steele, "Fantasy Islands: And Other Perfectly Legal Ways that Big Companies Manage to Avoid Billions in Federal Taxes," *Time*, November 16, 1998, p. 88.

5. James R. Morris, Wayne F. Cascio, and Clifford E. Young, "Downsizing After All These Years," *Organizational Dynamics*, Winter 1999, p. 85.

6. Assa Birati and Aharon Tziner, "Cost-Benefit Analysis of Organizational Interventions: The Case of Downsizing," *Journal of Business and Psychology*, Winter 2000, p. 285.

7. Oren Harari, "Layoffs: An Eternal Debate," *Management Review*, October 1993, p. 31.

8. Helene Rudzinski, "IT Outsourcing That Works," *UNISYS Exec*, July–August 2000, p. 34.

9. Frank Ostroff, *The Horizontal Organization: What the Organization of the Future Actually Looks Like and How It Delivers Value to Customers* (New York: Oxford University Press, 1999); Ann Majchrzak and Qianwei Wang, "Breaking the Functional Mind-Set in Process Organizations," *Harvard Business Review*, January 1998, p. 21.

10. Majchrzak and Wang, "Breaking the Functional Mind-Set," p. 95.

11. "The Right Look: How to Get the Most Out of Your Delegating Skills," *Executive Strategies*, January 1993, p. 7.

12. "The Power of POWERSHARING," *HR/OD*, July–August 1998, p. 2; Janet Purdy Levaux, "Delegating: Yes, Letting Go Is Hard to Do," *Investor's Business Daily*, January 1995, p. A3.

13. Barbara Ettore, "The Empowerment Gap: Hype vs. Reality," *Management Review*, July–August 1997, p. 13.

14. J. Steven Ott, *The Organizational Culture Perspective* (Chicago: Dorsey Press, 1989), pp. 20–48; Personal communication from Lynn H. Suksdorf, Salt Lake City Community College, October 1998.

15. Scott Hays, "'Ownership Cultures' Create Unity," *Workforce*, February 1999, pp. 60–64.

16. William C. Taylor, "At VeriFone It's a Dog's Life (and they love it), *Fast Company Handbook of the Business Revolution*, 1997, p. 17.

17. Dave Arnott, *Corporate Cults: The Insidious Lure of the All-Consuming Organization* (New York: AMACOM, 1999).

18. Daniel R. Denison, *Corporate Culture and Organizational Effectiveness* (New York: Wiley, 1990).

19. Louise Lee, "Tricks of E*Trade," *Business Week E.BIZ*, February 7, 2000, pp. 18–20.

20. Gary Hamel, "Reinvent Your Company," *Fortune*, June 12, 2000, pp. 97–118.

21. Charles A. O'Reilly III, Jennifer A. Chairman, and David F. Caldwell, "People and Organizational Culture: A Profile Comparison Approach to Assessing Person-Organization Fit," *Academy of Management Journal*, September 1991, pp. 487–516.

22. Charles D. Morgan, "Culture Change/Culture Shock," *Management Review*, November 1998, p. 13.

23. David A. Garvin, "Building a Learning Organization," *Harvard Business Review*, July–August 1993, p. 80.

24. "Are You Up to Speed on Knowledge Management?" *HRfocus*, August 2000, pp. 5–6.

25. Anita Lienert, "Plowing Ahead in Uncertain Times," *Management Review*, November 1998, p. 19.

26. Charles D. Morgan, "Culture Change/Culture Shock," *Management Review*, November 1998, p. 13.

27. Robert B. Reich, "Your Job Is Change," *Fast Company*, October 2000, p. 143.

28. Jerry Useem, "Dot-Coms: What Have We Learned?" *Fortune*, October 30, 2000, p. 104.

29. Alan H. Frohman, "Igniting Organizational Change from Below: The Power of Individual Initiative," *Organizational Dynamics*, Winter 1997, pp. 39–53.

30. Richard Pascale, Mark Millemann, and Linda Gioja, "Changing the Way We Change," *Harvard Business Review*, November–December 1997, pp. 126–139.

31. Kurt Lewin, *Field Theory and Social Science* (New York: Harper & Brothers, 1951).

32. Anna Muio, "GM Has a New Model for Change," *Fast Company*, December 2000, pp. 62, 64.

33. Paul Strebel, "Why Do Employees Resist Change?" *Harvard Business Review*, May–June 1996, p. 87.

34. Timothy A. Judge, et al., "Managerial Coping with Organizational Change: A Dispositional Perspective," *Journal of Applied Psychology*, February 1999, pp. 107–122.

35. H. James Harrington, *Business Process Improvement: The Breakthrough Strategy for Total Quality, Productivity, and Competitiveness* (New York: McGraw-Hill, 1991).

36. Bill Breen and Cheryl Dahle, "Field Guide for Change," *Fast Company*, December 1999, p. 384.

37. Jeffrey Pfeffer, *The Human Equation: Building Profits by Putting People First* (Boston, MA: Harvard Business School Press, 1998), pp. 126–128.

38. Nicholas DiFonzo and Prashnat Bordia, "A Tale of Two Corporations: Managing Uncertainty During Organizational Change," *Human Resource Management*, Fall–Winter 1998, pp. 295–303.

39. Ed Oakley and Doug Krug, *Enlightened Leadership* (New York: Simon & Schuster, 1993).

40. Rick Maurer, "Transforming Resistance," *HRfocus*, October 1997, p. 10.

41. Clayton M. Christensen and Michael Overdorf, "Meeting the Challenge of Disruptive Change," *Harvard Business Review*, March–April 2000, pp. 66–76; Christensen, "Should You Fear Disruptive Technology?" *Fortune*, April 3, 2000, pp. 249–250.

42. Christensen and Overdorf, "Meeting the Challenge," p. 73.

43. Carol A. Reeves and David A. Bednar, "Defining Quality: Alternatives and Implications," *Academy of Management Review*, July 1994, p. 419.

44. Joseph A. Defo, "Six Sigma: Road Map for Survival," *HRfocus*, July 1999, pp. 11–12.

253

Staffing and Human Resource Management

Based in Montreal, Québec (Canada) Quebecor World Inc. is the world's largest printing company. It encompasses 160 printing plants located in 14 countries and employs 43,000 people. Quebecor World Inc., recognized the necessity of not only looking at its pricing and manufacturing/quality processes to maximize efficiency and profits, but to also look at the customer service processes.

Based on extensive surveys and conversations with customers, it became apparent that the printing industry was becoming increasingly competitive, and that similarity of equipment was leveling the playing field. As a consequence, customers expected competitive pricing and high quality from all printers. Because the company could no longer compete on price and quality alone, "We asked ourselves what's going to differentiate this company from other companies in the printing market?" recalls Marc Shapiro, Quebecor World's Senior Vice President of Human Resources. "If it wasn't equipment, pricing and quality it had to be our people. So we decided that customer service was going to be the huge differentiator to give Quebecor World a competitive advantage and we embarked upon the largest training initiative ever attempted at Quebecor World.

During one of the sessions, Quebecor employees participate in a team-building cooking exercise. The Team Banquet challenges customer service representatives to design, prepare, and serve a banquet meal within two hours without any instruction. The team-building exercise encourages participants work together to come up with focused solutions in a short time.

OBJECTIVES

After studying this chapter and doing the exercises, you should be able to:

1 Describe the components of organizational staffing.

2 Be aware of the legal aspects of staffing.

3 Explain the importance of strategic human resource planning.

4 Present an overview of recruitment and selection.

5 Present an overview of employee orientation, training, and development.

6 Explain the basics of a fair and reliable method of evaluating employee performance.

7 Summarize the basics of employee compensation.

Chapter 10

During the last session, participants make presentations to senior management that demonstrate they learned and how they will apply it back on the job. Students receive a certificate after completing the entire program.

An advisory team composed of representatives from all levels within the company ensures relevant training that reflects current business trends. It reviews case studies for accuracy and applicability to the real world of printing. Curriculum is continuously improved to mirror business trends.[1]

The customer service training program at Quebecor illustrates one important way in which human resource management contributes to company productivity and competitiveness. This final chapter about organizing and staffing deals with the heart of human resources management—staffing the organization. Staffing requires many subactivities, including recruitment and selection, training, development, and evaluation.

THE STAFFING MODEL

Describe the components of organizational staffing.

In the model in Exhibit 10-1 the staffing process flows in a logical sequence. Although not every organization follows the same steps in the same sequence, staffing ordinarily proceeds in the way this section will discuss. The arrows pointing to Retention in the model suggest that a major thrust of staffing is to retain valuable employees, and that any aspect of staffing can contribute to retention. For example, selecting the right person for the job increases the probability that he or she will enjoy the job and stay with the firm.

Human resource specialists are engaged in all phases of staffing. Line managers, however, have the ultimate responsibility for staffing their own units. Typically specialists work with managers to help them make better staffing decisions. For example, in addition to your prospective manager or team leader, a human resource specialist may interview you for a job. Most of the techniques described in this chapter have some applicability for organizations of all sizes. However, because large organizations have more resources than small ones, large organizations can engage more fully in most aspects of the staffing model.

LEGAL ASPECTS OF STAFFING

Be aware of the legal aspects of staffing.

Federal, state, provincial, and local laws influence every aspect of organizational staffing. Managers and human resource specialists must keep the major provisions of these laws in mind whenever they make decisions about any phase of employment.

Exhibit 10-2 summarizes major pieces of U.S. federal legislation that influence various aspects of staffing—not just employee selection. Exhibit 10-3 presents highlights of comparable Canadian legislation. Managers need to be aware that such legislation exists, and also be familiar with the general provisions of each law or executive order. When a possible legal issue arises, the manager should review

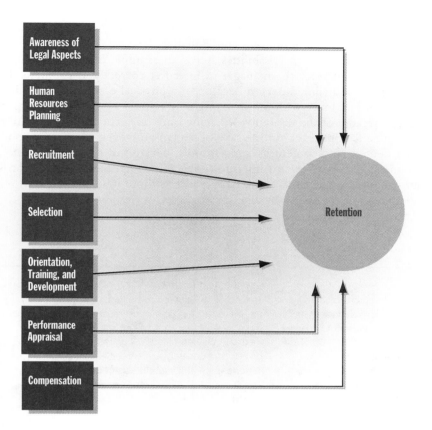

EXHIBIT 10-1

The Organization Staffing Model

Under ideal circumstances, organization staffing would proceed through the stages as shown, and would improve employee retention. Terminating employees might also be considered part of staffing.

257

the relevant legislation in depth and confer with a company specialist in employment law.

A key aspect of implementing the spirit and letter of employment discrimination law in the United States has been affirmative action programs. To comply with the Civil Rights Act of 1964, employers with federal contracts or subcontracts must develop such programs to end discrimination. **Affirmative action** consists of complying with antidiscrimination law and correcting past discriminatory practices. Under an affirmative action program, employers actively recruit, employ, train, and promote minorities and women who may have been discriminated against by the employer in the past. As a result, they are underrepresented in certain positions. Part of an affirmative action plan might include a career development program for women to help them qualify for management positions.

A national debate continues over whether any person in a competitive situation deserves a preference because of race, ethnicity, or sex. The opposing point of view to affirmative action programs is that race, ethnicity, or sex should not be a factor in making employment or business decisions. For example, a job candidate should not be given an edge over other applicants because she is a Hispanic female. What is your opinion on this issue?

A misperception of affirmative action views it as preferences or goals. Affirmative action can often be accomplished through recruitment in minority areas or publications geared toward affected minorities. Candidates thus flow naturally to

affirmative action

An employment practice that complies with antidiscrimination law and correcting past discriminatory practices.

disability

A physical or mental condition that substantially limits an individual's major life activities.

the firm without having to establish a quota such as "hiring only a Hispanic woman for our next opening as a credit analyst."

The Americans with Disabilities Act is an example of employment law that presents a challenge for the manager to interpret correctly. It prohibits discrimination against a qualified person because of a physical or mental disability. A job candidate or employee with one arm might be refused a position as a forklift truck operator because of the disability of having only one arm. (Two arms are needed to operate a forklift truck for the sake of safety.) However, the same person could not be denied employment as a receptionist because of having only one arm—assuming he or she were qualified to work as a receptionist. In the words of an employment law specialist, "The ADA protects those who are able to do the job. It doesn't guarantee the right to a job."[2]

EXHIBIT 10-2

Major U.S. Federal Antidiscrimination Legislation and Agreements

---

Civil Rights Act of 1964

Title VII of the Civil Rights Act of 1964 prohibits discrimination in all employment decisions on the basis of race, sex, religion, color, or national origin. Sexual harassment is in violation of Title VII.

Equal Employment Opportunity Commission

The Equal Employment Opportunity Commission (EEOC) administers Title VII and investigates complaints about violations. In addition, it has the power to issue guidelines for interpretation of the act. The EEOC's guidelines are not federal law. Instead, they are administrative rules and regulations.

Civil Rights Act of 1991

According to this act, victims of discrimination have rights to compensatory and punitive damages as well as jury trial. In general, in cases of intentional discrimination, the act shifts the burden of proof from employee to employer. Under earlier civil rights legislation, employees could only receive reinstatement, back pay, and attorneys' fees. The act places limits on how much employees can collect in compensatory and punitive damages. The amount depends on the size of the employer, with limits ranging from $50,000 to $300,000.

Age Discrimination in Employment Act, 1967

This act applies to employers with at least 25 employees. As later amended, it prohibits discrimination against people 40 years or older, in any area of employment, because of age. The act ended mandatory retirement for most employees covered by its provisions. Many employees laid off during downsizings have claimed to be victims of age discrimination.

Pregnancy Discrimination Act of 1978

This act broadens the definition of sex discrimination to cover pregnancy, childbirth, and related medical conditions. It also prohibits employers from discrimination against pregnant women in employment benefits if they are capable of performing their job duties. This act applies to employers with more than 21 employees.

Equal Pay Act, 1963

This act prohibits employers from paying unequal wages on the basis of sex. Equal pay must be paid for equal work, regardless of sex. Yet the act still allows employers to pay men and women different wages if the difference is based on ability or seniority.

Americans with Disabilities Act of 1990

The Americans with Disabilities Act (ADA) is designed to protect disabled and chronically ill people from discrimination in employment, public accommodations, transportation, and telecommunications. The act applies to employers with at least 15 employees.

A **disability** is defined as a physical or mental condition that substantially limits an individual's major life activities. Among the physical impairments covered by the ADA are severe vision problems, severe hearing problems, wheelchair confinement, muscular dystrophy, epilepsy, and severe physical disfigurement. Among the mental disabilities included are mental illness, alcoholism, and drug addiction. People who experienced these problems in the past cannot be discriminated against if they can perform the job.

If an employee can perform the essential functions of a job (even with special equipment), he or she should be considered qualified. Employers must accommodate the known disabilities of applicants and employees, unless the accommodations would impose "undue hardship" on the firm.

Family and Medical Leave Act, 1993

The Family and Medical Leave Act applies to employers having 50 or more employees. It requires the employer to provide up to 12 weeks of unpaid, job-protected leave to eligible employees for certain family and medical leave reasons such as caring for a newborn, newly adopted, or seriously ill child. The leave can also be used to take care of an employee's spouse or parent, or to take medical leave for the employee's own illness. The employer must also maintain the employee's health coverage during the leave.

Questions surrounding the interpretation of the ADA focus on what really constitutes a disability. Although the legal definition of a disability presented in Exhibit 10-2 may appear reasonably clear, confusion still exists. A stressed-out worker, for example, may claim to be disabled. The EEOC has stated that it intends to continue to interpret the definition of a disability as broadly as possible, and read court decisions narrowly. Furthermore, several U.S. Supreme Court decisions emphasized that the definition of a disability must be decided on a case-by-case basis. EEOC specialists are also directed to use the definition of disability that provides ADA coverage for people with a record of disability from which they have recovered totally or partially.[3] A former or present alcoholic with the drinking problem under control could therefore not be denied a job, or job transfer, on the basis of alcoholism alone.

STRATEGIC HUMAN RESOURCE PLANNING

3

Staffing begins with a prediction about how many and what types of people will be needed to conduct the work of the firm. Such activity is referred to as **strategic human resource planning**. It is the process of anticipating and providing for the movement of people into, within, and out of an organization to support the firm's business strategy. Management attempts, through planning, to have the right number and right kinds of people at the right time.

Explain the importance of strategic human resource planning.

Business strategy addresses the financial priorities of the organization with respect to identifying what business the firm should be in, product direction, profit targets, and so forth. Human resource planning addresses the question "What skills are needed for the success of this business?" Planning helps identify the gaps between current employee competencies and behavior and the competencies and behavior needed in the organization's future. Strategic human resource planning consists of four basic steps:[4]

strategic human resource planning
The process of anticipating and providing for the movement of people into, within, and out of an organization to support the firm's business strategy.

1. *Planning for future needs.* A human resource planner estimates how many people, and with what abilities, the firm will need to operate in the foreseeable future.
2. *Planning for future turnover.* A planner predicts how many current employees are likely to remain with the organization. The difference between this number and the number of employees needed leads to the next step.

EXHIBIT 10-3

Major Canadian Federal and Provincial Employment Antidiscrimination Legislation

---

Canadian Federal Equal Pay for Equal Work Legislation

The Canadian federal government has had pay equity (equal pay for equal work) legislation since the 1950s. The legislation prohibits paying different wages to men and women who perform the same or substantially similar work. Examples include janitors and housekeepers, and orderlies and nurses' aides.

Employment-Equity Legislation, 1995 (Ontario, Canada)

Much employment legislation in Canada is at the provincial rather than the national level. In 1995, the New Democratic Party introduced employment-equity legislation. It requires most employers to meet targets for employment of specified groups, including racial minorities, women, aboriginal people, and the handicapped.

Commission on the Rights of People (Québec, Canada)

The Québec Charter of Human Rights and Freedoms was adopted in 1975. The *Commission des droits de la personne* (rights of people) is responsible for seeing that situations jeopardizing human rights and freedoms are corrected. The charter provides that every person has a right to full and equal recognition and exercise of his or her human rights and freedoms, without distinction, exclusion, or preference based on such factors as race, color, ethnic or national origin, pregnancy, sexual orientation, age, religion, political convictions, language, social condition, or handicap. Citizens who feel their rights have been violated can file complaints through channels provided by the Québec government.

3. *Planning for recruitment, selection, and layoffs.* The organization must engage in recruitment, employee selection, or layoffs to attain the required number of employees. A major choice between the commitment strategy in which the firm seeks to develop its own human capital and the secondary strategy of acquiring human capital in the market must be made. Most firms find a balance between training and promoting current employees, and hiring needed talent from the outside.

4. *Planning for training and development.* An organization always needs experienced and competent workers. This step involves planning and providing for training and development programs that ensure the continued supply of people with the right skills.

Strategic business plans usually involve shifting around or training people. Human resource planning can therefore be an important element in the success of strategies. Human resource planning can also be a strategic objective in itself. For example, one strategic objective of Pepsi Cola International is the development of talented people. Human resource planning contributes to attaining this objective by suggesting on- and off-the-job experiences to develop talent.

4   RECRUITMENT

Present an overview of recruitment and selection.

recruitment

The process of attracting job candidates with the right characteristics and skills to fill job openings.

Recruitment is the process of attracting job candidates with the right characteristics and skills to fit job openings. Similar recruitment methods are used for traditional and contingent workers (see Chapter 8). The preferred recruiting method is to begin with a large number of possible job candidates and then give serious consideration to a much smaller number. However, if few candidates are available, the recruiter must be less selective or not fill the position. In this section we describe the major aspects of recruitment.

Purposes of Recruitment

A major purpose of recruiting and selection is to find employees who fit well into the culture of the organization. Most job failures are attributed to workers being a "poor fit" rather than because of poor technical skills or experience. The poor fit often implies poor relationships with coworkers. A person–organization fit occurs when the characteristics of the individual complement the organizational culture. The person–organization fit is usually based on a mesh between the person's values and those of the organization.[5] For example, a person who values technology and diversity among people—and is qualified—would be a good candidate to work for Compaq.

Another important purpose of recruiting is to sell the organization to high-quality prospective candidates. Recruiters must select candidates who can function in one job today and be retrained and promoted later, as company needs dictate. Flexible candidates of this type are in demand; therefore, a recruiter may need to sell the advantages of his or her company to entice them to work there.

Job Descriptions and Job Specifications

A starting point in recruiting is to understand the nature of the job to be filled and the qualifications sought. Toward this end, the recruiter should be supplied with job descriptions and job specifications. The job description explains in detail what the job holder is supposed to do. It is therefore a vital document in human resource planning and performance appraisal. An exception is that in some high-level positions, such as CEO, the person creates part of his or her own job description. Refer back to Exhibit 8-2 for a sample job description.

A **job specification** (or person specification) stems directly from the job description. It is a statement of the personal characteristics needed to perform the job. A job specification usually includes the education, experience, knowledge, and skills required to perform the job successfully. Both the job description and the job specification should be based on a careful **job analysis**, which is the process of obtaining information about a job by describing its tasks and responsibilities. The procedure requires a systematic investigation of the job through interviews, direct observations, and often completing a form. The data from job analysis become part of the job description. For example, suppose the job analyst studies the position of construction supervisor. Assume the analyst observes that the supervisor spends considerable time settling squabbles about which worker is responsible for certain tasks. Part of the job description would read, "Resolves conflict among tradespeople about overlapping job responsibilities."

Many firms see the tools of job descriptions, job specifications, and job analysis decrease in relevance. Organizations often expect workers to occupy flexible roles rather than specific positions, to meet the need for rapid change. An example of flexibility might be a worker whose role is to learn new job-related software, whereas a job description might mention specific software that must be mastered. Because companies need workers to carry out these more flexible roles, they must focus on job competencies. A communications competency, for example, would include basic skills such as writing, speaking, and making presentations.[6]

Recruiting Sources

The term *recruitment* covers a wide variety of methods for attracting employees to the firm, even through such methods as a manager handing out business cards to people she meets while skiing. Recruiting sources can be classified into four categories:

1. *Present employees.* As a standard recruiting method, companies post job openings so the current employees may apply. Managers also recommend current employees for transfer or promotion. A human resources information system can identify current employees with the right skills and competencies, which minimizes the need to reject unqualified internal applicants.
2. *Referrals by present employees.* For established firms, present employees can be the primary recruiters. Satisfied employees may be willing to nominate relatives, friends, acquaintances, and neighbors for job openings. During periods of labor shortages, employee referral programs become more popular; some companies even offer cash bonuses for referring employees who stay with the firm for a specified period of time. The effectiveness of current employees in the recruiting process comes from their ability to explain the culture of the firm to prospects, such as pointing out that the company expects its employees to work hard and long.[7]
3. *External sources other than online approaches.* Potential employees outside an organization can be reached in many ways. The best known of these methods is a recruiting advertisement, including print, radio, and sometimes television. Other external sources include (a) placement offices, (b) private and public employment agencies, (c) labor union hiring halls, (d) walk-ins (people who

job specification
A statement of the personal characteristics needed to perform the job.

job analysis
Obtaining information about a job by describing its tasks and responsibilities and gathering basic facts about the job.

show up at the firm without invitation), and (d) write-ins (people who write unsolicited job-seeking letters). Labor union officials believe that they simplify the hiring process for employers because only qualified workers are admitted to the union.

An increasingly popular recruiting source that also achieves a social responsibility goal is to recruit from among former welfare recipients who have participated in state-supported training. Companies generally aim this type of recruiting at entry-level workers during a tight labor market (labor shortage).

4. *Online recruiting including company Web sites.* The Internet now provides a standard source of recruiting job candidates. It offers hundreds of Web sites free to job candidates, and sometimes to employers. Online recruiting includes listing open positions on company Web sites and on job boards, and surfing sites for possible candidates.[8] Many online recruiting services operate in the same way as an employment agency with employers paying a fee. A key part of the service is the job board for posting openings, to which candidates submit their credentials. An example is Adecco Job Shop. The employer-paid online service screens candidates and claims to provide high-quality job candidates. Online job fairs provide another recruiting source. In an online job fair, a Web site such as Monster Board (http://www.monster.com) brings together recruiters and job seekers in a particular region or industry, such as the graphics art industry. Surfing directly for candidates could include going to newsgroups, chat rooms, and online clubs.

A factor contributing to the rapid growth of recruiting on the Net is that millions of job seekers every day surf the Net to explore job openings. The overloading of candidates has led some recruiters and job seekers, however, to take online recruiting less seriously. Because of the immense number of people surfing the Web for jobs, many job seekers and employers have turned to smaller, niche sites that focus on a particular industry. For example, Telecomcareers.net deals with positions in the telecommunications field.

Exhibit 10-4 lists some specific Web sites for recruiting. Online recruiting does not make other recruiting sources obsolete or ineffective. About 12 percent of positions are filled through e-cruiting. For example, top-level management positions are almost always filled through executive search firms or word of mouth. Finding employees or finding a job is best done through a variety of methods mentioned here.

Global Recruiting

Global recruiting presents unique challenges. Multinational businesses must have the capability to connect with other parts of the globe to locate talent. Company recruiters must meet job specifications calling for multiculturalism (being able to conduct business in other cultures) on top of more traditional skills. To fill international positions, the recruiter may have to develop overseas recruiting sources. The recruiter may also require the assistance of a bilingual interviewer to help assess the candidate's ability to conduct business in more than one language.

SELECTION

Selecting the right candidate for a job is part of a process that includes recruitment. Exhibit 10-5 shows the steps in the process. A hiring decision is based on

Web Site	Web Address
Adecco Job Shop	http://www.adecco.com
Best Internet Recruiter	http://www.bestrecruit.com
Best Jobs in the USA Today	http://www.bestjobsusa.com
Career Mosaic	http://www.careermosaic.com
Career Web	http://www.cweb.com
Christian & Timbers	http://www.ctnet.com (specializes in high-tech positions)
E-Span Résumé Bank	http://www.espan.com
Eurojobs	http://www.eurojobs.com
Fenwick Partners	http://www.fenwickpartners.com (specializes in high tech positions)
FlipDog.com	http://www.flipdog.com
Hire.com	http://www.hire.com
Hispanstar*	http://www.hispanstar.com (for employers searching for Hispanic workers, and workers looking to fill such positions)
Job Center	http://www.jobcenter.com
JobOptions	http://www.joboptions.com
Job World	http://www.job.world.com
The Monster Board	http://www.monsterboard.com; http://www.monster.com/recruit
Nationjob Network	http://www.nationjob.com
World Hire	http://www.worldhire.com

EXHIBIT 10-4

A Sampling of Web Sites for Employee Recruitment

263

From an employer's perspective, certain Web sites are recruiting tools. From the perspective of the job seeker, or the job browser, the same Web sites are a source of finding a job. Employers and job seekers should consult multiple Web sites because each site is likely to contain many positions and job seekers not found in the other sites.

information gathered in two or more of these steps. For instance, a person might receive a job offer if he or she was impressive in the interview, scored well on the tests, and had good references. Another important feature of this selection model allows for an applicant to be rejected at any point. An applicant who is abusive to the employment specialist might not be asked to fill out an application form.

Careful screening of job applicants has always been important because competent employees are the lifeblood of any firm. Judicial rulings add another reason for employers to evaluate candidates carefully. According to the doctrine of *negligent hiring and retention*, an employer can be liable for the job-related misdeeds of its employees, whether the wrongs affect customers or coworkers.[9] For example, if a supervisor with a pre-employment history of sexual harassment sexually

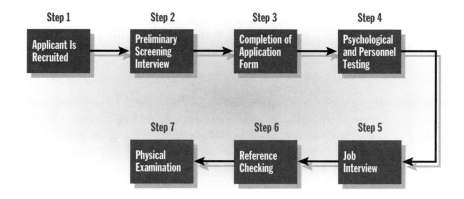

EXHIBIT 10-5

A Model for Selection

The selection process generally proceeds in the steps as indicated at the right, yet many exceptions in terms of which steps are included and in what order can occur. For example, some employers do not use psychological and personnel testing, and others have candidates complete the application form first.

harasses another employee during working hours, the employer might be considered negligent for having hired the supervisor. Employers can also be held liable for retaining an employee who commits physically harmful acts.

Preliminary Screening Interview

Selection begins as soon as candidates come to the attention of the recruiter. If candidates come close to fitting the job specifications, a brief screening interview follows, often by telephone. The purpose of the screening interview is to determine whether the candidate should be given further consideration. One area of disqualification would be for the candidate to demonstrate such poor oral communication skills over the phone that the person is excluded from consideration for a job requiring considerable customer contact. "Knockout" questions are sometimes used for quickly disqualifying candidates. Assume a person applying for a supervisory position in a nursing home is asked, "How well do you get along with senior citizens?" A candidate who responds, "Very poorly" is immediately disqualified.

Candidates who pass the screening interview are asked to fill out a job application form. Sometimes this process is reversed, and a screening interview takes place after the candidate successfully completes the application form.

Job Application Forms

Job application forms are a standard part of any selection procedure. They serve two important purposes. First, they furnish basic biographical data about the candidate, including his or her education, work experience, and citizenship. Second, they provide information that could be related to success on the job. A sloppily completed application form *could* indicate poor work habits, whereas a carefully completed form *could* indicate careful work habits.

Job application forms and employment interviewers should not ask direct or indirect questions that could be interpreted as discriminatory. Discussing the following topics in a job interview could be a violation of antidiscrimination laws:[10]

1. Race
2. Religion
3. Sex (male or female)
4. Pregnancy
5. Number of children
6. Ages of children
7. Marital status
8. Child-care plans
9. Height or weight
10. Disability
11. Age
12. Criminal record
13. Union affiliation
14. Workers' compensation claims on previous job
15. Medical problems (except information about medical history that can be taken by a medical specialist as part of the medical exam).

Questions about any of these topics must be job-related in order to avoid any accusation of discrimination. A *job-related* question or selection device deals with behavior and skills that are required for job success. Asking an applicant for a child-care specialist position whether he or she has ever been convicted of child molestation is job-related.

Employers often inquire about grade-point average either on the application form or the interview, particularly for entry-level jobs. The extent to which grade point average is related to success on the job has been intensely debated for probably 100 years. The bulk of evidence indicates a slight positive relationship between GPA and job performance for many different types of jobs.[11] Employers in favor of collecting information about GPA believe it reflects a student's problem-solving ability and effort. Many other employers focus more on interpersonal skills and practical experience than grade point average. Which school an applicant attended is often considered when evaluating grade point average.

Psychological and Personnel Testing

Hundreds of different tests are used in employment testing, and such testing is standard practice in about one-half of firms. All tests are psychological tests in the sense that measuring human ability is an important part of psychology. This book uses the term *personnel testing* as well as *psychological testing*, because many people think psychological tests deal with personality and personnel tests deal with job skills.

Many employers still use paper-and-pencil tests, whereas many others have shifted to computer-based testing. An example is credit card and financial services giant Capital One, which uses online testing for staffing its 8,000 call-center operator positions. Using online testing, overall cost per hire dropped 45 percent, while the pass rate increased by 30 percent without sacrificing the quality of new hires. The group of tests includes the job application form, a math test, a biographical information form, and a role-playing call simulation. Applicants listen to a CD-ROM program that plays customer situations. Applicants role play as call-center operators and answer multiple-choice questions as to how they would respond.[12]

Types of Psychological and Personnel Tests

The five principle types of psychological and personnel tests are achievement, aptitude, personality, honesty and integrity, and interest.

1. *Achievement tests* sample and measure an applicant's knowledge and skills. They require applicants to demonstrate their competency on job tasks or related subjects. The test just mentioned about dealing with customer situations is an achievement test. The most widely used achievement tests relate to computer skills: typing/data entry, word-processing software, and spreadsheet analysis.

2. *Aptitude tests* measure the potential for performing satisfactorily on the job, given sufficient training. Mental ability tests, the best-known variety of aptitude tests, measure the ability to solve problems and learn new material. Mental ability tests measure such specific aptitudes as verbal reasoning, numerical reasoning, and spatial relations (the ability to visualize in three dimensions). Many National Football League teams still use the Wonderlic Personnel Test, a brief test of mental ability, to help screen draftees. The highest scores on the mental ability tests are required for quarterbacks.

3. *Personality tests* measure personal traits and characteristics that could be related to job performance. The use of personality tests still sparks controversy, but research during the past decade shows positive connection between certain personality tests and subsequent job performance. Critics express concern that these tests invade privacy and are too imprecise to be useful. Nevertheless, personality factors can profoundly influence job performance. Exhibit 10-6 lists the major personality factors related to job performance.

   Personality tests were included in three studies that followed participants from early childhood to retirement. Conscientiousness, one of the

EXHIBIT 10-6

The Big Five Personality Factors

Many psychologists believe that the basic structure of human personality is represented by what they call the Big Five factors. These factors influence job performance. Conscientiousness, for example, is related to the tendency to produce quality work. Furthermore, these factors can be measured by psychological tests.

I. **Extraversion.** Extraversion (which is the same as extroversion) relates to whether a person is social, gregarious, assertive, talkative, or active.

II. **Emotional stability.** This factor relates to whether a person is anxious, depressed, angry, embarrassed, emotional, or worried.

III. **Agreeableness.** This factor relates to whether a person is courteous, flexible, trusting, good-natured, cooperative, forgiving, soft-hearted, or tolerant.

IV. **Conscientiousness.** This factor relates to whether a person is careful, thorough, responsible, organized, or prepared. This factor also relates to whether a person is hard-working, achievement-oriented, and persevering.

V. **Openness to experience.** This factor relates to whether a person is imaginative, cultured, curious, original, broad-minded, intelligent, or artistically sensitive.

major personality factors, was found to be a good predictor of career success as measured by compensation and promotions, as well as personal satisfaction. Also, having tendencies toward emotional instability was negatively related to compensation and promotions.[13] Industrial psychologist Richard Hagburg believes that personality tests combined with interviews can lead to 85 percent accuracy in predicting the leadership style and strengths of managers.[14]

4. *Honesty and integrity tests* are designed to measure a person's honesty or integrity as it relates to job behavior. (Honesty relates most specifically to lying, whereas integrity refers to sticking with your principles.) These tests are frequently used in workplaces such as retail stores, banks, and warehouses, where employees have access to cash or merchandise. Other types of work in which employees may potentially damage computers or access secret documents also call for a prediction of employee honesty. A major factor measured by integrity tests is social conscientiousness. People who score high on this personality factor show a much greater likelihood of following organizational rules. Despite controversy over their use, honesty and integrity tests are widely used. Years of experience with integrity and honesty tests indicate that these tests can help identify job candidates with a propensity to steal and engage in other counterproductive behavior (such as computer hacking).[15]

5. *Interest tests* measure preferences for engaging in certain activities, such as mechanical, clerical, literary, or managerial work. They also measure a person's interest in specific occupations, such as accountant, veterinarian, or sales representative. Interest tests are designed to indicate whether a person would enjoy a particular activity or occupation. They do not attempt, however, to measure a person's aptitude for it.

Validity and Equal Employment Opportunity

The EEOC insists that selection tests be scientifically accurate, job-related, and not discriminatory against any group. These rules also apply to other selection instruments, including application forms and interviews. A specific provision requires a validity study when a selection procedure shows an adverse impact on any race, sex, or ethnic group. A *validity study* is a statistical and scientific method of seeing if a selection device does predict job performance. Do high scorers perform well on the job? Do low scorers tend to be poor performers?

Thousands of studies have been conducted about the ability of tests to predict job performance. Some studies explore how well groups of tests used in combination predict job performance. These studies are considered the most valuable because, in practice, employment tests are often used in combinations referred to as test batteries. Considerable disagreement surrounds the issue of whether employment tests contribute to the selection process. Nevertheless, it appears that, used as intended, employment testing does improve the accuracy of selection decisions. As a result, productivity improves.

The most consistent finding about the effectiveness of psychological tests in predicting job performance stems from a long series of studies concerning general intelligence and conscientiousness. In general, employees who have good problem-solving ability and are conscientious are likely to perform well in most jobs.[16] (These findings assume that the employee also has the necessary education and job skills. Yet for basic jobs, the ability to learn and dependability are more important than experience and already existing skills.) General problem-solving ability is measured by mental ability tests, and conscientiousness by a Big Five personality test. A straightforward explanation of these findings is that a bright person will learn quickly, and a conscientious person will try hard to get the job done.

The Job Interview

The interview that follows testing is more thorough and comprehensive than the screening interview. The topics covered in a job interview include education, work experience, special skills and abilities, hobbies, and interests. Interviewers frequently use the candidate's résumé as a source of topics. For example, "I notice you have worked for four employers in three years. Why is that?" Testing results may also provide clues for additional questioning. If a candidate scored low on a scale measuring conscientiousness, the interviewer might ask about the candidate's punctuality and error rate.

Employment interviews are more valid when the interviewer is trained and experienced. Validity may also increase when several candidates are interviewed for each position, because comparisons can be made among the applicants. In general, the higher the level of the position, the more candidates are interviewed. Southwest Airlines, for example, interviews many more people for a pilot's position than for a baggage handler.

Job interviews serve a dual purpose. The interviewer tries to decide whether the interviewee is appropriate for the organization. At the same time, the interviewee tries to decide whether the job and organization fit him or her. An important approach to helping both the organization and the individual to make the right decision is to offer a **realistic job preview**, a complete disclosure of the potential negative features of a job to a job candidate. For example, an applicant for a help-desk position might be told, "At times customers will scream and swear at you because a computer file has crashed. Around holiday time many frustrated customers go ballistic." Telling job applicants about potential problems leads to fewer negative surprises and less turnover.[17]

Exhibit 10-7 presents guidelines for conducting a job interview. Several of the suggestions reflect a screening approach referred to as **behavioral interviewing** because the answers to many of the questions reveal behaviors that would be either strengths or weaknesses in a given position. Assume that in response to the

realistic job preview
A complete disclosure of the potential negative features of a job to a job candidate.

behavioral interviewing
A style of interviewing in which the interviewer asks questions whose answers reveal behaviors that would be either strengths or weaknesses in a given position.

EXHIBIT 10-7

Guidelines for Conducting an Effective Selection Interview

1. **Prepare in advance.** Prior to the interview, carefully review the applicant's job application form and résumé. Keep in mind several questions worthy of exploration, such as "I notice you have done no previous selling. Why do you want a sales job now?"

2. **Find a quiet place free from interruptions.** Effective interviewing requires careful concentration. Also, the candidate deserves the courtesy of an uninterrupted interview.

3. **Take notes during the interview.** Take notes on the content of what is said during the interview. Also, record your observations about the person's statements and behavior. For example, "Candidate gets very nervous when we talk about previous work history."

4. **Use a brief warm-up period.** A standard way of relaxing a job candidate is to spend about five minutes talking about neutral topics, such as the weather. This brief period can be extended by asking about basic facts, such as the person's address and education.

5. **Ask open-ended questions.** To encourage the employee to talk, ask questions that call for more than a one- or two-word answer. Sometimes a request for information—a statement like "Tell me about your days at business school"—works like an open-ended question.

6. **Follow an interview format.** Effective interviewers carefully follow a predetermined interview format. They

ask additional questions that are based on responses to the structured questions.

7. **Give the job candidate encouragement.** The easiest way to keep an interviewee talking is to give that person encouragement. Standard encouragements include "That's very good," "How interesting," "I like your answer," and "Excellent."

8. **Dig for additional details.** When the interviewee brings up a topic worthy of exploration, dig for additional facts. Assume the interviewee says, "I used to work as a private chauffeur, but then I lost my driver's license." Noticing a red flag, the interviewer might respond: "Why did you lose your license?"

9. **Make very limited use of a stress interview.** The purpose of a stress interview is to see how well the interviewee responds to pressure. Among the stress tactics are to insult the interviewee, to ignore him or her, or to stare at the interviewee and say nothing. These tactics create so much ill will that they are hardly worth pursuing. Besides, a job interview is stressful enough.

10. **Spend most of the interview time listening.** An experienced job interviewer spends little time talking. It is the interviewee who should be doing the talking.

11. **Provide the candidate ample information about the organization.** Answer any relevant questions.

open-ended question "What excites you on the job?" the candidate says, "Helping a coworker solve a difficult problem." The behavior indicated could be good teamwork.

Reference Checking and Background Investigation

reference check

An inquiry to a second party about a job candidate's suitability for employment.

A **reference check** is an inquiry to a second party about a job candidate's suitability for employment. The two main topics explored in reference checks are past job performance and the ability to get along with coworkers. Concerns about negligent hiring are causing the comeback of the reference check as an important part of the screening process. Former and prospective employers have a *qualified privilege* to discuss an employee's past performance. As long as the information is given to a person with a legitimate interest in receiving it, discussion of an employee's past misconduct or poor performance is permissible under law.[18]

Employers can often reduce their legal liability for reference checks by outsourcing the process. The Fair Credit Reporting Act provides limited legal immunity to employers who hire third-party investigators. This legal immunity is limited to suits alleging defamation, invasion of privacy, of negligence in conducting the investigation.[19]

Despite such rulings, many past employers are hesitant to provide complete references for two key reasons. First, job applicants have legal access to written references unless they specifically waive this right in writing (Privacy Act of 1974). Second, people who provide negative references worry about being sued for libel.

Here are a few recommended questions for checking references:[20]

- Is _____ eligible to be rehired? If not, is this because your company has a general policy on rehiring employees or is there another reason?
- What, if anything, distinguishes _____ from others who do the same type of work?
- Is it difficult to find candidates similar to _____?

Background investigations are closely related to reference checks, except that they focus on information from sources other than former employers. Areas investigated include driving record, possible criminal charges or convictions, creditworthiness, disputes with the IRS, and coworkers' and neighbors' comments about a candidate's reputation.

Background investigations are used for two major reasons. One is that so many job candidates present untrue information in résumés and job interviews. In general, about one-third of résumés contain distorted information. A study conducted by Reid Psychological Systems, indicated that 95 percent of college students admitted they would lie to get a job, and 41 percent said they already have.[21] The other major reason for the widespread use of background investigations is that former employers who are concerned about potential lawsuits release limited information. Background checks are important also because of the potential hazards of negligent hiring.

Physical Examination and Drug Testing or Impairment Testing

The physical examination remains a key part of pre-employment screening. The exam gives some indication as to the person's physical ability to handle the requirements of particular jobs. For example, a person with a history of four heart attacks would be a poor candidate for a high-stress managerial position. The physical exam also provides a basis for later comparisons. This step lessens the potential for an employee to claim that the job caused a particular injury or disease. For example, after one year on the job, an employee might claim that the job created a fusion of two vertebrae. If the pre-employment physical showed evidence of two fused vertebrae before the employee was hired, the employer would have little to fear from the claim.

The importance of the physical examination continues to increase since the passage of the Americans with Disabilities Act. As long as the candidate can perform the essential aspects of the job, including the employer making reasonable accommodations, he or she cannot be disqualified. However, if the person's disability prevents him or her from performing key aspects of the job, the person could be disqualified physically. For example, a person with vision in only one eye might lack the depth perception required to be a helicopter pilot. An employer can also deny employment to a disabled person if having the individual in the workplace poses a threat to his or her safety or the safety of others. If safety is an issue, the applicant might be offered a less hazardous position.

About two-thirds of large companies test all job applicants for use of illegal drugs. (Executives as well as entry-level workers can be drug abusers.) During a worker shortage, however, more employers will forego drug testing. Testing for substance abuse includes blood analysis, urinalysis, analysis of hair samples, observations of eyes, and examination of skin for punctures. Tendencies toward drug abuse can also be measured by honesty and integrity tests. Scores in the dishonest range trigger testing for physical evidence of drug abuse. Many companies test job candidates and current employees for abuse of prescription drugs because at least 25 to 30 percent of drug abuse in the workplace now involves prescription drugs.[22]

Some people raise the concern that inaccurate drug testing may unfairly deny employment to worthy candidates. A strong argument in favor of drug testing, however, is that employees who are drug abusers may create such problems as lowered productivity, lost time from work, and misappropriation of funds. Accident and absenteeism rates for drug (as well as alcohol) abusers are substantial, and they also experience more health problems.

impairment testing

An evaluation of whether an employee is alert enough for work.

As a movement away from the possible indignity and inaccuracy of drug testing, many employers have shifted to **impairment testing**, an evaluation of whether an employee is alert enough for work. A typical impairment test would have the applicant perform a visual task such as following a light. Performing such as task is extremely difficult if not mentally alert. The impairment test focuses on the candidate's ability to perform a task. Failing the impairment test could be attributed to problems that a drug test would miss such as fatigue, stress, and alcohol use. Impairment testing is job related and requires no bodily fluids, nothing of a demeaning nature.[23]

Cross-Cultural Selection

As with cross-cultural recruitment, most of the selection guidelines and techniques already mentioned can be applied cross-culturally. Many selection devices, such as widely used personnel tests, are published in languages besides English, especially Spanish. Managers and employment interviewers gathering information about job candidates from other countries should familiarize themselves with key facts about the other culture. For example, in France a *grand école* is a high-prestige college of business that qualifies graduates for positions in the best firms. An interviewer unfamiliar with the French culture might miss the significance of an interviewee talking about his diploma from a *grand école*.

An example of adapting selection techniques to cross-cultural requirements took place at a Japanese-American manufacturer of automobile parts. Management practices at the 80 percent Japanese-owned firm emphasized interpersonal skill, team orientation, and high product quality. The U.S.-based company was hiring for assembly jobs Americans who would fit the Japanese organizational culture. Work simulations (or work samples) proved to be the most effective selection device. It was found that applicant characteristics important in a Japanese culture (such as team and quality orientation) could be measured by the simulation. Trained observers rated the candidates on various factors including the following:[24]

- Attention to maintenance and safety
- Team attitude and participation
- Work motivation and involvement
- Quality orientation

After being recruited, job candidates pass through all the selection screens, such as the physical exam, before being hired. After making the hiring decision and applicant acceptance, human resource specialists and new employees complete all the necessary forms, such as those relating to taxes and benefits. Next comes orientation.

ORIENTATION, TRAINING, AND DEVELOPMENT

Most firms no longer operate under a "sink or swim" philosophy when it comes to employee learning. Instead, employees receive ample opportunity to become oriented to the firm. Later the firm trains and develops them.

Present an overview of employee orientation, training, and development.

Employee Orientation

A new employee usually begins his or her new job by attending an orientation program. An **employee orientation program** more formally acquaints new employees with the company. Part of the orientation may deal with small but important matters, such as telling the employee how to get a parking sticker. Large firms offer elaborate orientation programs conducted by human resource specialists. The program may include tours of the buildings, talks by department heads, videotape presentations, generous supplies of printed information, and visits to the company Web site.

employee orientation program
A formal activity designed to acquaint new employees with the organization.

Employee orientation also conveys to new employees the specific nature of their job and expectations in terms of performance. It is also valuable to hold periodic discussions of this same topic during the employee's time with the firm. In some firms, a *buddy system* is part of the orientation. A buddy, a peer from the new employee's department, shows the new employee around and fills in information gaps.

Walt Disney Corporation emphasizes the importance of thoroughly orienting new employees. Managers at Disney believe in making an up-front investment to help new employees become assimilated into the company. Disney provides insight for new cast members (employees) into how the firm operates, and information about the corporate family they are joining. Employees also receive a careful explanation of how their job fits into company strategy.[25] For example, the entry-level worker who parades around as Minnie Mouse supports the corporate strategy of bringing happiness to people.

Another aspect of orientation is informal socialization. In this process, coworkers introduce new employees to aspects of the organizational culture. Coworkers might convey, for example, how well motivated a new employee should be or the competence level of key people in the organization. The disadvantage of informal orientation is that it may furnish the new employee with misinformation.

A study conducted on the effectiveness of an employee orientation program included 116 newly hired employees in a large educational institution. These employees worked in 80 different departments and held 70 different job titles. The results of the study suggested that an employee orientation program helps employees become socialized, or learn about and adapt to new jobs, roles, and the corporate culture. Employees attending the orientation program became much more socialized with respect to goals and values, the history, and people than employees who did not attend the training. Employees attending the program were also more likely to develop an emotional commitment to the institution.[26] The emotional commitment in turn improved the retention rate.

Training and Development

Training and development deal with systematic approaches to improve employee skills and performance. **Training** is any procedure intended to foster and enhance learning among employees and particularly directed at acquiring job skills. Rapid changes in technology and the globalization of business have spurred the growth of training programs. Training programs exist to teach hundreds of different skills such as equipment repair, performance appraisal, software utilization, and budget preparation. Training can develop both hard skills (technical, scientific, and numerical) as well as soft skills (interpersonal skills and attitudes). The accompanying Management in Action explains the role of soft skills training in a competitive work environment.

A substantial amount of skills training in industry is delivered through computers, including the Internet. Among the terms referring to learning over the Internet are online learning, e-learning, and e-training. **Computer-based training** (or **Internet-based training**) is a learning experience based on the interaction between the trainee and a computer. The computer provides a stimulus or prompt, to which the trainee responds. The computer then analyzes the response and provides feedback to the student. A question in a customer service course might ask trainees to evaluate the following response to a customer complaint: "If you don't like my answer, go speak to my boss." A message would then appear suggesting that the trainee take more ownership of the problem. Close to 30 percent of all information technology-related and business skill courses outside of schools are now technology-based according to IDC Research.[27]

Despite the substantial contribution and growth of e-training, many students learn better when they can interact with people such as fellow students and instructors. Nonverbal cues, so important for many types of learning, are minimal at best when interacting with software.

Development is a form of personal improvement that usually consists of enhancing knowledge and skills of a complex and unstructured nature. For example, a development program might help managers become better leaders. A recent trend in management and leadership development focuses on helping the manager/leader become a better lifelong learner. In concrete terms, lifelong learning might encompass staying abreast of current developments in the outside world that could affect the profitability of the firm. A manager in a pharmaceutical firm might notice that the population is aging, and many of these aging people want to appear and act youthful. The manager would then invest more resources in developing lifestyle drugs that help people have more fun in life through such means as retaining more hair, lessening wrinkles, and enhancing sexuality.

Managers play an important role in most types of training and development, particularly with respect to on-the-job training and development. We return to the top of the manager as a teacher in discussions about mentoring in Chapter 11 and coaching in Chapter 16.

Most of this text and its accompanying course could be considered an experience in management training and development. The next paragraphs describe two vital aspects of training and development for employees and managers: needs assessment and the selection of an appropriate training program.

Needs Assessment

Before embarking on a training program, an organization needs to determine what type of training is needed. Such an assessment generally benefits from including a job analysis and asking the managers themselves, their managers, and group

---

training

Any procedure intended to foster and enhance learning among employees, particularly directed at acquiring job skills.

computer-based training (Internet-based training)

A learning experience based on the interaction between the trainee and a computer.

development

A form of personal improvement that usually consists of enhancing knowledge and skills of a complex and unstructured nature.

Management *in Action*

S o f t - S k i l l s   T r a i n i n g   R e c e i v e s   A t t e n t i o n

The pounding of red-hot steel into piston rods at Trinity Forge plant in Mansfield, Texas, can be deafening and nerve-wracking. Until a few years ago, so was employee supervision, according to Trinity's human resource manager. "We've had some front-line supervisors who were ignorant about how to handle anything," Steve Menchaca said.

Managers at the 200-worker factory rarely spoke with those working other shifts or in other departments and poorly handled workers' suggestions in meetings. When things went wrong, Menchaca said, "They always found the easiest thing to do was shout and throw things around."

But flying clipboards and screaming fits are no longer the norm at Trinity Forge. Despite complicated new technologies at the shop, plant supervisors today are more adept at employee oversight and can solve a problem without blowing a gasket as things bog down, Menchaca said.

It's not just a result of anger control. Four years of intense, specialized management training at the plant has raised the professional standards of supervision, Menchaca said. Production is up, and workers have more control over their destinies. The turnaround is attributed to the development of interpersonal "soft skills" that many training organizations and consultants credit with improving workplace environments and employee-worker relationships.

Soft-skills training can be a key to maintaining a market edge, said JoAn Weddle, director of small business development for enterprise excellence at the University of Texas at Arlington. "Any other competitive advantage is easy for a competitor to pick up and duplicate," Weddle said. "With this low unemployment rate for the employees in-house, you want to keep them and keep them committed to the company."

Companies are finding that teams of workers with better interpersonal skills, even when their technical skills aren't as sharp, are more efficient than teams comprised of technically skilled workers who don't cooperate," said Rad Hadsall, a Dale Carnegie instructor.

Source: "Soft Skills' Demand Growing: Tight Labor Market Requires Companies to Cultivate the Loyalty of Skilled Workers," Knight Ridder, April 23, 2000.

members about the managers' need for training. Also, the trainer observes the managers performing their regular duties to identify areas for improvement. Training and development needs can also be identified for the entire organization, or portions of it. For example, top management at a U.S. Steel plant in Pennsylvania believed that workers at all levels needed more information so they could adapt to a competitive steel business. The program trained every member of the plant's 2,400 employees in every aspect of U.S. Steel's operations, including such topics as processing orders, controlling costs, and fine points about market economics. Susan Forman, the supervisor for training and organizational development at the plant said, "I wanted to establish a partnership, and in a partnership, all the partners need to have the same information in order to make quality decisions."[28]

Despite the importance of matching training and development programs to specific individual and organizational needs, universal training needs also require attention. The training would include elements such as communication, motivation, decision making, coaching, and time management.

Selecting an Appropriate Training Program

After needs are assessed, they must be carefully addressed by appropriate training and development programs. A program must often be tailored to fit company requirements. The person assigning employees to training and development programs must be familiar with their needs for training and development, know the content of various programs, and enroll employees in programs that will meet their needs. Exhibit 10-8 presents a sample listing of training and development programs.

As part of a current trend, nonmanagers participate in training and development usually reserved for managers and future managers. The rationale is that workers assigned to teams manage themselves to some extent. They also deal directly with many managerial activities, such as selection interviewing and budgeting.[29]

In addition to training and development programs, substantial learning takes place outside of the classroom or away from the computer. Many employees learn job skills and information by asking each other questions, sharing ideas, and observing each other. Such learning is spontaneous, immediate, and task specific. Much **informal learning** takes place in meetings, on breaks, and in customer interactions. A nationwide survey found that up to 70 percent of employee learning takes place informally.[30] At Siemens, a high-technology company, managers found that software developers acquired considerable job information by congregating in the company cafeteria. Some companies have now installed high round tables around the company so workers can informally exchange ideas in addition to small talk.

informal learning

Any learning that occurs in which the learning process is not determined or designed by the organization.

---

6   PERFORMANCE APPRAISAL

Explain the basics of a fair and reliable method of evaluating employee performance.

Up to this point in the staffing model, employees have been recruited, selected, oriented, and trained. The next step is to evaluate performance. A **performance appraisal** is a formal system for measuring, evaluating, and reviewing performance. A performance appraisal system or technique must meet the same legal standards of fairness as selection devices. One such aspect requires categories of evaluation to be job related, such as rating a worker on creativity only if his or her job requires creative thinking.

The traditional appraisal involves a manager who evaluates an individual group member. The current emphasis on team structures changes performance

performance appraisal

A formal system for measuring, evaluating, and reviewing performance.

EXHIBIT 10-8

A Sample Listing of Training Programs versus Development Programs

Training programs listed in the left column are often included in a program of management development. The programs on the right, however, are rarely considered to be specific skill-based training programs.

Training Programs	Management Development
World-class customer service	Effective team leadership
Fundamentals of human resources	Strategic leadership
Introduction to human resources law	Gaining competitive advantage
Salary administration	Effective knowledge management
Preventing and controlling sexual harassment	Strategic diversity
Telemarketing skills	Developing cultural sensitivity
Understanding financial statements	Open book management
Getting started in e-commerce	Principle-centered leadership
Fundamentals of e-tailing	Retaining valued employees
Accident prevention	Developing a winning corporate culture
ISO 9000 certification	Becoming a charismatic leader
Effective interviewing	Strategic human resources planning

appraisals in two major ways. One, groups as well as individuals are now subject to regular evaluation. Another change comes in the widespread use of multirating systems whereby several workers evaluate an individual. The most frequently used multirater system is **360-degree feedback**, in which a person is evaluated by most of the people with whom he or she interacts.

An appraisal form for a manager might incorporate input from the manager's manager, all group members, other managers at his or her level, and even a sampling of customers when feasible. Self-assessment is also included. The manager's manager would then synthesize all the information and discuss it with him or her. Dimensions for rating a manager might include "gives direction," "listens to group members," "coaches effectively," and "helps the group achieve key results." Rating an employee on paper forms often takes about 45 minutes. With a computerized system, the time can often be reduced to about 30 minutes per rater.

The rationale for using 360-degree feedback for performance appraisal is based on its ability to present a complete picture of performance. This technique is used as much for management and leadership development as for performance appraisal. An industrial psychologist or human resource specialist counsels the manager in ways to improve on negative ratings of his or her leadership behavior and attitudes.

Some people object to 360-degree feedback. Key criticisms include the perception by the person being rated that the feedback is inaccurate, and that the raters do not understand the job.[31] Another common concern is that ratings reflect petty office politics; people who like you give you high ratings and people who dislike you use the feedback as an opportunity for revenge.

PhotoDisc, a Seattle-based digital imaging company, provides a basic example of 360-degree performance evaluations. The company uses 360-degree feedback to obtain a complete picture and save managers some time. Following a simple form, evaluators rate employees on a scale of 1 to 5 in areas that PhotoDisc considers to be its core values. The employees actually choose the six coworkers who will evaluate them. Reviewers complete a form on computer, and a software program synthesizes the comments into a well-organized report.

Managers, who provide further input, can more easily find the time to complete the evaluations. Report in hand, managers sit down with each employee to discuss areas for improvement and achievements. Managers still prepare year-end evaluations, but they often make use of the 360-degree information.[32]

Purposes of Performance Appraisal

Performance appraisals serve a number of important administrative purposes and can also help the manager carry out the leadership function. A major administrative purpose of performance appraisals is to decide whether an employee should receive merit increases and the relative size of the increases. The appraisal process also identifies employees with potential for promotion. High-performing teams can be identified as well. Employee reviews are widely used to provide documentation for discharging, demoting, and downsizing employees who are not meeting performance standards.

Performance appraisals help managers carry out the leadership function in several ways. Productivity can be increased by suggesting areas for needed improvement. Also, the manager can help employees identify their needs for self-improvement and self-development. Appraisal results can be used to motivate employees by providing feedback on performance. Finally, a performance

360-degree feedback

A performance appraisal in which a person is evaluated by a sampling of all the people with whom he or she interacts.

275

appraisal gives employees a chance to express their ambitions, hopes, and concerns, thereby enhancing career development.

Performance appraisals also help managers assess the effectiveness of previous steps in the staffing model. For example, if most employees are performing well, recruitment, selection, and training are probably adequate.

Design of the Performance Appraisal System

traits

Stable aspects of people, closely related to personality.

behavior

In performance appraisal, what people actually do on the job.

results

In performance appraisal, what people accomplish, or the objectives they attain.

Organizations currently use a number of different formats and methods of performance appraisal designed to measure traits, behavior, or results. **Traits** are stable aspects of people, closely related to personality. Job-related traits include enthusiasm, dependability, and honesty. **Behavior**, or activity, is what people do on the job. Job-related behavior includes working hard, keeping the work area clean, maintaining a good appearance, and showing concern for quality and customer service. **Results** are what people accomplish, or the objectives they attain. Under a system of management by objectives, a performance appraisal consists largely of reviewing whether people achieved their objectives.

At first glance, measuring performance on the basis of results seems ideal and fair. Critics of the results method of appraisal, however, contend that personal qualities are important. A performance-appraisal system that measures only results ignores such important traits and behavior as honesty, loyalty, and creativity. Many managers believe that people with good qualities will achieve good results in the long run.

Software-based performance appraisals tend to focus on results and actions rather than personality traits. As a consequence, employees are more likely to view them as fair. The software-based appraisal systems provide objective facts, such as "processed 34% more medical insurance claims than the average claims examiner." The facts can be used to create individual development plans and to help employees improve performance and focus on achieving key organizational goals.[33]

Many performance-appraisal systems attempt to measure both results and behavior or traits. Exhibit 10-9 shows a portion of a peer-rating system that includes both behavior and results. A group of peers indicates whether a particular aspect of job performance or behavior is a strength or a *developmental opportunity*. The initials under "peer evaluations" refer to coworkers doing the evaluation. The person being evaluated then knows who to thank or blame for the feedback. In addition to indicating whether a job factor is a strength or an opportunity, raters can supply comments and developmental suggestions. The results of the peer ratings might then be supplemented by the manager's ratings to achieve a total appraisal.

Major findings of years of research on performance appraisals of various types indicate that employees are the most satisfied with the system when they participate in the process. Participation can take a number of forms such as jointly setting goals with the manager, submitting a self-appraisal as part of the evaluation, and having the opportunity to fully discuss the results.[34]

Many workers dislike having their performance evaluated, and many managers dislike evaluating workers. Some managers and researchers therefore propose eliminating performance appraisals. Such a move would be tantamount to abolishing grades in school. One alternative to performance appraisals is for managers to have face-to-face conversations with workers about their performance on a regular basis. Managers make written note of any problems that workers experience, which creates the necessary documentation to support any necessary

EXHIBIT 10-9

Peer Evaluation of a Customer Service Technician

PERSON EVALUATED: Chris Marina						
SKILL CATEGORIES AND EXPECTED BEHAVIORS	PEER EVALUATIONS FOR EACH CATEGORY AND BEHAVIOR					
Customer Care	TR	JP	CK	JT	CJ	ML
Takes ownership for customer problems	O	S	S	S	S	S
Follows through on customer commitments	S	S	S	S	S	S
Technical Knowledge and Skill						
Engages in continuous learning to update technical skills	O	S	S	S	S	O
Corrects problems on the first visit	O	O	S	S	S	S
Work Group Support						
Actively participates in work group meetings	S	S	S	S	O	S
Backs up other work group members by taking calls in other areas	S	O	O	S	S	S
Minimal absence	S	O	S	S	O	S
Finance Management						
Adheres to work group parts expense process	S	S	S	O	S	S
Passes truck audits	S	S	S	O	S	S

Note: S refers to a strength; O refers to a developmental opportunity.

The person being evaluated here receives input from six different coworkers. Should a person observe that two or more people perceive a developmental opportunity, it could be time for a change in behavior.

discipline or termination.[35] In reality, regular conversations that accommodate documentation of poor performance simply translate into an informal system of performance appraisal, not its replacement.

COMPENSATION

Compensation, the combination of pay and benefits, is closely related to staffing. A major reason compensation requires so much managerial attention is that it constitutes about two-thirds of the cost of running an enterprise. Here we look at several types of pay and employee benefits. Chapter 12 will describe how compensation is used as a motivational device.

Summarize the basics of employee compensation.

Types of Pay

Wages and salary are the most common forms of pay. Wages are payments to employees for their services, computed on an hourly basis or on the amount of work produced. Salary is an annual amount of money paid to a worker and does not depend directly on output or hours worked. Nevertheless, future salary is dependent to some extent on how well the worker produced in the previous year. Many workers are eligible for bonuses or incentives to supplement their salary.

Skill-based pay is another way of establishing pay levels. Under a pay-for-knowledge-and-skills system, managers calculate starting pay based on the knowledge and skill level required for a given job. Subsequent increases depend on the worker's mastering additional skills and knowledge specified by the firm. Skill-based pay is popular with work teams because members must be multiskilled.

Many managers and human resource specialists like skill-based pay because it encourages widespread learning. Skill-based pay is used most frequently in manufacturing settings.

Competency-based pay is an extension of skill-based pay. The former is based on the demonstration of competencies, skills, and behaviors the organization identifies as critical to achieving competitive advantage. Such competencies would include having e-commerce capability and being multicultural. Competency-based pay is typically used with knowledge workers.[36]

Another recent development in salary administration is **broadbanding**, in which the company reduces the number of pay grades and replaces them with several pay ranges (or broad bands) that are based more on performance and skills rather than the position. For example, a multiskilled employee exceeding goals might receive 115 percent to 135 percent of a target pay range. A new employee or one not achieving goals might receive 80 percent to 95 percent of the target pay range. Broadbanding fits the modern, flexible organization because employees are encouraged to move to jobs where they can develop their careers and add value to the firm. The point is that employees take their salaries with them from job to job instead of being paid according to the range for a given job.[37]

Employee Benefits

An **employee benefit** is any noncash payment given to workers as part of compensation for their employment. Employee benefits cost employers about 35 percent of salaries. Therefore an employee earning $40,000 per year in salary probably receives a combined salary and benefit package of $54,000. Under ideal circumstances, employee benefits should be linked to business strategy, meaning that benefits should reward employees for achieving key business goals. A long-standing example is that some companies only offer tuition assistance for courses that directly improve job performance. Honda of America would thus reimburse an engineer for studying the chemistry of fuel, but would not reimburse an engineer for a course in acupuncture.

A substantial number of firms offer a **flexible benefit package** that allows employees to select a group of benefits tailored to their preferences. Flexible compensation plans generally provide employees with one category of fixed benefits—minimum standards such as medical and disability insurance. The second category is flexible, with a menu of benefits from which each employee is allowed to select, up to a certain total cost. An employee who prefers less vacation time, for instance, might choose more life insurance.

Exhibit 10-10 presents a representative list of employee benefits, organized by type and frequency. Organizations vary considerably in the benefits and services they offer employees. No one firm is likely to have the same portfolio of benefits, particularly for nonstandard benefits such as back massage services, or on-company-premises dry-cleaning.

Compensation, including pay and benefits, plays a major role in attracting and retaining valued employees in general, and particularly during a labor shortage. Even when a firm is downsizing, key employees will be recruited and retained by juggling benefits. Companies often attempt to attract desirable employees with incentives like a $5,000 signing bonus or a company-paid vehicle. On the other hand, some key employees receive bonuses for staying with a firm during periods when many employees are switching firms.

broadbanding
In salary administration, basing pay more on the person than the position, thus reducing the number of pay grades.

employee benefit
Any noncash payment given to workers as part of compensation for their employment.

flexible benefit package
A compensation plan that allows employees to select a group of benefits tailored to their preferences.

A major benefit offered to professional employees as an inducement to stay is a career development program designed to plot a person's future with the firm and also give career advice. Assisting workers in developing their careers fits the new employment relationship, as described by the CEO of Merck & Co., the pharmaceutical firm: "The company is responsible for providing the environment in which people can achieve their full potential, and employees are responsible for developing their skills."[38]

As with pay, benefits are more likely to help the company achieve its goals when the benefits are linked in some way to good performance. For example, only above-average performers might be offered flexible work arrangements.[39]

EXHIBIT 10-10

Most Frequent Employee Benefits

279

Employers find that the right package of benefits for an individual worker will increase the chances he or she will stay with the firm for a relatively long time.

Seven Most Frequent Health-Care Benefits
Dental insurance (96%)
Life insurance (95%)
Prescription program (91%)
Mail-order prescription program (79%)
Preferred provider organization (78%)
Mental health insurance (76%)
Employee assistance program (66%)

Seven Most Frequent Financial Benefits
Onsite parking (94%)
Payroll deductions (94%)
Direct deposit (92%)
Educational assistance (81%)
Defined-contribution retirement plan (72%)
Automobile allowance/expenses (59%)
Incentive bonus plan (59%)

Seven Most Frequent Family-Friendly Benefits
Dependent care flexible spending account (62%)
Flextime (51%)
Compressed work weeks (27%)
Telecommuting (26%)
Job sharing (22%)

Bring child to work in emergency (21%)
Child-care referral service (17%)

Seven Most Frequent Personal Services
Professional development opportunities (seminars, conferences, courses, etc.) (93%)
Professional memberships (76%)
Casual dress days (every day) (44%)
Casual dress days (one per week) (43%)
Organization-sponsored sports teams (40%)
Food services/subsidized cafeteria (30%)
Club memberships (27%)

Seven Infrequent Benefits of All Types
Car-pooling subsidy (3%)
Company-supported child-care center (3%)
Company-supported elder-care center (1%)
Subsidize cost of elder care (1%)
Already prepared take-home meals (1%)
Naptime during the workday (1%)
Pet health insurance (1%)

Source: "What Benefits Are Companies Offering Now?" *HRfocus*, June 2000, p. 6.

SUMMARY OF KEY POINTS

1 **Describe the components of organizational staffing.** The staffing model consists of seven phases: awareness of the legal aspects of staffing; strategic human resources planning; recruitment; selection; orientation, training, and development; performance appraisal; and compensation. All phases can influence employee retention.

2 **Be aware of the legal aspects of staffing.** Legislation affects all aspects of staffing. Exhibits 10-2 and 10-3 summarize key legislation relating to equal employment

opportunity. Managers should be generally familiar with these laws. Affirmative action consists of complying with antidiscrimination law and correcting past discriminatory practices.

3 **Explain the importance of strategic human resource planning.** Strategic human resource planning provides for the movement of people into, within, and out of the organization. At the same time, it relates these activities to business strategy.

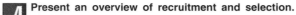

4 **Present an overview of recruitment and selection.** Recruitment is the process of attracting job candidates with the right characteristics and skills to fit job openings and the organizational culture. External and internal sources are used in recruiting, including expanded use of online recruiting.

Selecting the right employees helps build a firm and minimizes the problem of negligent hiring. Selecting the right candidate from among those recruited may involve a preliminary screening interview, completion of an application form, psychological and personnel testing, a job interview, reference checking, and a physical examination. The five types of psychological and personnel tests used most frequently in employee selection are achievement, aptitude, personality, honesty and integrity, and interest tests. Most job interviews are semistructured. They follow a standard format, yet they give the interviewer a chance to ask additional questions. Reference checks play an important role in helping employers prevent the problem of negligent hiring.

5 **Present an overview of employee orientation, training, and development.** An employee orientation program helps acquaint the newly hired employee with the firm. Training includes any procedure intended to foster and enhance employee skills. Development is a form of personal improvement that generally enhances knowledge and skills of a complex and unstructured nature. A needs assessment should be conducted prior to selecting training and development programs.

6 **Explain the basics of a fair and reliable method of evaluating employee performance.** A performance appraisal is a standard method of measuring, evaluating, and reviewing performance of individuals as well as teams. A recent appraisal technique, the 360-degree appraisal, involves feedback from many people. Performance appraisals serve important administrative purposes, such as helping managers make decisions about pay increases and promotions. Appraisals also help managers carry out the leadership function. Appraisal systems measure traits, behavior, and results, with some systems taking into account more than one factor.

7 **Summarize the basics of employee compensation.** Workers are typically paid salaries, bonuses, and sometimes payment for job skills. Broadbanding, which results in fewer pay grades, supports the modern, less hierarchical organization. Employee benefits are a major part of compensation. Flexible benefit packages allow employees to select a group of benefits tailored to their preferences. Compensation is a major factor in recruiting and retaining employees.

KEY TERMS AND PHRASES

Affirmative action, *257*

Disability, *258*

Strategic human resource planning, *259*

Recruitment, *260*

Job specification, *261*

Job analysis, *261*

Realistic job preview, *267*

Behavioral interviewing, *267*

Reference check, *268*

Impairment testing, *270*

Employee orientation program, *271*

Training, *272*

Computer-based training (Internet-based training), *272*

Development, *272*

Informal learning, *274*

Performance appraisal, *274*

360-degree feedback, *275*

Traits, *276*

Behavior, *276*

Results, *276*

Broadbanding, *278*

Employee benefit, *278*

Flexible benefit package, *278*

QUESTIONS

1. Why should a manager who does not work in the human resources department be familiar with the various aspects of staffing?

2. Which one of the business strategies described in Chapter 5 is the most closely tied in with staffing? Explain your answer.

3. What have you learned about staffing that you might apply to your own job search?

4. The U.S. Supreme Court is scheduled to decide whether repetitive motion disorder is a disability covered under the Americans with Disabilities Act. If repetitive motion disorder is classified as a disability, what would be the implications for employers?

5. With online training gaining momentum, what do you predict will be the future of classroom training in industry and government?

6. During downturns in business, companies often reduce benefits (such as free snacks and beverages, and neck massages) to reduce the number of workers to be downsized. Evaluate the merits of reducing benefits for many people to save the jobs of a few?

7. Would you want most of your salary increase to be based on the results of a 360-degree survey? Explain your reasoning.

CRITICAL THINKING QUESTIONS

1. The Americans with Disabilities Act was supposed to help disabled people find employment. Yet 11 years after the act was passed, the unemployment rate for physically disabled people remains about the same. Find out what went wrong. A good place to look is in journals such as *HR Management and Workforce*.

2. What would be the advantages and disadvantages to the organization and individuals if a company abolished performance appraisals?

SKILL-BUILDING EXERCISE: The Selection Interview

Assume the role of the manager or employment interviewer of the call center for Gateway Computer. The call center provides support to customers who already own Gateway computers. After thinking through the job demands of a call center representative, conduct a 15-minute interview of a classmate who pretends to apply for the call center rep position. Before conducting the interview, review the guidelines in Exhibit 10-7. Other students on your team might observe the interview and then provide constructive feedback.

INTERNET SKILL-BUILDING EXERCISE: Recruiting on the Net

Place yourself in the role of a manager who is recruiting qualified job applicants to fill one or more of the following positions: (a) sales representative of machine tools, (b) customer service supervisor who speaks English and Spanish, (c) Web site developer. Use the Internet to conduct your search for a pool of candidates. A good starting point might be the following Web sites: http://www.monster.com/recruit; http://www.careermosaic.com; http://www.espan.com; http://www.worldhire.com; and http://www.nationjob.com. Remember, in this exercise you are looking for job candidates, not a position for yourself. Try to determine whether you can locate any job applicants without paying an employer fee.

CASE PROBLEM 10-A: Labor Squeeze at Brittany Meadows

Brittany Meadows is a well-established nursing home in western New York, in operation since 1946. Brittany Meadows began small, taking care of a handful of wealthy senior citizens whose physical status made it difficult for them to live independently. The nursing home continues to expand as the proportion of the population that includes people in their seventies, eighties, and nineties increases.

As Maria Stetson, the chief executive of Brittany Meadows recently noted, "Elder care is one of the fastest-growing industries in the United States. Many people are living so long that they eventually get to a point where they need assisted living because of physical and intellectual problems. Another factor favoring elder care is that a smaller proportion of families today accept the responsibility of caring for older family members in their homes."

Stetson then pointed out that despite the increased demand for continuing care services at Brittany Meadows and other nursing homes in the region, growth is stifled. The nursing home finds it difficult to recruit the staff it needs to take care of its residents. Concern about the staffing problem led to a conference on the subject.

"Filling vacant positions is the single biggest problem we're facing," said Carl Young, president of the New York Association of Homes and Services for the Aging, which sponsored the meeting of about 30 service providers. In a recent report, the association detailed shortages of certified nurse assistants at 92 percent of nursing homes in New York, 82 percent of home health agencies, and 70 percent of adult care facilities.

Stetson noted that although Brittany Meadows pays higher than average wages, the pay for nurse assistants and other care providers is much lower than for work in most other fields. An entry-level nursing aid is paid about $17,500 per year, which is about one-half the average wage for full-time workers. Stetson added, "The work is physically and mentally demanding, and you really have to like taking care of older people. This is not a glamour field."

Few workers consider entering health care as a career, said Millie Gupta, vice president for medical and clinical services at Brittany Meadows. "Young people are going after the biggest check," Gupta said. "They don't want to hear about retirement plans or health care."

Stetson and Gupta have increased their staff recruiting efforts in recent months. Brittany Meadows now has a Web site that includes an employment section. Gupta admitted, however that the Web site has been ineffective in drawing applicants because few workers in continuing care are online yet. The nursing home advertises in local newspapers, and places ads on supermarket bulletin boards. Any staff member who successfully recruits a new staff member receives a gift certificate covering dinner for two. "We haven't tried spot ads during the Super Bowl, or used sky writing yet. But those methods could be next," joked Stetson.

The New York State Department of Labor is looking to help by assembling a marketing staff to organize elder care recruiting programs, said Vilma Burgos-Torres, of the employer services division. Burgos-Torres encourages employers to use the labor department to publicize their needs. With advances in information technology, the state can send a message about job openings to people collecting unemployment benefits by printing it on their check stubs.

Other ways to alleviate the staffing crunch are available. In the March report, titled "The Staffing Crisis in New York's Continuing Care System," the association of homes and services recommends better pay and benefits, increased third-party reimbursement, better employee training, and more child care options as a way to retain workers.

Questions for Discussion

1. How would you evaluate the thoroughness of the recruiting effort used by Brittany Meadows so far?
2. To what extent might compensation be blocking the recruiting efforts of Brittany Meadows as well as other nursing homes?
3. Offer a creative suggestion to Brittany Meadows for finding an effective recruiting source for nursing home personnel.

Source: Adapted from David Tyler, "Nursing Homes Eager for Workers," *Rochester Democrat and Chronicle*, July 13, 2000, p. 1D.

CASE PROBLEM 10-B: The Captive Workforce

Leah Shaffer is the president of Ceramics Limited, a manufacturer of ceramic photo and picture frames decorated with hand painting. The frames, sold through a California distributor to arts and crafts shops and through a New York distributor to retail stores, enjoy a steady demand throughout the United States. Some export sales to Canada, England, and Italy as well as Web sales that continue to trickle in also add to overall sales. The biggest challenge facing the business these days is finding competent, reliable workers who stay with the company long enough to be productive. Worker turnover has resulted in being unable to fill many orders, along with high costs of recruiting, selecting, and training employees.

So far Shaffer and her two partners, Harvey Phillips and Sue McDonald, continue to struggle with their workforce problem. One morning Phillips and McDonald arrive to find a photocopy of a newspaper article on their desk, with a handwritten note from Shaffer on the top, stating simply, "Harvey and Sue, maybe we should move in this direction. Best, Leah." An abridgment of the article follows:

Like many Americans with in-demand work skills, Lee Gibbs didn't have to go looking for a job—employers sought him out. And he was easy to find. After completing a seven-year drug sentence at a state prison in Lockhart, Texas, Gibbs walked out with more than the traditional $50 and a bus ticket. He had $8,000 in a bank account, expertise in electronic component boards, and a new job starting at more than $30,000 per year.

"They were calling me, offering me jobs even before I got out," said Gibbs, freed from prison over the summer. "With the money I had saved, I was able to get a vehicle, buy clothes for work, pay the first and last month's rent on an apartment, and put down a telephone deposit."

Thirty-year-old Gibbs became marketable through a prison work program run by a Marietta-based company, U.S.

Technologies, with subsidiaries that use prison inmates for outsourcing contracts with private companies.

With more Americans than ever behind bars and businesses shopping for workers from a tight labor pool, there is renewed debate over the pros and cons of having "cons" contributing to free-market enterprises. For most of this century, prison work programs have been sharply restricted by concerns about unfair competition and use of inmates as "slave labor." Questions have also arisen about whether criminals deserve to receive training, pay, and job experience.

Yet according to the U.S. Attorney General, the programs can be a force for good. Wages can go to the victims' restitution funds, prison recidivism (return rates) might be reduced, and there could be "another engine" for the national economy.

At the Putnamville (Indiana) Correctional Facilities, 20 inmates earn $7.95 per hour producing Hoosier Hickory Historic Furniture for sale to customers seeking a rustic relic of yesteryear. The hourly wage is not all profit. The workers must pay for room and board, taxes, restitution for victims and outstanding fines. In contrast to the work for Hoosier Hickory, most prison industry programs are barred from selling their products to private buyers. Those that do must follow a strict set of regulations, including a requirement that inmates be paid wages similar to those in private industry.

"For a lot of these people, this is the first job they've held," said Ken Smith, chief executive officer of U.S. Technologies. "They learn work habits. They have to get up, shower and shave and show up for work on time; they have to show initiative, they have to meet goals, they have to stay out of trouble."

In Florida, PRIDE Enterprises, a nonprofit company that started in 1985 training and employing prison inmates to perform useful jobs with a goal of reducing prison recidivism, employs 4,000 inmates in 51 operations. Their jobs range from making eyeglasses to data entry. Pamela Jo Davis, the PRIDE Enterprises president, says studies show that less than 13 percent of the organization's inmate workers landed back in prison, compared to a national rate of about 60 percent.

Inmate work programs are popular with prison officials who see them as a way to reduce idleness that leads to problems. "That's 200 inmates that are not just slogging around on the compound," Russell Smith, assistant superintendent at Liberty Correctional, said of the PRIDE operation there.

Curious about other perspectives on prison labor, Leah Shaffer turned to the Internet, where she located the World Socialist Web site (http://wsw.org). After reading the article, she forwarded it by e-mail to Philips and McDonald. The article explained that 80,000 inmates in the United States are employed in commercial activity, some earning as little as 21 cents per hour. The Federal Prison Industries (FPI) program sponsored by the U.S. government employs 21,000 inmates. FPI inmates manufacture a wide variety of products including clothing, file cabinets, electronic equipment, and military helmets that are sold to federal agencies and private companies. FPI sales have risen to $600 million annually, with more than $37 million in profits.

The report continued to explain that prisoners now manufacture everything from blue jeans to auto parts to electronics and furniture. Honda pays prison labor $2 an hour for the same work for which unionized autoworkers receive about $25 per hour. Toys R Us employed inmates to restock shelves, and Microsoft employed them to pack and ship software. Clothing made in California and Oregon prisons competes successfully with apparel made in Latin America and Asia.

The World Socialist Web site points out that the growth of prison labor contributes directly to the elimination of the jobs for other workers. For instance, Lockhart Technologies, Inc., closed its plant in Austin, Texas, laying off its 150 workers so that it could open shop in a state prison in Lockhart. The prisoners assemble circuit boards for blue-chip companies such as IBM, Compaq, and Dell. Lockhart does not pay health or any other benefits. The company is required to pay the prison the federal minimum wage for each laborer, but the inmates keep only 20 percent of the minimum wage.

One day after Philips and McDonald had sifted through the reports, they joined Shaffer for lunch to discuss the possibilities of Ceramics Unlimited hiring prison inmates to make some of their frames.

"Wait a minute," warned Phillips. "Before we start looking for prisoners to make our frames, we first have to understand what our distributors and ultimate customers would think. Some of them might be upset, particularly if they are strongly oriented toward workers' rights."

Shaffer replied, "I'm not suggesting that hiring inmates as part of our workforce is a perfect solution to our problems. We could use some reliable, low-priced labor. Yet I think we should at least make some preliminary inquires. Why don't we get in touch with PRIDE Enterprises or Federal Prison Industries?"

Discussion Questions

1. If Ceramics Limited does hire prison labor, what selection procedures should they use?
2. What other recruiting sources might Ceramics Limited use to find workers to build their frames?
3. What ethical issues does Ceramics Limited need to address with respect to hiring prison labor?

Sources: Adapted from Dan Sewell, "Opportunity Knocks for Inmates with Job Skills: Businesses Tap into Jail Population to Fill Positions in a Tight Labor Market," Associated Press, October 18, 1998; Charles Hoskinson, "More Prisons Use Inmates to Perform Labor," Associated Press, December 7, 1998; Alan Whyte and Jamie Baker, "Prison Labor on the Rise in U.S.," *World Socialist Web Site*, available at http://www.wsws.org/articles/2000/may2000/pris-m08.shtml, May 8, 2000.

ENDNOTES

1. Jennifer Koch Laabs, "Serving Up a New Level of Customer Service at Quebecor," *Workforce*, March 2001, pp. 40–41.

2. Quoted in Gail Dutton, "The ADA at 10," *Workforce*, December 2000, p. 42.

3. Dutton, "The ADA at 10," p. 44.

4. James A. F. Stoner and R. Edwards Freeman, *Management*, 4th ed. (Upper Saddle River, NJ: Prentice Hall, 1989), p. 331; Peter Bamberger and Ilan Meshoulam, *Human Resource Strategy: Formulation, Implementation, and Impact* (Thousand Oaks, CA: Sage, 2000).

5. Daniel M. Cable and Timothy A. Judge, "Interviewers' Perceptions of Person-Organization Fit and Organizational Selection Decisions," *Journal of Applied Psychology*, August 1997, p. 331; Lin Grensing-Pophal, "Hiring to Fit Your Corporate Culture: Don't Let Cultural Fit Supersede Other Considerations," *HR Magazine*, August 1999, pp. 50–54.

6. Carla Johnson, "Refocusing Job Descriptions," *HR Magazine*, January 2001, pp. 68–69.

7. Kerri Koss Morehart, "How to Create an Employee Referral Program That Really Works," *HRfocus*, January 2001, pp. 3–4.

8. "Online Recruiting: What Works, What Doesn't," *HRfocus*, March 2000, pp. 1, 11–15.

9. Ann Marie Ryan and Maria Lasek, "Negligent Hiring and Defamation: Areas of Liability Related to Pre-Employment Inquiries," *Personnel Psychology*, Spring 1991, pp. 291–308.

10. Philip Ash, "Law and Regulation of Preemployment Inquiries," *Journal of Business and Psychology*, Spring–Summer 1991, pp. 291–308.

11. The evidence is reviewed in Philip L. Roth and Philip Bobko, "College Grade Point Average as a Personnel Selection Device: Ethnic Group Differences and Potential Adverse Impact," *Journal of Applied Psychology*, June 2000, p. 399.

12. Gilbert Nicholson, "Automated Assessments for Better Hires," *Workforce*, December 2000, pp. 102, 104.

13. Timothy A. Judge et al., "The Big Five Personality Traits, General Mental Ability, and Career Success Across the Life Span," *Personnel Psychology*, Autumn 1999, pp. 621–652.

14. Cited in Cora Daniels, "Does This Man Need a Shrink?" *Fortune*, February 5, 2001, p. 206.

15. Leonard D. Goodstein and Richard I. Lanyon, "Applications of Personality Assessment to the Workplace: A Review," *Journal of Business and Psychology*, Spring 1999, p. 317.

16. Orlando Behling, "Employee Selection: Will Intelligence and Conscientiousness Do the Job?" *Academy of Management Executive*, February 1998, pp. 77–86; Goodstein and Lanyon, "Applications of Personality Assessment," p. 295.

17. Robert D. Bretz Jr., and Timothy A. Judge, "Realistic Job Previews: A Test of the Adverse Self-Selection Hypothesis," *Journal of Applied Psychology*, April 1998, pp. 330–337.

18. Marlene Brown, "Reference Checking: The Law Is on Your Side," *Human Resource Measurements* (a supplement to the December 1991 *Personnel Journal*, Wonderlic Personnel Test, Inc.); Charlotte Garvey, "Outsourcing Background Checks," *HR Magazine*, March 2001, pp. 95–104.

19. Garvey, "Outsourcing Background Checks," p. 95.

20. "Top Reference-Checking Questions," *Manager's Strategy File* (special supplement to *WorkingSMART*), 2001.

21. Studies reported in "Avoiding 'Truth or Dare' in Reference Checks," *HRfocus*, May 2000, p. 5.

22. Jane Easter Bahis, "Drugs in the Workplace," *HR Magazine*, February 1998, pp. 81–87.

23. Evelyn Beck, "Is the Time Right for Impairment Testing?" *Workforce*, February 2001, p. 70.

24. Kevin G. Love et al., "Selection Across Two Cultures: Adapting the Selection of Assemblers to Meet Japanese Performance Standards," *Personnel Psychology*, Winter 1994, pp. 837–846.

25. Alice M. Starcke, "Building a Better Orientation Program," *HR Magazine*, November 1996, p. 108.

26. Howard J. Klein and Natasha A. Weaver, "The Effectiveness of an Organizational-Level Orientation Training Program in the Socialization of New Hires," *Personnel Psychology*, Spring 2000, pp. 47–66.

27. Eilene Zimmerman, "Better Training Is Just a Click Away," *Workforce*, January 2001, p. 36.

28. Marc Adams, "Training Employees as Partners," *HR Magazine*, February 1999, p. 65.

29. Robert M. Fulmer, "The Evolving Paradigm of Leadership Development," *Organizational Dynamics*, Spring 1997, p. 70.

30. Nancy Day, "Informal Learning Gets Results," *Workforce*, June 1998, p. 31.

31. Jai Ghorpade, "Managing Five Paradoxes of 360-Degree Feedback," *Academy of Management Executive*, February 2000, pp. 140–150.

32. Carol A. L. Dannhauser, "How'm I Doing?" Performance Appraisals Don't Have to Be Painful," *Working Woman*, December–January 1999, p. 38.

33. Gail Dutton, "Making Reviews More Efficient and Fair," *Workforce*, April 2001, p. 76.

34. Brian D. Cawley, Lisa M. Keeping, and Paul E. Levy, "Participation in the Performance Appraisal Process and Employee Reactions: A Meta-Analytic Review of Field Investigations," *Journal of Applied Psychology*, August 1998, pp. 615–633.

35. Dayton Fandray, "The New Thinking in Performance Appraisals," *Workforce*, May 2001, p. 40.

36. Valerie L. Williams and Jennifer E. Sunderland, "New Pay Programs Boost Retention," *Workforce*, May 1999, p. 38.

37. Sandra L. O'Neill, "Aligning Pay with Business Strategy," *HR Magazine*, August 1993, pp. 79-86; Williams and Sunderland, "New Pay Programs," p. 38.

38. Aaron Bernstein, "We Want You to Stay, Really," *Business Week*, June 22, 1998, p. 68.

39. Jennifer Laabs, "Demand Performance for Benefits," *Workforce*, January 2000, pp. 42–46.

Leadership

Early on a mid-March morning in North Sioux City, South Dakota, Ted Waitt comes home. Walking quickly across a small courtyard he opens the door to Gateway's manufacturing plant. Inside the lunchroom, hundreds of people welcome him back. And while the folks here—assembly-line workers, freight operators, shipping managers, call-center reps, quality inspectors—have eight-hour shifts ahead of them, their mood is celebratory. Rock music blares from the speaker system. Friends jostle and call out to one another from across the room. Posters splayed all over the plant's walls pronounce, TED IS COMING!

On one that reads WELCOME BACK, TED in two-foot letters, workers have scribbled small notes to Waitt, yearbook style. "We're so glad to have you back. Rock on!" declares one message. "A great day for Gateway," another says. Still another reads: "The captain has come back to mind the ship and crew. Can't have the ship afloat without the captain." (Waitt had left his position as CEO for a year to play a less active role in the company as chairman. The outsider appointed as his successor proved to be unpopular with Gateway employees.)

As Waitt enters the room, a plant supervisor shouts over the crowd, "Ted is in the house!" The music shifts to Smash Mouth's "All Star." As the chorus throbs, "Hey now, you're a rock star . . ." Waitt steps up on to a small makeshift stage at the center or the cafeteria. The room is suddenly quiet—listening, waiting. Then softly, almost shyly, in a low throaty voice, Waitt says, "It's good to be home."

Here in this prairie town, where he was born and raised, met his

OBJECTIVES

After studying this chapter and doing the exercises, you should be able to:

1 Differentiate between leadership and management.

2 Describe how leaders are able to influence and empower team members.

3 Identify important leadership characteristics and behaviors.

4 Describe the leadership continuum, Theory X and Theory Y, Leadership Grid, situational, and entrepreneurial styles of leadership.

5 Describe transformational and charismatic leadership.

6 Explain the leadership role of mentoring.

7 Identify the skills that contribute to leadership.

Chapter 11

wife, had his four kids, and built Gateway from nothing, Waitt is more than just the CEO. As one plant worker, shouting above the crowd tells it: "He's our hero."[1]

leadership

The ability to inspire confidence and support among the people who are needed to achieve organizational goals.

The CEO and business founder just described illustrates one of the most important types of leaders in business, the charismatic leader who inspires employees to work hard to achieve company objectives. People who can accomplish this feat practice **leadership**, the ability to inspire confidence and support among the people who are needed to achieve organizational goals.[2]

Leadership can be exercised in many settings such as business, government, education, nonprofit firms, and sports. This chapter focuses on leadership in business firms, which is important at every organizational level. As George B. Weathersby explains, increasingly the productivity and profitability of every business team, operating department, corporate division, two-person service firm, and franchise operation is the true and lasting foundation of a strong economy in a city, state, nation, and region.[3] Effective leadership contributes to achieving these results. The success of the world's best companies is often attributed primarily to their leadership rather than physical assets.

Executives seeking candidates for management jobs list leadership skills as the top attribute they want. Approximately 47 percent of executives in a survey listed leadership first, followed by communication skills at 35 percent.[4] Successful professionals, regardless of their job titles, generally possess leadership capabilities. In order to cope with frequent change and to solve problems, people exercise initiative and leadership in taking new approaches to their job. Furthermore, in the modern organization, people slip in and out of leadership roles such as a temporary assignment as a task force leader.

In this chapter we describe the characteristics and behaviors of leaders in organizations, as well as useful leadership theories, and key leadership skills. You will also have the opportunity to read case histories of three effective leaders.

1   THE LINK BETWEEN LEADERSHIP AND MANAGEMENT

Differentiate between leadership and management.

Today's managers must know how to lead as well as manage, or their companies will become extinct. (You will recall that leadership—along with planning, organizing, and controlling—is one of the basic functions of management.) Three representative distinctions between leadership and management follow:[5]

- Management is more formal and scientific than leadership. It relies on universal skills, such as planning, budgeting, and controlling. Management is a set of explicit tools and techniques, based on reasoning and testing, that can be used in a variety of situations.
- Leadership, by contrast, involves having a vision of what the organization can become. Leadership requires eliciting cooperation and teamwork from a large network of people and keeping the key people in that network motivated, using every manner of persuasion.
- Management involves getting things done through other people. Leadership places more emphasis on helping others do the things they know need to be done to achieve the common vision.

Exhibit 11-1 presents a list outlining the difference between leadership and management. Effective leadership and management are both required in the modern workplace. Managers must be leaders, but leaders must also be good managers. Workers need to be inspired and persuaded, but they also need assistance in developing a smoothly functioning workplace.

The difference between leadership and management can be illustrated by the sports business team of Vince McMahon, the chairman of the World Wrestling Federation, and Linda E. McMahon, the president and CEO of WWF. The outgoing and slick Vince McMahon is the creative muscle, or leader, behind the WWF. Linda McMahon, in contrast, quietly runs the day-to-day operation and is the key manager. A friend of the couple comments, "Vince is the type to walk in and say he wants an office in Nairobi by Monday. Linda would be the one to put it together."[6]

Exhibit 11-2 presents an overview of the link between leadership and management. It also highlights several of the major topics presented in this chapter. The figure illustrates that, to bring about improved productivity and morale, managers do two things. First, they use power, authority, influence, and personal traits and characteristics. Second, they apply leadership behaviors and practices.

Leader	Manager
Visionary	Rational
Passionate	Consulting
Creative	Persistent
Flexible	Problem-solving
Inspiring	Tough-minded
Innovative	Analytical
Courageous	Structured
Imaginative	Deliberative
Experimental	Authoritative
Independent	Stabilizing
Shares knowledge	Centralizes knowledge

Sources: Genevieve Capowski, "Anatomy of a Leader: Where Are the Leaders of Tomorrow?" *Management Review,* March 1994, p. 12; David Fagiano, "Managers vs. Leaders: A Corporate Fable," *Management Review,* November 1997, p. 5.

EXHIBIT 11-1

Leaders vs. Managers

The difference between leaders and managers lies in the emphasis of certain behaviors. It is important not to regard managers as all being stodgy and unimaginative, whereas leaders are all inspirational and creative.

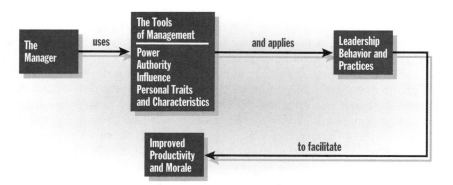

EXHIBIT 11-2

The Links Between Management and Leadership

Management and leadership are both applied to improve productivity and morale.

Source: Adapted from John R. Schermerhorn, Jr., *Management for Productivity,* 4th ed. (New York: Wiley, 1993).

2

Describe how leaders are able to influence and empower team members.

power

The ability or potential to influence decisions and control resources.

authority

The formal right to get people to do things or the formal right to control resources.

THE LEADERSHIP USE OF POWER AND AUTHORITY

Leaders influence people to do things through the use of power and authority. **Power** is the ability or potential to influence decisions and control resources. Powerful people have the potential to exercise influence, and they exercise it frequently. For example, a powerful executive might influence an executive from another company to do business with his or her company. **Authority** is the formal right to get people to do things or the formal right to control resources. Factors within a person, such as talent or charm, help them achieve power. Only the organization, however, can grant authority. To understand how leaders use power and authority, we examine the various types of power, influence tactics, and how leaders share power with team members. Understanding these different approaches to exerting influence can help a manager become a more effective leader.

Types of Power

Leaders use various types of power to influence others. However, the power exercised by team members, or subordinates, acts as a constraint on how much power leaders can exercise. The list that follows describes the types of power exercised by leaders and sometimes by group members.[7]

1. *Legitimate power* is the authentic right of a leader to make certain types of requests. These requests are based on internalized social and cultural values in an organization. It is the easiest type of influence for most subordinates to accept. For example, virtually all employees accept the manager's authority to conduct a performance appraisal. Legitimate power has its limits, however, as described later under "subordinate power."
2. *Reward power* is a leader's control over rewards of value to the group members. Exercising this power includes giving salary increases and recommending employees for promotion.
3. *Coercive power* is a leader's control over punishments. Organizational punishments include assignment to undesirable working hours, demotion, and firing. Effective leaders generally avoid heavy reliance on coercive power, because it creates resentment and sometimes retaliation.
4. *Expert power* derives from a leader's job-related knowledge as perceived by group members. This type of power stems from having specialized skills, knowledge, or talent. Expert power can be exercised even when a person does not occupy a formal leadership position. An advertising copywriter with a proven record of writing winning ad slogans has expert power. A widely used form of expert power is the control of vital information. If a person controls information other people need, power will flow to that person. Having valuable contacts, such as knowing people prepared to invest in start-up companies, is a form of controlling vital information.
5. *Referent power* refers to the ability to control based on loyalty to the leader and the group members' desire to please that person. Having referent power contributes to being perceived as charismatic, but expert power also enhances charisma.[8] Some of the loyalty to the leader is based on identification with the leader's personal characteristics. Referent power and charisma are both based on the subjective perception of the leader's traits and characteristics.
6. *Subordinate power* is any type of power that employees can exert upward in an organization, based on justice and legal considerations. For example, certain categories of workers cannot be asked to work overtime without compensation.

Power Flows Down ↓	Zone of Indifference	Zone of Noncompliance	Power Flows Up ↑
	Orders are acceptable; employees do not exercise subordinate power, but comply with requests and orders.	Orders are unacceptable; employees exercise subordinate power and refuse to comply.	

EXHIBIT 11-3

Subordinate Power and the Zone of Indifference

One source of group members' power is refusing to comply with orders they believe are unreasonable. In organizations where hierarchy is deemphasized, group members are likely to have a broader zone of noncompliance.

289

Group members can always exercise expert power, but subordinate power restricts the extent to which power can be used to control them. As Exhibit 11-3 shows, when subordinates perceive an order as being outside the bounds of legitimate authority, they rebel.

Legitimate orders lie within a range of behaviors that the group members regard as acceptable. A legitimate order from above is acceptable to employees and falls within the **zone of indifference**. That zone encompasses those behaviors employees do not mind following. If the manager pushes beyond the zone of indifference, the leader loses power. For example, few group members would accept an order to regularly carry out actions that harm the environment, such as dumping toxins.

Through subordinate power, group members control and constrain the power of leaders. Legal rights contribute to subordinate power. For example, an employee has the legal right to refuse sexual advances from the boss.

zone of indifference

The psychological zone that encompasses acceptable behaviors employees do not mind following.

Influence Tactics

In addition to various types of power, leaders use many other influence tactics to get things done. Eight frequently used influence tactics follow.

1. *Leading by example* means that the leader influences group members by serving as a positive model of desirable behavior. A manager who leads by example shows consistency between actions and words. For example, suppose a firm has a strict policy on punctuality. The manager explains the policy and is always punctual. The manager's words and actions provide a consistent model.

2. *Leading by values* means the leader influences people by articulating and demonstrating values that guide the behaviors of others. Using values to influence others is similar to the organizational culture guiding behavior. According to Manuel London, the ideal values for a leader to pursue would be mutual respect, trust, honesty, fairness, kindness, and doing good.[9] William Clay Ford, Jr., the 44-year-old chairman of Ford Motor Co., attempts to influence all Ford workers to embrace environmental values, and pursues plans to retire engines that emit carbon-monoxide by the end of his tenure as chairman.[10]

3. *Assertiveness* refers to being forthright in your demands. It involves expressing what you want done and how you feel about it. William Clay Ford, Jr., for example, would be assertive in saying, "All these horrible accidents we had with the Ford Explorer make me angry. Innocent people have been killed, and I want no more auto safety problems on our record." Assertiveness, as this example shows, also refers to making orders clear.

4. *Rationality* means appealing to reason and logic. Strong leaders use this tactic frequently. Rational persuasion is important today because many managers

work in situations in which they do not have extensive formal authority, but must rely on persuasion and teamwork. Rationality is also important when a manager must manage across different functions (outside of the department).[11] Pointing out the facts of a situation to group members in order to get them to do something is an example of rationality. For example, a middle-level manager might tell a supervisor, "If our department goes over budget this year, we are likely to be cut further next year." Knowing this information, the supervisor will probably become more cost conscious.

5. *Ingratiation* refers to getting somebody else to like you, often through the use of political skill. A typical ingratiating tactic would be to act in a friendly manner just before making a demand. Effective managers treat people well consistently to get cooperation when it is needed.

6. *Exchange* is a method of influencing others by offering to reciprocate if they meet your demands. Leaders with limited expert, referent, and legitimate power are likely to use exchange and make bargains with subordinates. A manager might say to a group member, "If you can help me out this time, I'll go out of my way to return the favor." Using exchange is like using reward power. The emphasis in exchange, however, is that the manager goes out of his or her way to strike a bargain that pleases the team members.

7. *Coalition formation* is a way of gaining both power and influence. A **coalition** is a specific arrangement of parties working together to combine their power, thus exerting influence on another individual or group. Coalitions in business are a numbers game—the more people you can get on your side, the better. For example, a manager might band with several other managers to gain support for a major initiative such as merging with another company.

8. *Joking and kidding* are widely used to influence others on the job.[12] Good-natured ribbing is especially effective when a straightforward statement might be interpreted as harsh criticism. In an effort to get an employee to order office supplies over the Internet, one manager said, "We don't want you to suffer from technostress. Yet you're the only supervisor here who still orders office supplies by telephone, paper memos, and carrier pigeon." The supervisor smiled and proceeded to ask for help in learning how to execute orders for office supplies over the Internet.

coalition

A specific arrangement of parties working together to combine their power, thus exerting influence on another individual or group.

Which Influence Tactic to Choose

Leaders are unlikely to use all the influence tactics in a given situation. Instead, they tend to choose an influence tactic that fits the demands of the circumstances. Researchers found support for this conclusion in a study of 125 leaders employed by a bank. To determine the influence tactics the leaders used, the researchers asked the leaders' superiors and subordinates to complete a questionnaire. The study found that in crisis situations the leaders used more expert power, legitimate power, referent power, and upward influence than in noncrisis situations. (Upward influence refers to using power to get higher-ranking people to act on one's behalf.) The study also concluded that the leaders were less likely to consult with subordinates in a crisis situation than in a noncrisis situation.[13]

Employee Empowerment and the Exercise of Power

Chapter 9 emphasized empowerment as a way of distributing authority in the organization. Empowerment is similarly a way for leaders to share power. When leaders share power, employees experience a greater sense of personal effectiveness and job ownership. Sharing power with group members enables them to feel better about themselves and perform at a higher level. Empowered employees perform better to a large extent because they become better motivated. The extra motivation stems from a feeling of being in charge. An important use of empowerment is to enhance customer service. As employees acquire more authority to take care of customer problems, these problems can be handled promptly, or sometimes right on the spot.

A key component of empowerment is the leader's acceptance of the employee as a partner in decision making. Because the team member's experience and information are regarded as equal to those of the leader, he or she shares control. Both the leader and team member must agree on what is to be accomplished. The partnering approach to empowerment builds trust between the employee and the leader.[14]

Empowerment also makes possible *grass-roots leadership* whereby top-level managers encourage workers throughout the organization to make decisions and provide ideas for improving the company. Ford Motor Company has been going through organizational change that features more people throughout the firm making important decisions. Ford views grassroots leadership as the best approach for creating a nimbler business. David Murphy, vice president of human resources explains, "We want people at all levels who will take risks, who are prepared to coach and counsel, and who can make decisions. We can't afford to wait for decisions to come down from the top. If we did, the consumer would be [angry] about having to wait so long—and would be gone before those decisions even got made."[15]

CHARACTERISTICS, TRAITS, AND BEHAVIORS OF EFFECTIVE LEADERS   **3**

Understanding leadership takes an understanding of leaders as individuals. This section will highlight findings about the personal characteristics and behaviors of effective managerial leaders. *Effective*, in this context, means that strong leaders create both high productivity and morale, as Exhibit 11–2 illustrates.

Identify important leadership characteristics and behaviors.

Characteristics and Traits of Effective Leaders

Possessing certain characteristics and traits does not in itself guarantee success. Yet effective leaders differ from others in certain respects. Studying leadership traits is also important because a person who is perceived to embody certain traits is more likely to be accepted as a leader. For example, people see managers whom they believe to be good problem solvers as able to help overcome obstacles and create a better workplace.

An assessment of the characteristics and behaviors of leaders translates into the idea that these same positive attributes of a leader will facilitate his or her effectiveness in comparable settings. For example, when executives are selected for high-tech companies, the attributes of drive, intelligence, and vision can be even more important than e-business experience.[16] Hundreds of human qualities can enhance leadership effectiveness in some situations. Here we present a sampling of factors relevant to many work settings.[17]

1. *Drive and achievement motive, and passion.* Leaders are noted for the effort they invest in their work and the passion they have for work and work associates. Drive also includes **achievement motivation**—finding joy in accomplishment

achievement motivation

Finding joy in accomplishment for its own sake.

for its own sake. High achievers find satisfaction in completing challenging tasks, attaining high standards, and developing better ways of doing things. At the same time effective leaders are passionate about what they are achieving. Two executive placement specialists who studied hundreds of successful business leaders concluded, "What was clear with everyone we sat down with was they were passionate about what they were doing. They love to talk about it. Also, the job today is so enormously demanding that you have to have a high energy level. They work an average of 65 hours per week."[18]

power motivation

Definition to come?

2. *Power motive.* Successful leaders exhibit **power motivation**, a strong desire to control others and resources or get them to do things on your behalf. A leader with a strong power need enjoys exercising power and using influence tactics. Only a manager who uses power constructively could be promoted rapidly in a modern, well-managed corporation. Bill Gates of Microsoft exemplifies a power-obsessed leader who aggressively pursues a market domination strategy.

3. *Self-confidence.* Self-confidence contributes to effective leadership in several ways. Above all, self-confident leaders project an image that encourages subordinates to have faith in them. Self-confidence also helps leaders make some of the tough business decisions they face regularly.

4. *Trustworthiness and honesty.* Leadership is undermined if people don't trust the leader. Trust is regarded as one of the major leadership attributes. Continuing waves of downsizings, coupled with generous compensation boosts to executives, have eroded employee trust and commitment in many organizations. Effective leaders know they must build strong employee trust to obtain high productivity and commitment. A major strategy for being perceived as trustworthy is to make your behavior consistent with your intentions. Practice what you preach and set the example. Let others know of your goals and invite feedback on how well you are achieving them.

open-book company

A firm in which every employee is trained, empowered, and motivated to understand and pursue the company's business goals.

Closely related to honesty and integrity is being open with employees about the financial operations and other sensitive information about the company. In an **open-book company** every employee is trained, empowered, and motivated to understand and pursue the company's business goals.[19] In this way employees become business partners.

To help you link the abstract concept of trust to day-by-day behavior, take the self-quiz in Exhibit 11-4. You might use the same quiz in relation to any manager you have worked for.

5. *Good intellectual ability, knowledge, and technical competence.* Effective leaders are good problem solvers and knowledgeable about the business or technology for which they are responsible. (As mentioned previously, at the highest levels of executive leadership, certain personal characteristics sometimes might be more important than technical knowledge.) The leader's skills at obtaining, using, and sharing useful knowledge are crucial to success in the information age.[20] Technical competence, or knowledge of the business, often translates into close attention to details about products. Barry Sternlich, the chair and CEO of Starwood Hotels & Resorts Worldwide Inc., makes suggestions for and gives his final approval to such details as bed covers, drapes, and carpet style. An amateur painter, he believes that emphasis on achieving the right look and feel is crucial to his business strategy.[21]

The accompanying Management in Action illustrates how intimate knowledge of the details of the business, as well as passion, is essential for certain leadership settings.

Management in Action

The High-Flying Captain Deborah McCoy

They didn't talk about flying in Deborah McCoy's family when she was growing up in St. Matthews, near Louisville, Kentucky. A plane crash had killed her father, a military flier, before she even had a chance to know him. But if aviation took one life, it gave her another—her own—and McCoy, 44, made the best of it. She is top pilot at Continental Airlines, where's she's known as Capt. Deborah McCoy, and the first woman to head flight operations for a major U.S. carrier, working at the company's Houston headquarters. She oversees the hiring, training, and flight operations for approximately 5,200 pilots and 8,700 flight attendants.

"Captain McCoy is one of the best and brightest in the business. In addition to being a superior pilot, she's an analytical thinker who knows how to get results," said Gordon Bethune, chair and chief executive officer of Continental Airlines.

Her career, based on a love of flying, took root during childhood vacations, lying in the grass of her grandmother's farm and watching the silver planes high above, dragging their contrails like banners through the summer sky. Her message to young girls who think they might like to fly one day: "Don't limit your options to being a flight attendant; consider traffic control, airplane mechanics, airport management, or even taking the controls. So many people misunderstand what the airline business is about. Young women coming out of high school, they can do it, and I can tell them all the steps of how to do it. I'd like my experience to be something that motivates all the young women out there and lets them know what the job is about."

McCoy decided to find out what it was about for herself at age 18, when she headed out to Bowman field for her first lesson. "It was a cold, sleety day," McCoy recalled. "Nobody knew I was out there doing this. So then the instructor said, 'Why don't you take the airplane off?'"

Her surprise turned to real fear a little while later as the wide-eyed teen and her instructor headed back in for a landing. "The door I thought I had closed wasn't really closed all the way, and the seat belt I thought was buckled wasn't. As we came over an expressway, my door popped open and I heard this terrible noise—bam, bam, bam! I thought, oh, no. I'm going to die and nobody knows I'm here." She didn't die, though, and she even gave the lessons another try with a different instructor. "It was a beautiful day," she said. "It was clear and pretty and smooth, and I fell in love with it."

McCoy's first assignment came in 1979 as first officer of a DC-9, six years after the hiring of the first female pilot. It was still a time when some male pilots objected to flying with women, when some airlines insisted that female pilots not wear makeup and keep their hair tied back under their caps so the passengers wouldn't get nervous.

But McCoy said she never encountered resistance because she was a woman. "In the pilot world you have to prove yourself by your ability to fly the airplane; that standard is the same whether you're a man or a woman," she said. "I can honestly say I never really experienced any kind of glass ceiling because there were always people here who encouraged me to take on new challenges."

Source: David Goetz, "Airline Names Woman to Head Flight Operations," Gannett News Service, October 11, 1999.

EXHIBIT 11-4

Behaviors and Attitudes of a Trustworthy Leader

The following behaviors and attitudes characterize leaders who are generally trusted by their group members and other constituents. After you read each characteristic, indicate whether this behavior or attitude is one you have developed already, or does not fit you at present.

	Fits Me	Does Not Fit Me
1. Tells people he or she is going to do something, and then always follows through and gets it done	☐	☐
2. Is described by others as being reliable	☐	☐
3. Keeps secrets and confidences well	☐	☐
4. Tells the truth consistently	☐	☐
5. Minimizes telling people what they want to hear	☐	☐
6. Is described by others as "walking the talk"	☐	☐
7. Delivers consistent messages to others in terms of matching words and deeds	☐	☐
8. Does what he or she expects others to do	☐	☐
9. Minimizes hypocrisy by not engaging in activities he or she tells others are wrong	☐	☐
10. Readily accepts feedback on behavior from others	☐	☐
11. Maintains eye contact with people when talking to them	☐	☐
12. Appears relaxed and confident when explaining his or her side of a story	☐	☐
13. Individualizes compliments to others rather than saying something like "You look great" to a large number of people	☐	☐
14. Does not expect lavish perks for himself or herself while expecting others to go on an austerity diet	☐	☐
15. Does not tell others a crisis is pending (when it isn't) just to gain their cooperation	☐	☐
16. Collaborates with others to make creative decisions	☐	☐
17. Communicates information to people at all organizational levels	☐	☐
18. Readily shares financial information with others	☐	☐
19. Listens to people and then acts on many of their suggestions	☐	☐
20. Generally engages in predictable behavior	☐	☐

Scoring: These statements are mostly for self-reflection, so no specific scoring key exists. However, the more statements that fit you, the more trustworthy you are—assuming you are answering truthfully. The usefulness of this self-quiz increases if somebody who knows you well answers it for you to supplement your self-perceptions.

6. *Sense of humor.* An effective sense of humor is an important part of a leader's job. In the workplace, humor relieves tension and boredom, defuses hostility, and helps build relationships with group members. Claudia Kennedy, as a former three-star Army general and the Army's chief intelligence officer, occupied a key leadership position. During an interview for a magazine article, she mentioned that although she had no regrets, her demanding career precluded time for a husband and children. The reporter commented, "You could still get married." Kennedy retorted, "Well certainly—put my phone number in this article."[22]

7. *Emotional intelligence.* Effective leaders demonstrate good emotional intelligence, the ability to manage themselves and their relationships effectively.

Emotional intelligence broadly encompasses many traits and behaviors related to leadership effectiveness, including self-confidence, empathy, passion for the task, and visionary leadership. Being sensitive to the needs of others (and not insulting or verbally abusing them) is another part of emotional intelligence.[23]

Leaders sometimes fail because of glaring deficits in emotional intelligence. When Frank Lorenzo took over Eastern Airlines (which he later led into bankruptcy), the animosity that developed between him and union bosses grew so great that it hastened the airline's demise.[24]

Behaviors and Skills of Effective Leaders

Traits alone are not sufficient to lead effectively. A leader must also behave in certain ways and possess key skills. As Chapter 1 described, managers need sound conceptual, interpersonal, technical, and political skills. The following actions or behaviors are linked to leadership effectiveness. Recognize, however, that behaviors are related to skills. For example, in giving emotional support to team members a leader uses interpersonal skills. An effective leader:

1. *Is adaptable to the situation.* Adaptability reflects the contingency viewpoint: A strategy is chosen based on the unique circumstances at hand. For instance, if a leader were dealing with psychologically immature subordinates, he or she would have to supervise them closely. Mature and self-reliant subordinates would require less supervision. Also, the adaptive leader selects an organization structure best suited to the situation. The circumstances would determine, for example, whether the manager chooses a brainstorming group or a committee.

   Another important aspect of adaptability is for a leader to be able to function effectively in different situations, such as leading in a manufacturing or office setting.

   The ability to size up people and situations and adapt tactics accordingly is a vital leadership behavior. It stems from an inner quality called insight or intuition—a direct perception of a situation that seems unrelated to any specific reasoning process.

2. *Demands high standards of performance for group members.* Effective leaders consistently hold group members to high standards of performance, which raises productivity. Setting high expectations for subordinates becomes a self-fulfilling prophecy. People tend to live up to the expectations set for them by their superiors. Setting high expectations might take the form of encouraging team members to establish difficult objectives.

3. *Provides emotional support to group members.* Supportive behavior toward subordinates usually increases leadership effectiveness. A supportive leader frequently gives encouragement and praise. The emotional support generally improves morale and sometimes improves productivity. Being emotionally supportive comes naturally to the leader who has empathy for people and who is a warm person.

4. *Gives frequent feedback and accepts feedback.* Giving group members frequent feedback on their performance is another vital leadership behavior. The manager rarely can influence the behavior of group members without appropriate performance feedback. Feedback helps in two ways. First, it informs employees of how well they are doing, so they can take corrective action if needed. Second, positive feedback encourages subordinates to keep up the good work.

The effective leader also listens to feedback from group members, and acts on positive suggestions, much like 360-degree feedback. One study looked at the annual administrations of a program in which 252 managers conducted feedback sessions with the work group. The researchers found that managers who met with their direct reports and discussed the feedback improved in terms of ratings by group members. Managers who only read the feedback reports without participating in these group discussions showed much less improvement.[25]

5. *Demonstrates a strong customer orientation.* Effective leaders show commitment to satisfying the needs of customers and clients. Their strong customer orientation helps inspire employees toward satisfying customers. John Chambers the CEO and chair of Cisco Systems is a prime example. He spends one third of his working hours visiting customers, earning a reputation as a leading salesperson for the Internet.

6. *Recovers quickly from setbacks.* Effective managerial leaders are resilient: They bounce back quickly from setbacks such as budget cuts, demotions, and being fired. Leadership resiliency serves as a positive model for employees at all levels when the organization confronts difficult times. During such times effective leaders sprinkle their speech with clichés such as "Tough times don't last, but tough people do," or "When times get tough, the tough get going." Delivered with sincerity, such messages are inspirational to many employees.

7. *Plays the role of servant leader.* Some effective leaders believe that their primary mission is to serve the needs of their constituents. Instead of seeking individual recognition, servant leaders see themselves as working for the group members. The servant leader uses his or her talents to help group members. For example, if the leader happens to be a good planner, he engages in planning because it will help the group achieve its goals.[26] H. Ross Perot, the business executive who ran for president of the United States twice, said he would become a servant leader if elected to office. Many academic administrators see themselves as servant leaders; they take care of administrative work so instructors can devote more time to teaching and scholarship. To be an effective servant leader, a person needs the many leadership traits and behaviors described in this chapter.

4   LEADERSHIP STYLES

Describe the leadership continuum, Theory X and Theory Y, Leadership Grid, situational, and entrepreneurial styles of leadership.

leadership style

The typical pattern of behavior that a leader uses to influence his or her employees to achieve organizational goals.

Another important part of the leadership function is **leadership style**. It is the typical pattern of behavior that a leader uses to influence his or her employees to achieve organizational goals. Several different approaches to describing leadership styles have developed over the years. Most of these involve how much authority and control the leader turns over to the group.

First, this section will describe two classical approaches for categorizing leadership styles. We will then discuss the Leadership Grid® styles of leadership, followed by the situational theory of leadership, which emphasizes its contingency nature. We will also describe the entrepreneurial leadership style. The skill-building exercise at the end of the chapter gives you a chance to measure certain aspects of your leadership style.

The Leadership Continuum

The leadership continuum, or classical approach, classifies leaders according to how much authority they retain for themselves versus how much they turn over to a group. Three key points on the continuum represent autocratic, participative, and free-rein styles of leadership. Exhibit 11-5 illustrates the leadership continuum.

Autocratic Leadership Style

Autocratic leaders retain most of the authority for themselves. They make decisions in a confident manner and assume that group members will comply. An autocratic leader is not usually concerned with the group members' attitudes toward the decision. Autocratic leaders are considered task-oriented because they place heavy emphasis on getting tasks accomplished. Typical autocratic leaders tell people what to do, assert themselves, and serve as models for group members.

Autocratic leaders are not inevitably mean and insensitive, yet many are difficult people. One of the most demanding, insensitive leaders of a successful enterprise is Robert Crandall, the retired chairman of American Airlines. His uncompromising attitude made him disliked by labor unions, pilots, and nonflight personnel. Crandall cursed incessantly and regularly called weekend meetings with managers.[27]

Participative Leadership Style

A **participative leader** is one who shares decision making with group members. Three closely related subtypes of participative leaders include consultative, consensus, and democratic. *Consultative leaders* confer with subordinates before making a decision. However, they retain the final authority to make decisions. Consensus leaders encourage group discussion about an issue and then make a decision that reflects the general opinion (consensus) of group members. All workers who will be involved in the consequences of a decision have an opportunity to provide input. A decision is not considered final until all parties involved agree with the decision. *Democratic leaders* confer final authority on the group. They function as collectors of opinion and take a vote before making a decision.

Participative leadership takes many forms, including the employee involvement typical of teams in an organization practicing quality management. The grassroots approach to leadership at Ford, described in the section about empowerment, is an example of a systematic approach to participative leadership.

Free-Rein Leadership Style

The **free-rein leader** turns over virtually all authority and control to the group. Leadership is provided indirectly rather than directly. Group members presented with a task must determine on their own the best way to perform it. The leader

autocratic leader

A task-oriented leader who retains most of the authority for himself or herself and is not generally concerned with group members' attitudes toward decisions.

297

participative leader

A leader who shares decision making with group members.

free-rein leader

A leader who turns over virtually all authority and control to the group.

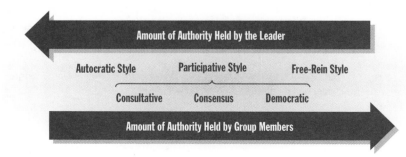

EXHIBIT 11-5

The Leadership Continuum

According to the leadership continuum, the autocratic style gives the leader the most authority, whereas the free-rein style gives group members most of the authority.

does not get involved unless requested. Subordinates are allowed all the freedom they want as long as they do not violate company policy. In short, the free-rein leader delegates completely.

Theory X and Theory Y

Autocratic and participative leaders see people differently. This difference in perception is the basis for the Theory X and Theory Y explanation of leadership style, as summarized in Exhibit 11-6. Douglas McGregor developed these distinctions to help managers critically examine their assumptions about workers. Theory X and Theory Y form part of the foundation of the human relations approach to management.

Although Theory X and Theory Y tend to get less and less ink in management books today, the ideas are still relevant. Many leaders and managers stop to examine the assumptions they make about group members in order to manage more effectively. In contrast, leaders and managers who do not assess their assumptions might make errors in attempting to lead others. For example, a manager might wrongly assume that group members are all motivated primarily by money.

Leadership Grid Leadership Styles

Several approaches to understanding leadership styles focus on two major dimensions of leadership: tasks and relationships. The best known of these approaches is the **Leadership Grid**. It is based on different integrations of the leader's concern for production (tasks) and people (relationships). As Exhibit 11-7 shows, grid terms are levels of concern on a scale of 1 to 9, with concern for production listed first and concern for people listed second. The Leadership Grid is part of a comprehensive program of leadership training and organizational development.

Leadership Grid

A visual representation of different combinations of a leader's degree of concern for task-related issues.

EXHIBIT 11-6

Theory X and Theory Y

According to Douglas McGregor, leadership approaches are influenced by a leader's assumptions about human nature. Managers make two contrasting assumptions about workers: **Theory X Assumptions.** Managers who accept Theory X believe that:

1. The average person dislikes work and will avoid it if possible.
2. Because of this dislike of work, most people must be coerced, controlled, directed, or threatened with punishment to get them to put forth enough effort to achieve organizational objectives.
3. The average employee prefers to be directed, wishes to shirk responsibility, has relatively little ambition, and puts a high value on security.

Theory Y Assumptions. Managers who accept Theory Y believe the statements in the list that follows. Equally important, these managers diagnose a situation to learn what type of people they are supervising.

1. The expenditure of physical and mental effort in work is as natural as play or rest for the average human being.
2. People will exercise self-direction and self-control to achieve objectives to which they are committed.
3. Commitment to objectives is related to the rewards associated with their achievement.
4. The average person learns, under proper conditions, not only to accept but to seek responsibility.
5. Many employees have the capacity to exercise a high degree of imagination, ingenuity, and creativity in the solution of organizational problems.
6. Under the present conditions of industrial life, the intellectual potential of the average person is only partially utilized.

Source: Adapted from Douglas McGregor, *The Human Side of Enterprise* (New York: McGraw-Hill, 1960), pp. 33–48.

Concern for production is rated on the Grid's horizontal axis. Concern for production includes results, bottom line, performance, profits, and mission. Concern for people is rated on the vertical axis, and it includes concern for group members and coworkers. Both concerns are leadership attitudes or ways of thinking about leadership. The Grid identifies seven styles, yet a leader's approach could fall into any of 81 positions on the Grid.

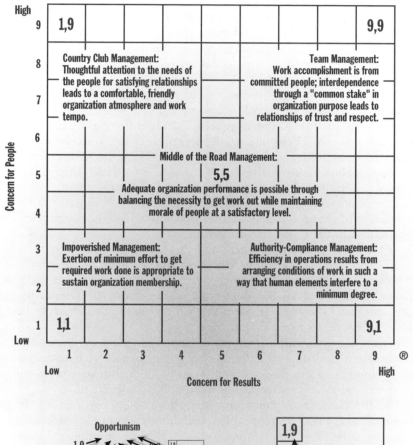

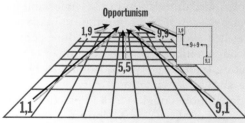

In Opportunistic Management, people adapt and shift to any Grid style needed to gain the maximum advantage. Performance occurs according to a system of selfish gain. Effort is given only for an advantage for personal gain.

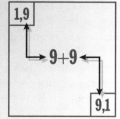

9+9 Paternalism/Maternalism
Reward and approval are bestowed to people in return for loyalty and obedience; failure to comply leads to punishment.

Source: The Leadership Grid® Figure, Paternalism Figure, and Opportunism Figure from *Leadership Dilemmas—Grid Solutions,* by Robert R. Blake and Anne Adams McCanse (formerly The Managerial Grid by Robert R. Blake and Jane S. Mouton). Houston: Gulf Publishing Company, (Grid Figure: p. 29, Paternalism Figure: p. 30, Opportunism Figure: p. 31). Copyright 1991 by Scientific Methods, Inc. Reproduced by permission of the owners.

situational leadership model

An explanation of leadership that matches leadership style to the readiness of group members.

task behavior

The extent to which the leader spells out the duties and responsibilities of an individual or group.

relationship behavior

The extent to which the leader engages in two-way or multi-way communication.

readiness

In situational leadership, the extent to which a group member has the ability and willingness or confidence to accomplish a specific task.

The developers of the grid argue strongly for the value of team management (9,9). According to their research, the team management approach pays off. It results in improved performance, low absenteeism and turnover, and high morale. Team management relies on trust and respect, which help bring about good results.[28]

The Situational Leadership Model

In another major perspective on leadership, effective leaders adapt their style to the requirements of the situation. The characteristics of the group members comprise one key requirement. The **situational leadership model** of Paul Hersey and Kenneth H. Blanchard explains how to match leadership style to the readiness of group members.[29] The situational leadership training program is widely used in business because it offers leaders practical suggestions for dealing with everyday leadership problems.

Basics of the Model

Leadership in the situational model is classified according to the relative amount of task and relationship behavior the leader engages in. **Task behavior** is the extent to which the leader spells out the duties and responsibilities of an individual or group. **Relationship behavior** is the extent to which the leader engages in two-way or multi-way communication. It includes such activities as listening, providing encouragement, and coaching. As Exhibit 11-8 shows, the situational model places combinations of task and relationship behaviors into four quadrants. Each quadrant calls for a different leadership style.

The situational leadership model states there is no one best way to influence group members. The most effective leadership style depends on the readiness level of group members. **Readiness** in situational leadership is defined as the extent to which a group member has the ability and willingness or confidence to accomplish a specific task. The concept of readiness is therefore not a characteristic, trait, or motive—it relates to a specific task.

Readiness has two components, ability and willingness. Ability is the knowledge, experience, and skill an individual or group brings to a particular task or activity. Willingness is the extent to which an individual or group has the confidence, commitment, and motivation to accomplish a specific task.

Within the context of situational leadership theory, as a group member's readiness increases, a leader should rely more on relationship behavior and less on task behavior. When a group member becomes ready, a minimum of task or relationship behavior is required of the leader. Notice that in the readiness condition R4 (as shown in Exhibit 11-8), the group member is able and willing or confident. The manager therefore uses a delegating leadership style (quadrant 4). He or she turns over responsibility for decisions and implementation.

For an example of how the situational model might work in practice, consider the leadership and management approach used by Lois Melbourne, the CEO of TimeVision Inc. of Irving, Texas, in selecting a new salesperson. When the company needed to add to its 20-person sales staff, Melbourne assigned the task to two of her salespeople. They created the job specification, posted it online, reviewed résumés, conducted interviews, and made the final recommendation. A TimeVision manager did not get involved until salary negotiations, and Melbourne did not see the sales rep until her first day on the job. Melbourne used the *delegating* leadership style because she believed that her salespeople were competent and motivated enough to handle this personnel assignment by themselves.[30]

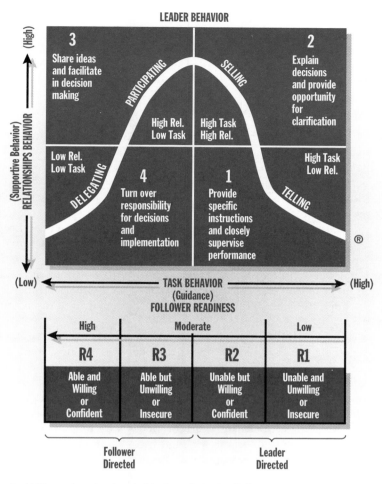

EXHIBIT 11-8

The Situational Model of
Leadership

301

Evaluation of the Situational Model

The situational model represents a consensus of thinking about leadership behavior in relation to group members: Competent people require less specific direction than do less competent people. The situational model also supports common sense and is therefore appealing. A manager can benefit from the model by attempting to diagnose the readiness of group members before choosing the right leadership style.

The model presents categories and guidelines so precisely that it gives the impression of infallibility. In reality, leadership situations are less clear-cut than the four quadrants suggest. Also, the prescriptions for leadership will work only some of the time. For example, many supervisors use a telling style with unable and unwilling or insecure team members (R1) and still achieve poor results.

The Entrepreneurial Leadership Style

Interest in entrepreneurial leadership continues to grow as start-up companies and other small enterprises become an important source of new employment. Corporate giants like AT&T and GE continue to shrink in terms of number of people employed, often outsourcing both manufacturing and services to smaller companies. Small businesses account for 47 percent of all sales in the United States.

Managers who initiate one or more innovative business enterprises show some similarity in leadership style. In overview, they tend to be task-oriented and charismatic. Entrepreneurs often possess the following personal characteristics and behaviors:

1. *A strong achievement need.* Entrepreneurs have stronger achievement needs than most managers. Building a business is an excellent vehicle for accomplishment. The high achiever shows three consistent behaviors and attitudes. He or she (a) takes personal responsibility to solve problems, (b) attempts to achieve moderate goals at moderate risks, and (c) prefers situations that provide frequent feedback on results (readily found in starting a new enterprise).[31]

2. *High enthusiasm and creativity.* Related to the achievement need, entrepreneurs are typically enthusiastic and creative. Their enthusiasm in turn makes them persuasive. As a result, entrepreneurs are often perceived as charismatic by their employees and customers. Henry Yeun, a past winner of the National Entrepreneur of the Year Award, says that an entrepreneurial leader is "genetically inclined to be an optimist."[32] Some entrepreneurs are so emotional that they are regarded as eccentric.

3. *Always in a hurry.* Entrepreneurs are always in a hurry. When engaged in one meeting, their minds typically begin to focus on the next meeting. Their flurry of activity rubs off on subordinates and others around them. Entrepreneurs often adopt a simple style of dressing to save time. A male entrepreneur may wear slip-on shoes so he doesn't have to bother with laces in the morning. A female entrepreneur may wear an easy-to-maintain short haircut.

4. *Visionary perspective.* Successful entrepreneurs carefully observe the world around them, in constant search for their next big marketable idea. They see opportunities others fail to observe. One example is Andy Taylor, who founded Enterprise Rent-a-Car. The opportunity he saw was to build a car rental agency that specialized in renting cars to airline travelers and people whose car was being repaired. Enterprise is now a major player in the car rental business.

5. *Uncomfortable with hierarchy and bureaucracy.* Entrepreneurs, by temperament, are not ideally suited to working within the mainstream of a bureaucracy. Many successful entrepreneurs are people who were frustrated by the constraints of a bureaucratic system. Once the typical entrepreneur launches a successful business, he or she would be wise to hire a professional manager to take over the internal workings of the firm. The entrepreneur would then be free to concentrate on making sales, raising capital, and pursuing other external contacts.

6. *A much stronger interest in dealing with customers than employees.* One of the reasons entrepreneurs have difficulty with bureaucracy is that they focus their energies on products, services, and customers. Some entrepreneurs are gracious to customers and moneylenders but brusque with company insiders.

The preceding list implies that it is difficult to find a classic entrepreneur who is also a good organizational manager. Many successful entrepreneurs therefore hire professional managers to help them maintain what they (the entrepreneurs) have built. Dineh Mohajer, the cofounder of Hard Candy, the upscale cosmetics firm, hired a professional manager to help her manage the enterprise she created.

Leadership styles relate directly to the leadership behavior of adaptability to the situation. After the Hay/McBer consulting firm studied the leadership styles of 3,871 executives, they revealed that leaders who achieve the best results do not stick with one leadership style. The effective executive selects the best style to fit a given situation, much like a golf player selecting the most appropriate club for a particular shot. The study looked at styles similar to the styles and influence tactics already mentioned in this chapter including coercive, authoritative, or democratic. An example of a leader fitting his style to the situation was "Tom," the vice president of marketing for a pizza chain. The chain was floundering, and the company held regular meetings to attempt to repair the damage. So Tom made a decisive move.

During a meeting he made an impassioned plea for his colleagues to think about pizza from the customer's perspective, and to strive for convenience. With his enthusiasm and clear vision, Tom filled a leadership vacuum at the company. Convenience became part of the mission statement, and it motivated pizza store operators to make buying pizza easier for customers. One such convenience was operating kiosks on busy street corners. Tom's shift to an authoritative styled saved the company.[33]

TRANSFORMATIONAL AND CHARISMATIC LEADERSHIP   **5**

Describe transformational and charismatic leadership.

The study of leadership often emphasizes the **transformational leader**—one who helps organizations and people make positive changes in the way they do things. Transformational leadership combines charisma, inspirational leadership, and intellectual stimulation. It plays an especially critical role in the revitalization of existing business organizations. The transformational leader develops new visions for the organization and mobilizes employees to accept and work toward attaining these visions. Research indicates that the transformational style of leader, in contrast to a more traditional leader, actually does improve business-unit performance.[34] This section will describe how transformations take place, the role of charisma, how to become charismatic, and the downside of charismatic leadership.

transformational leader

A leader who helps organizations and people make positive changes in the way they do things.

How Transformations Take Place

The transformational leader attempts to overhaul the organizational culture or subculture. To bring about the overhaul, transformations take place in one or more of three ways.[35] First, the transformational leader raises people's awareness of the importance and value of certain rewards and how to achieve them. In addition to pointing out the pride workers would experience if the firm became number one in its field, the leader would highlight the accompanying financial rewards.

Second, the transformational leader gets people to look beyond their self-interests for the sake of the work group and the firm. Such a leader might say, "I know you would like more support workers. But, if we don't cut expenses, we'll all be out of a job." Third, the transformational leader helps people go beyond a focus on minor satisfactions to a quest for self-fulfillment. He or she might explain, "I know that a long lunch break is nice. But, just think, if we get this project done on time, we'll be the envy of the company."

During the downturn in high-technology firms during 2001–2002, many leaders of these firms attempted to become transformational leaders. A good example is Ted Waitt of Gateway, described in the introduction to this chapter.

Upon his return, Waitt changed the management team, and refocused the company on the path that had brought it success in the past: emphasizing direct sales of computers to consumers.

The Link Between Charisma and Transformational Leadership

charisma

The ability to lead or influence others based on personal charm, magnetism, inspiration, and emotion.

Transformational leaders typically have **charisma**, the ability to lead or influence others based on personal charm, magnetism, inspiration, and emotion. To label a leader as charismatic does not mean that everybody shares that opinion. Even the most popular and inspiring leaders are perceived negatively by some members of their organization. Exhibit 11-9 presents glimpses of well-publicized managers who are perceived by many to have charisma.

Transformational and charismatic leaders have the characteristics and behaviors described at the start of the chapter. The list that follows presents transformational leaders' qualities that relate specifically to charisma.[36]

EXHIBIT 11-9

Examples of Charismatic Leadership

The leaders mentioned here are perceived as charismatic by many work associates. To the right of each person mentioned is an example of their charismatic behavior, or its impact on others.

Leader and Organization	Sample of Charismatic Behavior or Reactions from Others
Kim Polese, CEO and cofounder of Marimba Inc., an Internet software company	Mobbed by autograph seekers at trade shows, she grabs the spotlight when possible. Takes risks by investing money in new personnel before business orders have been received. Her charm and wisdom attract investors.
Steve Jobs, cofounder of Apple Computer Inc., and now CEO. Also CEO of Pixar Animation Studios	Projects great visions which inspire people to work 80 hours per week, and gets wealthy investors, including Bill Gates, to pour millions into his ventures. A folk hero among thousands of information technology fans. His followers admire Jobs even when Apple stumbles.
Willy C. Shih, digital imaging executive at Eastman Kodak Co.	So excited about his products that he often snaps digital images of visitors and follows up by sending them e-mails of these images. Combines personal flair with excellent marketing strategy.
Martha R. Ingram, CEO of Ingram Industries, Inc., wholesale distributor of books and other information products	Uses her gracious southern charm to win the confidence of customers, as she cuts billion-dollar deals to strengthen the Ingram empire.
Herb Kelleher, CEO, Southwest Airlines (retired)	Engages in zany antics such as singing and dancing on the job, and kissing both male and female employees to encourage fun on the job. Projects personal belief that a positive attitude toward customer service leads to competitive advantage. His approach to leadership and the success of his company, along with his personality, have made him a favorite of management experts. He is cited and quoted in hundreds of articles and books about management.

1. *Vision.* Charismatic leaders offer an exciting image of where the organization is headed and how to get there. A vision is more than a forecast, because it describes an ideal version of the future for an organization or organizational unit.

2. *Extraversion and agreeableness.* A study based on leaders in more than 200 organizations found that transformational leaders scored high on the personality traits of extraversion and agreeableness (from the five-factor model described in Chapter 10). Being extraverted and agreeable contributes to transformational leadership, but is of course not sufficient to make one a transformational leader.

3. *Masterful communication style.* To inspire people, charismatic and transformational leaders use colorful language and exciting metaphors and analogies. The CEO of Coca-Cola (and his predecessors) tells people, "We give people around the world a moment of pleasure in their daily lives." Another key aspect of the communication style of transformational leaders is that they tell captivating stories that relate to the goals of the firm. For example, some leaders use the fairy tale "The Three Little Pigs" to illustrate how business firms must make products and services stronger to withstand competitive force.

4. *Inspires trust.* People believe so strongly in the integrity of charismatic leaders that they will risk their careers to pursue the leader's vision.

5. *Helps group members feel capable.* A technique that charismatic leaders often use to boost their followers' self-images is to let them achieve success on relatively easy projects. The group members are then praised and given more-demanding assignments.

6. *Energy and action orientation.* Similar to entrepreneurs, most charismatic leaders are energetic and serve as a model for getting things done on time.

7. *Intellectual stimulation to others.* Transformational leaders actively encourage group members to look at old problems or methods in new ways. They emphasize getting people to rethink problems and reexamine old assumptions.

8. *Inspiring leadership.* Partly as a result of the seven preceding characteristics, transformational and charismatic leaders emotionally arouse people to the point that they want to achieve higher goals than they thought of previously. In short, the charismatic leader stands as an inspiration to many others.

A new perspective believes transformational and charismatic leaders exert their biggest impact on the performance of a firm during conditions of uncertainty. Uncertain conditions would include disruptive technology eating into market share, or a firm facing charges of unfair competition. The importance of charismatic leadership during times of uncertainty was indicated by the opinions of senior executives in large corporations.[37] However, this study should not be interpreted to mean that charismatic leadership is valuable *only* in an uncertain environment.

Developing Charisma

Managers can improve their image as charismatic by engaging in favorable interactions with group members through a variety of techniques.[38] A starting point is to *use visioning.* Develop a dream about the future of your unit and discuss it with others. *Make frequent use of metaphors.* Develop metaphors to inspire the people around you. A commonly used one after the group has experienced a substantial setback is to say, "Like the phoenix, we will rise from the ashes of defeat." It is important to *inspire trust and confidence*. Get people to believe in your competence by making your accomplishments known in a polite, tactful way.

Remember to *make others feel capable* by giving out assignments on which others can succeed, and lavishly praising their success. *Be highly energetic and goal oriented* so your energy and resourcefulness become contagious. To increase your energy supply, exercise frequently, eat well, and get ample rest. It is important to *express your emotions frequently*. Freely express warmth, joy, happiness, and enthusiasm. *Smile frequently*, even if you are not in a happy mood. A warm smile indicates a confident, caring person, which contributes to perceptions of charisma. *Make everybody you meet feel important*. For example, at a company meeting shake the hand of every person you meet.

A relatively easy characteristic to develop is to *multiply the effectiveness of your handshake*. Shake firmly without creating pain, and make enough eye contact to notice the color of the other person's eyes. When you take that much trouble, you project care and concern. Finally, *stand up straight and use nonverbal signs of self-confidence*. Practice good posture and minimize fidgeting and speaking in a monotone.

The Downside of Charismatic Leadership

Charismatic business leaders are seen as corporate heroes when they can turn around a failing business or launch a new enterprise. Nevertheless, this type of leadership has a dark side. Some charismatic leaders manipulate and take advantage of people, such as by getting them to invest retirement savings in risky company stock. Some charismatic leaders are unethical and lead their organizations toward illegal and immoral ends. People are willing to follow the charismatic leader down a quasi-legal path because of his or her charisma. Frank Lorenzo, the former top executive at Eastern Airlines (now defunct) and Continental Airlines, had charismatic appeal to some people. He was able to attract enough followers to support his plan to crush the labor unions at both airlines and sell off valuable assets. Lorenzo ultimately walked away from a financially troubled Continental, manipulating a settlement of $30 million for himself.

6   THE LEADER AS A MENTOR

Explain the leadership role of mentoring.

mentor

A more experienced person who develops a protégé's abilities through tutoring, coaching, guidance, and emotional support.

Another vital part of leadership is directly assisting less experienced workers to improve their job performance and advance their careers. A **mentor** is a more experienced person who develops a protégé's abilities through tutoring, coaching, guidance, and emotional support. The idea of mentoring traces back to ancient Greece when a warrior entrusted his son to the tutor Mentor. Although never out of style, mentoring is more important than ever as workers face complex and rapidly changing job demands.

The mentor, a trusted counselor and guide, is typically a person's manager or team leader. However, a mentor can also be a staff professional or coworker. A mentor is usually somebody who works for the same employer, yet many people are advised and coached by somebody outside their organization. Mentors are typically within the field of expertise of the protégé, but can also come from another specialty. For example, an accountant might be mentored by a manufacturing manager. A leader can be a mentor to several people at the same time, and successful individuals often have several mentors during their career.

Helping the protégé solve problems is an important part of mentoring. Mentors help their protégés solve problems by themselves and make their own discoveries. A comment frequently made to mentors is, "I'm glad you made me think through the problem by myself. You put me on the right track." A mentor can also give specific assistance in technical problem solving. If the mentor knows more about the new technology than the protégé, he or she can shorten the person's learning time. Many developments in information technology are likely to be taught by a coworker serving as a mentor, because a manager often has less current technology knowledge than a group member.

Mentoring has traditionally been an informal relationship based on compatibility between two personalities. As with other trusted friends, good chemistry should exist between the mentor and the protégé. Many mentoring programs assign a mentor to selected new employees. One study found that 31 out of 79 supervisor protégés were assigned a mentor.[39] Many formal mentoring programs began during the push for affirmative action in the 1970s. In the current era, formal mentors often supplement the work of managers by assisting a newcomer to acquire job skills and understand the organization culture.

Many career-minded people hire their own outside coaches to substitute for or supplement other forms of mentoring. The coach acts essentially like a personal trainer for one's career. The business coach listens carefully and gives emotional support and objective feedback to the client.[40] As such, the paid coach is much like a mentor. For higher-level managers, the company often pays for the coach because coaching can be a valuable form of leadership development. Here is an example of advice given to his middle-manager client by a business coach:

> I've watched you in action as a leader, and I've spoken to a few of your direct reports. Your biggest issue as a leader is that you are losing the personal touch. You spend far too much time sorting through e-mail and doing analytical work. You need to get out and communicate more directly with your team.

Mentoring has been noted for its importance in helping minorities advance in their careers. A study of 280 minority senior managers making at least $100,000 in annual salary found that those with supportive superiors and coworkers (part of mentoring) showed faster total compensation growth and progressed more rapidly through the organization. The study also found that it was important for the mentor to be sufficiently highly placed in the organization to make an impact. The director of the study listed several actions that can help minority managers (as well as majority managers) advance:[41]

- Develop or build on good relationships with superiors and request feedback on performance at least once a year.
- Find and identify an informal mentor who is willing to be an advocate for your upward mobility within the organization, help you learn the informal rules of the workplace, and help you make valuable contacts.
- Identify the informal rules of the company that are helpful in navigating through the organization. (An example would be "Never turn down a request from upper management.")
- Build a set of self-management skills, including the ability to overcome potential roadblocks, remain focused on tasks, and assign priorities to tasks. (See Chapter 17.)

The link between the behaviors and competencies just mentioned and mentoring is that the leader/mentor can help the protégé achieve them. Being a good mentor therefore enables the leader to develop group members.

Mentors have similarly played a critical role in the success of women in organizations. Long-term research by the nonprofit organization, Catalyst, concludes that to succeed, women need visibility (being noticed by key people), networking, and mentoring. So a leader who wants a woman to advance, should be her mentor, or help her find another mentor.[42]

7   LEADERSHIP SKILLS

Identify the skills that contribute to leadership.

As already explained, leadership involves personal qualities, behaviors, and skills. A skill refers to a present capability, such as being able to resolve conflict or create a vision statement. Many of these leadership skills have been mentioned or implied throughout the book. A prime example would be the five general skills for managers described in Chapter 1: technical, interpersonal, conceptual, diagnostic, and political. For example, to exercise strategic leadership a manager would need to have strong conceptual skills. To inspire people, a leader would need interpersonal skills, and to negotiate well, he or she would need good political skills. To be an effective face-to-face leader, the manager would need coaching skills, as described in Chapter 16.

The leadership roles presented in Chapter 1 directly associated with leadership skills are as follows: negotiator, coach, team builder, technical problem solver, and entrepreneur. The following checklist provides some additional skills that can contribute to leadership effectiveness, depending on the people and the task.

- Sizing up situations in order to apply the best leadership approach
- Exerting influence through various approaches such as rational persuasion, inspirational appeal, and being assertive
- Motivating team members through such specific techniques as goal setting and positive reinforcement
- Motivating people from diverse cultures and nations
- Resolving conflict with superiors and group members
- Solving problems creatively in ways that point group members in new directions
- Developing a mission statement that inspires others to perform well

As implied by this discussion, leadership involves dozens of different skills. An effective manager's toolkit combines various skills according to the leader's needs and the situation. Holding a leadership position offers a wonderful opportunity for personal growth through skill development.

SUMMARY OF KEY POINTS

1 Differentiate between leadership and management. Management is a set of explicit tools and techniques, based on reasoning and testing that can be used in a variety of situations. Leadership is concerned with vision, change, motivation, persuasion, creativity, and influence.

2 Describe how leaders are able to influence and empower team members. Power is the ability to get other people to do things or the ability to control resources. Authority is the formal right to wield power. Six types of power include legitimate, reward, coercive, expert, referent (stemming from charisma), and subordinate. Through subordinate power, team members limit the authority of leaders. To get others to act, leaders also use tactics such as leading by example, leading by values, assertiveness, rationality, ingratiation, exchange, coalition formation, and joking and kidding.

Empowerment is the process of sharing power with team members to enhance their feelings of personal effectiveness. Empowerment increases employee motivation, because the employee is accepted as a partner in decision making.

3 **Identify important leadership characteristics and behaviors.** Certain personal characteristics are associated with successful managerial leadership in many situations, including the following: drive and achievement motive, and passion; power motive; self-confidence; trustworthiness and honesty; good intellectual ability, knowledge, and technical competence; sense of humor; and emotional intelligence.

Effective leaders need to demonstrate adaptability, stable performance, and high standards of performance, and provide emotional support to group members. They should give and accept feedback, exhibit a strong customer orientation, recover quickly from setbacks, and perhaps be a servant leader.

4 **Describe the leadership continuum, Theory X and Theory Y, Leadership Grid, situational, and entrepreneurial styles of leadership.** Leadership style is the typical pattern of behavior that a leader uses to influence employees to achieve organizational goals. Autocratic leaders attempt to retain most of the authority. Participative leaders share decision making with the group. One subtype of participative leader is the consultative leader, who involves subordinates in decision making but retains final authority. A consensus leader also involves subordinates in decision making and bases the final decision on group consensus. A democratic leader confers final authority on the group. Free-rein leaders turn over virtually all authority and control to the group.

The distinctions between Theory X and Theory Y are made to help managers critically examine their assumptions about workers. According to Theory X assumptions, people basically dislike work and need to be controlled. According to Theory Y assumptions, people enjoy their work and want to be self-directing.

The Leadership Grid classifies leaders according to how much concern they have for both production and people. Team management, with its high emphasis on production and people, is considered the ideal.

The situational leadership model explains how to match leadership style to the readiness of group members. The model classifies leadership style according to the relative amount of task and relationship behavior the leader engages in. Readiness refers to both ability and willingness to accomplish a specific task. As group member readiness increases, a reader should rely more on relationship behavior and less on task behavior. When a group member becomes very ready, however, minimum task or relationship behavior is required.

Entrepreneurial leaders are generally task-oriented and charismatic. They have a strong achievement need, high enthusiasm and creativity, and a visionary perspective. They are uncomfortable with hierarchy and bureaucracy and are always in a hurry.

5 **Describe transformational and charismatic leadership.** The transformational leader helps organizations and people make positive changes. He or she combines charisma, inspirational leadership, and intellectual stimulation. Transformations take place through such means as pointing to relevant rewards, getting people to look beyond self-interest, and encouraging people to work toward self-fulfillment. Charismatic leaders provide vision and masterful communication. They can inspire trust and help people feel capable, and they are action-oriented. Some charismatic leaders are unethical and use their power to accomplish illegal and immoral ends.

6 **Explain the leadership role of mentoring.** Mentoring is more important than ever as workers face complex and rapidly changing job demands. Mentors can be higher-ranking individuals, coworkers, or people outside the organization or from another specialty. Mentors help protégés solve problems by themselves and make their own discoveries. Mentoring can share an informal or formal relationship, and has been noted for its importance in helping minorities and women advance their careers.

7 **Identify the skills that contribute to leadership.** To be an effective leader, a manager must possess a wide variety of skills, many of which are described throughout this chapter and this book. Among these diverse skills are exerting influence, motivating others, and solving problems creatively.

KEY TERMS AND PHRASES

Leadership, *286*

Power, *288*

Authority, *288*

Zone of Indifference, *289*

Coalition, *290*

Achievement motivation, *291*

Power motivation, *292*

Open-book company, *292*

Leadership style, *296*

Autocratic leader, *297*

Participative leader, *297*

Free-rein leader, *297*

Leadership Grid, *298*

Situational leadership model, *300*

Task behavior, *300*

Relationship behavior, *300*

Readiness, *300*

Transformational leader, *303*

Charisma, *304*

Mentor, *306*

QUESTIONS

1. Describe how a businessperson could be an effective leader yet an ineffective manager. Also describe how a businessperson could be an effective manager yet an ineffective leader.

2. If Ted Waitt of Gateway is such an inspiring leader, why has the company struggled with many of the same problems as other manufacturers of desktop computers?

3. Which influence tactics do you think would be particularly well suited to influencing an intelligent and well-educated person? Explain your reasoning.

4. Identify and describe the behavior of a public figure who appears to have low emotional intelligence. Do you think the person can be helped?

5. Many career counselors believe that if a person spends too many years working for a large corporation, he or she becomes unable to exercise entrepreneurial leadership. Why might this observation be true?

6. For what type of leadership situation might a transformational leader be inappropriate?

7. New hires for technical and professional positions at many companies are assigned a mentor, in addition to having a manager. In what way might this practice be less effective than finding a mentor by oneself?

CRITICAL THINKING QUESTIONS

1. Leaders in prominent positions, such as Bill Gates at Microsoft, are liked by many people yet disliked by many others. Many Web sites are dedicated to negative comments about Gates, and cartoon depictions of him are often unfriendly. How do you think prominent leaders deal with such criticism and negative portrayals?

2. Suppose you believed that you would be more effective as a leader if you were more charismatic. What would be a realistic action plan for you to begin this month to become more charismatic?

SKILL-BUILDING EXERCISE: What Style of Leader Are You?

Directions: Answer the following questions, keeping in mind what you have done, or think you would do in the scenarios and attitudes described.

	Mostly True	Mostly False
1. I am more likely to take care of a high-impact assignment myself than turn it over to a group member.	___	___
2. I would prefer the analytical aspects of a manager's job rather than working directly with group members.	___	___
3. An important part of my approach to managing a group is to keep the members informed almost daily of any information that could affect their work.	___	___
4. It is a good idea to give two people in the group the same problem, and then choose what appears to be the best solution.	___	___
5. It makes good sense for the leader or manager to stay somewhat aloof from the group, in order to make a tough decision when necessary.	___	___
6. I look for opportunities to obtain group input before making a decision, even on straightforward issues.	___	___
7. I would reverse a decision if several of the group members presented evidence that I was wrong.	___	___
8. Differences of opinion in the work group are healthy.	___	___

9. I think that activities to build team spirit, like the team fixing up a poor family's house on a Saturday, are an excellent investment of time.

10. If my group were hiring a new member, I would like the person to be interviewed by the entire group. ____ ____

11. An effective team leader today uses e-mail for about 98 percent of communication with team members. ____ ____

12. Some of the best ideas are likely to come from the group members rather than the manager. ____ ____

13. If our group were going to have a banquet, I would seek input from each member on what type of food should be served. ____ ____

14. I have never seen a statue of a committee in a museum or park, so why bother making decisions by committee if you want to be recognized? ____ ____

15. I dislike it intensely when a group member challenges my position on an issue. ____ ____

16. I typically explain to group members how (what method they should use) to accomplish an assigned task. ____ ____

17. If I were out of the office for a week, most of the important work in the department would get accomplished anyway. ____ ____

18. Delegation of important tasks is something that would be (or is) very difficult for me. ____ ____

19. When a group member comes to me with a problem, I tend to jump right in with a proposed solution. ____ ____

20. When a group member comes to me with a problem, I typically ask that person something like, "What alternative solutions have you thought of so far?" ____ ____

Scoring and Interpretation: The answers in the participative/team-style leader direction are as follows:
Mostly True: 3, 6, 7, 8, 9, 10, 12, 13, 17, 20
Mostly False: 1, 2, 4, 5, 11, 14, 15, 16, 18, 19

Skill development: The quiz you just completed is also an opportunity for skill development. Review the 20 questions and look for implied suggestions for engaging in participative leadership. For example, question 20 suggests that you encourage group members to work through their own solutions to problems. If your goal is to become an authoritarian leader, the questions can also serve as useful guidelines. For example, question 19 suggests that an authoritarian leader looks first to solve problems for group members.

INTERNET SKILL-BUILDING EXERCISE: Charisma Tips from the Net

A section in this chapter offered suggestions for becoming more charismatic. Search the Internet for additional suggestions and compare them to the suggestions in the text. Be alert to contradictions, and offer a possible explanation for them. You might want to classify the suggestions into two categories: those dealing with the inner person, and those dealing with more superficial aspects of behavior. A suggestion of more depth would be to become a visionary, and a suggestion of less depth would be to wear eye-catching clothing.

Use a search phrase such as "How to become more charismatic." An all-encompassing phrase such as "developing leadership effectiveness" is unlikely to direct you to the information you need. You might consult a search engine and look for information about developing charisma.

CASE PROBLEM 11-A: "Carly" Attempts a Big Overhaul at Hewlett-Packard

Carly Fiorina, the chair and CEO of Hewlett-Packard (HP), has been designated by *Fortune* magazine as the most powerful woman in business for three consecutive years. To her, "A Company is an organic, living, breathing thing, not just an income sheet and balance sheet. You have to lead with that in mind." The criteria for being designated a powerful woman include the size and importance of the woman's business in the global economy, her clout outside the company, her career accomplishments (past, present, and potential), as well as her influence on mass culture and society.

Fiorina holds an MBA from the University of Maryland and an M.S. from MIT. She once worked as a secretary at HP before joining AT&T in its Washington office, where she sold phone systems to the government.

Fiorina left an executive position at Lucent Technologies in fall 1999, and became the first female CEO of a major corporation—America's 13th largest, with close to $50 billion in annual sales. Fiorina is intent on transforming HP by inspiring 90,000 employees to change their ways of thinking and working to excel in the Internet age. In her definition, "Power is the

311

ability to change things." At the top of her agenda, Fiorina says, is promoting e-services—technologies that help companies with their own e-commerce initiatives.

When Fiorina was appointed as the new CEO of Hewlett-Packard, she insisted, "My gender is interesting, but it is not the story here." She preferred that the focus be on her considerable achievements as an executive with AT&T and its Lucent Technologies spinoff. From a purely business standpoint Fiorina was a logical choice to take over HP coming off a remarkable run as president of the Global Services division at Lucent. The division had $20 billion per year in sales. Fiorina shared responsibility for reengineering Lucent into a technology high flyer from what was once the telephone manufacturing division of AT&T. Similar to many major high-tech companies, Lucent's fortunes declined substantially in 2000. During her 20 years of technology experience, Fiorina had developed a track record of growing large businesses.

At HP, Fiorina faces a series of challenges as a company renowned for its engineering capability takes on fleet competitors like Dell and Sun Microsystems. As Fiorina assumed her new responsibilities, she said, "Clearly, we need to reinvigorate our sense of speed, our sense of urgency." Part of her leadership strategy is to help HP become more nimble and to compete more effectively in e-commerce. At the same time, Fiorina wants to retain Hewlett-Packard's greatest organizational strengths: its deep engineering roots and its dependability.

Another task CEO Fiorina has assumed is to craft a vision of HP as an Internet company that can pull together a vast range of products from inkjet cartridges to supercomputers for any customer that has to compete in the online and off-line worlds. "It's not rocket science that we have to be innovating at a rapid rate," says Fiorina. By 2001 Fiorina had forged deals with Yahoo and Oracle, signaling that she is serious about making HP a true Internet company.

Fiorina also sees the need for modifying the HP culture, which has overly emphasized teamwork and respect for coworkers. In recent years it translated into a bureaucratic, consensus-style culture with a sharp disadvantage in the Net-speed era. A consultant to HP says, "They have this ready, aim-aim-aim, fire culture. These days it has to be aim, fire, re-aim, re-fire." Fiorina believes that disposing of the counterproductive habits while retaining the good shouldn't be a problem. She plans to use a scalpel, not a machete. "Our people are very proud and smart. So, first, you reinforce the things that work, and then appeal to their brains to address what doesn't."

As a leader, Fiorina has a personal touch that inspires intense loyalty. She's known for giving balloons and flowers to employees who land big contracts. When the wife of a senior executive fell ill, Fiorina helped make sure she got medical service, doctors, and medical support. In addition to leadership ability, Fiorina is known for savvy marketing and sales techniques. She is also adept at pressing customers for an explanation of the real nature of their problem, so as to sell them what they need rather than what they ask for. An example is that a customer might be asking for the wrong type of server to solve their problem.

A key challenge Fiorina and her company faced in 2001, was dealing with a business downturn in the high-technology sector intensified by the September 11 attacks. She said, "Frankly, it was like somebody turned out the lights." Consumer spending had been lower than expected, "and our enterprise customers—responding to the growing economic uncertainty—have become increasingly cautious about information technology spending." Several times later that year, Fiorina continued to blame a slumping economy for less-than-anticipated sales growth. Company employees and outside financial analysts wondered what steps Fiorina and her management team might take to reenergize HP during a softening economy.

In 2001 Fiorina implemented a sweeping reorganization of the company. Hewlett-Packard had a 60-year-old decentralized structure, in which each product (such as PCs or printer cartridges) operated somewhat like a small company. Fiorina divided the company into three product development groups: printers, computers, and digital appliances. She divided sales and marketing into three groups: consumers, corporate markets, and consulting services. Far fewer HP managers now have direct contact with Fiorina.

Considerable confusion resulted from the sweeping changes in organization structure. A computer reseller said, "It's beyond my ability to communicate our frustration. It's painful to watch them screw up million-dollar deals." A sales representative from a company that sells Internet-related hardware that works with HP equipment reports going on a customer call at which sixteen HP staffers showed up. "The customer asked who in the room was from HP—and then said only three could stay."

Discussion Questions

1. How would you characterize Fiorina's leadership style?
2. Give Fiorina advice for changing Hewlett-Packard's organization structure.
3. Advise the HP board of directors on how much time Carly Fiorina should b e given to achieve her plans for improving the company.

Source: Patricia Sellers, "The 50 Most Powerful Women in Business: Secrets of the Fastest-Rising Stars," *Fortune*, October 16, 2000, pp. 131–132; Karl Taro Greenfield, "What Glass Ceiling?" *Time*, August 2, 1999, p. 72; Peter Burrows and Peter Elstrom, "The Boss," *Business Week*, August 2, 1999, pp. 76–84; http://www.time.com/time/digital50/17.html (accessed January 8, 2001); "Hewlett-Packard, Gateway Warn of Profits Downturn," Associated Press, January 12, 2001; Peter Burrows, "HP's Woes Are Deeper Than the Downturn," *Business Week*, May 7, 2001, p. 48.

CASE PROBLEM 11-B: The Sensational Michael Dell

Back in 1984, 19-year-old Michael Dell borrowed $1,000 to start a computer company from his University of Texas dormitory room. Today he is the fourth richest person in the United States, and the richest person in Texas. During a recent interview in a New York City hotel lobby, he calmly described how his computer company outperformed bigger rivals Compaq and IBM. "It makes you wonder whether we're doing well because we're doing a good job or because our competitors aren't doing a good job," Dell said in his monotone voice.

When photographed, Dell is usually wearing a business suit, and he lacks the eccentricities people often expect in an information-technology visionary. He is soft-spoken and does not enjoy small talk. He works standing at a podium desk, absorbed in and invigorated by his work. Dell is married with four children.

Through 2000, company sales were growing at a 50-percent annual rate, and Dell Computer stock has had one of the most rapid climbs in the history of American business (up by 63,000 percent in the 1990s). For these reasons Dell has been labeled as one of the most successful entrepreneurs in American history. Recently, Dell returned to the University of Texas to speak to an entrepreneurship class. A student asked the young multibillionaire, "Why don't you just sell out, buy a boat, and sail off to the Caribbean?" Dell stared at him and replied, "Sailing's *boring*. Do you have any idea how much fun it is to run a billion-dollar company?"

At age 36, Dell is the youngest and longest-serving chief of a big computer company, and he is the most imitated technology manager. (Other companies have imitated his direct selling and mass customization of computers.) Dell Computer has just edged out Compaq as the number-one U.S. seller of desktop computers. One after another, his biggest competitors—IBM, Hewlett-Packard, and Compaq—have been pounded by price-cutting wars in the computer business. As a result, they have been forced into profound changes in how they make and sell computers. Dell's strategy of selling most of its computers directly to the customer and eliminating the middle person has become an industry standard.

Having started out as a mail-order company, Dell deploys a direct salesforce to largely cut out the retailers, specialty stores, and distributors who can drive up prices. Annual sales total nearly $26 billion, making the company the world's biggest direct seller of computers. Dell Computer builds machines as customers order them. So instead of stockpiling products for distributors, the company can buy parts like disk drives and memory chips at the last minute. Inventory turnover at the company is seven days, compared with an industry average of about 80 days. The method saves money because component prices tend to fall many times

throughout the year. Dell often shares the savings with its customers. Dell's army of sales representatives are intensely devoted to selling Dell machines, typically working 70 hours per week. The reps with the biggest accounts earn six-figure incomes.

The lowest-priced Dell Computer is $900, including the monitor. Commenting on lower-priced machines, Dell says, "If you look at a lot of these low-priced machines, they might appear as a brilliant strategy to expand the market. But many of these machines are stockpiled older models that don't run a lot of new software."

As a college freshman, Dell began buying surplus PCs from dealers and embellishing them with graphics cards and other parts that appealed to the computer-savvy buyer. He sold $180,000 in computers in his first month of business, essentially by spotting a market niche. Dell says, "I saw that you'd buy a PC for about $3,000, and inside that PC was about $600 worth of parts." Dell hired a small staff and began selling his machines over the phone and through the mail. Several years later he created the industry's first on-site service program, in which the repair technician visits your office or home. Dell says, chuckling, "That was a pretty important plus because we didn't have any stores." Consumed by his business, Dell decided to postpone completing his formal education. Shortly after his 23rd birthday, Dell took his company public.

Dell Computer encountered troubles in 1993 when the company attempted to sell computers through retail stores and unsuccessfully launched its first laptops. To rebound, the company quickly refocused on its roots, and hired top industry managers to help run what had become a multibillion-dollar direct-sales business. A management consultant said, "Michael realized he needed professionals to run the company, so that he could continue to be a visionary." In 1996, Dell began a highly successful initiative of selling more powerful business machines, called servers, that run networks of desktops.

The company continues to expand its staff to fit its growth, and to prosper even when and where the computer industry runs into trouble. During the depths of the Asian economic crisis, Dell Computer was able to make money in the Far East, where sales were up by 77 percent in 1998. Dell explains that the cost and price advantages of the direct model allow for profit in any kind of market.

Dell's latest drive is boosting sales over the Internet. The company is already the biggest online seller of computers, with a remarkable $11 million per day in sales just three years after launching the Web store. The company is also trying to help its name catch up with its explosive sales. Recognizing that its image may not be as familiar as IBM or Compaq, Dell launched a major advertising campaign. Dell says in his laid-back manner, "We do see an opportunity to grow much faster in the market. Our focus is on the possibility, not just revenues."

Michael Dell believes that he built his successful enterprise by keeping his mind clearly focused on doing business instead of making money. He has concentrated on one major task: building high-quality computers and selling them at a lower price. He sees himself as a methodical person who squeezes the maximum out of an idea, and then tirelessly executes the idea. (Dell's foray into retail selling was an exception.) "I'm not a deal junkie," says Dell.

During the downturn in PC sales in 2001, Dell Computer continued to prosper despite a revenue decline of about 4 percent. To help sustain profits during this period, the management team headed by Dell laid off several thousand workers. Dell emphasizes, however, that a primary reason for the continuing prosperity of his company is that the Dell manufacturing system does not have the drag of expensive inventory characteristic of other computer makers.

Dell suggests that for an entrepreneur to stay on top, "The essential thing to do is to identify where and when you need help. You also have to change your role as your company grows, prioritizing what you have to do versus having others execute tasks at the detail level. If you have a good

strategy with sound economics, the real challenge is to get people excited about what you're doing. A lot of businesses get off track because they don't communicate an excitement about being part of a winning team that can achieve big goals. If a company can't motivate its people and it doesn't have a clear compass, it will drift."

Although he rarely talks about his private life to the press, Dell offered these comments about work/life balance: "I understand the limits of my effectiveness in terms of how many hours I work. I keep my work life and family life in healthy balance."

Discussion Questions

1. Identify three leadership behaviors or practices of Michael Dell by citing specific information from the case.

2. Identify three leadership traits or personal characteristics of Michael Dell by citing specific information from the case.

3. What suggestions can you offer Michael Dell for becoming a more effective leader/manager?

Source: Scott S. Smith, "Dell On . . ." *Entrepreneur*, April 1999, pp. 121–123; David E. Kalish, "For Whom the Dell Tolls," Associated Press, August 24, 1998; "The Best Managers," *Business Week*, January 12, 1998, p. 64; "Dell's Weaker Profit on Target," *Rochester Democrat and Chronicle*, May 18, 2001, p. 10D.

ENDNOTES

1. Katrina Brooker, "I Can Save It: I Built This Company," *Fortune*, April 30, 2001, pp. 94, 95.
2. W. Chan Kim and Renee A. Maubourgne, "Parables of Leadership," *Harvard Business Review*, July–August 1992, p. 123.
3. George B. Weathersby, "Leadership at Every Level," *Management Review*, June 1998, p. 5.
4. Survey cited in "What Leadership Skills Do Executives Seek?" *Managers Edge*, November 1998, p. 1.
5. John P. Kotter, *A Force for Change: How Leadership Differs from Management* (New York: Free Press, 1990); David Fagiano, "Managers versus Leaders," *Management Review*, November 1997, p. 5.
6. Diane Brady, "Blood, Sweat, and a Lady Named Linda," *Business Week*, January 24, 2000, p. 161.
7. John R. P. French Jr., and Bertram Raven, "The Bases of Social Power," in Dorwin Cartwright and Alvin Zander (eds.), *Group Dynamics: Research and Theory* (New York: Harper & Row, 1960), pp. 607–623.
8. Jeffrey D. Kudisch et al., "Expert Power, Referent Power, and Charisma: Toward the Resolution of a Theoretical Debate," *Journal of Business and Psychology*, Winter 1995, p. 189.
9. Manuel London, *Principled Leadership and Business Diplomacy: Value-Based Strategies for Management Development* (Westport, CT: Quorum Books, 1999).
10. Frank Gibney Jr., "The Rebel Driving Ford," *Time*, May 14, 2001, pp. 42–44.
11. Work of Jay Conger cited in Perry Pascarella, "Persuasion Skills Required for Success," *Management Review*, September 1998, p. 68.
12. Andrew J. DuBrin, "Sex and Gender Differences in Tactics of Influence," *Psychological Reports*, 68 (1991), pp. 645–646.
13. Mark Mulder et al., "Power Situation, and Leaders' Effectiveness:

An Organizational Field Study," *Journal of Applied Psychology*, August 1986, pp. 556–570.
14. Frank J. Navran, "Empowering Employees to Excel," *Supervisory Management*, August 1992, p. 5.
15. Keith Hammonds, "Grassroots Leadership: Ford Motor Co." *Fast Company*, April 2000, p. 143.
16. John A. Byrne, "High-Tech Honchos Needn't Come from High Tech," *Business Week*, May 3, 1999, p. 166.
17. Orlando Behling, "Employee Selection: Will Intelligence and Conscientiousness Do the Job?" *Academy of Management Executive*, February 1998, pp. 77–86; Shelly A. Kirkpatrick and Edwin A. Locke, "Leadership: Do Traits Matter?" *Academy of Management Executive*, May 1991, pp. 48–60.
18. "In Search of Leadership: A Talk with Headhunters Turned Authors Citrin and Neff," *Business Week*, November 15, 1999, p. 172.
19. John Case, "HR Learns How to Open the Books," *HR Magazine*, May 1998, p. 72.
20. Dale Zand, *The Leadership Triad: Knowledge, Trust and Power* (New York: Oxford University Press, 1997), p. 23.
21. "At Starwood, The CEO Is in the Details," *Business Week*, November 20, 2000, p. 142.
22. Sandra McElwaine, "A Different Kind of War," *USA Weekend*, October 3–5, 1997, p. 6.
23. Daniel Goleman, "Leadership That Gets Results," *Harvard Business Review*, March–April 2000, p. 80.
24. Joel Stein, "Bosses from Hell," *Time*, December 7, 1998, p. 181.
25. Alan G. Walker and James W. Smither, "A Five-Year Study of Upward Feedback: What Managers Do With Their Results Matters," *Personnel Psychology*, Summer 1999, pp. 393–423.
26. Robert K. Greenleaf, "The Servant as Leader," available at http://www.stolaf.edu, May 27, 1977; Greenleaf, *The Power of Servant Leadership* (San Francisco: Berrett-Koehler Publishers Inc., 1998).

27. Stein, "Bosses from Hell," p. 181.
28. Robert R. Blake and Anne Adams McCanse, *Leadership Dilemmas—Grid Solutions* (Houston: Gulf Publishing, 1991).
29. Paul Hersey, Kenneth H. Blanchard, and Dewey E. Johnson, *Management of Organizational Behavior: Utilizing Human Resources*, 7th ed. (Upper Saddle River, NJ: Prentice Hall, 1996), pp. 188–227.
30. Mark Henricks, "Give It Away," *Entrepreneur*, May 2000, p. 117.
31. David C. McClelland, *The Achieving Society* (New York: Van Nostrand Reinhold, 1961).
32. Quoted in Gail Dutton, "Wanted: A Practical Visionary," *Management Review*, March 1998, p. 34.
33. Daniel Goleman, "Leadership That Gets Results," *Harvard Business Review*, March–April 2000, pp. 78, 83.
34. Jane M. Howell and Bruce J. Avolio, "Transformational Leadership, Transactional Leadership, Locus of Control, and Support for Innovation: Key Predictions of Consolidated-Business-Unit Performance," *Journal of Applied Psychology*, December 1993, pp. 891–902.
35. John J. Hater and Bernard M. Bass, "Superiors' Evaluations and Subordinates' Perceptions of Transformational and Transactional Leadership," *Journal of Applied Psychology*, November 1988, p. 695.
36. Alan J. Dubinsky, Francis J. Yammarino, and Marvin A. Jolson, "An Examination of Linkages Between Personal Characteristics and Dimensions of Transformational Leadership," *Journal of Business and Psychology*, Spring 1995, p. 315; Henry Mintzberg, "Covert Leadership: Notes to Managing Professionals," *Harvard Business Review*, November–December 1998, p. 140; Timothy A. Judge and Joyce E. Bono, "Five-Factor Model of Personality and Transformational Leadership," *Journal of Applied Psychology*, October 2000, pp. 751–765; Ann Wylie, "The Secrets Behind the Art of Storytelling," *Success Workshop* (a supplement to *Managers Edge*), November 1999, p. 2.
37. David A. Waldman et al., "Does Leadership Matter? CEO Leadership Attributes and Profitability Under Conditions of Perceived Environmental Uncertainty," *Academy of Management Journal*, February 2001, pp. 134–143.
38. Andrew J. DuBrin, *Personal Magnetism: Discover Your Own Charisma and Learn How to Charm, Inspire, and Influence Others* (New York: AMACOM, 1997), pp. 93–111; Roger Dawson, *Secrets of Power Persuasion: Everything You'll Ever Need to Get Anything You'll Ever Want* (Upper Saddle River, NJ: Prentice Hall, 1992), pp. 181–183; Monica Larner, "The Man Who Saved Ferrari," *Business Week*, March 8, 1999, pp. 74–75.
39. Bennett J. Tepper, "Upward Maintenance Tactics in Supervisory Mentoring and Nonmentoring Relationships," *Academy of Management Journal*, August 1995, p. 1195.
40. Douglas T. Hall, Karen L. Otazo, and George P. Hollenbeck, "Behind Closed Doors: What Really Happens in Executive Coaching," *Organizational Dynamics*, Winter 1999, pp. 48–49.
41. Survey conducted by Korn/Ferry International and Columbia University Business School reported in Jerry Langdon, "Minority Executives Benefit from Mentors," Gannett News Service, December 7, 1998.
42. "Mentors Crucial to Women's Success," Knight Ridder, April 22, 2001.

315

Motivation

The man who brought you aerobics wants to bring you a more healthful all-around lifestyle—and have the government pay you for it. The Texas physician who is a candidate to become the nation's next surgeon general is endorsing federal tax breaks to encourage more healthful behavior. Call it an aerobics and veggie deduction.

"We need a financial incentive to encourage Americans to take care of themselves," Dr. Kenneth Cooper said of the proposed tax deductions. Cooper, the man who coined the term "aerobics" 25 years ago, spoke to a conference of health officials in Columbia, South Carolina. Cooper presented his 15-point plan to Bush officials, which included the innovative tax proposal. His plan would give tax deductions of up to $1,000 per person just for taking care of oneself. Keep your body mass index under 25, and you get a $250 deduction. You also would get $250 for keeping your blood pressure below 140 and over 90, your cholesterol under 200, and for not smoking. "Up to 73 percent of diseases in this country are the result of an unhealthy lifestyle," Cooper said. "That will only change if people do it themselves."[1]

The unusual proposal by the physician/businessman and potential U.S. Surgeon General points to the challenge of finding an effective way to motivate people to achieve a goal. In this case the goal is a healthy society and reduced medical costs. For many managers, the purpose of motivation is to get people to work hard toward achieving company objectives. A working knowledge of motivation theory and techniques can help managers achieve good financial results. Understanding motiva-

OBJECTIVES

After studying this chapter and doing the exercises, you should be able to:

1 Explain the relationship between motivation and performance.

2 Present an overview of major theories of need satisfaction in explaining motivation.

3 Explain how goal setting is used to motivate people.

4 Describe the application of behavior modification to worker motivation.

5 Describe the role of financial incentives, including profit sharing and gainsharing, in worker motivation.

6 Explain the conditions under which a person will be motivated according to expectancy theory.

7 Describe how equity theory can be applied to motivate workers.

Chapter 12

tion is also important because low motivation contributes to low-quality work, superficial effort, indifference toward customers, and high absenteeism and tardiness.

The term *motivation* refers to two different but related ideas. From the standpoint of the individual, motivation is an internal state that leads to the pursuit of objectives. Personal motivation affects the initiation, direction, intensity, and persistence of effort. (A motivated worker gets going, focuses effort in the right direction, works with intensity, and sustains the effort.) From the standpoint of the manager, motivation is the process of getting people to pursue objectives. Both concepts have an important meaning in common. **Motivation** is the expenditure of effort to accomplish results. The effort results from a force that stems from within the person. However, the manager or team leader, or the group, can be helpful in igniting the force.

motivation

The expenditure of effort to accomplish results.

This chapter will present several theories or explanations of motivation in the workplace. In addition, it will provide descriptions of specific approaches to motivating employees. Exhibit 12-1 presents an overview of various motivation theories and techniques. Referring back to this figure will help you integrate the information in this chapter. All the ideas presented in this chapter can be applied to motivating oneself as well as others. For instance, when you read about the expectancy theory of motivation, ask yourself: "What rewards do I value strongly enough for me to work extra hard?"

1

Explain the relationship between motivation and performance.

THE RELATIONSHIP BETWEEN MOTIVATION, PERFORMANCE, AND COMMITMENT

Many people believe the statements "You can accomplish anything you want" and "Think positively and you will achieve all your goals." In truth, motivation is but

EXHIBIT 12-1

Overview of Motivation Theories and Techniques

In this chapter we present both theories and explanations of motivation, along with techniques based on them.

I.	Theories and explanations of motivation
	1. Motivation through need satisfaction
	a. Maslow's need hierarchy
	b. Satisfaction of needs such as achievement, power, affiliation, and recognition
	c. Herzberg's two-factor theory
	2. Goal theory
	3. Behavior modification
	4. Expectancy theory
	5. Equity theory
II.	Specific motivational techniques stemming from theories
	1. Recognition programs
	2. Positive reinforcement programs
	3. Motivation through financial incentives
	a. Linking pay to performance
	b. Profit sharing and gainsharing
	c. Employee stock ownership programs and stock option plans

one important contributor to productivity and performance. Abilities, skills, and the right equipment are also indispensable. An office supervisor at a bank desperately wanted to become chairperson of the board within three years. Despite the intensity of his motivation, he did not reach his goal. The factors against him included his lack of formal business education, limited conceptual skills, underdeveloped political skills, and inadequate knowledge of high finance. Furthermore, the current chairperson had no intention of leaving the post.

Exhibit 12-2 shows the relationship between motivation and performance. It can also be expressed by the equation $P = M \times A$, where P refers to performance, M to motivation, and A to ability. Note that skill and technology contribute to ability. For instance if you are skilled at using information technology, and you have the right hardware and software, you can accomplish the task of producing a Web site. *Commitment* in the diagram is essentially an extension of motivation. The committed employee works joyfully toward achieving organizational objectives. A study of about 30 prosperous business firms suggested that these organizations are able to sustain high performance levels because they achieve the emotional commitment of their workforces. Employees are treated well and rewarded, and as a result they become loyal dedicated workers who help give the firm a competitive advantage.[2] High motivation for a given task is different from emotional commitment that translates into intense motivation for a long period of time. The process works as follows:

Day-by-day motivation and good treatment of workers → Long-term worker motivation → Emotional commitment to the firm → Competitive advantage → Elevated profits and stock price

Group norms also contribute to both motivation and performance. If group norms and organizational culture encourage high motivation and performance, the individual worker will feel compelled to work hard. To do otherwise isolates the worker from the group and the culture. Group norms and an organizational culture favoring low motivation will often lower individual output.

A manager contributes to performance by motivating group members, improving their ability, and helping to create a positive work culture. Before studying specific explanations of motivation, do the self-assessment exercise found on page 000. Taking the quiz will give you a preliminary idea of your current level of knowledge about motivation.

319

$P = M \times A$

An expression of the relationship between motivation and performance, where P refers to performance, M to motivation, and A to ability.

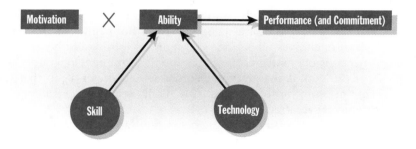

EXHIBIT 12-2

Motivation and Ability as Factors in Performance

Motivation does contribute substantially to performance, but not as directly as many people think.

2   MOTIVATION THROUGH NEED SATISFACTION

Present an overview of major theories of need satisfaction in explaining motivation.

320

need

A deficit within an individual, such as a craving for water or affection.

The simplest explanation of motivation is one of the most powerful: People are willing to expend effort toward achieving a goal because it satisfies one of their important needs. A **need** is a deficit within an individual, such as a craving for water or affection. Self-interest is thus a driving force. The principle is referred to as "What's in it for me?" or WIIFM (pronounced wiff'em). Reflect on your own experiences. Before working hard to accomplish a task, you probably want to know how you will benefit. If your manager asks you to work extra hours to take care of an emergency, you will most likely oblige. Yet underneath you might be thinking, "If I work these extra hours, my boss will think highly of me. As a result, I will probably receive a good performance evaluation and maybe a better-than-average salary increase.

People are motivated to fulfill needs that are not currently satisfied. The need-satisfaction approach requires two key steps in motivating workers. First, you must know what people want—what needs they are trying to satisfy. To learn what the needs are, you can ask directly or observe the person. You can obtain knowledge indirectly by getting to know employees better. To gain insight into employee needs, find out something about the employee's personal life, education, work history, outside interests, and career goals.

Second, you must give each person a chance to satisfy needs on the job. To illustrate, one way to motivate a person with a strong need for autonomy is to allow that person to work independently.

This section examines needs and motivation from three related perspectives. First, we describe the best-known theory of motivation, Maslow's need hierarchy. Then we discuss several specific needs related to job motivation and move on to another cornerstone idea, Herzberg's two-factor theory.

Maslow's Need Hierarchy

Maslow's need hierarchy

The motivation theory that arranges human needs into a pyramid-shaped model with basic physiological needs at the bottom and self-actualizing needs at the top.

Based on his work as a clinical psychologist, Abraham M. Maslow developed a comprehensive view of individual motivation.[3] **Maslow's need hierarchy** arranges human needs into a pyramid-shaped model with basic physiological needs at the bottom and self-actualization needs at the top. (See Exhibit 12-3.) Lower-order needs, called **deficiency needs**, must be satisfied to ensure a person's existence, security, and requirements for human contact. Higher-order needs, or **growth needs**, are concerned with personal development and reaching one's potential. Before higher-level needs are activated, the lower-order needs must be satisfied. The five levels of needs are described next.

deficiency needs

Lower-order needs that must be satisfied to ensure a person's existence, security, and requirements for human contact.

growth needs

Higher-order needs that are concerned with personal development and reaching one's potential.

1. *Physiological needs* refers to basic bodily requirements such as nutrition, water, shelter, moderate temperatures, rest, and sleep. Most office jobs allow us to satisfy physiological needs. Fire fighting is an occupation with potential to frustrate some physiological needs. Smoke inhalation can block need satisfaction.
2. *Safety needs* include the desire to be safe from both physical and emotional injury. Many operatives who work at dangerous jobs would be motivated by the prospects of obtaining safety. For example, computer operators who are suffering from cumulative trauma disorder would prefer a job that requires less intense pressure on their wrists. Any highly stressful job can frustrate the need for emotional safety.
3. *Social needs* are the needs for love, belonging, and affiliation with people. Managers can contribute to the satisfaction of these needs by promoting

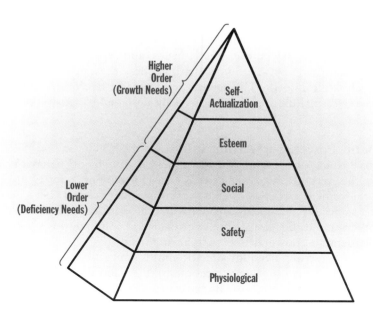

EXHIBIT 12-3
_____
Maslow's Need Hierarchy

As you move up the hierarchy, the needs become more difficult to achieve. Some physiological needs could be satisfied with pizza and a soft drink, whereas it might take becoming rich and famous to satisfy the self-actualization need.

teamwork and allowing people to discuss work problems with each other. Many employees see their jobs as a major source for satisfying social needs.

4. *Esteem needs* reflect people's desire to be seen by themselves and others as a person of worth. Occupations with high status are a primary source for the satisfaction of esteem needs. Managers can help employees satisfy their esteem needs by praising the quality of their work.

5. *Self-actualization needs* relate to the desire to reach one's potential. They include needs for self-fulfillment and personal development. True self-actualization is an ideal to strive for, rather than something that automatically stems from occupying a challenging position. Self-actualized people are those who are becoming all they are capable of becoming. Managers can help group members move toward self-actualization by giving them challenging assignments and the chance for advancement and new learning.

Maslow's need hierarchy is a convenient way of classifying needs and has spurred thousands of managers to take the subject of human motivation more seriously. Its primary value lies in recognition of the importance of satisfying needs in order to motivate employees. Furthermore, Maslow shows why people are difficult to satisfy. As one need is satisfied, people want to satisfy other needs or different forms of the same need. The need hierarchy has helped three generations of students understand that it is normal to be constantly searching for new satisfactions.

The need hierarchy is relevant in the current era because so many workers have to worry about satisfying lower-level needs. Despite the general prosperity, large business firms continue to downsize. Many of these downsizings come about because of consolidations and mergers designed to squeeze more profits out of the same sales volume.

Even if finding new employment is relatively easy, many workers feel their security is jeopardized when they have to worry about conducting a job search to pay for necessities.

322

Specific Needs People Attempt to Satisfy

Maslow's need hierarchy refers to classes of needs, and represents but one way of understanding human needs. The work setting offers the opportunity to satisfy dozens of psychological needs. This section will describe five of the most important of these needs, including programs specially designed to satisfy the recognition need.

Achievement, Power, and Affiliation

According to David McClelland and his associates, much job behavior can be explained by the strength of people's needs for achievement, power, and affiliation.[4] The achievement and power needs (or motives) have already been described in relation to leadership. The **affiliation need** is a desire to have close relationships with others and to be a loyal employee or friend. Affiliation is a social need, while achievement and power are self-actualizing needs.

A person with a strong need for affiliation finds compatible working relationships more important than high-level accomplishment and the exercise of power. Successful executives, therefore, usually have stronger needs for achievement and power than for affiliation. Workers with strong affiliation needs, however, typically enjoy contributing to a team effort. Befriending others and working cooperatively with them satisfies the need for affiliation.

Recognition

The workplace provides a natural opportunity to satisfy the **recognition need**, the desire to be acknowledged for one's contributions and efforts and to feel important. A manager can thus motivate many employees by making them feel important. Employee needs for recognition can be satisfied both through informal recognition and by formal recognition programs.

Praising workers for good performance relates closely to informal recognition. An effective form of praise describes the worker's performance rather than merely making an evaluation. Describing good performance might take this form: "You turned an angry customer into an ally who has referred new business to us." A straightforward evaluation would be "You did a great job with that angry customer." Even more effective would be to combine the two statements.

Although praise costs no money and only requires a few moments of time, many workers rarely receive praise. One researcher found that out of 1,500 workers surveyed, more than 50 percent said they seldom or never received spoken or written thanks for their efforts.[5] Managers therefore have a good opportunity to increase motivation by the simple act of praising good deeds. Other informal approaches to recognizing good performance include taking an employee to lunch, a handshake from the manager or team leader, and putting flowers on an employee's desk.

Formal recognition programs are more popular than ever as companies attempt to retain the right employees, and keep workers productive who worry about losing their jobs or having no private work area. Company recognition programs include awarding watches and jewelry for good service, plaques for good performance, and on-the-spot cash awards (around $25 to $50) for good performance. For example, FedEx authorizes its managers to make awards on the spot by giving employees a set of flags symbolizing a job well done, and a check for $50 to $100.

The more sophisticated recognition programs attempt to link recognition awards with performance and behavior tied to corporate objectives. At the

affiliation need

A desire to have close relationships with others and be a loyal employee or friend.

recognition need

The desire to be acknowledged for one's contributions and efforts and to feel important.

Prudential Insurance Company, the formal recognition program of the operations and technology function focuses on rewarding innovative, technology-based solutions for internal business clients.[6] For example, an information systems specialist who developed a way of minimizing sending repeated bills to deceased policyholders would be recognized.

Teams, as well as individuals, should receive recognition to enhance motivation. Motivation consultant Bob Nelson recommends that to build a high-performing team, the manager should acknowledge the success of all team members. As with individual recognition, a personal touch works best. Examples include a manager thanking group members for their involvement, suggestions, and initiatives. Holding a group luncheon for outstanding team performance is also a potential motivator.[7] We emphasize *potential* because team recognition does not take into account individual differences in preferences for rewards. For example, some employees object to group luncheons because it diverts time they might want to use for personal purposes.

In addition to motivating employees to work hard, reward and recognition programs have a positive impact on employee retention. Clive Metrick, specialist in human resource research, discovered from his surveys that, "Rewarding and recognizing positive results is an important factor in retaining employees." He also contends that these programs enhance motivation.[8]

Risk Taking and Thrill Seeking

Our discussion of motivation so far does not explain why some workers crave constant excitement on the job and are willing to risk their lives to achieve thrills. The willingness to take risks and pursue thrills is a need that has grown in importance in the high-technology era. Many people work for employers, start businesses, and purchase stock with uncertain futures. Both the search for giant payoffs and daily thrills motivates these individuals.[9]

A strong craving for thrills may have some positive consequences for the organization, including willingness to perform such dangerous feats as setting explosives, capping an oil well, controlling a radiation leak, and introducing a product in a highly competitive environment. However, extreme risk takers and thrill seekers can create problems such as being involved in a disproportionate number of vehicular accidents and making imprudent investments.

A manager can appeal to the need for risk taking and thrill seeking, and therefore enhance the motivation of a person so inclined by rewarding good behavior with adventuresome assignments such as the following:

- Dealing with an irate, hostile customer
- Working on a product development team under time constraints
- Repairing equipment under heavy time pressures and customer demands
- Attending dangerous team-building activities such as cliff hanging and race car driving

As a final note on how managers can focus on needs to motivate employees, consider these illustrative suggestions:[10]

- Workers with *achievement needs* typically show initiative and set personal goals, work well alone, take pride in a job well done, and seek recognition for their good work. You can best motivate them by seeking their input when defining work goals, giving them sufficient resources, showing them the final outcome of their work, and encouraging professional growth opportunities.

- Workers with strong *security needs* are likely to seek assurances, play it safe, look for clear instruction, and stick closely to a job description. You can best motivate them by offering predictable assignments, giving them clear instructions, avoiding sudden changes when possible, and offering frequent feedback. However, to encourage a little risk taking describe how others have succeeded by doing things in an unconventional way.

Herzberg's Two-Factor Theory

two-factor theory of work motivation

The theory contending that there are two different sets of job factors. One set can satisfy and motivate people, and the other set can only prevent dissatisfaction.

The study of the need hierarchy led to the **two-factor theory of work motivation**, which focuses on the idea of two different sets of job factors. One set of factors can satisfy and motivate people. The other can only prevent dissatisfaction.

Psychologist Frederick Herzberg and his associates interviewed hundreds of professionals about their work.[11] They discovered that some factors of a job give people a chance to satisfy higher-level needs. Such elements are satisfiers or motivators. A *satisfier* is a job factor that, if present, leads to job satisfaction. Similarly, a *motivator* is a job factor that, if present, leads to motivation. When a motivator is not present, the effect on motivation is neutral rather than negative. Herzberg's theory originally dealt with job satisfaction, but now it is also considered a theory of job motivation.

Individuals vary somewhat in the particular job factors they find satisfying or motivating. However, satisfiers and motivators generally refer to the content (the heart or guts) of a job. These factors are achievement, recognition, challenging work, responsibility, and the opportunity for advancement. All the factors are self-rewarding. The important implication for managers is that, as managers, they can motivate most people by providing an opportunity to do interesting work or to be promoted. The two-factor theory is thus the psychology that underlies the philosophy of job design through job enrichment and the job characteristics model, as described in Chapter 8.

Herzberg also discovered that some job elements are more relevant to lower-level needs than upper-level needs. Referred to as dissatisfiers, or hygiene factors, these elements are noticed primarily by their absence. A *dissatisfier* is a job element that, when present, prevents dissatisfaction; it does not, however, create satisfaction. People will not be satisfied with their jobs just because hygiene factors are present. For example, not having a handy place to park your car would create dissatisfaction. But having a place to park would not make you happier about your job.

Dissatisfiers relate mostly to the context of a job (the job setting or external elements). These include relationships with coworkers, company policy and administration, job security, and money. All these factors deal with external rewards. Money, however, does work as a satisfier for many people. Some people want or need money so much that high pay contributes to their job satisfaction. (See the discussion of financial incentives later in this chapter.) One reason that money can be a motivator is that high pay is often associated with high status and high esteem.

Exhibit 12-4 summarizes the major aspects of the two-factor theory of job motivation. The exhibit illustrates an important point: The opposite of satisfaction is no satisfaction—not dissatisfaction. Similarly, the opposite of dissatisfaction is no dissatisfaction—not satisfaction.

Herzberg's theory has had considerable influence on the practice of management and job design. The two-factor theory has prompted managers to

Satisfiers or Motivators		
{	Presence	Positive effect on motivation and satisfaction
	Absence	No negative effect on motivation or satisfaction

1. Achievement	4. Responsibility
2. Recognition	5. Advancement
3. Work itself	6. Growth

Dissatisfiers		
{	Presence	No positive effect on motivation or satisfaction
	Absence	Negative effect on motivation and satisfaction

1. Company policy	6. Relationships with peers
2. Supervision	7. Personal life
3. Relationship with supervisor	8. Relationships with subordinates
4. Work conditions	9. Status
5. Salary	10. Job security

EXHIBIT 12-4

The Two-Factor Theory of Work Motivation

ask, "What really motivates our employees?" Nevertheless, Herzberg's assumption—that all workers seek more responsibility and challenge on the job—may be incorrect. It is more likely that people in higher-level occupations strive for more responsibility and challenge. But even in a given occupational group, such as managers or production workers, not everybody has the same motivational pattern. One executive admitted to this author that she finds the status she receives as a company president to be highly motivational. Also, many workers are motivated by a secure job when they have heavy financial obligations.

MOTIVATION THROUGH GOAL SETTING

3

Explain how goal setting is used to motivate people.

Goal setting, including management by objectives (see Chapter 5), is a pervasive managerial activity. This section is concerned with the psychology behind goal setting; why and how it leads to improved performance.

Goal setting plays an important role in most formal motivational programs and managerial methods of motivating employees. The premise underlying goal theory is that behavior is regulated by values and goals. A *value* is a strongly held personal standard or conviction. It is a belief about something important to the individual, such as dignity of work or honesty. Our values create within us a desire to behave consistently with them. If an executive values honesty, the executive will establish a goal of trying to hire only honest employees. He or she would therefore make extensive use of reference checks and honesty testing.

With respect to planning, a goal has been defined as an overall condition one is trying to achieve. Its psychological meaning is about the same. A *goal* is what the person is trying to accomplish, or a conscious intention to act.

Edwin A. Locke and Gary P. Latham incorporated hundreds of studies about goals into a theory of goal setting and task performance.[12] Exhibit 12-5 summarizes some of the more consistent findings and the following list describes them.

EXHIBIT 12-5

The Basics of Goal Theory

Goals that meet the illustrated conditions have a positive impact on motivation, as revealed by a wide variety of research studies.

1. *Specific goals lead to higher performance than do generalized goals.* Telling someone to "do your best" is a generalized goal. A specific goal would be "Decrease the turnaround time on customer inquiries to an average of two working days."

2. *Performance generally increases in direct proportion to goal difficulty.* The harder one's goal, the more one accomplishes. An important exception occurs, however, when goals are too difficult. Difficulty in reaching the goal leads to frustration, which in turn leads to lowered performance. On the other hand, lofty goals can be inspirational. Author Nicholas Lore says that reasonable goals lead to dull, comfortable lives.[13] Even if you cannot achieve your dream goal right away, you can set smaller goals to make progress.

3. *For goals to improve performance, the employee must accept them.* If you reject a goal, you will not incorporate it into your planning. For this reason, it is often helpful to discuss goals with employees, rather than just imposing the goals on them. Participating in setting goals has no major effect on the level of job performance, except when it improves goal acceptance. Yet participation is valuable because it can lead to higher satisfaction with the goal-setting process.

    A study of pizza deliverers compared the contribution of assigned versus participative goal setting. All the deliverers were college students, whose average age was 21. At one store the employees participated in setting goals about making complete stops at intersections. At the other store, the pizza-delivery specialists were assigned a goal. Both groups significantly increased their number of complete stops at intersections, as measured by trained observers hiding behind nearby windows. A surprising finding was that the participative groups also increased the use of turn signals and safety belts.[14] Perhaps participating in goal setting made the deliverers feel more responsible.

4. *Goals are more effective when they are used to evaluate performance.* When workers know that their performance will be evaluated in terms of how well they attained their goals, the impact of goals increases. Management by objectives is built around this important idea.

5. *Goals should be linked to feedback and rewards.* Workers should receive feedback on their progress toward goals and be rewarded for reaching them.

Rewarding people for reaching goals is perhaps the best-accepted principle of management. Feedback is also important because it is a motivational principle within itself. The process of receiving positive feedback encourages us to repeat the behavior; receiving negative feedback encourages us to discontinue the behavior. A practical way of building more feedback into goal setting is to set achievable short-term goals. In this way, goal accomplishment gets measured more frequently, giving the goal setter regular feedback. Short-term goals also increase motivation because many people do not have the patience and self-discipline to work long and hard without seeing results.

6. *Group goal setting is as important as individual goal setting.* Having employees work as teams with a specific team goal, rather than as individuals with only individual goals, increases productivity. Furthermore, the combination of the compatible group and individual goals is more effective than either individual or group goals.

Despite the contribution of goals to performance, technically speaking, they are not motivational by themselves. Rather, the discrepancies created by what individuals do and what they aspire to do creates self-dissatisfaction. The dissatisfaction in turn creates a desire to reduce the discrepancy between the real and the ideal.[15] When a person desires to attain something, the person is in a state of mental arousal. The tension created by not having already achieved a goal spurs the person to reach the goal.

A criticism sometimes made of goal theory is that it applies mostly to non-complex tasks, such as doing laboratory experiments with Legos or delivering pizzas. In reality, goal setting does work for complex tasks. Executives regularly set strategic goals, such as global expansion in a specific time frame, to direct and inspire others.

BEHAVIOR MODIFICATION

4

The most systematic method of motivating people is **behavior modification**. It is a way of changing behavior by rewarding the right responses and punishing or ignoring the wrong responses. A reward is something of value received as a consequence of having attained a goal. This section will describe several key concepts and strategies of behavior modification (also referred to as OB Mod).

Key Concepts of Behavior Modification

The **law of effect** is the foundation principle of behavior modification. According to this principle, behavior that leads to positive consequences tends to be repeated. Similarly, behavior that leads to negative consequences tends not to be repeated. Perceptive managers rely on the law of effect virtually every day. Assume that a supervisor of a paint shop wants her employees to put on a face mask every time they use a spray gun. When she sees an employee using a mask properly, she might comment, "Good to see that you're wearing the safety mask today." If the supervisor noticed that an employee was not wearing a mask, she might say, "Please put down the spray gun, and go get your mask. If this happens again, I will be forced to suspend you for one day."

Behavior modification is generally associated with extrinsic rewards such as financial bonuses and prizes. However, intrinsic rewards are also used. A worker

---

Describe the application of behavior modification to worker motivation.

behavior modification
A way of changing behavior by rewarding the right responses and punishing or ignoring the wrong responses.

law of effect
The underlying principle of behavior modification stating that behavior leading to positive consequences tends to be repeated and that behavior leading to negative consequences tends not to be repeated.

might receive a more challenging assignment as a reward for performing well on the previous assignment.

Behavior Modification Strategies

The four behavior modification strategies—positive reinforcement, avoidance motivation, extinction, and punishment—can be used either individually or in combination.

1. *Positive reinforcement* increases the probability that behavior will be repeated by rewarding people for making the right response. The phrase "increases the probability" is noteworthy. No behavior modification strategy guarantees that people will always make the right response in the future. However, it increases the chance that they will repeat the desired behavior. The term *reinforcement* means that the behavior (or response) is strengthened or entrenched. For example, your response of placing your left pinky on the *a* of your keyboard is probably reinforced through thousands of successful attempts.

   Positive reinforcement is the most effective behavior modification strategy. Most people respond better to being rewarded for the right response than to being punished for the wrong response. The IBM decision to base sales representative's compensation in part on customer satisfaction illustrates rewarding the desired behavior to improve performance.

2. *Avoidance motivation (negative reinforcement)* rewards people by taking away an uncomfortable consequence. It is a method of strengthening a desired response by making the removal of discomfort contingent on the right response. Assume that an employee is placed on probation because of excessive absenteeism. After 20 consecutive days of coming to work, the employer rewards the employee by removing the probation. Because the opportunity for removing punishments is limited, negative reinforcement is not a widely used behavior modification strategy.

   Negative reinforcement or avoidance motivation is often confused with punishment. In reality, negative reinforcement is the opposite of punishment. It is rewarding someone by enabling him or her to avoid punishment.

3. *Extinction* is the weakening or decreasing of the frequency of undesirable behavior by removing the reward for such behavior. It is the absence of reinforcement. Extinction often takes the form of ignoring undesirable behavior. It works this way: Suppose an employee engages in undesirable behavior, such as creating a disturbance just to get a reaction from coworkers. If the coworkers ignore the disturbance, the perpetrator no longer receives the reward of getting attention and stops the disturbing behavior. The behavior is said to be extinguished.

   Extinction must be used with great care because in many instances it does not work. An employee may habitually come to work late. If the boss does not reprimand the employee, the employee's tardiness may strengthen. The employee may interpret the boss's attempt at extinction as condoning the behavior.

4. *Punishment* is the presentation of an undesirable consequence for a specific behavior. Yelling at an employee for making a mistake is a direct form of punishment. Another form of punishment is taking away a privilege, such as working on an interesting project, because of some undesirable behavior. In order to be effective, punishment not only tells people what not to do, it

teaches them the right behavior. When used appropriately, punishment can be a motivator for those punished and those observing the punishment. This means delivering it in a manner that is clearly impersonal, corrective, focused on a specific act, and relatively intense and quick.

Seventy-seven managers, each from a different organization, were interviewed to obtain their views on a variety of issues related to punishment. A consistent finding was that punishment is an effective learning tool. The punished workers learned what they did wrong and coworkers learned what type of performance and behavior would not be tolerated. Managers themselves learned more about following organizational policies and procedures.[16]

A serious disadvantage of punishment is that it may cause adverse consequences for managers and the organization. Employees who are punished often become defensive, angry, and eager to seek revenge. Many incidents of workplace violence, such as killing a former supervisor, occur after a mentally unstable employee has been fired—even when the dismissal is justified.

Successful Application of Positive Reinforcement

Behavior modification may take the form of an overall company program, such as a highly structured behavior modification program, or a rewards and recognition program. Managers use positive reinforcement more frequently, on an informal, daily basis. The following list presents suggestions for making effective use of positive reinforcement, whether as part of a company program or more informally.

1. *State clearly what behavior will lead to a reward.* The nature of good performance, or the goals, must be agreed to by both manager and group member. Clarification could take this form: "What I need are inventory reports without missing data. When you achieve this, you'll be credited with good performance."
2. *Use appropriate rewards.* An appropriate reward proves effective when it is valued by the person being motivated. Examine the list of rewards in Exhibit 12-6. Note that some have more appeal to you than do others. The best way to motivate people is to offer them their preferred rewards for good performance. Managers should ask employees what they are interested in attaining.
3. *Make rewards contingent on good performance.* Contingent reinforcement means that getting the reward depends on giving a certain performance. Unless a reward is linked to the desired behavior or performance it will have little effect on whether the behavior or performance is repeated. For example, saying "You're doing great" in response to anything an employee does will not lead to good performance. Yet if the manager reserves the "doing great" response for truly outstanding performance, he or she may reinforce the good performance.
4. *Administer rewards intermittently.* Positive reinforcement can be administered under different types of schedules. The most effective and sensible type is an intermittent schedule, in which rewards are administered often, but not always, when the appropriate behavior occurs. A reward loses its effect if given every time the employee makes the right response. Thus intermittent rewards sustain desired behavior for a longer time by helping to prevent the behavior from fading away when it is not rewarded.

In addition to being more effective, intermittent rewards are generally more practical than continuous rewards. Few managers have enough time to dispense rewards every time team members attain performance goals.

EXHIBIT 12-6

Rewards Suitable for Use in Positive Reinforcement

A large number of potential rewards can be used to motivate individuals and teams, and many of them are low-cost or no-cost. An important condition for a reward is the perception of its value by the individual being motivated. The viewpoint of the reward giver alone about the value of a reward is not sufficient.

Monetary
Salary increases or bonuses
Company-paid vacation trip
Discount coupons
Company stock
Extra paid vacation days
Bonus or profit sharing
Paid personal holiday (such as birthday)
Movie, concert, or athletic event tickets
Free or discount airline tickets
Discounts on company products or
    services
Gift selection from catalog
Race car driving camp

Job and Career Related
Challenging work assignment
Empowerment of employee
Change of job status from temporary to
    permanent
Promise of job security
Assignment to high-prestige team or
    project
Favorable performance appraisal
Freedom to choose own work activity
Promotion
Build fun into work
Do more of preferred task
Role as boss's stand-in when he or she
    is away
Contribution to presentations to top
    management
Job rotation
Learning seminars and continuous
    education
Encourage continuous learning
Opportunity to employees to set one's
    own goals

Food and Dining
Business luncheon paid by company
Company picnics
Department parties or special banquet
Holiday turkeys and fruit baskets

Recognition and Pride Related
Compliments
Encouragement
Inviting team to manager's home
Access to confidential information
Pat on back or handshake
Public expression of appreciation
Meeting of appreciation with executive
Flattering letter from customer
    distributed over e-mail
Note of thanks to individual
Open note of thanks distributed over
    e-mail
Employee-of-the-month award
Wall plaque indicating accomplishment
Special commendation
Visit to manager's office just to receive
    praise
Team uniforms, hats, T-shirts, or mugs
Designated parking space for outstanding
    performance

Status Symbols
Bigger desk
Bigger office or cubicle
Office or cubicle with window
Freedom to personalize work area
Private office
Assigned luxury model laptop computer

Time Off
Three-day weekend
Company time bank with deposits made for
    unusual effort or success
Personal leave days for events chosen by
    employee

Source: Dot Yandle, "Rewarding Good Work: What Do Your Employees Want? *Success Workshop* (A supplement to *Managers Edge*) May 1999, pp. 1–4; Bob Nelson, "The Power of I's: No-Cost Ways to Motivate Employees," *Success in Recruiting and Retaining,* Sample Issue, 2000, p. 2; "Do Incentive Rewards Work?" *HRfocus,* October 2000, pp. 1, 14–15; Neil Ruffolo, "Don't Forget to Provide Incentives for Your Middle Performers," *Workforce,* January 2000, pp. 62–63.

5. *Vary the size of the reward with the size of accomplishment.* Big accomplishments deserve big rewards, and small accomplishments deserve small rewards. Rewards of the wrong magnitude erode their motivational power. Also, people become embarrassed when praise is overly lavish.

6. *Administer rewards promptly.* The proper timing of rewards may be difficult because the manager is not present at the time of good performance. In this

case, a telephone call or a note of appreciation within several days of the good performance is appropriate.

7. *Change rewards periodically.* Rewards grow stale quickly; they must be changed periodically. A repetitive reward can even become an annoyance. How many times can one be motivated by the phrase "nice job"? Suppose the reward for making a sales quota is a CD player. How many CD players can one person use?

8. *Reward the team as well as the individual.* Janet Barnard conducted a study of rewards used by companies that were nominated for a national quality award. Many of the managers agreed that an effective reward process offered incentives to encourage teamwork, yet also let star performers shine. A results-oriented system, such as management by objectives, provides a good basis for determining who gets rewarded. The evaluation should be done by the project or team leader closest to the team's activities and best able to make a valid evaluation of both the team and its members.[17]

9. *Make the rewards visible.* When other workers notice the reward, its impact multiplies because the other people observe what kind of behavior is rewarded. Assume that you were informed about a coworker's exciting assignment, given because of high performance. You might strive to accomplish the same level of performance.

Behavior Modification Effectiveness

Behavior modification has a long history of improving productivity on the job. Fred Luthans and Alexander D. Sajkovic reviewed the quantitative research findings conducted with OB Mod over a 20-year period. The study indicated a substantial 17 percent average improvement in performance. The overall improvement in manufacturing settings was 33 percent and 13 percent in service settings. Another notable finding showed social reinforcers, such as recognition and positive feedback, to be as effective as monetary rewards.[18]

Behavior modification also proved effective in applications to improve attendance and punctuality, as well as safety. The accompanying Management in Action illustrates the application of OB Mod for improving safety, and at the same time gives you more insight into behavior modification in the workplace.

MOTIVATION THROUGH FINANCIAL INCENTIVES   **5**

A natural way to motivate workers at any level is to offer them financial incentives for good performance. Linking pay to performance improves the motivation value of money. Using financial incentives to motivate people fits behavior modification principles. Financial incentives, however, predate behavior modification. The paragraphs that follow discuss linking pay to performance, profit sharing and gainsharing, and employee stock ownership (and option) plans, and problems associated with financial incentives. Figure 12-7 outlines this information.

Describe the role of financial incentives, including profit sharing and gainsharing, in worker motivation.

Linking Pay to Performance

Financial incentives are more effective when they are linked to (or contingent upon) good performance. Linking pay to performance motivates people to work harder. Production workers and sales workers have long received contingent financial incentives. Many production workers receive, after meeting a quota,

Management *in Action*

Foamex Management Uses Behavior Modification to Improve Safety Training

Foamex, a flexible polyurethane foam manufacturer based in Lynwood, Pennsylvania, was committed to improving safety conditions and reducing worker compensation costs. So the company launched a behavior-modification safety training program. Marsh Risk Consulting designed the behavioral risk improvement (BRI) program to focus on changing employee behavior. Managers play a central role in the program by discussing it at each management staff meeting. Managers are also required to give positive reinforcement. The plant manager gives positive reinforcement to staff, the staff gives positive reinforcement to managers, and so on. Here are the key steps in the program:

1. *Assessment.* The first step was a study of Foamex's operations, its workforce demographics, work culture, and accident history for the past several years. This allowed the Marsh team to understand Foamex's processes and also ensure that its workforce was appropriate for behavioral-based safety training.
2. *Introduction.* Foamex appointed an improvement team of eight hourly workers—all volunteers—to be in charge of the program. Another team of 15 volunteer hourly employees was appointed to serve as observers, who then undergo extensive BRI training in positive reinforcement and corrective feedback, the cornerstone of the organizational behavior modification safety training program.
3. *Process improvement.* As part of the assessment phase, the company identified pinpoints—safety issues such as someone lifting improperly or using a cutting device unsafely. For example, Foamex has a rule that outside of the restrooms and the break room, everyone must wear eye protection at the facility. When establishing pinpoints,

observers establish baselines—how the company is doing without training. If a baseline for the behavior is 60 percent, the improvement team then sets an achievable goal such as 65 percent.

4. *Training.* Observers learned to make daily observations of behavior surrounding pinpoints using a 3×5 pinpoint card that lists in columns: the pinpoint, the safe behaviors, at-risk behaviors, positive reinforcement, and corrective feedback. A critical part of observer training is how to give corrective feedback in a way that does not offend the people they are observing. Employees receive training during weekly departmental safety meetings.
5. *Observation.* Every day, observers walk around the facility and mark on their cards where they see safe behaviors (such as workers wearing safety glasses) and when they see at-risk behaviors. When observers see a worker demonstrating a safe behavior pinpoint, they positively reinforce the behavior by, for example, saying "nice job." When they observe at-risk behaviors, they give corrective feedback. Observations are anonymous, and the pinpoint cards specify that employee names should not be recorded.
6. *Celebration.* When workers achieve pinpoint goals, the company celebrates with pizza lunches, desserts and drinks, free Blockbuster videos, T-shirts, and the like.

The benefits of the program to Foamex include a marked improvement in the attitude of employees toward safety and one another, increased communication between the hourly workforce and management and supervisory personnel, and a reduction in workers' compensation costs. Gary Archer, the environmental health and safety manager for Foamex, says that the two critical factors for success are employee ownership of the program and positive reinforcement. "I'm sold on doing this. If we don't tell people they're doing a good job, I don't believe people have the confidence that they are."

Source: Adapted from "How One Company Uses Behavior Mod to Improve Safety Training," *IOMA's Report on Managing Training and Development*, March 2001, pp. 4–6.

bonuses per unit of production. Most sales representatives receive salary plus commissions. Exhibit 12–8 presents a typical approach to linking employee pay to performance, a plan that is often referred to as *merit pay*. A cost-of-living adjustment is not considered merit pay because it is not related to performance.

Managers and others continue to fine-tune methods of linking pay to individual performance. A method now in use by many companies calculates base pay according to a variety of factors. Among them are ability to communicate, customer focus, dealing with change, interpersonal skills, and job knowledge. Managers are rated on employee development, team productivity, and leadership. Merit pay for both individual contributors and managers is based on actual results. Merit pay runs from 2 to more than 18 percent of total compensation.

An increasing effort of managers and compensation specialists to link pay to performance supports many business strategies. In other words, workers receive

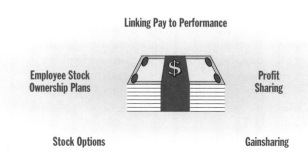

Linking Pay to Performance

Employee Stock Ownership Plans

Profit Sharing

Stock Options

Gainsharing

EXHIBIT 12-7

Several Approaches to Motivation Through Financial Incentives

Performance Level of Staff Members	Merit Increase (Percentage of Pay)
Demonstrate exceptional performance and make outstanding contributions during the year	4.75–5.50
Give consistently productive performance that meets all standards and exceeds some	3.75–4.74
Give consistently productive performance that meets expectations	2.00–3.74
Demonstrate performance that is not wholly satisfactory, even though some expectations may be met or even exceeded	1.00–1.99
Generally fail to meet key expectations and standards; substantial improvement is necessary and essential	0.00

EXHIBIT 12-8

Guidelines for Performance-Based Merit Increases at a Hospital

Merit pay is additional income earned for meeting performance standards.

financial incentives for performing in ways consistent with the business strategy. A company code-named Big Foods shifted its strategy from focusing mostly on profit to also focusing on gaining market share. The company incentive plan rewarded salespeople on a percent of gross margin of all product lines. The incentive plan prompted salespeople to emphasize selling mature product lines with the highest gross margins. To communicate the change in strategy, Big Foods management revised the incentive plan. The incentive award was now linked to the number of units sold rather than gross margin dollars. Also, products that the company wanted to introduce into the marketplace carried higher incentives.[19]

To help assure that performance-based rewards programs are aligned with the business strategy, two compensation specialists offer the following suggestions:[20]

- *Develop clear expectations.* Break down broad organizational goals into specific goals for each division, department, group, and team.
- *Create a clear line of sight.* Employees must see that their direct efforts will have a bearing on the results management seeks. At Big Foods, sales representatives were able to quickly redirect their sales effort to increase market share in the designated product lines in order to earn financial incentives.
- *Set achievable goals.* The same principle of goal theory applies: few people will be motivated to shoot for seemingly impossible goals.
- *Establish a credible measurement system.* In all types of performance-based rewards programs, quantitative measures of results work the best.
- *Empower employees.* Help employees achieve their goals by giving them the training and authority they need to perform well. Also, feed employees the information they need to succeed.
- *Make rewards meaningful.* The actual reward or incentive must be big enough to make a difference. In general incentives should be at least 15 percent to 25 percent of base pay.
- *Make payouts immediate.* Follow the rules for reinforcement here and elsewhere in using financial incentives. Minimize the time between achieving targets and receiving the payout. Avoid having workers wait six months or a year for their performance bonus.

Profit Sharing and Gainsharing

The pay plans mentioned so far link rewards to individual effort. Numerous organizations attempt to increase motivation and productivity through a companywide plan linking incentive pay to increases in performance. Here we describe profit sharing in general, and a specific form of sharing profits called gainsharing.

Profit Sharing

profit-sharing plan

A method of giving workers supplemental income based on the profitability of the entire firm or a selected unit.

Profit-sharing plans give workers supplemental income based on the profitability of the entire firm or a selected unit. The motivational principle is an employee belief in working harder to contribute to profitability because they will eventually share some of the profits. Ideally, all employees need to be committed to working for a common good. Employee contributions to profits may take a variety of forms such as product quantity, product quality, reducing costs, or improving work methods.

A profit-sharing plan based on participative management was developed at Honeywell's Commercial Avionics Division in Phoenix. The division needed to align its compensation plan to reward for performance. Instead of implementing an established incentive system the company formed an employee team to create a compensation program. The new risk-sharing (a type of profit-sharing) plan links 3.5 percent of all employees' pay to company profit. Workers can also receive an additional 5 percent when the company exceeds certain goals. Both management and employees are pleased with the program, and worker participation in building the plan enhanced acceptance of the new compensation system. After two years of operation, goals for profit and economic value added were exceeded by 10 percent.[21]

Gainsharing

Another approach to profit sharing focuses on productivity increases more directly attributable to worker ideas and effort. **Gainsharing** is a formal program that allows employees to participate financially in the productivity gains they have achieved. It is accomplished through establishing a payout formula and getting employees involved. Productivity gains are typically manufacturing related, but can also be in service, such as customer service. Rewards are distributed after performance improves. As in other forms of profit sharing, the participants can be the entire organization or a unit within the firm. Gainsharing is based on factors in the work environment that employees can control directly. Furthermore, rewards are shared with all members of the gainsharing unit, regardless of individual contribution toward productivity improvement.[22]

gainsharing
A formal program allowing employees to participate financially in the productivity gains they have achieved.

The formulas used in gainsharing vary widely, but share common elements. Managers begin by comparing what employees are paid to what they sell or produce. Assume that labor costs make up 50 percent of production costs. Any reductions below 50 percent are placed in a bonus pool. Part of the money in the bonus pool is shared among workers. The company's share of the productivity savings in the pool can be distributed to shareholders as increased profits. The savings may allow managers to lower prices, a move that could make the company more competitive.

The second element of gainsharing is employee involvement. Managers establish a mechanism that actively solicits, reviews, and implements employee suggestions about productivity improvement. A committee of managers and employees reviews the ideas and then implements the most promising suggestions. The third key element is employee cooperation. To achieve the bonuses for productivity improvement, group members must work harmoniously with each other. Departments must also cooperate with each other, because some suggestions involve the work of more than one organizational unit.[23]

Gainsharing plans have a history of more than 70 years of turning unproductive companies around and making successful companies even more productive. Lincoln Electric Co. of Cleveland, Ohio, is regularly cited as the ideal example of gainsharing. Lincoln manufactures and sells welding machines and motors. Its productivity rate is double to triple that of any other manufacturing operation that uses steel as its raw material and has 1,000 or more employees. The company offers no paid holidays or sick days, but has a no-layoff policy.

The Lincoln gainsharing plan rewards workers for producing high-quality products efficiently while controlling costs. All employees receive a base salary, and production workers also receive piecework pay (money in relation to units produced). A year-end bonus supplements the piecework pay based on increases in profits. Bonus payments are determined by merit ratings based on output, quality, dependability, and personal characteristics (such as cooperativeness).

The Gainsharing Inc. Web site (http://www.gainsharing.com) points to these four key advantages of this profit-sharing method:

- A dramatic increase in productive capacity, in record time. Most companies will achieve a productivity gain of 10 percent to 30 percent within 30 to 90 days after implementing gainsharing.
- The program achieves employee buy-in because they know exactly what benefit they will gain from performance improvement.
- Employees learn more about business fundamentals. Gainsharing programs illustrate how the different elements in a company must work together to achieve the performance on which bonuses are based.
- Unnecessary overtime is reduced. Because pay is based more on performance than on number of hours worked, employees find ways to get their work accomplished with a minimum of overtime.[24]

Employee Stock Ownership and Stock Option Plans

An increasingly popular way of motivating workers with financial incentives is to make them part owners of the business through stock purchases. Two variations of the same idea of giving workers equity in the business are stock ownership and stock option plans. Stock ownership can be motivational because employees participate in the financial success of the firm as measured by its stock price. If employees work hard, the company may become more successful and the value of the stock increases.

Under an *employee stock ownership plan (ESOP)* employees at all levels in the organization are given stock. The employer either contributes shares of its stock or the money to purchase the stock on the open market. Stock shares are usually deposited in employee retirement accounts. Upon retirement, employees can choose to receive company stock instead of cash. ESOPs are also significant because they offer tax incentives to the employer. For example, a portion of the earnings paid to the retirement fund are tax deductible.

Employee stock options are more complicated than straightforward stock ownership. Stock options give employees the right to purchase company stock at a specified price at some point in the future. If the stock rises in value, you can purchase it at a discount. If the stock sinks below your designated purchase price, your option is worthless. Thousands of workers in the information technology field, particularly in Silicon Valley, have become millionaires and multimillionaires with their stock options.

However, many of the 10 million workers in the United States who own stock options found their stock options to be worthless in the 2001–2002 era. When it came time to cash their options, the stock price was much less than option (striking) price. Furthermore, many workers who chose relatively small base pay and big options were especially disappointed when the stock market plunged. Stock options became sources of discouragement and anger rather than motivation. Another serious potential source of dissatisfaction with stock options is the tax owed on the gains at the time the employee exercises the option. If you hold the stock, and the price plunges you pay taxes on paper profits. Exhibit 12-9 shows you the arithmetic behind a stock option.

Problems Associated with Financial Incentives

Although financial incentives are widely used as motivators, they can create problems. A major problem is that workers may not agree with managers about the value of their contributions. Financial incentives can also pit individuals and

Brokerage sells 400 shares of company stock at $35 each (400 shares × $35)	= $14,000	
Brokerage deducts exercise price (400 shares × $10.57)	−4,228	
	$ 9,772	
Taxes withheld (28% for federal income tax + 17.56% for social security tax)	−3,475	
	$ 6,297	
Brokerage deducts fees/commissions/interest	−100	
	$ 6,197	
Brokerage pays profit to employee	$ 6,197	

Source: Carrington Nelson, "Exercising Your Stock Options," Gannett News Service, July 26, 1998.

EXHIBIT 12-9

How a Stock Option Works

Employee decides to exercise option for 400 shares at $10.57 each when stock reaches $35 per share.

337

groups against each other. The result may be unhealthy competition rather than cooperation and teamwork.

The most researched argument against financial rewards is that it focuses the attention of workers too much on the reward such as money or stocks. In the process, the workers lose out on intrinsic rewards such as joy in accomplishment. Instead of being passionate about the work they are doing, people become overly concerned with the size of their reward. One argument is that external rewards do not create a lasting commitment. Instead, they create temporary compliance, such as working hard in the short run to earn a bonus. A frequent problem with merit pay systems is that a person who does not receive a merit increase one pay period then feels that he or she has been punished. Another argument against financial incentives is that rewards manipulate people, as do bribes.[25]

Organizational theory specialist Jeffrey Pfeffer explains that people do work for money, but they work even more for meaning in their lives. Work brings people a meaningful type of fun. Pfeffer believes that people who ignore this truth are essentially bribing their employees and will pay the price in lack of loyalty and commitment. He illustrates his position with the SAS Institute, a successful software company that emphasizes excellent benefits and exciting work rather than financial incentives.[26]

In reality, workers at all levels want a combination of internal (intrinsic) rewards and financial rewards along with other external rewards such as praise. The ideal combination is to offer exciting (intrinsically motivating) work to people, and simultaneously pay them enough money so they are not preoccupied with matters such as salary and bonuses. Money is the strongest motivator when people have financial problems. Furthermore, people who find extreme joy in their work will leave one organization for another to perform the same work at much higher pay. Another practical problem is that even if a firm offers exciting work, great benefits, and wonderful coworkers, they usually need to offer financial incentives to attract quality workers.

EXPECTANCY THEORY

6

Explain the conditions under which a person will be motivated according to expectancy theory.

According to the **expectancy theory of motivation**, people will put forth the greatest effort if they expect the effort to lead to performance which in turn leads to a reward. Expectancy theory as applied to work has recently been recast as a theory called *motivation management*. As its basic premise, employees are motivated by what they expect will be the consequences of their efforts. At the same time, they must be confident they can perform the task.[27]

expectancy theory of motivation

The belief that people will expend effort if they expect the effort to lead to performance and the performance to lead to a reward.

A Basic Model of Expectancy Theory

Expectancy theory integrates important ideas found in the other generally accepted motivation theories. Exhibit 12-10 presents a basic version of expectancy theory. According to expectancy theory, four conditions must exist for motivated behavior to occur.[28]

Condition A refers *to expectancy*, which means that people will expend effort because they believe it will lead to performance. In this $E \rightarrow P$ expectancy, subjective probabilities range between 0.0 and 1.0. Rational people ask themselves, "If I work hard, will I really get the job done?" If they evaluate the probability as being high, they probably will invest the effort to achieve the goal. People have higher $E \rightarrow P$ expectancies when they have the appropriate skills, training, and self-confidence.

Condition B is based on the fact that people are more willing to expend effort if they think that good performance will lead to a reward, referred to as $P \rightarrow O$ instrumentality. It too ranges between 0.0 and 1.0. (*Instrumentality* refers to the idea that the behavior is instrumental in achieving an important end.) The rational person says, "I'm much more willing to perform well if I'm assured that I'll receive the reward I deserve." A cautious employee might even ask other employees if they received their promised rewards for exceptional performance. To strengthen a subordinate's $P \rightarrow O$ instrumentality, the manager should give reassurance that the reward will be forthcoming.

Condition C refers to *valence*, the value a person attaches to certain outcomes. The greater the valence, the greater the effort. Valences can be either positive or negative. If a student believes that receiving an A is important, he or she will work hard. Also, if a student believes that avoiding a C or a lower grade is important, he or she will work hard. Valences range from −1 to +1 in most versions of expectancy theory. A positive valence indicates a preference for a particular reward. A clearer picture of individual differences in human motivation spreads valences out over a range of −100 to +100.

Most work situations present the possibility of several outcomes, with a different valence attached to each. Assume that a purchasing manager is pondering whether becoming a certified purchasing manager (CPM) would be worth the effort. The list that follows cites possible outcomes or rewards from achieving certification, along with their valences (on a scale of −100 to +100).

- Status from being a CPM, 75
- Promotion to purchasing manager, 95
- Plaque to hang on office wall, 25

EXHIBIT 12-10

Basic Version of Expectancy Theory of Motivation

An individual will be motivated when:

A. The individual believes effort (E) will lead to favorable performance (*P*)—that is, when $E \rightarrow P$ (also referred to as expectancy).

B. The individual believes performance will lead to favorable outcome (*O*)—that is, when $P \rightarrow O$ (also referred to as instrumentality).

C. Outcome or reward satisfies an important need (in other words, valence is strong).

D. Need satisfaction is intense enough to make effort seem worthwhile.

- Bigger salary increase next year, 90
- Letters of congratulations from friends and relatives, 50
- Expressions of envy from one or two coworkers, −25

Valences are useful in explaining why some people will put forth the effort to do things with low expectancies. For example, most people know the chance of winning a lottery, becoming a rock star, or writing a best-selling novel is only one in a million. Nevertheless, a number of people vigorously pursue these goals. They do so because they attach an extraordinary positive valence to these outcomes (perhaps 100!).

Condition D indicates that the need satisfaction stemming from each outcome must be intense enough to make the effort worthwhile. Would you walk two miles on a hot day for one glass of ice water? The water would undoubtedly satisfy your thirst need, but the magnitude of the satisfaction would probably not be worth the effort. Similarly, an operative employee turned down a promotion to the position of inspector because the raise offered was only 50 cents per hour. The worker told his supervisor, "I need more money. But I'm not willing to take on that much added responsibility for twenty dollars a week."

Implications for Management

Expectancy theory has several important implications for the effective management of people. The theory helps pinpoint what a manager must do to motivate group members and diagnose motivational problems.[29]

1. *Individual differences among employees must be taken into account.* Different people attach different valences to different rewards, so a manager should try to match rewards with individual preferences. Behavior modification also makes use of this principle.
2. *Rewards should be closely tied to those actions the organization sees as worthwhile.* For example, if the organization values quality, people should be rewarded for producing high-quality work.
3. *Employees should be given the appropriate training and encouragement.* An investment in training will strengthen their subjective hunches that effort will lead to good performance.
4. *Employees should be presented with credible evidence that good performance does lead to anticipated rewards.* Similarly, a manager should reassure employees that good work will be both noticed and rewarded. As part of this implication, managers must listen carefully to understand the perceived link employees have between hard work and rewards. If instrumentality is unjustifiably low, the manager must reassure the employee that hard work will be rewarded.
5. *The meaning and implications of outcomes should be explained.* It can be motivational for employees to know the values of certain outcomes. If an employee who is interested in working on a special task force knows that assignment to the task force is linked to successful completion of a project, the employee will give special attention to the project.

EQUITY THEORY AND JOB MOTIVATION

Expectancy theory emphasizes the rational and thinking side of people. Similarly, another theory focuses on how fairly people think they are being treated in

7

Describe how equity theory can be applied to motivate workers.

equity theory

A theory of motivation in which employee satisfaction and motivation depend on how fairly the employees believe they are treated in comparison to peers.

comparison to certain reference groups. According to **equity theory**, employee satisfaction and motivation depend on how fairly the employees believe they are treated in comparison to peers. According to the theory, employees hold certain beliefs about the outcomes they receive from their jobs and the inputs they invest to obtain these outcomes.

The *outcomes* of employment include pay, benefits, status, intrinsic job factors such as interesting work, and anything else stemming from the job that workers perceive as useful. The *inputs* include all factors that employees perceive as their investment in the job or anything of value they bring to the job. Among such inputs are job qualifications, skills, education, effort, and cooperative behavior.

At the core of equity theory, employees compare their inputs and outcomes with others in the workplace.[30] When employees believe that they receive equitable outcomes in relation to their inputs, they generally express satisfaction. When workers believe they are being treated equitably, they are more willing to work hard. Conversely, when employees believe they are giving too much in comparison to what they are receiving from the organization, a state of tension and dissatisfaction ensues. The people used for reference are those whom the employee perceives as relevant for comparison. For example, a substance abuse counselor working at a family services center would make comparison with other substance abuse counselors in the same type of settings about whom he has information.

Comparisons are of two kinds. People consider their own inputs in relation to outcomes received, and they also evaluate what others are receiving for the same inputs. Equity is said to exist when an individual concludes that his or her outcome/input ratio is equal to that of other people. Inequity exists if the person's ratio is not the same. All these comparisons are similar to those judgments made by people according to expectancy theory—they are subjective hunches that may or may not be valid. The equity ratio is often expressed as follows:

$$\text{Equity occurs when } \frac{\text{Outcomes of Individual}}{\text{Inputs of Individual}} = \frac{\text{Outcomes of Others}}{\text{Inputs of Others}}$$

According to equity theory, the highest motivation occurs when a person's ratios equal those of the comparison person. For example, "Beth and I are both business graduates, we are both smart, we work incredibly hard, and we both get paid about the same." When people perceive an inequity, they are likely to engage in one of the following actions:

1. *Alter the outcomes.* The person who feels mistreated might ask for more salary or bonus, a promotion, or vacation time. Some people might even misappropriate company resources to get even, such as taking home company supplies for personal use.
2. *Alter the inputs.* A worker who feels treated inequitably might decrease effort or time devoted to work. The person who feels underpaid might engage in self-defeating behavior by using sick days to take care of personal business.
3. *Distort the perception.* To combat feelings of inequity, people can distort their perception of their own or others' inputs or outcomes. Recognizing that she is overpaid in comparison to coworkers, a bookkeeper might say, "I read *The Wall Street Journal* regularly, so I have much more financial knowledge than the other bookkeepers."
4. *Change the reference source.* A convenient way of restoring equity is to change to another reference source whose outcome/input ratio is similar to one's own. A person might be dissatisfied with his salary in comparison to the

average worker in his field. He might then say, "Many of the people included in the salary survey work in large cities. My cost of living is much lower in the city where I work."

5. *Leave the situation.* An extreme move taken by many people who feel treated inequitably is to quit a job. The person is then free to pursue greater equity in another position.

Equity theory looks good on the surface and has direct relevance for pay systems and employee retention. Even if other approaches to employee motivation, such as recognition and reward programs, are in place workers must still receive what they perceive to be equitable pay.

SUMMARY OF KEY POINTS

1 Explain the relationship between motivation, performance, and commitment. From the standpoint of the individual, motivation is an internal state that leads to the pursuit of objectives. From the standpoint of the manager, motivation is an activity that gets subordinates to pursue objectives. The purpose of motivating employees is to get them to achieve results and commitment. Motivation is but one important contributor to productivity and performance. Other important contributors are abilities, skills, technology, and group norms.

2 Present an overview of major theories of need satisfaction in explaining motivation. Workers can be motivated through need satisfaction, particularly because most people want to know "What's in it for me?" First, needs must be identified. Second, the person must be given an opportunity to satisfy those needs.

Maslow's need hierarchy states that people strive to become self-actualized. However, before higher-level needs are activated, certain lower-level needs must be satisfied. When a person's needs are satisfied at one level, he or she looks toward satisfaction at a higher level. Specific needs playing an important role in work motivation include achievement, power, affiliation, recognition, risk taking, and thrill seeking.

The two-factor theory of work motivation includes two different sets of job motivation factors: One set gives people a chance to satisfy higher-level needs. These are satisfiers and motivators. When present, they increase satisfaction and motivation. When satisfiers and motivators are absent, the impact is neutral. Satisfiers and motivators generally relate to the content of a job. They include achievement, recognition, and opportunity for advancement. Dissatisfiers are job elements that appeal more to lower-level needs. When they are present, they prevent dissatisfaction, but they do not create satisfaction or motivation. Dissatisfiers relate mostly to the context of a job. They include company policy and administration, job security, and money.

3 Explain how goal setting is used to motivate people. Goal setting is an important part of most motivational programs, and it is a managerial method of motivating group members. It is based on these ideas: (a) specific goals are better than generalized goals; (b) the more difficult the goal, the better the performance; (c) only goals that are accepted improve performance; (d) goals are more effective when used to evaluate performance; (e) goals should be linked to feedback and rewards; and (f) group goal setting is important.

4 Describe the application of behavior modification to worker motivation. Behavior modification is the most systematic method of motivating people. It changes behavior by rewarding the right responses and punishing or ignoring the wrong ones. Behavior modification is based on the law of effect: Behavior that leads to positive consequences tends to be repeated, and behavior that leads to negative consequences tends not to be repeated.

There are four behavior modification strategies. Positive reinforcement rewards people for making the right response. Avoidance motivation rewards people by taking away an uncomfortable consequence. Extinction is the process of weakening undesirable behavior by removing the reward for it. Punishment is the presentation of an undesirable consequence for a specific behavior. Punishment is often counterproductive. If used appropriately, however, it can be motivational.

Suggestions for the informal use of positive reinforcement in a work setting include (a) state clearly what behavior leads to a reward, (b) use appropriate rewards, (c) make rewards contingent on good performance, (d) administer intermittent rewards, (e) vary the size of rewards, (f) administer rewards promptly, (g) change rewards periodically, and (h) reward the team as well as the individual.

5 **Describe the role of financial incentives, including profit sharing and gainsharing, in worker motivation.** A natural way to motivate workers at any level is to offer financial incentives for good performance. Linking pay to performance improves the motivational value of financial incentives. Research has shown that pay is more often linked to quantity than quality of work.

Profit-sharing plans give out money related to company or large unit performance. Gainsharing is a formal program that allows employees to participate financially in productivity gains they have achieved. Bonuses are distributed to employees based on how much they decrease the labor cost involved in producing or selling goods. Employee involvement in increasing productivity is an important part of gainsharing.

Employee stock ownership plans set aside a block of company stock for employee purchase, often redeemable at retirement. Stock option plans give employees the right to purchase company stock at a spec-ified price at some future time. Both plans attempt to motivate workers by making them part owners of the business.

6 **Explain the conditions under which a person will be motivated according to expectancy theory.** Expectancy theory contends that people will expend effort if they expect the effort to lead to performance and the performance to lead to a reward. According to the expectancy model presented here, a person will be motivated if the person believes effort will lead to performance, the performance will lead to a reward, the reward satisfies an important need, and the need satisfaction is intense enough to make the effort seem worthwhile.

7 **Describe how equity theory can be used to motivate workers.** Equity theory explains how workers compare their inputs and outcomes with relevant people in the workplace. When employees believe that they are receiving equitable outputs in relation to their inputs, they are generally satisfied and motivated. When workers believe that they are giving too much in relation to what they are receiving from the organization, dissatisfaction ensues.

KEY TERMS AND PHRASES

Motivation, *318*

P = M x A, *319*

Need, *320*

Maslow's need hierarchy, *320*

Deficiency needs, *320*

Growth needs, *320*

Affiliation need, *322*

Recognition need, *322*

Two-factor theory of work motivation, *324*

Behavior modification, *327*

Law of effect, *327*

Profit-sharing plan, *334*

Gainsharing, *335*

Expectancy theory of motivation, *337*

Equity theory, *340*

QUESTIONS

1. What criticisms might you offer of the Behavioral Risk Improvement program at Foamex?
2. What information does this chapter have to offer the manager who is already working with a well-motivated team?
3. Some managers object to systematic approaches to motivating employees by expressing the thought, "Why should we have to go out of our way to motivate workers to do what they are paid to do?" What is your reaction to this objection?
4. Which of the motivation theories or methods described in this chapter do you think would have the most relevance for motivating executives? Explain.
5. Which of the motivation theories or methods described in this chapter do you think would have the most relevance for motivating welfare-to-work employees? (Welfare-to-work employees are those trained by the government so they can join the workforce.)
6. If internal motivation is important, why do many intrinsically motivating jobs (such as big business executive or professional basketball player) pay so much?
7. How could you use expectancy theory to increase your own motivation level?

CRITICAL THINKING QUESTIONS

1. Many business firms hire well-known sports coaches like Lou Holtz and Rick Pitino to give them advice about motivating managers and employees. The consultation often includes a motivational speech given to workers. How seriously should businesspeople take the motivational advice of sports coaches?

2. Suppose a person believes that he or she is not motivated enough to have a successful career. How might this person apply motivation theory to become more motivated?

SELF-ASSESSMENT EXERCISE: My Approach to Motivating Others

Describe how often you act or think in the way indicated by the following statements when attempting to motivate another person. Use the following scale: very infrequently (VI); infrequently (I); sometimes (S); frequently (F); very frequently (VF).

	VI	I	S	F	VF
1. I ask the other person what he or she is hoping to achieve in the situation.	1	2	3	4	5
2. I attempt to figure out whether the person has the ability to do what I need done.	1	2	3	4	5
3. When another person is heel-dragging, it usually means he or she is lazy.	5	4	3	2	1
4. I tell the person I'm trying to motivate exactly what I want.	1	2	3	4	5
5. I like to give the other person a reward up front so he or she will be motivated.	5	4	3	2	1
6. I give lots of feedback when another person is performing a task for me.	1	2	3	4	5
7. I like to belittle another person enough so that he or she will be intimidated into doing what I need done.	5	4	3	2	1
8. I make sure that the other person feels treated fairly.	1	2	3	4	5
9. I figure that if I smile nicely enough I can get the other person to work as hard as I need.	5	4	3	2	1
10. I attempt to get what I need done by instilling fear in the other person.	5	4	3	2	1
11. I specify exactly what needs to be accomplished.	1	2	3	4	5
12. I generously praise people who help me get my work accomplished.	1	2	3	4	5
13. A job well done is its own reward. I therefore keep praise to a minimum.	5	4	3	2	1
14. I make sure to let people know how well they have done in meeting my expectations on a task.	1	2	3	4	5
15. To be fair, I attempt to reward people about the same no matter how well they have performed.	5	4	3	2	1
16. When somebody doing work for me performs well, I recognize his or her accomplishments promptly.	1	2	3	4	5
17. Before giving somebody a reward, I attempt to find out what would appeal to that person.	1	2	3	4	5
18. I make it a policy not to thank somebody for doing a job he or she is paid to do.	5	4	3	2	1
19. If people do not know how to perform a task, their motivation will suffer.	1	2	3	4	5
20. If properly designed, many jobs can be self-rewarding.	1	2	3	4	5

Total Score _____

Scoring and interpretation: Add the numbers circled to obtain your total score.

90–100   You have advanced knowledge and skill with respect to motivating others in a work environment. Continue to build on the solid base you have established.

50–89   You have average knowledge and skill with respect to motivating others. With additional study and experience, you will probably develop advanced motivational skills.

20–49   To effectively motivate others in a work environment, you will need to greatly expand your knowledge of motivation theory and techniques.

Source: Adapted from David A. Whetton and Kim S. Cameron, *Developing Management Skills,* 3rd ed. (New York: Harper Collins, 1995), pp. 358–359.

SKILL-BUILDING EXERCISE: Identifying the Most Powerful Motivators

The class divides itself into small groups. Working alone, group members first attach a valence to all the rewards in Exhibit 12-6. Use the expectancy theory scale of –100 to +100. Next, do an analysis of the top 10 motivators identified by the group, perhaps by calculating the average valence attached to the rewards that at first glance were assigned high valences by most group members. After each group has identified its top 10 motivators, the group leaders can post the results for the other class members to see. After comparing results, answer these questions:

1. What appear to be the top three motivators for the entire class?
2. Do the class members tend to favor internal or external rewards?
3. Did career experience or gender influence the results within the groups?
4. Of what value to managers would this exercise be in estimating valences?

INTERNET SKILL-BUILDING EXERCISE: Recognition Programs

Recognition programs are such a widespread practice that you might want to learn more about them. Visit http://www .recognition.org, the National Association of Employee Recognition. Click on Recognition Strategies and search for at least two approaches to employee recognition not already mentioned in the text. Place yourself in the role of the manager in charge of motivation programs for your company. Critically evaluate the enthusiasm the National Association of Employee Recognition has for the programs it describes.

CASE PROBLEM 12-A: Rewards and Recognition at Tel-Service

Tel-Service is a fast-growing customer service and fulfillment firm based in New Jersey. The company's core business is responding to customer questions, complaints, and comments. Companies such as Sony, Tetley, and PR Newswire outsource much of their customer-service activities to Tel-Service. Any time a customer of a client company calls the toll-free number listed on the packaging and literature, they are actually reaching Tel-Service.

At Tel-Service headquarters, 300 employees respond to customer phone calls. In order to maintain high levels of customer satisfaction, Tel-Service employees are closely monitored. Workers are evaluated based on criteria such as courteousness, thoroughness, and calls answered per hour. A particular challenge is meeting performance standards when dealing with annoyed customers.

Up until one year ago, employee turnover at Tel-Service was unacceptably high. Employees stayed at the job for an average of only eight months. Considering that each new employee received two months of training, the eight-month average stay was particularly troublesome to management. Nathan Samuels, the director of operations at Tel-Service, knew that the high turnover had to be reduced. An increasing amount of money was invested in training staff, and less-skilled customer service representatives (CSRs) were responding to

customer inquiries. If the CSRs were doing a poor job, customers might complain, which could lead to Tel-Service losing a client. Samuels recognized that skilled customer service representatives were critical to the success of the firm.

Samuels decided that the first step in fixing the high turnover problem was to determine what was wrong in the first place. He decided to interview a sample of customer service representatives. Samuels thought that a good perspective on the problem could be reached by interviewing experienced employees and those less experienced. The sample consisted of those who had been working for the company for three years, and others who were barely out of training.

The interview questions focused mostly on the working atmosphere. Among the questions were "What do you enjoy about your work?" and "What could make your work time better?" Interviewees were encouraged to be frank, and it was made clear that there would be no repercussions from making negative comments. Based on the interviews, Samuels observed several themes:

- The more experienced employees remained because they needed the job. Most of these employees were not thrilled with the work, but they stayed with it to pay for necessities. Samuels reasoned that the motivation of this group of employees was not high enough to result in superior performance.

- The new employees were excited about the work but nervous about the horror stories told by their peers.
- Customer service representatives felt overworked and underappreciated by the rude and degrading customers they dealt with daily.

Based on these interview findings, Samuels believed he had a good grasp of the problems facing the customer service representatives. After reading a few leadership trade journals, Samuels decided that a rewards and recognition program might be enough to motivate the reps and make them feel appreciated. He decided to give some sort of reward to those employees who maintain a superior level of customer service. The reward would serve a dual function. First, it would motivate the CSRs to work harder to achieve their reward. Second, it would help the CSRs feel better appreciated by management to help compensate for the lack of appreciation by customers.

The plan was to hold an office party during the presentation of rewards. In this way, other employees in addition to the winner would receive something of value. After receiving approval from the CEO, Samuels decided that every three months one employee would win a vacation to Disney World. Tel-Service would pay for the accommodations and airfare. Samuels and the CEO thought that a reward of this magnitude would be motivational.

The customer service representatives were elated when they heard about the new program. Average performance based on the standards in use jumped 39 percent, including the number of telephone calls handled per hour. For the next three months not a single CSR left without giving notice. Several clients sent letters or e-mail messages explaining how satisfied their customers were with the telephone support.

During this same period, two large new accounts joined Tel-Service through recommendations from other firms.

When the first three months were completed, it was time to reward the winner and throw the party. Because not all representatives could leave the phones at the same time, coffee and cake were placed at a central location where the reps could serve themselves at breaks. During lunch hour, when the largest number or reps were off the phone, the winner was announced—Kristine Santora. Even though the competition was fierce, all employees were very proud of Santora. Samuels made sure to remind them that the start of the next contest was immediate, and everyone else had a chance to win. The fervor and motivation created three months prior was now fueled with new life.

After giving the reward of the Disney trip three times, Samuels phased down the program and replaced it with smaller, more personalized rewards like watches and sporting equipment. The office parties to celebrate the rewards were retained.

One year after the start of the program, CSR turnover at Tel-Service is approximately 15 percent, and the representatives appear happier in their jobs. According to Samuels, "I doubt we would have ever gotten the customer service rep problem under control without having implemented the reward and recognition program."

Discussion Questions

1. Identify the motivational techniques used by Samuels to enhance performance of the customer service reps.
2. What can Samuels do to keep the customer service staff motivated in the future?
3. Use expectancy theory to analyze why the reward and recognition program is working.

Source: Case prepared by Brian Romanko, Rochester Institute of Technology, November 2000.

C A S E   P R O B L E M   1 2 - B :   The Lonely Work-at-Homers

Missed package deliveries and phone calls, and the occasional barking dog were not exactly what Tom Galloway had in mind when he launched a digital printing business from his home a few years ago. His hopes were to roll out of bed each morning, start the coffee pot and PC and make a fortune without ever getting out of his pajamas. The reality was that within a few weeks, Galloway was buried under paperwork—e-mail messages—and lonely. After six months, he hung up his bathrobe for good. "It was such a pain," Galloway recalls.

Although he no longer works at home, Galloway still deals with that type of frustration, but now as a source of revenue. His new venture, a franchised chain of upscale, small

business-service centers called Your Office USA, targets people facing the same problems he did. Your Office is one among many firms serving the almost 40 million people in the United States who operate small businesses from home or are corporate telecommuters. Many of these people seek the professional services and social interaction characteristic of a traditional work environment.

Along with executive-suite operators such as HQ and Regus, Your Office positions itself as being a more elegant version of Kinko's. Superstores like Office Depot and Staples are looking to follow the lead of Kinko's by adding more in-house digital offerings.

Your Office is a subsidiary of IB Your Office, a $50 million-a-year company with more than 100 franchises in Europe and Asia. A company executive describes Your Office as a "superstore for the home-based entrepreneur." The 6,000-square-feet interiors have the familiar appearance of a corporate office: a receptionist area, long hallways with art on the wall, leading to individual offices and cubicles. Yet few corporate sites house such varied activity. For instance, in one room a customer trains security guards, an in another room a computer specialist is at a workstation.

Randolph Blatt, 41, of Raleigh, North Carolina, is one of those computer specialists. After working from home for four years, Blatt, who recruits computer professionals, became tired of the distractions. "I would get phone calls, and I had screaming babies in the background. I would duck into my laundry room to hide. It never worked. At Your Office, I regularly run into people, and I feel like I'm part of the world."

Your Office also hopes to serve millions of sales representatives who have lost their desks to downsizings and become corporate nomads, as well as on-the-go entrepreneurs who want satellite offices in several cities. By the hour, the day, or the month they can rent office space, hire a secretary, check their mailboxes or e-mail, or conduct a video-conference. Whenever New York City bankruptcy attorney Garret Rubin has to meet clients near the Brooklyn courts, he uses a nearby Your Office. "I wish my office were this nice," he says.

At any Kinko's outlet, day or night, graphic artists and bank presidents alike can access a uniform set of PCs, fax machines, color copiers, and printers to update résumés, create flyers, trade ideas, and confer with clients. "We're the intellectual meeting place in any community," claims Paul Orfalea, who started Kinko's in an old Santa Barbara, California, hamburger stand in 1970.

Susan Cummins, a Miami public relations expert, calls Kinko's "the only office social experience I connect with. It's like the office, but without the politics." To make things cozier, Kinko's has opened a few Citibank minibranches in its stores. At Your Office, franchisees hold pizza parties and holiday bashes to bring their disparate customers together.

Discussion Questions

1. What needs are the small business owners and telecommuters described in this case attempting to satisfy by frequenting the small-business service centers?

2. What recommendations would you have to the operators of the service centers to make their services even more attractive to small business owners and telecommuters?

3. What recommendations can you make to the small-business owners and telecommuters for obtaining more intrinsic satisfaction in their work?

Source: Daniel Eisenberg, "Offices by the Hour," *Time*, February 1, 1999, pp. 40–41. Used with permission of the publisher.

ENDNOTES

1. "Get Healthy—-and Get Deduction, Doctor Says," Knight Ridder Newspapers, April 8, 2001.
2. John Katzenbach, *Peak Performance: Aligning the Hearts and Minds of Your Employees* (Boston: Harvard Business School Press, 2000).
3. Abraham M. Maslow, "A Theory of Human Motivation," *Psychological Review*, July 1943, pp. 370–396; Maslow, *Motivation and Personality* (New York: Harper & Row, 1954), Chapter 5.
4. Michael J. Stahl, "Achievement, Power, and Managerial Motivation: Selecting Managerial Talent with Job Choice Exercise," *Personnel Psychology*, Winter 1983; David C. McClelland, *Power: The Inner Experience* (New York: Irvington, 1975).
5. Gerald Graham, "Motivating Entry-Level Workers," *WorkingSMART*, October 1998, p. 2.
6. Gillian Flynn, "Is Your Recognition Program Understood?" *Workforce*, July 1998, pp. 31–32.
7. Bob Nelson, "Does One Reward Fit All?" *Workforce*, February 1997, pp. 67–70.
8. "Well-Structured Employee Reward/Recognition Programs Yield Positive Results," *HRfocus*, November 1999, p. 1.
9. "What Makes Them Do It? *Time*, January 15, 1996, p. 60.
10. "Employee Motivation . . . Recognizing Workers' Needs," *Managers Edge*, March 1999, p. 1.
11. Frederick Herzberg, *Work and the Nature of Man* (Cleveland: World, 1966).
12. Edwin A. Locke and Gary P. Latham, *A Theory of Goal Setting and Task Performance* (Upper Saddle River, NJ: Prentice Hall, 1990).
13. "Set Outrageous Goals," *Executive Leadership*, June 2001, p. 7.
14. Timothy D. Ludwig and E. Scott Geller, "Assigned Versus Participative Goal Setting and Response Generalization: Managing Injury Control Among Professional Pizza Deliverers," *Journal of Applied Psychology*, April 1997, pp. 253–261.
15. P. Christopher Earley and Terri R. Lituchy, "Delineating Goal and Efficacy Effects: A Test of Three Models," *Journal of Applied Psychology*, February 1991, p. 83.
16. Kenneth D. Butterfield, Linda Kiebe Treviño, and Gail A. Ball, "Punishment from the Manager's Perspective: A Grounded Investigation and Inductive Model," *Academy of Management Journal*, December 1996, p. 1506.
17. Janet Barnard, "What Works in Rewarding Problem-Solving Teams?" *Compensation & Benefits Management*, Winter 1998, pp. 55–58.
18. Fred Luthans and Alexander D. Stajkovic, "Reinforce for Performance: The Need to Go Beyond Pay and Even Rewards," *Academy of Management Executive*, May 1999, pp. 52–54.
19. Thomas J. Hackett and Donald G. McDermott, "Seven Steps to Successful Performance-Based Rewards," *HRfocus*, September 1999, p. 11.
20. Hackett and McDermott, "Seven Steps," pp. 11–12.
21. Shari Caudron, "How Pay Launched Performance," *Personnel Journal*, September 1996, pp. 70–76.
22. Luis R. Gomez-Meija, Theresa M. Welbourn, and Robert M. Wiseman, "The Role of Risk Sharing and Risk Taking Under Gainsharing," *Academy of Management Review*, July 2000, p. 493; http://www.gainsharing.com.

23. Susan C. Hanlon, David C. Meyer, and Robert K. Taylor, "Consequences of Gainsharing: A Field Experiment Revisited," *Group and Organization Management*, 19, no. 1 (1994), pp. 87–111.

24. "Why Gainsharing Works Even Better Today Than in the Past," *HRfocus*, April 2000, p. 3

25. Alfie Kohn, "Why Incentive Plans Cannot Work," *Harvard Business Review*, September–October 1993, pp. 54–63; Bob Nelson, "Does One Reward Fit All?" *Workforce*, February 1997, p. 70.

26. Jeffrey Pfeffer, "Six Dangerous Myths About Pay," *Harvard Business Review*, May–June 1998, p. 110.

27. Thad Green, *Motivation Management: Fueling Performance by Discovering What People Believe About Themselves and Their Organizations* (Palo Alto, CA: Davies-Black Publishing, 2000).

28. Victor H. Vroom, *Work and Motivation* (New York: Wiley, 1964).

29. Walter B. Newsom, "Motivate Now!" *Personnel Journal*, February 1999, pp. 51–52.

30. J. Stacy Adams, "Toward an Understanding of Inequality," *Journal of Abnormal and Social Psychology*, 67 (1963), pp. 422–436; Jerald Greenberg, "Equity Theory and Workplace Status: A Field Experiment," *Journal of Applied Psychology*, December 1988, pp. 606–613.

Communication

It's 7:55 A.M. at PQ Systems. Each and every weekday, a simple message sounds off through employees' phone speakers: "Coffee's ready, coffee's ready." All 40 employees head to the company's training room and take seats in the chairs that form a big circle. By 8 A.M., it begins: a simple gathering, lasting 10 to 30 minutes, in which people openly talk about everything from financials to new product development to whose son or daughter just graduated from high school. "It gives us a sense of connectedness," says product manager Soren Gormley. "It's a great way to start the day."

Miles away, deep in the heart of Dallas, something similar takes place at Texas Nameplate. The company's biweekly DO-IT meetings—as in "daily operations innovation team"—bring together supervisors and team leaders from all areas of the operation. The sessions feature the usual one-way reporting, but they also demonstrate a level of sharing and helping across functional areas that most companies only dream of. "It's really cool to watch," says Linda Bush, who provided the leadership training that fosters genuine dialogue. "It's people taking responsibility for the overall good."[1]

OBJECTIVES

After studying this chapter and doing the exercises, you should be able to:

1 Describe the steps in the communication process.

2 Recognize the major types of nonverbal communication in the workplace.

3 Explain and illustrate the difference between formal and informal communication channels.

4 Identify major communication barriers in organizations.

5 Develop tactics for overcoming communication barriers.

6 Describe how to conduct more effective meetings.

7 Describe how organizational (or office) politics affect interpersonal communication.

Chapter 13

The communication sessions taking place in the two companies just mentioned illustrate the emphasis many successful companies place on an effective exchange of information among employees. So vital is communication that it has been described as the glue that holds the organization together. Poor communication is the number one problem in virtually all organizations and the cause of most problems. Communication problems can be immensely expensive. John O. Whitney says, "I have, as a manager or consultant in business turnarounds, observed losses totalling more than $1 billion in organizations where people, early in the game, either knew absolutely or had strong premonitions about the problem, but were intimidated, squelched, or ignored."[2]

Communication is an integral part of all managerial functions. Unless managers communicate with others, they cannot plan, organize, control, or lead. For example, a manager cannot communicate a vision without superior communication skills. Person-to-person communication is as much a part of managerial, professional, technical, and sales work as running is a part of basketball and tennis. Furthermore, the ability to communicate effectively relates closely to career advancement. Employees who are poor communicators are often bypassed for promotion, particularly if the job includes people contact.

The information in this chapter is designed to improve communication among people in the workplace. Two approaches are used to achieve this end. First the chapter describes key aspects of organizational communication, including communication channels and barriers. Second, the chapter presents many suggestions about how managers and others can overcome communication barriers and conduct effective meetings. We also study a subtle aspect of communications called office politics.

1 THE COMMUNICATION PROCESS

Describe the steps in the communication process.

communication

The process of exchanging information by the use of words, letters, symbols, or nonverbal behavior.

Anytime people send information back and forth to each other they are communicating. **Communication** is the process of exchanging information by the use of words, letters, symbols, or nonverbal behavior. Sending messages to other people, and having the messages interpreted as intended, generally proves to be complex and difficult. The difficulty arises because communication depends on perception. People may perceive words, symbols, actions, and even colors differently, depending on their background and interests.

A typical communication snafu took place at a quality-improvement meeting. The supervisor said to a technician, "Quality is in the eye of the beholder." The technician responded, "Oh, how interesting." Later the technician told the rest of the team, "It's no use striving for high quality. The boss thinks quality is too subjective to achieve." The supervisor's message—that the consumer is the final judge of quality—got lost in the process; communication failed.

Steps in the Communication Process

Exhibit 13-1 illustrates the complexity of the communication process. This diagram simplifies the baffling process of sending and receiving messages. The model of two-way communication involves four major steps, each subject to interference, or noise. The four steps are encoding, transmission, decoding, and feedback.

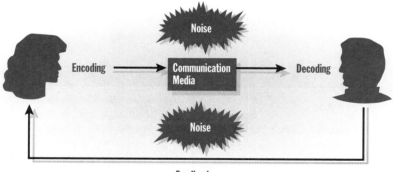

Encoding the Message

Encoding is the process of organizing ideas into a series of symbols, such as words and gestures, designed to communicate with the receiver. Word choice strongly influences communication effectiveness. The better a person's grasp of language, the easier it is for him or her to encode. Appropriate choices of words or any other symbol increase the chance that communication will proceed smoothly. The supervisor mentioned at the beginning of this section chose to use the somewhat vague phrase: "Quality is in the eye of the beholder." A more effective message might be: "Quality is measured by customer acceptance."

encoding

The process of organizing ideas into a series of symbols designed to communicate with the receiver.

Communication Media

The message is sent via a communication medium, such as voice, telephone, paper, or e-mail. Selecting a medium that fits the message contributes to its effectiveness. It would be appropriate to use the spoken word to inform a coworker that his shirt was torn. It would be inappropriate to send the same message through voice mail. Many messages in organizations are communicated nonverbally, through the use of gestures and facial expressions. For example, a smile from a superior in a meeting effectively communicates the message "I agree with your comment." Exhibit 13-2 presents additional ideas about choosing the best medium for your message.

Decoding the Message

In **decoding**, the receiver interprets the message and translates it into meaningful information. Barriers to communication often surface at the decoding step. People may interpret messages according to their psychological needs and motives. The technician mentioned earlier may have been looking for an out—a reason not to be so concerned about achieving high standards. So he interpreted the message in a way that minimized the need to strive for quality.

decoding

The communication stage in which the receiver interprets the message and translates it into meaningful information.

After understanding comes action—the receiver does something about the message. If the receiver acts in the manner the sender wants, the communication process is successful. From the manager's perspective, the success of a message is measured in terms of the action taken by a group member. Understanding alone is not sufficient. Many people understand messages but take no constructive action.

EXHIBIT 13-2

Choosing the Right Medium for Your Message

Several options exist for communicating an important message on the job. Before choosing an option, think of its major pros and cons.

Quick Telephone Call: On the positive side, a quick call is efficient. It is personal, informal, and allows for an exchange of ideas. A disadvantage is that phone calls are intrusive. You are asking the recipient to stop what he or she is doing, and the person may feel pressured into giving you an immediate response.

Face-to-Face Meeting: On the positive side, visiting a person at his or her work area can get a problem resolved quickly. On the negative side, you can annoy people by dropping by without an appointment. Making an appointment can also be disturbing because the person has to place you on his or her schedule. Dropping in on a high-ranking person may be unwelcome in a hierarchical organization.

E-mail: Sending a message by e-mail is excellent for wide distribution and provides a permanent record of your message. Your receiver also controls when to receive the message. A negative is that the tone of an e-mail message can be misinterpreted. Remember too, that once you hit the send button it is too late to change your mind. Also, with so many people sending e-mail, your message might get overlooked.

Hard-Copy Memo: Paper memos appear quite official, and are a standard part of organizational communications. You are also more likely to carefully compose and edit a hard-copy memo than an electronic one. Written memos, however, may appear stiff, and some people will misplace a written memo before or after reading it. A paper memo would appear out of date in most firms today.

Fax: A fax is generally used for the same purpose as any other hard-copy memo; however, it is now used primarily for transmitting factual information, and when a document with a personal signature is required. It can be an intrusive, interruptive form of communication if the fax machine is nearby the receiver.

Scheduled Meeting: If you schedule a meeting, you are in charge and you will be able to interact with several people about your issue. Holding a meeting dramatizes the importance of the topic. A disadvantage of a meeting is that some participants will be annoyed if the topic does not appear substantial enough to justify calling a meeting.

Source: Adapted from "The Right Medium for Your Message," *Working Smart*, January 1995, p. 5.

Feedback

The receiver's response to the sender's message is referred to as *feedback*. Without feedback it is difficult to know whether a message has been received and understood. The feedback step also includes the reactions of the receiver. If the receiver takes actions as intended by the sender, the message has been received satisfactorily.

Action represents a form of feedback, because it results in a message sent to the original sender from the receiver. Suppose a small-business owner receives this message from a supplier: "Please send us $450 within 10 days to cover your overdue account. If we do not receive payment within 10 days, your account will be turned over to a collection agent." The owner understands the message but decides not to comply, because the parts for which the $450 is owed were defective. The owner's noncompliance is not due to a lack of understanding.

Many missteps can occur between encoding and decoding a message. **Noise**, or unwanted interference, can distort or block the message. Later in the chapter the discussion of communication barriers will examine the problem of noise and how it prevents the smooth flow of ideas between sender and receiver.

noise

In communication, unwanted interference that can distort or block a message.

2   NONVERBAL COMMUNICATION IN ORGANIZATIONS

Recognize the major types of nonverbal communication in the workplace.

The most obvious modes of communication are speaking, writing, and sign language. (Many large business meetings today include an interpreter who signs for deaf members of the audience.) A substantial amount of interpersonal communication also occurs through **nonverbal communication**, the transmission of messages by means other than words. Body language refers to those aspects of nonverbal communication directly related to movements of the body such as gestures and posture.

Nonverbal communication usually supplements rather than substitutes for writing, speaking, and sign language. The general purpose of nonverbal communication is to express the feeling behind a message, such as nodding one's head vigorously to indicate an emphatic "yes." Nonverbal communication incorporates a wide range of behavior. Nevertheless, it can be divided into the following nine categories.[3]

1. *Environment.* The physical setting in which the message takes place communicates meaning. Included here would be office decor, type of automobile, and the restaurant or hotel chosen for a business meeting. What kind of message would you send to people if you drove to work in a Chevy Tahoe or a Land Rover?

2. *Body placement.* The placement of one's body in relation to someone else is widely used to transmit messages. Facing a person in a casual, relaxed style indicates acceptance. Moving close to another person also generally indicates of acceptance. Yet moving too close may be perceived as a violation of personal space, and the message sender will be rejected. Speechwriter and speaking coach Nick Morgan says that to effectively relate to an audience, you need a *kinesthetic connection* (effective movement of the body). This would include the other forms of nonverbal communication as well as moving around effectively. For example, vary the distance between yourself and your audience, and do not turn away from the audience to cue your next slide.[4]

3. *Posture.* Another widely used clue to a person's attitude is his or her posture. Leaning toward another person suggests a favorable attitude toward the message a person is trying to communicate. Tilting your head and leaning in indicates your concern and level of attention.[5] Leaning backward communicates the opposite. Standing up straight generally conveys self-confidence, while slouching can be interpreted as a sign of low self-confidence.

4. *Hand and body gestures.* Your hand and body movements convey specific information to others. Positive attitudes toward another person are shown by frequent gesturing. In contrast, dislike or disinterest usually produces few gestures. An important exception here occurs when some people wave their hands while in an argument, sometimes to the point of making threatening gestures. The type of gesture displayed also communicates a specific message. For example, moving your hand toward your body in a waving motion communicates the message "Come here, I like you" or "Tell me more." Palms spread outward indicate perplexity.

5. *Facial expressions and movement.* The particular look on a person's face and movements of the person's head provide reliable cues as to approval, disapproval, or disbelief.

6. *Voice quality.* Aspects of the voice such as pitch, volume, tone, and speech rate may communicate confidence, nervousness, and enthusiasm. People often judge intelligence by how a person sounds. Research suggests that the most annoying voice quality is a whining, complaining, or nagging tone.[6] Exhibit 13-3 provides some suggestions for developing impressive voice quality. Another aspect of voice quality is a person's accent. A study conducted in Texas found that job candidates with strong regional accents were less likely to be offered a high-prestige job or one with high public contact. The recommendation offered is to soften but not necessarily completely change a regional accent because a complete change could make a person feel unnatural.[7]

nonverbal communication

The transmission of messages by means other than words.

353

EXHIBIT 13-3

**How to Speak with an
Authoritative Voice**

A good voice alone will not make a businessperson successful. Yet, like clothing, voice quality should always add to a person's image, not subtract from it. Here are several practical suggestions, developed by voice coaches, for improving voice quality:

- **Avoid a nasal-sounding voice.** The only sounds that should come through the nose are the sounds of *m, n,* and *ng.* The rest of speech should be sounded in the mouth. There's an easy test to see if you talk through your nose: Say "that." Now, pinch your nose and say "that" again. You should notice no difference. If you sound like a duck when you pinch your nose and say "that," then you have a nasal voice. To solve this problem, throw open your mouth and repeat "that" as you yawn. This action will bring the vowel down into your mouth. With practice, you will sound the vowels in your mouth and lose the nasal tone.

- **Vary your tone.** If you speak in a monotone, your voice will sound mechanical. One way to overcome a monotone is to practice singing several of your typical presentations. This approach will help you develop skill in using vocal variety.

- **Decrease voice hesitations.** Vocal hesitations are a nonverbal clue to weakness and insecurity. When you hesitate between words, people may think you have not thought through your comments. This problem can be solved by slowing down your speech.

- **Avoid breathiness.** People who take a breath after almost every word appear anxious. To remedy breathiness, take the time to fill your lungs with air before speaking. Practice until you can speak two sentences without taking a breath.

- **Practice conveying commitment in the sound of your voice.** Tape yourself as you talk extemporaneously about a topic you care about, such as describing your fantasy goals in life. Replaying the tape, you will hear your voice move up and down the musical scale. The emotion shown reflects commitment.

Source: Adapted from Charles Livingston McCain, "Say It in the Voice of Authority," *Success,* May 1984, pp. 48, 51; and Roger Ailes and Jon Kraushar, "Are You a Communications Wimp?" *Business Week Careers,* June 1988, p. 76.

7. *Clothing, dress, and appearance.* The image a person conveys communicates such messages as "I feel powerful" and "I think this meeting is important." For example, wearing one's best business attire to a performance appraisal interview would communicate that the person thinks the meeting is important. Another important meaning of dress is that it communicates how willing the employee is to comply with organizational standards. By deviating too radically from standard, such as wearing a suit on "Dress Down" day, the person communicates indifference. As two researchers note, "Employees failing to maintain dress standards suffer consequences that range from insults and ridicule to termination."[8]

8. *Mirroring.* To mirror is to build rapport with another person by imitating his or her voice tone, breathing rate, body movement, and language. Mirroring relies 20 percent on verbal means, 60 percent on voice tone, and 20 percent on body physiology. A specific application of mirroring is to conform to the other person's posture, eye movements, and hand movements. The person feels more relaxed as a result of your imitation.

   Adjusting your speech rate to the person with whom you are attempting to establish rapport is another mirroring technique. If the person speaks rapidly, so do you. If the other person speaks slowly, you decelerate your pace. This technique could get confusing if you attempt to establish rapport simultaneously with two people who speak at different rates.

9. *Use of Time.* A subtle mode of nonverbal communication in organizations is the use of time. High-status individuals, such as executives, send messages about their power by keeping lower-ranking people waiting. Ambitious people attempting to get ahead are seldom late for appointments (in the American culture). However, a high-ranking official might be late for a meeting, and that same amount of lateness might be perceived as a symbol of importance or busyness. Looking at your watch is usually interpreted as a sign of boredom or restlessness. Yet when a high-status person looks at his or her watch in a two-person meeting, the action is likely to be interpreted as meaning, "Hurry up and make your point. You have used up almost all the time I can grant you."

Keep in mind that many nonverbal signals are ambiguous. For example, a smile usually indicates agreement and warmth, but at times it can indicate nervousness. Even if nonverbal signals are not highly reliable, they are used to judge your behavior, particularly in meetings.

ORGANIZATIONAL CHANNELS AND DIRECTIONS OF COMMUNICATION **3**

Messages in organizations travel over many different channels, or paths. Communication channels can be formal or informal and can be categorized as downward, upward, horizontal, or diagonal. As described in Chapter 2, the widespread use of e-mail and intranets has greatly facilitated sending messages in all directions.

Explain and illustrate the difference between formal and informal communication channels.

Formal Communication Channels

Formal communication channels are the official pathways for sending information inside and outside an organization. The organization chart formally indicates the channels messages are supposed to follow. By carefully following the organization chart, a maintenance technician would know how to transmit a message to the chairman of the board. In many large organizations, the worker may have to go through as many as eight management or organizational levels. Modern organizations, however, make it easier for lower-ranking workers to communicate with high-level managers.

In addition to being pathways for communication, formal channels are also means of sending messages. These means include publications such as newsletters and newspapers, meetings, written memos, e-mail, traditional bulletin boards, and electronic bulletin boards.

One important communication channel can be classified as both formal and informal. With *management by walking around*, managers intermingle freely with workers on the shop floor, in the office, with customers, and at company social events. By spending time in personal contact with employees, the manager enhances open communication. Because management by walking around is systematic, it could be considered formal. However, a manager who circulates throughout the company violates the chain of command. She or he, therefore, invites more informal communication.

formal communication channels
The official pathways for sending information inside and outside an organization.

Communication Directions

Messages in organizations travel in four directions: downward, upward, horizontally, and diagonally. Over time, an organization develops communication networks corresponding to these directions. A **communication network** is a pattern or flow of messages that traces the communication from start to finish.

communication network
A pattern or flow of messages that traces the communication from start to finish.

In *downward communication*, messages flow from one level to a lower level. For example, a supervisor gives orders to a team member, or top-level managers send an announcement to employees. An overemphasized downward communication sometimes occurs at the expense of receiving upward communication. A survey of employees from different companies indicated a concern about the quantity and quality of communications received from management. Consider the following employee complaint as representative:

> I still feel like I don't know what's going on around this company. I feel like decisions are being made and I never hear about it and when I do it's often too late.[9]

Upward communication transmits messages from lower to higher levels in an organization. Although it may not be as frequent as downward communication, it is equally important. Remember the $1 billion mistake mentioned at the outset of the chapter? Upward communication tells management how well messages have been received. The upward communication path also provides an essential network for keeping management informed about problems. Management by walking around and simply speaking to employees facilitate upward communication. Many companies develop their own programs and policies to facilitate bottom-up communication. Three such approaches follow:

1. *Open-door policy.* An open-door policy allows any employee to bring a gripe to top management's attention—without first checking with his or her immediate manager. The open-door policy can be considered a grievance procedure that helps employees resolve problems. However, the policy also enhances upward communication because it informs top management about problems employees are experiencing.
2. *Workout program at GE.* General Electric conducts three-day town meetings across the company, attended by a cross-section of about 50 company personnel—senior and junior managers, and salaried and hourly workers. Facilitators encourage the audience to express their concerns freely. Participants evaluate various aspects of their business, such as reports and meetings. They discuss whether each one makes sense and attempt to "work out" problems. By using upward communication, GE attempts to achieve more speed and simplicity in its operations.
3. *Complaint program.* Many organizations institute formal complaint programs. Complaints sent up through channels include those about supervisors, working conditions, personality conflicts, sexual harassment, and inefficient work methods.

Through *horizontal communication*, people send messages to others at the same organizational level. Horizontal communication frequently takes the form of coworkers from the same department talking to each other. Coworkers who fail to share information with and respond to each other are likely to fall behind schedules and miss deadlines. A lack of horizontal communication often contributes to duplication of efforts, and quality suffers. Another type of horizontal communication takes place when managers communicate with other managers at the same level.

Horizontal communication provides the basis for cooperation. People need to communicate with each other to work effectively in joint efforts. For example, they advise each other of work problems and ask each other for help when needed. Horizontal communication is especially important as the basis for the horizontal organization described in Chapter 9. Moreover, research evidence confirms the belief that extensive lateral communication enhances creativity. Exchanging and "batting around" ideas with peers sharpens imagination.[10]

Diagonal communication is the transmission of messages to higher or lower organizational levels in different departments. A typical diagonal communication event occurs when the head of the marketing department needs some pricing information. She telephones or sends an e-mail to a supervisor in the finance department to get his input. The supervisor, in turn, telephones a specialist in the data processing department to get the necessary piece of information. The marketing person has thus started a chain of communication that goes down and across the organization.

Informal Communication Channels

Organizations could not function by formal communication channels alone. Another system of communication, called an **informal communication channel**, is also needed. Informal communication channels form the unofficial network that supplements the formal channels. Most of these informal channels arise out of necessity. For example, people sometimes depart from the official communication channels to consult with a person with specialized knowledge. Suppose the manager of pension services in a bank was familiar with the methods of calculating exchange rates between the U.S. dollar and other currencies. Bank employees from other departments would regularly consult this manager when they faced an exchange-rate problem. Anytime two or more employees consult each other outside formal communication channels, an informal communication channel has been used. Two other major aspects of informal communication channels are chance encounters, and the grapevine and the rumors it carries.

Chance Encounters
Unscheduled informal contact between managers and employees can be an efficient and effective informal communication channel. John P. Kotter found in his study of general managers that effective managers do not confine their communications to formal meetings. Instead, they collect valuable information during chance encounters.[11] Spontaneous communication events may occur in the cafeteria, near the water fountain, in the halls, and on the elevator. For example, during an elevator ride, a manager might spot a purchasing agent and ask, "Whatever happened to the just-in-time inventory purchasing proposal?" In two minutes the manager might obtain the information that would typically be solicited in a 30-minute meeting. A chance encounter differs from management by walking around in that the latter is a planned event; the former occurs unintentionally.

The Grapevine and Rumor Control
The **grapevine** is the informal means by which information is transmitted in organizations. As such, it is the major informal communication channel. The term *grapevine* refers to tangled pathways that can distort information. This analogy tends to oversimplify its function. Management sometimes purposely uses the grapevine to disseminate information informally. For example, management might want to hint to employees that the plant will be closed unless the employees become more productive. Although the plans are only tentative, feeding them into the grapevine may result in improved motivation and productivity. Some important characteristics of the grapevine include the following:[12]

informal communication channel
An unofficial network that supplements the formal channels in an organization.

grapevine
The informal means by which information is transmitted in organizations.

357

- A substantial number of employees consider the grapevine to be their primary source of information about company events. The grapevine often creates a bigger impact on employees than do messages sent over formal channels. Messages received through formal communication channels often carry the perception of stale news.
- Information usually travels along the grapevine with considerable speed. The more important the information, the greater the speed. For example, information about the firing or sudden resignation of an executive can pass through the company in 30 minutes.
- Approximately three-fourths of messages transmitted along the grapevine are true. Because so many grapevine messages are essentially correct, employees believe most of them. Previous intermittent reinforcement supports this reliance on grapevine messages. Nevertheless, messages frequently become distorted and misunderstood. By the time a rumor reaches the majority of employees, it is likely to contain false elements. An example would be the case of a company CEO who gave a personal donation to a gay-rights group. The funds were to be used to promote local legislation in favor of equal employment opportunities for gay people. The last version of the story that traveled over the grapevine took this form: "The president has finally come out of the closet. He's hiring three gay managers and is giving some year-end bonus money to the Gay Alliance."
- Only about 10 percent of employees who receive rumors pass along the information to others. Those who do, however, usually communicate the information to several other employees, rather than to only one.

False rumors can be disruptive to morale and productivity. Some employees take actions that hurt the company and themselves in response to a rumor. Employees might leave a firm in response to rumors about an impending layoff. The valuable workers often leave first because they have skills and contacts in demand at other firms. Severe negative rumors dealing with products or services, especially about product defects or poisonings, must be neutralized to prevent permanent damage to an organization. Several years ago, a major soft drink company faced the false rumor of drug syringes in some beverage cans. The company recalled thousands of cans of the beverage and worked actively with the media to dispel the rumor. A child-care center lost 90 percent of its clients when a competitor started the rumor that a worker at the center had a prior conviction for child molestation. Widespread and severe rumors also led to bad press, loss of trust between management and staff, and increased employee job stress.[13]

In a study with public relations professionals, Nicholas DiFonzo and Prashant Bordia identified tactics for dealing with negative rumors about organizational change. The first broad strategy addresses how to *structure uncertainty*. Employees want clarification about uncertain events. Methods for structuring uncertainty include the following:

- State the procedures by which the upcoming changes will be decided. For example, members of senior management will confer with members of middle- and first-level management to decide which workers will be offered early retirement.
- State a time limit for the official message that contains full information. For example, "By July 1, all the details about outsourcing will be fully presented."

The second broad strategy combats rumors by *enhancing formal communication*. Employees naturally seek more information during times of intense rumors. Methods for enhancing formal communication include the following:

- Explain why you cannot comment or give full information. For example, during the preliminary stages of a merger, management is legally obligated to make no comment.
- Confirm the rumor. For example, "Yes, it is true. We are going to outsource the manufacture of all paper clips and staples."[14]

BARRIERS TO COMMUNICATION

Messages sent from one person to another are rarely received exactly as intended. Barriers exist at every step in the communication process. Exhibit 13-4 shows how barriers to communication influence the receipt of messages. The input is the message sent by the sender. Ordinarily, the message is spoken or written, but it could be nonverbal. Barriers to communication, or noise, affect *throughput*, the processing of input. Noise poses a potential threat to effective communication because it can interfere with the accuracy of a message. Noise creates barriers to effective transmission and reception of messages. The barriers may be related to the receiver, the sender, or the environment. The output in this model is the message as received.

Which messages are most likely to encounter barriers? Interference occurs most frequently when a message is complex, arouses emotion, or clashes with a receiver's mental set. An emotionally arousing message deals with such topics as money or personal inconvenience (e.g., being assigned a less convenient work schedule). A message that clashes with a receiver's usual way of viewing things requires the person to change his or her typical pattern of receiving messages. To illustrate this problem, try this experiment. The next time you order food at a restaurant, order the dessert first and the entrée second. The server will probably not hear your dessert order.

Low Motivation and Interest

Many messages never get through because the intended receiver is not motivated to hear the message or is not interested. The challenge to the sender is to frame the message in such a way that it appeals to the needs and interests of the receiver. This principle can be applied to conducting a job campaign. When sending a message, the job seeker should emphasize the needs of the prospective employer. An

> Identify major communication barriers in organizations.

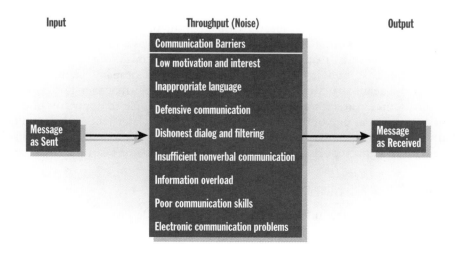

EXHIBIT 13-4

Barriers to Communication

Many factors make it difficult to get messages across as intended. A sampling of these barriers to communication is listed here.

example would be: "If I were hired, what problem would you like me to tackle first?" Many job seekers send low-interest messages of this type: "Would this job give me good experience?"

Sending a message at the right time contributes to motivation and interest. Messages should be sent at a time when they are most likely to meet with a good reception. Therefore a good time to ask for new equipment is early in the fiscal year before the budget is spent. Sending the message late in the fiscal year can also be effective. The manager might have some unspent money he or she does not want to return to the general fund.

Inappropriate Language

The language used to frame a message must be suited to the intended receivers. Language can be inappropriate for a host of reasons. Two factors of particular significance in a work setting—semantics and difficulty level—may affect appropriateness.

Semantics is the study of meaning in language forms. The message sender should give careful thought to what certain terms will mean to receivers. Take, for example, the term *productive*. To prevent communication barriers, you may have to clarify this term. Assume a manager says to the group members, "Our department must become more productive." Most employees will correctly interpret the term to mean "more efficient," but some employees will interpret it as "work harder and longer at the same rate of pay." Consequently, these latter employees may resist the message.

The *difficulty level of language* affects receiver comprehension. Communicators are typically urged to speak and write at a low difficulty level. At times, however, a low difficulty level is inappropriate. For instance, when a manager communicates with technically sophisticated employees, using a low difficulty level can create barriers. The employees may perceive the manager as patronizing and may tune him or her out. The use of jargon, or insider language, is closely related to difficulty level. When dealing with outsiders, jargon may be inappropriate; with insiders (people who share a common technical language), it may be appropriate. Jargon can help the sender establish a good relationship with the receivers.

Defensive Communication

defensive communication

The tendency to receive messages in a way that protects self-esteem.

An important general communication barrier is **defensive communication**—the tendency to receive messages in a way that protects self-esteem. Defensive communication also allows people to send messages to make themselves look good. People communicate defensively through the process of *denial*, the suppression of information one finds uncomfortable. It serves as a major barrier to communication because many messages sent in organizations are potentially uncomfortable. A middle manager learned that the company planned to shift entirely to a team structure and eliminate most middle manager positions. The human resources director advised him that he was eligible to apply for a business analyst position on one of the new teams. Two months later when asked about his decision about applying for a new position, the manager responded, "I would like to have four teams reporting to me, and change my title to team manager."

Dishonest Dialog and Filtering

Dialog that avoids the underlying issue forms a subtle communication barrier. When managers talk in generalities or do not pinpoint what they think is the real problem, communication remains incomplete and the real problem may not be solved. A manager might engage in dishonest dialog not because of a character flaw, but because the manager does not want to offend or stifle the creativity of a staff member. During a meeting, a marketing manager might make an inspiring presentation about how the business unit planned to take market share from a competitor. Dishonest dialog on the part of the CEO present might come in the form of compliments and encouragement when she really thought the plan lacked substance. With honest dialog, in contrast, the CEO asks penetrating questions like, "What weaknesses in our major competitor have you identified?" or "Just how are you going to make these gains?"[15]

A variation of dishonest dialogue is **filtering**, coloring and altering information to make it more acceptable to the receiver. Telling the manager what he or she wants to hear is a frequent type of filtering. Suppose an employee becomes aware of information that should be communicated to management, such as several incidents of sexual harassment in the office. The employee filters the truth to avoid dealing with the wrath of management.

filtering

Coloring and altering information to make it more acceptable to the receiver.

Insufficient Nonverbal Communication

Effective communicators rely on both verbal and nonverbal communication. If verbal communication is not supplemented by nonverbal communication, messages may not be convincing, as the following situation illustrates.

A customer service representative at a cable television station approached her manager with a preliminary proposal for increasing the number of subscribers. Her idea was to interview former customers who had dropped the service. With a blank expression on his face, the manager replied, "I see some merit in your idea. Work with it further." Two months later the manager asked the representative if she had completed the proposal. She replied that she had dropped the idea because "you seemed so unresponsive to my proposal."

Information Overload

Information overload, or **communication overload**, occurs when an individual receives so much information that he or she becomes overwhelmed. As a result, the person does a poor job of processing information and receiving new messages. Many managers suffer from information overload because of extensive e-mail in addition to the messages from office telephones, cellular telephones, voice mail, pagers, hard-copy correspondence, and trade magazines. Many managers receive about 150 e-mail messages daily. A study of workers in general found that they sent and received an average of 190 messages each day, most of them requiring at least some response.[16] The average e-mail user spends one hour per working day managing e-mail.[17]

information overload (or communication overload)

A condition in which an individual receives so much information that he or she becomes overwhelmed.

Poor Communication Skills

A message may fail to register because the sender lacks effective communication skills. The sender might garble a written or spoken message so severely that the receiver cannot understand it, or the sender may deliver the message so poorly that the receiver does not take it seriously. Communication barriers can also result from deficiencies within the receiver. A common barrier is a receiver who is a poor listener. Many messages left on voice mail systems are articulated so poorly that the receiver lacks enough information to act, including understanding the return telephone number.

Electronic Communication Problems

Advanced technology plays a fundamental role in communication in the workplace, yet it creates several communication problems. The problems associated with e-mail are representative of these barriers, particularly the problem of impersonality. Many people conduct business with each other exclusively by e-mail, thus missing out on the nuances of human interaction. Some managers and staff professionals discourage face-to-face meetings with workers who ask for help, and instead demand communication by e-mail. A human resource specialist at a major consulting firm said to a new business analyst asking for help, "I don't have time to meet with you to listen to your complaints. Send me an e-mail."

Face-to-face communication offers the advantage of a smile and an expression of sympathy through a nod of the head. When somebody asks or answers a question in person, it is easier to probe for more information than if the interaction took place through e-mail. Many people supplement their e-mail messages with *emoticons* to add warmth and humor. For example, a half "smiley" face is ;-). Because e-mail is much like any printed document, an electronic message can seem much harsher than a spoken message.

E-mail, in general, is better suited to communicating routine rather than complex or sensitive messages. According to an analysis of new etiquette for evolving technologies, when dealing with sensitive information it is better to deliver the message face to face or at least in a telephone conversation. In this way both parties can have questions answered and minimize misunderstandings.[18]

5   OVERCOMING BARRIERS TO COMMUNICATION

Develop tactics for overcoming communication barriers.

Most barriers to communication are surmountable. First, however, you must be aware that these potential barriers exist. Then as part of a strategy to overcome the barriers, you develop a tactic to deal with each one. For example, when you have an important message to deliver, make sure you answer the following question from the standpoint of the receiver: "What's in it for me?" The accompanying Management in Action explains how executives prefer face-to-face meetings for certain kinds of transactions. This section will describe 10 strategies and tactics for overcoming communication barriers. Exhibit 13-5 lists the strategies.

Understand the Receiver

To be an effective communicator, you must understand the receiver. Understanding the receiver provides a strategy that can assist in overcoming every communication barrier. For example, part of understanding the receiver comes from an awareness that he or she may be overloaded with information or be poorly motivated. Achieving understanding takes *empathy*, the ability to see things as another person does or to "put yourself in the other person's shoes."

Empathy leads to improved communication, because people more willingly engage in dialog when they feel understood. Managers especially need empathy to communicate with employees who do not share their values. A typical situation involves an employee who does not identify with company goals and is therefore poorly motivated. To motivate this employee, the manager might talk about

Management *in Action*

D e a l   M a k e r s   P r e f e r   t h e   H u m a n   T o u c h

A survey of 3,400 deal makers by Management Recruiters International shows that nothing beats a deal in a restaurant or a bar, according to about 60 percent of those surveyed. The survey also found the following tidbits about executive communication:

- Only six of 100 business owners conduct business at sporting events, although one of five admitted to having nothing against reaching an agreement with a client at a trade show, on an airplane, or in a hotel lobby.
- One in seven executives will break down and conduct business on the golf course.
- The one element of business deals remains unchanged: the vast majority of those meetings, wherever they occur, happen face to face.
- Few like Palm Pilot mail, e-mail, cell phone calls, or the nagging pager memos for serious business.

"Much of this depends, too, upon the level of involvement of the people," said Karen Bloomfield, senior director for a marketing company. "If people are exchanging information on a basic level, people are content and pleased to do that with e-mail. But if you're talking about a situation where it involves relationship building or something significant like recruitment where careers and lives are on the line, executives still have a desire to meet face-to-face." Bloomfield said those meetings often occur in bars or restaurants because they provide a neutral space and allow both parties to avoid the distractions of an office.

"The technology revolution means you are bombarded with e-mail, ringing telephones. It's just human nature to [want] personal contact."

Source: "Executives Shun Office for Closing Their Deals," Gannett News Service, January 1, 2001.

---

productivity leading to higher pay rather than to higher returns to stockholders. Empathy improves communication as it builds rapport with the other person. Rapport, in turn, substantially improves communication. You may notice that conversation flows smoothly when you achieve rapport with a work associate or friend.

Understand the receiver
Communicate assertively
Use two-way communication
Unite with a common vocabulary
Elicit verbal and nonverbal feedback
Enhance listening skills
Communicate to fit a global environment
Be sensitive to cultural differences
Be sensitive to gender differences
Engage in metacommunication

Effective Communication

EXHIBIT 13-5

Overcoming Communication Barriers

The chances of getting around the noise in the communication process increase when the sender uses specific strategies and tactics.

Empathy differs from sympathy. A manager might understand why an employee does not identify with company goals. The manager does not have to agree, however, that the company goals are not in the employee's best interests.

Communicate Assertively

Many people create their own communication barriers by expressing their ideas in a passive or indirect mode. If instead they explain their ideas explicitly and directly—and with feeling—the message is more likely to be received. Being assertive also contributes to effective communication because assertiveness enhances persuasiveness. When both sides are persuasive, they are more likely to find a shared solution.[19] Notice the difference between a passive (indirect) phrasing of a request versus an assertive (direct) approach:

Passive

Team member: *By any chance would there be some money left over in the budget? If there would happen to be, I would like to know.*

Manager: *I'll have to investigate. Try me again soon.*

Assertive

Team member: *We have an urgent need for a flatbed scanner in our department. Running to the document center to use their scanner is draining our productivity. I am therefore submitting a requisition for a scanner.*

Manager: *Your request makes sense. I'll see what's left in the budget right now.*

informative confrontation

A technique of inquiring about discrepancies, conflicts, and mixed messages.

Another use of assertiveness in overcoming communication barriers in the workplace is **informative confrontation,** a technique of inquiring about discrepancies, conflicts, and mixed messages.[20] Confronting people about the discrepancies in their message provides more accurate information. As a manager, here is how you might handle a discrepancy between verbal and nonverbal messages:

You're talking with a team member you suspect is experiencing problems. The person says, "Everything is going great" (verbal message). At the same time the team member is fidgeting and clenching his fist (nonverbal message). Your informative confrontation might be: "You say things are great, yet you're fidgeting and clenching your fist."

As another way of being assertive, you repeat your message and use multiple channels. Communication barriers sometimes prevent messages from getting through the first time they are sent. These barriers include information overload and the receiver's desire not to hear or see the information. By being persistent, your message is more likely to be received. An important message should be repeated when it is first delivered and repeated again one or two days later. Experienced communicators often repeat a message during their next contact with the receiver.

Repetition of the message becomes even more effective when more than one communication channel is used. Effective communicators follow up spoken agreements with written documentation. The use of multiple channels helps accommodate the fact that some people respond better to one communication mode than another. For example, a supervisor asked an employee why she did not follow through with the supervisor's request that she wear safety shoes. The employee replied, "I didn't think you were serious. You didn't send me an e-mail."

Use Two-Way Communication

Many communication barriers can be overcome if senders engage receivers in conversation. A dialog helps reduce misunderstanding by communicating feelings as well as facts. Both receiver and sender can ask questions of each other. Here is an example:

Manager: *I want you here early tomorrow. We have a big meeting planned with our regional manager.*

Employee: *I'll certainly be here early. But are you implying that I'm usually late?*

Manager: *Not at all. I know you come to work on time. It's just that we need you here tomorrow about 30 minutes earlier than usual.*

Employee: *I'm glad I asked. I'm proud of my punctuality.*

Two-way interaction also overcomes communication barriers because it helps build connections among people. According to management advisor Jim Harris, a challenge facing most companies is transforming traditional one-way, top-down communication into a flexible, two-way communication loop. A face-to-face communication style can be implemented by talking directly with employees instead of relying so heavily on e-mail and printed messages.[21] A manager who takes the initiative to communicate face to face with employees encourages two-way communication.

Unite with a Common Vocabulary

People from the various units within an organization may speak in terms so different that communication barriers are erected. For example, the information systems group and the marketing group may use some words and phrases not used by the other. Steve Patterson recommends that managers first identify the core work of a business, and then describe it in a shared business vocabulary.[22] All key terms should be clearly defined, and people should agree on the meaning. Assume that a company aims to provide "high-quality long-distance telephone service." Workers should agree on the meaning of high quality in reference to long distance. The various departments might retain some jargon, and their unique perspectives, but they would also be united by a common language.

Elicit Verbal and Nonverbal Feedback

To be sure that the message has been understood, ask for verbal feedback. A recommended managerial practice is to conclude a meeting with a question such as: "To what have we agreed this morning?" The receiver of a message should also take the responsibility to offer feedback to the sender. The expression "This is what I heard you say" is an effective feedback device. Feedback can also be used to facilitate communication in a group meeting. After the meeting, provide everyone in attendance with written follow-up to make sure they all left with the same understanding.

It is also important to observe and send nonverbal feedback. Nonverbal indicators of comprehension or acceptance can be more important than verbal indicators. For example, the manner in which somebody says "Sure, sure" can indicate if that person is truly in agreement. If the "Sure, sure" is a brush-off, the message may need more selling. The expression on the receiver's face can also be due to acceptance or rejection.

Enhance Listening Skills

active listening

Listening for full meaning, without making premature judgments or interpretations.

Many communication problems stem from the intended receiver not listening carefully. Unless a person receives messages as intended, he or she cannot get work done properly. Managers need to be good listeners because so much of their work involves eliciting information from others in order to solve problems. Reducing communication barriers takes active listening. **Active listening** means listening for full meaning, without making premature judgments or interpretations. An active listener should follow these six suggestions:[23]

1. *The receiver listens for total meaning of the sender's message.* By carefully analyzing what is said, what is not said, and nonverbal signals, you will uncover a fuller meaning in the message.

2. *The receiver forms an initial opinion about the information.* Assume that the information is not what the receiver wants to hear. An active listener will nevertheless continue listening.

3. *The receiver reflects the message back to the sender.* Show the sender that you understand by providing summary reflections such as "You tell me you are behind schedule because our customers keep modifying their orders."

4. *The sender and receiver both understand the message and engage in a concluding discussion.* In the preceding situation, the manager and the employee would converse about the challenges of making on-time deliveries despite changes in customer requirements.

5. *The receiver asks questions instead of making statements.* For example, do not say, "Maurice, don't forget that the Zytex report needs to be completed on Friday morning." Rather, ask, "Maurice, How is the Zytex report coming along? Any problems with making the deadline?" By asking questions you will start the type of dialog that facilitates active listening.

6. *The receiver does not blurt out questions as soon as the employee is finished speaking.* Being too quick to ask questions gives the impression that you were formulating your reply rather than listening. Before you ask a question, paraphrase the speaker's words. An example is, "So what you're saying is . . ." Then, ask your question. Paraphrasing followed by asking a question will often decrease miscommunication.

Communicate to Fit a Global Environment

The geographical dispersion of so many organizations creates a potential communication barrier. Managers in multinational corporations therefore need to develop a strategic communications program that cuts across the geographic distances between people. Good communications in general should take care of most problems created by geographic differences, yet here are a few additional considerations.

- *Make sure that stories transmitted on the grapevine support the corporate message.* In a cross-cultural environment, employees are likely to be extra-sensitive about whether top management from the parent company is being hypocritical. A German company needed to cut costs. Managers thought that the communications explaining the necessity of the cuts was adequate. In their cost-cutting initiatives, they decided not to replace an old company bus that shuttled employees from a remote spot in the parking lot up to headquarters. At the same time, the executives were receiving brand new Mercedes. A company official pointed out that all other communications about cost cutting was wasted. "All employees remembered was that the cost-cutting hit them (their bus was discontinued) and the executives received new luxury cars. Morale and employee support for cost containment sank," the official said.[24]

- *Choose effective media for global communications.* An effective strategic plan takes into consideration what medium (or media) should be used to communicate across countries. Some cultures respond more positively to information technology and written messages than do others. For example, Asian and Latin cultures respond much more favorably to personal forms of communication. As a consequence, personal ways of transmitting information, such as meetings and telephone calls, are more effective when communicating in those cultures.

- *Form a global communication advisory team.* A team composed of representatives from various countries comments upon the effectiveness of communications between the parent companies and the foreign affiliate. The team also makes suggestions for communications improvement, such as having a cultural translator pass judgment on the clarity of a message before it is transmitted globally.[25]

Be Sensitive to Cultural Differences

Another aspect of effective communications in a global environment requires sensitivity to cultural differences (as suggested by choosing the right medium for transmitting messages). The list that follows presents several ideas to help overcome cross-cultural communications barriers.

- *Be sensitive to the fact that cross-cultural communication barriers exist.* Awareness of these potential barriers alerts you to the importance of modifying your communication approach.

- *Show respect for all workers.* An effective strategy for overcoming cross-cultural communication barriers is to simply respect all others in the workplace. A key component of respect is to perceive other cultures as different from but not inferior to your own. Respecting other people's customs can translate into specific attitudes, such as respecting one coworker for wearing a yarmulke on Friday, or another for wearing native African dress to celebrate Kwanzaa. Another way of being respectful would be to listen carefully to the opinion of a senior worker who says the company should have converted to e-commerce a long time ago (even though you disagree).

- *Use straightforward language and speak clearly.* When working with people who do not speak your language fluently, speak in an easy-to-understand manner. Minimize the use of idioms and analogies specific to your language. A sales representative from Juárez, Mexico, was attending a company sales meeting in San Antonio, Texas. The sales manager said that the chief competitor was "over the hill." The sales representative was confused because he thought perhaps the competitor had relocated to a new town just "over the hill."

- *Observe cultural differences in etiquette.* Violating rules of etiquette without explanation can erect immediate communication barriers. A major rule of etiquette in many countries is that visitors address senior managers by their last names unless specifically invited to do otherwise. An outsider who attempts to act too informally toward a company official will create an immediate communication barrier.

- *Be sensitive to differences in nonverbal communication.* Be alert to the possibility that your nonverbal signal may be misinterpreted by a person from another culture. Hand gestures are especially troublesome. An engineer for a New Jersey company was asked a question by a German coworker. He responded OK by making a circle with his thumb and forefinger. The German worker stormed away because, in Germany, the same gesture is a personal insult and a vulgarity.[26]
- *Do not be diverted by style, accent, grammar, or personal appearance.* Although these superficial factors all relate to business success, they are difficult to interpret when judging a person from another culture. It is therefore better to judge the merits of the statement or behavior.[27] A brilliant individual from another culture may still be learning your language and may make basic mistakes in speaking your language.

Be Sensitive to Gender Differences

Despite the trend toward equality in organizations, numerous recent studies identify differences in communication styles between men and women. Awareness of these differences reduces potential communication barriers between men and women. Nevertheless, the differences described next represent stereotypes that overlook the fact that men and women vary among themselves in communication style. Differences in gender-related communication style include the following:[28]

- Women prefer to use communication for rapport building. In contrast, men prefer to use talk primarily as a means to preserve independence and status by displaying knowledge and skill.
- Men prefer to work out their problems by themselves, whereas women prefer to talk out solutions with another person.
- Women are more likely to compliment the work of coworkers, while men are more likely to be critical.
- Men tend to be more directive in their conversation, while women emphasize politeness.
- Women tend to be more conciliatory when facing differences, while men become more intimidating.
- Men are more interested than women in calling attention to their accomplishments or soliciting recognition. As a result, men are more likely to dominate discussion during meetings.

Understanding these differences can help you interpret the behavior of people, thus avoiding a communications block. For example, if a male team member is stingy with praise, remember that he is simply engaging in gender-typical behavior. Do not take it personally. If a female team member talks about a problem without looking for a quick solution, do not get frustrated. She is simply engaging in gender-typical behavior by looking for support.

A general suggestion for overcoming gender-related communication barriers is for men to improve communication by becoming more empathic (showing more empathy) listeners. Women can improve communication by becoming more direct.

Engage in Metacommunication

When confronted with a communication problem, one response attempts to work around the barrier, perhaps by using one of the methods already described.

A more typical response ignores the barrier by making no special effort to deal with the problem—a "take it or leave it" approach to communicating. Another possibility is to **metacommunicate**, or communicate about your communication to help overcome barriers or resolve a problem. If you as a manager faced heavy deadline pressures, you might say to a group member, "I might appear brusque today and tomorrow. Please don't take it personally. It's just that I have to make heavy demands on you because the group is facing a gruesome deadline."

Metacommunicating also helps when you have reached a communication impasse with another person. You might say, for example, "I'm trying to get through to you, but you either don't react to me or you get angry. What can I do to improve our communication?"

metacommunicate
To communicate about a communication to help overcome barriers or resolve a problem.

HOW TO CONDUCT AN EFFECTIVE MEETING   **6**

Describe how to conduct more effective meetings.

Much of workplace communication, including group decision making, takes place in meetings. When conducted poorly, meetings represent a substantial productivity drain. Most of the information presented in this chapter and in Chapter 6, which discussed decision making, applies to meetings. The following suggestions apply to those who conduct meetings. However, many also apply to participants. By following these suggestions, you increase the meeting's effectiveness as a communication vehicle.

1. *Meet only for valid reasons.* Many meetings lead to no decisions because they lacked a valid purpose in the first place. Meetings are necessary only in situations that require coordinated effort and group decision making. Memos can be substituted for meetings when factual information needs to be disseminated and discussion is unimportant.
2. *Have a specific agenda and adhere to it.* Meetings are more productive when an agenda is planned and followed carefully. People should see the agenda in advance so they can give some careful thought to the issues—preliminary thinking helps people arrive at more realistic decisions. In addition, assign maximum discussion times to the agenda items.
3. *Share decision-making authority.* A key attribute of an effective problem-solving meeting is authority sharing by the leader. Unless authority is shared, the members are likely to believe that the hidden agenda of the meeting is to seek approval for the meeting leader's tentative decision.
4. *Keep comments brief and to the point.* A major challenge facing the meeting leader is to keep conversation on track. Verbal rambling by participants creates communication barriers because other people lose interest. An effective way for the leader to keep comments on target is to ask the contributor of a non sequitur, "In what way does your comment relate to the agenda?"
5. *Encourage critical feedback and commentary.* Meetings are more likely to be fully productive when participants are encouraged to be candid with criticism and negative feedback. Openness helps prevent groupthink and also brings important problems to the attention of management.
6. *Strive for wide participation.* One justification for conducting a meeting is to obtain a variety of input. Although not everybody is equally qualified to voice a sound opinion, everyone should be heard. A skillful leader may have to limit the contribution of domineering members and coax reticent members to voice their ideas.
7. *Provide summaries for each major point.* Because many ideas are expressed in the typical meeting, so some members may have trouble following what has been accomplished. Summarizing key points can help members follow the discussion

and make better-informed decisions. Without summaries, participants sometimes do not know what, specifically, they are voting for or against.

8. *Strive for consensus, not total acceptance.* Few groups of assertive individuals will reach total agreement on most agenda items. Furthermore, disagreement is healthy because it can sharpen and refine decision making. It is more realistic to strive for consensus—a state of harmony, general agreement, or majority opinion. When consensus is achieved, each member should be willing to accept the plan because it is logical and feasible. Several approaches to achieving consensus were described in Chapter 6 in relation to group decision making. Also, strive for win-win solutions and plans instead of using such methods as majority rule and coin flipping. Another consensus-builder asks whether the group is ready to reach a decision. The question should be asked when it is apparent to you that a consensus solution is about to emerge; otherwise the question will disrupt problem solving and discussion.

9. *Congratulate members when they reach a decision.* Complimenting group members when they reach a decision reinforces decision-making behavior and increases the probability that consensus will be reached the next time the group faces a problem.

10. *Solve small issues ahead of time with e-mail.* Meetings can be briefer and less mundane when small issues are resolved ahead of time. E-mail is particularly effective for resolving minor administrative issues, and also for collecting agenda items in advance.

11. *Ensure that all follow-up action is assigned and recorded.* All too often, even after a decision has been reached, a meeting lacks tangible output. Distribute a memo summarizing who is responsible for taking what action and by what date.

7   ORGANIZATIONAL POLITICS AND INTERPERSONAL COMMUNICATION

Describe how organizational (or office) politics affects interpersonal communication.

organizational (or office) politics

Informal approaches to gaining power or other advantage through means other than merit or luck.

At various places in our study of management we mention political factors. For example, Chapter 1 describes political skill as essential to success as a manager, and Chapter 6 describes the role of political factors in decision making. Politics affects communication because so much interpersonal communication in organizations is politically motivated. Our communication is often shaped by a desire to gain personal advantage. As used here, **organizational politics** refers to informal approaches to gaining power or other advantage through means other than merit or luck. In recent years as managers rely more on personal influence and less on hierarchy, people tend to recognize the more positive aspects of organizational politics. For example, a team of management researchers defines political skill as "an interpersonal style that combines social awareness with the ability to communicate well. People who practice this skill behave in a disarmingly charming and engaging manner that inspires confidence, trust, and sincerity."[29]

In this section we describe a sampling of political tactics, classified as relatively ethical versus relatively unethical. We also mention what managers can do to control politics. The Management in Action about meetings in restaurants to make deals hinted at the use of political factors in conducting business.

Relatively Ethical Political Tactics

A political tactic might be considered relatively ethical if used to gain advantage or power that serves a constructive organizational purpose such as getting an influential executive on your side so you can implement a company wellness program. Five useful and relatively ethical tactics are described next.

1. *Develop power contacts.* After you have identified who the powerful people are in your organization, establish alliances with them. Cultivating friendly, cooperative relationships with organizational members and outsiders can advance the cause of the manager or professional. These people can support your ideas or directly assist you with problem solving. A modern use of power contacts is to schmooze with the information technology experts in your office who can help you resolve an urgent computer problem (such as retrieving seemingly lost data).[30]

2. *Be courteous, pleasant, and positive.* Having good human relations skills creates many more friends than enemies and can help you be chosen for good team assignments and stay off the downsizing list. It is widely acknowledged by human resource specialists that courteous, pleasant, and positive people are the first to be hired and the last to be fired (assuming they are also technically qualified).

3. *Create a positive image.* A positive image can be created through such means as keeping your voice calm and well-modulated, dressing fashionably, and matching your humor to others around you.[31] Speaking well is critical, and being courteous, pleasant, and positive (as already mentioned) also contributes to a positive image.

4. *Ask satisfied customers to contact your boss.* A favorable comment by a customer receives considerable weight because customer satisfaction is a top corporate priority. If a customer says something nice, the comment will carry more weight than one from a coworker or subordinate, because coworkers and subordinates might praise a person for political reasons. Customers' motivation, on the other hand, is assumed to be pure because they have little concern about pleasing suppliers.

5. *Send thank-you notes to large numbers of people.* One of the most basic political tactics, sending thank-you notes profusely, is simply an application of sound human relations. Many successful people (including Jack Welch of GE) take the time to send handwritten notes to employees and customers. Handwritten notes are warmer than e-mail messages, but both help create bonds with their recipients. In the words of Tom Peters, "The power of a thank you (note or otherwise) is hard—make that impossible—to beat.[32]

Relatively Unethical Political Tactics

In the ideal organization, each employee works harmoniously with work associates, all focused on achieving organizational goals rather than pursuing self-interest. Furthermore, everyone trusts each other. In reality not all organizations are ideal, and many people use negative political tactics to fight for political advantage. Downsizing can contribute to devious office politics because many people want to discredit others so that the other person is more likely to be "tapped" for termination. Here we describe four unethical political tactics.

1. *Back stabbing.* The despised yet widely practiced back stab requires that you pretend to be nice, but all the while plan someone's demise. A frequent form of back stabbing is to initiate a conversation with a rival, or someone you just dislike, about the weaknesses of a common boss. You encourage negative

commentary and make careful mental notes of what the person says. When these comments are passed along to the manager, the other person appears disloyal and foolish.

E-mail provides a medium for back stabbing. The sender of the message documents a mistake made by another individual and includes key people on the distribution list. A sample message sent by one manager to a rival began as follows: "Hi Ruth. Thanks for being so candid about why you think our corporate strategy is defective. I was wondering if you had any additional suggestions that you think would help the company compete successfully. . . ."

A useful counterattack to the back stab is to ask an open-ended question to justify his or her actions, such as, "I'm not sure I understand why you sent that e-mail about my not supporting the corporate strategy. Can you explain why you did that, and what made you think I do not support corporate strategy?"[33]

2. *Setting up another person to fail.* A highly devious and deceptive practice is to give another person an assignment with the hopes that he or she will fail and therefore be discredited. The person is usually told that he or she is being chosen to tackle this important assignment because of a proven capability to manage difficult tasks. (If the person does perform well, the "set up" will backfire on the manager.) A typical example of setting a person up to fail is to assign a supervisor to a low-performing unit, staffed mostly with problem employees who distrust management.

3. *Playing territorial games.* Also referred to as *turf wars*, territorial games involve protecting and hoarding resources that give one power, such as information, the authority to make decisions, and relationships with key people. A relationship is "hoarded" in such ways as not encouraging others to visit a key customer, or blocking a high performer from getting a promotion or transfer. For example, the manager might tell others that his star performer is mediocre to prevent the person from being considered a valuable transfer possibility. Other examples of territorial games include monopolizing time with clients, scheduling meetings so someone cannot attend, and shutting out coworkers from joining you on an important assignment.[34]

4. *Being unpredictable.* Some particularly devious executives behave unpredictably by design to keep people off guard. People are easier to control when they do not know whether you will be nice or nasty. In the words of business commentator Stanley Bing, "This quality of rampaging unpredictability is a well-known tool used by terrorists, authoritarian brainwashers, and those who wish to command and dominate others. It's used because it works better than straight-out intimidation, which can be anticipated and psychologically prepared for."[35]

Exercising Control of Negative Organizational Politics

Carried to excess, organizational politics can damage productivity and morale and hurt the careers of innocent people. The productivity loss stems from managers and others devoting too much time to politics and not enough time to useful work. A survey of 150 executives indicated that about one day each week is spent handling office politics, which includes everything from rivalries to bickering.[36] Just *being aware of the presence of organizational politics* can help a manager stay alert for its negative manifestations such as back stabbing. The politically aware manager carefully evaluates negative statements made by one group member about another.

Open communication can also constrain the impact of political behavior. For instance, open communication lets everyone know the basis for allocating resources, thus reducing the amount of politicking. If people know in advance how resources will be allocated, the effectiveness of kissing up to the boss will be reduced. *Avoiding favoritism* (giving the best rewards to group member you like the most) is a powerful way of minimizing politics within a work group. If trying to be the boss's pet is not effective, people are more likely to focus on good job performance to get ahead. Annette Simmons recommends that managers *find a way to talk about territorial games.* Addressing the issues and bringing them out in the open might make group members aware that their territorial behavior is under close observation.[37]

S U M M A R Y   O F   K E Y   P O I N T S

1 **Describe the steps in the communication process.** The communication process involves four basic elements, all of which are subject to interference, or noise. The process begins with a sender *encoding* a message and then *transmitting* it over a channel to a receiver, who *decodes* it. *Feedback* from receiver to sender is also essential. In successful communication, the receiver decodes the message, understands it, and then acts on it.

2 **Recognize the major types of nonverbal communication in the workplace.** The major modes of transmitting nonverbal messages are through the environment (physical setting); body placement; posture; hand and body placement; posture; hand and body gestures; facial expressions and movement; voice quality (including accent); and clothing, dress, and appearance. Mirroring—the use of nonverbal communication to establish rapport—is significant, as is timing.

3 **Explain and illustrate the difference between formal and informal communication channels.** Formal channels follow the organization chart. Management by walking around can also be considered a formal communication channel. Messages are transmitted in four directions: upward, downward, sideways, and diagonally. Informal channels are the unofficial network of communications that supplement the formal pathways. The grapevine is the major informal communication pathway, and it transmits rumors. Management can take steps to neutralize negative rumors, such as publicly discussing them.

4 **Identify major communication barriers in organizations.** Barriers exist at every step in the communication process. Among them are (1) low motivation and interest, (2) inappropriate language, (3) defensive communication, (4) dishonest dialog and filtering, (5) insufficient nonverbal communication, (6) information overload, (7) poor communication skills, and (8) electronic communication problems.

5 **Develop tactics for overcoming communication barriers.** To overcome communication barriers you must (1) understand the receiver, (2) communicate assertively, (3) use two-way communication, (4) unite with a common vocabulary, (5) elicit verbal and nonverbal feedback, (6) enhance listening skills, (7) communicate to fit a global environment, (8) be sensitive to cultural differences, (9) be sensitive to gender differences, and (10) engage in metacommunication (communicate about the communications).

6 **Describe how to conduct more effective meetings.** To improve communication effectiveness and the decision-making quality of meetings, follow these suggestions: (1) meet only for valid reasons; (2) adhere to a specific agenda; (3) share decision-making authority; (4) keep comments brief and to the point; (5) encourage critical feedback and commentary; (6) strive for wide participation; (7) provide summaries for major points; (8) strive for consensus; (9) congratulate members when they reach a decision; (10) solve small issues ahead of time with e-mail; and (11) ensure that follow-up action is assigned and recorded.

7 **Describe how organizational (or office) politics affects interpersonal communication.** Politics is related to communication because so much interpersonal communication in organizations is politically motivated. Relatively ethical political tactics include (a) develop power contacts, (b) be courteous, pleasant, and positive, (c) create a positive image, (d) ask satisfied customers to contact your boss, and (e) send thank-you notes to large numbers of people. Four relatively unethical political tactics are (a) back stabbing, (b) setting up another person to fail, (c) playing territorial games, and (b) being unpredictable.

KEY TERMS AND PHRASES

374

Communication, *350*

Encoding, *351*

Decoding, *351*

Noise, *352*

Nonverbal communication, *353*

Formal communication channels, *355*

Communication network, *355*

Informal communication channel, *357*

Grapevine, *357*

Defensive communication, *360*

Filtering, *361*

Information overload (or communication overload), *361*

Informative confrontation, *364*

Active listening, *366*

Metacommunicate, *369*

Organizational (or office) politics, *370*

QUESTIONS

1. Employers continue to emphasize good communication skills as one of the most important qualifications for screening career-school and business graduates. What are some of the reasons for this requirement?

2. How might understanding the steps in the communication process help managers and professionals do a better job?

3. What kind of facial expression do you think might make a person appear intelligent?

4. Several newspaper cartoons address the subject of one worker sending an e-mail to another worker in an adjoining cubicle or office. What is the justification for sending an e-mail to somebody such a short distance away?

5. Many telemarketers possess poor spoken communication skills, which makes them difficult to understand. What should telemarketing managers do about this problem?

6. Assume that you are a supervisor, and one of your direct reports tends to mumble and look in another direction when the two of you talk. Explain how you might use metacommunication to deal with this problem.

7. Why are political skills so important that they are classified as one of the five basic skills of managers (refer back to Chapter 1)?

CRITICAL THINKING QUESTIONS

1. As a research project, find some evidence that good communications by managers actually increase productivity.

2. If executives really spend one day a week dealing with office politics, how do they accomplish all the other tasks a manager is expected to accomplish?

SKILL-BUILDING EXERCISE: Listening Traps

Certain behavior patterns interfere with effective hearing and listening. After thinking carefully about each trap, check how well the trap applies to you: Not a Problem, or Need Improvement. To respond to the statements accurately, visualize how you acted in a recent situation that called for listening.

	Not a Problem	Need Improvement
• **Mind reader.** You receive limited information if you constantly think, "What is this person really thinking or feeling?"	___	___
• **Rehearser.** Your mental rehearsals for "Here's what I'll say next" tune out the sender.	___	___
• **Filterer.** You engage in selective listening by hearing only what you want to hear. (Could be difficult to judge because the process is often unconscious.)	___	___
• **Dreamer.** You drift off during a face-to-face conversation, which often leads you to an embarrassing "What did you say?" or "Could you repeat that?"	___	___

	Not a Problem	Need Improvement
• **Identifier.** If you refer everything you hear to your experience, you probably did not really listen to what was said.		
• **Comparer.** When you get sidetracked sizing up the sender, you are sure to miss the message.	—	—
• **Derailer.** You change the subject too quickly, giving the impression that you are not interested in anything the sender has to say.	—	—
• **Sparrer.** You hear what is said, but quickly belittle or discount it, putting you in the same class as the derailer.	—	—
• **Placater.** You agree with everything you hear just to be nice or to avoid conflict. By behaving this way you miss out on the opportunity for authentic dialog.	—	—

Interpretation: If you checked "Need Improvement" for 5 or more of the preceding statements, you are correct—your listening needs improvement! If you checked only 2 or fewer of the traps, you are probably an effective listener and a supportive person.

Source: Reprinted with permission from *Messages: The Communication Skills Book* (Oakland, CA: New Harbinger Publications, 1983).

INTERNET SKILL-BUILDING EXERCISE: Improving Your Nonverbal E-Mail Communication Skills

The purpose of this assignment is to search the Internet for emoticons—such as the ;-) for a wink and the :-) for a smile—and acronyms to incorporate nonverbal signals into your e-mail messages. Find a combination of 10 emoticons and acronyms using the Internet. Compare your list with that of a few classmates, and look for a rare one. **IM[H]O** it would be good to do it **ASAP**<g>. Your Internet search should help you decode the two acronyms and the last emoticon.

CASE PROBLEM 13-A: The Scrutinized Team Member Candidate

HRmanager.com is a human resources management firm that provides human resource services such as payroll, benefits administration, affirmative action programs, and technical training to other firms. By signing up with HRmanager, other firms can outsource part or all of their human resources functions. During its seven years of operation, HRmanager.com has grown from 3 to 50 employees, and to total revenues of $21 million last year.

Most of the work of the firm is performed by teams, led by a rotating team leader. Each team member takes an 18-month turn at being a team leader. CEO and founder Jerry Clune believes the four-person new ventures team is vital to the future of the company. In addition to developing ideas for new services, the team members are responsible for obtaining clients for any new service they propose that is approved by Clune. The new ventures team thus develops and sells new services. After the service is launched and working well, the sales group takes over responsibility for developing more clients.

As with other teams at HRmanager.com, the team members have a voice as to who is hired to join their team. In con-

junction with Clune, the new ventures team decided it should expand to five members. The team posted the job opening for a new member on an Internet recruiting service, ran classified ads in the local newspaper, and also asked present employees for referrals. One of the finalists for the position was Gina Cleveland, a 27-year-old business graduate. In addition to interviewing with Clune and the two company vice presidents, Cleveland spent one-half day with the new ventures team, breakfast and lunch included. About half of the time was spent in a team interview in which Gina sat in a conference room with the four team members.

The team members agreed that Cleveland appeared to be a strong candidate on paper. Her education and experience were satisfactory, her résumé was impressive, and she presented herself well during a telephone screening interview. After Cleveland completed her time with the new ventures team, the team leader, Lauren Nielsen suggested that the group hold a debriefing session. The purpose of the session would be to share ideas about Cleveland's suitability for joining the team. Nielsen commented, "It seems like we think that

Gina is a strong candidate based on her credentials and what she said. But I'm a big believer in nonverbal communication. Studying Gina's body language can give us a lot of valuable information. Let's each share our observations, about what Gina's body language tells us she is *really* like. I'll go first.

Lauren: I liked the way Gina looked so cool and polished when she joined us for breakfast. She's got all the superficial movements right to project self-confidence. But did anybody else notice how she looked concerned when she had to make a choice from the menu? She finally did choose a ham-and-cheese omelet, but she raised her voice at the end of the sentence when she ordered it. I got the hint that Gina is not very confident.

I also noticed Gina biting her lips a little when we asked her how creative she thought she was. I know that Gina said she was creative, and gave us an example of a creative project she completed. Yet nibbling at her lips like that suggests she's not filled with fire power.

Michael: I didn't make any direct observations about Gina's being self-confident or not, but I did notice something that could be related. I think Gina is on a power trip, which could indicate high or low self-confidence. Did anybody notice how Gina put her hands on her hips when she was standing up? That's a pure and clear signal of somebody who wants to be in control. Her hair cut is almost the same length and style as most women who made it to the top in *Fortune* 500 companies. I think she cloned her hairstyle from Carly Fiorina.

Another hint I get of Gina's power trip is the way she eyed the check in the restaurant at lunch. I could see it in her eyes that she really wanted to pay for the entire team. That could mean a desire to control, and show us that she is important. Do we want someone on the team with such a strong desire to control?

Brenda: I observed a different picture of Gina based on her nonverbal communication. She dressed just right for the occasion; not too conservatively, not too far business casual. It tells me she can fit into our environment. Did you notice how

well-groomed her shoes were? It says she is well organized and good at details. Her attaché case was a soft, inviting leather. If she were really into power and control she would carry a hard vinyl or aluminum attaché case. I see Gina as a confident and assertive person who could blend right into our team.

Larry: I hope that because I'm last, I'm not too influenced by the observations that you three have shared so far. My take is that Gina looks great on paper, but they she may have a problem in being a good team player. She's too laid back and distant. Did you notice her handshake? She gave me the impression of wanting to have the least possible physical contact with me. Her handshake was so insincere. I could feel her hand and arm withdrawing from me, as she shook my hand.

I also couldn't help noticing that Gina did not lean much toward us during the round table discussion. Do you remember how she would pull her chair back ever so slightly when we got into a heavy discussion? I interpreted that as a sign that Gina does not want to be part of a close-knit group.

Lauren: As you have probably noticed, I've been typing as fast as I can with my laptop, taking notes on what you have said. We have some mixed observations here, and I want to summarize and integrate them before we make a decision. I'll send you an e-mail with an attached file of my summary observations by tomorrow morning. Make any changes you see fit and get back to me. After we have finished evaluating Gina carefully, we will be able to make our recommendations to Jerry (Clune).

Discussion Questions

1. To what extent are the team members making an appropriate use of nonverbal communication to size up Gina Cleveland?
2. Which team member do you think made the most realistic interpretation of nonverbal behavior? Why?
3. Should Lauren, the team leader, have told Gina in advance that the team would be scrutinizing her nonverbal behavior? Justify your answer.

CASE PROBLEM 13-B: Just Call Me "Kat"

Katherine Matthews worked for many years in a variety of retail positions, including a three-year assignment as an assistant manager at a women's clothing store. Matthews was then involved in an automobile accident as the passenger in a friend's car. Although she was wearing a seat belt, Matthews was severely injured. Her right leg and ankle were broken when the door on her side caved in upon impact with a tree.

After four months of rehabilitation, Matthews walked well with the assistance of a cane. Yet she could not walk for long without enduring pain. Katherine, and the team of medical

specialists assisting her, agreed that an on-the-feet job was not appropriate for her in the foreseeable future. Katherine assessed her financial situation and decided she needed to return to work soon. Her disability payments were ending soon, and her savings were nearly gone.

To make the transition back to full-time employment in another field, Katherine signed on with OfficeTemps, a well-established temporary placement agency. Katherine explained that she sought work that was mentally challenging but not physically demanding on her right leg and ankle. After carefully assessing Katherine's capabilities and experiences, the employment interviewer, Jack Radison, created a computer file for her. Radison said, "I'll call you as soon as I find a suitable assignment."

One week later Radison called Katherine with good news. He had located a nine-month assignment for her as a telephone interviewer for a market research firm. The market research firm was hiring several people to conduct telephone interviews with dealers and retailers about the acceptability of a relatively new product, a personal air cooler. The cooler is about the size of the central processing unit on a personal computer, and would easily fit on a desk or adjacent to a television set. The air cooler evaporates water, thereby lowering the temperature by 12 degrees F (6.7 C) in a 7-foot area. Using an air cooler, a person would have less need for air conditioning. With the cooler operating, a person could either eliminate air conditioning, or set it at a higher temperature. The manufacturer of the cooler was interested in estimating the potential market for the product, now being sold primarily by mail order.

Katherine's task was to telephone specific people (usually store managers or owners) from a long list of names. Completing an interview would require about 30 minutes, and involved obtaining answers to 20 separate questions. Each market research interviewer was given a quota of six completed interviews per day.

As the interviewers perceived the task, a major challenge was to keep the interviewee on the line long enough to answer all the detailed questions. Quite often the interviewer had to dig for additional information (such as sales of room air conditioners and fans), or request that the interviewee search his or her files for appropriate information. The several interviewers also agreed that an even bigger challenge was to get through to the people on the list and get them to cooperate. Among the problems were reaching a voice mail system instead of the actual person, excuses about being too busy to be interviewed, and outright rejection and rudeness.

Following the script provided by the market research firm, Katherine began her pitch in this manner: "Hello, this is

Katherine from Garson Research Associates in Chicago. I'm asking for your cooperation to participate in an important study about an exciting new product, personal coolers. My interview should only take approximately 30 minutes. May we conduct the interview right now, or would you prefer another time in the next few days?"

Four weeks into the job, Katherine was behind quota by an average of two interviews per day. Feeling fatigued one day, she slipped into introducing herself as "Kat," the name used by family members and close friends. The interviewee prospect responded, "Oh sure, Kat, I can talk now." Two days later, Katherine made a personal call to a friend, thus prompted again to think of herself as "Kat." She inadvertently introduced herself as "Kat" to the next person on her list. Again, the prospective interviewee responded with enthusiasm: "Hey Kat, I'm ready to talk."

Prompted by the second cooperative response, Katherine then shifted to introducing herself as "Kat." The percentage of prospects willing to be interviewed jumped from 10 percent to 20 percent. Katherine explained this unusual result to her supervisor, who said that using a nickname and achieving good results was probably just a coincidence, that maybe she had simply become more confident. The increased confidence was therefore responsible for the higher success ratio in obtaining interviews.

Katherine responded, "I'm not so sure. There must be some other reasons that Kat gets more interviews than Katherine."

Discussion Questions

1. How can information about overcoming communication barriers help explain why "Kat" gets more interviews than "Katherine"?

2. How might the sex of the receiver be related to the different success ratios of "Kat" and "Katherine" in obtaining interviews?

3. Based on Kat's good results, what recommendations can you offer the research firm to help them increase the percentage of people who agree to be interviewed?

ENDNOTES

1. Tom Terez, "Can We Talk?" *Workforce*, July 2000, pp. 47–48.
2. John O. Whitney, *The Trust Factor: Liberating Profits and Restoring Corporate Vitality* (New York: McGraw-Hill, 1994).
3. Some of this information is based on Michael Argyle, *Body Communication*, 2nd ed. (Madison, CT: International Universities Press, 1990); Nick Morgan, "The Kinesthetic Speaker: Putting Action Into Words," *Harvard Business Review*, April 2001, pp. 112–120.
4. Morgan, "The Kinesthetic Speaker," p. 115.
5. Julia Boorstin, "Etiquette Tips: The Making of a Model Consultant," January 22, 2001, p. 158.
6. Jeffrey Jacobi, *The Vocal Advantage* (Upper Saddle River, NJ: Prentice-Hall, 1996).
7. Carla D'Nan Bass, "Strong Accent Can Hurt Chances for Employment," Knight Ridder, October 1, 2000.
8. Anat Rafeli and Michael G. Pratt, "Tailored Meetings: On the Meaning and Impact of Organizational Dress," *Academy of Management Review*, January 1993, p. 32.
9. "Managing Employee Opinions," *The Surcon Report*, July 1995, p. 2.
10. John J. Bush, Jr., and Alan L. Frohman, "Communication in a 'Network' Organization," *Organizational Dynamics*, Autumn 1991, pp. 23–26.

11. John P. Kotter, *The General Manager* (New York: The Free Press, 1991).

12. Alan Zaremba, "Working with the Organizational Grapevine," *Personnel Journal*, March 1989, p. 34.

13. Nicholas DiFonzo and Prashant Bordia, "How Top PR Professionals Handle Hearsay: Corporate Rumors, Their Effects, and Strategies to Manage Them," *Public Relations Review*, Summer 2000, p. 179.

14. DiFonzo and Bordia, pp. 182–185.

15. Ram Charan, "Conquering a Culture of Indecision," *Harvard Business Review*, April 2001, p. 77.

16. Gallup poll reported in Kirstin Downey Grimsley, "Message Overload Is Taking a Toll," *The Washington Post* story, June 1, 1998.

17. Gartner poll in John Yaukey, "E-Mail Out of Control for Many," Gannett News Service, May 8, 2001

18. "New Etiquette for Evolving Technologies: Using E-Mail and Voice Mail Effectively," *Business Education Forum*, October 1998, p. 8; Edward M. Hallowell, "The Human Moment at Work," *Harvard Business Review*, January–February 1999, pp. 58–66.

19. Jay A. Conger, "The Necessary Art of Persuasion," *Harvard Business Review*, May–June 1998, p. 86.

20. William Cormier and Sherilyn Cormier, *Interviewing Strategies for Helpers* (Monterey, CA: Brooks/Cole, 1990).

21. Jim Harris, "Listen and Respond: The Communication Two-Step," *Leadership* (American Association International), June 1998, p. 4.

22. Steve Patterson, "Returning to Babel," *Management Review*, June 1994, pp. 44–48.

23. Andrew E. Schwartz, "The Importance of Listening: It Can't Be Stressed Enough," *Supervisory Management*, July 1991, p. 7; "Train Yourself in the Art of Listening," *Positive Leadership*, p. 10, sample issue, 2001.

24. Charlene Marmer Solomon, "Communicating in a Global Environment," *Workforce*, November 1999, p. 51.

25. Solomon, "Communicating in a Global Environment," p. 56.

26. Roger E. Axtell, *Gestures: The Dos and Taboos of Body Language Around the World* (New York: Wiley, 1991).

27. David P. Tulin, "Enhance Your Multi-Cultural Communication Skills," *Managing Diversity*, 1, 1992, p. 5.

28. Deborah Tannen, *Talking from 9 to 5* (New York: William Morrow, 1994); Tannen, *You Just Don't Understand* (New York: Ballantine, 1990); John Gray, *Men Are from Mars, Women Are from Venus* (New York: HarperCollins, 1992).

29. Gerald R. Ferris, Pamela L. Perrewé, William P. Anthony, and David C. Gilmore, "Political Skill at Work," *Organizational Dynamics*, Spring 2000, p. 25.

30. Mildred L. Culp, "Work Productivity: Buddy-Up with Tech 'Fixers'," *WorkWise®* syndicated column, January 10, 1999.

31. "Office Politics a Positive," Gannett News Service, February 13, 2001.

32. Tom Peters, "Power," *Success*, November 1994, p. 34.

33. "Did You Leave This Knife Here?" *WorkingSMART*, March 1997, p. 1.

34. Annette Simmons, *Territorial Games: Understanding and Ending Turf Wars at Work* (New York: AMACOM, 1998).

35. Stanley Bing, "What Would Machiavelli Do?" *Fortune*, December 5, 199, pp. 222–223.

36. Survey reported in "Execs Regularly Must Soothe Staff," *Rochester Democrat and Chronicle*, December 31, 2000, p. 1G.

37. Simmons, *Territorial Games*, p. 218.

Teams, Groups, and Teamwork

What are the ingredients of a great restaurant? Superb cuisine, a special ambience, a chef with presence. Radius has those ingredients in abundance. Its modern French menu repeatedly wins raves from food critics. Its location, in a bank building in Boston's Financial District, is quite distinctive. And its co-owner and chef Michael Schlow keeps a high profile in Boston and New York City. But Radius's recipe for success includes a fourth ingredient: a real commitment to teamwork. Schlow says, "This restaurant is about creating something bigger than any of us could accomplish alone."

Greatness at Radius starts with great teamwork, and great teamwork starts in the kitchen. The Radius kitchen is made of stations: the meat station, the fish station, the garde-manger station, and the pastry station. Two people work at each station and take full responsibility for their part of the meal. In other words, the team at the meat station not only cooks the meat but also butchers it and seasons it—a sharp departure from the standard procedure at most restaurants.

Radius developed a series of meetings in which both the spirit and the practice of teamwork are reinforced. One weekly meeting focuses on frontline service. The sous-chef and the pastry chefs meet with the back waiters and the food runners (the waiters' support staff) to review dishes and procedures.

A daily meeting (the kitchen-staff session) focuses on behind-the-scenes operations. About 30 staffers gather around Schlow to discuss plans for the evening. Then the daily service meeting, led by restaurant management, includes all of the wait staff, the floor managers, and the

OBJECTIVES

After studying this chapter and doing the exercises, you should be able to:

1 Identify various types of teams and groups, including self-managed work teams and project groups.

2 Describe the characteristics of effective groups and teams.

3 Describe the stages of group development.

4 Specify key roles assumed by team and group members.

5 Summarize managerial actions for building teamwork.

6 Explain the actions and attitudes of an effective team player.

7 Point to the potential contributions and problems of teams and groups.

8 Describe the positive and negative aspects of conflict and how team leaders and managers can resolve conflict.

Chapter 14

hosts and hostesses. About 40 people gather in a large, rotunda-like lounge located in the restaurant's lower level. The general manager reviews that night's reservations: who the customers will be, their occupation, and whether they have been to Radius before. The wait staff is asked detailed questions about the food to be served.

The commitment to learning and teamwork at Radius contributes to its loyal following and a growing reputation in the industry. Jay Caputo, a 26-year-old line cook and a recent graduate of the Culinary Institute of America, recognized its commitment to quality. "The first time I walked into Radius, the whole atmosphere was beautiful," he says. "You could tell that people really believed in what they were doing. I knew this was the place for me."[1]

The emphasis on teamwork in the French restaurant just described underscores a major trend in modern organizations. Teams are used frequently to enhance organizational effectiveness. The heavy emphasis on teams and group decision making in the workplace increases the importance of understanding teams and other types of groups. (You will recall the discussion of group decision making in Chapter 6 and the mention of teams throughout the book.)

We approach an additional understanding of teams, groups, and teamwork here by presenting a handful of key topics: types of groups and teams, characteristics of effective work groups; stages in the development of groups, group member roles, building teamwork, and becoming a team player. We also describe the manager's role in resolving conflict that takes place within groups and between groups.

group

A collection of people who interact with each other, are working toward some common purpose, and perceive themselves to be a group.

TYPES OF TEAMS AND GROUPS

1

Identify various types of teams and groups, including self-managed work teams and project groups.

team

A special type of group in which members have complementary skills and are committed to a common purpose, a set of performance goals, and an approach to the task.

teamwork

A situation characterized by understanding and commitment to group goals on the part of all team members.

A **group** is a collection of people who interact with each other, are working toward some common purpose, and perceive themselves to be a group. The head of a customer service team and her staff would be a group. In contrast, 12 people in an office elevator would not be a group because they are not engaged in collective effort. A **team** is a special type of group. Team members have complementary skills and are committed to a common purpose, a set of performance goals, and an approach to the task. **Teamwork** is characterized by understanding and commitment to group goals on the part of all team members.[2]

Some groups are formally sanctioned by management and the organization itself, while others are not. A **formal group** is deliberately formed by the organization to accomplish specific tasks and achieve goals. Examples of formal groups include departments, project groups, task forces, committees, and quality teams. In contrast, **informal groups** emerge over time through the interaction of workers. Although the goals of these groups are not explicitly stated, informal groups typically satisfy a social or recreational purpose. Members of a department who dine together occasionally would constitute an informal group. Yet the same group might also meet an important work purpose of discussing technical problems of mutual interest.

All workplace teams share the common element of people who possess a mix of skills, working together cooperatively. No matter what label the team carries, its broad purpose is to contribute to a *collaborative workplace* in which people help each other achieve constructive goals. Through teams, workers collaborate with a high level of cooperation rather than compete with or prevent others from getting their work done. Here we describe five types of work groups even though they have many similarities. The groups are self-managing work teams, project teams, cross-functional teams, top management teams, and virtual teams.

As teams become more common in the workplace, organizations invest much effort into specifying the skills and knowledge needed to function effectively on a team, particularly a self-managing work team. Exhibit 14-1 presents a representative listing of team skills as perceived by employers.

Self-Managed Work Teams

A dominant trend in work group formation is to organize workers into teams with considerable authority to direct themselves. Many U.S. corporations use some form of team structure in their organizations, often a type of self-managed teams. Team structures are also prevalent in Canadian, European, and Asian industry. A **self-managed work team** is a formally recognized group of employees who are responsible for an entire work process or segment that delivers a product or service to an internal or external customer.[3] Other terms for self-managed work team include *self-directed work team, semi-autonomous team, production work team,* and *work team*. The difference in title sometimes refers to varying

formal group

A group deliberately formed by the organization to accomplish specific tasks and achieve goals.

informal group

A group that emerges over time through the interaction of workers.

381

self-managed work team

A formally recognized group of employees who are responsible for an entire work process or segment that delivers a product or service to an internal or external customer.

EXHIBIT 14-1

Team Skills

A variety of skills are required to be an effective member of various types of teams. Several different business firms use a skill inventory to help guide team members toward the competencies they need to become high-performing team members. Review each team skill listed and rate your skill level using the following classification:

S = strong (capable and comfortable with effectively implementing the skill)
M = moderate (demonstrated skill in the past)
B = basic (minimum ability in this area)
N = not applicable (not relevant to the type of work I do)

Communication Skills	Skill Level (S, M, B, or N)	**Thought Process Skills**	Skill Level (S, M, B, or N)
Speak effectively	___	Analyze issues	___
Foster open communications	___	Think "outside the box"	___
Listen to others	___	**Organizational Skills**	
Deliver presentations	___	Know the business	___
Prepare written communication	___	Use technical/functional expertise	___
Self-Management Skills		Use financial/quantitative data	___
Act with integrity	___	**Strategic Skills**	
Demonstrate adaptability	___	Recognize big picture impact	___
Engage in personal development	___	Promote corporate citizenship	___
Strive for results	___	Focus on customer needs	___
Commitment to work	___	Commit to quality	___
Thought Process Skills		Manage profitability	___
Innovate solutions to problems	___		
Use sound judgment	___		

amounts of authority held by the group. Self-managed work groups originated as an outgrowth of job enrichment. Working in teams broadens the responsibility of team members.

Small as well as large companies make use of this form of job design, as suggested by Radius, the French restaurant. Self-directed teams function in businesses as diverse as food processing, furniture manufacturing, telecommunications, insurance, government agencies, and health care.[4]

The key purposes for establishing self-managed teams are to increase productivity, enhance quality, reduce cycle time (the amount of time required to complete a transaction), and respond more rapidly to a changing workplace.

Method of Operation

Members of the self-managed work team typically work together on an ongoing, day-by-day basis, thus differentiating it from a task force or committee. The work team often assumes total responsibility or "ownership" of a product or service. A work team might be assigned the responsibility for preparing a merchandise catalog. At other times, the team takes on responsibility for a major chunk of a job, such as building a truck engine (but not the entire truck). The self-managed work team is taught to think in terms of customer requirements. The team member might ask, "How easy would it be for a left-handed person to use this tire jack?"

To promote the sense of ownership, management encourages workers to be generalists rather than specialists. Each team member learns a broad range of skills and switches job assignments periodically. Members of the self-directed work team frequently receive training in team skills. Cross-training in different organizational functions helps members develop an overall perspective of how the firm operates. Exhibit 14-2 presents the distinguishing characteristics of a self-managing work team. Studying these characteristics will provide insight into work teams.

The level of responsibility for a product or service contributes to team members' pride in their work and team. At best, the team members feel as if they operate a small business, with the profits (or losses) directly attributable to their efforts. An entry-level worker, such as a data-entry clerk in a government agency, is less likely to experience such feelings.

EXHIBIT 14-2

**Characteristics of a
Self-Managed Work Team**

1. Through empowerment, team members share many management and leadership functions, such as making job assignments and giving pep talks.
2. Members plan, control, and improve their own work processes.
3. Members set their own goals and inspect their own work.
4. Members create their own schedules and review their group performance.
5. Members often prepare their own budgets and coordinate their work with other departments.
6. Members typically order materials, keep inventories, and deal with suppliers.
7. Members hire their own replacements or assume responsibility for disciplining their own members.
8. Members assume responsibility for the quality of their products and services, whether provided to internal or external customers.

Source: Adapted from Richard S. Wellings, William C. Byham, and Jeanne M. Wilson, *Empowered Teams: Creating Self-Directed Work Groups That Improve Quality, Productivity, and Participation* (San Francisco: Jossey-Bass, 1991), p. 3.

Self–Managed Work Team Effectiveness

Self-managed work teams demonstrate a reasonably good record of improving productivity, quality, and customer service. About 50 percent of the time they result in productivity gains, yet effective teams can produce remarkable results. A representative example of the potential productivity gains from a self-managed work team took place at Monarch Marking Systems, based in Dayton, Ohio. The company manufactures labeling, identification, and tracking equipment. The teams trimmed the square footage needed in the assembly area by 70 percent, reduced past-due shipments 90 percent, and increased productivity 100 percent.[5]

Despite their potential contribution, self-managed work teams create challenges for managers. High-caliber employees are required for the team because they must be able to solve problems on their own and rely less on a supervisor. Effective contributors to a self-managed team must be multiskilled, and not all employees are willing or able to develop new skills. Another challenge for the manager, particularly the team leader, is being left with relatively little to do because the team is self-managing. In some firms, however, a middle-level manager might have overall responsibility for several teams. The team leaders become the direct reports, and the manager acts as a facilitator.

Project Teams

Project teams comprise the basic component of the project organization described in Chapter 9 in relation to a matrix form of organization. A **project team** is a small group of employees working on a temporary basis in order to accomplish a particular goal.[6] Here we present additional details about project teams to help you understand this important type of work group.

project team

A small group of employees working on a temporary basis in order to accomplish a particular goal.

1. Project managers operate independently of the normal chain of command. They usually report to a member of top-level management, often an executive in charge of projects. This reporting relationship gives project members a feeling of being part of an elite group. (A Management in Action feature in Chapter 9 describes the key role project managers play in the modern organization.)
2. Project managers negotiate directly for resources with the heads of the line and staff departments whose members are assigned to a given project. For example, a project manager might borrow an architectural technician from the building design department. For the team member who likes job rotation, project teams offer the opportunity for different exciting projects from time to time.
3. Project managers act as coordinators of the people and material needed to complete the project's mission, making them accountable for the performance of the people assigned to the project. Project members therefore feel a sense of responsibility to their project leader and their team.
4. Members of the project team might be from the same functional area or from different areas, depending on the needs of the project. The members of a new-product development team, for example, are usually from different areas. A cross-functional team might therefore be regarded as a special type of project team. An example of a project team with members from the same functional area would be a group of financial specialists on assignment to revise the company pension program.
5. The life of the project ends when its objectives are accomplished, such as adding a wing to a hospital or building a prototype for a new sports car. In contrast, most departments are considered relatively stable.

Project teams are found in almost every large company. The Speed Team at IBM (described in Case 14-A) can be considered a project team. The members worked full time at a project, and returned to their previous (or a comparable) position when the mission was accomplished.

From the standpoint of the work group, the project team offers an important advantage. Being part of a project encourages identification with the project, which often leads to high morale and productivity. A frequently observed attitude is "we can get this important job done." From the standpoint of the organization, a project team offers flexibility. If the project proves not to be worthwhile the project can be disbanded quickly, without having committed enormous resources like renting a separate building or hiring a large staff. If the new project is a big success, it can become the nucleus of a new division of the company or a major new product line. For example, Nissan Motor Corporation's venture into the SUV market began as a project.

One problem with project teams, as well as other temporary teams, is that people assigned to the project may be underutilized after the project is completed. Unless another project requires staffing, some of the project members may be laid off.

Cross-Functional Teams

It is common practice for teams to be composed of workers from different specialties. A **cross-functional team** is a group composed of workers from different specialties, at the same organizational level who come together to accomplish a task. (A cross-functional team might be considered a type of project team.) A cross-functional team fulfills its purpose by blending the talents of team members from different specialties as they work toward a task that requires such a mix. To perform well on a cross-functional team a person must think in terms of the good of the larger organization, rather than in terms of his or her own specialty. A typical application of a cross-functional team would be to develop a new product like a Net TV. Among the specialties needed on such a team would be computer science, engineering, manufacturing, industrial design, marketing, and finance. (The finance person would help guide the team toward producing a Net TV that could be sold at a profit.) When members from different specialties work together, they take into account each other's perspectives when making their contribution. For example, if the manufacturing representative knows that a Net TV must sell for about one-half the price of a personal computer, then he or she will have to build the device inexpensively. Using a cross-functional team for product development enhances communication across groups, thus saving time.

In addition to product development, cross-functional teams can improve quality, reduce costs, and run a company (in the form of a top-management team). Northwestern Mutual Life has been using cross-functional teams for various purposes almost as long as the company has been in business. In recent years a cross-functional team created the company's Web site (http://www.northwesternmutual.com). Most Northwestern cross-functional teams now include an individual who has no responsibility for the problem—who is not a stakeholder. The outside perspective is thought to be effective in stimulating the thinking of other team members.

The success of a cross-functional team requires collaboration among its members. Yet the research of Avan R. Jassawalla and Hemant C. Sashittal suggests that some members of new product cross-functional teams do not have the right interpersonal skills to collaborate. Also, some team members demonstrate difficulty committing to a common agenda. On a positive note, the likelihood of collaboration increases when team members agree on a common agenda and openly share concerns. The members must also share power and make a sincere effort to trust one another.[7]

Top-Management Teams

The group of managers at the top of most organizations is referred to as a team, the management team, or the top-management team. Yet as Jon R. Katzenbach observes, few groups of top-level managers function as a team in the sense of the definition presented earlier in this chapter.[8] The CEO gets most of the publicity, along with credit and blame for what goes wrong. Nevertheless, groups of top-level managers are teams in the sense that they make most major decisions collaboratively with all members of the top-management group included. Michael Dell (Dell Computers) exemplifies a highly visible CEO who regularly consults with trusted advisors before making major decisions.

The term *top-management team* has another less frequently used meaning. A handful of companies are actually run by a committee of two or more top executives who claim to share power equally. In this way they are similar to a husband-and-wife team running a household. An example of power sharing at the top to form a two-person team, then a three-person team, took place at Citigroup a few years ago. The arrangement did not work well because of bickering over who was really in charge of what. One executive, John Reed, finally retired, one executive, Sanford Weill, took charge. Some observers are skeptical that a company can really be run well without one key executive having the final decision. Can you imagine your favorite athletic team having two head coaches, or your favorite band having two leaders?

Virtual Teams

We hinted earlier at virtual teams in reference to the virtual office mentioned in Chapter 3. A **virtual team** is a small group of people who conduct almost all of their collaborative work by electronic communication rather than in face-to-face meetings. In the language of information technology, they engage in "cyber-collaboration" by conducting "cybermeetings." E-mail is the usual medium for sharing information and conducting meetings. Groupware is another widely used approach to conducting a cybermeeting. Using groupware, several people can edit a document at the same time, or in sequence. Videoconferencing is another technological advance that facilitates the virtual team. Electronic brainstorming, as described in Chapter 6, is well suited for a virtual team.

Most high-tech companies make some use of virtual teams. The trend toward forming cross-cultural teams from geographically dispersed units of a firm increases the application of virtual teams.[9] Strategic alliances in which geographically dispersed companies work with each other depend on virtual teams in many regards. The field technician in Iceland who holds a cybermeeting with her counterparts in South Africa, Mexico, and California realizes a significant cost savings over bringing them all together in one physical location. IBM makes some use of virtual teams in selling information technology systems, partially because so many IBM field personnel work from their homes, vehicles, and hotel rooms.

According to Lynn Newman, trust is a crucial component of virtual teams. Managers trust people to perform well without direct supervision. Team members

virtual team

A small group of people who conduct almost all of their collaborative work by electronic communication rather than in face-to-face meetings.

develop trust in their coworkers without the benefit of face-to-face meetings. Managers face the same challenge as that for assembling self-managed work teams: self-reliant and talented employees must be selected for the team.[10]

The accompanying Management in Action provides additional insights into virtual teams, especially from the perspective of information technology and finance.

2   CHARACTERISTICS OF EFFECTIVE WORK GROUPS

Describe the characteristics of effective groups and teams.

Groups, like individuals, possess characteristics that contribute to their uniqueness and effectiveness. As shown in Exhibit 14-3, these characteristics can be grouped into eight categories. Our description of work group effectiveness follows this framework.[11]

EXHIBIT 14-3

Work Group Characteristics Related to Effectiveness

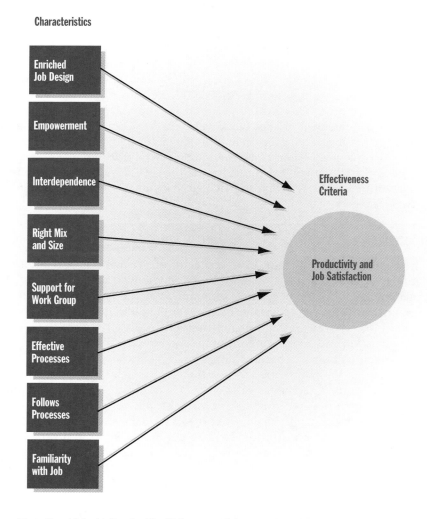

Characteristics

- Enriched Job Design
- Empowerment
- Interdependence
- Right Mix and Size
- Support for Work Group
- Effective Processes
- Follows Processes
- Familiarity with Job

Effectiveness Criteria

Productivity and Job Satisfaction

Source: Adapted from Michael A. Campion, Ellen M. Papper, and Gina Medsker, "Relations Between Work Team Characteristics and Effectiveness: A Replication and Extension," *Personnel Psychology*, Summer 1996, p. 431; David E. Hyatt and Thomas M. Ruddy, "An Examination of the Relationship Between Work Group Characteristics and Performance," *Personnel Psychology*, Autumn 1997, p. 579; Brian D. Janz, Jason A. Colquitt, and Raymond A. Noe, "Knowledge Worker Team Effectiveness: The Role of Autonomy, Interdependence, Team Development, and Contextual Support Variables, *Personnel Psychology*, Winter 1997, pp. 877–904; Bradley L. Kirkman and Benson Rosen, "Powering Up Teams," *Organizational Dynamics*, Winter 2000, pp. 48–52.

Management *in Action*

Nortel Networks Takes the Plunge into Virtual Teams

Dale Pratt doesn't share an office with her team members. She is not even in the same building or postal code (zip code). Pratt, director of HR for Nortel Networks Corporation, works at company headquarters in Ontario, Canada. But as a member of a virtual team, she has colleagues as far away as Europe and China.

Nortel Networks creates Internet technologies, with its 80,000 employees located in 150 countries. "We have to work in real time across the globe, really fast, and our employees have to be where our customers are," says Pratt. "For us, working with our virtual team is the same as other companies where people might sit together under a centralized roof. We simply use different tools to do our jobs every day."

Pratt trained her virtual team of 60 finance and legal employees on deal-making skills. To accommodate team members located throughout the world, Pratt chose an assortment of technology tools, beginning with group meeting software called Meeting Manager. Virtual participants on individual PCs and also on a teleconference line talk and listen to one another. She prepared charts that team members could view on their screens, and provided an electronic white board for random ideas and scribbling.

The meeting took place—in real time—from the team members' desktops at their various locations around the world. After scheduling the meeting on the company's intranet calendar and inviting participants by e-mail, Pratt secured charts from the meeting presenters and uploaded them onto the company's Meeting Manager, which allowed for group viewing. As chair of the meeting, Pratt controlled the order of the meeting and the viewing of the charts. Participants posed questions on the white board, which Pratt could see. She then addressed or answered the questions on the computer screen, or posed and took questions on the phone.

Pratt explains the phenomenal cost savings in not having to meet face-to-face. Nortel's IS department studied travel savings. The expense of travel comes not only from airfare and hotels but also in lost work time. Cutting travel budgets results in cost savings and greater efficiency.

Source: Charlene Marmer Solomon, "Managing Virtual Teams," *Workforce*, June 2001, pp. 60–65.

1. *Enriched job design.* Effective work groups follow the principles of job design embodied in job enrichment and the job characteristics model described in Chapter 8. For example, task significance and task identity are both strong. Group members therefore perceive their work as having high intrinsic motivation.

2. *A feeling of empowerment.* An effective group or team believes in its authority to solve a variety of problems without first obtaining approval from management. Empowered teams share four experiences: potency, meaningfulness, autonomy, and impact. *Potency* refers to teams members believing in themselves and exhibiting a confident, can–do attitude. Teams with a sense of *meaningfulness* collectively commit to their mission and see their goals as valuable and worthwhile. *Autonomy* refers to the freedom, discretion, and control the teams experience (the same as in job enrichment). A team experiences *impact*

when members see the effect of their work on other interested parties such as customers and coworkers.[12]

3. *Interdependent tasks and rewards.* Effective work groups are characterized by several types of group member dependencies on one another. Such groups show *task interdependence* in the sense that members interact and depend on one another to accomplish work. *Goal interdependence* refers to the linking of individual goals to the group's goals. Unless the task requires interdependence, such as building a motorcycle, a team is not needed. A member of a sales team might establish a compensation goal for herself, but she can realize this goal only if the other team members achieve similar success. *Interdependent feedback and rewards* also contribute to group effectiveness. Individual feedback and rewards should be linked to group performance to encourage good team play.

4. *Right mix and size.* A variety of factors relating to the mix of group members are associated with effective work groups. The diversity of group members' experience, knowledge, and education generally improves problem solving. Cultural diversity tends to enhance creativity by bringing various viewpoints into play. However, only when each team member enjoys high quality interactions can the full benefits of diversity be realized. The interactions relate to both the task itself (such as talking about improving a motorcycle starter) and social interactions (such as chatting about children during a break).[13]

    Groups should be large enough to accomplish the work, but when groups become too large, confusion and poor coordination may result. Also, larger groups tend to be less cohesive. Cross-functional teams, work teams, committees, and task forces tend to be most productive with 7–10 members. Another important composition factor is the quality of the group or team members. Bright people with constructive personality characteristics contribute the most to team effectiveness. A study involving 652 employees composing 51 work teams found that teams with members higher in mental ability, conscientiousness, extraversion, and emotional stability received higher supervisor ratings for team performance.[14] (Put winners on your team and you are more likely to have a winning team.) The group itself should have high emotional intelligence in the sense of being able to build relationships both inside and outside the team, and make constructive use of its emotion. Norms that establish mutual trust among group members contribute to an emotionally intelligent group.[15]

5. *Good support for the work group.* One of the most important characteristics of an effective work group is the support it receives from the organization. Key support factors include giving the group the information it needs, coaching group members, providing the right technology, and receiving recognition and other rewards. *Training* quite often facilitates work group effectiveness. The training content typically includes group decision making, interpersonal skills, technical knowledge, and the team philosophy. *Managerial support* in the form of investing resources and believing in group effort fosters effectiveness. A contributing factor to the success of the highly productive Kansas City Harley-Davidson plant is that workers say the higher-ups pay more than lip service to partnership: They pay attention in such ways as granting worker requests about funding for new equipment and machinery.

6. *Effective processes within the group.* Many processes (activities) take place within the group that influence effectiveness. One is the belief that the group can do the job, reflecting high team spirit. Effectiveness is also enhanced when workers provide *social support* to each other through such means as helping each other have positive interactions. *Workload sharing* is another process char-

acteristic related to effectiveness. *Communication and cooperation* within the work group also contributes to effectiveness. Collectively, the right amount of these process characteristics contributes to *cohesiveness*, or a group that pulls together. Without cohesiveness, a group will fail to achieve synergy.

7. *Follows processes and procedures.* Teams that can be trusted to follow work processes and procedures tend to perform better. Adhering to such processes and procedures is also associated with high-quality output. Although following processes and procedures might appear to be a routine expectation, many problems are created by workers who fail to do so. For example, a group might show a productivity dip if workers on a project fail to back up computer files and a computer virus or worm attacks.

8. *Familiarity with jobs, coworkers, and the environment.* Another important set of factors related to work group effectiveness is familiarity. It refers to the specific knowledge group members have of their jobs, coworkers, and the environment. Familiarity essentially refers to experience, and for many types of job experience—at least to the point of proficiency—is an asset. The contribution of familiarity is evident also when new members join an athletic team. Quite often the team loses momentum during the adjustment period.

To help you pull together information about the characteristics of effective work groups and teams, study the following summary of research conducted with professional-level workers in a financial services firm.

> The high-performing teams performed a variety of tasks that members perceived to be significant. They were allowed a high degree of self-management, were interdependent in terms of tasks, goals and feedback, and functioned as a single team. They tended to have members with complementary skills who were flexible in the tasks they performed. They were not too large for the tasks assigned them. They were well supported by the organization in terms of training, managerial support, and cooperation and communication from other teams. They had confidence in their teams' abilities, and members supported one another, communicated, cooperated, and fairly shared the workload.[16]

The characteristics of an effective work group or team should be supplemented by effective leadership. Team leaders must emphasize coaching more than controlling. Instead of being a supervisor, the leader becomes a team developer.

STAGES OF GROUP DEVELOPMENT   **3**

To understand the nature of work groups, one must understand what the group is doing (the content) and how it proceeds (the process). A key group process is how a group develops over time. To make this information meaningful, relate it to any group to which you belonged for at least one month. Understanding the stages of group development can lead to more effective group leadership or membership. We describe the five group stages next.[17] (See Exhibit 14-4.)

Describe the stages of group development.

Stage 1: Forming. At the outset, members are eager to learn what tasks they will be performing, how they can benefit from group membership, and what constitutes acceptable behavior. Members often inquire about rules they must follow. Confusion, caution, and being cordial toward each other typically characterize the initial phase of group development.

Stage 2: Storming. During this "shakedown" period, individual styles often come into conflict. Hostility, infighting, tension, and confrontation occur at this stage.

EXHIBIT 14-4

The Stages of Group Development

Most groups follow a predictable sequence of stages.

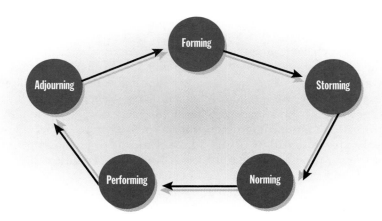

Members may argue to clarify expectations about their contributions. Coalitions and cliques may form within the group, and one or two members may be targeted for exclusion. Subgroups may form to push an agenda of interest to them. (Despite the frequency of storming, many workplace groups work willingly with one another from the outset, thus skipping stage 2.)

Stage 3: Norming. Overcoming resistance and establishing group standards of conduct (norms) follow the storm. Cohesiveness and commitment begin to develop. The group starts to come together as a coordinated unit, and harmony prevails. Norms stem from three sources: The group itself quickly establishes limits for members, often by effective use of glares and nods. For example, the team member who responds sarcastically to the group leader's suggestions might receive disapproving glances from other members. Norms may also be imposed that are derived from the larger organization and professional codes, such as that used by accountants and financial planners. A third source of norms might be an influential team member who inspires the group to elevate its performance or behavior. A team member might say, "Why stop at having the best safety record in this division. Let's be number one in the entire company."

Stage 4: Performing. When the group reaches the performing stage, it is ready to focus on accomplishing its key tasks. Issues concerning interpersonal relations and task assignment are put aside as the group becomes a well-functioning unit. Intrinsic motivation and creativity are likely to emerge as the group performs. At their best, members feel they are working "for the cause," much like a political campaign team or a team bringing a breakthrough product to market.

Stage 5: Adjourning. Temporary work groups disband after accomplishing their task. Those same group members, however, developed important relationships and understandings they can take with them should they be part of the same team in the future. Case 14-B describes an IBM team that began with an adjournment date in mind, yet stands prepared to continue its good work. The link between adjourning and forming shown in Exhibit 14-4 indicates that many groups do reassemble after one project is completed. The link between Stages 1 and 5 would not apply for a group that disbanded and never worked together again.

Helping the group move past the first three stages into performing poses a key managerial challenge. At times, leaders may need to challenge group members to spend less time on process issues and more time on task—getting the job done!

ROLES FOR TEAM AND GROUP MEMBERS

Another perspective on the group process is to identify team member roles.[18] The positive roles described here can help you identify areas of possible contribution in group or team effort.

Specify key roles assumed by team and group members.

- *Knowledge Contributor.* Being technically proficient, the knowledge contributor provides the group with useful and valid information. He or she is intent upon helping with task accomplishment and values sharing technical expertise with team members. Referring again to the Harley-Davidson example, the knowledge contributor role is emphasized for production technicians because they are expected to make suggestions for improving quality and productivity. The plant general manager says, "What we're trying to do is get the work force to run the factory."[19]

- *Process Observer.* A person occupying this role forces the group to look at how it is functioning, with statements such as: "We've been at it for two and one-half hours, and we have only taken care of one agenda item. Shouldn't we be doing better?" The process observer might also point to excellent team progress.

- *People Supporter.* A person occupying this role assumes some of the leader's responsibility for providing emotional support to teammates and resolving conflict. He or she serves as a model of active listening while others are presenting. The people supporter helps others relax by smiling, making humorous comments, and appearing relaxed. He or she supports and encourages team members even when disagreeing with them.

- *Challenger.* To prevent complacency and noncritical thinking, a team needs one or more members who confront and challenge bad ideas. A challenger will criticize any decision or preliminary thinking that is deficient in any way, including being ethically unsound. Effective interpersonal skills are required to be a challenger. Antagonistic, attack-style people who attempt the challenger role lose their credibility quickly.

- *Listener.* Listening contributes so substantially to team success that it comprises a separate role, even though other roles involve listening. If other people are not heard, the full contribution of team effort cannot be realized. As a result of being a listener, a team member or team leader is able to summarize discussion and progress for the team.

- *Mediator.* Disputes within the group may become so intense and prolonged that two people no longer listen or respond to each other. The two antagonists develop such polarized viewpoints that they are unwilling to move toward each other's point of view. Furthermore, they have moved beyond the point that conciliation is possible. At this point the team leader or a team member must mediate the dispute.

- *Gatekeeper.* A recurring problem in group effort is that some members may fail to contribute because other team members dominate the discussion. Even when the viewpoints of the timid team members have been expressed, they may not be remembered because one or two other members contribute so frequently to discussion. When the opportunity gate is closed to several members, the gatekeeper pries it open. He or she requests that a specific team member be allowed to contribute, or that the member's past contribution be recognized.

- *Take-Charge Leader.* Some teams cry out for direction because either a formal leader has not been appointed or the appointed leader is unusually laid-back. In such situations, a team member can assume the role of the take-charge leader. The problem could be that team members are hesitant to make even simple decisions or take a stand on controversial matters. A starting point for the take-charge leader is to encourage the team to define its mission and list its three main objectives.

A team leader who plays several of the roles just described is likely to be perceived as an *informal leader*, or a person who exercises leadership without having the formal title. The take-charge role is essentially an informal leader. Acting as an informal leader can often boost an individual's career; management may recognize those capabilities and choose the informal leader for a formal leadership position, such as a supervisor.

5   MANAGERIAL ACTIONS FOR BUILDING TEAMWORK

Summarize managerial actions for building teamwork.

The team player roles described previously point to actions the individual can take to become a team player. Here we highlight managerial actions and organizational practices that facilitate teamwork.[20] We use the term *managerial practices* to include team leader practices because many groups and teams do not use the title *team leader* for the person in charge. A department manager, for example, might be able to build teamwork. Good teamwork enhances, but does not guarantee, a successful team. For example, a group with excellent teamwork might be working on improving a service no longer valued by the company or customers. No matter what the output of the team, it will probably be ignored.

Gordon Bethune, the CEO who helped rebuild Continental Airlines from "worst to first" offers a good starting point for building teamwork. He maintains that the entire team must agree on what constitutes success. Every team member has to say: "Yes, that's it."[21] At Habitat for Humanity International everyone agrees on the cause of providing housing to low-income families—people who could not ordinarily afford a home. Another early step is to help team members believe they have an urgent, constructive purpose. A demanding performance challenge helps create and sustain the team.

Competing against a common enemy is one of the best-known methods of building team spirit. It is preferable that the adversary is external, such as an independent diner competing against franchised family restaurants. A primary strategy for teamwork promotes the attitude that working together effectively is an expected norm. Developing such a culture of teamwork generally proves difficult when a strong culture of individualism exists within the firm. The team leader can communicate the norm of teamwork by making frequent use of words and phrases that support teamwork. Emphasizing the words *team members* or *teammates*, and deemphasizing the words *subordinates* and *employees* helps communicate the teamwork norm. Exhibit 14-5 summarizes the key culture changes necessary to achieve teamwork.

Using the consensus decision-making style provides another way to reinforce teamwork. A sophisticated approach to enhancing teamwork, it feeds team members valid facts and information that motivate them to work together. New information prompts the team to redefine and enrich its understanding of the challenge it is facing, thereby focusing on a common purpose. A subtle yet potent method of building teamwork emphasizes the use of language that fosters cohesion and commitment. In-group jargon bonds a team and sets the group apart from others. For example, a team of computer experts says "Give me a core dump" to mean "Tell me your thoughts." The culture at Microsoft heavily emphasizes using hip jargon to build teamwork. Using the term *bandwidth* as a synonym for intelligence appears to have been invented by CEO Bill Gates.

Individual Culture	Team Culture
Workers compete against each other for recognition, raises, and resources.	Workers learn to collaborate with each other.
Workers are paid for their individual efforts.	Workers are rewarded based on own efforts plus efforts of teammates.
Supervisors use authoritarian leadership or management style.	Supervisors become facilitative; they coach workers rather than only giving orders.

Source: Adapted from "The 'Facts of Life' for Teambuilding," *Human Resources Forum,* February 1995, p. 3.

EXHIBIT 14-5

Developing a Culture of Teamwork

Teamwork is more likely to persist when the organization establishes a culture of teamwork.

393

To foster teamwork, the manager should minimize **micromanagement**, or supervising group members too closely and second-guessing their decisions. Micromanagement can hamper a spirit of teamwork (potency) because team members do not feel in control of their own work.

One high-impact strategy for encouraging teamwork rewards the team as well as individuals. The most convincing team incentive is to calculate compensation partially on the basis of team results. For a more general reward strategy, managers apply positive reinforcement whenever the group or individuals engage in behavior that supports teamwork. For example, team members who took the initiative to have an information-sharing session can be singled out and praised for this activity.

Team leaders encourage workers to communicate with each other and establish a norm of teamwork. Northwestern Mutual, as mentioned in regard to cross-functional teams, takes pride in its culture of teamwork. In this way, workers adjust easily to working on teams. The manager can publish a *team book* containing a one-page biography of teach team member. The biography can include a photo, a list of hobbies, personal interests, and family information. As team members look through the book, they become better acquainted with each other, leading to feelings of closeness.

Another option available to organizations for enhancing teamwork comes through experiential learning such as sending members to outdoor training. Participants acquire leadership and teamwork skills by confronting physical challenges and exceeding their self-imposed limitations. In rope activities, which are typical of outdoor training, participants attached to a secure pulley with ropes climb ladders and jump off to another spot. Another form of outdoor training for elite teams, a day at an auto-racing track, provides team members with an opportunity to drive at race car speeds in some kind of cooperative venture. All of these challenges require teamwork rather than individual effort, hence their contribution to team development. Outdoor training generally offers the most favorable outcomes when the trainer helps the team members comprehend the link between such training and on-the-job behavior.

Effective managers pick and choose from strategies as appropriate to build teamwork. Relying too heavily on one tactic, such as establishing a mission statement or outdoor training, limits the development of sustained teamwork.

micromanagement
Supervising group members too closely and second-guessing their decisions.

BEING AN EFFECTIVE TEAM PLAYER

6

Being an effective team player makes collaborative effort possible. Being an effective team player also affects managerial perceptions. A survey of business organizations in 34 industries indicates that employers rate "team player" as the most highly ranked

Explain the actions and attitudes of an effective team player.

workplace behavior. Approximately 40 percent of the managers surveyed ranked team player as number one among seven desirable traits.[22] Here we describe a number of skills, actions, and attitudes contributing to effective team play. For convenience, five are classified as task-related, and five as people-related. In reviewing these attributes, remember that all team situations do not have identical requirements.

Task-Related Actions and Attitudes

Task-related actions and attitudes focus on group or team work goals rather than on interpersonal relationships. An effective team player is likely to behave and think in the following ways:

1. *Possesses and shares technical expertise.* Most people are chosen to join a particular work team on the basis of their technical or functional expertise. Glenn Parker believes that using technical expertise to outstanding advantage requires a willingness and ability to share that expertise. It is also necessary for the technical expert to be able to communicate with team members in other disciplines who lack the same technical background.[23]

2. *Assumes responsibility for problems.* The outstanding team player assumes responsibility for problems. If he or she notices a free-floating problem (not yet assigned to a specific person), the team member says, "I'll do it." The task should be one suited for independent rather than coordinated activity, such as conducting research.

3. *Is willing to commit to team goals.* The exceptional team player will commit to team goals even if his or her personal goals cannot be achieved for now. For instance, the team member seeking visibility will be enthusiastic about pursuing team goals even if not much visibility will be gained.

4. *Is able to see the big picture.* As described in Chapter 1, a basic management skill is to think conceptually. Exceptionally good team players exhibit this same skill. In team efforts, discussion can get bogged down in small details. As a result, the team might temporarily lose sight of what it is trying to accomplish. The team player (or team leader) who can help the group focus on its broader purpose plays a vital role.

5. *Is willing to ask tough questions.* A **tough question** helps the group achieve insight into the nature of the problem it faces, what it might be doing wrong, and whether progress is sufficient. Tough questions can also be asked to help the group see the big picture. Asking tough questions helps the group avoid groupthink. Here is a representative tough question asked by a team member: "I've been to all our meetings so far. What in the world have we accomplished?"

6. *Is willing to try something new.* An effective team player experiments with new ideas even if the old method works relatively well. Trying something new leads to a spirit of inventiveness that helps keep the group vibrant. In one of the Harley-Davidson work teams, several of the workers designed a device to guide the brush in painting Harley's trademark striping. Although the more experienced manufacturing technicians had been successful with the hand-painting method, in the spirit of teamwork they were willing to try the new technique.

People-Related Actions and Attitudes

Outstanding team players cultivate a conscious awareness of their interpersonal relations within the group. They recognize that effective interpersonal relationships are important for task accomplishment. An outstanding team player is likely to do or think the following:

tough question

A question that helps the group achieve insight into the nature of a problem, what it might be doing better, and whether progress is sufficient.

1. *Trust team members.* The cornerstone attitude of the outstanding team player is to trust team members. If you do not believe that the other team members have your best interests at heart, it will be difficult to share opinions and ideas. Trusting team members includes believing that their ideas are technically sound and rational until proven otherwise. Another manifestation of trust is taking a risk by trying out a team member's unproven ideas.

2. *Share credit.* A not-to-be-overlooked tactic for emphasizing teamwork is to share credit for your accomplishments with the team. Sharing credit is authentic because other members of the team usually have contributed to the success of a project. Related to sharing credit, Steve Covey, best-selling author and consultant, says that teamwork is fostered when you don't worry about who gets the credit.[24] To the strong team player, getting the group task accomplished is more important than receiving individual recognition.

3. *Recognize the interests and achievements of others.* A fundamental tactic for establishing yourself as a solid team player is to recognize the interests and achievements of others. Let others know that you care about their interests by such means as asking, "How do my ideas fit into what you have planned?" Recognizing the achievements of others can be done by complimenting their tangible accomplishments.

4. *Listen actively and share information.* The skilled team player listens actively both inside and outside of meetings. As described previously, an active listener strives to grasp both the facts and feelings behind what is being said. Information sharing helps other team members do their job well and also communicates concern for their welfare. Information sharing can take many forms, such as bringing in news clips and magazine articles, informing teammates of useful Web sites, and recommending relevant books.

5. *Give and receive criticism.* The strong team player offers constructive criticism when needed, but does so diplomatically. A high-performance team demands sincere and tactful criticism among members. In addition to criticizing others in a helpful manner, the strong team player benefits from criticism directed toward him or her. A high-performing team involves give and take, including criticism of each other's ideas. The willingness to accept constructive criticism is often referred to as *self-awareness*. The self-aware team player insightfully processes personal feedback to improve effectiveness.

6. *Don't rain on another team member's parade.* Pointing out the flaws in another person's accomplishments, or drawing attention to your own achievements when somebody else is receiving credit, creates disharmony within the group. When a teammate is in the spotlight, allow him or her to enjoy the moment without displaying petty jealousy.

POTENTIAL CONTRIBUTIONS AND PROBLEMS OF TEAMS AND GROUPS   **7**

Given that teams and groups are such an integral part of how organizations function, it is easy not to look critically at their contribution. However, researchers, writers, and managerial workers themselves assess the contributions of groups, both the upside and downside, especially with teams.

Point to the potential contributions and problems of teams and groups.

Potential Contributions of Teams and Groups

Teams and groups make a contribution to the extent that they produce results beyond what could be achieved without a high degree of collaboration among workers. Considerable case history evidence supports the contribution of teams over independent effort. The previous discussion of self-managed work teams presented examples of this evidence. Teams tend to be the most useful as a form of organization under the following conditions:[25]

- When work processes cut across functional lines (as in new-product development)
- When speed is important (keeping the number of team meetings to a minimum)
- When the organization faces a complex and rapidly changing environment (as in developing toys and video games for the next holiday season)
- When innovation and learning have high priority (e-commerce)
- When the tasks to be accomplished require integration of highly interdependent performers (gathering inputs for a strategic plan).

When these conditions do not exist, the organization is better off assigning the task to more traditional groups, or to individuals working alone. Remember that a team is essentially a supergroup.

Potential Problems of Teams and Groups

Although the collaborative workplace enjoys a certain popularity, many concerns accompany the use of teams and groups. In Chapter 6, discussing problem solving and decision making, we described two problems with groups: time wasting and groupthink. Here we look at other problems: limited productivity gains, group polarization, social loafing, and career retardation.

Limited Productivity Gains

A major concern about teams is not that they are harmful, but that their effectiveness is overrated. Teams lead to increases in productivity, quality, and job satisfaction only some of the time, not nearly all the time. The Saratoga Institute, a firm that studies performance measurement, surveyed 61 U.S. companies about their approaches to team design, performance measurement, and compensation. Only one-half of the companies said they are achieving positive results in meeting their operating objectives. One of the major problems cited was the difficulty in measuring the output of teams. Also, just because a team improves a group process (such as better cooperation among members) it does not necessarily lead to a competitive advantage. The survey results just presented also have a positive spin. Half the companies surveyed did think teams were producing good results. Also, although only half the operating managers thought teams were working out well, 80 percent of the companies said their team approach was meeting corporate expectations.[26]

A manager can often improve the productivity of teams by helping the team develop some of the characteristics of an effective work group discussed earlier. Making a deliberate effort to develop teamwork alerts a team to what is needed and helps it realize its potential.

Group Polarization

group polarization

A situation in which post-discussion attitudes tend to be more extreme than pre-discussion attitudes.

During group problem solving, or group discussion in general, members often shift their attitudes. Sometimes the group moves toward taking greater risks, called the risky shift. At other times the group moves toward a more conservative position. The general term for moving in either direction is **group polarization**, a situation in which postdiscussion attitudes tend to be more extreme than prediscussion attitudes.[27] For example, as a result of group discussion members of an executive team become more cautious about entering a new market.

Group discussion facilitates polarization for several reasons. Discovering that others share our opinions may reinforce and strengthen our position. Listening to persuasive arguments may also strengthen our convictions. The "devil-made-me-do-it" attitude is another contributor to polarization. If responsibility is diffused, a person will feel less responsible—and guilty—about taking an extreme position.

Group polarization has a practical implication for managers who rely on group decision making. Workers who enter into group decision making with a stand on an issue may develop more extreme postdecision positions. For example, a team of employees who were seeking more generous benefits may decide as a group that the company should become an industry leader in employee benefits.

Social Loafing

An unfortunate by-product of group and team effort happens when an under-motivated person squeezes by without contributing a fair share. **Social loafing** is freeloading, or shirking individual responsibility, when a person is placed in a group setting and removed from individual accountability. Readers who have worked on group projects for courses may have encountered this widely observed dysfunction of collective effort.

Two motivational explanations of social loafing have been offered. First, some people believe that because they are part of a team, they can "hide in the crowd." Second, group members typically believe that others are likely to withhold effort when working in a group. As a consequence they withhold effort themselves to avoid being played for a sucker.

Tina L. Robbins conducted an experiment with college students in which they were given the opportunity to evaluate important proposals about student life. In the experimental group, a "confederate" told the group about his or her intention to put a lot of effort in the task or to hardly contribute. In the control (contrast) group, the students were not made aware of somebody working extra hard or contributing low effort. Students tended to work harder when they worked alone than when they had a partner contributing high effort. The results of the study demonstrated that social loafing can occur even when the task is thought-provoking, personally involving, and allows for unique contribution. Robbins concludes, "The performance of self-directed work teams or groups which are formed for the purpose of brainstorming, product idea generation, or for making proposal implementation decisions, may suffer the consequences of social loafing."[28]

As one approach to minimizing the effects of social loafing, a manager may ask group members to contribute to the evaluation of each other. Concerns about being evaluated as a freeloader by peers would prompt some people to work harder.

Career Retardation

A final concern about teams arises from focusing too much on group or team effort, rather than individual effort, which can retard a person's career. Some managers classify workers as team players versus leaders. (The perception is somewhat misleading because most effective leaders and managers are also good team players.) The element of truth in the perception is that a person who tries too hard to be a good team player might become a conformist and not seek individual recognition. People who do break away from the team and become higher-level managers are typically those known for independent thought and outstanding accomplishment.

social loafing

Freeloading, or shirking individual responsibility, when a person is placed in a group setting and removed from individual accountability.

For those who want to advance beyond being a team member, or team leader, it is important to be recognized for outstanding performance. As a team member, for example, volunteer to take on leadership roles such as chairing a team meeting or coordinating a special project. Bring a dossier of your individual accomplishments to your performance review. Every team has a most valuable player (MVP) who is still a good team player.

8   RESOLVING CONFLICT WITHIN TEAMS AND GROUPS

Describe the positive and negative aspects of conflict and how team leaders and managers can resolve conflict.

conflict

The simultaneous arousal of two or more incompatible motives.

Although harmony and collaboration are an important goal of groups and teams, some disagreement and dispute is inevitable. **Conflict** is the simultaneous arousal of two or more incompatible motives. It is often accompanied by tension and frustration. Whenever two or more people in the group compete for the same resource, conflict occurs. Two team members, for example, might both want to take the team's one laptop computer on business trips they are taking on the same date. Conflict can also be considered a hostile or antagonistic relationship between two people. Here we look at three aspects of conflict particularly relevant to managers and team leaders of small groups: cognitive versus affective conflict, consequences of conflict, and methods of conflict resolution.

Cognitive Versus Affective Conflict

Some conflicts within the group deal mostly with disagreements over how work should be done. They are referred to as task-oriented or *cognitive conflicts*, because they deal mostly with the intellect rather than emotions. Two group members, for example, might argue over whether it is better to use their limited advertising budget to buy space on the outside of a bus versus on the radio. **Cognitive conflict** focuses on substantive, issue-related differences. These issues are tangible and concrete and can be dealt with more intellectually than emotionally.

cognitive conflict

Conflict that focuses on substantive, issue-related differences and is dealt with more intellectually than emotionally.

Other conflicts within the group are more people-oriented. They occur because people have personality clashes, are rude to each other, or simply view many problems and situations from a different frame of reference. **Affective conflict** focuses on personalized, individually oriented issues. The conflict relates to subjective issues that are dealt with more emotionally than intellectually.[29] One symptom that affective conflict exists within the group is when, during a meeting, two people say to each other frequently, "Please let me finish. I'm still speaking."

affective conflict

Conflict that focuses on more personal or subjective issues and is dealt with more emotionally than intellectually.

Cognitive conflict is functional because it requires teams to engage in activities that foster team effectiveness. Team members engaged in cognitive conflict would critically examine alternative solutions and incorporate different points of view into their goals or mission statement. Because frank communication and different points of view are encouraged, cognitive conflict encourages innovative thinking. In contrast, affective conflict undermines group effectiveness by blocking constructive activities and processes. By such means as directing anger toward individuals and blaming each other for mistakes, affective conflict leads to cynicism and distrust.

The differences between cognitive and affective conflict are found in the executive suite as well as in lower-ranking organizational units. Allen C. Amason studied conflict as it relates to strategic decision making in top-management teams in the food-processing and furniture-making industries. Conflict was found to improve decision-making quality, and it was the cognitive dimension that accounted for the improvement. For example, the furniture company executives might argue over whether the company should sell nonassembled furniture to compete with its finished line of furniture. As a result of the strongly different opinions, they reach a decision that gains market share. Affective conflict, on the other hand, appeared to lower decision quality and affective acceptance (emotionally buying into a decision). The paradox uncovered is that conflict may improve decisions but it may hurt consensus and interpersonal relationships.[30]

Consequences of Conflict

Conflict results in both positive and negative consequences. The right amount of conflict may enhance job performance, but too much or too little conflict lowers performance. If the manager observes that job performance is suffering because of too much conflict, he or she should reduce it. If performance is low because employees are too placid, the manager might profitably increase conflict. For example, the manager might establish a prize for top performance in the group.

Positive Consequences of Conflict
Many managers and scholars believe that job conflict can have positive consequences. When the right amount of conflict is present in the workplace, one or more of the following outcomes can be anticipated.

1. *Increased creativity.* Talents and abilities surface in response to conflict. People become inventive when they are placed in intense competition with others.
2. *Increased effort.* Constructive amounts of conflict spur people to new heights of performance. People become so motivated to win the conflict that they may surprise themselves and their superiors with their work output.
3. *Increased diagnostic information.* Conflict can provide valuable information about problem areas in the department or organization. When leaders learn of conflict, they may conduct investigations that will lead to the prevention of similar problems.
4. *Increased group cohesion.* When one group in a firm is in conflict with another, group members may become more cohesive. They perceive themselves to be facing a common enemy.

Negative Consequences of Conflict
When the wrong amount or type of conflict exists, job performance may suffer. Some types of conflict have worse consequences than others. A particularly bad form of conflict is one that forces a person to choose between two undesirable alternatives. Negative consequences of conflict include the following:

1. *Poor physical and mental health.* Intense conflict is a source of stress. A person under prolonged and intense conflict may suffer stress–related disorders. Many acts of workplace violence stems from highly stressed employees or ex-employees who experienced conflict with supervisors or coworkers.
2. *Wasted resources.* Employees and groups in conflict frequently waste time, money, and other resources while fighting their battles. One executive took a personal dislike to one of his managers and therefore ignored his cost-saving recommendations.
3. *Sidetracked goals.* In extreme forms of conflict, the parties involved may neglect the pursuit of important goals. Instead, they focus on winning their conflicts. A goal displacement of this type took place within an information systems

group. The rival factions spent so much time squabbling over which new hardware and software to purchase that they neglected some of their tasks.

4. *Heightened self-interest.* Conflict within the group often results in extreme demonstrations of self-interest at the expense of the group and the larger organization. Individuals or groups place their personal interests over those of the rest of the firm or customers. One common result of this type of self-interest is hogging resources. A team member might attempt to convince the team leader to place him on an important customer troubleshooting assignment even though he knows his rival on the team is better qualified.

Methods of Conflict Resolution

Managers spend as much as 20 percent of their work time dealing with conflict. A leader who learns to manage conflict effectively can increase his or her productivity. In addition, being able to resolve conflict enhances one's stature as a leader. Employees expect their boss to be able to resolve conflicts. Here we describe the five basic styles or methods of resolving conflict: forcing, accommodation, sharing, collaboration, and avoiding. An effective manager will choose the best approach for the situation.

Forcing

The forcing, or competitive, style is based on the desire to win one's own concerns at the expense of the other party, or to dominate. Autocratic leaders such as Al Dunlap, formerly of Scott Paper and Sunbeam Corp., chose to resolve conflict in this way. Dunlap's bullying style of resolving conflict, combined with his extensive job cutting, led many employees to cheer when he was fired as CEO of Sunbeam. A person with a forcing style is likely to engage in win-lose ("I win, you lose") power struggles, resulting in poor teamwork.

Accommodation

The accommodative style favors appeasement, or satisfying the other's concerns without taking care of one's own. People with this orientation may be generous or self-sacrificing just to maintain a relationship. An irate customer might be accommodated with a full refund "just to shut him (or her) up." The intent of such accommodation might also be to retain the customer's loyalty.

Sharing

The sharing style is midway between domination and appeasement. Sharers prefer moderate but incomplete satisfaction for both parties. The result is compromise. The term *splitting the difference* reflects this orientation. The sharing style of conflict resolution is commonly used in such activities as purchasing a house or car. Within the work group, sharing might take the form of each team member receiving the same percentage salary increase rather than haggle over dividing the pool of money available for increases.

Collaboration

In contrast to the sharing style, collaboration reflects an interest in fully satisfying the desire of both parties. It is based on an underlying win-win philosophy, the belief that after conflict has been resolved both sides should gain something of value. For example, a small-company president might offer the management team more stock options if they are willing to take a pay cut to help the firm through rough times. If the firm succeeds, both parties have scored a victory.

All parties benefit from collaboration, or a win-win approach to resolving conflict. In addition, compliance with the solution occurs readily, and the relationship between those in conflict improves.

A conflict-resolution technique built into the collaboration style is *confrontation and problem solving*. Its purpose is to identify the real problem and then arrive at a solution that genuinely solves it. First the parties are brought together and the real problem is confronted.

Another collaborative approach involves asking what action can break an impasse. When a conflict reaches a point where progress has reached a standstill, one of the parties asks, "What would you like me to do?" The other side often reacts with astonishment and then the first party asks, "If I could do anything to make this situation okay in your eyes, what would that be?"[31] Frequently the desired action—such as "Treat me with more respect"—can be implemented.

Avoiding

The avoider combines uncooperativeness and unassertiveness. He or she is indifferent to the concerns of either party. The person may actually be withdrawing from conflict or relying upon fate. Managers sometimes use the avoiding style to stay out of a conflict between team members. The members are left to resolve their own differences.

Experience and research suggest that the cooperative approaches to resolving conflict (sharing and collaboration) work more effectively than the competitive approaches (forcing and accommodation). For example, a study conducted with 61 self-managing teams involved 489 employees from the production department of a leading electronics manufacturer. A cooperative (focus on mutual benefits or win-win) approach to conflict resolution led to confidence in skills for dealing with conflict. The heightened confidence in dealing with conflict, in turn, led to more effective performance as evaluated by managers.[32]

SUMMARY OF KEY POINTS

1 **Identify various types of teams and groups, including self-managed work teams and project groups.** Formal groups are deliberately formed by the organization, whereas informal groups emerge over time through worker interaction. Representative types of work teams include self-managed work teams, project teams, cross-functional teams, top-management teams, and virtual teams.

2 **Describe the characteristics of effective groups and teams.** Effective work group characteristics are well documented. Member jobs are enriched, and workers feel empowered to solve problems. Group members operate interdependently in terms of tasks and rewards. Culturally diverse members enjoy task and social interaction. The right size of the group as well as the intelligence and personality of group members and the emotional intelligence

of the group as a whole are all crucial factors. The work group requires good support from management. Effective group processes include team spirit, workload sharing, and communication and cooperation. Following work processes and procedures also aids effectiveness, as does familiarity with jobs and coworkers.

3 **Describe the stages of group development.** Groups usually go through predictable stages: forming, storming, norming, performing, and adjourning. A key managerial challenge is to get the group to the performing stage.

4 **Specify key roles assumed by team and group members.** Group member roles include knowledge contributor (technical expert), process observer, people supporter, challenger, listener, mediator, gatekeeper, and take-charge leader. A team member who plays several of the roles just mentioned is likely to be perceived as an informal leader.

5 **Summarize managerial actions for building teamwork.** Managers and leaders can enhance teamwork through many behaviors, attitudes, and organizational actions, including the following: get agreement on what success means for the group; give the team an urgent, constructive purpose; compete against a common adversary; use a consensus decision-making style; use in-group jargon; minimize micromanagement; keep the group small; create physical structures for interaction including idea sharing by computer; reward the team as well as individuals; publish a team book with details about members; and support outdoor training.

6 **Explain the actions and attitudes of an effective team player.** Task-related actions and attitudes of effective team players include: sharing technical expertise; assuming responsibility for problems; committing to team goals; seeing the big picture; asking tough questions; and trying something new. People-related actions and attitudes include trusting team members; sharing credit; recognizing others; listening and information sharing; giving and receiving criticism; and not downplaying the success of others.

7 **Point to the potential contributions and problems of teams and groups.** Teams and groups make a contribution when they lead to results that could not be achieved without collaboration. Evidence from both case histories and formal studies indicates that collective effort leads to enhanced productivity. Groups and teams also have potential problems. Sometimes they do not improve productivity; group polarization (taking extreme positions) may occur, and members may engage in social loafing (freeloading). Also, focusing too much on group or team effort instead of attaining individual recognition can retard a person's career.

8 **Describe the positive and negative aspects of conflict and how team leaders and managers can resolve conflict.** Although harmony and collaboration are important goals of groups and teams, some conflict is inevitable. Cognitive conflict focuses on substantive, issue-related differences. Affective conflict focuses on personalized, individually oriented issues that are dealt with more emotionally than intellectually. Cognitive conflict leads to such positive outcomes as creative problem solving. Positive consequences of conflict also include increased effort, obtaining diagnostic information, and increased group cohesion. Negative consequences of conflict include wasting resources and heightened self-interest.

Five major modes of conflict management have been identified: forcing, accommodation, sharing, collaboration, and avoiding. Each style is based on a combination of satisfying one's own concerns (assertiveness) and satisfying the concerns of others (cooperativeness). Confrontation and problem solving is a widely applicable collaborative technique of resolving conflict.

KEY TERMS AND PHRASES

Group, *380*

Team, *380*

Teamwork, *380*

Formal group, *380*

Informal group, *380*

Self-managed work team, *381*

Project team, *383*

Cross-functional team, *384*

Virtual team, *385*

Micromanagement, *393*

Tough question, *394*

Group polarization, *396*

Social loafing, *397*

Conflict, *398*

Cognitive conflict, *398*

Affective conflict, *398*

QUESTIONS

1. In your own words, describe the difference between a group and a team.

2. In what way do self-managing work teams negate some of the advantages of job specialization as described in Chapter 8?

3. Why is experience working on a cross-functional team particularly valuable for a person who aspires to a career in management?

4. Give an example of a *tough question* a manager might ask a team.

5. Provide two examples of interdependent (or collaborative) tasks in the workplace for which teams are well suited.

6. In what way might team-building exercises like rope climbing and white-water rafting be considered a form of job discrimination?

7. Many communities object to having cellular telephone towers erected in certain locations. To overcome these objections, some cellular telephone companies have erected, at their expense, silos and church steeples with cellular antennae hidden inside. Explain which method of conflict resolution this approach represents.

CRITICAL THINKING QUESTIONS

1. In what way does the position of a project manager resemble that of a general manager, including a CEO?

2. The U.S. Department of Commerce regularly publishes information about the productivity of workers. Can you find any data about the productivity of *teams*?

SKILL-BUILDING EXERCISE: The Trust Fall

Perhaps the most widely used team-building activity is the trust fall, which may be familiar to many readers. Nevertheless, each application of this exercise is likely to produce new and informative results. The class organizes itself into teams. In each team, each willing member stands on a chair and falls backwards into the arms of teammates. A less challenging alternative to falling off a chair is to simply fall backwards standing up. Those team members who for whatever physical or mental reason would prefer not to fall back into others, or participate in catching others, are excluded without being pressured. However, they can serve as observers. After the trust falls have been completed, a team leader gathers answers to the following questions, and then shares the answers with the rest of the class.

1. How does this exercise develop teamwork?
2. How does this exercise develop management or leadership skills?
3. What did the participants learn about themselves?

INTERNET SKILL-BUILDING EXERCISE: The Dale Carnegie Approach

Hundreds of consulting firms and training organizations offer team-building exercises, including Dale Carnegie Training®, the organization that became famous by offering training in public speaking, the development of self-confidence, and sales skills. Visit http://www.dalecarnegie.com to investigate what type of teamwork training Dale Carnegie offers. Compare the ideas of Dale Carnegie with those presented in the chapter. What similarities and differences do you see? What is your impression of the Dale Carnegie approach to building teamwork?

CASE PROBLEM 14-A: The Speed Team at IBM

Steve Ward, the vice president of business transformation and chief information officer at IBM, was dining with a few members of his approximately 200-member leadership council. During dinner he decided that saving time, such as making decisions faster, writing software faster, and completing projects faster, needed higher priority at IBM. If smaller telecommunications companies could continue to work faster than IBM, they would keep nibbling away at Big Blue's market share.

The morning after the leadership council dinner, the Speed Team was born. Ward contacted 21 IBMers and gave them an assignment: Get the 100,000-person information technology group moving faster than ever, with a focus on the rapid development of Web-oriented applications. At IBM, the IT group has high status and reports to the senior vice president of strategy.

The Speed Team's coleaders—Jane Harper, director of technology operations, and Ray Blair, director of e-procurement—had strong reputations for pushing projects forward at a blazing pace. The two leaders decided that the team should have a lifespan of approximately six months. "I think that we will have failed if the Speed Team is still together three years from now," explains Harper. "Our plan, when we started this, was to come together, look at what works, look at why projects get bogged down, create some great recommendations about how to achieve speed, get executive buy-in, and try to make those recommendations part of the fabric of the business."

Steve Ward built the Speed Team with IBM employees who had led breakthrough projects that were completed in an unusually short period of time. One example is Gina Poole, founder of developerWorks, a Web site to help IBM forge stronger relationships with software companies. She was drafted based on how quickly she was able to get the site up and running.

Members of the Speed Team shared success stories about how rapidly they accomplished projects in the past. They also shared information about how they were able to overcome barriers to speed, such as company rules that slowed down getting a new development accepted.

The Speed Team picked up some ideas about quick turn-around times by studying the IBM WebAhead lab that develops prototypes for new technologies. WebAhead employees work in a single shared-office setup, not unlike that of a business school computer lab—long tables of several employees arranged in rows. The overall atmosphere is casual. A sign on the door reads, "This is not your father's IBM." The lab's purpose is simple and liberating: "Our team is funded to do cool stuff for IBM," says Bill Sweeney, a WebAhead manager. "We don't have to think about increasing sales of a product line. We just have to think about the next important thing that might hit us." One of WebAhead's projects was to assemble a system for translating Web data into phone data. The project took less than two days, including going to lunch.

One of the secrets unlocked by the WebAhead team is that speed is its own reward. Employees were encouraged and energized when they saw their pet projects being deployed in weeks rather than months or quarters.

After examining many fast-moving projects, including e-procurement, the Speed Team began outlining what those projects had in common. It then created the "Success Factors for Speed," six attributes that all successful projects had in common: strong leaders, team members who were speed demons, clear objectives, a strong communication system, and a process carefully tailored to the requirements of the group. The general principle discovered by the Speed Team is that going faster is all about how you relate to time. If you treat time as a tangible (like money), you'll wind up moving faster.

The Speed Team decided that it needed a medium for gathering fast feedback, so the team held a weeklong online "town hall" meeting. The goal was to encourage other employees to contribute ideas about getting projects accomplished quickly. Some of the suggestions that filled the message boards of the online meeting confirmed what the Speed Team had learned. Many projects wind up in the breakdown lane because of overly rigorous measurement. The coordinator of the online meeting said, "People complained about breaking down 13-week projects into 13 phases and having to produce measurement reports at the end of each week."

The Speed Team also picked up some information about speed they did not discover on their own. Information overload at IBM was slowing people down. Newsletters, e-mail, and the intranet created duplication and mixed messages. The coordinator said, "We discovered through the online town hall a need to focus and funnel information to people, rather than pointing the fire hose at them."

Soon the Speed Team began implementing both its "quick hit" ideas and its long-term initiatives. Quick hits included things like creating a speed rating for employee-performance reviews and getting all leads to specify more clearly their time-oriented priorities. Long-term initiatives involved addressing the occasional disconnect between finance department employees who supervise the funding of company projects and those employees who actually run the projects. Sometimes by the time a project is ready for implementation, its funding has been cut.

Although the Speed Team specified a termination date, its members and its leaders believe its influence will not end. "These people will work together for years, whether you call them the Speed Team or not," says Ward. "Our evidence of success is that our changes have been adopted by the organization. People have begun to think about the need for speed in their work. We're no longer necessary. Our job was to be catalysts, and catalysts can't linger around."

Discussion Questions

1. What characteristics of an effective work group does the Speed Team appear to have?
2. To what extent was a team structure really necessary to carry out the mission of the Speed Team?
3. Should the Speed Team really adjourn at this point?

Source: Adapted from Scott Kirsner, "Faster Company," *Fast Company*, May 2000, pp. 162–172.

CASE PROBLEM 14-B: Building Cooperation at Ambitech

Ambitech, the biotechnology division of a larger firm, obtains the majority of its revenue from contracts with the federal government. As a consequence of being a federal contractor,

government auditors are present full-time at the Ambitech division. The auditors regularly evaluate the division's costs submitted to the government for reimbursement.

Over the years, a somewhat adversarial relationship developed between the auditors and the workers in the finance department of Ambitech. Many of the hard feelings stem from the auditors disallowing many costs the division submitted for reimbursement, such as apportioning too much overhead to the government project. The auditors question a considerable proportion of the costs submitted. From the auditors' perspective, they are performing well when they find costs not reimbursable under federal guidelines. Every dollar not reimbursed decreases government spending. A given item submitted for reimbursement could be rejected because of a lack of documentation, or because the cost is not eligible for payment under the government contract.

The finance department is challenged daily to provide additional documentation to support any charges under question, or to defend the charges. Because the federal guidelines about cost reimbursement are ambiguous, both parties will often interpret them in support of their position. Considerable haggling takes place over disputed charges.

After a dispute over charges arises, middle-level managers from the division and the government audit staff are called in to resolve the issue. Several managers from both groups have strong personalities, and they typically hold firmly to their positions. An Ambitech accounts payable supervisor noted, "I hate to see management get involved. It prolongs the battle over even simple issues."

Over the years, the relationship between the finance staff and the audit staff deteriorated to the point where few major issues reach resolution. Discouraged with all the conflict, the Ambitech division president called in a consultant to conduct a team-building workshop for the finance personnel and the audit staff. Before the workshop began, a management team from both parties was assembled in an effort to pinpoint the major issues. They identified about 100 issues, which were divided into three major categories:

1. A lack of trust and respect between the two groups
2. A need to improve communication
3. A lack of appropriate process to facilitate accomplishments of each group's mission and goals.

By the end of three hours of discussing these issues, workshop objectives were identified.

- Start building the foundation for an environment of trust and mutual respect.
- Improve the formal and informal communication channels between the finance and audit staffs.
- Share each group's mission and goals with each other, and identify common themes.
- Define roles and responsibilities for all workers involved.

- Identify opportunities for improving the work processes the two groups currently use.

In collaboration with the staff members, the consultant then established ground rules for the workshop. Participants were encouraged to listen generously, and seek understanding rather than victory. The consultant believed that staff members were using terms like "Gottcha" too frequently, signifying an adversarial relationship between the Ambitech and government groups. It was also suggested that participants make more frequent use of the term *I* rather than *we* when identifying a problem. In this way the individual workers would be taking more ownership of problems. Participants were instructed to share relevant conversations that took place outside the workshop, such as in the hallways or at the copy center.

Workshop participants were also told to "discuss the undiscussables," such as sensitive issues they hesitated to bring out into the open. The consultant also suggested that members be candid about expressing their feelings, even at the risk of not being politically correct. All workshop members were asked to be specific and provide data about problems, rather than toss out generalities.

At the beginning of the workshop, the mission statements for both groups were reviewed. The two facilitators (the head consultant and a colleague) pointed out the similarities of the statements, such as wanting to be an outstanding contributor within the larger organization.

For the first team-building exercise, all workshop participants were given a sheet of poster paper on which they were to draw (no words allowed) something about themselves that people they worked with did not know about them. The drawings were designed to be an icebreaker, and place the individuals in a more human light. On the same piece of paper, the participants were to write out their personal motto, or the words that guide their life, such as "Live and let live."

The objective of the second team-building exercise was to provide insight into each workshop participant's orientation toward trust. Each participant was instructed to move to side A or side B of the conference room. Side A was reserved for those individuals who inherently trusted people until they were given a reason not to trust. Side B was reserved for those individuals who did not trust people until the trust was earned. A finance specialist who chose side B said, "When I meet a government auditor, that person has to work pretty hard to win my trust."

The objective of the third team-building exercise was to look at which processes were working well in the interaction between the groups, and which processes were hindering the interaction. Participants were divided into various groups each consisting of a scribe, a timekeeper, a facilitator, and a recorder. Each team was then asked to brainstorm three improvement areas for both groups by identifying the behaviors and work practices each group should continue doing, do more of, or decrease. After the 10-minute brainstorming session was complete, all ideas were discussed. A tallying procedure was used to select the top three behaviors and work practices in each category for each group. These lists were combined and distributed to all workshop participants for reference after the session.

The final teambuilding exercise was aimed at process improvement. Workshop participants were divided into groups of 6–9 people. Each group was asked to brainstorm work processes that needed improvement. The tallying procedure was used again to select the top three areas for improvement, such as "Maybe the government auditors should provide input earlier on the whether an expense should be reimbursable, particularly for major expenses. This could cut down on disagreements."

Both sides were pleased with the outcome of the workshop. Of the 100 issues for consideration identified before the workshop, about 60 were resolved. At monthly meetings, the team reviews the status of process improvement areas and the issues yet to be resolved.

Discussion Questions

1. Evaluate the sources of conflict between the Ambitech finance specialists and the auditors in terms of cognitive versus affective.

2. Which approach to conflict resolution does the workshop illustrate? Explain your reasoning.

3. Identify a possible win-win outcome to the conflict between the groups in this case.

Source: Case researched by Leslie Genthner, Rochester Institute of Technology, May 2001.

E N D N O T E S

1. Gina Emparato, "Their Specialty? Teamwork," *Fast Company*, January–February 2000, pp. 54–56.
2. Jon R. Katzenbach and Douglas K. Smith, "The Discipline of Teams," *Harvard Business Review*, March–April 1993, p. 113.
3. Richard S. Wellings, William C. Byham, and Jeanne M. Wilson, *Empowered Teams: Creating Self-Directed Work Groups That Improve Quality, Productivity, and Participation* (San Francisco: Jossey-Bass, 1991), p. 3.
4. For case studies of self-managed work teams, see Dale E. Yeatts and Cloyd Hyten, *High-Performing Self-Managed Work Teams* (Thousand Oaks, CA: Sage, 1998).
5. Data in this paragraph are from Carla Johnson, "Teams at Work," *HR Magazine*, May 1999, p. 32.
6. Gregory M. Bounds and John A. Woods, *Supervision* (Cincinnati, OH: South-Western, 1998), p. 74.
7. Avan R. Jassawalla and Hemant C. Sashittal, "Building Cross-Functional New Product Teams," *Academy of Management Executive*, August 1999, pp. 50–63.
8. Jon R. Katzenbach, "The Myth of the Top Management Team," *Harvard Business Review*, November–December 1997, pp. 82–99.
9. Joseph J. Distefano and Martha L. Maznevski, "Creating Value with Diverse Teams in Global Management," *Organizational Dynamics*, Summer 2000, pp. 45–63.
10. Cited in Charlene Marmer Solomon, "Managing Virtual Teams," *Workforce*, June 2000, p. 64.
11. Based on literature reviews and original material in Michael A. Campion, Ellen M. Papper, and Gina Medsker, "Relations Between Work Team Characteristics and Effectiveness: A Replication and Extension," *Personnel Psychology*, Summer 1996, p. 431; David E. Hyatt and Thomas M. Ruddy, "An Examination of the Relationship Between Work Group Characteristics and Performance," *Personnel Psychology*, Autumn 1997, p. 579; Brian D. Janz, Jason A. Colquitt, and Raymond A. Noe, "Knowledge Worker Team Effectiveness: The Role of Autonomy, Interdependence, Team Development, and Contextual Support Variables," *Personnel Psychology*, Winter 1997, pp. 877–904; Bradley L. Kirkman and Benson Rosen, "Powering Up Teams," *Organizational Dynamics*, Winter 2000, pp. 48–52.
12. Kirkman and Rosen, "Powering Up Teams," pp. 48–52.
13. Priscilla M. Ellsass and Laura M. Graves, "Demographic Diversity in Decision-Making Group: The Experience of Women and People of Color," *Academy of Management Review*, October 1997, p. 968.
14. Murray R. Barrick et al., "Relating Member Ability and Personality to Work-Team Processes and Team Effectiveness," *Journal of Applied Psychology*, June 1998, pp. 377–391.
15. Vanessa Urch Druskat and Steven B. Wolff, "Building the Emotional Intelligence of Groups," *Harvard Business Review*, March 2001, pp. 80–90.
16. Campion, Papper, and Medsker, "Relations Between Work Team Characteristics and Effectiveness," p. 450.
17. J. Steven Heinen and Eugene Jacobsen, "A Model of Task Group Development in Complex Organizations and a Strategy for Implementation," *Academy of Management Review*, October 1976, pp. 98–111.
18. Glenn M. Parker, *Team Players and Teamwork: The New Competitive Business Strategy* (New York: AMACOM, 1992), pp. 40–52; "Lead or Lay Back? How to Play the Right Role on a Team," *Executive Strategies*, November 1999, p. 2.
19. Dan Fields, "Harley Plant Produces Teamwork," The Associated Press, June 22, 1998.
20. Katzenbach and Smith, "The Discipline of Teams," p. 112; John Syer and Christopher Connolly, *How Teamwork Works: The Dynamics of Effective Team Development* (London: McGraw-Hill, 1996); "Fly in Formation: Easy Ways to Build Team Spirit," *Executive Strategies*, March 2000, p. 6; Regina Fazio Maruca, ed., "Unit of One: What Makes Teams Work?" *Fast Company*, November 2000, pp. 109–142.
21. Shelia M. Puffer, "Continental Airlines' CEO Gordon Bethune on Teams and New Product Development," *Academy of Management Executive*, August 1999, p. 30.
22. "Team Player Gets Top Spot in Survey" (undated sample copy distributed by Dartnell Corporation, 1994), p. 3.
23. Glenn M. Parker, *Cross-Functional Teams: Working with Allies, Enemies, & Other Strangers* (San Francisco: Jossey-Bass Publishers, 1994), p. 3.
24. Steven Covey, "Team Up for a Superstar Office," *USA Weekend*, September 4–6, 1998, p. 10.
25. Russ Forrester and Allan B. Drexler, "A Model for Team-Based Performance," *Academy of Management Executive*, August 1999, p. 47.
26. Jac Fitz-Enz, "Measuring Team Effectiveness," *HRfocus*, August 1997, p. 3.
27. Gregory Moorhead and Ricky W. Griffin, *Organizational Behavior: Managing People and Organizations*, 4th ed. (Boston: Houghton Mifflin, 1995), pp. 52–62.

28. Tina L. Robbins, "Social Loafing on Cognitive Tasks: An Examination of the 'Sucker Effect,'" *Journal of Business and Psychology*, Spring 1995, p. 337.

29. Allen C. Amason, Wayne A. Hockwater, Kenneth R. Thompson, and Allison W. Harrison, "Conflict: An Important Dimension in Successful Management Teams," *Organizational Dynamics*, Autumn 1995, pp. 2–30.

30. Allen C. Amason, "Distinguishing the Effects of Functional and Dysfunctional Conflict on Strategic Decision Making: Resolving a Paradox for Top Management Teams," *Academy of Management Journal*, February 1996, pp. 123–148.

31. James A. Autry, *Love & Profit* (New York: Morrow, 1991).

32. Steve Alper, Dean Tjosvold, and Kenneth S. Law, "Conflict Management, Efficacy, and Performance in Organizational Teams," *Personnel Psychology*, Autumn 2000, pp. 625–642.

Essentials of Control

Bluemount Nurseries Inc., located in Monkton, Maryland, stocks 1,500 plant varieties. Nick Pindale, CFO and grandson-in-law of the founder, suspected that some plants yielded profits and some only losses. Unfortunately, Pindale wasn't sure which was which.

Pindale sought answers from an accounting technique called activity-based costing, or ABC. Dividing nursery tasks into categories such as potting and planting, he assigned costs to each. Then he determined which ones Bluemount performed cost effectively and which would be better outsourced, trimmed, or omitted. The information identified the most profitable plants and even helped provide documentation for a bank loan needed to boost production of money-making lines.

ABC helped Pindale determine that he could breed some plant varieties at about half the cost of buying from wholesalers. "Using those numbers, we were able to sit down with the bank and borrow to build a new propagation facility," he says. "They were really impressed with our figures and graphs, and that loan went straight to the bottom line."

Pindale cautions that communication is delicate in implementing ABC. Some Bluemount workers feared ABC would result in job cuts as tasks were automated. In fact, automation did take the place of some employees, but those workers were redeployed into activities that added value but were not suitable to automation. Making sure that employees understood the goals and techniques of ABC was essential to controlling dissent.

OBJECTIVES

After studying this chapter and doing the exercises, you should be able to:

1 Explain how controlling relates to the other management functions.

2 Understand the different types and strategies of control.

3 Describe the steps in the control process.

4 Explain the use of nonbudgetary control techniques.

5 Summarize the various types of budgets, and the use of budgets and financial ratios for control.

6 Explain how managers and business owners manage cash flow and control costs, and use nontraditional measures of financial performance.

7 Outline the basics of an information system.

8 Specify several characteristics of effective controls.

Chapter 15

Bluemount bloomed with ABC. "Five years later, not one of our original greenhouses is still standing," says Pindale of the 65-person nursery. "We've added state-of-the-art machinery in our potting line. And we've doubled in size."[1]

The story about the nursery attempting to weed out unprofitable plants and work activities illustrates how managers can boost productivity and profitability by implementing modern financial tools. Keeping track of critical information, such as which activities are profitable, is part of a control system. The control function of management involves measuring performance and then taking corrective action if goals are not being achieved.

As you will see in studying this chapter, controls make many positive contributions to the organization. Controlling aligns the actions of workers with the interests of the firm. Without the controlling functions, managers cannot know whether people are carrying out their jobs properly. Controls enable managers to gauge whether the firm is attaining its goals.

Controls often make an important contribution to employee motivation. Achieving the performance standards set in a control system leads to recognition and other deserved rewards. Accurate control measurements give the well-motivated, competent worker an opportunity to be noticed for good work.

In this chapter we emphasize the types and strategies of controls, the control process, budgets and controls, how managers manage cash flow and cut costs, and the use of information systems in control. Finally, we describe characteristics of effective controls.

1   CONTROLLING AND THE OTHER MANAGEMENT FUNCTIONS

Explain how controlling relates to the other management functions.

Controlling, sometimes referred to as the terminal management function, takes place after the other functions have been completed. Controlling is most closely associated with planning, because planning establishes goals and the methods for achieving them. Controlling investigates whether planning was successful.

The links between controlling and other major management functions are illustrated in Exhibit 15-1. Controlling helps measure how well planning, organizing, and leading have been performed. The controlling function also measures the effectiveness of the control system. On occasion, the control measures are inappropriate. For example, suppose one measure of sales performance is the number of sales calls made. Such a measure might encourage a sales representative to call on a large number of poor prospects, just to meet the performance standard. Spending more time with better prospects would probably boost the sales representative's effectiveness. More will be said about effective control measures later.

The planning and decision-making tools and techniques described in Chapter 7 also provide tools and techniques of control. For example, a Gantt chart keeps track of how well target dates for a project are being met. Keeping track is a control activity. If an event falls behind schedule, a project manager usually takes corrective action.

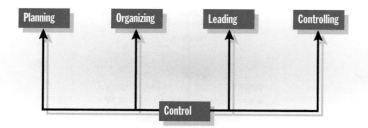

EXHIBIT 15-1

The Links Between Controlling and the Other Management Functions

The control function is extremely important because it helps managers evaluate whether all four major management functions have been implemented.

TYPES AND STRATEGIES OF CONTROL

2

Controls can be classified according to the time at which the control is applied to the activity—before, during, or after. Another important way of describing controls relates to the source of the control—external versus internal.

Understand the different types and strategies of control.

The Time Element in Controls

A **preventive control** (or precontrol) takes place prior to the performance of an activity. A precontrol prevents problems that result from deviation from performance standards. Preventive controls are generally the most cost-effective. A manufacturer that specifies quality standards for purchased parts establishes a precontrol. By purchasing high-quality parts, the manufacturer prevents many instances of machine failure. Precontrols are also used in human resource management. Standards for hiring employees are precontrols. For example, a company may require that all job candidates are nonsmokers. This preventive control helps decrease lost productivity due to smoking breaks and smoking-related illnesses.

preventive control
A control that takes place prior to the performance of an activity.

   Concurrent controls monitor activities while they are carried out. A typical concurrent control takes place when a supervisor observes performance, spots a deviation from standard, and immediately makes a constructive suggestion. For example, suppose a sales manager overhears a telemarketing specialist fail to ask a customer for an order. On the spot, the manager would coach the telemarketer about how to close an order.

concurrent control
A type of control that monitors activities while they are carried out.

   Feedback controls (or postcontrols) evaluate an activity after it is performed. Feedback controls measure history by pointing out what went wrong in the past. The process of applying the control may provide guidelines for future corrective action. Financial statements are a form of feedback control. If a financial report indicates that one division of a company lost money, top-level managers can then confer with division managers to see how to improve the situation. Identifying the most profitable plants at Bluemount Nurseries functioned as a feedback control.

feedback control
A control that evaluates an activity after it is performed.

   Exhibit 15-2 summarizes the three types of time-based controls. Most firms use a combination of preventive, concurrent, and feedback controls. An important part of a manager's job is choosing controls appropriate to the situation.

External Versus Internal Controls

Controls can be classified according to their underlying strategy. **External control strategy** is based on the belief that employees are motivated primarily

external control strategy
An approach to control based on the belief that employees are motivated primarily by external rewards and need to be controlled by their managers.

EXHIBIT 15-2

Three Types of Time-Based Controls

Controlling can take place before, during, or after an event or process. Preventive controls usually offer the biggest payoff to the organization.

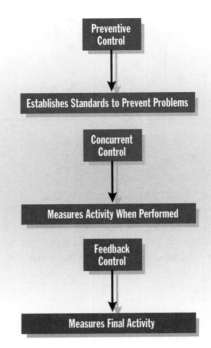

by external rewards and need to be controlled by their managers. Autocratic and Theory X management use an external control strategy. An effective external control system involves three steps. First, the objectives and performance standards need to be relatively difficult in order to gain optimum effort of team members and leave little leeway in performance. Second, the objectives and measures must be set in such a way that people cannot manipulate or distort them. For instance, top-level management should make its own investigation of customer satisfaction rather than take the word of field personnel. Third, rewards must be directly and openly tied to performance.

An external control strategy produces several different effects. On the positive side, employees may channel considerable energy into achieving objectives. Employees do so because they know that good performance leads to a reward. A tightly structured control system translates into a high degree of control over employee behavior.

External control can create problems, however. Employees may work toward achieving performance standards, but they may not develop a commitment to the firm. They may reach standards but not be truly productive. Reaching standards without being productive is sometimes referred to as "looking good on paper." Suppose the marketing and sales director of a telecommunications company establishes as a performance standard a high number of customers processed. To achieve this standard, the customer service manager instructs the customer service representatives, "Take care of as many calls as you can. And minimize the time customers are kept on hold." As a result, the customer service reps spend brief amounts of time on the phone attempting to resolve problems with most customers. Instead of customers being happy with customer service, many of them are dissatisfied with the abrupt treatment. The standard of taking care of more customers is met, yet at the same time customer service deteriorates.

Internal control strategy is based on the belief that employees can be motivated by building their commitment to organizational goals. Participative and Theory Y management use internal control strategy, as do self-managed work teams and other forms of empowerment. Part of the success of the development of Windows NT was attributed to an internal control strategy. Two hundred and fifty programmers, testers, and program managers worked to develop the software for personal computers. Control directed from the bottom up meant that professionals established controls for their own work.[2]

Building an effective internal control system requires three steps. First, group members must participate in setting goals. These goals are later used as performance standards for control purposes. Second, the performance standards (control measures) must be used for problem solving rather than for punishment or blame. When deviations from performance are noted, superiors and subordinates work together to solve the underlying problem. Third, although rewards should be tied to performance, they should not be tied to only one or two measures. An internal control strategy calls for evaluation of an employee's total contribution, not one or two quantitative aspects of performance.

Use of internal controls usually leads to a higher commitment to attain goals. Thus, they may direct greater energy toward task performance. Another good effect results from the encouragement of upward and horizontal flow of valid information about problems.

On the negative side, an internal control system may motivate employees to establish easy performance standards for themselves. Another problem occurs if the supervisor loses control over subordinates and feels powerless as a result. Finally, an internal control system creates some problems in providing equitable rewards if loose performance standards make good performance difficult to measure.

An internal control system is not necessarily good, and an external control system is not necessarily bad. Internal controls work satisfactorily for a high-caliber, well-motivated workforce. External controls compensate for the fact that not everybody is capable of controlling their own performance. If applied with good judgment and sensitivity, external control systems work quite well. The effective use of controls thus follows a contingency, or "if . . . , then . . . ," approach to management.

STEPS IN THE CONTROL PROCESS

The steps in the control process follow the logic of planning: (1) performance standards are set, (2) performance is measured, (3) performance is compared to standards, and (4) corrective action is taken if needed. The following discussion describes these steps and highlights the potential problems associated with each one. Exhibit 15-3 presents an overview of controlling.

Setting Appropriate Performance Standards

A control system begins with a set of performance standards that are realistic and acceptable to the people involved. A **standard** is a unit of measurement used to evaluate results. Standards can be quantitative, such as cost of sales, profits, or time to complete an activity. Standards can also be qualitative, such as a viewer's perception of the visual appeal of an advertisement. An effective standard shares the same characteristics as an effective objective (see Chapter 5). Exhibit 15-4 presents two of the performance standards established for a customer service representative unit within a telecommunications company.

---

internal control strategy

An approach to control based on the belief that employees can be motivated by building their commitment to organizational goals.

413

3

Describe the steps in the control process.

standard

A unit of measurement used to evaluate results.

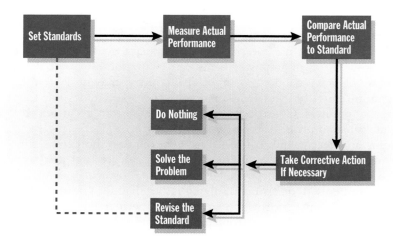

EXHIBIT 15-3

Steps in the Controlling Process

Controlling begins with setting meaningful standards that are accepted by the people doing the measuring and those being measured.

Historical information about comparable situations often provides the basis for setting initial standards. Assume a manufacturer wants to establish a standard for the percentage of machines returned to the dealer for repair. If the return rate for other machines with similar components is 3 percent, the new standard might be a return rate of no more than 3 percent.

At times, profit-and-loss considerations dictate performance standards. A case in point is the occupancy-rate standard for a hotel. Assume break-even analysis reveals that the average occupancy rate must be 75 percent for the hotel to cover costs. Hotel management must then set an occupancy rate of at least 75 percent as a standard.

Measuring Actual Performance

To implement the control system, performance must be measured. Performance appraisals are one of the major ways of measuring performance. Supervisors often make direct observations of performance to implement a control system. A simple example would be observing to make sure a sales associate always asks a customer, "Is there anything else I could show you now?" A more elaborate performance measure would be a 10-page report on the status of a major project submitted to top-level

EXHIBIT 15-4

Two Performance Standards Established for a Customer Service Operation

The performance standards shown here give customer service representatives precise targets for meeting organizational objectives. Performance evaluation is based on how well customer service representatives, individually and as a group, meet these standards.

CSR Objectives	Distinguished Performance (4 points)	Above-Standard Performance (3 Points)	Standard Performance (2 Points)	Below-Standard Performance (1 Point)
Customer Satisfaction	89% or higher overall customer satisfaction	86%–88% overall customer satisfaction	83%–85% overall customer satisfaction	<83% overall customer satisfaction
Calls Answered in 30 Seconds	Group consistently answers 80% or more of calls within 30 seconds.	Group consistently answers 75%–79% of calls within 30 seconds.	Group consistently answers 70%–74% of calls within 30 seconds.	Group consistently answers <70% of calls within 30 seconds.

management. The aspects of performance that accountants measure are manufacturing costs, profits, and cash flow (a statement of cash receipts and payments).

Measurement of performance is much more complex than it would seem on the surface. The list that follows presents three important conditions for effective performance measurement:[3]

1. *Agree on the specific aspects of performance to be measured.* Top-level managers in a hotel chain might think that occupancy rate is the best measure of performance. Middle-level managers might disagree by saying, "Don't place so much emphasis on occupancy rate. If we try to give good customer service, the occupancy rate will take care of itself. Therefore, let's try to measure customer service."

2. *Agree on the accuracy of measurement needed.* In some instances, precise measurement of performance is possible. Sales volume, for example, can be measured in terms of customer billing and accounts paid. The absolute number or percentage of customer returns is another precise measurement. In other instances, precise measurement of performance may not be possible. Assume top-level managers of the hotel chain buy the idea of measuring customer service. Quantitative measures of customer satisfaction—including the ratings that guests submit on questionnaires and the number of formal complaints—are available. However, many measurements would have to be subjective, such as the observation of the behavior of guests, including their spontaneous comments about service. These qualitative measures of performance might be more relevant than the quantitative measures.

3. *Agree on who will use the measurements.* In most firms, managers at higher levels have the authority to review performance measures of people below them in the chain of command. Few people at lower levels object to this practice. Another issue centers around the level of staff access to control reports. Line managers sometimes believe that too many staff members make judgments about their performance.

Comparing Actual Performance to Standards

After establishing standards and taking performance measurements, managers move on to the next step of actually comparing performance to standards. Key aspects of comparing performance to standards include measuring the deviation and communicating information about it.

Deviation in a control system indicates the size of the discrepancy between performance standards and actual results. It is important to agree beforehand how much deviation from the standard is a basis for corrective action. When using quantitative measures, statistical analysis can determine how much of a deviation is significant. Recall the 75 percent occupancy rate standard in the hotel example. A deviation of plus or minus 3 percent may not be considered meaningful but rather caused by random events. Deviations of 4 percent or more, however, would be considered significant. Taking corrective action only in the case of significant deviations applies the *exception principle*.

Sometimes a deviation as small as 1 percent from standard can have a big influence on company welfare. If a division fails by 1 percent to reach $100 million in sales, the firm has $1 million less money than anticipated. At other times, deviations as high as 10 percent might not be significant. A claims department might be 10 percent behind schedule in processing insurance claims. However, the claims manager might not be upset, knowing that all the claims will eventually be processed.

deviation

In a control system, the size of the discrepancy between performance standards and actual results.

415

When statistical limits are not available, it takes wisdom and experience to diagnose a random deviation. Sometimes factors beyond a person's influence lead to a one-time deviation from performance. In such a case, the manager might ignore the deviation. For example, a person might turn in poor performance one month because he or she faced a family crisis.

For the control system to work, the results of the comparison between actual performance and standards must be communicated to the right people. These people include the employees themselves and their immediate managers. At times, the results should also be communicated to top-level managers and selected staff specialists. They need to know about events such as exceptional deviations from safety and health standards. For example, nuclear power plants are equipped with elaborate devices to measure radiation levels. When a specified radiation level is reached or exceeded, several key people are notified automatically.

Taking Corrective Action

An evaluation of the discrepancy between actual performance and a standard presents a manager with three courses of action: do nothing, solve the problem, or revise the standard. Each of these alternatives may be appropriate, depending on the results of the evaluation.

Do Nothing

The purpose of the control system is to determine whether the plans are working. If the evaluation reveals that events are proceeding according to plan, no corrective action is required. Doing nothing, however, does not mean abdicating, or giving up, responsibility. A manager might take the opportunity to compliment employees for having achieved their objectives (thus increasing employee motivation), but do nothing about their approach to reaching objectives because performance measurements show it to be effective.

Solve the Problem

The big payoff from the controlling process concerns the correction of deviations from substandard performance. If a manager decides that a deviation is significant (nonrandom), he or she starts problem solving. Typically the manager meets with the team member to discuss the nature of the problem. Other knowledgeable parties might participate in the problem-solving process. At times, a significant deviation from a performance standard demands a drastic solution. A severe shortfall in cash, for example, might force a retailer to sell existing inventory at a loss.

Sometimes a manager can correct the deviation from a performance standard without overhauling current operations. An office manager in a group dental practice used a control model to measure the percentage of professional time allotted to patient care. The analysis revealed that nonbilled time exceeded 10 percent—an unacceptable deviation. The corrective action involved two steps. First, workers scanned dental records to find patients overdue for cleaning and checkups. Second, the office manager telephoned these people and asked whether they would like to schedule an appointment for cleaning and a checkup. The successful telemarketing campaign filled virtually all the slack time within 10 days.

Revise the Standard

Deviations from standard are sometimes attributable to errors in planning rather than to performance problems. Corrective action is thus not warranted because the true problem is an unrealistic performance standard. Consider an analogy to the classroom: If 90 percent of the students fail a test, the real problem could be an unrealistically difficult test.

Standards often must be revised because of changes in the task environment. A sudden shift in consumers' preference—from large to small sport utility vehicles (SUVs) for example—could necessitate the revision of standards. Planning for a new task can also create a need for revised standards. Performance quotas may be based on "guesstimates" that prove to be unrealistically difficult or overly easy to reach. A performance standard is too difficult if no employee can meet it. A performance standard may be too easy if all employees can exceed it. As Exhibit 15-3 shows, revising standards means repeating the control cycle.

NONBUDGETARY CONTROL TECHNIQUES

One way of classifying control techniques is to divide them into those based on budgets versus those not based on budgets. In this section we describe nonbudgetary techniques, and classify them into two types. **Qualitative control techniques** are methods based on human judgments about performance that result in a verbal rather than a numerical evaluation. For example, customer service might be rated as "outstanding" rather than as 4.75 on a 1-to-5 scale. **Quantitative control techniques** are methods based on numerical measures of performance. Rating customer services as 4.75 on a 1-to-5 scale rather than as "outstanding" would indicate a quantitative control measure.

Exhibits 15-5 and 15-6 summarize qualitative and quantitative control techniques, respectively. The purpose in listing them is primarily to alert you to their existence. Chapter 7 provided details about four of the quantitative control techniques described in Exhibit 15-6. When interpreting the results of an audit, it is necessary to evaluate carefully the systems and procedures used to provide the

417

qualitative control technique

A method of controlling based on human judgments about performance that result in a verbal rather than numerical evaluation.

4

Explain the use of nonbudgetary control techniques.

quantitative control technique

A method of controlling based on numerical measures of performance.

Technique	Definition	Key Features
Audit	Examination of activities or records to verify their accuracy or effectiveness	Usually conducted by someone from outside the area audited
External audit	Verification of financial records by external agency or individual	Conducted by an outside agency, such as a CPA firm
Internal audit	Verification of financial records by an internal group of personnel	Wide in scope, including evaluation of control system
Management audit	Use of auditing techniques to evaluate the overall effectiveness of management	Examines wide range of management practices, policies, and procedures
Personal observation	Manager's first-hand observations of how well plans are carried out	Natural part of manager's job
Performance appraisal	Formal method or system of measuring, evaluating, and reviewing employee performance	Points out areas of deficiency and areas for corrective action; manager and group member jointly solve the problem
Policy	General guideline to follow in making decisions and taking action	Indicates whether manager is following organizational intentions

EXHIBIT 15-5

Qualitative Control Techniques

The competence and ethics of people collecting information for qualitative controls influence the effectiveness of these controls.

EXHIBIT 15-6

Quantitative Control Techniques Used in Production and Operations

Quantitative control techniques are widely accepted because they appear precise and objective.

Technique	Definition	Purpose
Gantt chart	Chart depicting planned and actual progress of work on a project	Describes progress on a project
CPM/PERT	Method of scheduling activities and events using time estimates	Measures how well project is meeting schedule
Break-even analysis	Ratio of fixed costs to price minus variable costs	Measures organization's performance and gives basis for corrective action
Economic-order quantity (EOQ)	Inventory level that minimizes ordering and carrying costs	Avoids having too much or too little inventory
ABC analysis	Method of assigning value to inventory; A items are worth more than B or C items	Indicates where emphasis should be placed to control money
Variance analysis	Major control device in manufacturing	Establishes standard costs for materials, labor, and overhead, and then measures deviations from these costs

information. A poorly developed performance appraisal system, for example, might not detect deviations from performance. Another factor to investigate is the political motivation of the people conducting the audit. Are the auditors going out of their way to please management? Are they out to make management look bad? Or are they motivated only to be objective and professional?

Firms use controls to keep costs at acceptable levels, which trigger feedback when costs rise too high. In response, managers begin to reduce as many variable costs as possible. Details about cost reduction are presented later in the discussion of managing cash flow. Some firms implement preventive controls to guard against the need to trim costs. The use of temporary employees can be a preventive control. By hiring temporaries, a firm prevents a portion of payroll costs from reaching an unacceptable level. A firm pays a temporary worker only for the duration of the assignment. In contrast, permanent workers often remain on the payroll while between assignments because managers anticipate finding constructive work for them soon.

5 BUDGETS AND BUDGETARY CONTROL TECHNIQUES

Summarize the various types of budgets, and the use of budgets and financial ratios for control.

budget

A spending plan expressed in numerical terms for a future period of time.

When people hear the word budget, they typically think of tight restrictions placed on the use of money. The car-rental agency name Budget Rent-A-Car was chosen because of popular thinking that the adjective *budget* means conservative spending. In management, a budget does place restrictions on the use of money, but the allotted amounts can be quite generous. A **budget** is a plan, expressed in numerical terms, for allocating resources. The numerical terms typically refer to money, but they could also refer to such things as the amount of energy or the number of printer ribbons used. A budget typically involves cash outflow and inflow.

Virtually every manager assumes some budget responsibility, because a budget outlines a plan for allocating resources. Without budgets, keeping track of how much money is spent in comparison to how much money is available would be nearly impossible. Here we look at different types of budgets and how to use budgets for control. We also describe four other topics closely tied in with budgeting and control: managing cash flow and cost cutting, the balanced score-card, activity-based accounting, and the measurement of intellectual capital. Readers familiar with accounting and finance will find much of this information a review.

Types of Budgets

Budgets can be classified in many ways. For example, budgets are sometimes described as either fixed or flexible. A *fixed budget* allocates expenditures based on a one-time allocation of resources. The organizational unit receives a fixed sum of money that must last for the budget period. A *flexible budget* allows for variation in the use of resources on the basis of activity. Under a flexible budget, a sales department would receive an increased telephone budget if the department increased its telemarketing program. Any type of budget can be classified as fixed or flexible.

Many different types of budgets help control costs in profit and nonprofit firms. Brief descriptions of seven commonly used budgets follow. Most other budgets are variations of these basic types.[4]

Master Budget

A **master budget** consolidates the budgets of various units. Its purpose is to forecast financial statements for the entire company. Each of the separate budgets gives the projected costs and revenues for its own operations.

master budget
A budget consolidated from the budgets of various units.

Cash Budget

A **cash budget** presents a forecast of cash receipts and payments. The budget is compared against actual expenditures. The cash budget acts as an important control measure because it reflects a firm's ability to meet cash obligations. A firm that is working to capacity—such as a restaurant overflowing with customers—can still go bankrupt if its expenses are so high that even full production cannot generate enough revenue to meet expenses. (A typical problem is that the firm in this position has borrowed so much money that having a cash surplus becomes almost impossible. Principal and interest payments on the loans consume most of the cash receipts.)

Cash budgeting also serves the important function of showing the amount of cash available to invest in revenue-producing ventures. In the short term, businesses typically invest cash surpluses in stocks, bonds, and money market funds. In the long term, the cash is likely to be invested in real estate or in the acquisition of another company. Another long-range alternative is to use surplus cash to expand the business. Managers can also use cash surpluses to retire debt and consolidate ownership by buying up shares of the company owned by others.

cash budget
A forecast of cash receipts and payments.

Revenue-and-Expense Budget

A **revenue-and-expense budget** describes in dollar amounts plans for revenues and operating expenses. It is the most widely used, and most readily understood, type of budget. The sales budget used by business firms is a revenue-and-expense budget. It forecasts sales and estimates expenses for a given period of time. Many firms use a monthly revenue-and-expense budget. The monthly budgets are later converted into quarterly, semiannual, and annual budgets. Most revenue-and-expense budgets divide operating expenses into categories. Major operating expenses include salaries, benefits, rent, utilities, business travel, building maintenance, and equipment.

revenue-and-expense budget
A document that describes plans for revenues and operating expenses in dollar amounts.

production budget

A detailed plan that identifies the products or services that must be produced to match the sales forecast and inventory requirements.

materials purchase/ usage budget

A plan that identifies the raw materials and parts that must be purchased to meet production demands.

human resource budget

A schedule that identifies the human resource needs for a future period and the labor costs to meet those needs.

capital expenditure budget

A plan for spending money on assets used to produce goods or services.

Production Budget

After sales forecasts are established, the units needed from the production area must be estimated. A **production budget** is a detailed plan that identifies the products or services that must be produced or provided to match the sales forecast and inventory requirements. A production budget can be considered a production schedule.

Materials Purchase/Usage Budget

After production demands have been forecast, it is necessary to estimate the cost of meeting this demand. A **materials purchase/usage budget** is a plan that identifies the raw materials and parts that must be purchased to meet production demands. In a retail business a comparable budget specifies the merchandise that must be purchased to meet the anticipated sales demand.

Human Resource Budget

To satisfy sales and production demands, money must be allocated for the labor to accomplish the work. A **human resource budget** provides a schedule to identify the human resource needs for a future period and the labor (or personnel) costs to meet those needs. Of particular interest to management is whether the number of employees will have to be substantially increased or decreased to meet sales and production forecasts.

Capital Expenditure Budget

Organizations must invest in new equipment and buildings to stay in operation. A **capital expenditure budget** is a plan for spending money on assets used to produce goods or services. Capital expenditures are usually regarded as major expenditures and are tied to long-range plans. Capital expenditures include money spent for buildings, machinery, equipment, and major inventories. In a typical budgeting system, the planned purchase of a computer network would be included in the capital budget. The monthly payment for postage and private delivery companies would be an operating expense.

Suggestions for Preparing a Budget

Although budgets give the appearance of being factual, objective documents, judgment, and political tactics all enter into budget preparation. When preparing a budget, a manager can impress higher-ups if he or she tracks variables with care and makes sound assumptions. In contrast, if the manager allocates resources poorly or permits too much flab, he or she will lose credibility. A business newsletter offers these recommendations for preparing a sensible budget:[5]

- *Leave wiggle room.* Optimistic projections with little basis in reality will come back to haunt you. Bill Powell, CEO of Progress Industries in Newton, Iowa, recommends that you budget conservatively for income and liberally for expenses. Using this approach, you will be impressive if you contain costs and generate more revenue than you anticipated.
- *Research the competition.* Do some fact-finding to determine how your competitors at other firms arrive at their budget estimates. For example, find out how others adjust for inflation or an industry slump. "My managers who submit the best budgets show comparisons to the competition and explain to me how they can outperform and why," says Phil Joffe, chief operating officer at CalFarm Insurance Co.

- *Embrace reality.* Study the facts carefully, and take a historical perspective in arriving at the right estimates for any given financial period. For example, if your industry traditionally experiences high turnover, factor high turnover costs into your budget forecast.

Budgets and Financial Ratios as Control Devices

The control process relies on the use of budgets and financial ratios as measures of performance. To the extent that managers stay within budget or meet their financial ratios they perform according to standard.

Budgets and the Control Process
Budgets are a natural part of controlling. Planned expenditures are compared to actual expenditures, and corrective action is taken if the deviation is significant. Exhibit 15-7 shows a budget used as a control device. The nightclub and restaurant owner described in Chapter 7 operates with a monthly budget. The owner planned for revenues of $40,000 in March. Actual revenues were $42,500, a positive deviation. The discrepancy is not large enough, however, for the owner to change the anticipated revenues for April. Expenses were $150 over budget, a negative deviation the owner regards as insignificant. In short, the performance against budget looks good. The owner will take no corrective action on the basis of March performance.

Financial Ratios and the Control Process
A more advanced method of using budgets for control is to use financial ratio guidelines for performance. Three such ratios are presented here. In addition, we look at economic value added (EVA), another measure of financial performance.

Item	Budget	Actual	Over	Under
Revenues	$40,000	$42,500	$2,500	
Beginning inventory	3,500	3,500		
Purchases	19,250	19,000		$250
End inventory	3,000	3,000		
Cost of goods sold	19,750	19,500		
Gross profit	20,250	23,000		
Salaries expense	10,500	10,500		
Rent and utilities expense	1,500	1,500		
Miscellaneous expense	100	250	150	
Maintenance expense	650	650		
Total operating expenses	12,750	12,900		
Net income before tax	7,500	10,100		
Taxes (40%)	3,000	4,040		
Net income	$4,500	$6,060		

EXHIBIT 15-7

March Revenue-and-Expense Budget for Nightclub and Restaurant

Budget summary: Revenues and Net Income exceed budget by $2,500 and $1,560, respectively.

Note: Data analyzed according to *Generally Accepted Accounting Principles* by Jose L. Cruzet of Florida National College.

gross profit margin

A financial ratio expressed as the difference between sales and the cost of goods sold, divided by sales.

One commonly used ratio is **gross profit margin**, expressed as the difference between sales and the cost of goods sold, divided by sales:

$$\text{Gross profit margin} = \frac{\text{Sales} - \text{Cost of goods sold}}{\text{Sales}}$$

This ratio measures the total money available to cover operating expenses and to make a profit. If performance deviates significantly from a predetermined performance standard, corrective action must be taken.

Assume the nightclub owner needs to earn a 10 percent gross profit margin. For March, the figures are as follows:

$$\text{Gross profit margin} = \frac{\$42,500 - \$19,500}{\$42,500} = \frac{\$23,000}{\$42,500} = .54$$

Based on the gross profit margin financial ratio, the business performed better than planned. One could argue that the gross profit margin presents an overly optimistic picture of how well the business is performing. Another widely used financial ratio is the **profit margin**, or return on sales. Profit margin measures profits earned per dollar of sales as well as the efficiency of the operation. In the business press, the profit margin is usually referred to as simply the *margin* and calculated as profits divided by sales.

profit margin

A financial ratio measuring return on sales, or net income divided by sales.

$$\text{Profit margin} = \frac{\text{Net income}}{\text{Sales}} = \frac{\$6,060}{\$42,500} = .14 \text{ or } 14\%$$

A profit margin of 14 percent would be healthy for most businesses. It also appears to present a more realistic assessment of how well the nightclub in question performs as a business.

The last ratio described here is **return on equity**, an indicator of how much a firm is earning on its investment. It is the ratio between net income and the owner's equity, or

return on equity

A financial ratio measuring how much a firm is earning on its investment, expressed as net income divided by owner's equity.

$$\text{Return on equity} = \frac{\text{Net income}}{\text{Owner's equity}}$$

Assume that the owner of the nightclub and restaurant invested $400,000 in the restaurant, and that the net income for the year is $72,500. The return on equity is $72,500/$400,000 = .181 or 18.1 percent. The owner should be satisfied, because few investments offer such a high return on equity.

Another measure of financial health that works much like a financial ratio is **economic value added (EVA)**. EVA refers to how much more (or less) the company earns in profits than the minimum amount its investors expect it to earn. The minimum amount also known as the *cost of capital* represents what the company must pay the investors to use their capital. Cost of capital is also calculated as the overall percentage cost of the funds used to finance a firm's assets. If the sole source of financing were bonds that paid investors 10 percent, the cost of capital would be 10 percent. All earnings beyond the minimum are regarded as excess earnings.[6]

economic value added (EVA)

Measures how much more (or less) a company earns in profits than the minimum amount its investors expect it to earn.

For example, assume that investors give their company $2 million to invest and the investor's minimum desired return is 10 percent, or $200,000 per year. The company earns $300,000 per year. The EVA is $100,000 as follows:

Earnings: $300,000
Cost of capital: $200,000 (10% × $2 million capital)
Excess earnings: $100,000

Investors expect higher excess earnings when they invest in a risky venture, such as a company with unproven technology entering a new industry. An example might be manufacturing electronic communication systems for space stations. Investors willing to settle for lower excess earnings usually invest in a company with proven technology in a stable industry, such as construction supplies. EVA is a frequently used control measure because it focuses on creating shareholder value. For example, the bonus plan at Eli Lilly requires managers to attain continuous, year-to-year improvements in EVA.[7]

The ratios just presented offer a traditional view of the financial health of an organization because they emphasize earning a profit. The hundreds of failed dot-com companies in recent years reinforce the importance of actual profit. Many dot-com companies with revenues far below their expenses paid salaries and other expenses out of investor capital. Dozens of other dot-com companies did not pay their bills at all because they lacked the necessary cash. Without cash to pay bills and profits to pay investors, most companies eventually fail. Ratios such as profit margin and return on equity are therefore still relevant in today's economy.

MANAGING CASH FLOW AND COST CUTTING

Explain how managers and business owners manage cash flow and control costs, and use nontraditional measures of financial performance.

cash flow

Amount of net cash generated by a business during a specific period.

In addition to developing and monitoring the cash budget, many managers pay special attention to keeping cash on hand to prevent overreliance on borrowing and being perceived by investors as a firm in financial trouble. Both cash flow and controlling, or cutting, costs help meet these objectives. **Cash flow** is the amount of net cash generated by a business during a specific period. Although this definition appears straightforward, many other definitions of cash flow add to its complexity. A corporation's cash flow statement is divided into three sections, each specifying a different source of cash, with a fourth section that combines the first three.[8]

1. *Cash provided by (or used in) operating activities.* This section indicates how much cash a business uses (a loss), thereby containing clues to the health of earnings. Cash from operating activities is the heart of cash flow and includes subsections: net income, provision for uncollectible money owed the company, tax benefit from stock options, receivables, inventories, and accounts payable.
2. *Cash provided by (or used in) financing activities.* This section records cash from or paid to outsiders such as banks or stockholders.
3. *Cash provided by (or used in) investing activities.* Recorded here is the cash used to buy or received from selling stock, assets, and businesses, plus capital expenditures.
4. *Summary.* This revealing section lists cash at the beginning and end of the specific period, plus the change in cash position.

According to finance professor Ashok Robin, managers and accountants calculate cash flow differently.[9] See Exhibit 15-8. A company that writes off many income deductions will have a better cash flow. The more depreciation charges a company takes (as reflected in cash used in investing activities), the better its cash flow.

Firms with large cash flows make attractive takeover targets because acquiring firms are likely to use the cash to pay off the cost of the acquisition. A company

Cash Flow as Calculated by Accountants

Revenues	$15,000
Expenses	8,000
Depreciation	3,000
Taxable Income	4,000
Taxes at 40%	1,600
Net Income	2,400
Cash Flow	2,400 + 3,000 = $5,400 (Because you do not have to pay tax on the $3,000 depreciation, you can use it for other purposes.)

Cash Flow as Calculated by Managers

Revenues	$15,000
Expenses	8,000
Tax	1,600
Cash Flow	$5,400

that does not want to be taken over might deliberately lower its cash flow by taking on a lot of debt. A large cash flow for a business owner contributes to peace of mind because the owner can keep operating without borrowing during a business downturn.

Cash flow analysis is well accepted because it provides a more accurate picture of financial health than does sales volume. A company frequently makes a sale but then does not receive payment for a minimum of 30 days. Several years ago Sears, Roebuck and Co. enjoyed an impressive sales gain but its cash flow position was much less impressive. The problem developed from high delinquency rates on Sears credit cards—customers purchased more but not all paid their bills promptly. In some cases they failed to pay their bills at all. Sears added 18 million cardholders, but some later declared bankruptcy. The company established $393 million in reserves for credit card delinquencies, which also reduced cash flow.[10]

Cash flow analysis provides an important tool because it is less subject to distortion than is a statement of revenues. Many managers use the questionable accounting practice of classifying as "revenue" goods in the hands of distributors, which have not yet been sold, and contracts for which no money has yet been exchanged.

The ideal way to improve cash flow is to generate more revenue than expenses. However, generating more revenue can be an enormous challenge. Many companies therefore trim costs to improve cash flow. Even when revenues are increasing, some firms reduce costs to remain more competitive. As you may have noticed, the less cash you spend, the more you have on hand. Exhibit 15-9 presents a variety of measures companies use to reduce costs.

The Balanced Scorecard

Many researchers and managers abandoned their exclusive reliance on financial ratios and related indices to measure the health of a firm. Budgets reveal important, but incomplete, information. Managers continue to look for ways to overcome the limited view of performance sometimes created by budgets. An

Techniques Focused Mostly on People

- Minimize business travel by using e-mail, telephone, or videoconferencing when possible.
- Have business travelers fly coach instead of first class, and stay at budget hotels and motels.
- Establish per diem rates for meal allowances instead of an open-ended travel account substantiated by receipts.
- Keep offices, factories, and laboratories at the coolest or warmest temperature that does not lower morale or productivity, or damage equipment. Encourage employees to wear warm clothing in cold months, and light clothing in warm months.
- Establish a telecommuting program to reduce the demand for office space.
- Place frequent business travelers on hoteling status, whereby they do not have a permanent office or cubicle when in the office.
- Ask employees to conduct bimonthly brainstorming sessions to find ways to reduce costs. Offer rewards for the best savings.
- Keep on the payroll only those employees who contribute to the goals of the firm. Hire consultants and subcontractors instead of keeping on the payroll those employees whose skills are needed only occasionally.
- Establish a cadre of retired employees who can serve as temporary workers during peak periods.
- Drop customers who cost you money because of their constant demands for service despite modest purchases.
- Eliminate free coffee and food except for special occasions such as training or Saturday morning meetings.

Techniques Focused Mostly on Material and Equipment

- Compare prices on the Internet before committing to a purchase.
- When possible, send local paper messages by fax instead of mail or courier service. Delete obsolete files on floppy disks, and reuse the disks.
- To save on telephone bills, look to make calls to people in earlier time zones after 5 P.M. in your time zone to profit from the reduced evening rate.
- Use application service providers (ASPs) to provide information technology requirements instead of owning advanced hardware and software.
- Lease equipment when it is less expensive than owning (as with the ASP).
- Demand an immediate 5 percent price cut from all suppliers. (Asking for more is likely to lead to resistance and lower-quality supplies.)
- Hold a sale of surplus and obsolete equipment. At the same time sell the equipment over an Internet auction site.
- Centralize buying for a multilocation company, and ask managers to cart some supplies with them after a visit to headquarters.
- Subcontract manufacturing and services that can be done less expensively by other firms.
- Sell the corporate jet and limousines, and ask executives to fly on commercial airlines and drive their own vehicles for business (or take the bus or train).

Techniques Focused Mostly on Money Management

- Ask suppliers for discounts on early payments. If the discounts are not granted, pay all bills including taxes, utilities, and suppliers as late as possible without incurring a fee. In this way you rather than someone else is earning a return on the money.
- For small businesses share office expenses, including support services, with several other firms by renting a large office space together and dividing it into offices for each firm.
- Use activity-based costing to help trim costs that do not add value for customers.
- Consolidate advertising and marketing with one agency to earn volume discounts.
- Use a "sweep" checking account that places your unused balances in a relatively high-paying money market account overnight.

EXHIBIT 15-9

A Variety of Ways to Cut Costs

Saving money can greatly affect profit levels, so managers look for many ways to trim costs that do not damage productivity or morale. Annual savings range from a few hundred dollars to millions, depending on the measures used.

425

balanced scorecard

A set of measures to provide a quick but comprehensive view of the business.

accounting professor and a technology consultant worked with hundreds of companies to devise a **balanced scorecard**—a set of measures to provide a quick but comprehensive view of the business. Managers using the balanced scorecard do not rely on short-term financial measures as the only indicators of a company's performance. The balanced scorecard helps an organization set goals and measure performance from four perspectives that are vital to all businesses:[11]

1. *Financial.* How much do we earn? What do shareholders think of us?
2. *Customer service.* How do customers see us?
3. *Learning and growth.* Can we continue to improve and create value?
4. *Internal processes.* In what ways must we excel?

The balanced scorecard follows a strategy to the extent that it directs the company effort in the direction of achieving the four goals just mentioned. A balanced scorecard usually incorporates both financial yardsticks, such as return on equity, and operational yardsticks, such as customer satisfaction and the ability to innovate. Compensation is based on achieving all the factors included in the balanced scorecard. Exhibit 15-10 presents a composite balanced scorecard from 60 companies.

Duke Children's Hospital in Durham, North Carolina, successfully applies the balanced scorecard approach. Several years ago, the hospital faced a financial crisis, along with a reduction in the number of patient beds and low-quality patient care. When Jon Meilones, the newly appointed medical director, evaluated the situation, he found two major hospital groups pursuing different goals: (1) clinicians focused solely on providing the best medical care, and (2) administrators concerned about the worsening financial ratios. Meilones implemented a balanced scorecard to help the two groups focus on multiple goals.

The scorecard approach provides workers with report cards to show how well they perform in meeting goals, and to provide a complete picture of the organization. The report cards enabled the medical staff to evaluate where they could cut

EXHIBIT 15-10

The Balanced Scorecard for Measuring Business Unit Performance

Some companies use a balanced scorecard to evaluate the performance of their business units and to shape performance-based compensation. Here are the average weights assigned to the five types of performance measures in the balanced scorecard, as it is being used by 60 large firms surveyed by Towers Perrin, New York. Note that, on average, the companies assign "customer focus" a 19 percent weighting.

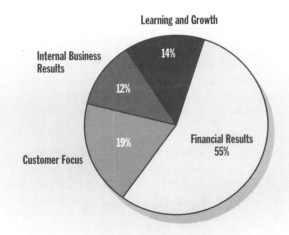

Learning and Growth 14%
Internal Business Results 12%
Customer Focus 19%
Financial Results 55%

Source: Adapted with permission from "Compensation: The Link to Customer Satisfaction," *Human Resources Forum,* a supplement to *Management Review,* October 1996, p. 3.

costs, and also empowered them to look for other ways to improve quality of care. Another set of report cards showed administrators that increasing nursing productivity does cut costs, but it also lowers quality of patient care and staff satisfaction.

From 1997 forward, Duke Children's Hospital created 10 balanced scorecards, reduced the average cost per patient case by 33 percent, reduced the average length of stay by 31 percent, and received the highest rating in customer satisfaction among 28 institutions.[12]

Activity-Based Costing

Concerns that conventional methods of measuring financial performance may be misleading prompt the use of another approach to understanding the true costs involved in conducting business. **Activity-based costing (ABC)** is an accounting procedure that allocates the costs of producing a product or service to the activities performed and the resources used. An activity-based cost system offers managers a more strategic approach to their business because it presents a comprehensive view of all the costs involved in making a product or service and getting it to market. In contrast, a more traditional cost system might focus most on costs such as labor, parts, and administrative overhead. By using activity-based costing managers can assess the productivity of products and business units by assigning costs based on the use of company-wide resources. The profitability of customers can also be assessed: Some customers use up so many resources they are not profitable to keep.[13] Is it worth selling a $35 pair of shoes to a customer who tries on 20 pairs before making a decision? Similarly, an industrial customer might be unprofitable because he or she takes too much time to serve. Recall how the nursery described at the opening of the chapter used ABC to identify its most profitable products and which products to discontinue.

How does activity-based costing work in practice? Let's assume a company introduces two new cell phone models. One phone is for use in autos and other general purposes. The other phone is a waterproof model targeted at people who are so attached to technology, or are in such demand, that they want a cell phone that works in the shower. The manufacturing cost is $100 for the conventional model and $130 for the shower model. However, the activity-based cost is $125 for conventional model and $400 for the shower model. The difference represents the resources used and the people consulted in order to make the shower model as safe as possible for its intended use. The wet-look model also requires extensive consultation with the legal staff to iron out any possible product liability claims.

activity-based costing (ABC)
An accounting procedure that allocates the costs of producing a product or service to the activities performed and the resources used.

Measurement of Intellectual Capital

Activity-based costing is but one advance in measuring the financial performance of a firm. A more radical approach regards employee brainpower as a major contributor to the wealth of an organization. This approach makes some attempt to measure **intellectual capital**, which is the value of useful ideas and the people who generate them. The difficult part, for example, comes in trying to attach a reliable value to a group of programmers and the software they produce. In traditional accounting methods, a fleet of company trucks would receive a higher valuation than the company's software. Intellectual assets are found throughout a firm. An office assistant who has a good feel for customer preference is also a valuable asset, even if difficult to measure. Setting such valuation raises a number of issues because the company does not own the office assistant who can leave at will.

intellectual capital
The value of useful ideas and the people who generate them.

Robert Howell, a professor of finance and accounting, believes that the real assets of a knowledge-intensive company are the know-how of its workforce, intellectual property (such as its patents), brand equity, and relationships with employees, customers, and suppliers. As a starting point as to how these might be valued, Howell says: "At a minimum, I would book as assets such costs as recruitment and training and development, and amortize them over some sort of employment life. Why aren't they as much of an asset as some piece of machinery?"[14]

The five companies with the highest knowledge capital as determined by some of the measures just described are: General Electric, Pfizer, Microsoft, Philip Morris, and Exxon Mobil.[15]

7 INFORMATION SYSTEMS AND CONTROL

Outline the basics of an information system.

information system (or management information system)

A formal system for providing management with information useful or necessary for making decisions.

An **information system (IS)**, or **management information system (MIS)**, is a formal system for providing management with information useful or necessary for making decisions. The IS is usually based on a mainframe computer, but recent advances allow some of these systems to be based on personal computers and servers. Many firms that decentralized their information systems later went back to using a large centralized corporate mainframe. A centralized system reduces duplication and helps integrate the different functions. Several developments in recent years contributed to the recentralization trend in information systems. The Internet explosion prompted businesses to connect their many networks. Companies put many essential applications on their intranets. Also, many companies found maintaining PCs on a network too expensive to be cost effective.[16] Furthermore, mainframe computers crash less frequently than smaller computers.

Widespread use of information systems can be found throughout all kinds of organizations, small businesses included. Advances in digital technology make accessing computers from remote locations easier than ever. With hand-held information tools (or personal digital assistants), field personnel, including technicians, can get information from a central source. Sales representatives equipped with laptop computers or personal digital assistants can access needed information from the home office in seconds. Simultaneously, they can feed back to marketing vital information about customer orders and preferences.

A managerial control based on valid information makes an effective IS an indispensable part of any control system. The next sections describe the basic elements of an information system, how it can function as a control, and the electronic monitoring of work.

Elements of an Information System

Establishing an information system usually involves four basic steps: (1) analyze the information requirements, (2) develop an information base, (3) design an information processing system, and (4) build controls into the system. See Exhibit 15-11.

Analyze Information Requirements

The first step in designing an information system is to research the kinds of decisions managers and specialists need help in making. A related step decides what type of information can best provide that help. For example, research might show that managers need help in making decisions about which employees are qualified for overseas assignments. The IS designed to help them would include data about

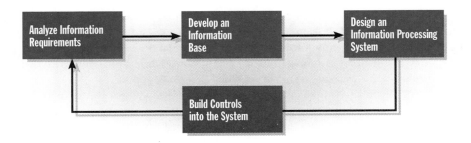

EXHIBIT 15-11

Basic Elements of an Information System

Although information systems are complex and must be built with the assistance of information technology specialists, these systems all contain certain basic elements.

429

each employee's travel preferences, foreign language skills, and ability to work without close supervision.

The people who use the data from the information system should decide on the information requirements, which means managers must give the IS specialists a clear picture of their information requirements. Providing carefully articulated requirements keeps users from getting stuck with an inadequate system; additionally, users are more committed to a system that they help select. Too often, when other people, such as systems analysts, decide on requirements, they make a wrong guess about what the users need. For example, the systems analyst may purchase software that is able to produce only limited information.

Develop an Information Base

A database of valid information forms the heart of any information system. Developing relevant information takes ingenuity. Sometimes, much of the information already exists in company records; it simply needs to be coded and stored in the IS. In other cases, information must be collected. In the overseas assignment example, managers and IS specialists might develop a questionnaire for job candidates to be completed both by the candidate and by the manager during interviews. The results could be combined with the company information about work performance.

A recent Internet-based contribution to developing an information base is *Webcasting*—software that brings information to your computer tailored to your individual needs. The information you want is delivered automatically to your desktop (and possibly to the company mainframe). The term *push technology* is used in relation to Webcasting because the information the manager needs is pushed through to him or her. Webcasting popularity failed to live up to expectations. One of the reasons for its limited demand is increasingly efficient search engines that make access to information relatively easy.

Design an Information Processing System

In this step, IS specialists design a system to collect, store, transmit, and retrieve information. Because specialized knowledge about computer systems is required to complete this step successfully, many firms use outside assistance. The total IS is a composite of a number of specific information systems. The same system that helps select candidates for overseas assignments cannot keep track of spare parts.

Build Controls into the System

At the beginning of this chapter, we mentioned that one part of the controlling function is to evaluate the control system. Building controls into the IS is a special case of this general principle. Most information systems look impressive on the surface because they involve modern electronic equipment. However, despite outward sophistication, an IS can generate invalid or outdated information. The information system for foreign assignments might generate a list of employees at the press of a few buttons. However, performance appraisal data entered inaccurately may result in an assignment list of people unqualified for overseas work. To use a tired cliché, "garbage in, garbage out."

Another type of control built into an information system is a control against misappropriation, or unauthorized use, of information. Controls preventing computer theft include an elaborate system of passwords and other security devices. Programs to counter computer viruses are another aspect of computer security. A *computer virus* is an unauthorized program, placed secretly into a computer, that destroys stored data and other programs. A virus can also be introduced into a system accidentally by a contaminated disk from an outside source.

Effective controls enable managers to pinpoint the deficiencies in an IS. Additionally, effective controls can be useful in updating the system as information requirements change. For example, a constructive by-product of preparations for the Year 2000 (Y2K) problem was substantial upgrades of many information systems. While IS specialists worked to prevent the potentially disastrous problem, other faulty aspects of systems were discovered and repaired. Numerous companies achieved more efficient inventory management systems as a result of becoming Y2K compliant.

Control Information Supplied by an Information System

The field of information systems keeps expanding. This growth is partly attributable to the increasing need for useful control information. The control information that can be generated by an information system is virtually unlimited. Exhibit 15-12 shows a sampling of what an IS keeps track of. A company-specific example is Southland Corp., which owns and franchises the 7-Eleven convenience stores. Its computerized information system tracks inventory and forecasts sales. The system can precisely track 2,300 items and help individual stores stock the right number of items such as Slurpees and low-fat turkey breast on pita. Another advantage of the information system is that it can help analyze sales trends on such factors as time of day, weather, and socioeconomic level of the neighborhood. A

EXHIBIT 15-12

Examples of Control Information Supplied by Information Systems

Information systems can:
- Report on sales of products by territory, sales representative, and customer category
- Supply inventory-level information by region, plant, and department
- Describe magazine subscribers by age, income, occupational level, and ZIP code
- Report turnover rates by age, sex, job title, and salary level
- Supply information about budget deviations by location, department, and manager
- Automatically compile financial ratios and compare them to industry standards
- Automatically compile production and operation control indexes and compare them from plant to plant
- Print out a summary of overdue accounts according to customer, and goods or services purchased
- Report hospital-bed occupancy rates according to diagnosis, sex, and age of patient
- Calculate, by subsidiary, the return on investment of cash surpluses
- Using the Internet, make price comparisons for goods and services

computer information system of this type can help the individual store manager and owner cope with the major problems of overstocking perishable items and understocking hot items—such as beer, soft drinks, and snacks in response to a major sports event on television.

The accompanying Management in Action describes how a major airline uses an information system to keep its planes in top shape and to satisfy its customers.

Computer-Aided Monitoring of Work

More and more, companies use their information systems for *computer-aided monitoring of work*. In this type of monitoring, a computer-based system gathers data about the work habits and productivity of employees. These systems capitalize on the networking of computer terminals to monitor the work of employees who use computer terminals in their jobs or who operate complex machine tools. Once the monitoring software is installed, the central computer processes information from each terminal and records the employee's efficiency and effectiveness.

Office workers, including those in frequent telephone contact with the public, are the most likely to be monitored. Word-processing specialists are measured by such factors as words keyed per minute, the number of breaks taken, and the duration of each break. The Internal Revenue Service uses an electronic monitoring system to evaluate workers who provide taxpayer assistance by telephone. AT&T uses electronic monitoring to evaluate operators, who must complete calls within a set time. Safeway Stores equips its trucks with small, computerized boxes that record truck speed, gas mileage, gear shifting patterns, and whether the truck strays from its route.

The major advantage of an electronic monitoring system is the close supervision it allows managers. Some employees welcome computerized monitoring because it supplements arbitrary judgments by supervisors about their productivity. Computerized work-monitoring systems have substantial disadvantages, however. Many argue that these systems invade employee privacy and violate their dignity. Moreover, electronic monitoring often contributes to low levels of job satisfaction, absenteeism, high turnover, and job stress.

CHARACTERISTICS OF EFFECTIVE CONTROLS   **8**

An effective control system improves job performance and productivity by helping workers correct problems. A system that achieves these outcomes possesses distinct characteristics. The greater the number of the following characteristics a given control system contains, the better the system will be at providing management with useful information and improved performance:

Specify several characteristics of effective controls.

1. *The controls must be accepted.* For control systems to increase productivity, employees must cooperate with the system. If employees are more intent on beating the system than on improving performance, controls will not achieve their ultimate purpose. For example, the true purpose of a time-recording system is to ensure that employees work a full day. If workers are intent on circumventing the system through such means as having friends punch in and out for them, the time-recording system will not increase productivity.

2. *The control measures must be appropriate and meaningful.* People tend to resist control measures that they believe do not relate to performance in a meaningful way. Customer service telephone representatives, for example, may

Management in Action

The IT Maintenance System at United Airlines

The average Boeing 747 uses about 400,000 mechanical parts, and the smaller 737 about 150,000. Multiply those kinds of numbers by a fleet of more than 600 sophisticated aircraft from a variety of manufacturers, and it's easy to understand why the 67 worldwide Maintenance Operations Centers of United Airlines are such busy places.

United constantly looks for ways to reduce costs, boost revenues, and improve customer satisfaction. Management relies more and more on information technology to meet these challenges. "Flight delays and cancellations are the bane of every airline," explains Brian Bauer, director of fleet operations for United's Information Services Division. "They take a toll on customer satisfaction and the bottom line. The ability of our mechanics to perform routine aircraft maintenance and identify and correct problems efficiently and quickly is essential. Our maintenance IT system provides our 10,000 aircraft maintenance technicians and engineers with fast access to timely information and parts to keep our fleet ready for revenue service every day."

It's not always an easy job. The airline performs about 50 complete aircraft engine overhauls each month. Every four years a United aircraft goes through "heavy maintenance," during which it is completely rebuilt. At any given time 35 to 40 aircraft are in heavy maintenance, literally being taken apart for replacement of crucial parts. In addition to maintaining its own fleet, United is also one of the largest third-party aircraft maintenance suppliers. Its technicians provide service for 77 other airlines, and for many military aircraft.

Three key IT systems keep United's maintenance operations running smoothly—and its planes in top shape and in the air: the Material Management System, the Job Instruction Card system, and the Electronic Data Distribution system.

United developed the Material Manager System (MMS) with the help of Unisys to streamline its supply chain. "MMS manages our parts supply chain from acquisition, to use, to purchase of new parts," Bauer says. As some 25,000 new parts are received into inventory each month, they are bar-coded and scanned into a data management system that resides on mainframe computers. "When inventory reaches a certain threshold, the system automatically reorders parts through electronic interfaces with our vendors. It also enables us to track parts either by individual unit or by quantity from source to consumption," says Bauer.

Aircraft maintenance follows a strict schedule determined by manufacturers' recommendations, an airline's own maintenance specifications, and Federal Aviation Administration (FAA) safety requirements. United combines all these data in a system called Job Instruction Card (JIC), which technicians use to print predetermined lists of the necessary tasks, tools, and parts for any maintenance or repair activity. When a plane is due for scheduled maintenance, the system prints out a JIC list for that particular aircraft.

Sometimes a technician must first consult a manufacturer's maintenance manual for guidance before servicing an aircraft. Instead of dealing with cumbersome paper manuals, United technicians simply log onto the airline's Electronic Document Distribution (EDD) system, which provides quick online access to approximately 1.5 million pages of digitized, up-to-date manufacturers' maintenance manuals.

"EDD gives descriptions and graphics of parts and tools associated with a particular repair or maintenance activity," Bauer explains. "And because EDD is linked to the parts inventory system, the technician simply clicks on a description or graphic and the system will point to the part in the inventory system and automatically predraw it." For example, if a

Boeing 737 needed a passenger seat replaced, the technician could call up the appropriate section of the manual and click on a graphic of the seat or highlight a written description of an installation step to see a list of the required parts and tools. The technician then instructs EDD to predraw the parts and tools from inventory.

"Together these information systems allow our technicians to operate in a nearly paperless environment," says Bauer. The integration of the systems also reduced United's inventory costs, allowing United to remove approxi-

mately $400 million in inventory over a 20-year period as it moves toward a just-in-time inventory system.

The airline's maintenance IT systems provided benefits across the board, but the greatest impact was felt in customer service. "Our fleet has a reliability index of about 97 percent," says Bauer. "Because maintenance-related delays are less likely, United passengers are the ultimate beneficiaries."

Source: Helene Rudzinski, "More Than the Sum of the Parts," *UNISYS Exec*, March–April 2000, pp. 36–38.

object to a control measure based primarily on the amount of inquiries processed. Experienced operators contend that giving the right assistance to fewer callers would be a better measure of performance. A classic example of the difference between a meaningful and a nonmeaningful control follows:

> At one point Continental Airlines was doing poorly. A contributing problem, according to Adam M. Pilarski, an aviation consultant and economist, was that the company was using a set of inappropriate incentives, such as rewarding pilots for saving fuel. In response to these standards, pilots were flying airplanes at slow speeds and rationing their use of air conditioning. As a result, many business passengers who were arriving late and sweaty decided to switch to other airlines, creating losses for Continental. A new incentive was introduced to pay every employee a monthly bonus if the airline was among the industry leaders in on-time performance. A dramatic turnaround took place. Business travelers returned to Continental and the airline is now profitable and an industry leader. The point of this story is that in terms of an airline becoming more profitable, on-time performance is a more effective control standard than saving fuel.[17]

3. *An effective control measure provides diagnostic information.* If controls are to improve performance, they must help people correct deviations from performance. A sales manager might be told that he or she was performing well in all categories except selling to small-business owners. This information might prompt the manager to determine what services the company sells that would have more appeal to small businesses.

4. *Effective controls allow for self-feedback and self-control.* A self-administering control system saves considerable time. Employees can do much of their own controlling if the system permits them access to their own feedback. An example is a system whereby clients complain directly to the employee instead of going to management.

5. *Effective control systems provide timely information.* Controls lead to positive changes in behavior if the control information is available quickly. It is more helpful to give workers daily rather than monthly estimates of their performance against quota. Given day-by-day feedback, an employee can make quick

adjustments. If feedback is withheld until the end of a month or a quarter, the employee may be too discouraged to make improvements.

6. *Control measures are more effective when employees have control over the results measured.* People rebel when held responsible for performance deviations beyond their control. For example, a resort hotel manager's profits might fall below expectations because of a factor beyond his or her control such as a sudden shift in weather that results in cancellations.

7. *Effective control measures do not contradict each other.* Employees are sometimes asked to achieve two contradictory sets of standards. As a result, they resist the control system. Employees told to increase both quantity and quality, for example, may experience confusion and chaos. A compromise approach would be to improve quality with the aim of increasing net quantity in the long run. Care taken in doing something right the first time results in less rework. With less time spent on error correction, eventually the quantity of goods produced increases.

8. *Effective controls allow for random variations from standard.* If a control allows for random variations that do not differ significantly from the standard, then it is more effective. An ineffective way of using a control system is to quickly take action at the first deviation from acceptable performance. A one-time deviation may not indicate a genuine problem. It could simply be a random or insignificant variation that may not be repeated for years. For example, would you take action if a team member exceeded a $3,000 travel expense allowance by $2.78?

9. *Effective controls are cost-effective.* Control systems should result in satisfactory returns on investment. In many instances they don't because the costs of control are too high. Having recognized this fact, some fast-food restaurants allow employees to eat all the food they want during working hours. The cost of trying to control illicit eating is simply too high. (This policy provides the added benefit of building worker morale.)

10. *A cross-functional team's measurement system must empower the team instead of top management retaining the power.* The growing prominence of teams in organizations often requires that control measures for teams be given special consideration. Traditional performance measures may inhibit empowerment because team members do not have full control. One suggestion is for teams to create measures that track the process of delivering value. An example is that a product-development team might decide to measure the number or percentage of new parts to be used in a product. The rationale is that the more parts a product contains, the greater the possibility for malfunction.[18]

A creative use of controls is to loosen them in order to enhance creativity. As described in Chapter 6, creativity often flourishes in a permissive atmosphere in which people do not feel overly constrained. Mark Maletz and Nitin Nohria conducted a research project about the company atmosphere and entrepreneurial activity. (You will recall that creativity is an important characteristic of the entrepreneur.) The research project focused on *whitespace*, defined as the large territory in a company where rules are vague, authority and strategy unclear, and budgets nonexistent. Furthermore, in this type of environment, entrepreneurial activity that reinvigorates a company can flourish. For example, a manager, operating in whitespace, developed a new line of business for a bank on his own without top management's knowledge or approval. After the entrepreneurial deed is accomplished, top management is informed. The study also found that senior executives most effectively nurture whitespace projects by setting aside their traditional planning, organizing, and controlling techniques.[19]

SUMMARY OF KEY POINTS

1 Explain how controlling relates to the other management functions. Controlling is used to evaluate whether the manager is effective in good job planning, organizing, and leading. Controls can also be used to evaluate control systems.

2 Understand the different types and strategies of control. Controls can be classified according to the time when they are applied. Preventive controls are applied prior to the performance of an activity. Concurrent controls monitor activities while they are being carried out. Feedback controls evaluate and prompt corrective action after activity performance.

Controls can also be classified according to their underlying strategy. An external control strategy is based on the assumption that employees are motivated primarily by external rewards and need to be controlled by their managers. An internal control strategy assumes that managers can motivate employees by building commitment to organizational goals.

3 Describe the steps in the control process. The steps in the controlling process include setting standards, measuring actual performance, comparing actual performance to standards, and taking corrective action if necessary. To measure performance, agreement must be reached on the aspects of performance to be measured, the degree of accuracy needed, and who will use the measurements.

The three courses of action open to a manager are to do nothing, to solve the problem, or to revise the standard. Taking corrective action on significant deviations only is called the exception principle.

4 Explain the use of nonbudgetary control techniques. Nonbudgetary control techniques can be qualitative or quantitative. Qualitative techniques include audits, personal observation, and performance appraisal. Quantitative techniques include Gantt charts, PERT, and economic-order quantity. Loosening controls can sometimes enhance creativity. Cost cutting is closely tied to the control function.

5 Summarize the various types of budgets, and the use of budgets and financial ratios for control. A budget is a spending plan for a future period of time, expressed in numerical terms. A fixed budget allocates expenditures based on a one-time allocation of resources. A flexible budget allows variation in the use of resources based on the level of activity. Seven widely used types of budgets are (1) master budgets, (2) cash budgets, (3) revenue-and-expense budgets, (4) production budgets, (5) materials purchase/usage budgets, (6) human resource budgets, and (7) capital expenditure budgets.

Budgets function as a natural part of controlling. Managers use budgets to compare planned expenditures to actual expenditures, and they take corrective action if the deviation is significant. Three key financial ratios are gross profit margin, profit margin, and return on equity. Economic value added (EVA) is another useful way of measuring the financial performance of a firm.

6 Explain how managers and business owners manage cash flow and control costs, and use nontraditional measures of financial performance. Closely tied in with the cash budget is the special attention managers pay to cash flow. Cash flow measures how much actual cash is available for conducting business. The three sections of a cash-flow statement are cash provided by (or used in) operating activities, financing activities, and investing activities. A firm that writes off many income deductions will have a bigger cash flow. Many companies trim costs to improve cash flow.

Many researchers and managers no longer rely exclusively on financial ratios and related indices to measure the health of a firm. Instead, they use a balanced scorecard that measures the various aspects of an organization's performance.

Activity-based costing offers another approach to measuring financial performance that goes beyond traditional measures. The method focuses on the activities performed and the resources used to deliver a product or service. Another approach to determining a firm's wealth measures intellectual capital or the brainpower of a firm.

7 Outline the basics of an information system. An information system (IS), or management information system (MIS), is a formal system for providing management with information useful or necessary for making decisions. To develop an IS, first analyze the information requirements, then develop an information base, design an information processing system, and build controls into the system. An IS tracks a wide range of data used for control purposes. The data warehouse is a type of information system used in the retailing industry to collect important data from various sources.

Information systems are also used for the electronic monitoring of the work habits and productivity of employees. Although the method helps managers monitor employee performance, it has met with considerable criticism. Electronic monitoring works best when its results are used for constructive feedback.

8 Specify several characteristics of effective controls.

An effective control system results in improved job performance and productivity, because it helps people correct problems. An effective control measure is accepted by workers, appropriate, provides diagnostic information, allows for self-feedback and self-control, and provides timely information. It also allows employees some control over the behavior measured, does not embody contradictory measures, allows for random variation, and is cost-effective. Teams can sometimes select their own relevant control measures.

KEY TERMS AND PHRASES

Preventive control, *411*

Concurrent control, *411*

Feedback control, *411*

External control strategy, *411*

Internal control strategy, *413*

Standard, *413*

Deviation, *415*

Qualitative control technique, *417*

Quantitative control technique, *417*

Budget, *418*

Master budget, *419*

Cash budget, *419*

Revenue-and-expense budget, *419*

Production budget, *420*

Materials purchase/usage budget, *420*

Human resource budget, *420*

Capital expenditure budget, *420*

Gross profit margin, *422*

Profit margin, *422*

Return on equity, *422*

Economic value added (EVA), *422*

Cash flow, *423*

Balanced scorecard, *426*

Activity-based costing (ABC), *427*

Intellectual capital, *427*

Information system
(or management information system), *428*

QUESTIONS

1. Why don't managers who are great controllers generally receive as much publicity as managers who are great leaders?

2. In several companies, a performance standard for maintenance technicians is to have relatively few demands for service from the manufacturing department. Explain the logic behind this performance standard.

3. Why is it so difficult for managers and financial analysts to assign a precise value to intellectual capital?

4. How does EVA give a company a more accurate picture of its profitability?

5. How can you apply cash flow analysis to better control your personal finances?

6. Provide an example of how feedback from customers can be used as part of a control system.

7. How can a manager use the Internet as an information system?

CRITICAL THINKING QUESTIONS

1. Tony works full-time as a computer-repair technician who makes on-site repairs for individuals and small businesses. He says his gross profit margin is 94% because last year his total revenues were $100,000 and his expenses were $6,000. "I'm actually doing better than Microsoft. They talk about gross profit margins of 80%," says Tony. What is wrong with Tony's estimate of his gross profit margin?

2. Identify three types of cost cutting that hurt companies financially, such as reducing customer service. To answer this question, use your imagination but also obtain some input from an experienced manager.

SKILL-BUILDING EXERCISE: Financial Ratios

Jessica Albanese invested a $50,000 inheritance as equity in a franchise print and copy shop. Similar to well-established national franchises, the shop also offers desktop publishing, fax, and computer graphics services. Jessica's revenue-and-expense statement for her first year of operation follows:

Item	Financial Result
Revenues	$255,675
Beginning inventory	15,500
Purchases	88,000
End inventory	14,200
Cost of goods sold	89,300

Gross profit	166,375
Salaries expense	47,000
Rents and utilities expense	6,500
Miscellaneous expense	1,100
Maintenance expense	750
Total operating expenses	55,350
Net income before taxes	111,025
Taxes (40%)	44,410
Net income	66,615

Working individually or in small groups, compute the following ratios: gross profit margin, profit margin (return on sales), and return on equity. Groups might compare answers. Discuss whether you think that Jessica is operating a worthwhile business.

INTERNET SKILL-BUILDING EXERCISE: Analyzing Profit Margins

Imagine yourself as a potential investor in companies of your choice. Your Internet assignment is to obtain future earnings estimates for six companies in which you might choose to invest. For each of these companies, calculate their profit margin (net income divided by sales). Earning estimates might simply state profits that can be interpreted as net income. You can most likely find the earnings estimates you seek by trying these Web sites:

First Call available at http://www.thomsoninvest.net
I/B/E/S available at http://www.fool.com
Zacks Investment Research available at http://www.zacks.com

If these sites are not accessible, find other sources of earnings estimates using your favorite search engines.

CASE PROBLEM 15-A: The Squeeze on Palm

Not too long ago, Carl J. Yankowski, the chief executive of Palm was in his glory. The highly esteemed marketing executive stood at the helm of a company with a 75 percent share of the growing market for personal digital assistants. Consumers bought 13 million units during a five-year span. Furthermore, Palm licensed its operating system to several competitors.

Then came trouble. A series of management miscalculations, tough competition, and weak market conditions left the company in turmoil. Sales plunged, with mounting losses and Palm bleeding cash. At the same time Palm needed millions to update its technology to fend off a renewed challenge from Microsoft. A research analyst commented, "This company got into trouble so fast it makes your head spin."

Investors ran away from Palm. By June 2001 the stock price plunged more than 90 percent from its high. Some analysts believe that Palm may be a candidate for takeover, with Apple Computer Inc. and IBM as potential buyers.

Like many telecommunication firms, Palm was caught off-guard by the industry slowdown in Fall 2000. Coming off

five consecutive quarters of triple-digit growth in the number of units sold, Palm increased production in late November 2000 to meet what it thought would be a continued growth in demand. However, as consumers became more reluctant to make discretionary purchases in January 2001, sales of low-end Palm models softened. At the same time, competitors began to nibble into Palm's market share. Colorful, low-price models—such as those made by Handspring—made successful inroads into the market.

Another setback for Palm came when hand-held makers using the Microsoft PocketPC operating systems began to attract buyers with more powerful personal digital assistants and clearer screens. The PocketPC-based systems quickly grabbed 26 percent of the U.S. market for hand-helds in the $350 range and up. The most profitable palm-size computers are found in this market. Palm was making about $150 profit on each sale of the top-of-the-line $399 V compared with only $26 for the $149 entry-level m100 model.

Delayed product availability also created problems for

Palm. To compete with a new Handspring model, Yankowski moved up the announcement of two new Palm models to replace the best-selling Palm V line to March 2001. But after the product rollout was postponed until mid-May, Palm sales plunged.

As Yankowski ponders what to do next, he must trim ambitious growth plans and possibly sell a part of the company. "We are taking a hard look at more or less dramatically changing our business model," he concedes. Raising funds is a top priority. Palm's cash reserve was $700 million but it is rapidly dwindling. One plan to sell the new San Jose, California, site it recently bought for new headquarters for $238 million ran into a soft real estate market.

Palm management cancelled its acquisition of enterprise software developer Extended System Inc. The purpose of the deal was to give Palm an edge in the corporate market for hand-held network software. In contrast, Microsoft committed $300 million on new technology to gain a chunk of the market.

The management team notes that the new m500s and m505s are again helping to boost Palm's U.S. revenues. Yet Yankowski realizes that these new sales alone cannot rescue the company. He admits that Palm is a "work in progress."

Discussion Questions

1. What are your recommendations with respect to cost-cutting for Palm to help boost profitability?
2. Which business strategy (review Chapter 5) do you recommend for Palm?
3. Calculate the profit margins for the Palm V and the Palm m100 models.

Source: Adapted from Cliff Edwards, "Palm's Market Starts to Melt in Its Hands," *Business Week*, June 4, 2001, p. 42.

CASE PROBLEM 15-B: How Well Is EFTEK Doing?

EFTEK is a package engineering and design company, whose primary product is called the Water Ballast/Rinser System. The system helps soft drink bottling companies cope with the problem of top-heavy plastic bottles that tend to tip over before being filled at the plant. The result is that these bottles cannot be run through filling lines at anywhere near the speeds and efficiencies normally associated with glass or base-cup-equipped plastic bottles.

The heart of the patented system is injection of rinse water into the bottles in quantities sufficient to act as ballast. The bottles can then be moved on standard glass conveyor lines at speeds in excess of 1,000 per minute. The bottles are then emptied of rinse water, rinsed again, and then filled and capped.

The enhancement pays for itself financially in less than six months, making it appealing to cost-conscious managers at major bottlers like Coca-Cola, PepsiCo, and Perrier. A group of financial analysts estimates the potential market for the ballaster in the United States and Canada to be 4,000 packagers of beverage products, plus another 6,000 units internationally. A portion of projected financial information for EFTEK for the next fiscal year follows.

Units Sold	150
NET SALES	$21,235,500
Cost of Goods	8,167,500
GROSS PROFIT	13,068,000
Gross Margin	61.5%

Discussion Questions

1. Do you think EFTEK has a product that meets customer requirements?
2. Apply financial ratio analysis to decide whether EFTEK is projected to have outstanding financial results.

Source: *Letter from the Publisher*, Berkshire Information Services, Inc., One Evertrust Plaza, Jersey City, N.J. 07032. E-mail: berkshire@growth.com.

ENDNOTES

1. Mark Henricks, "Beneath the Surface," *Entrepreneur*, October 1999, p. 108, 113.
2. C. Pascal Zachary, *Showstopper! The Breakthrough Race to Create Windows NT and the Next Generation of Microsoft* (New York: The Free Press, 1994).
3. Richard O. Mason and E. Burton Swanson, "Measurement for Management Decision: A Perspective," *California Management Review*, Spring 1979, pp. 70–81.
4. Belverd E. Needles Jr., Henry R. Anderson, and James C. Caldwell, *Principles of Accounting*, 4th ed. (Boston: Houghton Mifflin, 1990), pp. 1099–1113.
5. "Master the Art of Budget Projection," *WorkingSMART*, March 1999, p. 6.
6. Don Delves, "EVA® for the non-MBA," *HRfocus*, December 1998, p. 7.
7. "Eli Lilly Is Making Shareholders Rich. How? By Linking Pay to EVA," *Fortune*, September 9, 1996, p. 173.
8. Anne Tergesen, "The Ins and Outs of Cash Flow," *Business Week*, January 22, 2001.
9. Personal communication from Ashok J. Robin, Rochester Institute of Technology, 1999.
10. De'Ann Weimer, "Put the Comeback on My Card," *Business Week*, November 10, 1997, pp. 120–121.

11. Robert S. Kaplan and David P. Norton, "Using the Balanced Score-card as a Strategic Management System," *Harvard Business Review*, January–February 1996, pp. 75-77;

12. Angela Padgett, "Life in the Balance," *sas com*, January/February 2001, pp. 28–31.

13. Robin Cooper and Robert S. Kaplan, "The Promise—and Peril—of Integrated Cost Systems," *Harvard Business Review*, July–August 1998, p. 111.

14. Thomas A. Stewart, "Accounting Gets Radical," *Fortune*, April 16, 2001, p. 188. The discussion of intellectual capital is based on the entire article, pp. 184–194.

15. Stewart, "Accounting Gets Radical," p. 192.

16. David Kirkpatrick, "Back to the Future with Centralized Computing," *Fortune*, November 10, 1997, p. 96.

17. Adam Pilarski, "Computers—Headache or Panacea?" *Business Forum*, Spring–Fall 1997, p. 75; updated in Shelia M. Puffer, "Continental Airlines' CEO Gordon Bethune on Teams and New Product Development," *Academy of Management Executive*, August 1999, p. 31.

18. Christopher Meyer, "How the Right Measures Help the Team Excel," Harvard *Business Review*, May–June 1994, p. 96.

19. Marck C. Maletz and Nitin Nohria, "Managing in the Whitespace," *Harvard Business Review*, February 2001, pp. 102–111.

Managing Ineffective Performers

Charlie Henderson, the manager of a suburban branch of the Motor Vehicle Department, enjoyed the changes in the culture of the MVD during the past decade. For many years the majority of people who had personal contact with the Motor Vehicle Department perceived its employees as callous and indifferent. The attitude of many employees seemed to be, "If you don't like doing business with us, it's your tough luck. We have no competition." During the last decade, MVD emphasized treating citizens like valued customers. Most of the MVD employees now smile at customers, and say hello and thank you.

Henderson worries, however, about Diane Stephano, a specialist who gathers credentials from first-time applicants for an operator's license. Aside from receiving written complaints about Stephano's impatience with customers, Henderson observed her in several harsh dialogs with them. Henderson mentioned several times to Stephano that she needs to be more patient and understanding with applicants. A recent incident in which a teenage girl left the bureau crying prompted a face-to-face meeting with Stephano in Henderson's office.

Henderson began the meeting by asking: "Diane, how well have you been getting along with our customers—and taxpayers—lately?"

"Nothing too bad, Charlie," replied Diane. "We've got a lot of nice people out there, and I treat them pretty well. But some of those other people have a bad attitude, and I let them have it right back."

"Hold on, Diane," said Charlie. "Am I hearing correctly that how a citizen treats you determines your behavior toward that person?"

OBJECTIVES

After studying this chapter and doing the exercises, you should be able to:

1 Identify factors contributing to poor performance.

2 Describe the control model for managing ineffective performers.

3 Know what is required to coach and constructively criticize employees.

4 Understand how to discipline employees.

5 Develop an approach to dealing with difficult people, including cynics.

6 Explain the recommended approach to terminating employees.

Chapter 16

442

Diane said, "I guess you could say that. I'm a citizen too, and I have the right to be treated with the highest respect."

Charlie replied, "It appears we might have an opportunity here for improvement. Applicants for a first-time license, and their parents, are usually nervous about the situation. Like that girl who ran away crying. She must have been pretty nervous. As a DMV employee who deals directly with customers, it is your responsibility to control the situation and be positive."

"Are you saying, Charlie, that the customers have more rights than I do? That I have a responsibility to them, and they don't have a responsibility to me?"

"I can see that you are upset with some of the customers. But keep in mind that the Motor Vehicles Department pledges itself to a high level of customer service. So our job is helping and pleasing citizens. I cannot control whether these same people are committed to being civil toward us."

"I'm getting to see your point a little," said Diane. "Maybe I could be a little friendlier in spots."

**ineffective job
performance**

*Job performance that lowers
productivity below an acceptable standard.*

The interchange between the supervisor and the MVD specialist illustrates another important responsibility of a manager: coaching employees whose performance and behavior fall below acceptable levels. Managerial control requires dealing constructively with **ineffective job performance**, defined as performance that does not meet standards for the position. Ineffective performers are also referred to as problem employees because they create problems for management.

Ineffective performers lower organizational performance directly by not accomplishing their fair share of work. They also lower organizational productivity indirectly. Poor performers decrease the productivity of their superiors by consuming managerial time. Additionally, the productivity of coworkers is often decreased because coworkers must take over some of the ineffective performer's tasks.

The consequences of ineffective performance are enormous. For example, one set of factors contributing to poor performance is employee deviancy. It includes behaviors such as stealing, cheating, and substance abuse. These factors produce organizational losses estimated to range from $7 billion to $230 billion annually.[1] In this chapter, we address ineffective performance as a control problem for which the manager can take corrective actions. However, control of performance might also involve effective leading, motivating, and staffing.

1   FACTORS CONTRIBUTING TO INEFFECTIVE PERFORMANCE

Identify factors contributing
to poor performance.

Employees are or become ineffective performers for many different reasons. The cause of poor performance can be rooted in the person, the job, the manager, or the company. At times, the employee's personal traits and behaviors create so much disturbance that he or she is perceived as ineffective. Performance is sometimes classified as ineffective, or substandard, because of an arbitrary standard set by management. For example, Enron managers meet twice a year to classify the performance of workers over the past six months. Employees are rated on a five-point scale, with the top 5% designated superior; next 30% excellent; 30% strong; 20% satisfactory; and 15% needs improvement. Any employee described as needing improvement has six months to reach standard performance, or be dismissed. Employees refer to this system as rank and yank.[2] A problem with labeling the bottom 15% as needing improvement is that a company might have a large number of talented people, with even the lowest 15% doing satisfactory work.

Exhibit 16-1 summarizes factors that can contribute to ineffective performance. Factors not listed here can also be contributors. These factors fall into one of four categories: personal, or related to the job, manager, or company. Usually, the true cause of ineffective performance is a combination of several factors. Assume that an employee is late for work so frequently that his or her performance becomes substandard. The contributing factors in this situation could be the worker's disrespect for work rules, an unchallenging job, and an unduly harsh supervisor. One factor may be more important than others, but they are all contributors.

A manager and a company can contribute significantly to ineffective performance through improper implementation of the various functions of management. For example, with poor planning and leadership, workers receive little guidance and may drift into poor work habits. Too much supervision can also cause problems. A system of tight controls can create enough stress to lower performance.

The following list expands on how the factors listed in Exhibit 16-1 are related to ineffective performance:

EXHIBIT 16-1

Factors Contributing to Ineffective Performance

Dozens of factors can lower job performance. The factors listed contribute to the majority of ineffective performance.

Factors Related to the Employee

Insufficient mental ability and education
Insufficient job knowledge
Job stress or burnout
Low motivation and loafing
Technological obsolescence
Excessive absenteeism and tardiness
Emotional problem or personality disorder
Alcoholism and drug addiction
Tobacco addiction or withdrawal symptoms
Conducting outside business on the job
Family and personal problems
Physical limitations
Preoccupying office romance

Factors Related to the Manager

Inadequate communication about job
    responsibilities
Inadequate feedback about job
    performance
Inappropriate leadership style
Bullying or intimidating manager

Factors Related to the Job

Ergonomics problems and cumulative
    trauma disorder
Repetitive, physically demanding job
    including heavy travel
Built-in conflict
Substandard industrial hygiene
A "sick" building

Factors Related to the Organization

Organizational culture that tolerates poor
    performance
Counterproductive work environment
Negative work group influences
Violence or threats of violence
Sexual harassment

The Employee

- *Insufficient mental ability and education.* The employee lacks the problem-solving ability necessary to do the job. Poor communication skills are included here such as not being able to read instructions or speak clearly to customers and coworkers.
- *Insufficient job knowledge.* The employee is a substandard performer because he or she comes to the job with insufficient training or experience.
- *Job stress and burnout.* Severe short-term stress leads to errors in concentration and judgment. As a result of prolonged job stress, an employee may become apathetic, negative, and impatient. He or she can no longer generate the energy to perform effectively.
- *Low motivation and loafing.* An employee who is poorly motivated will often not sustain enough effort to accomplish the amount of work required to meet standards. Closely related to low motivation is goofing off and loafing. Sixty-three percent of human resource managers who responded to a survey said that employees are spending too much time surfing the Net or engaging in some other diversionary activity, such as making personal phone calls and running personal errands during working hours.[3]
- *Technological obsolescence.* The employee does not keep up with the state of the art in his or her field. He or she avoids using new ideas and techniques and becomes ineffective.
- *Excessive absenteeism and tardiness.* The employee is often not at work for a variety of personal or health reasons. Lost time leads to low productivity.
- *Emotional problem or personality disorder.* The employee may have emotional outbursts, periods of depression, or other abnormal behaviors that interfere with human relationships and work concentration. Cynical behavior may lower the performance of an entire work group if the negative attitude spreads to others.
- *Alcoholism and drug addiction.* The employee cannot think clearly because his or her mental or physical condition has been temporarily or permanently impaired by alcohol or other drugs. Attendance is also likely to suffer.
- *Tobacco addiction or withdrawal symptoms.* The employee who smokes is often fatigued and takes so many cigarette breaks that his or her work is disrupted. Sick leave may also increase. Even workers who stop smoking may suffer performance problems for a while. Recent quitters report depression, anxiety, lower job satisfaction, more job tension, and increased short-term absence.[4]
- *Conducting outside business on the job.* The employee may be an "office entrepreneur" who sells merchandise to coworkers or spends time on the phone and e-mail working on investments or other outside interests. Time spent on these activities lowers productivity.
- *Family and personal problems.* The employee is unable to work at full capacity because of preoccupation with an off-the-job problem such as a marital dispute, conflict with children, a broken romance, or indebtedness.
- *Physical limitations.* Job performance decreases as a result of injury or illness. For example, in the United States, lower-back problems account for approximately 8 million lost workdays a year and is a major source of worker compensation claims.[5]
- *Preoccupying office romance.* For many people, a new romance is an energizing force that creates positive stress, resulting in a surge in energy directed toward

work. For others, an office romance becomes a preoccupation that detracts from concentration. Time spent together in conversation and long lunch breaks can lower productivity.

The Job

- *Ergonomics problems and repetitive motion disorder.* If equipment or furniture used on the job contributes to fatigue, discomfort, or injury, performance problems result. For example, if an employee develops neck pain and eyestrain from working at a poorly designed computer configuration, performance will suffer. As described in Chapter 8 about job design, repetitive motion disorder, including carpal tunnel syndrome, is a major problem stemming from poorly designed or poorly utilized computer equipment.
- *Repetitive, physically demanding job.* A repetitive, physically demanding job can cause the employee to become bored and fatigued, leading to lowered performance.
- *Built-in conflict.* The nature of the job involves so much conflict that job stress lowers performance. The position of collection agent for a consumer-loan company might fit this category.
- *Night-shift work assignments.* Employees assigned to all-night shifts suffer many more mental lapses and productivity losses than those assigned to daytime or evening shifts.
- *Substandard industrial hygiene.* Excessive noise, fumes, uncomfortable temperatures, inadequate lighting, high humidity, and fear of injury or contamination engender poor performance.
- *A "sick" building.* In some office buildings a diverse range of airborne particles, vapors, and gases pollute the indoor environment. The result can be headaches, nausea, and respiratory infections. Performance suffers and absenteeism increases.[6]

The Manager

- *Inadequate communication about job responsibilities.* The employee performs poorly because he or she lacks a clear picture of what the manager expects.
- *Inadequate feedback about job performance.* The employee makes a large number of errors because he or she does not receive the feedback—early enough or at all—to prevent them.
- *Inappropriate leadership style.* The employee performs poorly because the manager's leadership style is inappropriate to the employee's needs. For example, an immature employee's manager gives him or her too much freedom and the result is poor performance. This employee needs closer supervision. Related to leadership style is the problem of some managers unwittingly setting up a group member to fail. The manager perceives a given group member as mediocre, and that person lives down to the manager's expectations, perhaps because the group member loses some self-confidence.[7]
- *Bullying or intimidating manager.* Many employees perceive that they are intimidated and bullied by their managers to the point that they cannot work effectively. Bullying and intimidation go far beyond being firm and setting high

standards. They include such behaviors as publicly insulting group members, frequent yelling, and insensitivity toward personal requests, such as time off to handle a severe personal problem.[8]

The Company

- *Organizational culture that tolerates poor performance.* Suppose an organization has a history of not imposing sanctions on employees who perform poorly. When managers demand better performance, many employees may not respond to the new challenge.
- *Counterproductive work environment.* The employee lacks the proper tools, support, budget, or authority to accomplish the job. An example would be a sales representative who does not have an entertainment budget sufficient to meet customers' expectations.
- *Negative work group influences.* Group pressures restrain good performance or the work group penalizes a high-performance worker. Similarly, peer group social pressure may cause an employee to take overly long lunch breaks, neglecting job responsibilities. A study conducted in 20 organizations showed that antisocial behaviors such as lying, spreading rumors, loafing, and absenteeism were more frequent when coworkers exhibited the same behavior.[9]
- *Intentional threats to job security.* A company, for example, makes excessive work demands on an employee in the context of a veiled threat that the job will be eliminated unless the extra work is done. Performance suffers as the worker becomes fearful and anxious.
- *Violence or the threat of violence.* Employees witness violent behavior in the workplace such as physical assaults, knifings, shootings, or threats of violence. Many employees not directly affected are nevertheless distracted and fearful, leading to lowered productivity.
- *Sexual harassment.* The employee who is sexually harassed usually experiences enough stress to decrease concentration and performance in general. The person who commits sexual harassment and is under investigation for or charged with the act is likely to experience stress and preoccupation about the charges.

behavior mismatch

A condition that occurs when one person's actions do not meet another's expectations.

Many performance problems just described can be viewed from the perspective of a **behavior mismatch**. Such a mismatch happens when one person's actions do not meet another's expectations.[10] In the present context, it is the group member's actions and the manager's expectations. A lack of understanding between the manager and the group member that stems from their different perspectives leads to different expectations. The perception of poor performance results from differing views and expectations.

Assume that a group member is experiencing the problem of a personal bankruptcy. His perception is that because he has personal problems, less should be expected of him. Perhaps he believes that 75 percent of his usual productivity is adequate performance. Yet his supervisor perceives him as not meeting job expectations.

You are invited to take the self-quiz in Exhibit 16-2 to ponder tendencies of your own that could ultimately contribute to substandard performance. Many sports figures, elected officials, and business executives experience the problems pinpointed in the questionnaire.

2   THE CONTROL MODEL FOR MANAGING INEFFECTIVE PERFORMERS

Describe the control model for managing ineffective performers.

The approach to improving ineffective performance presented here follows the logic of the control process shown in Exhibit 16-3. Problem identification and

EXHIBIT **16-2**

The Self-Sabotage
Questionnaire

Directions: Indicate how accurately each of the following statements describes or characterizes you, using a five-point scale: (0) very inaccurately, (1) inaccurately, (2) midway between inaccurately and accurately, (3) accurately, (4) very accurately. Consider discussing some of the questions with a family member, close friend, or work associate. Another person's feedback may prove helpful in providing accurate answers to some of the questions.

Answer

1. Other people have said that I am my worst enemy. _____
2. If I don't do a perfect job, I feel worthless. _____
3. I am my own harshest critic. _____
4. When engaged in a sport or other competitive activity, I find a way to blow a substantial lead right near the end. _____
5. When I make a mistake, I can usually identify another person to blame. _____
6. I have a sincere tendency to procrastinate. _____
7. I have trouble focusing on what is really important to me. _____
8. I have trouble taking criticism, even from friends. _____
9. My fear of seeming stupid often prevents me from asking questions or offering my opinion. _____
10. I tend to expect the worst in most situations. _____
11. Many times I have rejected people who treat me well. _____
12. When I have an important project to complete, I usually get sidetracked, and then miss the deadline. _____
13. I choose work assignments that lead to disappointments even when better options are clearly available. _____
14. I frequently misplace things such as my keys, then get very angry at myself. _____
15. I am concerned that if I take on much more responsibility people will expect too much from me. _____
16. I avoid situations, such as competitive sports, where people can find out how good or bad I really am. _____
17. People describe me as the "office clown." _____
18. I have an insatiable demand for money and power. _____
19. When negotiating with others, I hate to grant any concessions. _____
20. I seek revenge for even the smallest hurts. _____
21. I have a blinding ego. _____
22. When I receive a compliment or other form of recognition, I usually feel I don't deserve it. _____
23. To be honest, I choose to suffer. _____
24. I regularly enter into conflict with people who try to help me. _____
25. I'm a loser. _____

Total score _____

Scoring and interpretation: Add your answers to all the questions to obtain your total score. Your total score provides an approximate index of your tendencies toward being self-sabotaging or self-defeating. The higher your score, the more probable it is that you create conditions to bring about your own setbacks, disappointments, and failures. The lower your score, the less likely it is that you are a self-saboteur.

0–25: You appear to have few tendencies toward self-sabotage. If this interpretation is supported by your own positive feelings toward your life and yourself, you are in good shape with respect to self-defeating behavior tendencies. However, stay alert to potential self-sabotaging tendencies that could develop at later stages in your career.

26–50: You may have some mild tendencies toward self-sabotage. It could be that you do things occasionally that defeat your own purposes. A person in this category, for example, might write an angry memo to an executive expressing disagreement with a decision that adversely affects his or her operation. Review actions you have taken during the past six months to decide if any of them have been self-sabotaging.

51–75: You show signs of engaging in self-sabotage. You probably have thoughts, and carry out actions, that could be blocking you from achieving important work and personal goals. People whose scores place them in this category characteristically engage in negative self-talk that lowers their self-confidence and makes them appear weak and indecisive to others. For example, "I'm usually not good at learning new things." People in this range frequently experience another problem. They sometimes sabotage their chances of succeeding on a project just to prove that their negative self-assessment is correct.

76–100: You most likely have a strong tendency toward self-sabotage. (Sometimes it is possible to obtain a high score on a test like this because you are going through an unusually stressful period in your life.) You might discuss your tendencies toward undermining your own achievements with a mental health professional.

problem solving lie at the core of this approach. The control process for managing ineffective performers is divided into the eight steps illustrated in Exhibit 16-3, and should usually be followed in sequence. This section will describe each of these steps in detail. Another key method of improving ineffective performance—employee discipline—receives separate attention later in the chapter.

Two cautions are in order in using the control model for improving ineffective performance. First, the model may need slight modification to follow company procedures. Company policy, for example, might establish certain procedures about documenting poor performance and reporting it immediately to higher levels of management. Second, the control process is designed to deal with mental illness. An employee who suddenly begins to neglect the job because of a sudden change in personality should be referred immediately to a human resource specialist. (The personality change could be related to depression or a bipolar disorder that results in wide mood swings.) The specialist, in turn, will make an appropriate referral to a mental health professional.

Define Performance Standards

Penalizing employees for not achieving performance standards without first carefully communicating those standards is unfair. Therefore, the first step in the control model for managing ineffective performers is to clearly define what is expected of employees. (This step matches the step labeled "Set Standards" in the controlling process shown in Exhibit 16-3.) Performance standards are commonly established by such means as job descriptions, work goals, production quotas, and formal discussions of what is to be accomplished in a position.

Detect Deviation from Acceptable Performance

Detection is the process of noting when an employee's performance deviates from an acceptable standard. Managers use the various control measures described in Chapter 15 to detect deviations from acceptable performance. For performance to be considered ineffective or poor, it must deviate significantly from the norm.

EXHIBIT 16-3

The Control Model for Managing Ineffective Performers

The most systematic and effective method for bringing ineffective performance up to standard is to follow the control process, referred to in this application as the control model.

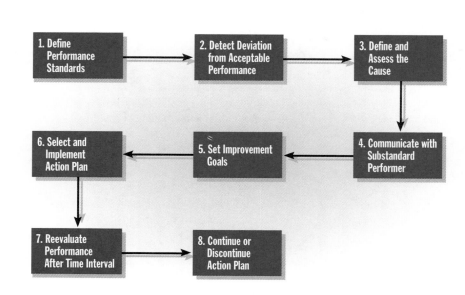

1. Define Performance Standards
2. Detect Deviation from Acceptable Performance
3. Define and Assess the Cause
4. Communicate with Substandard Performer
5. Set Improvement Goals
6. Select and Implement Action Plan
7. Reevaluate Performance After Time Interval
8. Continue or Discontinue Action Plan

At times, quantitative measures can be used to define ineffective performance. For some jobs, ineffective performance might begin at 30 percent below standard. For other jobs, the cutoff point could be 20 or 50 percent, or any other percentage of deviation that fits the situation. What percentage of deviation from standard do you think would be acceptable for a quality inspector? For a loan specialist in a bank?

Personal observation plays a key role in detecting ineffective performance. One reason that observation is so important is that it is a concurrent control. By the time quantitative indicators of poor performance have been collected, substantial damage may have been done. Assume a bank manager observes that one of the loan officers is taking unduly long lunch hours on Fridays. Upon return, the officer appears to be under the influence of alcohol. Eventually, this unacceptable behavior will show up in quantitative indicators of performance. However, it might take a year to collect these data.

Define and Assess the Cause

At this stage the manager attempts to diagnose the real cause of the problem. Following the logic of Exhibit 16-1, the primary contributor to the problem could be a personal factor or a factor related to the job, the company, or the manager. A discussion with the employee (the next step in the control mode) may be necessary to reveal the major cause of the problem. For example, an office assistant was absent so frequently that her performance suffered. She claimed that extensive photocopying made her sick. The supervisor investigated further and called in the company health and safety expert. A medical examination confirmed that the office assistant was allergic to the trace fumes from the toner in the large-volume photocopier. After the office assistant was reassigned, her attendance became satisfactory.

Communicate with the Substandard Performer

After detecting unacceptable performance or behavior, the manager must communicate concern to the worker. At times, a simple discussion will suffice. At other times, a more sensitive form of feedback may be necessary. **Confrontation** means dealing with a controversial or emotional topic directly. Confrontation is necessary whenever the employee does not readily admit to experiencing a problem.

Managers often avoid confrontation for several reasons. They may have limited skill in criticizing employees. Or, they may prefer not to deal with the anger and resentment that confrontation is likely to trigger. A third reason is not wanting to make the employee feel uncomfortable.

A recommended confrontation technique is to communicate an attitude of concern about the confronted person's welfare. To use this technique, confront the person in a sincere and thoughtful manner. Using the words *care* and *concern* can be helpful. For instance, a manager might begin by saying: "The reason I'm bringing up this problem is that I care about your work. You have a good record with the company, and I'm concerned that your performance has slipped way below its former level."

confrontation
Dealing with a controversial or emotional topic directly.

Set Improvement Goals

The fifth step in the control model is to set improvement goals. An **improvement goal** is one that, if attained, will correct unacceptable deviation from a performance standard. The goals should be documented on paper or electronically. Improvement

improvement goal
A goal that, if attained, will correct unacceptable deviation from a performance standard.

goals should have the same characteristics as other objectives (see Chapter 5). Above all, improvement goals should specify the behavior or result that is required. Vague improvement goals are not likely to cause changes in performance.

An example of a specific improvement goal is: "During this month, nine of your ten customer service reports must be in on time." This specific goal is likely to be more effective than a general improvement goal, such as "Become more prompt in submitting customer service reports."

If the ineffective performer expresses an interest in improvement, joint goal setting is advisable. By providing input into goal setting, the substandard performer stands a good chance of becoming committed to improvement. At times, managers need to impose improvement goals on substandard performers, especially in cases involving a motivation problem. If substandard employees were interested in setting improvement goals, they would not have a motivation problem.

Select and Implement an Action Plan

The setting of improvement goals leads logically to the selection and implementation of action plans to attain those goals. Much of the art of remedying ineffective performance is contained in this step. Unless appropriate action plans are developed, no real improvement is likely to take place. Many attempts at improving substandard performance fail because the problem is discussed and then dropped. Thus the employee has no concrete method of making the necessary improvements.

Types of Action Plans

An action plan for improvement can include almost any sensible approach tailored to the specific problem. An action plan could be formulated to deal with every cause of ineffective performance listed in Exhibit 16-1.

Action plans for improving ineffective performance can be divided into two types. One type is within the power of the manager to develop and implement. Plans of this type include coaching, encouraging, and offering small incentives for improvement. The other type of action plan is offered by the organization or purchased on the outside, and include training programs, stress management programs, and stays at alcoholism-treatment centers. Exhibit 16-4 lists a selection of feasible corrective actions.

When attempting to improve ineffective performance resulting from a variety of personal problems, the preferred action plan for many managers is to refer the troubled worker to an **employee assistance program (EAP)**. The EAP is an organization-sponsored service to help employees deal with personal and job-related problems that interfere with job performance. An employee assistance program is staffed by professionals who specialize in dealing with particular problems. Many companies that do not have an EAP of their own refer employees to such a program that serves firms in the area.

When supervisors refer employees to the EAP, workplace problems should be the focus. The supervisor should not say, "I am encouraging you to go to the EAP. The EAP can help you with any personal problems you may have." Say instead, "I encourage you to go to the EAP. The EAP may be able to help you solve your workplace problems."[12] The second approach usually creates less defensiveness than the first.

Employees and their families use assistance programs to cope with a variety of personal and family problems and illnesses. Among them are alcoholism and other

employee assistance program (EAP)

An organization-sponsored service to help employees deal with personal and job-related problems that hinder performance.

substance abuse, financial and legal difficulties, emotional problems, chronic illness such as AIDS or cancer, compulsive gambling, and weight control. Employees also use EAPs to deal with job-related concerns such as work stress, chronic job dissatisfaction, and sexual harassment.

Implementation of the Action Plan

After the action plan is chosen, it must be implemented. As shown in Exhibit 16-3, implementation begins in step 6 and continues through step 8. The manager utilizes the approaches listed under "Managerial Actions and Techniques" in Exhibit 16-4. Human resources specialists outside the manager's department usually implement organizational programs.

An important part of effective implementation is continuation of the remedial program. Given the many pressures facing a manager, it is easy to forget the substandard performer who needs close supervision or a motivational boost. Often, a brief conversation is all that is needed.

EXHIBIT 16-4 | 451

Corrective Actions for Ineffective Performers

When attempting to bring ineffective performers up to standard or beyond, managers can either take action by themselves or refer employees to a company program designed to help them with performance problems.

Managerial Actions and Techniques

- **Coaching.** The manager points out specifically what the performer could be doing better or should stop doing. In daily interaction with the team members, the manager makes suggestions for improvement. One estimate is that coaching takes approximately 85 percent of the time a manager spends on performance improvement.[11]

- **Closer supervision.** The manager works more closely with the subordinate, offering frequent guidance and feedback.

- **Reassignment or transfer.** The manager reassigns the ineffective performer to a position that he or she can handle better.

- **Use of motivational techniques.** The manager attempts to improve employee motivation by using positive reinforcement or some other motivational technique.

- **Corrective discipline.** The manager informs the employee that his or her behavior is unacceptable and that corrections must be made if the worker is to remain employed by the firm. The employee is counseled as part of corrective discipline.

- **Temporary leave.** The manager offers the employee an opportunity to take a leave of absence for a specified time in order to resolve the problems causing the poor performance.

- **Lower performance standards.** If performance standards have been too high, the manager lowers expectations of the team member. Consultation with higher management would probably be necessary before implementing this step.

- **Job rotation.** If ineffective performance results from staleness or burnout, changing to a different job of comparable responsibility may prove helpful.

Organizational Programs

- **Employee assistance programs (EAPS).** The employee is referred to a counseling service specializing in rehabilitating employees whose personal problems interfere with work.

- **Wellness programs.** The organization encourages employees to participate in specialized programs that help them stay physically and mentally healthy. By doing so, employees may prevent or cope with health problems—such as heart disease or an eating disorder—that interfere with job performance or lead to absenteeism. The wellness program usually includes stress management.

- **Career counseling and outplacement.** The employee receives professional assistance in solving a career problem, including being counseled on finding a job outside the firm.

- **Job redesign.** Specialists in human resource management and industrial engineering redesign job elements that could be causing poor performance. For example, the job is changed so that the employee has less direct contact with others, leading to reduced conflict.

- **Training and development programs.** The employee is assigned to a training or development program linked directly to his or her performance deficiency. For example, a reserved sales representative receives assertiveness training.

Reevaluate Performance After a Time Interval

Step 7 in the controlling process helps ensure that the process is working. In this step the manager measures the employee's current performance. If the remedial process is working, the team member's performance will move up toward standard. The greater the performance problem, the more frequent the reevaluations of performance should be. In instances of behavior problems, such as alcoholism, weekly performance checks are advisable.

Formal and Informal Reviews

A reevaluation of performance can be formal or informal. A formal progress review takes the form of a performance appraisal session. It might include written documentation of the employee's progress and samples of his or her work. Formal reviews are particularly important when the employee has been advised that dismissal is pending unless improvements are made. Reviews are critical to avoid lawsuits over a dismissal.

The first level of informal review consists of checking on whether the employee has started the action plan. For example, suppose a reserved sales representative agreed to attend an assertiveness training program. One week later, the manager could ask the rep, "Have you signed up for or started the training program yet?"

The next level of informal review is a discussion of the employee's progress. The manager can ask casual questions such as, "How much progress have you made in accounting for the missing inventory?" Or the manager might ask, "Have you learned how to use the new diagnostic equipment yet?"

Positive Reinforcement and Punishment

If the employee makes progress toward reaching the improvement goal, positive reinforcement is appropriate. Rewarding an employee for progress is the most effective way of sustaining that progress. The reward might be praise, encouragement, or longer intervals between review sessions. The longer time between reviews may be rewarding because the employee will feel that he or she is "back to normal."

Giving rewards for making improvement generally proves more effective than giving punishments for not making improvement. Yet if the problem employee does not respond to positive motivators, some form of organizational punishment is necessary. More will be said about punishment in the discussion about employee discipline.

Continue or Discontinue the Action Plan

Step 8 in the control model for managing ineffective performers is making the decision whether to continue or discontinue the action plan. This step can be considered the feedback component of the control process. If the performance review indicates the employee is not meeting improvement goals, the action plan is continued. If the review indicates goal achievement, the action plan is discontinued.

An important part of using the control model to manage ineffective performers is realizing that positive changes may not be permanent. Performance is most likely to revert to an unacceptable level when the employee is faced with heavy job pressures. For instance, suppose an employee and a manager formulated an action plan to improve the employee's work habits. The employee's performance improved as a result. When the employee is under pressure, however, his or her work may once again become badly disorganized. The manager should then repeat the last five steps of the process, beginning with confrontation.

COACHING AND CONSTRUCTIVE CRITICISM

Most performance improvement takes place as a result of a manager dealing directly with the worker not meeting standards. The usual vehicle for bringing about this improvement is **coaching**. It is a method for helping employees perform better, which usually occurs on the spot and involves informal discussion and suggestions. Workplace coaching is much like coaching on the athletic field or in the performing arts. Coaching involves considerable **constructive criticism**, a form of criticism designed to help people improve. The same technique is sometimes referred to as constructive *direction* because the intent is to help people and set them in the right direction. To be a good coach, and to criticize constructively, requires considerable skill.

Business psychologists James Waldroop and Timothy Butler point out that good coaching is simply good management. Coaching requires the same skills that contribute to effective management such as keen observation skills, sound judgment, and an ability to take appropriate action. Also, coaching shares one goal of effective management: to make the most of human resources.[13] The following suggestions will help you improve your coaching skill if practiced carefully:

1. *Focus feedback on what is wrong with the work and behavior rather than the employee's attitude and personality.* A major principle of employee coaching is to focus on the substandard work behavior itself, not the person or his or her attitudes. When the feedback attacks a person's self-image, he or she is likely to become hostile. A defensive person is more likely to focus on getting even rather than getting better. Another way to upset the person being coached is to exaggerate the nature of the poor performance, such as saying, "You've committed the same mistake 100 times," when you have only observed the mistake four times.

2. *Listen actively and empathize.* An essential component of coaching employees requires careful listening to both their presentation of facts and feelings. Your listening will encourage the employee to talk. As the employee talks about his or her problem, you may develop a better understanding of how to improve performance. As you listen actively, the opportunity to show empathy will arise naturally. Suppose the employee blames being behind schedule on the servers being down so frequently. You might show empathy by saying, "Yes, I know it is frustrating to have a computer breakdown when faced with a deadline. Yet we all have to deal with this problem."

3. *Ask good questions.* An effective workplace coach asks questions that help people understand their needs for improvement. Start the coaching question by asking a question, thereby encouraging the person being coached to be an active participant immediately. Consultant Marilyn J. Darling says that effective coaching is based on asking good questions. She notes that the simpler the question, the better.

   - What are you trying to accomplish?
   - How will you know if you have succeeded?
   - What obstacles do you believe are stopping you?
   - How can I help you succeed?[14]

Know what is required to coach and constructively criticize employees.

coaching

A method for helping employees perform better, which usually occurs on the spot and involves informal discussion and suggestions.

constructive criticism

A form of criticism designed to help improve performance or behavior.

These questions contribute to active listening because they are open ended. An open-ended question requests that the person provide details rather than a Yes or No response. "What obstacles do you believe are stopping you?" is open ended because the worker must point to obstacles to answer the question. A closed question on the same topic would be "Are there any obstacles stopping you?" Such a question fails to promote dialog.

4. *Engage in joint problem solving.* Work together to resolve the performance problem. One reason joint problem solving is effective is that it conveys a helpful and constructive attitude on the part of the manager. Another is that the employee often needs the superior's assistance in overcoming work problems. The manager is in a better position to address certain problems than is the employee.

5. *Offer constructive advice.* Constructive advice can be useful to the employee with performance problems. A recommended way of giving advice is first to ask an insightful question. You might ask the employee, "Could the real cause of your problem be poor work habits?" If the employee agrees, you can then offer some specific advice about improving work habits.

   As part of giving advice it is more effective to suggest that a person do something rather than *try* to do something. For example, it is more persuasive to say, "Be at out staff meetings on time," than to say "Try to be at our staff meetings on time." "Trying" something gives a person an excuse not to succeed.

6. *Give the poor performer an opportunity to observe and model someone who exhibits acceptable performance.* A simple example of modeling would be for the manager to show the employee how to operate a piece of equipment properly. A more complex example of modeling would be to have the poor performer observe an effective employee making a sale or conducting a job interview. In each case the ineffective performer should be given opportunities to repeat the activity.

7. *Obtain a commitment to change.* Ineffective performers frequently agree to make improvements but are not really committed to change. At the end of a session, discuss the employee's true interest in changing. One clue that commitment may be lacking is when the employee too readily accepts everything you say about the need for change. Another clue is agreement about the need for change but with no display of emotion. In either case, further discussion is warranted.

8. *When feasible, conduct some coaching sessions outside of the performance review.* The coaching experience should focus on development and improvement whereas the performance review is likely to be perceived by the ineffective performer as a time for judging his or her performance. Despite perception, performance reviews should include an aspect of development.

Business (or executive) coaching described in Chapter 11 often takes the form of mentoring. This type of coaching supplements coaching received from a manager. Sometimes a company hires the coach because a high-level worker is having performance problems. At other times, an executive or other worker hires a coach to help develop skills needed for career advancement. Or the coach might be hired to present a fresh perspective on a problem the person faces, such as giving insight into whether to accept a job transfer.

4   EMPLOYEE DISCIPLINE

Understand how to discipline employees.

Up to this point, the chapter emphasized positive approaches to improving substandard performance. At times, however, using the control model requires a manager to discipline employees in an attempt to keep performance at an acceptable level. It is also part of an effective manager's role to be willing to take harsh and unpopular action when the situation requires such behavior. **Discipline**, in a general sense, is punishment used to correct or train. In organizations, discipline can be divided into two types.

Summary discipline is the immediate discharge of an employee because of a serious offense. The employee is fired on the spot for rule violations such as stealing, fighting, or selling illegal drugs on company premises. In unionized firms, the company and the union have a written agreement specifying which offenses are subject to summary discipline.

Corrective discipline allows employees to correct their behavior before punishment is applied. Employees are told that their behavior is unacceptable and that they must make corrections if they want to remain with the firm. The manager and the employee share the responsibility for solving the performance problem. The controlling process for managing ineffective performers includes corrective discipline. Steps 4 through 7 in Exhibit 16–3 are based on corrective discipline.

In a recent development in discipline, the group or team assumes some of the disciplinary activity that was formerly the manager's sole responsibility. Sharing responsibility for discipline reflects the empowerment of teams to carry out managerial functions. An experiment conducted with 231 members of 41 work groups indicated that managers and group consensus decisions (the group as a whole) show similarities in what they consider to be fair discipline for the same offense. For example, both managers and the group as an entity might recommend a one-week suspension for one employee harassing another.[15] The same study also concluded that groups are capable of making valid and fair decisions about poor performance of group members.

Taking disciplinary action is often thought of in relation to lower-ranking employees. Managers, professionals, and other salaried employees, however, may also need to be disciplined.

The paragraphs that follow will describe three other aspects of discipline. First, we describe the most widely used type of corrective discipline, progressive discipline. Second, we explain the rules for applying discipline. Third, we examine the positive consequences of discipline to the organization.

Progressive Discipline

Progressive discipline is the step-by-step application of corrective discipline, as shown in Exhibit 16–5. The manager confronts and then coaches the poor performer about the performance problem. If the employee's performance does not improve, the employee is informed in writing that improvements must be made. The written notice often includes a clear statement of what will happen if performance does not improve. The "or else" could be a disciplinary layoff or suspension. If the notice is ignored and the disciplinary action does not lead to improvement, the employee may be discharged.

Progressive discipline, an old concept, continues to be widely used for two key reasons. First, it provides the documentation necessary to avoid legal liability for firing poorly performing employees. Second, many labor-management agreements require progressive discipline because of the inherent fairness of the step-by-step procedure.

Rules for Applying Discipline

This chapter discussed discipline as it relates to the correction of ineffective performance. However, discipline is more frequently used to deal with infractions of

discipline
Punishment used to correct or train.

summary discipline
The immediate discharge of an employee because of a serious offense.

corrective discipline
A type of discipline that allows employees to correct their behavior before punishment is applied.

progressive discipline
The step-by-step application of corrective discipline.

EXHIBIT 16-5

Steps in Progressive Discipline

Progressive discipline is a standard practice that remains important because it gives the worker a chance to improve, and it documents poor performance. Should discharge be necessary, it would be more difficult for the employee to claim unfair treatment and wrongful discharge.

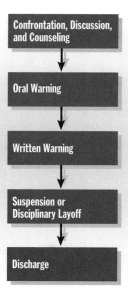

Confrontation, Discussion, and Counseling

Oral Warning

Written Warning

Suspension or Disciplinary Layoff

Discharge

policy and rules. The employee in these situations may not necessarily be a poor performer. The administration of discipline, whether for poor performance or infractions, should adhere to certain time-tested rules. Before applying these rules, a manager in a unionized firm must make sure they are compatible with the employee discipline clauses in the written union agreement.

The red–hot–stove rule offers an old-fashioned but still valid principle in administering discipline. According to the *red–hot–stove rule*, employee discipline should be the immediate result of inappropriate behavior, just as a burn is the result of touching a very hot stove. The employee should receive a warning (the red metal), and the punishment should be immediate, consistent, and impersonal. A manager should keep this rule and those that follow in mind when disciplining employees. Several of these suggestions incorporate the red–hot–stove rule.

1. *All employees should be notified of what punishments will be applied for what infractions.* For example, paralegals might be told that discussing the details of client cases with outsiders, a violation of company policy, will result in discharge.
2. *Discipline should be applied immediately after the infraction is committed.* As soon as is practical after learning of a rule violation, the manager should confront the employee and apply discipline.
3. *The punishment should fit the undesirable behavior.* If the punishment is too light, the offender will not take it seriously. If, on the other hand, it is too severe, it may create anxiety and actually diminish performance.
4. *The manager should focus attention on the unsatisfactory behavior or performance, not on the person's attitudes or traits.* A core principle of discipline and punishment is for the person administering the discipline to point out what results are unacceptable rather than insulting or diagnosing the group member's personality. Thus the manager would say, "Your store received five consecutive below–average customer service ratings." The same manager should not say, "You couldn't care less about customer service."
5. *Managers should be consistent in the application of discipline for each infraction.* Every employee who violates a certain rule should receive the same punishment.

Furthermore, managers throughout the organization should impose the same punishment for the same rule violation.

6. *Disciplinary remedies should be applied impersonally to offenders.* "Impersonal" in this context implies that everybody who is a known rule violator should be punished. Managers should not play favorites.

7. *Documentation of the performance or behavior that led to punishment is required.* Justification for the discipline must be documented in substantial detail. Documentation is essential for defending the company's action in the event of an appeal by the employee or the union or in the case of a lawsuit.

8. *When the discipline is over, return to usual work relations.* The manager should not hold a grudge or treat the rule violator as an outcast. How the person who violated the rule is treated could become a self-fulfilling prophecy. Treating the person who was disciplined as an outcast may make that person feel alienated, causing his or her performance to deteriorate. If the person is treated as someone who is expected not to commit mistakes, he or she will most likely try to live up to that expectation.

Positive Consequences of Punishment

Conventional wisdom is that punishment should be avoided in the workplace or used only as a last resort because of its negative side effects. Workers who are punished may become anxious, fearful, revengeful, and even violent. More recent evidence, however, suggests that punishment perceived in certain ways can actually benefit the organization.[16]

A key factor in whether punishment is beneficial is the employee's *belief in a just world*, or that people get the rewards and punishments they deserve. Employees who believe in a just world are likely to accept punishment when they violate rules or perform poorly because they believe they deserve to be punished. As a consequence, they do not complain about punishment, and might even spread the word that the organization is fair.

When employees observe that another employee has been punished justly (fairly), they will often rally on the side of management. The employees may think that the offending employee deserved the punishment. In some instances, other employees may desire that a rule violator be punished because it fits their sense of justice.

Just punishment also informs employees that certain types of misconduct will not be tolerated, as documented in an interview study conducted with 77 managers from different organizations. Many managers therefore regard punishment as an opportunity to promote *vicarious learning* (in this sense, learning through others).[17] For example, if one employee receives a 10-day suspension for racial harassment, other employees learn that the organization takes racial harassment seriously.

difficult person
An individual whose personal characteristics disturb other people.

DEALING WITH DIFFICULT PEOPLE, INCLUDING CYNICS

5

Develop an approach to dealing with difficult people, including cynics.

Although to this point, the chapter focused on dealing with substandard performers, another group of employees may perform adequately yet be annoying and waste managers' time. At times their performance slips below standard because they divert their energy from accomplishing work. A person in this category is often referred to as a **difficult person**, an individual whose personal characteris-

457

tics disturb other people. Two frequently found types of difficult employees are disgruntled workers and passive-aggressive workers.

Disgruntled workers are angry and often see themselves as victims. They justify their feelings by blaming work associates including supervisors, coworkers, and customers. Typically they isolate themselves from those around them.[18] Extremely disgruntled employees with low emotional stability may engage in workplace violence. The passive-aggressive worker, on the other hand, expresses anger and hostility by such means as neglecting to take care of an emergency or sitting silently in a meeting without making a contribution.

Other types of difficult people include whiners and complainers, know-it-alls, bullies, pessimists, and poor team players. Here we describe tactics for dealing with difficult people in general, and then highlight cynics because their numbers appear to be rising.

Tactics for Dealing with Difficult People

Much of the advice about dealing with difficult people centers around certain tactics, as described next. It will often be necessary to use a combination of these tactics to help a difficult person become more cooperative. The more the difficult behavior is an ingrained personality pattern, the more difficult it will be to change. In contrast, it is easier to change difficult behavior that stems from the pressures of a given situation. For example, a worker might be sulking because he was not appointed as team leader rather than being a long-term passive-aggressive personality. The list that follows describes eight tactics for dealing with a variety of difficult people.

- *Stay focused on the issues at hand.* A general strategy for dealing with difficult people is not to react specifically to the problem-maker's antics and instead stay focused on work issues. Describe the behavior you want changed, and explain why the behavior is disruptive. Pause for a moment, then wait for a response. Acknowledge what the person says, then state what needs to be changed, such as "Please stop giving customers an exasperated look and a loud exhale when they make a special request." Ask how the difficult person will make the change, and then get a commitment to change. (Notice the good coaching technique.)
- *Take the problem person professionally, not personally.* A key principle in dealing with difficult people is not to take what they do personally. Difficult people are not necessarily out to "get" the manager or coworker. You or somebody else might just represent an obstacle, or a stepping stone for them to get their way.[19] Remind yourself that you are paid to do your job, and dealing with difficult people is part of it. As you learn to take insults, slights, and back stabbing professionally rather than personally, you will experience less stress and harassment.
- *Use tact and diplomacy.* Team members who irritate you rarely do annoying things on purpose. Tactful actions on your part can sometimes take care of these problems without your having to go through the controlling process. For example, close your door if a team member is busily engaged in conversation outside your office. When subtlety does not work, you may have to confront the person. Incorporate tact and diplomacy into the confrontation. For example, as you confront a team member, point out one of his or her strengths.
- *Use humor.* Nonhostile humor can often be used to help a difficult person understand how his or her behavior annoys or blocks others. The humor should point to the person's unacceptable behavior but not belittle him or her. You might say to a subordinate who is overdue on a report: "I know we are

striving for zero defects in our company. But if you wait until your report is perfect before submitting it, we may not need it anymore." Your humor may help the team member realize that timeliness is an important factor in the quality of a report.

- *Give recognition and attention.* Difficult people, like misbehaving children, are sometimes crying out for attention. Give them recognition and attention, and their difficult behavior will sometimes cease. For example, in a staff meeting, mention the person's recent contributions to the department. If the negative behavior is a product of a deeper-rooted problem, recognition and attention by themselves will not work. The employee may have to be referred for professional counseling.
- *Listen and then confront or respond.* When discussing the problem with the difficult person, allow the individual a full expression of feelings. Next, acknowledge your awareness of the situation, and confront the person about how you size up the situation. Finally, specify what you would like changed, such as: "Please stop complaining so much about factors beyond our control." Avoid judging the person ("You *shouldn't* be like that") or generalizing ("You *always* act this way").[20]
- *Stand fast and do not make unwarranted concessions.* A variety of difficult people, but particularly bullies, expect you to sacrifice your position or standards such as breaking the rules just for them. If a person insults you, don't laugh it off or sidestep the remarks. Instead, say, "That's not called for. I cannot let your lack of professionalism pass unnoticed." If you are not intimidated, and do not appear insecure, the difficult person is less likely to keep pushing for the advantage.[21]
- *Boost the difficult worker's self-confidence.* Many workers who complain and make excuses frequently or exhibit other forms of difficult behavior are suffering from low self-confidence. They may not stay focused on work because of fear of failure. Assign these employees an easy task, so they can succeed and begin to build self-confidence. Then move up the scale with a more difficult task. Administer praise and recognition after each success.[22]

Dealing with Cynical Behavior

Many employees carry extremely negative attitudes toward their employers, and these negative attitudes often take the form of cynicism. Much of the cynicism appears to be a reaction to top-level management actions such as boosting their own compensation substantially while laying off lower-ranking workers to save money. Hiring so many contract and temporary workers at the expense of offering full-time employment also leads to cynicism. Cynics are classified as difficult people because they express their cynicism more negatively and persistently than do others. Cynicism is usually expressed by finding something negative about even the best intentions of others. A recent investigation into the topic concludes that workplace cynicism is shown on any of three dimensions:

- *A belief that the organization lacks integrity* (The cynic might say, "Our advertising is a pack of lies.")
- *A negative affect toward the organization* (Cynics frequently make such comments as, "This company is the pits," or "Who in his right mind would join this company today?")
- *Tendencies toward disparaging and critical behaviors directed at the organization that are consistent with these beliefs* (The cynic might use a competitor's consumer product and brag about it.)[23]

Managers may not want to suppress dissent, but too much cynicism in the workplace can lower the morale of others and interfere with recruiting positive people. Cynicism can also be distracting enough to harm productivity. One promising approach to dealing with cynics is to use the reinforcement strategy of extinction. Ignore cynical comments, and move on to another subject. If the cynic is seeking attention by being cynical, the lack of response will defeat the purpose of the sarcastic comments.

Cynical commentary can sometimes be reduced by demanding evidence to support harsh comments. Ask for the facts behind the opinion. A cynic might say, "I doubt there will be any money in the bonus pool this year. As usual, top management is taking care of themselves first and leaving little money for the rest of us." You might respond, "I seriously doubt top management is going to deny us raises. Where did you get your information?" As in dealing with most difficult people, changing the individual substantially is unlikely. However, you can work toward enough improvement to bring about a more positive working relationship.[24]

To help you better understand how being difficult can hurt a person's career, and how seriously many companies take the problem of difficult people, study the accompanying Management in Action.

6   TERMINATION

Explain the recommended approach to terminating employees

When corrective actions fail to improve ineffective performance, an employee is likely to be terminated. The company may also assist the person in finding new employment. Termination is considered part of the control process because it is a corrective action. It can also be considered part of the organizing function because it involves placing people.

termination

The process of firing an employee because of poor job performance, unacceptable behavior, or interpersonal problems.

Termination is the process of firing an employee because of poor job performance, unacceptable behavior, or interpersonal problems. Termination is regarded as the last alternative. It represents a failure in staffing and in managing ineffective performers. Nevertheless, to maintain discipline and control costs, a firm is often forced to terminate nonproductive employees. When substandard performers are discharged, it communicates the message that adequate performance must be maintained. Thus, a firing can also be valuable because it may increase the productivity of employees who are not fired.

Termination usually takes place only after the substandard performer has been offered the types of help described throughout this chapter. In general, every feasible alternative—such as retraining and counseling—should be attempted before termination. A manager must also accumulate substantial written documentation of substandard performance. Appropriate documentation includes performance appraisals, special memos to the file about performance problems, and statements describing the help offered the employee.

wrongful discharge

The firing of an employee for arbitrary or unfair reasons.

If these steps are not documented, the employer can be accused of wrongful discharge. **Wrongful discharge** is the firing of an employee for arbitrary or unfair reasons. Many employers face wrongful discharge suits. Court rulings in the last decade increasingly prohibited the termination of employees when good faith, fair dealing, and implied contracts were at issue.

due process

In relation to employee rights, giving a worker a fair hearing before he or she is dismissed.

Another way of looking at wrongful discharge is to consider the idea that employees have certain rights in relation to preserving their jobs. According to **due process**, employees must be given a fair hearing before being dismissed. This process includes the right to progressive discipline and the right to present one's side of the story to management.

Management *in Action*

K a r y l   I n n i s   H e l p s   t h e   " S m a r t   B u t s "

Karyl Innis deals with so many Smart Buts that she is trademarking the phrase. The 52-year-old career strategist and CEO of The Innis Co. in Dallas, Texas, is routinely asked by employers to shave the rough edges of promising management talent. A corporate executive will say, 'Karyl, I've got an employee who's so bright and so smart, but . . .' After that there's always something like, 'Nobody will work with him because he leaves bodies in his wake' or 'Nobody knows she's in the same room because she won't open her mouth.'"

Once these Smart Buts would have been shunted aside to let more suitable protégés pass them by. But today's tight labor market has employers scrambling for executive talent and trying to coax the most from the employees they have. With fewer sages to mentor younger employees, companies turn to outside consultants such as Innis for that guiding light.

"Companies are shoehorning people into executive slots. They force-fit people who aren't ready and then get disastrous results," says Innis, sitting in her 17th floor offices in One Galleria Tower. "Our coaching bridges the gap between who people are and who they need to be." Recasting workers into new internal roles is her company's fastest-growing segment.

In a nutshell, Innis tells people to know what they want and how to figure out where to find it. "Careers don't just happen. They don't just fall into your lap," says Innis. "We spend a lot of time building clarity around what people really want. There are still those who want a corporation to take care of them—create, cast, and define them. The new rule is you cast and define yourself."

While working as the manager of staffing for Motorola, Innis learned about Smart Buts—people who didn't get the job or promotion. "They were bright and smart, but they weren't right for it," she says. "They were head down, pencil up and worked diligently, but they weren't able to express their contributions or worth even to their immediate bosses. It wasn't that they were undervalued. They were valued in a silo," she says, moving her hands vertically. "Their supervisors couldn't see how their skills could apply outside that."

Innis is fond of telling people that while they have to emphasize their strengths, they also must realistically assess their shortcomings. "There's an arrogance in not knowing how you affect others," Innis says. "That's where our Smart Buts most often fall down. They are so focused on task, task, task and producing good results that they don't realize the style they've adopted is affecting people in a highly negative way."

Source: "Fine-Tuning Up-and-Comers," Knight Ridder, February 11, 2001.

In recognition of the delicate human relations and legal problems involved in firing poor performers, some firms turn to specialists to help them avoid lawsuits from dismissed workers. Others firms look to lower the risk of retaliation through employee violence. A consultant who specializes in firing people for other companies admits the work is difficult. In his words:

It's not like, "Oh man, I get to fire someone today." It's the hardest thing because you're actually changing someone's life.[25]

After an employee is fired, the manager must deal with the questions and feelings of the group members within the unit. Often these people were close friends of the terminated employee. Be honest with the other employees, but do not bad-mouth the terminated worker. Avoid being too specific to avoid a lawsuit about defamation of character. Emphasize how performance factors led to the discharge. Allow coworkers to express their feelings and concerns in a group setting or one-on-one with you, the manager.[26]

To minimize major errors in firing an employee, also follow these guidelines:

- *Never fire an employee when you are angry.* Words said in anger may be too harsh, and could also reveal a prejudice, such as, "I'm getting rid of you, Harry, because we need some fresh young thinkers in this department."
- *Never fire anyone based on second-party information.* For your own legal protection you should have first-hand knowledge and evidence of the employee's unsatisfactory, immoral, or illegal behavior.
- *Be direct and clear in your language.* Inform the employee explicitly that he or she is being fired and why. Yet ease the blow with a few reassuring phrases such as, "I am sorry this job did not work out for you. Good luck in your next job."[27]

SUMMARY OF KEY POINTS

1 Identify factors contributing to poor performance. Job performance is ineffective when productivity falls below a standard considered acceptable at a given time. Ineffective performers consume considerable managerial time. The causes of poor job performance can be rooted in the employee, the job, the manager, or the company. Usually, ineffective performance is caused by a combination of several factors.

2 Describe the control model for managing ineffective performers. The approach to improving ineffective performance presented in this chapter is a controlling process. It consists of eight steps that should be followed in sequence: (1) define performance standards, (2) detect deviation from acceptable performance, (3) define and assess the cause, (4) confront the substandard performer, (5) set improvement goals, (6) select and implement an action plan for improvement, (7) reevaluate performance after a time interval, and (8) continue or discontinue the action plan.

Corrective actions for ineffective performers are divided into managerial actions and techniques, and organizational programs. Managerial actions include close supervision and corrective discipline. Organizational programs include career counseling, outplacement, and job redesign.

3 Know what is required to coach and constructively criticize employees. Coaching and constructive criticism are useful approaches to managing poor performers. Coaching consists of giving advice and encouragement. Most coaching includes constructive criticism. Skill is required to coach ineffective performers and criticize them constructively. Another approach to coaching is to hire a business (or executive) coach to assist in elevating performance, particularly with respect to interpersonal relationships.

4 Understand how to discipline employees. The controlling process may also call for discipline. Summary discipline is the immediate discharge of an employee who commits a serious offense. Corrective discipline gives employees a chance to correct their behavior before punishment is applied. Both the manager and the employee share the responsibility for solving the performance problem. Corrective discipline involves counseling.

The major type of corrective discipline is called progressive discipline. It represents a step-by-step application of corrective discipline. The manager confronts the ineffective performer about the problem and then coaches him or her. If the employee's performance does not improve, the employee is given a written warning. If this fails, the employee is suspended or given a disciplinary layoff. The next step is discharge.

The red-hot-stove rule refers to administering discipline right away. The situation should include a warning; consistent, impersonal punishment should be administered immediately after the infraction is committed.

Punishment can help an organization because many employees believe that a rule violator should be punished. Also, punishment emphasizes that certain types of misconduct will not be tolerated.

5 Develop an approach to dealing with difficult people, including cynics. When dealing with difficult people, stay focused on the issue at hand, and take the problem professionally, not personally. Also use humor, tact, and diplomacy, while giving recognition and attention. Listen to the difficult person and confront the person about how you size up the situation. Also, explain the importance of teamwork. Boost the difficult person's self-confidence by starting with an easy task to perform. One approach to dealing with cynics is to ignore cynical comments. However, the cynic might also be challenged to support the basis for his or her cynicism.

 Explain the recommended approach to terminating employees. Termination should take place only after the substandard performer has been offered the type of help built into the control model. Documentation of poor performance is required. Coworkers should be offered a performance-based explanation of why the substandard performer was terminated. Never fire anyone based on second-hand information.

KEY TERMS AND PHRASES

Ineffective job performance, *442*

Behavior mismatch, *446*

Confrontation, *449*

Improvement goal, *449*

Employee assistance program (EAP), *450*

Coaching, *453*

Constructive criticism, *453*

Discipline, *455*

Summary discipline, *455*

Corrective discipline, *455*

Progressive discipline, *455*

Difficult person, *457*

Termination, *460*

Wrongful discharge, *460*

Due process, *460*

QUESTIONS

1. What is the link between managing ineffective performers and organizational productivity?
2. Explain which levels (or types) of managers are the most likely to be involved with managing ineffective performers.
3. How can a person avoid becoming a substandard performer?
4. Which negative consequences to the organization do cynics create?
5. In what type of job might being a difficult person not be much of a liability?
6. Why should management be willing to rehabilitate employees through an employee assistance program when so many workers have been downsized in recent years?
7. Which human resource management technique, discussed in another chapter of this book, would be helpful in giving Smart Buts the feedback they need?

CRITICAL THINKING QUESTIONS

1. What problems might be created by assuming that the bottom 10 percent, or bottom 5 percent, of the company workforce contains ineffective performers?
2. Conduct library or Internet research to obtain fresh information on how alcohol and drugs contribute to substandard performance. Report your findings to the class.

SKILL-BUILDING EXERCISE: The Sick Building Audit

You and one or two other classmates have been assigned to a sick-building task force. Your task is to identify potential pollutants in or around a specific building that could possibly lower productivity. You might use your school as a subject of study, an office building, or a large retail store. Consult a source of information on potential pollutants, such as Michelle Conlin, "Is Your Office Killing You?" *Business Week,* June 5, 2000, pp. 114–128. Also, ask questions of people you encounter in the building. One of dozens of possibilities is second-hand smoke from smokers outside being sucked back into the building by revolving doors. After conducting your audit, decide whether the building in question is sick. Do you have any recommendations for the building maintenance department?

INTERNET SKILL-BUILDING EXERCISE: Can This Employee Be Salvaged?

To learn more about when employee termination is advisable or inadvisable, visit the Business Resource Center's Web site at http://www.morebusiness.com. Check out their free interactive questionnaire (choose Templates, Business Checklists), which asks a manager 29 questions to determine whether salvaging an ineffective performer is feasible. The site also offers guidelines on wrongful discharge to managers and future managers. You might ask the 29 questions about an ineffective performer you observed in action, including a present or former coworker. Readers with supervisory experience might answer the questions about a present or former direct report.

CASE PROBLEM 16-A: The Preoccupied Business Analyst

Harold Gupta is the team leader for a group of business analysts that provides data on real estate trends for a variety of businesses such as real estate developers, home builders, home improvement chains, and several government agencies. The work of the business analysts requires considerable concentration and attention to detail. The analysts obtain much of their data from telephone interviews, as well as newspapers, computerized databases, and trade magazines. After assembling the data, the analyst prepares a coherent report. The analyst submits the report to Gupta who edits the report, and returns it to the analyst for final revision.

Gupta's real estate data team consistently meets its productivity goals and receives satisfactory reviews from the company. With only six people on the team, however, each member must meet his or her individual quota for the team to meet its quota of salable reports. Currently, Gupta faces concerns about Randy Murphy, an analyst who has been with the team for one year. Murphy's reports arrive at the last minute, and many contain errors such as incorrect mathematical calculations and conclusions that do not fit the data. Also, Murphy is slow in revising his reports after Gupta edits them.

Gupta mentioned the dual problem of errors and lateness several times to Murphy in recent months. Each time Randy replies, "Sorry about that Harold. The problem won't happen again." Harold felt relieved to know that Randy at least acknowledged the problem, so he believed Randy would overcome the problems.

While editing a recent report submitted by Randy one week late, Harold noticed that Randy reached the opposite conclusion supported by the data. He reported a 15 percent projected increase in the demand for housing in the suburbs of Baton Rouge, Louisiana, in the period under forecast. The data actually showed a decrease of 15 percent. Harold decided it was time to review Randy's performance problems with him face-to-face, so he asked Randy to meet with him in his office.

"Randy, it looks like we have a problem," said Harold. "You are still late with your reports, and their quality is deteriorating. The incorrect conclusion on the Baton Rouge report was serious. I assume you remember the e-mail I sent you about your miscalculation."

Randy commented, "But Harold, I just substituted a plus sign for a minus sign. You review all my reports, so an error like that will most likely be caught."

In an annoyed tone, Harold said, "Terrible excuse. As a professional you are responsible for your work. You cannot count on me or anybody else to catch your mistakes. Can you image the damage to the reputation of our firm if an error like that got into the hands of a client?

"But the bigger problem is: *Why* are you making mistakes and being late so frequently Randy? Up to a few months ago, you were doing above-average work. Have you lost interest in your job? What's up?"

"Actually, plenty is up," said Randy. "I've been plagued with personal problems lately. I've run my four credit cards up to the max, and I'm having troubles making even the minimum payments. My orthopedist tells me I may need orthoscopic surgery on my knee to get rid of some cartilage fragments. It could put my future as a soccer player in doubt."

"Those are big problems Randy," responded Harold. "Any others?"

"Yes, the big one. My fiancée dumped me two months ago. She tells me that she needs more space, that she wants to explore the world a little more before getting tied down. So she left. Put all those problems together, and you can see why I am not performing at my best. I don't think its fair of the company to expect a good employee who faces a sudden bunch of problems to produce like his life was normal. I see myself as temporarily disabled and protected under the ADA [Americans with Disabilities Act]."

Harold cradled his face in his hands, and then replied, "I am sorry that you are facing so many personal problems. I will try to help you, but you are responsible for producing high-quality, prompt work. Let me think this over, and we will talk some more later."

Discussion Questions

1. How would you evaluate Gupta's coaching technique so far?
2. What should Gupta do next?
3. Should Randy be excused from meeting standards because he is troubled by personal problems? Explain your reasoning.
4. You be the employment law specialist. Is Randy covered under the ADA? (See Chapter 10.)
5. What advice can you offer Randy?

C A S E   P R O B L E M   1 6 - B :   Revenge Has Its Price

Caryn Andersen was the senior secretary to the regional vice president of an insurance company, a position she held for six years. In Caryn's contacts with other regional offices she discovered that her counterparts were promoted to executive assistants. Caryn wanted to be an executive assistant because the position would give her more status, salary, and vacation time. She approached Dana Leonard, her manager, and requested a promotion to executive assistant.

Dana liked the idea, and asked Caryn to draft a job description that would increase her level of responsibilities, including work on special assignments. Dana reviewed the description with Caryn, contacted the headquarters human resource department, and secured the reclassification. After the reclassification, Caryn could not understand why Dana was placing more demands on her time and requesting that she accomplish more things independently. Dana in turn could not understand why Caryn was blocking his requests because it was she who had asked for the promotion.

Caryn would openly complain, "What good is it to be an executive assistant and get more vacation time? Every time I turn around, Dana has some new project for me. I never get to take the vacation time I have." Caryn soon began bad-mouthing Dana. She would answer his calls and say such things as, "I don't know where Dana is. He never tells me anything anymore."

Caryn's disgruntlement continued, and she stopped providing Dana with the information she was supposed to. Twice when Dana asked her to set up a meeting at a designated time, she neglected to inform the people who were supposed to attend. When Dana returned after waiting futilely for the others, Caryn denied telling Dana that she had set up the meeting.

On one occasion, Caryn scheduled several people to meet with Dana but did not tell him about it until the last minute when a group suddenly appeared at his office. Caryn insisted to Dana, "I told you this meeting was scheduled. Don't you listen to me anymore?" Her rhetorical question was asked in front of the guests who had arrived for the meeting.

Caryn insisted that all the information sent to Dana had to be reviewed by her first, and that e-mail messages for Dana be sent to her for forwarding. Even hard-copy items were plucked from Dana's in-box and reviewed. Caryn would then openly pass judgment on the contents. Once she told a manager reporting to Dana that a promotion for one of her people would most certainly be approved by Dana. Yet Dana had not yet read the request.

One day the company president telephoned Dana, and Caryn took the opportunity to describe Dana's inability to run his operation. Upon speaking to Dana, the president said, "Muzzle her or fire her. I don't care which." Later that day, Dana confronted Caryn: "Ever since your promotion, your performance and attitude have deteriorated. Worse yet, your loyalty to me and the organization have vanished. You wanted a promotion to executive assistant. You wanted all the advantages that went along with the position.

"Two things you didn't take into account. First, in order to attain that level, we expected a higher caliber of work. Not only did you not give us that, your performance deteriorated. Second, your constant harping about my work amounts to insubordination. I am recommending that you be demoted to an entry-level position in the staff support (central clerical pool) center. After one year of good performance, you may reapply for the position of senior secretary."

Caryn was stunned. She left for home for the day to decide on her options.

Discussion Questions

1. How might Dana have done a more effective job of managing Caryn as an ineffective performer?
2. What factors contributed most strongly to Caryn's ineffective performance?
3. Would Dana have been justified in firing Caryn when he found out that she told the president that Dana was having difficulty running his operation? Why or why not?

E N D N O T E S

1. Figures updated in 2001 from Sandra L. Robinson and Rebecca J. Bennett, "A Typology of Deviant Workplace Behaviors: A Multidimensional Scaling Study," *Academy of Management Journal*, April 1995, p. 555; Jane Easter Bahis, "Drugs in the Workplace," *HR Magazine*, February 1998, p. 82.
2. John Greenwald, "Rank and Fire," *Time*, June 18, 2001, pp. 38–40.

3. Brenda Park Sunoo, "This Employee May Be Loafing. Can You Tell?" *Personnel Journal*, December 1996, pp. 54–62.

4. Michael R. Manning, Joyce S. Osland, and Asbjorn Osland, "Work-Related Consequences of Smoking Cessation," *Academy of Management Journal*, September 1989, p. 606.

5. Joseph J. Martocchio, David A. Harrison, and Howard Berkson, "Connections Between Lower Back Pain, Interventions, and Absence from Work: A Time-Based Meta-Analysis," *Personnel Psychology*, Autumn 2000, p. 496.

6. Michelle Conlin, "Is Your Office Killing You?" *Business Week*, June 5, 2000, pp. 114–128.

7. Jean-François Manzoni and Jean-Louis Barsoux, "The Set-Up-to-Fail Syndrome," *Harvard Business Review*, March–April 1998, pp. 101–113.

8. Harvey A. Hornstein, *Brutal Bosses and Their Prey* (New York: GP Putnam's Sons, 1996); http://www.myboss.com.

9. Sandra L. Robinson and Anne M. O'Leary-Kelly, "Monkey See, Monkey Do: The Influence of Work Groups on the Antisocial Behavior of Employees," *Academy of Management Journal*, December 1998, pp. 658–672.

10. Rebecca Mann, *Behavior Mismatch: How to Manage "Problem" Employees Whose Actions Don't Match Your Expectations* (New York: AMACOM, 1993).

11. Kenneth H. Blanchard, "How to Turn Around Department Performance," *Supervisory Management*, March 1992, p. 3.

12. Jonathan A. Segal, "I'm Depressed—Accommodate Me!" *HR Magazine*, February 2001, p. 148.

13. James Waldroop and Timothy Butler, "The Executive as Coach," *Harvard Business Review*, November–December 1996, p. 111.

14. Marilyn J. Darling, "Coaching Helps People Through Difficult Times," *HR Magazine*, November 1994, p. 72.

15. Robert C. Liden et al., "Management of Poor Performance: A Comparison of Manager, Group Member, and Group Disciplinary Decisions," *Journal of Applied Psychology*, December 1999, p. 846.

16. Gail A. Ball, Linda Klebe Treviño, and Harry P. Sims Jr., "Just and Unjust Punishment: Influence on Subordinate Performance and Citizenship," *Academy of Management Journal*, April 1994, pp. 300–301.

17. Kenneth B. Butterfield, Linda Klebe Treviño, and Gail A. Ball, "Punishment from the Manager's Perspective: A Grounded Investigation and Inductive Model," *Academy of Management Journal*, December 1996, pp. 1493.

18. Paul Falcone, "Welcome Back Disgruntled Workers," *HR Magazine*, February 2001, p. 133.

19. "Help! I'm Surrounded by Difficult People," *WorkingSMART*, March 25, 1991, p. 2.

20. Sam Deep and Lyle Sussman, *What to Say to Get What You Want* (Reading, MA: Addison-Wesley, 1991).

21. "Fighting off Bullies," *WorkingSMART*, September 1997, p. 1.

22. "How to Deal with 'Problem' Workers," *Positive Leadership*, sample issue 2001, p. 6.

23. James W. Dean Jr., Pamela Brandes, and Ravi Dharwadkar, "Organizational Cynicism," *Academy of Management Review*, April 1998, pp. 341–352.

24. "Shut Down a Cynic," *WorkingSMART*, September 1997, p. 1.

25. Martha Irvine, "Terminator Consultants Hired So They Can Fire," Associated Press, November 2, 1998.

26. Robert McGarvey, "After the Fire," *Entrepreneur*, September 1995, p. 80.

27. Steve Lauer and B. Jack Gebhardt, *Now Hiring* (New York: AMACOM, 1997).

Enhancing Personal Productivity and Managing Stress

Joe Greulich, the director of MIS at Roberts Express, Akron, Ohio, says, "We're a high-speed delivery service, so our revenue is based on our ability to manage time. We ship freight—quickly and on time. And we're proud of our record. We complete 96 percent of our jobs within 15 minutes of our estimated time of arrival. We gear every element of our business toward time.

"We've set up our salary structures to match our speed objectives because we believe that people will accomplish tasks rapidly when they're given the incentive to do so. For example, up to 60 percent of my salary is pegged to how quick Windows pops up on our computers. We also keep track of each customer assistance team's on-time record for pickup and delivery. The people on a customer assistance team can make up to 16 percent of their salary in bonuses, depending on how prompt the team's deliveries have been.

"Perhaps the most important principle that we've learned is that you should never sacrifice humanity for speed. We track how long employees are on the phone and award bonus points if they take calls speedily. That gives them an incentive to handle customer calls quickly. But we found that, as a result of this policy, employees were giving short shrift to our truck drivers, who also call in for help. So we've hired a person whose sole mission is to talk to truck drivers about problems they encounter on the road."[1]

OBJECTIVES

After studying this chapter and doing the exercises, you should be able to:

1 Identify techniques for improving work habits and time management.

2 Identify techniques for reducing procrastination.

3 Understand the nature of stress, including its consequences.

4 Explain how stress can be managed effectively.

Chapter 17

The manager just described reinforces a key point about operating a business successfully. Excellent work habits, including choosing an optimal speed in performing tasks, elevates productivity. At the same time, the manager takes into account human considerations to help workers in need, thereby preventing some forms of stress.

In this chapter we describe methods for both improving productivity and managing stress, because the two are as interlocked as nutrition and health. If you are well organized, you will avoid much of the negative stress that stems from feeling that your work and life are out of control. If your level of stress is about right, you will be able to concentrate better on your work and be more productive.

The emphasis in this final chapter of the book is about managing yourself rather than managing other people or managing a business. Unless you have your work under control, and effectively manage stress, it is unlikely you can be an effective manager or leader.

1   ## IMPROVING YOUR WORK HABITS AND TIME MANAGEMENT

Identify techniques for improving work habits and time management.

High personal productivity leads to positive outcomes such as higher income, more responsibility, and recognition. Furthermore, in an era of work streamlining and downsizings based on company consolidations, the demand for high productivity among managerial workers has never been higher. Productivity enhancers, such as daily planners, sell at record rates. High job productivity also allows you to devote more worry-free time to your personal life. In addition, high productivity helps reduce the stress experienced when a person's job is out of control.

Here we describe improving productivity by improving work habits and time management. In the next section productivity improvement is approached from the perspective of reducing procrastination.

Develop a Mission, Goals, and a Strong Work Ethic

A major starting point in becoming a better organized and more productive person is to have a purpose and values that propel you toward being productive. In the words of Steven Covey, without a personal mission statement, you have nothing to plan and act for.[2] Assume that a person says, "My mission in life is to become an outstanding office supervisor and a caring, constructive spouse and parent." The mission serves as a compass to direct that person's activities (such as getting done on time) to developing a reputation that will lead to promotion to supervisor. Goals are more specific than mission statements, and support the mission statement, but the effect is the same. For example, the person in question might set a goal one day to respond to 75 different customer inquiries that have accumulated on the Internet by the end of the day. Accomplishing that amount of work today would be one more step toward being promoted to supervisor.

work ethic

A firm belief in the dignity and value of work.

Closely related to establishing goals is to have a strong **work ethic**—a firm belief in the dignity and value of work. Developing a strong work ethic may lead to even higher productivity than goal setting alone. For example, one might set the goal of earning a high income. It would lead to some good work habits, but not necessarily to a high commitment to quality. A person with a strong work ethic believes in quality, is highly motivated, and minimizes time-wasting activities.

Clean Up Your Work Area and Sort Out Your Tasks

People sometimes become inefficient because their work area is messy. They waste time looking for things and neglect important papers. So to get started improving personal productivity, clean up your work area and sort out what tasks you need to accomplish. Cleaning up your work area includes your briefcase, your file of telephone numbers, your hard drive, and your e-mail files. Having loads of e-mail messages stacked in your Inbox, Sent, and Deleted files can easily lead to overlooking important new messages. Weeding out your mailing list is also important. Ask to be removed from the distribution of paper and e-mail that is of no value. Rebel against being spammed.

Prepare a To-Do List and Assign Priorities

A to-do list lies at the heart of every time management system. In addition to writing down tasks you need to do, assign priorities to them. A simple categorization, such as top priority versus low priority, works well for most people. In general, take care of top-priority tasks before low-priority ones. There are so many things to do on any job that some very low-priority items may never get done. Keep your to-do list on a desk calendar or a large tablet or in your computer. A word processing file may suffice, but more advanced software for work scheduling is also available. Small slips of paper in various locations tend to be distracting and often get misplaced. Plan the next day's activities at the end of each workday, thereby giving yourself a fresh plan of attack for the next day including discharging today's unfinished work.[3]

Many workers today use daily planners to serve as a to-do list. A planner typically divides the day into 15-minute chunks and leaves room for the daily to-do list. Some planning systems are linked to a person's mission, thus giving an extra impetus to accomplishing tasks. No matter how elaborate the system that incorporates the humble to-do list, it will not boost productivity unless the items are referred to frequently. An exception is that some well-organized people plan their to-do list in their head. As they move through the day, they keep working the list.

Taking care of a small, easy-to-do task first—such as getting a refill for a ballpoint pen—has a hidden value. It tends to be relaxing because it gives you the emotional lift of having accomplished at least one item on your list. Also, accomplishing small tasks helps reduce stress.

Streamline Your Work

The most important new work habit and management principle is **work streamlining**—eliminating as much low-value work as possible and concentrating on activities that add value for customers or clients. To streamline work, justify whether every work procedure, memo, report, meeting, or ceremonial activity contributes value to the firm. Group luncheon meetings away from the office might be cut in half, giving staff members more time during the day to conduct urgent work. Another example of work streamlining would be to decrease the number of holiday cards sent to work associates.

work streamlining
Eliminating as much low-value work as possible and concentrating on activities that add value for customers or clients.

Work at a Steady Pace

Although a dramatic show of energy (as in "pulling an all-nighter") is impressive, the steady worker tends to be more productive in the long run. The spurt employee creates many problems for management; the spurt student is in turmoil at examination time or when papers are due. Managers who expend the same amount of effort day-by-day tend to stay in control of their jobs. When a sudden problem or a good opportunity comes to their attention, they can fit it into their schedule.

Working at a steady pace often means always working rapidly. To be competitive most organizations require that work be accomplished rapidly. Consultant Price Pritchett advises, "So you need to operate with a strong sense of urgency. Accelerate in all aspects of your work, even if it means living with a few more ragged edges. Emphasize *action*. Don't bog down in endless preparation trying to get things perfect before you make a move. Sure, high quality is crucial, but it must come quickly. You can't sacrifice speed."[4]

Minimize Time Wasters

An important strategy for improving personal productivity is to minimize time wasters. Each minute invested in productive work can save you from working extra hours. A major time waster is interruptions from others. When doing intellectually demanding work, getting the appropriate flow of thought is difficult. When interrupted, people lose momentum and must launch themselves again.[5] The definition of what constitutes an *interruption* is tricky. A coworker asking you to participate in a basketball pool is certainly an interruption, but socializing with him or her you might strengthen your network. Some executives feel that a demand from a customer should never be classified as an interruption. A sudden demand from a boss might also *not* be classified as an interruption.

Exhibit 17-1 presents a list of significant ways to reduce wasted time. Many of the other suggestions in this chapter can also help you save time directly or indirectly.

Concentrate on One Task at a Time

Productive managers develop their capacity to concentrate on the problem facing them at the moment, however engulfed they are with other obligations. Intense concentration leads to sharpened judgment and analysis and also decreases the chances of making major errors. Another useful by-product of concentration is reduced absentmindedness. The person who concentrates on the task at hand allows less chance of forgetting what he or she intended.

To assist their concentration levels on the task at hand, some people use *performance cues*, or items to concentrate on when under pressure.[6] For example, when facing a difficult customer your performance cue might be a smile. Say to yourself, "I must smile now." Smiling is effective because it helps reduce the difficult customer's hostility. Another performance cue might be taking notes when major points come up in your conversation with a group member. Taking notes forces you to concentrate intently on the message sender. Your performance cue is, "When she says something of special importance, I will jot down the idea on paper."

Concentrate on High-Output Tasks

To become more productive on the job or in school, concentrate on tasks in which superior performance could have a large payoff. For a manager, a high-output task would be to develop a strategic plan for the department. For a student, a high-output task would be to think of a creative idea for an independent study project. Expending your work effort on high-output items is analogous to looking for a good return on investment for your money. The high-output strategy also follows the Pareto principle, described in Chapter 7.

Do Creative and Routine Tasks at Different Times

To improve productivity, organize your work so you do not shift between creative and routine tasks. For many people it is best to work first on creative tasks because they require more mental energy than routine tasks. A minority of people prefer to get minor paperwork and e-mail chores out of the way so they can get to the pleasure of doing creative tasks. Whichever order you choose, it is important not to interrupt creative (or high-output) tasks with routine activities such as sorting mail or rearranging the desk.

Stay in Control of Paperwork, E-Mail, and Voice Mail

No organization today can accomplish its mission unless paperwork, including the electronic variety, receives appropriate attention. If you handle paperwork improperly, your job may get out of control. Once your job is out of control, the

EXHIBIT 17-1

Ways to Prevent and Overcome Time Wasting

Wasted time is a major productivity drain, so it pays to search for time wasters in your work activities. The following list suggests remedies for some of the major time wasters in the workplace.

1. Use a time log for two weeks to track time wasters.
2. Minimize daydreaming on the job by forcing yourself to concentrate.
3. Avoid the computer as a diversion from work, such as sending jokes back and forth to network members, playing video games, and checking out recreational Web sites during working hours.
4. Batch tasks together such as returning phone calls or responding to e-mail messages. For example, in most jobs it is possible to be productive by reserving two or three 15-minute periods per day for taking care of e-mail correspondence.
5. Socialize on the job just enough to build your network. Chatting with coworkers is a major productivity drain and one of the reasons so many managers work at home part of the time when they have analytical work to get done.
6. Be prepared for meetings, such as having a clear agenda and sorting through the documents you will be referring to. Make sure electronic equipment is in working order before attempting to use it during the meeting.

7. Keep track of important names, places, and things, to avoid wasting time searching for them.
8. Set a time limit for tasks after you have done them once or twice.
9. Prepare a computer template for letters and computer documents that you send frequently. (The template is essentially a form letter, especially with respect to the salutation and return address.)
10. When you only have to provide routine information, telephone people before and after normal working hours, leaving a message on their voice mail. (This saves conversation time.)
11. Avoid perfectionism, which leads you to keep redoing a project. Let go and move on to another project.
12. Make use of bits of time; for instance, 5 minutes between appointments. Invest those 5 minutes in sending a business e-mail, or revise your to-do list. (Note the exception to the batch principle.)
13. Minimize procrastination, the number-one time waster for most people.

Source: Suggestions 4, 5, and 6 are based on Stephen R. Covey with Hyrum Smith, "What If You Could Chop an Hour from Your Day for Things That Matter Most?" *USA Weekend*, January 22–24, 1999, pp. 4–5.

stress level will increase greatly. Invest a small amount of time in paperwork and electronic mail every day. The best time to take care of routine correspondence is when you are at less than peak efficiency but not overfatigued. Reserve your high-energy periods for high-output tasks.

Avoid becoming a paper shuffler or frequently rereading e-mail messages. The ideal is to handle a piece of paper or an e-mail message only once. When you pick up a hard-copy memo or read an electronic one, take some action: throw it away or delete it, route it to someone else, write a short response to the sender, or flag it for action later. Loose ends of time can be used to take care of the flagged memos.

Staying in control of voice mail and answering machine messages is also important to stay productive. Stacked up voice-mail messages will often detract from your ability to concentrate on other work. Not returning voice mail messages promptly also creates the problem of perceived rudeness and poor customer service. Disciplining yourself to answer voice mail messages in batches, as described in Exhibit 17-1, will help you manage these messages productively.

Make Effective Use of Office Technology

Many managerial workers boost their productivity by making effective use of office technology. Yet the productivity gains are not inevitable. Just because a person can receive rapidly transmitted e-mail messages from all over the world, and can produce exquisite pie charts, increased sales and decreased costs do not always follow. Boosting your personal productivity is contingent upon choosing equipment that truly adds to productivity and does not drain too much time for purposes of learning and bringing it back and forth to the repair shop.

A major reason many workers do not achieve productivity gains with information technology is that they do not invest the time saved in other productive activity. If sending a batch of e-mail messages instead of postal mail saves you two hours, you will only experience a productivity gain if the two hours are then invested in a task with a tangible output, such as searching for a lower-cost supplier. Another problem is that some workers will duplicate their activities such as telephoning another person to find out if they were able to retrieve a file sent by e-mail.

Office technology devices are attractive and intriguing. It is also important to know when simple mechanical or handwritten procedures are faster than office technology. For example, the simple 3×5 index card remains a powerful low-technology way of preparing and executing a to-do list. Managers and professionals who move from one location to another may find it a time waster to access a computer just to check their daily list. Even a palm-size computer can be more disruptive than simply glancing at an index card attached to a pocket calendar. A complaint some people have about large $8\frac{1}{2} \times 11$ planners is they are cumbersome to lug around unless you are carrying an attaché case.

Bill Marriott, the CEO of Marriott International, exemplifies a successful executive who knows when low technology is the method of choice. He keeps his schedule, usually drawn up three months ahead in collaboration with an administrative assistant, on a 3×5 index card that he carries in his left breast pocket, which enables him to glance at it several times a day.

Practice the Mental State of Peak Performance

peak performance

A mental state in which maximum results are achieved with minimum effort.

To achieve maximum potential productivity one must transcend ordinary levels of concentration and devotion to duty. That occurs in **peak performance**, a mental state in which maximum results are achieved with minimum effort. Peak performers remain mentally calm and physically at ease when challenged by difficult problems. They focus intensely and stay involved, much like they would be in playing the best tennis games of their lives. You may have experienced the state of peak performance when totally involved with a problem or task. At that moment, nothing else seems to exist.

To achieve peak performance, you must continually work toward being mentally calm and physically at ease. Concentrate intensely, but not so much that you choke. In addition to frequent practice, peak performance can be achieved through visualization. In *visualization* you develop a mental image of how you would act and feel at the point of peak performance. For example, imagine yourself making a flawless presentation to top-level management about the contributions of your department. Psychologist Charles Garfield observed that people who achieve peak performance typically have an important mission in life—such as building a top-quality company.[7]

Take Naps

A fast-growing trend for increasing personal productivity is to take a nap of about 15 to 30 minutes designed to recharge the individual. Well-placed naps actually enhance rather than diminish productivity, and they are also an excellent stress reducer. You can combat procrastination by taking a brief nap before beginning an uncomfortable task.

According to one researcher, "The remarkable aspect of prophylactic napping, or napping in advance of an extended period of work, is that the benefits of the nap, even one of only 25 minutes duration, can be evident in performance hours afterward."[8] Naps can also prevent industrial disasters by overcoming grogginess before it leads to an accident such as the *Exxon Valdez* oil spill. Even better, with the proper amount of sleep, napping is much less necessary. According to the National Sleep Foundation, most adults need 8 hours of sleep to produce high-quality work. However, most adults average 6 hours and 57 minutes of sleep per night.[9] Again, individual differences are a major factor. Many successful people require less sleep, which allows them more time for work, life, and recreation.

In recognition of the importance of napping as a productivity booster and stress reducer, some firms offer napping areas for their employees.[10] Nevertheless, the organizational napper must use discretion in napping so as not to be perceived as sleeping on the job. Toward this end, some workers nap in their cars or in a storeroom during lunch break. In companies where the organization accepts such behavior, some employees nap with their heads resting on their desks or work tables during breaks.

Put Extra Effort into Managing Multiple Priorities

A major time-management problem for employees is dealing with multiple demands placed on them from a variety of people. Clerical support personnel, for example, might support 10 workers, each of whom thinks he or she has a personal assistant. One approach to this problem is to let the people served know how you prioritize work. Among these priority systems are (a) first come, first served, (b) giving top priority to work for major customers, and (c) giving top priority to work that goes to top-level management. The worker facing multiple demands can allocate certain times of the day or week to each assigned project. For example, Thursday morning is for budget preparation, and Monday afternoon is for processing expense account vouchers.

Build Flexibility into Your System

A time management system must allow some room for flexibility. How else could you handle unanticipated problems? If you work 50 hours per week, build in a few hours for taking care of emergencies. If your plan is too tight, delegate some tasks to others or work more hours. Perhaps you can find a quicker way to accomplish several of your tasks. Finally, to avoid staleness and stress, your schedule must allow sufficient time for rest and relaxation.

The Management in Action presents an inside peek at the work habits of one of the best-known businesspersons of all time. As you will see, he would strongly endorse most of what you have read so far in this chapter.

2   UNDERSTANDING AND REDUCING PROCRASTINATION

Identify techniques for reducing procrastination.

procrastination

The delaying of action for no good reason.

The number-one time waster for most people is **procrastination**, the delaying of action for no good reason. Reducing procrastination pays substantial dividends in increased productivity, especially because speed can give a company a competitive advantage. Many people regard procrastination as a laughable weakness, particularly because procrastinators themselves joke about their problem. Yet procrastination has been evaluated as a profound, debilitating problem.[11] Exhibit 17-2 gives you an opportunity to think about your own tendencies toward procrastination, so get to it without delay. Here we consider why people procrastinate, and what can be done about the problem.

Why People Procrastinate

People procrastinate for many different reasons, with some of them being deep-rooted emotional problems, and others more superficial and related directly to the work. Here we look at six major reasons for procrastination.

1. Some people fear failure or other negative consequences. As long as a person delays doing something of significance, he or she cannot be regarded as having performed poorly on the project. Other negative consequences include looking foolish in the eyes of others or developing a bad reputation. For instance, if a manager delays making an oral presentation, nobody will know whether he or she is an ineffective speaker.
2. Procrastination may stem from a desire to avoid uncomfortable, overwhelming, or tedious tasks.
3. People frequently put off tasks that do not appear to offer a meaningful reward. Suppose you decide that your computer files need a thorough updating. Even though you know it should be done, having a completely updated directory might not be a particularly meaningful reward to you.
4. Some people dislike being controlled. When a procrastinator does not do things on time, he or she has successfully rebelled against being controlled by another person's time schedule.
5. People sometimes are assigned tasks they perceive to be useless or needless, such as rechecking someone else's work. Rather than proceed with the trivial task, the individual procrastinates.

Management *in Action*

Work Habits of the World's Richest Person

Many people have heard or read that the personal fortune of Microsoft chairman Bill Gates (estimated at $80 billion in June 2001) exceeds the gross domestic product of many nations, including Israel. Less well known about Gates is that his work habits contribute to his success as an executive. In addition to being the wealthiest person in the world, he is also considered to be one of the hardest-working businesspersons.

Bill Gates's work habits were scrutinized by a business magazine reporter who trailed him on a five-day business trip to India and South Africa. Sixteen-hour days were the norm for Gates, filled with customer meetings, audiences with heads of state, press interviews, photo sessions, speeches, and some autograph signing. Wedged in between were a few banquets at which Gates pushed his ideas, pep talks to local Microsoft workers, conferences with business partners, staged confabs with school children, and a few police-escorted motorcades.

Gates devotes about one-quarter of his work time each year to what he calls "evangelism"—trips to preach the Microsoft gospel. He measures his effectiveness by the number of events and meetings he can squeeze in. In reflecting on his 25,000-mile trip to India and South Africa, Gates said, "It was a great trip. The guys filled up my time really well."

A distinguishing characteristic about the Gates management style is how well he manages his time. Hardly a waking moment is squandered, whether he is roaming about as a high-tech ambassador, or back at headquarters plotting business strategy, or poring over tiny details of Microsoft's product development efforts. In recent years Gates also spent time helping build the argument that his company is not a monopoly. He takes an almost macho attitude about his schedule, leaving only the tiniest cracks in the day for eating, chatting with people, or simply chilling out. What little

spare time he did have on the trip in question he spent either catching up on his e-mail with a portable PC or hastily preparing for the next meeting.

During the trip he left no time for sightseeing other than what he could observe out the windows of the white Mercedes-Benzes that shuttled him between airports, hotels, and government offices. Nevertheless, Gates is intensely curious about the places he visits. He studies about each destination en route, reading books and magazine articles recommended by the heads of local subsidiaries. Once on the ground, he probes his escorts with endless questions, and concentrates intently on what they have to offer. These seemingly casual conversations often lead to direct action. Says Gates:

> I never realized that there are 14 distinct written and spoken languages in India. Now that I understand that, we're going to invest a whole lot more in localizing our products. And the raw software talent that you see there really grabs you. A billion people is a lot of people, and even though the country is really poor, there are a lot of talented people with world-class educations, and companies that are as forward-looking and capable as anywhere. I came back quite enthused about taking some of our software development overload here and moving it over there.

Recognizing that he is hero-worshipped at the company, Gates sets a vivid and pragmatic example of what he describes as a Microsoftian work ethic. His grueling schedule is just one not-so-subtle hint of what he expects from his employees. (A joke floats around Microsoft that the company has a flexible work schedule. You can work 16 hours a day, any days you choose.)

Another key work habit of Bill Gates is that he completes one task before starting another, and avoids working on two tasks at once. He won't even watch CNN Headline News while working out on a bicycle in his gym. However, once off the bike, Gates is likely to study the news intensely.

Gates always stays focused on the true purpose of his evangelical trips: to sell more software. Although he enjoyed meeting with the chiefs of state of South Africa and India, more important to Gates was conducting business. He held discussions with Indian government officials about the necessity of lowering taxes and import duties, enforcing stricter copyright laws, and modernizing the country's aging

telecommunications infrastructure. He also held business discussions with leading bankers in South Africa.

Commenting on the output of his trips, Gates said, "Believe me, I've got plenty to do already, so I wouldn't come on these trips if I didn't think I was getting something out of it that really helps Microsoft sell software."

Sources: Adapted from Brent Schlender, "On the Road with Chairman Bill." Reprinted from the May 26,1997 issue of *Fortune* by special permission; copyright 1997, Time, Inc. Also included is information from Susan B. Garland, "A Tough Sell, But Not Impossible," *Business Week*, January 18, 1999, p. 44; http://www.webho.com.

6. A curious reason for procrastination is to achieve the stimulation and excitement that stems from rushing to meet a deadline. For example, some people enjoy fighting their way through traffic or running through an airline terminal so they can make an appointment or airplane flight barely on time. They appear to enjoy the rush of adrenaline, endorphins, and other hormones associated with hurrying.[12]

Approaches to Reducing and Controlling Procrastination

Procrastination often becomes a strong habit that is difficult to change. Nevertheless, the following strategies and tactics can be helpful in overcoming procrastination:

1. *Break the task down into smaller units.* By splitting a large task into smaller units, you can make a job appear less overwhelming. Subdividing the task is referred to as the "Swiss-cheese method" because you keep putting little holes into the overall task. This approach is useful, of course, only if the task can be done in small pieces.

2. *Make a commitment to others.* Your tendency to procrastinate on an important assignment may be reduced if you publicly state that you will get the job done by a certain time. You might feel embarrassed if you fail to meet your deadline.

3. *Reward yourself for achieving milestones.* A potent technique for overcoming any counterproductive behavior pattern is to give yourself a reward for progress toward overcoming the problem. Make your reward commensurate with the magnitude of the accomplishment.

4. *Calculate the cost of procrastination.* You can sometimes reduce procrastination by calculating its cost. Remind yourself, for example, that you might lose out on obtaining a high-paying job you really want if your résumé and cover letter are not ready on time. The cost of procrastination would include the difference in the salary between the job you do find and the one you really wanted. Another cost would be the loss of potential job satisfaction.

5. *Use subliminal messages about overcoming procrastination.* For example, software called MindSet flashes positive, reinforcing messages across your computer

EXHIBIT 17-2

Procrastination Tendencies

477

Circle yes or no for each item:

1.	I usually do my best work under the pressure of deadlines.	Yes	No
2.	Before starting a project, I go through such rituals as sharpening every pencil, straightening up my desk more than once, and discarding bent paper clips.	Yes	No
3.	I crave the excitement of the "last minute rush."	Yes	No
4.	I often think that if I delay something, it will go away, or the person who asked for it will forget about it.	Yes	No
5.	I extensively research something before taking action, such as obtaining five different estimates before getting the brakes repaired on my car.	Yes	No
6.	I have a great deal of difficulty getting started on most projects, even those I enjoy.	Yes	No
7.	I keep waiting for the right time to do something, such as getting started on an important report.	Yes	No
8.	I often underestimate the time needed to do a project, and say to myself, "I can do this quickly, so I'll wait until next week."	Yes	No
9.	It is difficult for me to finish most projects or activities.	Yes	No
10.	I have several favorite diversions or distractions that I use to keep me from doing something unpleasant.	Yes	No

Total yes responses _____

The greater the number of yes responses, the more likely it is that you have a serious procrastination problem. A score of 8, 9, or 10 strongly suggests that procrastination lowers your productivity.

screen. The user can adjust the frequency and duration of the suggestions. The message can flash by subliminally (below the level of conscious awareness) or remain on screen for a few seconds. The antiprocrastination message reads: "My goals are obtainable. I am confident in my abilities. I make and keep deadlines." The same effect can be achieved by posting notes in your work and living areas, encouraging you to get something done by a particular time. For example, "The plan for recycling laser print cartridges is due September 15, and YOU CAN DO IT!!!!!"

6. *Counterattack.* Another way of combating procrastination is to force yourself to do something uncomfortable or frightening. After you begin, you are likely to find that the task is not as onerous as you thought. Assume you have been delaying learning a foreign language even though you know it will help your career. You remember how burdensome it was studying another language in school. You grit your teeth and remove the cellophane from the audiocassette for the target language. After listening for five minutes, you discover that beginning to study a foreign language again is not nearly as bad as you imagined.

7. *Post a progress chart in your work area.* The time and activity charts presented in Chapter 7 can be applied to combating procrastination. As you chart your progress in achieving each step in a large project, each on-time accomplishment will serve as a reward, and each missed deadline will be self-punishing. The constant reminder of what needs to be accomplished by what date will sometimes prod you to minimize delays. Exhibit 17-3 presents a basic version of a chart for combating procrastination.

EXHIBIT 17-3

A Time and Activity Chart to Combat Procrastination

Charting key tasks and their deadlines, along with your performance in meeting the deadlines, can sometimes help overcome procrastination.

	Deadlines for Task Accomplishment					
Task to Be Accomplished	Jan 1	Jan 31	Feb 15	Feb 28	Mar 15	Mar 31
Expense reports	Did it					
Real estate estimates		Blew it				
Web site installed			One day late			
Replace broken furniture				Made it		
Plan office picnic					On time	
Collect delinquent account						Blew it

3

Understand the nature of stress, including its consequences.

THE NATURE OF STRESS AND BURNOUT

Job stress and its related condition, job burnout, contribute to poor physical and mental health. Employee stress is a source of discomfort and a major concern to managers and stockholders. The American Institute of Stress reports that stress costs U.S. businesses between $200 billion and $300 billion a year in lost productivity, increased workers' compensation claims, turnover, and health care costs.[13] In order to effectively prevent and control stress, you first need to understand the nature and cause of these conditions. A good starting point in understanding stress symptoms is to take the self-quiz presented in Exhibit 17-4.

stress

The mental and physical condition that results from a perceived threat that cannot be dealt with readily.

As used here, **stress** is the mental and physical condition that results from a perceived threat that cannot be dealt with readily. Stress is therefore an internal response to a state of activation. The stressed person is physically and mentally aroused. Stress ordinarily occurs in a threatening or negative situation, such as being fired. However, stress can also be caused by a positive situation, such as receiving a major promotion.

A person experiencing stress displays certain symptoms indicating that he or she is trying to cope with a stressor (any force creating the stress reaction). These symptoms can include a host of physiological, emotional, and behavioral reactions.

Physiological symptoms of stress include increased heart rate, blood pressure, breathing rate, pupil size, and perspiration. If these physiological symptoms are severe or persist over a prolonged period, the result can be a stress-related disorder, such as a heart attack, hypertension, migraine headache, ulcer, colitis, or allergy. Stress also leads to a chemical imbalance that adversely affects the body's immune system. People experiencing emotional stress may experience difficulty shaking a common cold or recovering from sexually transmitted disease. In general, any disorder classified as psychosomatic is precipitated by emotional stress.

Emotional symptoms of stress include anxiety, tension, depression, discouragement, boredom, prolonged fatigue, feelings of hopelessness, and various kinds of defensive thinking. Behavioral symptoms include nervous habits, such as facial twitching, and sudden decreases in job performance due to forgetfulness and errors in concentration or judgment. Increased use of alcohol and other drugs may also occur.

Not all stress is bad. People require the right amount of stress to keep them mentally and physically alert. If the stress is particularly uncomfortable or distasteful, however, it will lower job performance—particularly on complex, demanding jobs. An example of a stressor that will lower job performance for most people is a bullying, abrasive manager who wants to see the employee fail. It is a person's perception of something (or somebody) that usually determines whether it acts as

EXHIBIT **17-4**

The Stress Questionnaire

Here is a brief questionnaire to give a rough estimate of whether you are facing too much stress. Apply each question to the last six months of your life. Check the appropriate column.

Mostly Yes	Mostly No	
☐	☐	1. Have you been feeling uncomfortably tense lately?
☐	☐	2. Do you frequently argue with people close to you?
☐	☐	3. Is your romantic life very unsatisfactory?
☐	☐	4. Do you have trouble sleeping?
☐	☐	5. Do you feel lethargic about life?
☐	☐	6. Do many people annoy or irritate you?
☐	☐	7. Do you have constant cravings for candy and other sweets?
☐	☐	8. Is your consumption of cigarettes or alcohol way up?
☐	☐	9. Are you becoming addicted to soft drinks, coffee, or tea?
☐	☐	10. Do you find it difficult to concentrate on your work?
☐	☐	11. Do you frequently grind your teeth?
☐	☐	12. Are you increasingly forgetful about little things, such as mailing a letter or responding to an e-mail?
☐	☐	13. Are you increasingly forgetful about big things, such as appointments and major errands?
☐	☐	14. Are you making far too many trips to the lavatory?
☐	☐	15. Have people commented lately that you do not look well?
☐	☐	16. Do you get into verbal fights with others too frequently?
☐	☐	17. Have you been involved in more than one break-up with a friend lately?
☐	☐	18. Do you have more than your share of tension headaches?
☐	☐	19. Do you feel nauseated much too often?
☐	☐	20. Do you feel light-headed or dizzy almost every day?
☐	☐	21. Do you have churning sensations in your stomach far too often?
☐	☐	22. Are you in a big hurry all the time?
☐	☐	23. Are far too many things bothering you these days?
☐	☐	24. Do you hurry through activities even when you are not rushed for time?
☐	☐	25. Do you often feel that you are in the panic mode?

Scoring

0–6	Mostly Yes answers: You seem to be experiencing a normal amount of stress.
7–16	Mostly Yes answers: Your stress level seems high. Become involved in some kind of stress management activity, such as the activities described in this chapter.
17–25	Mostly Yes answers: Your stress level appears to be much too high. Seek the help of a mental health professional or visit your family doctor (or do both).

a positive or negative stressor. For example, one person might perceive an inspection by top-level managers to be so frightening that he is irritable toward team members. Another manager might welcome the visit as a chance to proudly display her department's high-quality performance.

After prolonged exposure to job stress, a person runs the risk of feeling burned out—a drained, used-up feeling. **Job burnout** is a pattern of emotional, physical, and mental exhaustion in response to chronic job stressors. Cynicism, apathy, and indifference are the major behavioral symptoms of the burned-out worker. Hopelessness is another key symptom of burnout, with the worker often

job burnout

A pattern of emotional, physical, and mental exhaustion in response to chronic job stressors.

feeling that nothing he or she does makes a difference. Correspondingly, burnout involves losing a sense of the basic purpose and fulfillment of your work.[14] Supervisors are more at risk for burnout than other workers because they deal primarily with the demands of other people.[15]

Negative stress typically lowers job performance, yet many people perform well when experiencing stress, such as the heroic airplane pilot who safely lands a damaged jetliner filled with passengers. An extensive review of research about job stress concludes that stress is less likely to lower performance when employees have high levels of self-esteem and commitment to the organization. Not being a Type A personality (described later) also helps a worker cope with stress.[16]

Factors Contributing to Stress and Burnout

Factors within a person, as well as adverse organizational conditions, can cause or contribute to stress and burnout. Personal life stress and work stress also influence each other. Work stress can create problems—and therefore stress—at home. And stress stemming from personal problems can lead to problems—and therefore stress—at work. Because stress is additive, if you have considerable personal stress you will more susceptible to job stress, and vice versa.

Factors Within the Individual

Hostile, aggressive, and impatient people find ways of turning almost any job into a stressful experience. Such individuals are labeled Type A, in contrast to their more easygoing Type B counterparts. In addition to being angry, the outstanding trait of Type A people is their strong sense of time urgency, known as "hurry sickness." This sense of urgency compels them to achieve more and more in less and less time. Angry, aggressive (usually male) Type A people are more likely than Type Bs to experience cardiovascular disorders. In one study, Type A behavior was measured among 250 police workers and firefighters. A seven-year follow-up indicated that Type A people were more likely to have experienced cardiovascular disorders, including a fatal heart attack.[17]

Although Type A behavior is associated with coronary heart disease, only some features of the Type A personality pattern may be related to cardiac disorders. The adverse health effects generally stem from hostility, anger, cynicism, and suspiciousness in contrast to impatience, ambition, and drive. Recognize also that not every hard-driving, impatient person is correctly classified as Type A. Managers who love their work and enjoy other people are not particularly prone to heart disease.

locus of control

The way in which people look at causation in their lives.

Another notable personality characteristic related to job stress is **locus of control**, the way in which people look at causation in their lives. People who believe that they have more control over their actions than do external events are less stress prone. For example, a 50-year-old person with an internal locus of control might lose his job and say, "I don't care if a lot of age discrimination in business exists. I have many needed skills and many employers will want me. Age will not be an issue for me in finding suitable employment." This man's internal locus of control will help him ward off stress related to job loss. A 50-year-old with an external locus of control will experience high stress because the person believes that he or she is helpless in the face of job discrimination. A study about job stress and locus of control among 288 managers concluded that managers who possess a high internal locus of control should be selected for stressful positions.[18]

People who have high expectations are likely to experience job burnout at some point in their careers, because they may not receive as many rewards as they are seeking. People who need constant excitement also face a high risk of job burnout, because they bore easily and quickly.

Adverse Organizational Conditions

Under ideal conditions, workers experience just enough stress to prompt them to respond creatively and energetically to their jobs. Unfortunately, high stress levels created by adverse organizational conditions lead to many negative symptoms. A major contributor to job stress is work overload. Demands on white-collar workers appear to be at an all-time high, as companies attempt to increase work output and decrease staffing at the same time.

Entrepreneurs are particularly susceptible to work overload stress, as demonstrated in a study of 169 male and 56 female business owners from 12 small towns in Ontario. An entrepreneur was defined as a person who both owns and operates a service, retail, wholesale, or manufacturing business. Entrepreneurs scored higher on the workload scale of the Job Stress Questionnaire than did previously tested white-collar, blue-collar, and professional groups.[19]

Job frustrations caused by such factors as parts shortages, excessive politics, or insufficient funds can create job stress. Extreme conflict with other workers or with management is also a stressor. Having heavy responsibility without the right amount of formal authority upsets many employees. Another annoyance is short lead times—too little notice to get complex assignments accomplished. A powerful stressor today is job insecurity due to the many mergers and downsizings. Worrying about having one's job outsourced to another region, country, or a subcontractor is also a stressor.

According to the **job demand–job control model**, workers experience the most stress when the demands of the job are high, yet they have little control over the activity.[20] (See Exhibit 17-5.) A customer-service representative with limited authority who has to deal with a major error by the firm would fit this category. In contrast, when job demands are high and the worker has high control, the worker will be energized, motivated, and creative. A branch manager in a successful business might fit this scenario.

Interactions with customers can be a major stressor, according to interviews with 93 employees. Stressful events frequently cited include customers losing control, using profanity, badgering employees, harassing employees, and lying. The employees interviewed said that these adverse interactions with customers negatively affected the quality of their work environment.[21] Part of the problem is that the sales associate often feels helpless when placed in conflict with a customer. The sales associate is told that "the customer is always right." Furthermore, the store manager usually sides with the customer in a dispute with the sales associate.

Related to adverse customer interaction is the stressor of having to control the expression of emotion to please or avoid displeasing a customer. Imagine having to smile at a customer who belittles you or makes unwanted sexual advances. Alicia A.

job demand–job control model

A model demonstrating the relationship between high or low job demands and high or low job control. It shows that workers experience the most stress when the demands of the job are high yet they have little control over the activity.

EXHIBIT 17-5

The Job Demand-Job Control Model

A worker is likely to experience the most job stress when he or she exercises low control over a job with high demands.

	Low Job Demands	High Job Demands
Low Control	Passive Job	High-strain Job
High Control	Low-strain Job	Active Job

emotional labor

The process of regulating both feelings and expressions to meet organizational goals.

Grandey defines **emotional labor** as the process of regulating both feelings and expressions to meet organizational goals.[22] The process involves both surface acting and deep acting. Surface acting means faking expressions such as smiling, whereas deep acting involves controlling feelings such as suppressing anger toward a customer you perceive to be annoying or hostile. Sales workers and customer service representatives carry the biggest emotional labor among all workers because so often they have to fake facial expressions and feelings, so as to please customers.

Engaging in emotional labor for prolonged periods of time can lead to job dissatisfaction, stress, and burnout. A contributing cause is that faking expressions and emotion takes a physiological toll. Workers who engage in emotional labor may also develop cardiovascular problems and weakened immune systems.

Absence of ample positive feedback and other rewards is strongly associated with job burnout. As a consequence of not knowing how well they are doing and not receiving recognition, employees often become discouraged and emotionally exhausted. The result is often—but certainly not always—job burnout.

Adverse conditions do not exist in all organizations. However, enough of these problems are present to make long-term stress and burnout a serious problem. Many employers recognize that workers often suffer from stressful conditions and therefore take constructive action to lessen the problem. At Merck, for example, employees were assigned to teams devoted to solving problems such as complaints about overwork, inadequate training, and poor new-hire screening. The team analyzed and reorganized work so that workers perceived they had more control over their workloads and schedules.

In one area of the company, payroll employees felt dissatisfied with heavy amounts of overtime. Based on problem-solving discussions, team leaders discovered that most of the payroll work was more critical earlier in the week than toward the end. Among the solutions proposed were reducing commuting time by allowing employees to work at home more often, and implementing compressed work weeks. Merck provided the hardware and software needed to input data from home. After implementing the solutions to problems, turnover slowed from 45 percent to 32 percent, and overtime costs and absenteeism decreased. Workload pressures were eased by slashing overtime and commute time.[23]

4   STRESS MANAGEMENT TECHNIQUES

Explain how stress can be managed effectively.

As the Merck example illustrates, organizations can play a major role in preventing and remedying stress by correcting the kinds of conditions we have discussed and by offering wellness programs and work/life programs. This chapter, however, emphasizes what individuals can do to deal with stress and burnout. Techniques for managing job stress can be divided into three categories: control, symptom management, and escape.[24]

Methods for Control and Reduction of Stress

The five control techniques described next consist of both actions and mental evaluations that help people take charge in stressful situations.

1. *Get social support.* Few people can go it alone when experiencing prolonged stress. Receiving social support—encouragement, understanding, and friendship—from other people is an important strategy for coping successfully with job stress.
2. *Improve your work habits.* You can use the techniques described for improving your personal productivity to reduce stress. People typically experience stress

when they feel themselves losing control of their work assignments. Conscientious employees are especially prone to negative stress when they cannot get their work under control.

3. *Develop positive self-talk.* Stress-resistant people are basically optimistic and cheerful. This kind of positivism can be learned by switching to positive self-talk instead of thinking many negative thoughts.

4. *Hug the right people.* Hugging is now being seriously regarded as vital for physical and mental well-being. People who do not receive enough quality touching may suffer from low self-esteem, ill health, depression, and loneliness. Conversely, quality touching may help people cope better with job stress. The hugging, however, has to represent loving and caring.

5. *Simplify your life by getting rid of unessential activities.* Andrew Weil, the natural health guru, recommends that you downsize your life. He believes that significant stress stems from the complexity of our lives. Our material possessions contribute to this complexity. Many people have too many physical objects that require attention and maintenance. Weill recommends that you get rid of what you can spare.[25] You will gain greater control of your life situation by having less clutter. Note, however, that an oversimplified life can also be an impoverished life, creating stress of its own.

6. *Demand less than perfection from yourself.* By demanding less than 100 percent performance from yourself, you will fail less frequently in your own perceptions. Not measuring up to one's own unrealistically high standards creates a considerable amount of stress. Few humans can operate with zero defects or ever achieve Six Sigma perfection!

Symptom Management

This category of stress management refers to tactics that address the symptoms related to job stress. Dozens of symptom management techniques have been developed, including the following:

1. *Make frequent use of relaxation techniques.* Learning to relax reduces the adverse effects of stress. The **relaxation response** is a general-purpose method of learning to relax by yourself. The key ingredient of this technique is to make yourself quiet and comfortable. At the same time, think of the word one (or any simple chant or prayer) with every breath for about 10 minutes. The technique slows you down both physiologically and emotionally. An extremely easy relaxation method is to visualize yourself in an unusually pleasant situation, such as floating on a cloud, walking by a lake, or lying on a comfortable beach. Pick any fantasy that you find relaxing.

2. *Get appropriate physical exercise.* Physical exercise helps dissipate some of the tension created by job stress, and it also helps the body ward off future stress-related disorders. A physically fit, well-rested person can usually tolerate more frustration than can a physically run-down, tired person. One way in which exercise helps combat stress is that it releases endorphins. These morphine-like chemicals are produced in the brain and act as painkillers and antidepressants. Workers who travel frequently particularly need physical exercise because travel can damage the body, producing such symptoms as muscle cramps and even blood clots from long airplane trips. More information about the benefits of physical exercise is presented in Exhibit 17-6.

3. *Try to cure hurry sickness.* People with hurry sickness should learn how to relax and enjoy the present for its own sake. Specific tactics include having at least

relaxation response
A general-purpose method of learning to relax by yourself.

EXHIBIT 17-6

The Benefits of Physical Exercise

- Increases energy
- Reduces feelings of tension, anxiety, and depression
- Improves sleep
- Improves concentration
- Enhances self-esteem and self-confidence
- Helps you lose weight or maintain a healthy weight
- Reduces the risk of heart disease, or improves cardiac function if you have had a heart attack or bypass
- Reduces the risk of colon cancer

- Lowers high blood pressure and the risk of stroke
- Controls blood sugar levels if you have, or are at risk for, diabetes
- Improves bone density and lowers the risk of osteoporosis and fractures as you get older

Sources: The American Heart Association, the American College of Sports Medicine, Shape Up America!, The American Academy of Family Physicians, and National Cattlemen's Beef Association. As compiled by Shari Roan, "The Theory of Inactivity," *The Los Angeles Times,* March 9, 1998.

one idle period every day; eating nutritious, not overly seasoned foods to help decrease nervousness; and finding enrichment in an area of life not related to work.

Escape Methods of Stress Management

Escape methods are actions and reappraisals of situations that provide the stressed individual some escape from the stressor. Eliminating the stressor is the most effective escape technique. For example, if a manager is experiencing stress because of serious understaffing in his or her department, that manager should negotiate to

EXHIBIT 17-7

Stress Busters

- Take a nap when facing heavy pressures. "Power napping" is regarded as one of the most effective techniques for reducing and preventing stress.
- Give in to your emotions. If you are angry, disgusted, or confused, admit your feelings to yourself. Suppressing your emotions adds to stress.
- Take a brief break from the stressful situation and do something small and constructive like washing your car, emptying a wastebasket, or getting a haircut.
- Get a massage because it can loosen tight muscles, improve your blood circulation, and calm you down.
- Get help with a stressful task from a coworker, boss, or friend.
- Concentrate on reading, surfing the Internet, a sport, or a hobby. Contrary to common sense, concentration is at the heart of stress reduction.

- Have a quiet place at home and have a brief idle period there every day.
- Take a leisurely day off from your routine.
- Finish something you have started, however small. Accomplishing almost anything reduces some stress.
- Stop to smell the flowers, make friends with a young child or elderly person, or play with a kitten or puppy.
- Strive to do a good job, but not a perfect job.
- Work with your hands, doing a pleasant task.
- Find somebody or something that makes you laugh, and have a good laugh.
- Minimize drinking caffeinated or alcoholic beverages. Drink fruit juice or water instead.

receive authorization to hire additional help. Mentally blocking out a stressful thought is another escape technique, but it may not work in the long run.

A useful method of escaping stress is to identify your work skills, and then find work to match those skills. Assessing your skills and preferences can help you understand why you find some tasks or roles more stressful than others.[26] For example, many people enter the computer field without having appropriate skills and interests for that type of work. When they are asked to perform such tasks as coding for nine hours in one day, they become stressed out, because they lack the right aptitude and interest for such work.

Given that you could probably locate 30,000 articles, books, and Internet comments on the subject of job stress, we have not mentioned every possible approach to managing stress. To prevent information overload, study Exhibit 17-7 to get a few more ideas on reducing stress, and reinforce a few suggestions made already.

SUMMARY OF KEY POINTS

1 Identify techniques for improving work habits and time management. One way of increasing your personal productivity is to improve your work habits and time management skills: develop a mission, goals, and a strong work ethic. Clean up your work area and sort out your tasks. Prepare a to-do list and assign priorities. Also, streamline your work; work at a steady pace; minimize times wasters; and concentrate on one task at a time. Concentrate on high-output tasks; do creative and routine work at different times; and stay in control of paperwork, e-mail, and voice mail. Making effective use of office technology is essential. Strive to achieve peak performance, take naps, and put extra effort into managing multiple priorities.

2 Identify techniques for reducing procrastination. Avoid procrastinating by understanding why you procrastinate and taking remedial action, including the following: break the task down into smaller units, make a commitment to others, reward yourself for achieving milestones, calculate the cost of procrastination, use subliminal messages, counterattack against an uncomfortable task, and post a progress chart.

3 Understand the nature of stress, including its consequences. Stress is the mental and physical condition that results from a perceived threat that cannot be dealt with readily. Job burnout is a pattern of emotional, physical, and mental exhaustion in response to chronic job stressors. Hopelessness is another key symptom of burnout. Key stress symptoms include tension, anxiety, and poor concentration and judgment. Job stress is caused by factors within the individual such as Type A behavior and an external locus of control. A variety of adverse organizational conditions, including work overload and low control over a demanding job, contribute to stress. People with high expectations are candidates for burnout. Limited rewards and lack of feedback from the organization contribute to burnout.

4 Explain how stress can be managed effectively. Methods of preventing and controlling stress and burnout can be divided into three categories: attempts to control stressful situations, symptom management, and escapes from the stressful situation. Specific tactics include eliminating stressors, getting sufficient physical exercise, using relaxation techniques, curing hurry sickness, getting emotional support from others, and improving work habits.

KEY TERMS AND PHRASES

Work ethic, *472*

Work streamlining, *473*

Peak performance, *476*

Procrastination, *478*

Stress, *482*

Job burnout, *483*

Locus of control, *484*

Job demand–job control model, *485*

Emotional labor, *486*

Relaxation response, *487*

QUESTIONS

1. What is your mission in life? If you do not have a mission, how might you develop one?
2. How can an employee be well organized yet unproductive?
3. Many people complain that they have suffered a productivity loss after their hand-held computer crashed. How might these people have planned for the crash?
4. How can a person determine whether answering e-mail is an important part of the job or a productivity drain?

5. How can a person use achieving a state of peak performance to reduce stress?
6. Why is heavy business travel a negative stressor for so many managers, yet a source of enjoyment and excitement for others?
7. Although this chapter is mostly about managing oneself, how might a manager use the information to help group members?

CRITICAL THINKING QUESTIONS

1. Assume you are the human resource director for a large, diversified company and you want to develop a tentative policy about employee napping to boost productivity and reduce stress. Perhaps you might want to call in a few other managers to help you refine the policy. Plan for such possibilities as (a) how many members of a department or team are allowed to nap at the same time, (b) if you have a formal napping room, who is allowed to nap in the room at the same time, and (c) the priority napping has in relation to taking care of urgent tasks.
2. Which factors, or variables, influence how much work stress is good for a person? Support your answer with research.

SKILL-BUILDING EXERCISE: Good and Bad Ways to Reduce Stress

The purpose of this exercise is to help participants understand the difference between constructive and less constructive ways of reducing stress. The materials needed for the exercise are a white board, a black board, an overhead projector, or a computerized method of projecting information on a screen.

For 10 minutes, participants suggest as many techniques as possible for managing or reducing stress that they are willing to share with class members. (Some class members might have ways of reducing stress they would prefer to keep private.) Participants speak one at a time. As each new technique is suggested, the audience shouts either "Good" or "Bad." Based on majority opinion, the moderator places the technique in the Good or Bad column.

A good technique is defined roughly as one that produces almost all benefits. A bad technique is one that produces short-lived benefits such as a "high," followed by negative side effects. (An example would be getting drunk to escape a major problem.) For some or all of the techniques, people should justify their classification as Good or Bad.

After the techniques are listed for all to see, the class discusses any conclusions about the difference between good and bad techniques. The group also discusses why knowing the difference is important.

Source: Adapted from Robert E. Epstein, "Stress Busters: 11 Quick, Fun Games to Tame the Beast," *Psychology Today,* March/April 2000, p. 34.

INTERNET SKILL-BUILDING EXERCISE: Boosting and Lowering Productivity on the Internet

The number of people online continues to grow substantially throughout the world. Gather into small teams or work individually to identify 10 ways in which the Internet can increase personal productivity and reduce stress either on the job or at home. Also identify several ways in which the Internet can decrease personal productivity or increase stress. To supple- ment your own thinking, you might search the Internet for ideas on how the Internet is supposed to boost productivity. Also, look for negative comments about the ability of the Internet to boost productivity. However, the negative are more likely to be found in hard copy than online.

CASE PROBLEM 17-A: Meridian Workers Go Surfing

Jimmy Linn is the director of logistics at Meridian Furnishings, a furniture manufacturer based in Charlotte, North Carolina. Logistics plays a major role in company operations because virtually all the furniture Meridian manufactures is packed and shipped to customers. Late deliveries pose a chronic problem in the furniture industry, so Meridian management attempts to gain a competitive edge by making shipments as promised. At times the logistics group must make particularly rapid deliveries to compensate for manufacturing delays.

All employees in the logistics division work at computers for such varied tasks as keeping track of deliveries and the location of trucks, e-mail, word processing, and budget preparation. In addition, logistics workers search the Internet for information such as road conditions, shipping rates for truckers and the railroad, and changes in government regulations about shipping.

Linn now faces a concern that many logistics workers at Meridian are slipping into a pattern of sometimes using the Internet for recreational purposes. For example, while walking around the office, Linn noticed several instances of travel agency and sports Web sites on computer monitors. Meridian's explicit written policy about Internet use states that Web access and e-mail are company resources to be used for business purposes only. The policy also stipulates that violators could be subject to disciplinary action. Little discussion ever takes place about the Internet policy since it was originally established.

Before bringing the potential problem of Internet misuse to the attention of employees, Linn decided to obtain more information. To help determine the extent of the problem, he hired a consultant who specializes in monitoring employee use of the Internet. The consultant, Suzanne Schuster, studied server logs that record all the Internet activity on a network, indicating who visited what Web site, how long they stayed, what they looked at, what they searched for, and which Web site they visited next. Schuster also retrieved old e-mail messages for auditing.

Her findings indicated some Internet and e-mail misuse, but not an alarming pattern of substantial neglect of work. Among the activities revealed by the report were that, on average, employees were spending about 30 minutes per day surfing the Web for purposes not directly related to Meridian business. The diversionary visits to Web sites included reading the news, making travel arrangements, visiting job search sites, company recruitment ads, playing video games, and the occasional visit to pornographic sites. About 10 percent of e-mail messages were nonwork-related, including sending messages to friends, and forwarding jokes to other Meridian employees.

Although not stunned by the evidence, Linn decided to confront employees about the problem. First, he held a meeting with his four supervisors to review the consultant's findings. Schuster attended the meeting to present the findings in detail, and answer questions. The supervisors offered various reactions to the findings. One supervisor thought the company should begin to impose strong sanctions on any employee violating the Internet policy. Another thought the recreational use of the Internet was not substantial enough to bother bringing to the attention of employees. A third supervisor thought that the company should monitor Web use regularly, and punish only the severe violators. The fourth supervisor suggested that the company hold an information-gathering session with employees to go beyond the statistical report.

Linn, impressed with the idea of an information-gathering session, scheduled a town hall meeting with all interested employees for 4 P.M. the following Friday. Every eligible employee attended the meeting, and most contributed input to the situation of nonwork-related use of the Internet. Several employees explained why the recreational use of Web sites probably helps the company.

A logistics technician said, "I spend much less time on my surfing breaks than the time the smokers use up on their smoking breaks outside the building. Since I'm not a caffeine addict either, I don't take breaks to feed my habit. Besides, the few moments I spend surfing the net or reading an e-mail joke give me the energy I need to dig back into work."

An office assistant contributed this input, "With all due respect to company policy, the so-called nonwork use of the Web and e-mail is a low-cost stress reducer. When I'm having a stressful day, I browse one of my favorite online stores. Five minutes of walking down the virtual isles of Abercrombie and Fitch lowers my stress level like magic. In some of those high-tech companies, you get a back rub at your desk with a real masseur if you're stressed out. That would cost Meridian a lot more, and take much more time than a few minutes of surfing the Web."

The most senior supervisor said, "Employees always find a way to spend a few minutes not working. It could be a trip to the water cooler, a chat at the copy machine, or watching birds outside the window. So now it's surfing. Except for a few workaholics nobody puts in 100 percent effort on the job. Even top execs have been known to take an afternoon off for golf."

Linn ended the meeting with these words: "Thanks so much for your candor and your useful input. We're going to study our Internet policy a little further and then get back to you." As he left the meeting Linn pondered whether some of his employees were making excuses for surfing, or actually using the Internet to enhance productivity.

Discussion Questions

1. What is your opinion of the effectiveness of using Web surfing to relieve stress?

2. What is your opinion of the effectiveness of using Web surfing to enhance productivity?

3. What policy recommendations can you make to the logistics division of Meridian about the nonwork use of Web surfing and e-mail?

Source: Adapted from: Alan Cohen, "No Web for You," *Fortune Small Biz*, October 2000, pp. 44–56.

488

CASE PROBLEM 17-B: The Busy Office Manager

Mike Powers looked at the kitchen clock and said to his wife, Ruth, "Oh no, it's 7:25. It's my turn to drop off Jason and Gloria at the child-care center. Jason hasn't finished breakfast, and Gloria is still in her pajamas. Can you get Gloria dressed for me?"

Ruth responded, "Ok, I'll help Gloria, but today is your turn to take care of the children. I have a client presentation at 8:30 this morning. I need to prepare for a few more minutes."

"Forget I asked," said Mike. "I'll take care of it. Once again I'll start my day in a frenzy, late for child care, and just barely making it to work on time."

"Why didn't you get up when the alarm rang the first time?" asked Ruth.

"Don't you remember, we talked until one this morning? It seems like we never get to talk to each other until midnight," Mike replied.

After getting Jason and Gloria settled at the child-care center, Mike dashed off to the public accounting firm where he worked as the office manager. After greeting several staff members, Mike turned on his computer to check his e-mail. Ann Gabrielli, one of the partners in the firm, left the following message: "See you today at 11:30 for the review of overhead expenses. Two other partners will be attending."

Mike quickly looked at his desk calendar. According to his calendar, the meeting was one week from today. Mike called Gabrielli immediately and said, "Ann, my apologies. My schedule says that the meeting is one week from today at 11:30, not today. I'm not ready with the figures for today's meeting."

"My calendar says the meeting is today," said Gabrielli harshly. "I'm ready for the meeting and so are Craig and Gunther (the other partners). This isn't the first time you've gotten your weeks mixed up. The meeting will go on, however poorly you have to perform."

"I'll be there," said Mike. "It's just a question of reviewing some figures that I've already collected."

After putting down the phone, Mike calculated that he had about 2 hours and 40 minutes in which to prepare a preliminary report on reducing overhead. He then glanced at his desk calendar to see what else he had scheduled this morning. The time looked clear except for one entry: "PA/LC."

"What is PA/LC?" thought Mike. "I can't imagine what these initials stand for. Wait a minute, now I know. The initials stand for performance appraisal with Lucy Cruthers, our head

bookkeeper. I'm not ready for that session. And I can't do it this morning. Mike then sent Cruthers an e-mail message, suggesting that they meet the following week at the same time.

Cruthers answered back immediately. She wrote that she would not be able to meet the following week because that was the first day of her vacation. Mike sent her another note: "I'll get back to you later with another date. I don't have time now to make plans."

Next, Mike informed the department assistant, Lois Wang, that he had to hurriedly prepare for the 11:30 meeting. Mike asked for her cooperation in keeping visitors away the rest of the morning.

He then retrieved his computer directory to look for the file on overhead expenses that he began last week. As he scanned the directory, he found only three files that might be related to the topic: COST, EXPENSES, and TRIM. Mike reasoned that the file must be one of these three.

Mike retrieved the file, COST. It proved to be a summary of furniture expenses for the firm. Upon bringing EXPENSES up on the screen, Mike found that it was his expense account report for a business trip he took seven months ago. TRIM was found to be a list of cost estimates for lawn-care services.

Agitated, and beginning to sweat profusely, Mike asked Lois Wang to help him. "I'm stuck," he pleaded. "I need to find my file for the overhead expense analysis I was doing for the partners. Do you recall what I named the file? Did I give it to you on disk?"

"Let me see if I can help," said Wang. "We''ll search your directory together." Wang scanned about 100 files. "What a clutter," she sighed. You ought to clean out your files sometime soon. Here's a possibility, PTR."

"I doubt it," said Mike. "'PTR' stands for partner. I'm looking for a file about overhead expenses."

"But you are preparing the file for the partners, aren't you?"

Lois proved to be right. The PTR file contained the information Mike sought. Within 30 minutes he completed the spreadsheet analysis he needed. He then prepared a brief memo explaining his findings. With 20 minutes left before the presentation, Mike asked Lucy if she could run off three copies in a hurry. Lucy explained that the photocopier was not operating and offered to print out three additional copies from Mike's computer files.

"Bring them into my meeting with the partners as soon as you can," said Mike. "I've run out of time."

On the way to the meeting, Mike exhaled a few times and consciously relaxed his muscles to overcome the tension accumulated from preparing the report under so much pressure. Mike performed reasonably well during the meeting. The partners accepted his analysis of overhead expenses and said they would study his findings further. As the meeting broke up at 12:30, the senior partner commented to Mike, "If you had gotten your weeks straight, I think you would have presented your analysis in more depth. Your report was useful, but I know you are capable of doing a more sophisticated analysis."

After returning from lunch, Mike revised his daily planner again. He noticed a Post-it™ note attached to the light on his desk. The entry on the slip of paper said, "Racquetball, Monday night with Ziggy."

"Not again," Mike said to himself in a groan of agony. "Tonight I've got to get Jason and Gloria to bed. Ruth has a class scheduled for her course in Japanese. I'll have to call Ziggy now. I hope he's in his office."

Mike left an URGENT message on Ziggy's e-mail, offering his apologies. He thought to himself, "I hope Ziggy won't be too annoyed. This is the second time this year I've had to reschedule a match at the last moment."

Mike returned from lunch at 2:00 P.M. He decided to add more details to the overhead expense report he had prepared for the partners. By 4:00 P.M. Mike was ready to begin the tasks outlined on his daily planner. At that point Lois Wang walked into Mike's office and announced, "There's a representative here from AccountTemps. She said she was in the build-ing so she decided to drop in to talk about their temporary employment services."

"Might as well let her in," said Mike. "We will be hiring some temporary bookkeepers soon. AccountTemps has a good reputation. It's getting too late to do much today anyway."

Mike made it to the child-care center by 5:45 and packed Jason and Gloria into the family minivan. Gloria, the eldest child, asked if the family could eat at Hardee's this evening. Mike said, "OK, but I'll have to stop at an ATM first. I don't have enough cash on hand to eat out. We'll stop at the ATM then stop by the house and see if Mom wants to eat out tonight before class."

Mike and the children arrived home at 6:15 and asked Ruth if she would like to have a family dinner at Hardee's this evening.

"I have about one hour to spare before class," said Ruth. "Why not? By the way, how was your day?"

"My day?" asked Mike with a sigh. "I just fell one day farther behind schedule. I'll have to do some paperwork after the children are asleep. Maybe we can watch the late-night news together this evening. We should both be free by then."

Discussion Questions

1. What time management mistakes does Mike appear to be making?
2. What does Mike appear to be doing right from the standpoint of managing time?
3. What suggestions can you offer Mike to help him get his schedule more under control?
4. What evidence do you find that Mike is experiencing negative stress?

E N D N O T E S

1. Jill Rosenfeld, ed., "It's About Time," *Fast Company*, November 1999, p. 152.
2. Ed Brown, "The 'Natural Laws' of Saving Time," *Fortune*, February 1, 1999, p. 138.
3. Edwin C. Bliss, "The Productive Way to End Each Day," *Manager's Edge*, December 2000, p. 1.
4. Price Pritchett, *The Employee Handbook of New Work Habits for a Radically Changing World* (Dallas, TX: Pritchett & Associates, Inc., undated).
5. Robert E. Kelley as cited in *Manager's Edge*, sample issue, 2001.
6. Shane Murphy, *The Achievement Zone: Eight Skills for Winning All the Time from the Playing Field to the Boardroom* (New York: G. P. Putnam's Sons, 1996).
7. Ingrid Lorch-Bacci, "Achieving Peak Performance: The Hidden Dimension," *Executive Management Forum*, January 1991, pp. 1–4.
8. Donald J. McNerney, "Napping at Work: You Snooze, You Win!" *HRfocus*, March 1995, p. 3.
9. Harriet Johnson Brackey, "Snoozing Studies Alarm Experts," *Knight Ridder*, July 6, 1998.
10. Lisa Lee Freeman, ed., "Dozing for Dollars," *Working Woman*, October 1999, pp. 71–72.
11. Robert Boice, *Procrastination and Blocking: A Novel, Practical Approach* (Westport, CT: Greenwood Publishing Group, 1996).
12. "When to Procrastinate and When to Get Going," *WorkingSMART*, March 1992, pp., 1–2.
13. William Atkinson, "When Stress Won't Go Away," *HR Magazine*, December 2000, p. 106.
14. Lin Grensing-Pophal, "HR, Heal Thyself," *HR Magazine*, March 1999, p. 84.
15. Cynthia L. Cordes and Thomas Dougherty, "A Review and an Integration of Research on Job Burnout," *Academy of Management Review*, October 1993, p. 644.
16. Steve M. Jex, *Stress and Job Performance: Theory, Research, and Implications for Managerial Practice* (Thousand Oaks, CA: Sage, 1998).
17. John Schaubroeck, Daniel C. Ganster, and Barbara E. Kemmer, "Job Complexity, 'Type A' Behavior, and Cardiovascular Disorder: A Prospective Study," *Academy of Management Journal*, April 1994, pp. 426–439.
18. M. Afzalur Rahim, "Relations of Stress, Locus of Control, and Social Support to Psychiatric Symptoms and Propensity to Leave a Job," *Journal of Business and Psychology*, Winter 1997, pp. 159–174.
19. Julie Aitken Harris, Robert Saltsone, and Maryann Fraboni, "An Evaluation of the Job Stress Questionnaire with a Sample of Entrepreneurs," *Journal of Business and Psychology*, Spring 1999, pp. 447–455.

490

20. Marilyn L. Fox, Deborah J. Dwyer, and Daniel C. Ganster, "Effects of Stressful Job Demands and Control on Physiological and Attitudinal Outcomes in a Hospital Setting," *Academy of Management Journal*, April 1993, pp. 290–292.

21. James D. Brodzinski, Robert P. Scherer, and Karen A. Goyer, "Workplace Stress: A Study of Internal and External Pressures Placed on Employees," *Personnel Administrator*, July 1989, pp. 77–78.

22. Alicia A. Grandey, "Emotion Regulation in the Workplace: A New Way to Conceptualize Emotional Labor," *Journal of Occupational Health Psychology*, 5, no. 1 (2000), pp. 95–110.

23. Jennifer Laabs, "Overload," *Workforce*, January 1999, pp. 34–35.

24. Janina Latack, "Coping with Job Stress: Measures and Future Direction for Scale Development," *Journal of Applied Psychology*, August 1986, pp. 522–526; David Antonioni, "Two Strategies for Responding to Stressors: Managing Conflict and Clarifying Work Expectations," *Journal of Business and Psychology*, Winter 1996, pp. 287–295; Gail Dutton, "Cutting Edge Stressbusters," *HRfocus*, September 1998, pp. 11–12.

25. Andrew Weil, "Beating Stress," *USA Weekend*, December 26–28, 1997, p. 4.

26. Atkinson, "When Stress Won't Go Away," pp. 108–109.

Glossary

achievement motivation Finding joy in accomplishment for its own sake.

action plan The specific steps necessary to achieve a goal or objective.

active listening Listening for full meaning, without making premature judgments or interpretations.

activity In the PERT method, the physical and mental effort required to complete an event.

activity-based accounting (ABC) An accounting procedure that allocates the costs of producing a product or service to the activities performed and the resources used.

administrative management The use of management principles in the structuring and managing of an organization.

affective conflict Conflict that focuses on more personal or subjective issues and is dealt with more emotionally than intellectually.

affiliation need A desire to have close relationships with others and be a loyal employee or friend.

affirmative action An employment practice that complies with antidiscrimination law and correcting past discriminatory practices.

alternative workplace A combination of nontraditional work practices, settings, and locations that supplements the traditional office.

anchoring In the decision-making process, placing too much value on the first information received and ignoring later information.

authority The formal right to get people to do things or the formal right to control resources.

autocratic leader A task-oriented leader who retains most of the authority for himself or herself and is not generally concerned with group members' attitudes toward decisions.

B

balance of trade A measure of the dollar volume of a country's exports relative to its imports over a specified time period.

balanced scorecard A set of measures to provide a quick but comprehensive view of the business.

behavior In performance appraisal, what people actually do on the job.

behavior mismatch A condition that occurs when one person's actions do not meet another's expectations.

behavior modification A way of changing behavior by rewarding the right responses and punishing or ignoring the wrong responses.

behavioral interviewing A style of interviewing in which the interviewer asks questions whose answers reveal behaviors that would be either strengths or weaknesses in a given position.

bounded rationality The observation that people's limited mental abilities, combined with external influences over which they have little or no control, prevent them from making entirely rational decisions.

brainstorming A group method of solving problems, gathering information, and stimulating creative thinking. The basic technique is to generate numerous ideas through unrestrained and spontaneous participation by group members.

break-even analysis A method of determining the relationship between total costs and total revenues at various levels of production or sales activity.

broadbanding A compensation system in which the company reduces the number of pay grades based on job position, replacing them with broader pay ranges that reward performance.

budget A spending plan expressed in numerical terms for a future period of time.

bureaucracy A rational, systematic, and precise form of organization in which rules, regulations, and techniques of control are specifically defined.

capital expenditure budget A plan for spending money on assets used to produce goods or services.

cash budget A forecast of cash receipts and payments.

cash flow Amount of net cash generated by a business during a specific period.

centralization The extent to which authority is retained at the top of the organization.

charisma The ability to lead or influence others based on personal charm, magnetism, inspiration, and emotion.

coaching A method for helping employees perform better, which usually occurs on the spot and involves informal discussion and suggestions.

coalition A specific arrangement of parties working together to combine their power, thus exerting influence on another individual or group.

cognitive conflict Conflict that focuses on substantive, issue-related differences and is dealt with more intellectually than emotionally.

communication The process of exchanging information by the use of words, letters, symbols, or nonverbal behavior.

communication network A pattern or flow of messages that traces the communication from start to finish.

communication overload (or information overload) A condition in which an individual receives so much information that he or she becomes overwhelmed.

company intranet A Web site designed only for company employees, often containing proprietary information.

compressed work week A full-time work schedule that allows 40 hours of work in less than five days.

computer-based training (Internet-based training) A learning experience based on the interaction between the trainee and a computer.

computer goof-offs Employees who spend so much time attempting new computer routines and accessing information of questionable value that they neglect key aspects of their jobs.

concurrent control A type of control that monitors activities while they are carried out.

conflict The simultaneous arousal of two or more incompatible motives.

conflict of interest A situation that occurs when one's judgment or objectivity is compromised.

confrontation Dealing with a controversial or emotional topic directly.

constructive criticism A form of criticism designed to help improve performance or behavior.

contingency approach to management A perspective on management that emphasizes that no single way to manage people or work is best in every situation. It encourages managers to study individual and situational differences before deciding on a course of action.

contingency plan An alternative plan to be used if the original plan cannot be implemented or a crisis develops.

contingent workers Part-time or temporary employees who are not members of the employer's permanent workforce.

corporate culture (organizational culture) The system of shared values and beliefs that actively influence the behavior of organization members.

corporate social consciousness A set of consciously held shared values that guide decision making.

corporate social performance The extent to which a firm responds to the demands of its stakeholders for behaving in a socially responsible manner.

corrective discipline A type of discipline that allows employees to correct their behavior before punishment is applied.

creativity The process of developing novel ideas that can be put into action.

critical path The path through the PERT network that includes the most time-consuming sequence of events and activities.

cross-functional team A group composed of workers from different specialties at the same organizational level who come together to accomplish a task.

cultural sensitivity Awareness of local and national customs and their importance in effective interpersonal relationships.

culture shock Physical and psychological symptoms that can develop when a person is placed in a foreign culture.

cumulative trauma disorders Injuries caused by repetitive motions over prolonged periods of time.

customer departmentalization An organization structure based on customer needs.

data mining The extraction of useful analyses from the mass of information available to firms.

decentralization The extent to which authority is passed down to lower levels in an organization.

decision A choice among alternatives.

decision-making software Any computer program that helps a decision maker work through problem-solving and decision-making steps.

decision tree A graphic illustration of the alternative solutions available to solve a problem.

decisiveness The extent to which a person makes up his or her mind promptly and prudently.

decoding The communication stage in which the receiver interprets the message and translates it into meaningful information.

defensive communication The tendency to receive messages in a way that protects self-esteem.

deficiency needs Lower-order needs that must be satisfied to ensure a person's existence, security, and requirements for human contact.

delegation Assigning formal authority and responsibility for accomplishing a specific task to another person.

departmentalization The process of subdividing work into departments.

development A form of personal improvement that usually consists of enhancing knowledge and skills of a complex and unstructured nature.

deviation In a control system, the size of the discrepancy between performance standards and actual results.

difficult person An individual whose personal characteristics disturb other people.

disability A physical or mental condition that substantially limits an individual's major life activities.

discipline Punishment used to correct or train.

disruptive technology Innovations by small or lesser-known companies that create an entirely new market and jeopardize the position of industry leaders by introducing a new kind of product or service.

diversity A demographic and/or cultural mixture of people with different group identities within the same work environment.

diversity training Training that attempts to bring about workplace harmony by teaching people how to get along better with diverse work associates.

downsizing The slimming down of operations to focus resources and boost profits or decrease expenses.

due process In relation to employee rights, giving a worker a fair hearing before he or she is dismissed.

economic order quantity (EOC) The inventory level that minimizes both administrative costs and carrying costs.

economic value added (EVA) Measures how much more (or less) a company earns in profits than the minimum amount its investors expect it to earn.

emotional intelligence The ability to connect with people and understand their emotions.

emotional labor The process of regulating both feelings and expressions to meet organizational goals.

employee assistance program (EAP) An organization-sponsored service to help employees deal with personal and job-related problems that hinder performance.

employee benefit Any noncash payment given to workers as part of compensation for their employment.

employee network groups Employees within a company who affiliate on the basis of race, ethnicity, sex, sexual orientation, or physical ability to discuss ways to succeed in the organization.

employee orientation program A formal activity designed to acquaint new employees with the organization.

empowerment The process by which managers share power with group members, thereby enhancing employees' feelings of personal effectiveness.

encoding The process of organizing ideas into a series of symbols designed to communicate with the receiver.

entrepreneur A person who initiates and operates an innovative business

entropy A concept of the systems approach to management that states that an organization will die without continuous input from the outside environment.

equity theory A theory of motivation in which employee satisfaction and motivation depend on how fairly the employees believe they are treated in comparison to peers.

ethically centered management An approach to management that emphasizes that the high quality of an end product takes precedence over its scheduled completion.

ethics The study of moral obligation, or separating right from wrong.

event In the PERT method, a point of decision or the accomplishment of a task.

expectancy theory of motivation An explanation of motivation that states that people will expend effort if they expect the effort to lead to performance and the performance to lead to a reward.

expected time The time that will be used on the PERT diagram as the needed period for the completion of an activity.

expected value The average return on a particular decision being made a large number of times.

external control strategy An approach to control based on the belief that employees are motivated primarily by external rewards and need to be controlled by their managers.

extranet A Web site that requires a password to enter.

feedback control A control that evaluates an activity after it is performed.

filtering Coloring and altering information to make it more acceptable to the receiver.

first-level managers Managers who supervise operatives (also known as first-line managers or supervisors).

flat organization structure A form of organization with relatively few layers of management, making it less bureaucratic.

flexible benefit package A compensation plan that allows employees to select a group of benefits tailored to their preferences.

flexible working hours A system in which employees must work certain core hours but can choose their arrival and departure times.

formal communication channels The official pathways for sending information inside and outside an organization.

formal group A group deliberately formed by the organization to accomplish specific tasks and achieve goals.

free-rein leader A leader who turns over virtually all authority and control to the group.

functional departmentalization An arrangement that defines departments by the function each one performs, such as accounting or purchasing.

gainsharing A formal program allowing employees to participate financially in the productivity gains they have achieved.

Gantt chart A graphic depiction of the planned and actual progress of work over the life of the project.

global start-up A small firm that comes into existence by serving an international market.

grapevine The informal means by which information is transmitted in organizations.

gross profit margin A financial ratio expressed as the difference between sales and the cost of goods sold, divided by sales.

group A collection of people who interact with each other, are working toward some common purpose, and perceive themselves to be a group.

group decision The process of several people contributing to a final decision.

group polarization A situation in which postdiscussion attitudes tend to be more extreme than prediscussion attitudes.

groupthink A psychological drive for consensus at any cost.

growth needs Higher-order needs that are concerned with personal development and reaching one's potential.

Hawthorne effect The phenomenon in which people behave differently in response to perceived attention from evaluators.

heuristics A rule of thumb used in decision making.

horizontal structure The arrangement of work by teams that are responsible for accomplishing a process.

human resource budget A schedule that identifies the human resource needs for a future period and the labor costs to meet those needs.

human resources approach to management A perspective on management that emphasizes managing people by understanding their psychological makeup and needs.

impairment testing An evaluation of whether an employee is alert enough for work.

improvement goal A goal that, if attained, will correct unacceptable deviation from a performance standard.

ineffective job performance Job performance that lowers productivity below an acceptable standard.

informal communication channel An unofficial network that supplements the formal channels in an organization.

informal group A group that emerges over time through the interaction of workers.

informal learning Any learning that occurs in which the learning process is not determined or designed by the organization.

information overload (or communication overload) A condition in which an individual receives so much information that he or she becomes overwhelmed.

information system (or management information system) A formal system for providing management with information useful or necessary for making decisions.

informative confrontation A technique of inquiring about discrepancies, conflicts, and missed messages.

intellectual capital The value of useful ideas and the people who generate them.

internal control strategy An approach to control based on the belief that employees can be motivated by building their commitment to organizational goals.

Internet-based training (or computer-based training) A learning experience based on the interaction between the trainee and a computer.

intuition An experience-based way of knowing or reasoning in which weighing and balancing evidence are done unconsciously and automatically.

job analysis Obtaining information about a job by describing its tasks and responsibilities and gathering basic facts about the job.

job burnout A pattern of emotional, physical, and mental exhaustion in response to chronic job stressors.

job characteristics model A method of job enrichment that focuses on the task and interpersonal dimensions of a job.

job crafting The physical and mental changes individuals make in the task or relationship aspects of their job.

job demand–job control model A model demonstrating the relationship between high or low job demands and high or low job control. It shows that workers experience the most stress when the demands of the job are high and they have little control over the activity.

job description A written statement of the key features of a job, along with the activities required to perform it effectively.

job design The process of laying out job responsibilities and duties and describing how they are to be performed.

job enlargement Increasing the number and variety of tasks within a job.

job enrichment An approach to including more challenge and responsibility in jobs to make them more appealing to most employees.

job involvement The degree to which individuals identify psychologically with their work.

job rotation A temporary switching of job assignments.

job sharing A work arrangement in which two people who work part time share one job.

job specialization The degree to which a job holder performs only a limited number of tasks.

job specification A statement of the personal characteristics needed to perform the job.

judgmental forecast A qualitative forecasting method based on a collection of subjective opinions.

just-in-time system A system to minimize inventory and move it into the plant exactly when needed.

knowledge management The ways and means by which a company leverages its knowledge resources to generate business value.

lateral thinking A thinking process that spreads out to find many alternative solutions to a problem.

law of effect The underlying principle of behavior modification stating that behaviors leading to positive consequences tends to be repeated and that behavior leading to negative consequences tends not to be repeated.

Leadership Grid A visual representation of different combinations of a leader's degree of concern for task-related issues.

leadership style The typical pattern of behavior that a leader uses to influence his or her employees to achieve organizational goals.

learning organization An organization that is skilled at creating, acquiring, and transferring knowledge.

locus of control The way in which people look at causation in their lives.

management The process of using organizational resources to achieve organizational objectives through planning, organizing and staffing, leading, and controlling.

management by objectives (MBO) A systematic application of goal setting to help individuals and firms be more productive.

management information system (or information system) A formal system for providing management with information useful or necessary for making decisions.

manager A person responsible for the work performance of group members.

maquiladora A manufacturing plant close to the U.S.–Mexico border that is established specifically to assemble American products.

Maslow's need hierarchy The motivation theory that arranges human needs into a pyramid-shaped model with basic physiological needs at the bottom and self-actualizing needs at the top.

master budget A budget consolidated from the budgets of various units.

materials purchase/usage budget A plan that identifies the raw materials and parts that must be purchased to meet production demands.

materials requirement planning A computerized manufacturing and inventory control system designed to ensure that materials handling and inventory control are efficient.

matrix organization A project structure superimposed on a functional structure.

mentor A more experienced person who develops a protégé's abilities through tutoring, coaching, guidance, and emotional support.

metacommunicate To communicate about communication to help overcome barriers or resolve a problem.

micromanagement Supervising group members too closely and second-guessing their decisions.

middle-level managers Managers who are neither executives nor first-level supervisors, but who serve as a link between the two groups.

milestone chart An extension of the Gantt chart that provides a listing of the subactivities that must be completed to accomplish the major activities listed on the vertical axis.

mission The firm's purpose and where it fits into the world.

modified work schedule Any formal departure from the traditional hours of work, excluding shift work and staggered work hours.

moral intensity The magnitude of an unethical act.

moral laxity A slippage in moral behavior because other issues seem more important at the time.

motivation The expenditure of effort to accomplish results.

multicultural worker An individual who is aware of and values other cultures.

multiculturalism The ability to work effectively and conduct business with people from different cultures.

multinational corporation (MNC) A firm with operating units in two or more countries in addition to its own.

need A deficit within an individual, such as a craving for water or affection.

noise In communication, unwanted interference that can distort or block a message.

nominal group technique (NGT) A group decision-making technique that follows a highly structured format.

nonprogrammed decision A decision that is difficult because of its complexity and the fact that the person faces it infrequently.

nonverbal communication The transmission of messages by means other than words.

office (organizational) politics Informal approaches to gaining power or other advantage through means other than merit or luck.

open-book company A firm in which every employee is trained, empowered, and motivated to understand and pursue the company's business goals.

operating plans The means through which strategic plans alter the destiny of the firm.

operational planning Planning that requires specific procedures and actions at lower levels in an organization.

organization structure The arrangement of people and tasks to accomplish organizational goals.

organizational (or office) politics Informal approaches to gaining power or other advantage through means other than merit or luck.

organizational culture (corporate culture) The system of shared values and beliefs that actively influence the behavior of organization members.

outsourcing The practice of hiring an individual or another company outside the organization to perform work.

$P = M \times A$ An expression of the relationship between motivation and performance, where P refers to performance, M to motivation, and A to ability.

paradigm The perspectives and ways of doing things that are typical of a given context.

Pareto diagram A bar graph that ranks types of output variations by frequency of occurrence.

participative leader A leader who shares decision making with group members.

peak performance A mental state in which maximum results are achieved with minimum effort.

498

performance appraisal A formal system for measuring, evaluating, and reviewing performance.

pet-peeve technique A creativity training (or problem-solving) exercise in which the group thinks up as many complaints as possible about every facet of the department.

policies General guidelines to follow in making decisions and taking action.

power The ability or potential to influence decisions and control resources.

power motivation A strong desire to control others or get them to do things on your behalf.

preventive control A control that takes place prior to the performance of an activity.

problem A discrepancy between ideal and actual conditions.

procedure A customary method for handling an activity. It guides action rather than thinking.

procrastinate To delay in taking action without a valid reason.

procrastination The delaying of action for no good reason.

production budget A detailed plan that identifies the products or services that must be produced to match the sales forecast and inventory requirements.

product-service departmentalization The arrangement of departments according to the products or services they provide.

profit margin A financial ratio measuring return on sales, or net income divided by sales.

profit-sharing plan A method of giving workers supplemental income based on the profitability of the entire firm or a selected unit.

program evaluation and review technique (PERT) A network model used to track the planning activities required to complete a large-scale, nonrepetitive project. It depicts all of the interrelated events that must take place.

programmed decision A decision that is repetitive, or routine, and made according to a specific procedure.

progressive discipline The step-by-step application of corrective discipline.

project organization A temporary group of specialists working under one manager to accomplish a fixed objective.

project team A small group of employees working on a temporary basis in order to accomplish a particular goal.

qualitative control technique A method of controlling based on human judgments about performance that result in a verbal rather than numerical evaluation.

quantitative approach to management A perspective on management that emphasizes use of a group of methods in managerial decision making, based on the scientific method.

quantitative control technique A method of controlling based on numerical measures of performance.

readiness In situational leadership, the extent to which a group member has the ability and willingness or confidence to accomplish a specific task.

realistic job preview A complete disclosure of the potential negative features of a job to a job candidate.

recognition need The desire to be acknowledged for one's contributions and efforts and to feel important.

recruitment The process of attracting job candidates with the right characteristics and skills to fill job openings.

reengineering The radical redesign of work to achieve substantial improvements in performance.

reference check An inquiry to a second party about a job candidate's suitability for employment.

relationship behavior The extent to which the leader engages in two-way or multi-way communication.

relaxation response A general-purpose method of learning to relax by yourself.

results In performance appraisal, what people accomplish, or the objectives they attain.

return on equity A financial ratio measuring how much a firm is earning on its investments, expressed as net income divided by owner's equity.

revenue-and-expense budget A document that describes plans for revenues and operating expenses amounts.

role An expected set of activities or behaviors stemming from a job.

rule A specific course of action or conduct that must be followed. It is the simplest type of plan.

S

satisficing decision A decision that meets the minimum standards of satisfaction.

scientific management The application of scientific methods to increase individual workers' productivity.

self-managed work team A formally recognized group of employees who are responsible for an entire work process or segment that delivers a product or service to an internal or external customer.

situational leadership model An explanation of leadership that matches leadership style to the readiness of group members.

small-business owner An individual who owns and operates a small business.

social leave of absence An employee benefit that gives select employees time away from the job to perform a significant public service.

social loafing Freeloading, or shirking individual responsibility, when a person is placed in a group setting and removed from individual accountability.

social responsibility The idea that firms have obligations to society beyond their obligations to owners or stockholders and also beyond those prescribed by law or contract.

span of control The number of workers reporting directly to a manager.

stakeholder viewpoint The viewpoint on social responsibility contending that firms must hold themselves responsible for the quality of life of the many groups affected by the firm's actions.

standard A unit of measurement used to evaluate results.

stockholder viewpoint The traditional perspective on social responsibility that a business organization is responsible only to its owners and stockholders.

strategic human resource planning The process of anticipating and providing for the movement of people into, within, and out of an organization to support the firm's business strategy.

strategic planning A firm's overall master plan that shapes its destiny.

strategy The organization's plan, or comprehensive program, for achieving its vision, mission, and goals.

stress The mental and physical condition that results from a perceived threat that cannot be dealt with readily.

suggestion program A formal method for collecting and analyzing employees' suggestions about processes, policies, products, and services.

summary discipline The immediate discharge of an employee because of a serious offense.

SWOT analysis A method of considering the strengths, weaknesses, opportunities, and threats in a given situation.

synergy A concept of the systems approach to management that states that the whole organization working together will produce more than the parts working independently.

systems perspective A way of viewing aspects of an organization as an interrelated system.

 T

tactical planning Planning that translates a firm's strategic plans into specific goals by organizational unit.

task behavior The extent to which the leader spells out the duties and responsibilities of an individual or group.

team A special type of group in which members have complementary skills and are committed to a common purpose, a set of performance goals, and an approach to the task.

team leader A manager who coordinates the work of a small group of people, while acting as a facilitator and catalyst.

teamwork A situation characterized by understanding and commitment to group goals on the part of all team members.

techno–obsessive Individuals obsessed with technological devices.

telecommuting An arrangement with one's employer to use a computer to perform work at home or in a satellite office.

termination The process of firing an employee because of poor job performance, unacceptable behavior, or interpersonal problems.

territorial departmentalization An arrangement of departments according to the geographic area served.

360-degree feedback A performance appraisal in which a person is evaluated by a sampling of all the people with whom he or she interacts.

time–series analysis An analysis of a sequence of observations that take place at regular intervals over a period of time (hourly, weekly, monthly, and so forth).

top–level managers Managers at the top one or two levels in the organization.

total quality management (TQM) A management system for improving performance throughout a firm by maximizing customer satisfaction, making continuous improvements, and relying heavily on employee involvement.

tough question A question that helps the group achieve insight into the nature of a problem, what it might be doing wrong, and whether progress is sufficient.

training Any procedure intended to foster and enhance learning among employees, particularly directed at acquiring job skills.

traits Stable aspects of people, closely related to personality.

transformational leader A leader who helps organizations and people make positive changes in the way they do things.

transnational corporation A special type of MNC that operates worldwide without having one national headquarters.

transnational team A work group composed of multinational members whose activities span multiple countries.

two–factor theory of work motivation The theory contending that there are two different sets of job factors. One set can satisfy and motivate people, and the other set can only prevent dissatisfaction.

unity of command The classical management principle stating that each subordinate receives assigned duties from one superior only and is accountable to that superior.

vertical thinking An analytical, logical process that results in few answers.

virtual office An arrangement in which employees work together as if they were part of a single office despite being physically separated.

virtual team A small group of people who conduct almost all of their collaborative work by electronic communication rather than in face-to-face meetings.

vision An idealized picture of the future of an organization.

Web master An individual responsible for the creation and maintenance of a company's Web site.

whistle blower An employee who discloses organizational wrongdoing to parties who can take action.

work ethic A firm belief in the dignity and value of work.

work streamlining Eliminating as much low-value work as possible and concentrating on activities that add value for customers or clients.

wrongful discharge The firing of an employee for arbitrary or unfair reasons.

zone of indifference The psychological zone that encompasses acceptable behaviors employees do not mind following.

Index

NOTE: The letter *e* after a page number refers to exhibits.

A

ability, 300, 319
absenteeism, 212
accommodation, conflict resolution and, 400
accomplishments, rewards and, 330
accountability, 202, 233–234
achievement motivation, 291–292, 302, 323
achievement tests, 265
achievers, high, 204
action orientation, 305
action plans, 115, 131, 450–451, 451e, 452–453
active listening, 366; questions and, 453–454
activities: low-volume and no-value, 231; performance appraisals measures of, 276; PERT, 179; unessential, stress and, 483
activity-based costing (ABC), 427; example, 409–410; reductions and, 231
adaptability, leadership and, 295
Adecco Job Shop, 262
Adler, Paul S., 223–224
administrative management, 17
administrators, 4–5
advice, constructive, 454
affective conflict, 398–399
affiliation: in e-commerce, 128; need for, 322
affirmative action, 257–258
Age Discrimination in Employment Act (1967), 258e
agendas, 162, 369
agreeableness, charismatic leadership and, 305
Allinson, Robert Elliott, 89

alternative solutions, 142
alternative workplaces, 211
Amabile, Teresa M., 153, 154
Amason, Allen C., 398
Amazon.com, 119–120, 126, 206–207, 237e
American Airlines, 157
American Institute of Stress, 478
Americans with Disabilities Act (1990), 258–259, 258e, 269
analysis paralysis, 146
anchoring, 147–148
antidiscrimination laws, 257, 258e, 259e, 264
appearance, nonverbal communication and, 354
aptitude tests, 265
Archer, Gary, 332–333
Armstrong, Michael, 239
assertiveness, 289, 308, 364
AT&T, 206, 212, 239
authority, 162, 222. *See also* power
autocratic leaders, 297, 412
automation, 201
autonomy, 203, 387
avarice, 93
avoidance, 401
avoidance motivation, 328
awareness, of organizational politics, 372
Axicom Corp., 239, 240

B

back stabbing, 371–372
background investigations, 269
Baker, David, 59
balance of trade, 36
balanced scorecard, 424, 426–427, 426e
bandwidth, 392
Barnard, Janet, 331
Barrett, Craig R., 221
Bauer, Brian, 432–433

behavior modification: effectiveness of, 331; at Foamex, 332–333; law of effect and, 327–328; positive reinforcement for, 329–331; strategies for, 328–329. *See also* coaching

behavioral interviewing, 267–268

behaviors: mismatches of, 446; performance appraisals measures of, 276; for positive reinforcement, 329

benefits, 278–279, 279e

Berry, Tim, 88

best practices, 21, 22e

Bethune, Gordon, 293, 392

Bezos, Jeff, 119, 120

bias, 91

Bildman, Lars, 93

bills of materials, 186

Bing, Stanley, 372

biological approach to job design, 198–199, 199e

Blanchard, Kenneth H., 300

Bloomfield, Karen, 363

Bluemont Nurseries Inc., 409–410

Boatman, Beth, 232

body placement, nonverbal communication and, 353

Bordia, Prashant, 358

bounded rationality, 143–144

brainstorming, 155, 156–157; electronic, 157, 385; on job enrichment program, 204; rules for, 156e

branding, 141

break-even analysis, 182–183, 182e

breaking the rules, 152

Brett, Jeanne, 39

Bridgestone/Firestone Inc., 89

broadband access, 68e

broadbanding (compensation system), 278

Bromberg, Joyce, 137

budgets: about, 418–419; and financial ratios as control devices, 421–423, 421e; preparation suggestions for, 420–421; types of, 419–420

bureaucracies, 222; advantages and disadvantages of, 223–224; entrepreneurs and, 302; organization principles in, 222; organization structure of, 223e; orientation to, 225e. *See also* matrix organizations

Burke, Kathy, 100, 210

burnout, 479–481

Bush, Linda, 349

business ethics, 86–88. *See also* ethics

business strategy, 117; activities of, 117–118; competitive advantage and sustainability of, 120; example, 119–120; nature of, 118e; operational effectiveness and, 117; trade-offs and, 118; variety of, 124–128, 125e. *See also* strategic planning

Butler, Timothy, 453

call centers, information technology and, 76

Canada, staffing legislation of, 256, 259e

capability, charismatic leadership and, 306

capital expenditure budgets, 420

Caputo, Jay, 380

career development, 275–276, 279

career retardation, 397–398

caring attitudes, organizational culture and, 236

carpal tunnel syndrome, 208

cash budgets, 419

cash flow, 423–424, 424e

Cassar, Kenneth, 172

Catalyst, 307–308

cause-mentality, creativity and, 155

cell phones, Web-enabled, 61, 68e

centralization, 235

certainty, decision making and, 148–149

challengers, 391

challenges, creativity and, 154

Chambers, John, 296

chance encounters, 357

change: degree of, organizational culture and, 236; disruptive technology and, 245–246; gaining support for, 243–245; at individual level *vs.* organizational level, 241–242; management of, 241; resistance to, 242–243; total quality management and, 246–247; unfreezing-changing-refreezing model of, 242, 242e

charisma, 303, 305–306

charismatic leadership, 304–306, 304e

Charles Schwab, 155, 245

Chicago, City of, 231–232

chief executive officers (CEOs), 240

chief knowledge officers (CKOs), 239

Christensen, Clayton M., 245–246

Cisco Systems Inc., 65, 238, 246, 296

Citigroup, 385

Civil Rights Act (1964), 257, 258e

Civil Rights Act (1991), 258e

clients: relationships with, 201. *See also* customers

clock punchers, 204

clothing, nonverbal communication and, 354

coaches, 11, 307, 308

coaching, 453–454; example, 461

coalitions, leadership and, 290

Coca-Cola, 141, 155

codes of conduct, written organizational, 104

coercive power, 288

cognitive conflict, 398–399

cognitive intelligence, 145, 146

cohesiveness, effective work groups and, 389

collaboration, 400–401; workplace, 381
collections, global managerial workers and, 36–37
Commission on the Rights of People (Québec, Canada), 259e
commitment, 318–319, 454, 476
committees, 388
communication: barriers, 359–362, 359e; charismatic leadership and, 305; direct authority for, job enrichment and, 202; directions of, 355–357; effective work groups and, 389; examples, 349; formal, 355; informal, 357–359; information technology and, 63; for meetings, 369–370; nonverbal, 352–355; organizational channels and, 355; organizational politics and, 370–373; process, 350–352, 351e; strategies for effective, 362–369, 363e; for teamwork, 393
communication media, 351, 352e, 364
communication networks, 355
communication overload, 361
communication skills, 361–362
community redevelopment projects, 100–101
company intranets, 64, 428
compensation, 277; benefits, 278–279; pay types, 277–278
competency-based pay, 278
competitive advantage, 62, 237
competitors: international trade, 44–45; team building and, 392
complaint programs, 356
compliments, 370
compressed work weeks, 211
computer-aided monitoring of work, 431
computer-based training, 272
computer equipment: automation and, 201; dot.com collapse and, 75
computer goof-offs, 65–66
computer software, achievement tests on, 265
concentration, productivity and, 471
conceptual skills, 14, 308
concurrent controls, 411; observation as, 449
confidential information, 92
conflict: cognitive vs. affective, 398–399; creativity and, 154; decision making and, 149; negative consequences of, 399–400; positive consequences of, 399
conflict resolution: leadership and, 308; methods of, 400–401
conflicts of interest, 92
confrontation, 449; problem solving and, 401
conscientiousness tests, 266, 267
consensus building: in group problem solving, 162–163; in meetings, 370; teamwork and, 392

consensus leaders, 297
consequences, ethics and, 86
constructive criticism, 453–454
consultative leaders, 297
consumer orientation, leadership and, 296
Continental Airlines, 293, 392
Continental Insurance Company, 197
contingency approach to management, 20–21
contingency plans, 116–117
contingent workers, 216
controlling, 7; external vs. internal strategies for, 411–413; ineffective job performances, 446, 448–453, 448e; nonbudgetary techniques for, 417–418, 417e, 418e; roles for, 12; self-sabotage questionnaire and, 447e; steps in, 412–417, 413e
controls: budgets and, 418–423; cash flow and, 423–428; characteristics of effective, 431, 433–434; example, 409–410; information systems and, 428–431; locus of, 480; over schedules, job enrichment and, 202; time-based, 411, 412e
Conway, Craig A., 151
Cooper, Kenneth, 317
cooperation, 356–357, 389
core competencies, 127–128
corporate culture, 235. See also organizational culture
corporate espionage, 93
corporate resources, misuse of, 92–93
corporate social consciousness, 95
corporate social performance, 97
corrective discipline, 455
Cortland, Russ and Maggie, 171–172
cost leadership, as business strategy, 125
cost of capital, 422
costs: cutting techniques for, 425e; effective controls and, 434; Internet and control of, 72; PERT estimates for, 181–182; for procrastination, 476. See also activity-based costing; cash flow
Cotsakos, Charles Christos, 238
courtesy, office politics and, 371
Cousins, Thomas G., 100–101
Covey, Steve, 395, 468
coworker familiarity, effective work groups and, 389
Crandall, Robert, 297
creative tasks, 471
creative-thinking skills, 153–154
creativity: about, 150–152; appropriate physical surroundings for, 158; conditions for, 153–154; conflict and, 399; effective controls and, 434; entrepreneurial leadership and, 302; managerial and organizational practice to foster, 154–155; organizational programs for improving, 155–158; personality for, 152–153; problem-solving and, 308;

roles for, 159; self-help techniques for improving, 158–159
creativity training, 155–156
credit, team players' sharing of, 395
crisis, decision making and, 149
critical path, for PERT, 180
criticism: constructive, 453–454; team players and, 395
cross-cultural communication, 367–368
cross-cultural hiring, 270–271
cross-cultural skills and attitudes, 46e
cross-functional teams, 384–385, 388, 434
cross-generational diversity, 52
cross-training, 382
cultural diversity, 46
cultural sensitivity, 33–35, 34e
cultural strength/influence, in organizational culture, 236–237
culture shock, 38
cumulative trauma disorders, 208–209
currency inflation/devaluation, global managerial workers and, 36
customer departmentalization, 227
customer service, information technology and, 63, 66
customers: employee stress and, 481; entrepreneurs and, 302; order progress information for, 76; satisfied, 371. *See also* clients
cyberethics, 93–94
cybermeetings, 63, 385
cynical behavior, 459–460

D

Daimler/Chrysler, 237e, 238
Dana Corp., 157
Darling, Marilyn J., 453
data analysis, information technology and, 64
data mining, 75
database, for e-commerce, 70
Davis, Bob, 99
Dayton-Hudson, 245
decentralization, 233, 234–235
decision making: bounded rationality and, 143–144; creativity in, 150–159; ethical, 94; in groups, 159–165; influences on, 144–150, 144e; shared, for meetings, 369; software for, 64; steps in, 139–144, 140e. *See also* group decisions; quantitative decision making
decision trees, 184, 185e
decisions, 137; compliments for making, 370; eleven greatest business-related, 141; implementation of, 143; nonprogrammed *vs.* programmed, 138–139
decisiveness: measures of, 146e; personality and, 145–146
decoding messages, 351; sender's empathy and, 362–364
Deere & Co., 240

defensive communication, 360
deficiency needs, 320
delegating leadership style, 300
delegation, 233–234
Dell, Michael, 141, 143, 385
Dell Computer, 127, 186
demand-driven pull system, 189
democratic leaders, 297
demographic diversity, 46
denial, communication and, 360
departmentalization, 224; customer, 227; functional, 224, 226, 226e; product–service, 227, 227e; territorial, 226–227, 226e
depreciation, cash flow and, 423
development: definition of, 272; example, 273; opportunities for, 276
deviations, 414
diagnostic information, 399, 433, 449
diagnostic skills, 15, 308
diagonal communication, 357
dialog, dishonest, 360–361
Diamond Technology Partners Inc., 59
dictation software, 66
difficult persons, 457–458; cynical behavior of, 459–460; tactics for dealing with, 458–459
difficulty level of language, communication and, 360
DiFonzo, Nicholas, 358
digital imaging, 68e
Diners Club Card, 141
direct foreign investment, 41
disability, definition of, 258e, 259
discipline, 454–455; rules for applying, 455–457
discussion, planning for change and, 243
disgruntled workers, 458. *See also* difficult persons
Disney, Walt, 141
disruptive technology, 245–246
dissatisfiers, 324, 325e
disturbance handlers, 12
diversification of goods and services, 127
diversity, 45–46; characteristics of, 47e; companies with excellent performance in management of, 49e; competitive advantage of, 47–49; corporate policies on, 50; creativity and, 155; effective work groups and, 388; leadership and, 308; organizing practices to encourage, 49; relative, organizational culture and, 236; scope of, 47
diversity training, 51–52
documentation, of disciplinary actions, 457
Dodge-Regupol Inc., 99
domestic products, 33
domination, as business strategy, 125–126
Domino's Pizza, 127
downsizing, 101–102, 230–231. *See also* layoffs

downward communication, 356
dress, nonverbal communication and, 354
Drucker, Peter, 2, 14
drug testing, 270
due process, 460
Duffield, David A., 151
Duke Children's Hospital, Durham, N.C., 426
dumpster diving, 93
Dunlap, Al, 400
DuPont, Center for Creativity and Innovation, 155–156
duties, ethics of, 86–88
Dutton, Jane E., 207

E

e-commerce: essentials, 68e; forecasts of impact of, 176e; global presence for, 77; marketing with, 67; purchasing with, 68–69, 71; quantitative planning for, 171–172; reengineering and, 232; success factors in, 76–77; Wright & Filippis, 70–71
e-mail, 62, 63; brainstorming using, 157; as communication barrier, 362; control of, 471–472; meetings and, 370; pagers, 61; virtual teams and, 385
e-tailing. *See* e-commerce
Eastern Airlines, 295
Eastman Kodak, Xiamen, China factory, 31
Eaton Consulting Group, 44
economic crises in other countries, global managerial workers and, 35–36
economic forecasting, 175
economic order quantity (EOQ), 186–188
economic value added (EVA), 421–423
effective questions, 244
effort, conflict and, 399
electronic brainstorming, 157
Ellison, Larry, 93
Emerson Electric, 9
emotional expression, 306
emotional intelligence, 146–147, 294–295
emotional labor, 481–482
emotional support. *See* support
empathy, 147, 362–364, 368, 453
employee assistance program (EAP), 450–451
employee benefits, 278–279, 279e
Employee Internet Management software, 74
employee network groups, 51
employee orientation program, 271
employee self-service, 65
employee stock options, 336, 337e
employee stock ownership plans (ESOP), 336
employee talent, telecommuting and, 213
employees: control over control measures by, 434; discipline for, 454–457; duties and rights of, in bureaucracies, 222–223; electronic surveillance of, 72–75; empowerment of, 290–291; expectancy theory of motivation and, 339; gainsharing and, 335; layoff-survivor, 231; personal welfare of, decision making and, 149; strength of growth need for, 203e, 204
Employment-Equity Legislation (Canada, 1995), 259e
empowerment, 64, 233–234, 290–291, 387–388
encoding messages, 351
energy, charismatic leadership and, 305, 306
English language, 52
enterprise servers, 68e
enthusiasm, entrepreneurs and, 302
entrepreneurs, 5, 12; effective controls and, 434; leadership and, 308; leadership style of, 301–302; organizational culture and, 238; overload stress and, 481
entropy, 20
environment: creative, 153–154, 158; effective work groups and, 389; nonverbal communication and, 353
environmental cleanliness, 88
environmental management, 98
environmentally friendly policies, 44
Equal Employment Opportunity Commission, 258e, 266
Equal Pay Act (1963), 258e
equity theory, 339–341
ergonomics, 198–199, 207–209, 208e
espionage, corporate, 93
esteem needs, 321
ethical reasoning inventory, 87e
ethically-centered management, 89
ethics, 85; benefits from, 102–103; for business, 86–88; confrontations about deviations from, 105; contributors to problems in, 90–91; decision making and, 94; definition of, 86; formal mechanisms for monitoring, 103–104; leadership by example and, 104; political tactics and, 370–372; temptations and violations of, 91–94; training programs in, 105; values and, 88–89; widespread communication on, 104; written codes of conduct and, 104
etiquette, cultural differences in, 367
E★Trade, 238
European Union (EU), 32
evaluation: of decision making, 143; for planning, 113e, 116. *See also* feedback
events, PERT, 179
excellence, decision making and, 149–150
exception principle, 414
exchange, leadership and, 290
executive communication, 363

expectancy theory, 337–339, 338e
expected time, for PERT, 180, 181
expected value, for decision trees, 184, 185e
expert power, 288
expertise: creativity and, 153–154; team players and, 394
exporting, 40
external control strategies, 411–412
external stakeholders, 96
external threats and opportunities, 114
extinction, behavior modification and, 328
extranets, 63
extraversion, charismatic leadership and, 305
Exxon Mobil, 125–126, 237e, 428

facial expression and movement, nonverbal communication and, 353
Fair Credit Reporting Act, 268–269
Family and Medical Leave Act (1993), 258e
favoritism, organizational politics and, 373
Federal Trade Commission, U.S., 33
FedEx, 322
feedback: coaching and, 453; communication and, 352; of decision making, 143; direct, 201; goals and, 326–327; information technology and, 433–434; interdependent, 388; job enrichment and, 203, 204; leadership and, 295–296; in meetings, 369; for planning, 113e, 116; stress and, 482; verbal and nonverbal, 365–366
feedback controls, 411
figurehead role, 11
filtering, communication and, 361
financial benefits, of change, 243–244
financial incentives, 331, 333e; employee stock options, 336, 337e; employee stock ownership plans, 336; gainsharing, 335–336; merit pay, 331, 333e, 334–335; problems with, 336–337; profit-sharing plans, 334–335
financial ratios, control process and, 421–423, 421e
financial resources, 5–6
financial success, organizational culture and, 237
financing, cash flow and, 423
first-level managers, 3–4
fixed budgets, 419
flat organization structures, 229
flexibility: decision making and, 146; personal productivity and, 474
flexible budgets, 419
flexible job benefits package, 278–279

flexible job competencies, recruitment for, 261
flexible working hours (flextime), 100, 209–211, 210e
Foamex, behavioral risk improvement program at, 332–333
focus, as business strategy, 128
Follett, Mary Parker, 17
follow-up activities, after meetings, 370
force, conflict resolution using, 400
Ford, William Clay, Jr., 289
Ford Motor Company, 89, 191, 247
forecasting, 173–175
foreigners, global managerial workers as, 37
formal communication channels, 355–357; rumor control and, 358–359
formal groups, 380, 381
formation, group, 389–390
free-rein leaders, 297–298
freedom, creativity and, 154
fulfillment seekers, employees as, 204
functional departmentalization, 224, 226, 226e
functional managers, 4
future staffing needs, 259
future turnover, 259
future work requirements, 231

gainsharing, 335–336
Gainsharing Inc. Web site, 335
Gantt, Henry, 17
Gantt charts, 176–177, 177e
Garfield, Charles, 473
Garino, Jason, 71
gatekeepers, 391
Gates, Bill, 141, 292, 392, 475–476
Gateway, 126, 285–286
gender differences, communication and, 368
General Electric (GE), 247, 356, 428
general managers, 4
gestures, nonverbal communication and, 353
Giannecchinni, Lindy, 99
Gilbreth, Frank and Lillian, 17
Gillett, Frank, 78
Gillette Sensor for Women razor, 140
Gilmartin, Raymond V., 48
Gispan, Jonathan, 230
global diversification, 127
global e-commerce presence, 77
global managerial workers, 35; balance of trade and, 36; collections and, 36–37; culture shock and, 38; currency inflation/devaluation and, 36; economic crises in other countries and, 35–36; example, 29–30; as foreigner, 37; human rights violations and, 38; intel-

lectual property and other merchandise piracy and, 39; negotiating style differences and, 38–39. *See also* international management
global mergers, 41
global recruiting, 262
global start-ups, 41–42
globalization, 45, 45e. *See also* international trade; multinational corporations
gluttony, 93
goals, 326e; basic theory of, 326e; guide to establishing, 131e; improvement, 449–450; interdependent, 388; leadership and, 308; motivation through setting, 325–327; organizational, 130; personal, 468; sidetracked, conflict and, 399–400
Gormley, Soren, 349
grade-point averages, job application forms and, 264–265
Grandey, Alicia A., 481
grapevine, 357–359
grass-roots leadership, 291
Graves, Samuel B., 102, 103
greed, 93
Green, Greg, 43
green economy, 44
GreenMan Technologies, 99
Greenspan, Alan, 187
Greulich, Joe, 467
Greyhound Lines, Inc., 122
gross profit margin, 422
group decisions, 159–161; on goals, 327; steps in, 162e
group members: and proposal review, 130–131; roles for, 391–392
group norms, motivation, performance and, 319
group problem solving: general method for, 161–163; nominal group technique for, 163–165
groups, 380–381; conflict and, 398–401; development stages for, 389–390, 390e; polarization in, 396–397; potential contributions of, 395–396; potential problems of, 396–398. *See also* teams; work groups
groupthink, 160, 161
groupware, virtual teams and, 385
growth needs, 320
Gulati, Ranjay, 71

Habitat for Humanity, 392
Hadsall, Rad, 273
Hagburg, Richard, 266
Hamel, Gary, 121–122, 238
hand-held PCs, 61
handshakes, charismatic leadership and, 306

Hard Candy, 153
Harley-Davidson, 388, 394
Harris, Jim, 365
Hawthorne effect, 18
Hay/McBer, 302
health care, disruptive technology and, 245
Henderson, Charlie, 441
Herzberg, Frederick, 201, 324–325, 325e
heuristics, 144
Hewlett-Packard, 100, 132, 141, 210, 245–246
Hickey, Fred, 187
hierarchy, entrepreneurs and, 302
high-speed product delivery, 127
High Tech Strategist, The (Hickey), 187
Hitt, Michael, 60
Hofstede, Geert, 35
honesty: leadership and, 292; tests for, 266, 270
Honeywell, 247, 334–335
horizontal communication, 356–357
horizontal job loading, 206
horizontal organization structures, 229e, 232–233, 232e
hosting, Web sites, 68e
hoteling, 215
HotOffice Virtual Office Service, 213
Howell, Robert, 428
hugging, stress reduction and, 483
human relations skills, 371
human resources, 5–6; budgets for, 420; as management approach, 17–19; staffing and, 256
human rights, global managerial workers and, 38
humor, leadership and sense of, 294
hurry sickness, stress and, 483–484

IBM: domination of, 125, 126; on knowledge management, 239; mainframe computer decision of, 141; Mobility Initiative, 212; organizational culture of, 237e; project teams at, 384
idea quotas, 155, 157
image, positive, 371
imitation, 126
impact, empowerment and, 387–388
impairment testing, 270
implementation, of decisions, 143
improvement goals, 449–450
In the Age of the Smart Machine (Zubroff), 75
income deductions, cash flow and, 423
ineffective job performance: company factors in, 446; control model for management of, 446, 448–453, 448e; difficult persons and, 457–460; discipline for, 454–457; employee factors

in, 444–445; example, 441–442; factors in, 442–443, 443e; job factors in, 445; manager factors in, 445–446; self-sabotage questionnaire, 447e; termination for, 460–462

inequities, motivation and, 340–341

influence tactics, 289–290; leadership and, 308

informal communication channels, 357–359

informal groups, 380, 381

informal leaders, 392

informal learning, 274

informal socialization, 271

information: access to, 63–64; overload, 361; quality and accessibility of, 147–148; resources for, 5–6; sharing in teams, 395

information systems (IS): control and, 428; control information from, 430–431, 430e; elements of, 428–430, 429e

information technology: e-commerce essentials, 69e; example, 59; external relationships and, 67–71; internal operations and, 71–76; job enrichment and, 202; management and, 21; managers and, 60; negative consequences of, 65–67; organization structure and, 233; positive consequences of, 61–65, 62e; success factors, 76–77

informative confrontations, 364

Ingram, Martha R., 304e

Ingram Micro, 72, 73e

ingratiation, leadership and, 290

Innis, Karyl, 461

innovation, organizational culture and, 236, 240

inputs, equity theory and, 340

inspirational leadership, 303, 305, 308

instrumentality, expectancy theory of motivation and, 338

integrity: ethics and, 88; tests for, 266, 270

Intel, 72, 221

intellectual abilities, leadership and, 292

intellectual capital, 427–428. See also knowledge contributors; knowledge workers

intellectual property piracy, 39. See also knowledge management

intellectual stimulation, 303, 305

interdependent tasks, 388

interest, communication and, 359–360

interest tests, vocational, 266

intermittent rewards, positive reinforcement and, 329

internal capabilities, determination of, 114

internal control strategies, 412

internal stakeholders, 96

international management, 30; cultural differences and, 33–35, 34e; example, 31; trade agreements among countries, 32–33. See also under global

international trade, 43, 44–45; English language for, 52; U.S., 37e

Internet: e-commerce essentials, 68e; e-commerce marketing, 67; e-commerce purchasing, 68–69; forecasts of impact of, 176e; global start-ups and, 41–42; increased visibility with, 71; instability and chaos with, 75; integration with old economy, 69, 71; internal operations and, 71–76; netiquette tips, 93e; pure players on, 67; recruitment and, 262; surfing on, 65–66, 75

Internet-based training, 272

interpersonal skills, 14, 308; of team players, 394–395

interruptions, definition of, 471

intranets, company, 64, 428

intuition, decision making and, 145

inventory control techniques, 186–190; economic order quantity, 186–188; just-in-time system, 188–190; materials requirement planning, 186; for overproduction, 187

inventory file records, 186

investing, cash flow and, 423

iron law, stakeholder perspective and, 96

Isdell, Neville, 155

J

J. S. Smucker Co., 122

Jassawalla, Avan R., 384

job analysis, for recruitment, 261

job application forms, 264–265

job burnout, 479–481

job characteristics model, 203–204, 203e

job competency, 261

job crafting, 207

job demand–job control model, 481, 481e

job descriptions, 200, 200e, 260–261

job design: ergonomics and, 207–209; example, 197; job crafting and, 206–207; modified work schedules and, 209–216; types of, 198–200, 199e

job enlargement, 206

job enrichment, 201–203, 202e; effective work groups and, 387; job characteristics model of, 203–204, 203e; program implementation guidelines, 204–205; self-managed work teams and, 382

job interviews, 267–268, 268e

job involvement, 205, 205e

job rotation, 206

job sharing, 215

job specialization, 200–201, 201

job specifications, for recruitment, 260–261

Jobs, Steve, 304e
joking, as influence tactic, 290
judgmental forecasts, 173
Jupiter Communications, 67, 172
just-in-time (JIT) system, 188–190
just world, discipline and belief in, 457

kanbans, in just-in-time system, 189
Karat, Clare-Marie, 202–203
Katzenbach, Jon R., 385
Kelleher, Herb, 304e
Kennedy, Claudia, 294
kidding around, as influence tactic, 290
kinesthetic connections, 353
Kmart, 125
Knight, Charles F., 9
knowledge capital, 427–428. *See also*
    intellectual property piracy
knowledge contributors, 125, 391
knowledge management (KM), 239–240,
    292
knowledge workers, 14
Koch Industries, 206–207
Kotter, John P., 357
Krinick, Bob, 99
Krispy Kreme, 126
Kroc, Ray, 141

ladder climbers, 204
Lange, Wendy, 99
laptop computers, 61, 428
Larson, Allen, 52
lateral communication, 356–357
lateral thinking, 152–153
Latham, Gary P., 325
law of effect, behavior modification and,
    327–330
layoffs, 75, 231, 260. *See also* downsizing
leaders: autocratic, 297; behaviors and
    attitudes of, 294e, 295–296; free-rein,
    297–298; informal, 392; managers *vs.*,
    287e; as mentors, 306–308; participa-
    tive, 297; take-charge, 391–392; trans-
    formational and charismatic, 303–306
leadership, 7; about, 286; effective,
    291–296; by example, 289; manage-
    ment and, 286–287, 287e; power and
    authority and, 288–290; roles for,
    11–12; skills for, 308. *See also* leader-
    ship styles
leadership activity, direction of, organiza-
    tional culture and, 239
leadership continuum, 296–298, 297e
leadership grid, 298–300, 299e
leadership styles, 296–303; classical,
    296–298, 297e; entrepreneurial,
    301–302; leadership grid, 298–300,

299e; situational, 300–301, 301e; The-
    ory X and Theory Y, 298
learning, job enrichment and, 202
learning organizations, 239–240
leaves of absence, social, 100
legislation on staffing, 256–259, 258e,
    259e
legitimate power, 288
Levi Strauss, 240
Lewin, Kurt, 242
liaisons, role of, 10
licensing, in world markets, 40
lifelong learning, 272
Lincoln Electric Co., Cleveland, Ohio,
    335
line functions, in bureaucracies, 223
line managers, staffing and, 256
listeners, 391, 395
listening skills, 366, 453
littering, ethics and, 88
Living Benefits, Inc., 152
L.L. Bean, 206
local assembly and packaging, in world
    markets, 40
local business concepts, laws, and cus-
    toms, 43
local markets, global enterprise and, 42
local talent, in world markets, 43
local warehousing and selling, in world
    markets, 40
Locke, Edwin A., 325
Lockheed Martin Corporation, 103–104,
    230
locus of control, 480
Loftin, Jennifer, 65
London, Manuel, 289
Lore, Nicholas, 326
Lorenzo, Frank, 295, 306
low-volume activities, 231
Luthans, Fred, 331

m-commerce, 68e
Maletz, Mark, 434
management: best practices for, 21, 22e;
    classical approach to, 16–17; contin-
    gency approach to, 20–21; controlling
    and other functions of, 410, 411e; def-
    inition of, 2; of diversity, 45–49; effec-
    tive work groups support by, 388;
    environmental, 98; ethically-centered,
    89; expectancy theory of motivation
    and, 339; functions of, 6–8; human
    resources approach to, 17–19; influ-
    ence on managerial roles, 13; informa-
    tion technology and, 21; international,
    30, 32–35; of knowledge, 239–240,
    292; layers of, information technology
    and, 64; leadership and, 286–287,
    287e; levels of, 1–3, 3e; process of,

5–8, 6e; quantitative approach to, 19; responsibilities in bureaucracies, 223; systems perspective for, 19–20; teamwork facilitation by, 392–393; by walking, 355. *See also* managers

management by objectives (MBO), 130–132

management information systems (MIS), 428–430, 429e

Management Recruiters International, 363

management team, for international trade, 44–45

managerial workers. *See* global managerial workers; wired managerial workers

managers: creativity for, 152; definition of, 2; information technology and, 60; leaders *vs.*, 287e; levels and sample job titles, 3e; organizational culture and, 240; performance appraisals alternatives for, 276–277; positive roles for, creativity and, 155; roles for, 8, 10–13, 10e; self-managed work teams and, 383; skills development of, 15–16; skills of, 13–15; span of control and, 229; of teleworkers, 214; traditional *vs.* modern, 13e; types of, 4–5. *See also* global managerial workers; wired managerial workers

maquiladoras, 40

margin, 422

Marimba, 77–78

marketing, e-commerce, 67

Marriott, Bill, 472

Marsh Risk Consulting, 332

Maslow, Abraham M., 19, 320

Maslow's need hierarchy, 17, 19, 320–321, 321e

Mastej, Jeff, 70, 71

master budgets, 419

master production schedules, 186

materials purchase/usage budgets, 420

materials requirement planning (MRP), 186

matrix organizations, 228, 229e

McCoy, Deborah, 293

McDonald's, 141

McGregor, Douglas, 18, 298

McMahon, Linda E., 287

McMahon, Vince, 287

McNamara, Frank, 141

McNamee, Roger, 187

meaningfulness, empowerment and, 387

mechanistic approach to job design, 198, 199e

mediators, 391

meetings: communication for, 369–370; virtual, 387

Meilones, Jon, 426

Melbourne, Lois, 300

Mellon Bank, 128

Menchaca, Steve, 273

mental ability tests, 265

mentors, leaders as, 306–308

merchandise piracy, global managerial workers and, 39

Merck & Co., 279

merit pay, 333, 333e

Merrill Lynch, 245

Messman, Jack L., 62

metacommunication, 368–369

metaphors, charismatic leadership and, 305

Metrick, Clive, 323

Mickey and Minnie Mouse, 141

micromanagement, 393

Microsoft, 125, 237e, 392, 428. *See also* Gates, Bill

middle-level managers, 3

milestone charts, 176, 177, 178e

minorities: affirmative action and, 257; mentoring and, 307

mirroring, nonverbal communication and, 354

mission, 121, 121e; peak performance and, 473

mission statements: leadership and, 308; personal, 468

modeling, good behavior, 454

modified work schedules, 209; alternative workplaces, 211; compressed work weeks, 211; flexible working hours, 209–211, 210e; hoteling and, 215; job sharing, 215; part-time and temporary work, 215–216; sharing office spaces and, 215; shift work, 216; telecommuting, 212–214

Mohajer, Dineh, 153, 302

Monarch Marking Systems, 383

monitoring, 12; of business environment, time spent on, 8e; employee work electronically, 72–75; information technology, 77; of work, computer-aided, 431. *See also* controlling

Monster Board, 262

moral intensity, 86

moral laxity, 90

Morgan, Charles D., 239, 240

Morgan, Nick, 353

motivation, 147; achievement needs and, 323; affiliation needs and, 322; behavior modification and, 327–331; communication and, 359–360; creativity and, 153–154; equity theory and, 339–341; example, 317–318; expectancy theory of, 337–339; financial incentives for, 331, 333, 336–337; gainsharing and, 335–336; goal setting and, 325–327; Herzberg's two-factor theory of, 324–325, 325e; job design and, 198, 199e; job enrichment and, 201, 203–205; leadership and,

291–292, 308; Maslow's need hierarchy and, 320–321; need satisfaction and, 320; performance, commitment and, 318–319; performance appraisals and, 275; profit-sharing plans, 334–335; recognition need and, 322–323; risk taking and, 323; security needs and, 323; theories about, 318, 318e
motivators, 324, 325e
Motorola Corp., 247
multicultural workers, 33–35, 43–44, 367–368
multiculturalism, 14
multinational corporations (MNCs), 30, 262, 366–367. *See also* international management; international trade
multiple inputs, 121–122

naps, 473
NASA decision making, Challenger explosion and, 160
National Highway Traffic Safety Association, 89
National Security Agency, 76
National Sleep Foundation, 473
navigation, as business strategy, 128
needs: for affiliation, 322; motivation and satisfaction of, 320; for recognition, 322–323; for risk taking, 323–324. *See also* Maslow's need hierarchy
negative reinforcement, behavior modification and, 328
negligent hiring and retention doctrine, 263–264, 268, 269
negotiation: leadership and, 308; managers and, 11; of organizational goals and objectives, 131; planning and, 243; styles, global managerial workers and, 38–39
Nelson, Bob, 323
netiquette tips, 93e
Newman, Lynn, 385
Nidetch, Jean, 141
9th Circuit Court of Appeals, U.S., on employee surveillance, 74–75
no-value activities, 231
Nohria, Nitin, 434
noise: communication and, 352, 359; trauma and, 209
nominal group technique (NGT), 163–165, 163e
nonprogrammed decisions, 138–139
nonstop (Internet) service, 68e
nonverbal communication, 352–355; cultural differences in, 368; for feedback, 365–366; insufficient, 361; training and, 272
Nortel Networks Corporation, 387

North American Free Trade Agreement (NAFTA), 32
Northwestern Mutual Life, 384, 393
Nutt, Paul C., 139

OB Mod, behavior modification effectiveness at, 331
objectives, 130, 131e
obligations, ethics of, 86–88
Ochalek, Bill, 242
office politics, 370; control of negative, 372–373; ethical tactics in, 370–371; unethical tactics in, 371–372
Okumura, Tetsushi, 39
Olive, Ron, 183
Olsen, John, 78
online addiction, 66
online recruiting, 262, 263e
open-book companies, 292
open communication, 372
open-door policy, 356
Open Plan software, 181
operating cash, 423
operating plans, 128, 129
operational planning, 10, 113
operations: information technology and, 71–76, 73e; research on, 19; of self-managed work teams, 382
operatives, 200
opportunities, analyzing corporate, 124
optimism, decision making and, 146
optimum decisions, 143
Oracle Corp., 93
OrderZone.com, 68
organization structures: of bureaucracies, 222–224, 223e; communication channels in, 355; decentralized, 233, 234–235; definition of, 222; delegation and, 233–234; of departmentalization, 224, 226–227, 226e, 227e; downsizing, 230–231; empowerment and, 233–234; example of change in, 221; flat, 229; horizontal, 229e, 232–233, 232e; of matrix organizations, 228, 229e; systems view of, 20e
organizational culture, 235; consequences and implications of, 237–239, 238e; descriptions of, 237e; dimensions of, 235–237; as learning organization, 239–240; managing and controlling, 240; motivation, performance and, 319
organizational politics, 370; control of negative, 372–373; ethical tactics in, 370–371; unethical tactics in, 371–372
organizational staffing. *See* staffing
organizational support. *See* support
organizing, 7, 10
orientation programs, 271

outcomes: equity theory and, 340;
expectancy theory and, 339
outdoor training, for teamwork, 393
outsourcing, 76, 231–232. *See also* down-sizing
overconfidence, 148, 174, 175
Overdorf, Michael, 245–246
overhead, telecommuting and, 212
overload, change and, 244
Owen, Robert, 17
ownership, organizational culture and, 236

$P = M \times A$, 319, 319e
pagers, e-mail, 61
paperwork, control of, 471–472
paradigms, 152
Pareto diagrams, 190–191, 190e
Parker, Glenn, 394
part-time work, 215–216
participation: in goal-setting, 326; in meetings, 369; in performance appraisals, 276; in planning for change, 243
participative leaders, 297. *See also* empowerment
partners, international trade, 44–45
Pascarella, Perry, 88–89
passive-aggressive workers, 458. *See also* difficult persons
Patterson, Steve, 365
Pauker, Anne M., 197
pay: Canadian legislation on, 259e; merit, 333; types of, 277–278; U.S. legislation on, 258e
paycheck cashers, 204
peak performance, 472–473
peer evaluations, 276, 277e
peoplepalooza, 125
PeopleSoft, Inc., 151
Pepsi Cola International, 260
perceptual/motor approach to job design, 199, 199e
perfectionism, decision making and, 146
performance: cues for, 470; goal setting and, 326; measures of, 413–414; motivation, ability and, 319e; motivation, commitment and, 318–319; peak, 472–473; positive reinforcement and, 329. *See also* ineffective job performance
performance appraisals, 274–275; design of, 276–277; goals and, 326; ineffective performance and, 452; MBO and, 131; purpose of, 275–276
performance standards: comparison of actual performance to, 414–415; corrective action to meet, 415–416; defining, 448; detecting deviations

from, 448–449; leadership and, 295; setting, 412–413, 413e
Perot, H. Ross, 296
person-organization fit, 238, 260
personal computers, 428
personal digital assistants, 61, 428
personal productivity: clean work area for, 470; concentration and, 470; creative *vs.* routine tasks and, 471; flexibility and, 474; goals and, 468; high-output tasks and, 471; mission statement and, 468; multiple priorities and, 473–474; naps for, 473; office technology and, 472; paperwork, e-mail, voice mail control and, 471–472; peak performance for, 472–473; work ethic and, 468; work streamlining and, 469–470; workpace for, 470
personality, decision making and, 145
personality tests, 265–266, 266e
personnel testing, for recruitment, 265–267; cross-cultural, 270
PERT (program evaluation and review technique), 178–181, 179e; complex applications of, 181–182
pessimism, decision making and, 146
pet-peeve technique, 156
Peters, Tom, 371
Pfeffer, Jeffrey, 337
Pfizer, 428
Philip Morris, 428
Phillips, Charles I., 151
philosophical principles, ethics and, 86–88
PhotoDisc, 275
physical examinations, job selection and, 269
physical exercise, 483, 484e
physical resources, 5–6
physiological needs, 320
Piaget, SWOT analysis for, 123–124
Pincura, John, 70, 71
Pindale, Nick, 409–410
Pitney Bowes, 50
planning, 6–7, 111–112; action plans for, 115; budget development for action plans, 115–116; for change, 243; for contingencies, 116–117; contribution of, 112; control of, 116; defining present situation for, 114; establishing goals and objectives for, 114–115; forecasting for, 115; general framework for, 112–114, 113e; implementation of, 116. *See also* quantitative decision making
pleasant attitude, office politics and, 371
Polese, Kim, 77–78, 304e
policies, 128, 129
politics: change and, 244; decision making and, 148; leadership and, 308; skills for, 15. *See also* organizational politics
Porter, Michael, 117, 128

positive attitude, office politics and, 371
positive reinforcement: application of, 329–331, 330e; behavior modification and, 328; improvement goals and, 452; leadership and, 308
posture, nonverbal communication and, 353
potency, empowerment and, 387
Pottruck, David, 155
Potts, Mike, 99
power, 288–289. *See also* empowerment
power contacts, 371
power motivation, leadership and, 292
power sharing, 385
PQ Systems, 349
praise, recognition need and, 322
Pratt, Dale, 387
Pregnancy Discrimination Act (1978), 258e
prejudice, 91
preliminary screening interview, 264
preventive controls, 411
priceline.com, 128
priorities, personal productivity and, 470
Pritchett, Price, 471
Privacy Act (1964), 269
problem solving: creativity in, 150–159; in groups, 159–165; joint, 454; leadership and, 292, 308; mental-ability tests and, 267; at Steelcase, 137–138; steps in, 139–144, 140e. *See also* decision making
problems, 137; alternatives to, 142; diagnosis of, 140; indicators of, 139–140. *See also* decisions
procedures, 128, 130; effective work groups and, 389; work streamlining and, 470–471
process mentality, 233
process observers, 391
processes, effective work groups and, 388–389
procrastination, 474, 476–477, 477e, 478e; decision making and, 150
Procter & Gamble, 141
product differentiation, 126
production budgets, 420
production work teams, 381–382, 382e
productivity: example, 467–468; information technology and, 62; new company-wide-software and, 60; performance appraisals and, 275; personal, 468–476; teams or groups and, 396; telecommuting and, 212
products, diversification of, 42–43
product–service departmentalization, 227, 227e
profit margin, 422, 423; Internet and, 74, 75
profit-sharing plans, 334–335
program evaluation and review technique

(PERT), 178–181, 179e; complex applications of, 181–182
programmed decisions, 138–139
progressive discipline, 455, 456e
project organizations, 228
project teams, 383–384
prudence, quantitative forecasting and, 174
Prudential Insurance Company, 100, 322–323
psychological testing, for recruitment, 265–267
psychology, job enrichment and, 203
punishment: behavior modification and, 328–329; improvement goals and, 452; positive consequences of, 457. *See also* discipline
purchasing, online, 68–69, 71
pure players, 67
push technology, 429

qualified privileges, employee's past performance and, 268
qualitative control techniques, 416–417, 416e, 449
qualitative forecasting, 173
quality, six sigma and, 247
quantitative approach to management, 19
quantitative control techniques, 416–417, 417e, 449
quantitative decision making: break-even analysis, 182–183, 182e; decision trees, 184, 185e; example, 171–172; forecasting methods, 172–176; Gantt charts, 176–177, 177e; inventory control techniques, 186–190; milestone charts, 176, 177, 178e; Pareto diagrams and, 190–191, 190e; PERT, 178–182, 179e
quantitative forecasting, 173–175
Quebecor World Inc., 255–256
questions, active listening and, 453–454

Radius (restaurant), 379–380
Ramon, Kathy, 171–172
rapport, communication and, 363
rationality, leadership and, 289–290, 308
Ray, Michael L., 151–152
Raytheon, 74
reach, in e-commerce, 128
readiness, 300
realistic job previews, 267
realities, analyzing, 121, 122
recallability, quantitative forecasting and, 174–175
recognition needs, 322–323
recruitment, 260–262

red-hot-stove rule, 456–457
redefinition, industry, 127
Reebok International, Ltd., 85
Reed, John, 385
reengineering, 233
reference checks, 268–269
referent power, 288
refreezing, change and, 242, 242e
Reid Psychological Systems, 269
relationship behavior, 300
relaxation response, 483
repetition, communication and,
    364
repetitive motion disorders, 66, 209
resilience, leadership and, 296
resources: allocation and rewards of, 236;
    control over, 11, 202; creativity and,
    154; PERT estimates for, 181–182
responsibility, 223, 394. *See also* social
    responsibility
results, performance appraisals measures
    of, 276
retention, 256
return on equity, 422, 423
revenue-and-expense budgets, 419
reward power, 288
rewards: expectancy theory and, 339;
    goals and, 326–327; interdependent,
    388; for positive reinforcement,
    329–331; for procrastination control,
    476; stress and, 482; for teamwork,
    393. *See also* motivation
richness, in e-commerce, 128
rigidity, decision making and, 146
risk-sharing plans, 335
risk takers/taking, 204; creativity and,
    155; decision making for, 148–149;
    motivation and, 323–324; personality
    and, 145
Robbins, Tina L., 397
Roberts Express, Akron, Ohio, 467
Robin, Ashok, 423
Rodek, Jeffrey R., 72
role models, organizational culture and,
    240
roles, 8
routine tasks, 471
rules, 128, 130; breaking, 152
rumor control, 357–359
Russo, J. Edward, 140

S

safety needs, 320; motivation and, 324
Sajkovic, Alexander D., 331
salaries, 277
sales forecasting, 175
Saratoga Institute, 396
Sashittal, Hemant C., 384
satisficing decisions, 143
satisfiers, 324, 325e

scheduling control, job enrichment and,
    202
Schlow, Michael, 379
Schmitz, Joerg, 44
Schultz, Howard, 111
scientific management, 16–17
Scott, H. Lee, Jr., 114, 115
Scrap Tire Management Council, 99
Sears, Roebuck and Co., 141, 424
security needs, 320; motivation and, 324
selection, for staffing, 262–264, 263e;
    background investigations, 269; cross-
    cultural techniques, 270–271; drug
    testing, 270; job application forms,
    264–265; job interview, 267–268,
    268e; physical examinations, 269; pre-
    liminary interview, 264; psychological
    and personnel testing, 265–267; refer-
    ence checks, 268–269
self-actualization needs, 321
self-assessment, 275
self-awareness, 147
self-confidence, 292, 306
self-directed work teams, 381–382, 382e
self-dissatisfaction, goals and, 327
self-efficacy, decision making and, 146
self-image, charismatic leadership and,
    305
self-interest, conflict and, 400
self-managed work teams, 381–382, 382e
self-regulation, 147
self-sabotage questionnaire, 447e
self-talk, positive, 483
semantics, communication and, 360
semi-autonomous teams, 381–382, 382e
servant leaders, 296
setbacks, leadership and, 296
setting up others for failure, 372
sexual harassment, 92, 92e
Shapiro, Marc, 255
shared office spaces, 215
shared workload, effective work groups
    and, 389
sharing, conflict resolution using, 400
shift work, 216
Shih, Willy C., 304e
Shurtleff, Jill, 140
Siau, Keng L., 157
SilentRunner (Internet traffic monitoring
    software), 179e
Simmons, Annette, 373
Simon, Herbert A., 143–144
situational leadership model, 300–301,
    301e
six sigma/Six Sigma, 247
skills: job enrichment and, 203; motiva-
    tion, performance and, 319; pay based
    on, 277–278
small-business owners, 5
small-business servers, 68e
Smucker, Richard K., 122

social conscientiousness tests, 266, 267
social leaves of absence, 100
social loafing, 397
social needs, 320–321
social responsibility, 85, 94–95; benefits
    from, 102–103; community redevel-
    opment projects, 100–101; compas-
    sionate downsizing, 101–102;
    corporate social performance and, 97;
    environmental management, 98;
    example, 99; initiatives, 98; leadership
    by example and, 104; social leaves of
    absence, 100; stockholder *vs.* stake-
    holder viewpoint of, 95–97; training
    programs in, 105; whistle blowers and,
    101; widespread communication on,
    104; work/life programs, 98, 98e, 100
social skills, 147
socialization, informal, 271
soft-skills training, 273
software: decision-making, 64; employee
    surveillance, 74; illegally copying, 91;
    for performance appraisals, 276; quan-
    titative planning, 172, 173e; for virtual
    teams, 385; voice recognition, 66
Sonoma County Stable and Livestock, 99
Sony Corporation, 240
Southwest Airlines, 117–118, 125, 237,
    237e, 267
span of control, 229
spokesperson role, 11
Sprint PCS, 66
staff functions, in bureaucracies, 223
staffing, 7; compensation, 277–279; coor-
    dinator for, 10–11; employee orienta-
    tion and, 271; legal aspects of,
    256–259; model of, 256, 257e; per-
    formance appraisals and, 274–277;
    recruitment, 260–262; selection
    process for, 262–271; strategic human
    resource planning, 259–260; training
    and development for, 272–274
stakeholder viewpoint of social responsi-
    bility, 96–97, 96e
standards. *See* performance standards
Starbucks Corp., 111, 127–128
start-ups, global, 41–42
status quo, decision making and, 148, 150
Staud, John, 39
stealing, 91
Steelcase, 137–138
Stello, Jeff, 213
Sternlich, Barry, 292
stockholder viewpoint of social responsi-
    bility, 95–97
strategic alliances, 126; in world markets,
    40–41
strategic human resource planning,
    259–260
strategic inventory, 123e
strategic planners, 10

strategic planning, 112–113, 117,
    120–122; example, 119–120. *See also*
    business strategy
strengths, corporate, 124
stress, 478–480; conflict and, 399; control
    and reduction methods for, 467–468,
    482–483; escape methods for,
    484–485, 484e; individual factors in,
    480–481; organizational factors in,
    481–482; questionnaire, 479e; symp-
    tom management, 483–484
subcontracting. *See* outsourcing
subliminal messages, procrastination con-
    trol and, 476–477
suboptimum decisions, 143
subordinate power, 288–289, 289e
success, determination of, 114
suggestion programs, 155, 157
summaries of major points: in group
    problem solving, 162; in meetings,
    369–370
summary, cash flow, 423
summary discipline, 455
Sun Microsystems, 158
supervising: time spent on, 8e. *See also*
    management
suppliers, information technology and, 63
support: for change, 243–245; effective
    work groups and, 388–389; emotional,
    295; organizational, creativity and,
    155; stress reduction and, 482;
    team/group role with, 391; teamwork,
    392–393, 393e
SWOT analysis, 121, 122–124
sympathy, empathy *vs.*, 364
synergy, 20
systems perspective, 19–20, 20e

tactical planning, 113
take-charge leaders, 391–392
Target Stores, 245
task behavior, 300
task delegator, role of, 11
task forces, 388
task identity, job enrichment and, 203
task mentality, 233
task significance, job enrichment and, 203
task specialization, in bureaucracies, 222
tasks: high-output, 471; interdependent,
    388; prioritizing, 470
Taylor, Frederick W., 17, 19, 198
Taylor, Sam, 77
team books, 393
team builders/building, 11–12, 308;
    example, 255–256
team goals, team player and, 394
team leaders, 5
team members, 391–392
team players, 12; effective, 393–395

teams: conflict and, 398–401; cross-functional, 384–385; potential contributions of, 395–396; potential problems of, 396–398; project, 383–384; self-managed work, 381–383; skills of, 381e; top-management, 385; transnational, 41; types of, 380–381; virtual, 63, 385–386. *See also* groups; work teams

teamwork: about, 380–381; example, 379–380; management practices supporting, 392–393, 393e

technical problem solvers, 12, 308

technical skills: leadership and, 292, 308; for management, 13–14

techno-obsessives, 66

technological forecasting, 175

technology: as communication barrier, 362; disruptive, 245–246; effective use of, 472. *See also* information systems; information technology

telecommuting, 212–214

telemarketing, employee monitoring in, 72

teleworkers, 212

temporary work, 215–216

tension, creativity and, 154

terminal management function, 410. *See also* controlling

termination, 460–462

territorial departmentalization, 226–227, 226e

territorial games, 372, 373

Texas Nameplate, 349

thank-you notes, 371

theft, 91

Theory X, 17, 18, 298, 298e; external control strategy of, 412

Theory Y, 17, 18, 298, 298e

thinking outside the box, 152

Thomas, H. Roosevelt, Jr., 51

threats, analyzing corporate, 124

360-degree feedback, 275

3M: creativity support at, 155; suggestion program, 157

throughput, communication, 359

time, usage of, nonverbal communication and, 355

time-series analysis, 174, 174e

to-do lists, 470

Ton Yang Indonesia (TYI), 85

top-level managers, 2–3

top-management teams, 385

Total Flex, 197

total quality management (TQM), 246–247

tough questions, team players and, 394

Toyota, 189

Toys R Us, 152

trade-offs, business strategy and, 118

training and development, 272; effective work groups and, 388; expectancy theory and, 339; needs assessment for, 272–273; organizational culture and, 240; outdoor, for teamwork, 393; planning for, 260; program selection for, 274, 274e

traits, performance appraisals measures of, 276

transformational leaders, 303–304. *See also* charismatic leadership

transnational corporations, 30

transnational teams, 41

trauma disorders, cumulative, 208–209

travel and expense reporting, information technology and, 65

Trinity Forge, 273

trust: charismatic leadership and, 305, 306; by team players, 395; virtual teams and, 385–386

trustworthiness, leadership and, 292

two-factor work motivation theory, 324–325, 325e

two-way communication, 365

Tyabji, Hatim, 236

uncertainty: change and, 244; decision making and, 148–149; structuring, 358

unethical behavior, 90–91; confrontations about, 105

unfair work environments, 91

unfreezing, change and, 242, 242e

uninterruptible power supplies (UPSs), 68e

unique experiences, job enrichment and, 202

United Airlines, information technology maintenance system at, 432–433

United States: international trade highlights, 37e; staffing legislation, 256, 258e

United States Central Intelligence Agency, employee surveillance, 74

United States Postal Service, disruptive change and, 246

United States Supreme Court, on disability claims, 259

unity of command, bureaucracies and, 222

unpredictability, office politics and, 372

upward communication, 356

U.S. Steel, training and development at, 273

utilitarianism, 86

valences, expectancy theory of motivation and, 338–339

validity studies, on psychological tests, 266–267

values: decision making and, 149–150; empathy and, 362–363; ethics and, 88–89; leading by, 289; motivation and, 325; organizational culture and, 236. *See also* decision trees; economic value added
Vance, Mike, 154
Vantive Corporation, 151
vaporized companies, 69
VeriFone, Inc., 236
Vermont Crafters Inc., 171–172, 183, 188
vertical job loading, 206
vertical thinking, 152–153
viatical settlements, 152
vicarious learning, discipline and, 457
videoconferences, 63; virtual teams and, 385
virtual corporations, 212
virtual office, 63
virtual teams, 63, 385–386; example, 387
virtue ethics, 88
virtuous circle, 103
vision, 121, 121e; charismatic leadership and, 305; entrepreneurs and, 302
visualization: crisis management and, 149; peak performance and, 473
vocabulary, communication and, 365
voice: authoritative speaking, 354e; quality of, nonverbal communication and, 353
voice mail, control of, 471–472
voice recognition software, 66

Waddock, Sandra A., 102, 103
wages, 277
Waitt, Theodore W., 126, 285–286, 303–304
Wal-Mart: action plans for, 115; corporate social consciousness and, 95; forecasting for, 115; general framework for planning, 114; goals and objectives of, 114–115; inventory control at, 186; strategic planning by, 112–113; work streamlining at, 470–471
Waldroop, James, 453
Walt Disney Corporation, 271
Warner-Lambert, 126
wasted resources, conflict and, 399
wasted time, 471, 471e
Watson, Thomas, Jr., 141
weaknesses, corporate, 124
Weathersby, George B., 286
Web-enabled cell phones, 61, 68e
Web master, 67
Web sites, 62; analysis of, 68e. *See also* computer goof-offs; Internet
Webcasting, 429
Websense, 74
Weddle, JoAn, 273

Weight Watchers, 141
Weil, Andrew, 483
Weill, Sanford, 385
Weinbach, Larry, 149
Wells Fargo & Co., 69, 71
Wendy's International, 52
whistle blowers, 101
whitespace, corporate, 434
Whitney, John O., 350
Whyte, Glen, 161
willingness, readiness and, 300
wired managerial workers, 66–67
Wireless Application Protocol (WAP), 68e
women: affirmative action and, 257; communication styles of, 368; mentoring and, 307–308
Wonderlic Personnel Test, 265
Woodruff, Robert, 141
work ethic, 468
work groups, 386–389, 386e. *See also* groups; work teams
work habits, stress reduction and, 482–483
work pace, 471
work schedules, example, 197
work streamlining, 470–471
work teams, 381–382, 382e, 388. *See also* groups; work groups
working relationships, change and, 245
workload sharing, effective work groups and, 389
workout programs, 356
world markets, 40–42; success factors, 42–45
World Trade Organization, 32
Wrights & Filippis, 70–71; focus of, 128
wrongful discharge, 460
Wrzesniewski, Amy, 207

Xerox Corporation, 128, 155

Zahar, Shaker A., 44
Zarella, Ronald L., 149
zone of indifference, 289, 289e
Zubroff, Shoshanna, 75

Essentials of Management

6 EDITION

Andrew J. DuBrin

Professor of Management
College of Business
Rochester Institute of Technology

THOMSON
™
SOUTH-WESTERN

Australia · Canada · Mexico · Singapore · Spain · United Kingdom · United States

Essentials of Management, Sixth Edition
Andrew J. DuBrin

Editor-in-Chief: Jack W. Calhoun
Team Leader: Michael Roche
Acquisitions Editor: Joseph A. Sabatino
Developmental Editor: Emma F. Guttler
Marketing Manager: Rob Bloom
Production Editor: Starratt E. Alexander
Manufacturing Coordinator: Rhonda Utley
Production House: Trejo Production
Printer: Transcontinental Printing, Inc.
Peterborough, Ontario
Design Project Manager: Rik Moore
Internal Designer: Rik Moore
Cover Design: Rik Moore
Cover Illustration: Greg Hargreaves, © Artville, LLC
Photography Manager: Deanna Ettinger

Library of Congress Cataloging-in-Publication Data
DuBrin, Andrew J.
       Essentials of management / Andrew J. DuBrin. — 6th ed.
           p.   cm.
       Includes bibliographical references and index.
       ISBN 0-324-11467-2
       1. Management   I. Title.
HD31.D793   2002
658—dc21
                                                                    2001058171